In a Nut

Bed and Breakfast

a **Fisherman's Cottage** on the East Coast where you can watch whales and the world's highest tides.

a **Mountain Chalet** on the West Coast with a panoramic view of the Pacific Ocean and mountain ranges.

a **Prairie Ranch** near the Rocky Mountains foothills where you can watch the annual branding.

a **Penthouse in the City** where groups of young people are welcomed if they want to sleep on the carpeted terrace.

a **Traditional Victorian Home** full of antiques and paintings with a gracious staircase and plenty of oak and walnut woodwork.

a **Remote Home** which can only be reached by plane or boat or kayak, located in the heart of Canada's newest National Park on the West Coast.

a **Downtown Metropolitan Residence** where they serve Champagne in bed for breakfast and the New York Times along with it.

an **Indian Home** owned by a family specializing in Indian Lore. Choose to sleep in a tipi or a trapper's tent.

a **Typical Canadian Farm** where guests are invited to help with chores and feed animals, and where they serve huge homecooked meals from own produce.

a **Moored Ship** where you can fall asleep by the restful lullaby of the waves washing against the hull.

a **Northwest Territories Home** where you can join freighter canoeing trips with Inuit hunters and eat Arctic Char and Muskox meat.

a **Modern Residential Home** on the West Coast with its private beach and a boat for charter.

a **Skating Home** where you can put on your skates inside the back door and walk over to the longest outdoor skating rink in the world.

an **Old Sea Captain's Cabin** a base for deep sea fishing, clam digging and enjoying lobster suppers.

an **Isolated Prairie Farm** where you can sit and relax in wide open spaces and tranquil surroundings and listen to the wheat grow.

a **Hiker's Home** on the famous Bruce Trail where they offer to move your car to the end of your hike and drop it off at some other B&B location.

a **Wilderness Tours Home** in the Whitewater Capital of Canada where you can find something more comfortable than roughing it in the outdoors after a long canoeing trip.

a **Theatre Home** around the corner from Shakespeare or Shaw Festivals where you can walk home after a late performance.

a **Ski Home** by major slopes or groomed trails; sip hot cider by the fireplace after a day on the slopes.

a **Houseboat** on a private island with a large screened deck, offering a unique environment of simple elegance.

a **Haida Home** in a village with old totem poles, where the host will gladly share his knowledge of native foods, culture and history.

The Canadian Bed & Breakfast Guide

GERDA PANTEL

Revised and Enlarged Fifth Edition

Chicago Review Press

Dedication

To my parents,
the late Alfons Kemper and Hedy Kemper,
who brought their family to Canada,
but themselves never had a chance to discover
how beautiful this country really is.

The Canadian Bed & Breakfast Guide

Chicago Review Press Incoporated
814 North Franklin Street
Chicago, Illinois 60610

Acknowledgements

Many thanks to my husband Ted for being so understanding,
and for helping me with the computer.

Thank you to Joan and John Huiberts of Crawford Bay, BC
for permission to use their house on the cover.

Typesetting by E.H. Pantel

Printed and bound in Canada

ISBN-1-55652-064-6

Contents

What is Bed & Breakfast?

Bed & Breakfast is the next best thing to staying with realtives or friends.

The Bed & Breakfast concept is growing rapidly in Canada. More and more people are taking advantage of this new phenomenon. More and more people are being introduced to it by chance, and they love it.

In an age of expensive travelling, one can still find comfortable and reasonable accommodation located in private homes across Canada from coast to coast. These homes offer a short-term, overnight stay for a paying guest in comfortable, cosy and friendly surroundings, close to chosen travel routes and places of interest, and they offer a hearty breakfast.

Bed & Breakfast is very popular in Britain and Europe. There, local hosts will even go to the railway station and ask arriving visitors if they are looking for accommodation - they will display a sign in their window saying "Zimmer frei" or "Room available".

In Canada, the Bed & Breakfast concept was pioneered in Cape Breton Island around 1972. It all started, more or less, with farmers and rural families offering their country home atmosphere to city travellers for a change and a rest away from the "rat race". Bed & Breakfast flourished shortly in Montreal during Expo. Today, there are Bed & Breakfast places in virtually every city and town from coast to coast.

Bed & Breakfast is an alternative to staying in a hotel room. It is geared to that certain type of traveller who is interested in getting to know people and places through personal contact. This all amounts to a unique change of pace and a more original way of travelling. It provides adventure and a relaxed atmosphere. Above all, it provides assistance and advice on a personal basis and an opportunity to make new and lasting friends.

Bed & Breakfast hosts are people who are interested in sharing their genuine hospitality in a family atmosphere, and at the same time enriching their own lives through cultural exchange and friendship. Their homes are neat, clean and cosy, but not necessarily luxurious. Their homes may be a modest fisherman's cottage on the east coast or a cosy mountain chalet in the west; an apartment suite in a metropolis or a ranch in the prairies; an historic mansion in a rural setting, an old family farm house, or a contemporary residence in suburbia. The hosts' main concern, above all, is to make guests feel welcome and comfortable and to help them have a wonderful holiday.

Many B & B places are members of a local Bed & Breakfast organization or agency or are affiliated with the local Chamber of Commerce and Provincial Department of Tourism. These organizations establish guidelines and a basis for good standards and also act as a referral system within the local area when a room is already booked.

About The Canadian Bed & Breakfast Guide

The Canadian Bed & Breakfast Guide has been compiled for easy and quick reference for use with Official Standard Canadian Road Maps. These are available from Tourist Departments in the individual provinces or from the Canadian Government Office of Tourism, Ottawa (see Index).

Visitors to Canada will find that "mileage" shown along the roads and on the maps are in Kilometers, thus distances to each individual B&B home are shown in approximate kilometer in The Guide (1 mile = 1.6 km)

The Author does not arrange for reservations. Guests are responsible for contacting individual hosts or agencies. Only a few of the homes have been visited by the Author on her personal travels from coast to coast. Listings should not be taken as a recommendation; all the information was supplied by the hosts in response to a questionaire, and has been transfereed to this book as acccurately as possible. Hosts are listed under their postal address only and not under area or district. All of the homes operate the year round, unless otherwise stated.

Most hosts would appreciate advance notice. **It is suggested that guests contact the hosts ahead of time, either by letter or phone.** When on route, travellers should stop by early afternoon, decide how far they will travel that day, choose a B&B, and then phone from a nearby booth or tourist office. The hosts will appreciate the consideration and if they are booked for the night, they may be able to refer the traveller to another B&B in the area. When a room is waiting, it provides for far more relaxed travel.

Rates are shown in Canadian Currency. It is assumed that hosts will honor the prices shown in the latest edition of The Canadian Bed & Breakfast Guide. These rates are set by individual hosts or B&B organization. A small tax charge may be added to the room rate according to local provincial regulations.

Small children should bring their own sleeping bags to be used as bedding. Arrival and departure times vary and should be arranged by the hosts and guests at the time of first contact. Only when hosts have provided in-house-pet information, it has been indicated in this publication. If this is important, always check beforehand when making the reservation.

If you know of a B&B host who would like to be included in the next edition of the Guide, please use the tear-out form provided in the back. The Guide is up-dated and revised periodically. Many new entries could not be included in this edition, due to space limitations and questionaire response after the requested due date.

The Author would like to hear about your travels experience with The Canadian Bed & Breakfast Guide, as well as suggestions for any changes that would make the Guide more useful.

If there is no listing in a place of your choice, write or drop in to the local Chamber of Commerce Office and/or the local Tourist Bureau and inquire about any B&B's in that particular area.

The photos included in The Canadian Bed and Breakfast Guide were selected at random and will be rotated in future editions according to the availability of book space.

How to use The Canadian Bed & Breakfast Guide

1) Refer to the Official Standard Canadian Road Map of the province you are visiting and for the route you plan to take.

2) Determine the place or area where you would like to stay in a Bed & Breakfast home. (If on route or planning a trip, decide how many km/miles you want to travel on a specific day and then determine the place or area where you would like to stay in a B&B)

3) Look for the chosen location in The Canadian Bed & Breakfast Guide. All locations are listed in alphabetical order according to province. Nearby larger places are shown in brackets throughout the Guide for each listing.

   A "see also" reference will direct you to another B&B location either in the immediate or general geographic area where you are looking for a B&B.

   Example: Hamilton
   (see also Burlington, Waterdown ... etc)

   This means that there are also B&B homes in Burlington and/or Waterdown (both places are located in the immediate geographic area of Hamilton) which may be contacted in case the Hamilton homes(s) are booked.

4) If there is no reference of a place you are looking for, consult your map again and look for a nearest larger place; then find it in the book and use the "see also reference" method described above. It could be that a small change in your route will find you another place to stay and perhaps a look at an interesting part of the country you hadn't thought of visiting.

5) Refer to the handy key on the flaps for interpretation of signs and symbols in the individual listing, and use the key for handy bookmarks.

6) Where applicable, use a toll-free telephone number for reserving a B&B room.

British Columbia

(including Queen Charlotte Islands)

For ferry crossing schedules and information to Vancouver Island, Gulf
Islands and Queen Charlotte Islands contact:
B.C. Ferries Corporation   (604) 386-3431
818 Broughton St., Victoria, BC   V8W 1E4   (604) 669-1211

Vancouver Island

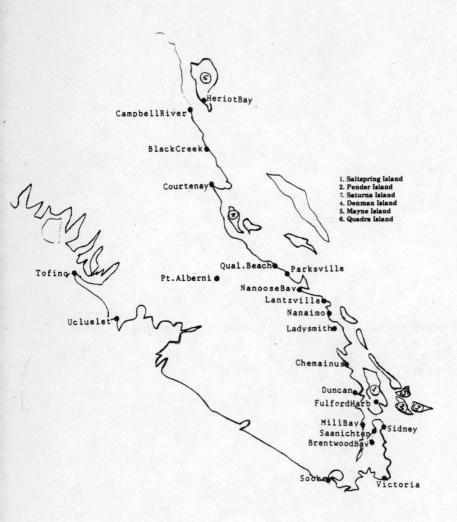

CampbellRiver●
HeriotBay●
BlackCreek●
Courtenay●

1. Saltspring Island
2. Pender Island
3. Saturna Island
4. Denman Island
5. Mayne Island
6. Quadra Island

Tofino●
Pt.Alberni●
Qual.Beach●
Parksville●
NanooseBay●
Lantzville●
Nanaimo●
Ladysmith●
Ucluelet●

Chemainus●
Duncan●
FulfordHarb●
MillBay●
Saanichten●
Sidney●
BrentwoodBay●
Sooke●
Victoria●

B.C Mainland

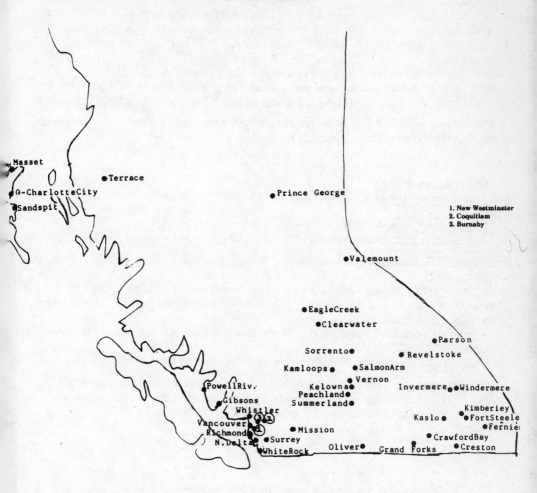

Masset

Terrace

Q-CharlotteCity

Sandspit

Prince George

1. New Westminster
2. Coquitlam
3. Burnaby

Valemount

EagleCreek

Clearwater

Parson

Sorrento

Revelstoke

Kamloops

SalmonArm

Vernon

PowellRiv.

Kelowna

Invermere

Windermere

Gibsons

Peachland

Whistler

Summerland

Vancouver

Kaslo

Kimberley

Richmond

FortSteele

Mission

Fernie

N.Delta

Surrey

CrawfordBay

WhiteRock

Oliver

Grand Forks

Creston

Black Creek
(on Vancouver Island, near Courtenay; see also Campbell River, Quathiaski Cove)

Bohn, Elaine and Ron (Country Comfort)   ⌐ CC
8214 Island Hwy, Box 3, Black Creek, BC   V0R 1C0   ☎ (604) 337-5273

Located on Hwy 19.
$25 S $45D $10Child(age 6-12)   (Special rates for longer stay)   ► 4
● Choice, homebaked   ♠ Rural, modern home, patio, orchard   ■ 2D (upstairs)
⊢ 2D   ⌐ 1Sh.w.g.   ★ TV,F,LF, freezer for fish   ⊛ Restricted smoking,
controlled pets
↔ General store, restaurants, pizza take-out, bus stop, fresh fruit stand
⇔ Prov. Park, beach, golfing, boat marina with fish guides, tennis court, trail rides, Mt.
Washington and Forbidden Plateau, popular ski and hiking facilities, shopping center

☞ Relax in modern home. Convenient location for travellers headed to Prince Rupert
via Port Hardy ferry. There is a cat in residence.

Brentwood Bay
(on Vancouver Island near Victoria; see also Mill Bay, Sooke)

Merritt, Harvey and Jean   ⌐ CC
746 Sea Drive, RR1, Brentwood Bay, BC   V0S 1A0   ☎ (604) 652-9370

Located 1.5 km west of Brentwood Bay off Wallace and Woodward Drives.
$98S $98D   ► 2
● Cont.   ♠ Rural, near village, res., acreage, view, patio, quiet, oceanfront
■Separate cottage   ⊢ 1Q   ⌐ Private   ★ Separate entrance, parking, rowing dinghy
for guests   ⊛ Smoking, children, pets   ∿ German
↔ Butchart's Gardens, Village of Brentwood Bay, marina (Guides and boat rental for
fabulous salmon fishing
⇔ City of Victoria, Sidney, Malahat Drive, parks, southern part of Vancouver Island

☞ Waterfront Cottage with adjacent bathhouse and dock is located on property
separately from main house. Enjoy the luxury of quiet time in this unique setting and
watch the resident Harbour Seal, the great Blue Heron and Bald Eagles.

B&B Travel Tip: *Do remember that you are entering a private house as a
guest – (even though you are paying something) – the hosts are still doing you a
favour by inviting you into their homes and you must observe whatever house rules
exist. If you keep this in mind, your stay will be very enjoyable.*

Campbell River

(on Vancouver Isle; see also Courtenay, Duncan, Quadra Isle, Black Creek

Bright, Valerie and George (Willow Point Guest House)   ⌐ CC
2460 South Island Hwy, Campbell River, BC   V9W 1C6   ☎ (604) 923-1086

Located on Island Hwy. Coming from south look for sign on left just past Gas Station.
$30-40S $40-50D $15Add.person   ► 7A
● Full, homebaked   ♠ Res., sub., oceanview   ■ 3D (upstairs)   �':' 2T,2D,1P
⚲ 1Sh.w.g., 1ensuite   ★ F,TV, parking   ⚘ Rest. smoking, children min. age 12
↔ Walks on beach across the road, fish from new salt water sport fishing pier
⟺ Elk Falls Prov. Park (trails through old growth forest), Strathcona Parks (highest
point of island), whale-watching, Telegraph Cove, Valley of a Thousand Faces, Quadra
Island and Rebecca Spit Marine Park (picnic sites, ocean swimming and fishing)

☞ Widely travelled hosts in newer home with breathtaking views of the mountains
and Discovery Passage. From the Bay window watch cruise ships going by. There are two
cats in the house.

Johnson, Peter (Campbell River B&B)   ⌐ B&B
302 Birch St., Campbell River, BC   V9W 2S6   ☎ (604) 287-4213

From Hwy 19 in Campbell River turn left at 3rd Ave and go to house up hill.
$25S $40D   ► 10
● Cont.   ♠ Res., older, sub., acreage, view, oceanfront, patio, sundeck, quiet   ■ 4D
�':' 1S,3D,1Q   ⚲ Sh.w.h.   ★ TV,KF, parking   ⚘ Smoking, pets, children min. age 12
↔ Neighborhood Pub, downtown Campbell River, beach, restaurants, tennis
⟺ Great skiing, super salmon fishing (charters arranged by host)

☞ Centrally located and charming older home nestled in an acre of dogwood trees.

Chemainus

(on Vancouver Island near Duncan; see also Victoria, Saltspring Isle)

Mitchell, Ross and Joyce (The Mitchell House)   ⌐ CC
2877 Fuller Lake Rd., RR1, Chemainus, BC   V0R 1K0   ☎ (604) 246-3513

Located south of Chemainus and 14 km. north of Duncan.
$25S $34-36D $10Child   ⚟ Meals   ► 4A,2Ch
● Full, homebaked   ♠ Rural, acreage, view, patio, quiet   ■ 2D (upstairs)   �':' 2D
⚲ Sh.w.h.   ★TV, parking   ⚘ Non-smokers preferred, pets, children min age 6
↔ "Heritage Country Crafts" shop on property (local quality handcrafted articles in
rustic surrounding), Fuller Lake recreation area (swimming boating, tennis, golfing,
fishing), Fuller Lake Arena
⟺ "Chemainus City of Murals", Duncan "City of Totems", shopping, local Art Gallery

☞ BC Cedars, landscaped lawns and a profusion of flowers provide attractive setting
and homey atmosphere. Parents and hockey tournament players are welcome.

Clearwater
(mear 100-Mile House north of Kamloops; see also Eagle Creek)

Kintzinger, Henry and Erika (Omas Bed & Breakfast)   ⌐ CC
229 Schmidt Rd, Box 4074, RR2,Clearwater, BC V0E 1N0   ☎ (604) 674-3467

On Hwy 5West from Jasper take Hwy 11. From Vancouver take the Coquihalla Toll
Hwy East. From Kamloops take Hwy 5 East. Located in Clearwater off the old North
Thompson Hwy. Follow signs.
$25S $30D $10Child   ► 5A,2Ch
● Full, homebaked   🏠 Rural, acreage, quiet, large sundeck   ■ 1S,2D,1F
⊢4T,1R   ⌐ 2Private   ★ TV,F,LF   ♥   🖐 Restricted smoking   ≈ German
↔ Walk in the woods or cross-country skiing, Clearwater Shopping Centre, Dutch Lake,
canoeing, North Thompson Prov. Park,
⇔ Wells Gray Wilderness Park, Trophy Mountains, Alpine Area, downhill skiing,
Spahats Falls, golf course, tennis court

☞ Old fashioned hospitality in new house set in a quiet wooded area close to the
famous Wells Gray Park. Ideal stop between Edmonton,Jasper and Vancouver. Well
travelled hosts are knowledgeable about the area. Pick-up from bus and train station.

Coquitlam
(Vancouver; see also White Rock, Surrey, Richmond, New Westminster)

Loven, Galen & S. Wydeman (Bakerview B&B)
405 Mariner Way, Coquitlam, BC V3C 5A4   ☎ (604) 942-4129

From Hwy 1 across Port Mann Bridge, take 1st exit to Hwy 7, bearing left so as to travel
north towards Mariner Way exit. Follow signs to Mariner Way. Maps and detailed
directions will be sent.
$25S $40D   🍽 Meals   ► 4
✚ May 1-Oct.15   ● Full, homebaked   🏠 Res, sub., view, patio   ■ 2D (upstairs)
⊢2Q,1P   ⌐ 1Sh.w.h., 1ensuite   ★ TV,F   🖐 Smoking, pets, children min. age 12
↔ Park and nature trails
⇔ Vancouver Game Farm, Golden Ears Park (beaches, watersports), two major
shopping centres with cinemas and restaurants, Vancouver City Centre, museums,
concert halls, US border crossing at Blaine (Wash)

☞ New home situated on the eastern outskirts of Greater Vancouver, overlooking
Coquitlam River Valley, the Golden Ears Mountains and Mount Baker
(Washington/US). Hosts are classical music lovers and gourmet cooks. Breakfast served
on sun-deck, weather permitting.

Courtenay
(on Vancouver Island near Comox; see also Denman, Campbell River, Black Creek)

Drew, Betty and Ivan (The Dahlia Patch)   ⌐ B&B
RR3, 3675 Minto Rd., Courtenay, BC   V9N 5M8   ☎ (604) 336-8345

From Courtenay, take Island Hwy 19 south to light at Royston (5 km). Turn towards
Cumberland and proceed 2 Km, turn right onto Minto St and house on left.
$30S $40D $10Child   (Seniors discounts available)   ► 6A
✚ May-Oct.   ● Full   ♠ Rural, older, acreage, patio, quiet   ■ 3D   ⊨ 2D,2T
⌐1Private,1Sh.w.g.   ★ Separate entrance, TV in guest room   ⊎ Non-smokers
preferred   ♥   ⌇ French understood
⇔ Comox Lake, swimming, boating, Forbidden Plateau, hiking, Mt Washington, Miracle
Beach Prov. Park, salmon and trout fishing, sailing, golfing, shopping centers

☞ Early retired school-teachers in ivy-clad house with spacious lawns, colourful garden
and situated on 10 acres of pasture and evergreen forest. A quiet resting place for hot
summer days. There is a dog in the house.

Nelson, Mary (Greystone Manor)   ⌐ B&B
4014 Haas Rd., RR6, C2, Site 684, Courtenay, BC   V9N 5M8   ☎ (604) 338-1422

From Island Hwy south of Courteneay (3 km), turn onto Hilton and then immediately
left onto Haas Rd and house on right.
$35S $45D $10Add. person $5Child   ► 6A
● Full, homebaked   ♠ Rural, older, view, oceanfront, patio, quiet, acreage   ■ 3D
⊨ 2S,2D   ⌐ Sh.w.g.   ★ F   ⊎ Pets, nonsmokers preferred
↪ Comox Bay, rural setting with walking trails
⇔ Courtenay Youth Music Centre, downhill and cross-country skiing, Fillberg Lodge,
Campbell River salmon fishing, ferry to mainland

☞ Relax in quiet comfort on Comox Bay overlooking Denman and Hornby Islands
with beautiful view of Mainland coastal mountains in the distance. Special ski packages
and mystery weekends available.

Cranbrook
(see also Kimberley, Fort Steele, Creston, Fernie)

Crawford Bay
(near Nelson; see also Creston, Kimberley, Fort Steeles, Kaslo)

Huiberts, Joan & John Edwards (Wedgwood Manor)　　　　✔ B&B
Box 135, Crawford Bay, BC　V0B 1E0　　　　　　　　☎ (604) 227-9233

From Nelson go east on Hwy 3A cross Kootenay Lake by ferry and drive 8.5 km east to
Crawford Bay. From Creston go north on Hwy 3A along Kootenay Lake to Crawford Bay
$40S　$45D　$7.50Child　$15Add.person　　　　　　▶ 10A,2Ch
● Full,homebaked　🏠 Rural, hist., acreage, view, patio, quiet　■4D (upstairs)
⬻4D,1Q,1 cot　⌐ 1ensuite,1private,2shw.g.　★ 3F, private guest lounge, bicycles for
guests, honeymoon & anniversary specials　🖐 Pets
↤ Crawford Bay beach on 90-mile long Kootenay Lake, swimming (water still pure
enough to drink), canoe along pristine shoreline, fish for record rainbow trout, excellent
walking and hiking from doorstep, guided nature tours available, bicycle and explore the
local back roads, Harrison Memorial church next door (handy for wedding party)
⇔ Kootenay Lake Ferry (longest free ride in NA), Ainsworth (sumptuous hot springs
and cavern), mine tours, paddlewheel cruises, historic town of Kaslo, Nelson (unique
dining and shopping), "The Glass House" built entirely of glass bottles

🐾 1900 built Manor is situated on a 55-acres estate overlooking a small valley at the
foot of the Purcell Mountains and is furnished with pieces from the Victorian era with a
library lounge and front veranda providing pleasant atmosphere. Much of the fresh food
comes straight from the Manor gardens, and "Breakfast in Bed" is available. Stretch out
in a hammock and absorb the peace and silence of a country day.

Creston
(near US border (Idaho); see also Kaslo, Fort Steele, Kimberley, Crawford Bay)

Orr, Audrey and Cecil (Rising Sun Guest Ranch)
3246 Riverview Rd., RR1, Creston, BC　V0B 1G0　　　　☎ (604) 428-4886

From Creston take Hwy 21 to Mallory Rd. Turn left and continue to ranch.
$25S　$30D　$10Child　🍴 Meals　　　　　　　　▶ 8A,2Ch
● Full, homebaked　🏠 Ranch, quiet, patio, isolated　■ 4D　⬻ 2T,2D,1Q,R
⌐ 2Private, 2sh.w.g.　★ F,LF,TV in guest room, separate entrance

↤ Golf course, river, swimming, trail
rides, hiking in private and secluded
woods, cross country skiing

⇔ Kootenay Lake, fishing, boating,
Kootenay Skyway Summit, Ghost
towns, Ainsworth Hot Springs, Creston
Wildlife Management Area, Slocan
Valley, US Border

🐾 Guest ranch offers country
atmosphere with homemade meals.

Denman Island
(near Courtenay on Vancouver Island)

Okrainec, Bob and Mary Ann (Denman Island Guest House)
Box 9, Denman Island, BC V0R 1T0   ☎ (604) 335-2688

From Nanaimo travel north on Hwy 19 to Buckley Bay. Take 10 minute ferry ride to
Denman Island (hourly service) and follow the main road (Denman Rd) for 0.8 km. Look
for B&B sign on gate.
$30S $35-45D $10Add.person   ▣ Meals   ► 10
● Full   ♠ Small farm, hist., view, sundecks, porches   ■ 6D,F   ⊢ D,T,S
⌐ Sh.w.g.   ★ TV   ⑭ Pets
↪ General store, ocean beach (watersports and beachcombing), hiking bicycling
⇔ Ferry to Hornby Island, Helliwell Park, Tribune Bay, Filongley Prov. Park.

☛ Turn-of-the-Century island farmhouse located in Georgia Strait with unique rural
atmosphere and spectacular view. Seafood specialties served in licenced dining room.

Tait, Hamish and Graeme   ✓ B&B
Scott Rd., Denman Island, BC V0R 1T0   ☎ (604) 335-2640

Take Hwy 19 north from Nanaimo to Buckley Bay ferry dock. Take ferry and proceed up
the hill. Turn left at junction. Follow West Rd for 3.7 km to another junction and
continue to the left (N.W.Rd) 0.2 km. Turn left and look for driveway on right.
$20S $30D $10Child   ▣ Meals   ► 4
● Full   ♠ Rural, 15-acres, patio   ■ 2D   ⊢ 4S,cot   ⌐ Sh.w.h.   ★ TV,F,
separate entrance, facilities for the handicapped   ♥   ⊷ some French, Swahili
↪ Ocean beach, fresh water lake (trout fishing)
⇔ Many beaches, Hornby Island (ferry), Salmon fishing, craft shop, tennis court

☛ Island home in peaceful surroundings and beautiful view of Baynes Sound, Beaufort
Range and Forbidden Plateau (locally known as The Glacier). Enjoy over 2500 daffodils
in spring time. There are pets in the house.

Duncan
(on Vancouver Island near Victoria; see also Chemainus, Mill Bay)

Hignell, Val and Dave (Sahtlam Lodge)   ✓ B&B
5720 Riverbottom Rd., RR2, Duncan, BC V9L 1N9   ☎ (604) 748-7738

From Hwy 1, take Old Lake Cowichan Rd to Riverbottom Rd, then 8 km to lodge.
$40-50S $50-60D   ● $4.50Each   ▣ Meals   ► 8A
●Full   ♠Farm, hist., riverfront, view, quiet, isolated, large veranda   ■4D(upstairs),
also rustic cabins for families   ⊢4T,3D,3R   ⌐2Sh.w.g.   ★F   ⑭Children, pets
↪ River swimming and tubing on 2 private beaches, seasonal white water sports, winter
steelhead fishing (drift boat and guide available)
⇔ Chemainus (Festival of Murals), Cowichan Sweater shops, Gulf Island Ferries

☛ Old-fashioned holiday lodge, situated in quiet and tranquil surroundings in secluded
valley of the warm, lake-fed Cowichan River. Grand veranda excellent for river gazing.

Oliver, Judy & Frank (Grove Hall Estate B&B)
6159 Lakes Road, Duncan, BC   V9L 4J6

⌐ B&B
☎ (604) 746-6152

Phone for directions. Located on Quamichan Lake and 5min off TC Hwy.
$75S (and up) $95D (and up)
► 6A
● Full   ♠ Hist., sub., large acreage, view, lakefront, patios, quiet, isolated, tennis
court   ■ 3D (upstairs)   ⊢ 2S,2Q (including antique Chinese wedding bed)
⌐ 2Sh.w.g.   ★ F, separate entrance, TV in billard room, parking   ⊕ Restricted
smoking, pets, children
↪ Lakefront garden paths for quiet walks, feed swans while down at the lake, old
gardens on expansive property
⇔ Chemainus (famous town with murals, tea house, Canadian Arts and Crafts and
antique shops), B.C. Forest Museum and old steam train ride, Cowichan and Maple Bay
quaint waterfront areas, three golf courses

☞ Very spacious mansion restored and newly decorated was built by the famous BC
architect Samuel Maclure. Hosts have spent many years in the Orient and have collected
many antiques and artifacts. Rooms are named "Singapore", "Siamese", "Arabian
Rooms" and "Indonesion Suite".

Eagle Creek
(near 100-Mile House; see also Clearwater, Valemount)

Bradshaw, Al and Joyce (Minac Lodge)
Eagle Creek, BC   V0K 1L0

⌐ CC
☎ (604) 397-2416

Take Hwy 97 to Canim Lake turn-off, turn right to Forest Grove Esso and right again
(paved all the way).
$32.50S $3.50D $8Child   ●Extra   ▣ Meals
► 12
● Full   ♠ Rural, acreage, view, patio, lakefront, quiet   ♠ S,D (upstairs),also cabin
⊢ 3T,2D,2R, cot, crib   ⌐ Ensuite   ★ F,TV, parking   ⊕ Pets
↪ Walking and hiking trails, motor/pedal/row boating, canoeing, swimming in beach
⇔ Pro Golf Course, groomed ski trails, fishing, hunting, Canim Falls(local Art),

☞ Cariboo hospitality in lodge with dining room. Hunting/fishing guides available.
Dog sled trips in winter can be arranged. Transportation and pick-up is available.

B&B Travel Tip: *Contacting the B&B hosts ahead of time is a big advantage. You will not only have a bed waiting for you that night, but you have already
"broken the ice." The hosts will be welcoming you at the door and you are not a
stranger any more.*

Fernie
(near Cranbrook; see also Fort Steele, Kimberley, Invermere, Windermere)

Delahunt, Doug and Mance (Rocky Mountain B&B)   ✔ CC
48 Coal Creek Rd., Box 2317, Fernie, BC   V0B 1M0   ☎ (604) 423-4865

Located in the SE corner of B.C. in the Rocky Mountains on Hwy 3, the scenic
Crowsnest Highway crossing Southern B.C.
$30S $45D $5-10Child   ► 4A,2-3Ch
● Full   ♠ Rural, res., view, patio, quiet   ■ 3D (main and upper level)   ⤙ 1K,1S,2T,
cot   ⌐ 1Sh.w.g., 1ensuite   ★ F,TV in guest room, LF, parking   ⑱Smoking, pets
⤳some French

↪ Charming golf course, renowned
Snow Valley Ski Area, horse stables and
hiking trails, mountain stream and
developed nature trail

☛ Modern log alpine-style home
situated at the edge of town with
privacy and relaxed viewing of the
Rocky Mountains and surrounding
countryside from front and side sun
decks. Location is an ideal stop-over
between Calgary/Lethbridge and the
Southern B.C. interior. There is a cat in
the house.

Fort Steele
(near Cranbrook; see also Kimberley, Invermere, Windermere, Crawford Bay, Fernie)

Termuende, Bob and Orma (Wild Horse Farm)   ✔ CC
Box 7, Fort Steele, BC   V0B 1N0   ☎ (604) 426-6000

Located on Hwy 93/95 directly across from Fort Steele Heritage Park.
$48-67S $58-77D $13Add.person   ▣ Meals   (Deposit required)   ► 8A
✿ Summer ● Full, homebaked   ♠ Farm, country mansion, hist., view, screened
veranda, quiet   ■ 2D,1Ste,1F (main and upper floor)   ⤙ 2T,1Q (Canopy),1K,P, cot
⌐ 1Ensuite, 2private   ★ F,TV in guest sitting room, separate entrance
↪ Fort Steele Historic Park, cross-country ski trails
⇔ Many beautiful lakes for fishing, boating and water-sports, hiking and riding trails
abound, Kimberley, Cranbrook, golfing, tennis, dining and shopping, Alpine ski areas

☛ Spacious half-log, vine-covered mansion on secluded, treed estate adjoining
Provincial Heritage Park was built in the early 1900 looks up to The Purcell Mountains.

Fulford Harbour

(on Salt Spring Island near Victoria; see also Duncan, Pender Isle, Saturna Isle)

Yardley, Sue and Jonathan (Southdown Farm)   ✔ B&B
1121 Beaver Point Rd, RR1, Fulford Harbour, BC   V0S 1C0   ☎ (604) 653-4322

Take ferry from Swartz Bay to Salt Spring Island Ferry Terminal at Fulford Harbour.
Drive 4.8 km to farm on Beaver Point Road.
$60S $55-85D – $5Child(age 5-12) $15Add. person   (Off-season Rates)   ► 10
● Full   🏠 Farm, hist. river valley view, patio, quiet, isolated   ■ 2D,1S (plus
separate cottage with 2D)   ⊢ 2S,1D,3Q, cot, crib   ⌐ Ensuite, jacuzzi   ★ F,KF,LF,
woodstove, separate entrance, facilities for the handicapped, riding lessings in private
ring   ♥   ✋ Restricted smoking

↔ Park valley walks, beaches, pony rides

⇔ Ruckle Prov. Park, Fulford Harbour, Victoria and Nanaimo ferris to Vancouver

🐎 1911 heritage farmhouse renovated by architect host and situated in a beautiful valley of gently undulating farmland on Gulf Island in the Strait of Georgia. Very appealing soft climate and friendly atmosphere. Children most welcome. Ferry pick-up available.

Gibsons

(near Vancouver; see also Powell River)

Beyser, Gunter and Marcelina (Sunshine Coast Country Hideaway)   ✔ CC
1148, RR4, Reid Rd., Gibsons, BC   V0N 1V0   ☎ (604) 886-7261

Take BC Ferries to Langdale or drive along the Sunshine Coast from Vancouver or
Powell River. Phone for detailed directions.
$35S $45D $10Child $10Add.person   ► 2A,2Ch
✚ starting July 1989   ● Full, homebaked   🏠 Village, rural, res., bungalow, acreage,
patio, quiet   ■ 1Ste   ⊢ 1D,1R   ⌐ Private   ★ TV,KF, separate entrance,
badminton, table tennis, fully equipped tent for children   ♥   ⁓ German, Tagalog
⇔ Ferry, Tourist Information Booth

🐎 Home is situated on a park-like acreage between majestic firs and cedars.
Accommodation is in a self-contained suite. Continental or NA breakfast served in suite,
dining room or deck. Kennel and dog sitting provided. There are pets in the house.

Bulger, Mrs. G (Bulger's By The Sea)   ✓ B&B
RR2, Box 37/8, Gibsons, BC   V0N 1V0   ☎ (604) 886-7164

Take ferry from Horseshoe Bay near Vancouver (35min ride). Drive through Gibsons to
Lower Rd and then 8.5 km to Bayview Rd and look for 3rd driveway and sign.
$36S $42D $80F   ► 4A,2Ch
● Full   ♠ Rural, split-level, acreage, oceanfront   ■ 2D,1F, and cottage   2S,2D,
cot   ⌐1Private, 1sh.w.h.   ★ F,,TV in guest room, separate entrance, parking
⊕Small controlled pets only
↪ Lovely beach, very good restaurant, store, Post Office
⇔ Golf Course, marina and boat charters, shopping, dining, library

☞ Enjoy the beautiful Sunshine Coast Beach at doorstep and the spectacular sunsets
from lovely garden.

Cattanach, Ian and Barbara   ✓ B&B
S18, C7, RR2, Hanbury Rd., Gibsons, BC   V0N 1V0   ☎ (604) 885-5444

Drive 12 km north of Gibsons and then 1 km past golf course to Lockyer Rd. Turn right,
then left on Hanbury Rd. From Vancouver drive to Horseshoe Bay and take ferry to
Langdale).
$25S $35D– $5Child   ► 6A,4Ch
● Full   ♠ Farm, quiet   ■ 3D (upstairs)   ⊨2T,1Q,P, crib   ⌐1Sh.w.g.   ★ TV
in guest room   ♥
↪ Wooded trails for hiking
⇔ Beach, picnic site, Sunshine Coast Golf Course, Gibsons

☞ Unique and beautiful rustic log home situated in quiet rural area along Sunshine
Coast. Plenty of room for RV's. Great place for children.

Grand Forks
(near Osoyos; see also Oliver)

Mason, Mrs. Audrey (Grandma's B&B)   ✓ B&B
586 Central Ave., Grand Forks, BC   V0H 1H0   ☎ (604) 442-3061

Located on Hwy 3 at the lights in Grand Forks and on the corner of Central & Sixth
Streets.
$25S $30D $2.50AChild   ► 6A,2Ch
● Choice   ♠ Downtown, res., older   ■ 1D,1Ste,1F (upstairs)   ⊨2T,2D, cot, crib
⌐1Private, 1ensuite   TV in guest room, separate entrance, parking   ⊕ Smoking,
drinking
↪ Center of village, park, museum, art gallery, shopping
⇔ Spokane (Washington)

☞ Heritage home in the centre of this historic town, full of mining relics and
Doukhobor memorabilia. There is a dog in the house.

Walsh, Patrick and Pauline (The School House)   ✓ B&B
Box 2772, Grand Forks, BC V0H 1H0   ☎ (604) 442-2897

Located 8.5 km west of Grand Forks on Hwy 3. Watch for sign.
$30S $40D $5Child $15Add.person   ▣ Meals   ► 3
✚ Full, homebaked   ♠ Farm, renovated 1-room schoolhouse, acreage, view, quiet
1D (cottage)   ⊷ 1Q(waterbed)   ⁈ Private   ★ TV in guest room, parking   ♥
🖐Restricted smoking
↪ Hiking trail
⇔ Christina Lake, secluded swimming spots on Granby River

🐾 Renovated Heritage Russian house on 54-acre farm with a view from the east porch
of Grand Forks Valley and facing out onto aviaries of exotic birds and apple orchard with
grazing sheep and peacocks roaming free. Hosts offer romantic dinners served in the
schoolhouse (specialty Roast Pheasant, gourmet trimmings; all homegrown products).

Heriot Bay
(on Quadra Island near Campbell River; see also Powell River)

Kenyon, Janice and Ross Henry (Hyacinthe Bay B&B)   ✓ CC
Box 343, Heriot Bay, BC V0P 1H0   ☎ (604) 285-2126

Home is 15 min from ferry terminal - phone for directions.
$30S $50D $10Child   ► 2A,2Ch
●Full   ♠Rural, acreage, view, patio, quiet, oceanfront   ■1D and loft   ⊷2T,2P
⁈1Private   ★F,sundeck with hot tub   🖐Smoking, pets   ᰛFrench, German
↪ Ocean beach for beachcombing, clamming,swimming, canoeing, kayacking, dinghy
sailing, explore Quadra Island
⇔ Ferry from Campbell River, Rebecca Spit, lighthouse at Cape Mudge, Kwakiutl Indian
Museum, hiking trails

🐾 Island retreat, with spectacular views to make an eagle jealous, located in the heart
of salmon fishing country. Gourmet breakfast served on the deck next to the hottub.
Hosts love to sail. There is a possibility of exploring the sea on hosts's 32-ft Aloha
sailboat. Picnic lunches provided.

> **B&B Travel Tip:** *Breakfast is almost always memorable! Most hosts will
> ask in the evening what you would like for breakfast and at what time (you can
> sleep in if you wish!). Go ahead and tell them if you would like porridge or some-
> thing special. You will be pleasantly surprised.*

Invermere
(north of Kimberley; see also Fort Steele, Parson, Windermere, Fernie)

Andrews, Dawne and Bill (Home-Inn)   ✓ CC
1610-8th Ave., Box 462, Invermere, BC V0A 1K0   ☎ (604) 342-9699

Coming from West on Trans Canada Hwy 1 take Hwy 95 south at Golden. From the East
(Banff) on Trans Canada Hwy 1 take Hwy 93 south to Radium Hot Springs and then
Hwy 95 to Invermere. Go straight through town on main street past Invermere Inn
around an"S"turn, down Beach Ave. Before RR track, make sharp right turn up to 8th
Ave and right to 1st house on left.
$40S $50D $75Apt   ► 6
● Full, homebaked   🏠 Village, view, patio, sundeck   ■ 1D (plus fully equipped
studio/apt for 4)   ⊨ 2D,2R,1P   ⌐ 2Private   ★ 2F,LF,KF, separate entrance, TV in
guest living room, parking   🖐 Non-smoking preferred   ～ some French

↔ Kinsmen Beach, tennis, historic
walk and town center with shops,
excellent dining

⇔ Golfing, crystal clear mineral Hot
Springs, beautiful Lake Windermere
with all watersports, Kootenay
Nat.Park (wilderness and hiking areas),
Panorama Ski Resort (downhill and
cross-country), heli-skiing, hunting,
fishing

☞ Cosily decorated chalet-type home
is situated on a quiet residential street
in pretty little mountain town with
beautiful scenery all around. Formerly from the big City, hosts enjoy sharing the peace
and magic of the Columbia Valley with the fresh invigorating mountain air.

Kamloops
(near Salmon Arm; see also Sorrento)

Bentz, Lynn and Trevor (Park Place B&B)   ✓ CC
730 Yates Rd., Kamloops, BC V2B 6C9   ☎ (604) 554-2179

Phone for directions.
$30S $40D $10Add.person   ► 4
● Full   🏠 Sub., bungalow, acreage, view, swimming pool, patio, quiet,
riverfront   ■1S,2D (main and lower floor)   ⊨ 1S,2D   ⌐Sh.w.g.   ★LF,KFTV in
guest room, separate entrance   🖐Smoking, child min. age 14, leashed pets outdoor only
↔ Boating, hiking, fishing, swimming, shopping, tennis, racket courts
⇔ Waterslide, lakes, paddlewheeler river boat cruise "Wanda Sue", Provincial Parks

☞ Comfortable home with solar-heated inground pool and lots of privacy by the river.
There is a dog in the house. Facilities for RV parking.

Farquharson, Ian and Darlene ✔ B&B
1994 High Schylea Dr., Kamloops, BC   V2E 1K9   ☎ (604) 372-3769

Phone for directions.
$25S $35D   ► 4A
✤ Summer   ● Full   🏠 Res., sub, acreage, view, sundeck, quiet   ■ 2D (garden level)   ⊨2T,1D   ⫚ Private   ★ TV,LF   Ⓦ Smoking, children, pets
↔ Hiking trails, golfing, tennis, waterslides
⇔ Downtown, Todd Mountain skiing, Wildlife Park, boating, fishing

☛ Attractive ranch-style home with country atmosphere. Magnificient view of Kamloops and the Thompson River Valley.

Imeson, Evelyne and Brett ✔ B&B
492 Sentinel Court, Kamloops, BC   V2E 2G6   ☎ (604) 374-0841

Take Hwy 5A south off Hwy 1, turn left at Summit Dr, then right at Monteith and at Sentinel.
$25S $30D   🍽 Meals   ► 4A
● Full, homebaked   🏠 Res., view, quiet, verandas   ■ 2D,1S   ⊨2T,1Q,1S
⫚3Private   ★ Air,TV,KF,LF,F separate entrance, parking   Ⓦ Smoking, pets, children   ∞Swedish, some French
↔ Park across the street, golfing
⇔ Aberdeen Shopping Mall, restaurants, numerous fishing lakes, skiing

☛ Relax and enjoy the view from the verandas surrounding two sides of the house.

Matter, John and Kitty (Matter House) ✔ CC
225 McGill Rd., Kamloops, BC   V2C 1M2   ☎ (604) 374-8011

From Trans Canada Hwy 1 take Exit Summit Dr west onto Columbia St and the exit at McGill.
$30S $45D $10Child $10Add.person   ► 5
✤Summer   ●Full   🏠Res., split-level, view, patio, quiet   ■2D   ⊨2T,1Q,1P
⫚2Private   ★Air,TV in guest room, parking   ⓌSmoking,pets not inside   ∞German
↔ Retaurants, shopping centre

☛ Cozy home in quiet residential area with beautiful view of Kamloops River and the Mountains. Warm and friendly atmosphere. Airport/bus pick-up available.

Tangen, Mrs. Terry
5354 Sunrise Dr., Kamloops, BC   V2C 5H4   ☎ (604) 573-3997

Phone for directions when in the area.
$30S $40D $5Child   ▣ Meals   ► 4
● Choice, homebaked   ♠ Res., ranch-style, view, balcony, patio, quiet   ■ 2D
╼2D   ⌐2Private   ★ Air,TV,F, parking, facilities for the disabled
♥   ⊕Non-smoking and non-drinking preferred
↔ Good hiking from property
⇔ Downtown Kamloops, large shopping Center, golfing, fishing, waterslides, Shuswap
lakes resort and recreational area

☞ Comfortable and spacious home is situated on the morning side of the mountain in
a well developed residential area on a large lot with an abundance of trees (some fruit
trees). Lovely view from bright and cheerful rooms, one opening up onto the balcony.
The air is fresh even on the hottest day. There is a small lap dog in residence.

Kaslo
(near Nelson; see also Kimberley, Crawford Bay)

Frary, Tony and Candace (Frary House)   ↙ B&B
Box 884, Kaslo, BC   V0G 1M0   ☎ (604) 353-7134

Located west of Hwy 31 on Thomson Rd, 8 km south of Kaslo and 13 km north of
Ainsworth Hot Springs. Follow signs.
$30S $40D   (Family rates available)   ▣ Meals   ► 6
● Full, homebaked   ♠ Rural, acreage, view, quiet   ■ 3D   ╼ 2T,1D,1Q,1P, cot
⌐Sh.w.g.   ★ Guest sitting room with fridge, separate entrance, parking
⊕Smoking, pets
↔ Fletcher Falls and beach on Kootenay Lake, wooded trails, mountain wilderness
hiking, cross-country skiing
⇔ Ainsworth Hot Springs, historic towns of Kaslo & Nelson, Kokanee Glacier Park,
Cody's Caves, Purcell Mountain Wilderness Conservation, Selkirk, New Denver ghost
town, world's longest free ferry ride on Kootenay Lake, golfing, fishing

☞ Large comfortable informal Swiss Chalet-style Frary house situated alongside
Fletcher Creek in a secluded wooded setting with spectacular view of the rugged
snow-capped Purcell Mountains across Kootenay Lake, which is one of the largest bodies
of clear, fresh water in the world. Scrumptious breakfasts include well-loved scones made
from an old family recipe. Bring comfortable walking shoes or your canoe or your
mountain-bike or skis.

Kelowna
(see also Vernon, Salmon Arm, Summerland)

Davidson, Norma and Don
3070 Boucherie Rd., Kelowna, BC   V1Z 2G7   ☎ (604) 769-5197

Located just off Hwy 97 South. Phone for directions.
$30S $35D $5Add.person   ► 4A,2Ch
● Full   ♠ Sub., bungalow, acreage, view, quiet, large sundeck   ■ 2D (main and lower
level)   ⊷ 2D   ⌐ 2Sh.w.h.   ★ TV,F,LF, parking   ⊛ Smoking, pets

↔ Neighborhood shopping centre, wineries and tours

⇔ Kelowna City centre, beaches, golfing, wterslides, hiking, restaurants, downhill and cross-country skiing, fishing, Provincial Parks

☛ Quiet and comfortable home with panoramic view of Okanagan Lake and mountains surrounded by fruit trees. Friendly hosts will serve breakfast on sundeck, weather permitting.

Graham, Pat (The Gables Country Inn & Tea House)   ⬑ B&B
2405 Bering Rd., Box 1153, Kelowna, BC   V1Y 7P8   ☎ (604) 768-4468

Located 1 block off Hwy 97 and 10 km south of Kelowna. Turn off Highway at Old
McDonald's Farm (Bering Rd) and go 1 block to Old Okanagan Highway.
$35S $40-45D $5Child $15Add.person   ► 6
● Homebaked   ♠ Village, older, acreage, view, patio, swimming pool   ■ 3D
⊷ 1D,1Q,2T   ⌐ 1Private, 1sh.w.g.   ★ F,TV in guest room, window seat, dormer or
bay window in each room, parking   ♥   ⊛ Smoking, pets
↔ Waterslide, recreation parks, orchards, shopping restaurants, bus at door
⇔ Excellent beaches, winery tours, hiking, golfing, downhill and cross-country skiing

☛ Charmingly-restored "Ann of Green Gables" heritage home with pine, brass,
antiques. Relax by the huge country fireplace or on the old-fashioned verandah.

B&B Travel Tip: *Traditionally, B&B is overnight accommodation only, but
nowadays people stay longer, sometimes even up to a week.*

Jarman, Robin and Celia (View to Remember)   ✔ B&B
1090 Trevor Dr., Kelowna, BC   V1Z 2J8   ☎ (604) 769-4028

Located just off Hwy 97 south. On arrrival in Kelowna phone for directions.
$30-35S $35-40D $5-10Child $15Add.person   ► 2-5
● Full, homebaked   ♠ Semi-rural, res., bungalow, view, patio, quiet   ■ 1D,1F
↵ 2D,1R,1P   ⏧ 1Sh.w.g., 1private   ★ F,TV, separate entrance, parking   ♥
Ⓦ Non-smoking preferred, drinking   ⌇ some German
↪ Neighborhood shopping centre, Prov. Park (walking, ski trails and fabulous views)
⇔ Golfing, winery (tours), large water slide, The Okanagan Lake (boat rentals, beaches),
historic Father Pondosy Mission, Last Mountain and other downhill ski resorts

☞ Friendly hosts, originally from Australia, invite guests to very warm atmosphere in
quiet and relaxing home, decorated with antiques and with a spectacular view of
orchards, lake and mountains.

Moelaert, John and Tasha (The Cat's Meow)   ✔ B&B
5299 Chute Lake Rd., Kelowna, BC   V1Y 7R3   ☎ (604) 764-7407

From downtown follow road which starts as Pandosy, then becomes Lakeshore Dr and
in turn becomes Chute Lake Rd. Look for sign on left.
$35S $40-45D   ► 4A
● Choice   ♠ Sub., acreage, sundeck, quiet   ■ 2D   ↵ 1D,1Q   ⏧ 1Ensuite
★TV,F, parking   Ⓦ Smoking, children, pets   ⌇ Dutch, Spanish
↪ Hiking trails through field and forest, panoramic view of Okanagan Lake
⇔ Downtown, beach, boat rentals, Okanagan Game Farm, various estate wineries,
golfing and tennis, Vernon, Penticton

☞ Large modern custom-built home is nestled among Ponderosa Pines in beautiful
Okanagan Mission district, a peaceful and quiet residential area. There is a Siamese cat,
called"Tasha" in the house.

Kimberley
(near Cranbrook; see also Fort Steele, Invermere, Crawford Bay)

Driver, Larry (Larry's B&B)
34-101 Ave., Kimberley, BC   V1A 1A3   ☎ (604) 427-4489

Phone for directions.
$20S $30D   🍽 Meals   ► 4-6
● Choice, homebaked   ♠ Res., older, patio, quiet   ■ 2 (upstairs)   ↵ 1Q,2S,1P
waterbed, crib   ⏧ 2Sh.w.g.   ★ TV,LF, off street parking, BETA movie machine
Ⓦ Non- smokers preferred
⇔ Kimberley Gardens and Mine (tours), North Star and Sullivan Ski slopes, Alpine
Slide, St. Mary's Alpine Prov. Park, Fairmont Hotsprings, Purcell Mountains for hiking

☞ Large home and large yard in quaint"Bavarian City"of the Rockies with Bavarian
Alpine architecture in a beautiful mountain setting and world's largest Cuckoo Clock in
the Kimberley Platzl Pedestrian Mall. Airport transportation can be arranged.

Ladysmith

(on Vancouver Island between Duncan and Nanaimo)

Trieger, S.& Betty Nickerson (Aneverly-By-The-Sea)   ✔ All Seas.B&B
3012 Yellow Point Rd., RR3, Ladysmith, BC V0R 2E0   ☎ (604) 722-3349

On Vancouver Island, follow Hwy l south out of the City to major intersection at
Southgate Mall and continue to first street. Turn left and follow Cedar Rd to bridge, turn
right. Continue on Cedar Rd 13 km to fork in road. Take left fork (Yellow Point Rd) and
travel another 13 km to house with long driveway on left.
$35S $45D $5Child $10Add.person   🍽 Meals   ► 4A,2Ch
● Full. homebaked   🏠 Rural, acreage, view, quiet, oceanfront   ■ 1S,1D,1Ste
(upstairs)   ⊨ 1S,1D,1R   ⺊ Sh.w.g.   ★ KF,LF,F,TV in guest room, computer
(modem and word-processing)   ⌇ some French and German
↔ Walks on rock beach, tidepools, clams, fishing, boating, canoeing, crabbing
⇔ Excellent restaurants, (gourmet and seafood), English pub, Nanaimo, Ladysmith,
Malaspina College, open ocean fishing and boating, hiking trails

☛ Year round privacy, peace and quiet - ideal place for artists, writers or anyone
wanting to think, create or just relax in harmony with nature. Hosts are involved with
computer networking on environmental issues world-wide. There is a cat in residence..

Lantzville

*(on Vancouver Island near Nanaimo; see also Parksville, Qualicum Beach, Pt.
Alberni, Nanoose Bay)*

Bartell, Lorraine and Jake   ✔ CC
7610 Lantzville Rd., S15, Box 11, Lantzville, BC V0R 2H0   ☎ (604) 390-4525

Phone for directions.
$25S $40-45D $5Child (over age 5) $5Add.person   ► 5
● Full   🏠 Sub., view, oceanfront, patio, quiet   ■ 1S,2D   ⊨ 1S,1D,1Q cot, crib
⺊ Sh.w.g.   ★ F,KF,LF,RV space, separate entrance, quiet sitting room   ♥
↔ Sandy beach, safe yard for children, swimming, health club
⇔ Fishing and boating, theatre, Mainland ferries, Wilderness Parksunique shopping,
Artisan Studio, Art Gallery

☛ Relaxing atmosphere with spectacular view from each window. Location is excellent
as a base for day trips to North, West and South of Island.

Masset
(on Queen Charlotte Islands; see also Sandspit, Queen Charlotte City)

Feller, Eliane and Charly (Alaska View Lodge)
Box 227, Tow Hill Rd., Masset, BC V0T 1M0

↙ CC

☎ (604) 626-3751

From Skidgate landing on QCI drive on paved highway along scenic coastline north to Masset. Situated 12.6 km from Masset Causeway.
$45S $55D   ▣ Meals   ▶ 4
● Full, homebaked   ♠ Rural, bungalow, acreage, view, quiet, oceanfront, isolated
2D (upstairs)   ⊢ 4S   ⏱ Sh.w.h.   ★ LF, parking   ⊛ Children, pets   ∾ French, Swiss-German
↔ Rainforest located on property, beach, Sangan and Chown rivers
⇔ Haida villages of Masset, Port Clements and Tlell, see the "Golden Spruce" and "old Haida Canoe", Rose Spit Ecological Reserve, climb Tow Hill or pick agates at Agate Beach

☞ Enjoy a truly memorable experience in a pleasant comfortable room with balcony and magnificient view of the ocean, Alaska on the horizon, bald eagles, seals, whales or look for an elusive Japanese glass float amidst miles of sun-bleached driftwood. There is a dog in the house.

Suna, Vladimir and Carol Sharpe (Harbourview Lodging)
Box 441, Masset, BC V0T 1M0

↙ CC

☎ (604) 626-5109

Take ferry from Prince Rupert to Skidegate (6 hours) and drive to Masset along the scenic Coastline Highway. Located next to Masset Harbour. (Phone BC Ferries)
$40-45S $45-50D   (Family rates available)   ● Extra   ▶ 4A,2Ch
● Compl. tea or coffee   ♠ Res., view, oceanfront, quiet   ■ 2D   ⊷ 2D,2R
⏱ Sh.w.g.   ★ TV in guest room, sauna, parking   ⊛ Pets   ∾ German, Czech
↔ Marina, Delkatia Wildlife Sanctuary, Ed Jones Haida Museum, hospital, gift shops
⇔ Beaches, Naikoon Prov. Park, walking at Rose Spit, hiking up Tow Hill, Trail to Golden Spruce(far banks of Yakoun River), logging camp at Juskatla

☞ Young host family in ver convenient location. Enjoy a visit in the largest town on the Charlottes. Kayaking and Wilderness trips can be arranged from here.

> **B&B Travel Tip:** *You can stay in a B&B when attending a wedding in another town. Many churches have lists of B&B's located nearby.*

Mayne Island
(near Saltspring Isle; see also Duncan, Victoria, Sidney, Surrey,Saanichton)

Crumblehulme, Brian and Mary (Fernhill Lodge)
Box 140, Mayne Island, BC   V0N 2J0   ☎ (604) 539-2544

Take Gulf Island Ferry from Tsawwassen or from Swartz Bay to Mayne Island. From ferry
dock follow Village Bay Rd to stop sign, turn right.
$35S (and up $50D (and up) $8Child (age 5-12)   ◙ Meals   ► 16
● Choice   ♠ Rural, Herb Garden, view   ■ 6   ⊷ 8D (and sleeping loft in F)
⌐6Ensuite   ★ Separate entrance, facilities for the disabled   ⊛ Pets, smoking
↪ Beaches, tennis courts, store, cycling, hiking
⇔ Lighthouse overlooking Active Pass, galleries, restaurant and pub

🖙 Gulf Island rustic farmhouse in nature lovers' paradise located in the middle of
Mayne Island with rooms re-created in Early "European", "Canadian or "American".
Enjoy herb plants and products, browse through the books or stroll in garden. Hosts will
meet ferry by prior arrangements. Bike rental, fishing charters available. Licenced
dining room on premises House specialty: "historical" and "nostalgic" meals. "

Somerville, Karen and Ken (Gingerbread House)   ↙ CC
Campbell Bay Rd., Mayne Island, BC   V0N 2J0   ☎ (604) 539-3133

Mayne Island is accessible by daily ferry service from both Tsawwassen and Swartz Bay
and interconnect from other Gulf Islands. Phone for directions.
$54-90S $59-95D $20Add.person   ◙ Meals   (Senior mid-week discounts)   ► 9
◘ Easter-Thanksgiving   ● Full, homebaked   ♠ Rural, histo., acreage, view, patio,
quiet, oceanfront, isolated   ■ 4D   ⊷ 3D,2T,1R   ⌐ 2Private, 2sh.w.h.   ★ F,
separate entrance, library, mooring and dockage facilities   ⊛ Restricted smoking, pets,
children min age 12 (not suitable for small children)
↪ Beautiful beach, boating, fishing, tennis, cycling, hiking
⇔ Discover Mayne Island, small airport for light planes

🖙 Elaborately ornamented Gothic-design cottage, built around the turn-of-the
Century, with fully modern services, but retaining the original woods and authentic style
and sitting high on the shore of Campbell Bay, a sheltered pocket inlet with the most
beautiful beach sites on the Gulf Island. Fine dining nightly for guests featuring local
farm fresh products. "Two-nights Get-A-Way Specials" available.

*B&B Travel Tip: You can go B&B all year around. Of course, it is most
popular when on vacation. And there are many more B&B's available in the summertime.*

Mill Bay

(on Vancouver Island near Duncan; see also Victoria, Fulford Harbour, Saltspring Isle, Sooke, Brentwood Bay)

Boan, Margaret and Bruce (Seaside Manor) ✔ B&b
580 Kilmalu Rd., RR2, Box 1, Mill Bay, BC V0R 2P0   ☎ (604) 743-2252

From Victoria take Hwy 1 north to Mill Bay. Continue through traffic lights at Kilmalu Rd. Turn right and go to intersection of Hollings and Wiskey Point Rds. Do not turn, continue onto gravel into trees and turn right into first driveway.
$40S $45D   ► 5
●Homebaked   ♠Rural, acreage, oceanfront, patio, quiet   ⊷1S,2D(upstairs)
⊷1S,2D   ⌐Sh.w.g.   ★Reading library for guests   ⓌSmoking, pets   ⌇Spanish

↤ Ocean Bay, quiet back roads for walking

⇔ Victoria, City of Totems and worlds largest hockey stick, BC Forest Museum, Chemainus (village of murals), Cowichan Bay (fishing village, sailing, fishing), Golf and Country Club, Butchart Gardens

☛ Beautiful tudor-style home on wooded acreage and tranquil Mill Bay, south part Vancouver Island. Enjoy a scrumptious breakfast on the sundeck overlooking the sea and rose garden. Watch seals and waterbirds in the Bay, and relax in quiet country atmosphere. There is a cat in the house.

Clarke, Clifford and Barbara (Pine Lodge Farm) ✔ B&B
3191 Mutter Rd., Mill Bay, BC V0R 2P0   ☎ (604) 743-4083

Take Island Hwy to Kilmalu Rd., turn east to Telegraph Bay Rd. Go north to Meredith, turn right and then left on Mutter Rd.
$35S $65D $10Child (under age 12)   ▣ Meals   ► 14A,4Ch
● Full,homebaked   ♠ 30-acres farm, hist., view, patio, quiet   ■ 7D   ⊷ 2T,6D,2R
⌐ 7Ensuite   ★ Air,TV,F, parking   Ⓦ Pets, restricted smoking
↤ Walking trails through maples, firs, cedars, dogwood, alder, hemlock and stately arbutus, pond with rainbow trout, fields and farm animals
⇔ Cowichan Bay resort area, City of Duncan, fishing, hiking, City of Victoria

☛ Charming Pine lodge built on the hillside overlooking the ocean with majestic arbutus trees and breath-taking views of sea and islands. Antiques and Collectables for sale in restored 1-room schoolhouse on premises.

Mission
(near Vancouver)

Brunger, Hans & Margita (Morningside)
8378 Aster Terrace., Mission, BC   V2V 5V7   ☎ (604) 820-0110

On Lougheed Hwy (No 7), turn north on Stave Lake Rd., go up to high ridge, turn left on Cherry Ave and continue to Aster Terrace (across from school). Map avail.
$20S $35D   ▥ Meals   ► 5A
● Choice, homebaked   🏠 Res., view, patio, quiet   ■ 1S,2D (ustairs)   ⊶ 1S,2D
⌐2Sh.w.g. ★ TV,F,LF   Ⓦ Smoking, children, pets   ⋙ French, German, Polish, some Spanish
↪ Westminster Abbey (Benedictine), Leisure Centre, excellent fishing, boating
⇔ Downtown Vancouver, Mt Baker (USA), Harrison Hot Springs and Lake, Cultus Lake

📢 Congenial and well travelled hosts in their recently built retirement home. Enjoy breakfast on upper deck with a panoramic view of Fraser Valley and Mt Baker. 14' fishing boat can be available for guests.

Nanaimo
(on Vancouver Island; see also Lantzville, Parksville, Qualicum Beach, Duncan)

May, Ken and Shirley   ✔ B&B
2415 Cosgrove Cr., Vancouver Isle, Nanaimo, BC   V9S 3N9   ☎ (604) 758-1423

Take ferry from Horseshoe Bay (W.Van) to Departure Bay and Rt 19 north.
$28S $38D $5Child(under age 12)   ▥ Meals   ► 4
● Choice, homebaked   🏠 Sub., res., deck, patio, quiet   ■ 2D,F   ⊶ 2D,P
⌐1Private   ★ LF, TV in guest room, parking, picnic lunches packed   ♥
Ⓦ Smoking, drinking, children min. age 2   ⋙ French
↪ Golfing at rear of property, beaches, swimming, tennis courts
⇔ Boating, fishing, ferries to Newcastle and Gabriola Islands, Parksville

📢 Friendly hospitality in home located close to Departure Bay. Hosts will pick up guests from ferry or bus depot. There is a cat in residence.

Molnar, Catherine (Carey House B&B)
750 Arbutus Ave., Nanaïmo, BC   V9S 5E5   ☎ (604) 753-3601

Turn left off Trans Canada Hwy at Townsite Ave, after passing downtown. Arbutus is 3rd Ave on right. To ensure booking please phone or write.
$25SS $40-45D   ▥ Meals   ► 4A
● Choice, homebaked   🏠 Res., quiet, older   ■ 2D   ⊶ 2D   ⌐ 1Sh.w.g.
Ⓦ Pets, smoking persons allergic to dogs and cats
⇔ Downtown Nanaimo, ferry and bus terminal, golf course, good restaurants, museums, wildlife sanctuary, chemainus murals

📢 Scottish hospitality. Centrally located quiet residential area surrounded by beautiful gardens. Hosts are seasoned world travellers. There are pets in the house.

Smith, Cameron and Evelyn ✔ CC
2359 Wild Dove Rd., Nanaimo, BC V9T 3T2 ☎ (604) 758-3974

Phone for directions.
$30S $35D ▶ 4
● Choice 🏠 Res., split-level, patio, quiet ■ 2D ⊨ 2T,1D,1P ⌐ 1Private,
1sh.w.h. ★TV in guest room, LF, parking
↪ Bus stop and excellent public transportation, small nature park
↔ Shopping Mall, downtown Nanaimo, ocean and beachs, craft shops

📞 Attractive home on a quiet street with friendly hospitality and gracious hosts.

Nanoose Bay
(on Vancouver Island near Nanaimo; see also Parksville, Lantzville)

Chapman, Lee and Leone (Oceanside) ✔ All Seas.B&B
Box 26, Blueback Dr., RR2, Nanoose Bay, BC V0R 2R0 ☎ (604) 468-9241

Located 25 km north of BC Ferry dock at Nanaimo on Rt 19. Turn right at Northwest
Bay Rd and follow signs for 7 km to 3161 Dolphin Drive in Schooner Cove.
$45S $55-60D $70-110Ste $40Cabin $15Add.person ▣ Meals ▶ 4A,2Ch
✚ May-Oct. ● Full, homebaked 🏠 Rural, acreage, view, patio, oceanfront, quiet
■2D,1Ste,cottage on beach ⊨ 2T,2D,1Q,1K,R, crib, cot ⌐ 1Private, 1sh.w.h.
★F,KF,LF, TV in guest room, separate entrance ♥
↪ Sandy beach, swimming, fishing, sailing, kayacking, marina, restaurant and pub
↔ Children's recreational park, Cathedral Grove, Little Qualicum and Englishman River
Falls, Qualicum Fish Hatchery, Nanaimo Ferry dock

📞 Modern home surrounded by tall evergreens, arbutus and rhododendrons with a
spectacular view of ocean, islands and mountains and located in Schooner Cove area.
Hosts are world travellers and enjoy conversation, good food and boating.

Wilkie, Marj and Herb (The Lookout)
Box 71, Blueback Dr., RR2, Nanaimo, BC V0R 2R0 ☎ (604) 468-9796

Travel north on Island Hwy 19 from Departure Bay Ferrie. Turn right at Nanoose Bay
traffic light (Petro Can Stn), and follow signs. Look for house on left side .5 km before
Cove at 3381 Dolphin Dr.
$40S $50D $65Ste ▣ Meals ▣ not Nov.5-Feb.28 ● Choice 🏠 Res., view,
wrap-around decks, quiet ■ 1S,1D,1Ste (main and upper level) ⊨ 1S,2Q,1R, cot
⌐ 1Sh.w.h.,1ensuite ★ F,KF,LF,TV in guest room, balconies,
parking ♥ ⊕Restricted smoking, pets
↪ Delightful walks through woods or by the ocean, Schooner Cove and Marina,
Fairwinds Golf Club, beaches, fishing, golfing
↔ Nanaimo, Parksville, Qualicum Beach, Courtenay, Comox

📞 Well travelled hosts in lovely West Coast Contemporary cedar home in natural rock
and bush setting; very quiet and secluded location with a spectacular panoramic view of
Georgia Straits and many of the islands.

New Westminster

(Vancouver; see also Surrey, White Rock, Langley, Ladner)

Field, Ethel (Royal City B&B)   ⌐ CC
127 Queen's Ave., New Westminster, BC   V3L 1J4   ☎ (604) 521-5733

Located in Queen's Park area. PHone for directions.
$35S $45D $10Child   ► 4A,1Ch
● Full, homebaked   🏠 Res., hist., riverview, sundeck   ■ 2D (upstairs)   ⊢ 2D,1Q
⊓ 1Sh.w.h.   ★ TV, parking, grand piano for musical guests   🐾 Pets
↔ Rapid transit to downtown Vancouver, shopping mall, adventure playground
⇔ International Airport, beaches, Vancouver Island Ferry, Deer Lake, Burnaby, BCIT
(Institute of Technology)

🐾 Grand old Heritage home, formerly the N. Nelson Mansion and built in 1912, with beamed ceilings, stained glass windows. Hosts enjoy sharing their comfortable place with guests. Delicious muffins are a house specialty. There is a dog and a cat inhouse.

Gilgan, June and Gordon (Gilgan's B&B)
333 Third St., New Westminster, BC   V3L 2R8   ☎ (604) 521-8592

From East: Off Hwy 1, take Second Brunette Exit and go to Columbia, turn right and continue to McBride. Turn left at Royal and then right on Third St. From South: On Hwy 99A cross Patullo Bridge. Turn right to Royal and right again.
$30S $40-60D $10Child   ► 4A,3Ch
● Full (Gourmet)   🏠 Res., older, patio, quiet, heated outdoor swimming pool, hot tub   ■ 1D,1Ste (in large cool basement)   ⊢ 1D,2Q,1R   ⊓ Sh.w.g.   ★ F, separate entrance, parking   🐾 Pets, smoking

↔ Fine restaurants, Skytrain to Vancouver, museums, parks and playgrounds

⇔ International Airport, Grouse Mountain (North Vancouver), U.B.C., Museum of Anthropology, Lower Mainland attractions

🐾 Queen Anne-style house built in 1907, competely renovated under supervision of an architect, and situated in established neighbourhood.

Kelly, Mrs. Theresa (The Kelly House B&B)   ✓ B&B
230-3rd St., New Westminster, BC   V3L 2R6   ☎ (604) 522-6564

From Hwy 1 take the New Westminster South cut-off and continue into City center to
Royal Ave. Proceed to 3rd St, turn right. House is on left side.
$25S $40D   ▶ 5A
●Cont.   ♠Res., hist., patio, quiet, central   ■1S,2D(upstairs)   ⊷5S,sofa   ⌐Sh.w.g.
★LF,TVin guest sitting room, parking ⓦSmoking,children,pets
↪ LRT Station to Vancouver,"Restaurant Row," heritage sights, churches
⇔ City Center, ferries to Vancouver Island, Fraser Valley

☞ Turn of the Century home in the exclusive Queens Park area, carefully refurbished
over the years and has old time atmosphere along with modern conveniences. There is a
cat in residence.

O'Connor, Donna and Michael (Phillips House)
323 Queens Ave., New Westminster, BC   V3L 1K1   ☎ (604) 522-8937

Phone for directions.
$40S $50-60D $10Child $10Add.person   ▣ Meals   ☎ 4

● Full, choice   ♠ Res., hist., quiet, wrap-around veranda   ■ 1D,1Ste (upstairs)
⊷1D,1Q   ⌐ 1Private, 1ensuite   ★ LF, parking   ♥   ⓦ Smoking
↪ Beautiful city park, skytrain rapid Transit to downtown Vancouver, fine dining,
Westminster Quay (riverside, shops, marina, restaurants
⇔ Ocean and beaches, Stanley Park, lower mainland attractions

☞ Grand and restored Heritage home, designed by City's most prestigious architect of
the Victorian era, exhibits the asymmetrical Queen Anne character with wide veranda's
corbeled brick chimneys and spacious halls with high ceilings. Home is often included in
Heritage Home Tours. There are pets in the house.

North Delta
(near New Westminster; see also Richmond, Surrey, White Rock)

Lahmer, Sheila and Allan (Delta View)   ✓ B&B
8036 Modesto Drive, North Delta, BC   V4C 4B1   ☎ (604) 594-2797

Located near Hwy 91 and River Rd. Phone for directions.
$25S $40D $5-10Child $10Add.person   ▶ 4
● Full, homebaked   ♠ Res., sub, split-level, acreage, swimming pool, view, patio,
quiet   ■ 1S,1D,F   ⊷ 1S,1D,1P(D)   ⌐ Private   ★ LF,TV in guest room, separate
entrance, parking   ♥   ⓦ Smoking, pets   ⋙ some French
↪ Delta Nature Reserve, Sungod Aquatic Centre and Arena, Fraser River, shopping
⇔ US Border, Vancouver Int.Airport, ferries to Vancouver Island, downtown Vancouver,
public markets, golfing, beaches, museums

☞ Spacious home in sunny Delta situated very conveniently to the Metropolitan
attractions and Lower Mainland. Enjoy the large secluded garden and heated pool.

Oliver

(near Penticton; see also Summerland, Grand Forks)

Wendt, Fred and Mary (Surprise Ranch)   ✔ B&B
S/50-C/9 RR2, Oliver, BC   V0H 1T0   ☎ (604) 498-2698

Located 5 km south of the Radio Observatory on the White Lake Rd (off Hwy 97) south
of Penticton.
$25S $35D $5Child $10Add.person   🍽 Meals   ► 9
✚ April-Oct.31   ● Full,homebaked   🏠 Farm, ranch-style, acreage, view, patio, quiet,
isolated   ■ 2D,1F   ↤ 4S,1D,1Q,1P   ⌐ Sh.w.g.   ★ TV in guest room
🚭 Smoking, pets
↔ cycling, walking, bird-watching
⇔ Dominion Astophysical Radio Observatory, wineries, lakes, Game Farm, golfing,
Penticton beaches

☞ Spacious farm home situated among pine trees and overlooking small quiet valley.
There are lots of farm animals including a large herd of European Wild Boars. The area
is famous for wild flowers (April-June). There are pets in the house.

Parksville

(on Vancouver Island; see also Qualicum Beach, Port Alberni, Nanaimo, Lantzville)

Chilton, Bob and Marg   ✔ B&B
19 Jenkins Place, Box 591, Parksville, BC   V0R 2S0   ☎ (604) 248-6846

From Island Hall go north to lights at Pym St. Turn left to Jenkins Place, turn left.
$30S $40-50D   (Children's rates)   🍽 Meals   (Reservation please)   ► 6
● Choice, homebaked   🏠 Downtown, res., patio, quiet   ■ 3D (upstairs)
↤2D,1Q, cot   ⌐ 1Private, 1sh.w.g.   ★ TV,LF,F, parking   ❤   🚭 Pets
↔ Georgia Pacific Mall, Community Park, tennis court, excellent fishing, beach, marina

☞ Attractive, modern home with country tranquility in town. Ideal location for day
trips to Long Beach Cathedral Grove and Tofino on the West Coast.

Hutchins, Jim and Jeanne (Hutchin's French Creek B&B)   ✔ B&B
RR3, S323, C49, Parksville, BC   V0R 2S0   ☎ (604) 752-5146

From Sandpiper Estate, off Island Hwy, go up Drew Rd, turn right to 1280 Gilley.
$35S $40D   ► 4A
✚ Feb.-Oct.   ● Choice   🏠 Res., patio, quiet, balcony   ■ 2D   ↤ 1D,1Q
(waterbed)   ⌐ 1Ensuite, 1private   ★ TV,F, parking   🚭 Pets
↔ French Creek Marina, beach
⇔ Cathedral Grove with huge trees, Englishman River Falls, Coombs Country Market
(with goats on roof), Rathtrevor Beach

☞ Located in the Sandpiper subdivision of French Creek in garden setting. Fishing
charters can be arranged. There is a Senior Poodle in residence.

Kern, Dea and Art (Marina View B&B)   ✔ CC
895 Glenhale Cr., Box 577, Parksville, BC   V0R 2S0   ☎ (604) 248-9308

Travel through Parksville past French Creek Market Place and turn right on Wright Rd
and left on Glenhale Cr. Look for sign at driveway.
$35S $45-50D $15Add.person   ► 7
✪ April-Sept   ● Res., split-level, view, oceanfront, quiet, patio   ■ 3D(upstairs)
■T,D,R   ⌐ Ensuite, sh.w.g.   ★ TV in guest room, separate entrance, parking
⊛Smoking, pets, not suitable for small children   ～ French, some German

↔ French Creek Marina, excellent
fishing, beachcombing, restaurant,
laundromat, store, bakery

⇔ Englishman River and Qualicum
River Falls, Cathedral Grove Prov. Park
(large trees), beaches, golfing

☛ Waterfront home in the heart of
vacationland with large deck
overlooking the Strait of Georgia,
islands and mountains beyond. Watch
the Alaska Cruise Ships sail by and
catch a glimpse of seals and otters
frolicking neary the shore and admire
the spectacular sunsets.

Parson
(near Golden; see also Invermere, Windermere)

Kelly-McArthur, Marilyn and Bryan (Taliesin Guest House)   ✔ CC
Box 101, Parson, BC   V0A 1L0   ☎ (604) 348-2247

Follow Hwy 95 south of Golden or north of Radium to Beards Creek Rd and continue for
1.2 km to Spence Rd. Turn right and take first turn. Sign posted.
$30S $40D   ▣ Meals   ► 10
● Full, homebaked   ♠ Rural, log home, mountain view, quiet, isolated   ■ 2S,2D
(upstairs)   ⊢ 2S,2D, bunks   ⌐ 1Sh.w.h., 1sh.w.g.   ★ TV,F,LF   ♥   ⊛ Smoking,
pets   ～ some French and German
↔ Enjoy the peaceful mountains, bird-watching, nature-appreciation, hiking
⇔ Canoeing, whitewater-rafting, Bugaboo Glacier, Yoho and Kootenay Nat. Parks,
Radium Hotsprings, Invermere Resort, windsurfing, swimming, fishing

☛ Log Cabin commanding spectacular views of the Columbia River Valley, the Purcell
and Rocky Mountains from its serene location on the Forested Columbia Valley benches.

Peachland

(near Kelowna; see also Summerland)

Ross, Mary and Tom (The Place)
S-13A,C-1 RR1, Peachland, BC   V0H 1X0   ☎ (604) 767-2155

From stoplight in Peachland go south and turn at Renfrew Rd. From Summerland go
north 20 km and turn left on Renfrew Rd to house on left side (No 6347).
$25S $35D   ► 4A
● Choice, homebaked   ♠ Village, ranch-style, view, patio   ■ 2D   ⊶ 2T,1D
⊓2Private   ★ TV,F, parking   ⑯ Smoking, drinking, children, pets
↔ Beaches, swimming boating, fishing, golfing, cross-country skiing
⇔ Cities of Kelowna, Penticton and Summerland

☞ Spacious home on large property with unparalelled view of Okanagan Lake and
mountains from garden deck surrounding the entire house. Hosts are seasoned B&B
travellers and know exactly what B&B guests are looking for. Delicious home-made
breads, scones, muffins and fruits served in season.

Pender Island

(near Saltspring Island; see also Fulford Harbour, Saturna Isle)

Baird, Bill and Louise (Billou)   ✓ CC
40 Anchor Way, RR1, Pender Island, BC   V0N 2M0   ☎ (604) 629-6207

Located on Thieve's Bay, and 40 min (BC Ferry) from Swartz Bay on Vancouver Island.
Call BC Ferries for schedule information.
$35S $50-55D   ► 4
Homebaked   ♠ Rural, view, quiet, oceanfront   ■ 2D   ⊶ 2T,1Q   ⊓ 1Sh.w.g.
★TV,F,KF, parking   ⑯ Pets
↔ Beach walks, marked hiking trails, boating, especially suited for outdoor enthusiasts.
⇔ Golf course, craft shop, restaurants, seasonal salmon fishing and eagle watching

☞ Contemporary cedar Island home overlooking Swanson Channel in the Pacific
Ocean. This secluded Gulf Island retreat has an idyllic setting with spectacular sunsets.

Gill, Joe and Jose (Ashley Downs)   ✓ CC
Hoosen Rd. RR1, Pender Island, BC   V0N 2M0   ☎ (604) 629-6459

On Pender Island, take Otter Bay Rd left onto Bedwell Harbor Rd. Turn right after
passing church on left and turn right onto Hoosen Rd. Look for house on right side.
$38S $65D   ► 4A
● Full   ♠ Rural, island home, acreage, 2 patios, quiet, trout pond   ■ 2D (upstairs)
⊶ 2T,1Q   ⊓ 1Sh.w.g.   ★ F, separate entrance   ⑯ Smoking, children, pets
↔ Great hiking and bicycling trails with wonderful views of other islands
⇔ Various beaches, Bedwell Harbour Resort with marina and Browning pub, swimming
pool, tennis courts, craft shops

☞ Quite unusual home with an old-world look, is a replica of an Old English Tavern
with a peek-a-boo view of the sea. Pond at rear of house is stocked with trout.

Port Alberni
(on Vancouver Island; see also Parksville, Qualicum Beach, Lantzville)

Farn, Mildred and Maurice (Port Alberni B&B)   ✓ B&B
4651 Elizabeth St., Port Alberni, BC   V9Y 6L8   ☎ (604) 724-1553

Phone for directions.
$25S $35D $10Add.person   ► 5
● Full (British-style)   ♠ Downtown, res., hist., view, patio swimming pool, quiet
■1S,1D(upstairs) ⊷2T,1D ⌐Sh.w.h. ★TV,parking ⍟Restricted smoking
↪ Harbour Quay ("Lady Rose"trips), marina (boat rentals, public swimming), excellent
restaurants, Pulp Mill (tours), golf course, Art Centre, museum, churches, bus depot
⇔ Sproat and Great Central Lakes, Robertson Creek Hatchery, Mount Arrowsmith,
Cathedral Grove, little Qualicum Stamp and Della Falls

☛ Irish/English hosts in conveniently located home just off the main road which leads
to the West Coast of Vancouver Island. Fishing boat charters can be arranged.

Parks, S.   ✓ B&B
3765 Morgan S.Cresc., Port Alberni, BC   V9Y 6B9   ☎ (604) 723-5475

From Nanaimo, take Hwy 19 north and Hwy 4 west to Port Alberni.
$25S $35D   ► 2-4
✖ June-Sept ● Full ♠ Res., patio, quiet ■ 1D,F ⊷ 1D,P ⌐ Sh.w.h.
  ★F,TV, parking
↪ Shopping Mall, city bus route, walking on the beach, hiking, whale watching, Lady
Rose ferry trip down Alberni Inlet
⇔ Robertson Creek (fish Hatcheries), McMillan Park Cathedral Grove, McMillan Paper
Mill, Martin Mars Water Bombers on Sproat Lake, fishing, swimming, trail to Della Falls
(for experienced hikers), golfing

☛ Ideal location from which to make trips to west coast of Vancouver Island.

Van Beek, Lavana and John (Stirling House)   ✓ CC
7941 Stirling Arm Dr., Port Alberni, BC   V9Y 7L7   ☎ (604) 724-1089

Leave Pacific Rim Hwy west of Port Alberni. Turn left on 2nd Rd onto McCoy Lake Rd
past orange bridge. Turn left again onto Stirling Arm Dr to house on right.
$30S $40D $10-15Child(free under age 6)   ► 4A,2Ch
● Choice, homebaked and homegrown   ♠ Farm, view, large sundeck, quiet
■ 2D,F ⊷ 1S,1D, large futon ⌐ 1sh.w.h. ★ TV,KF,LF ⍟ Smoking, pets
∾German, Dutch, some French
⇔ Downtown Port Alberni, Robertson Creek Salmon Hatchery, harbour and"MV Lady
Rose"trips to Ucluelet and Bamfield, hiking trails, family skiing

☛ Cozy country home with genuine musical Grand Father Clock (1896). Hostess is a
certified Reflexologist. Good location for day trips to west coast of island and Pacific Rim
National Park. Products from organic gardening. There are friendly pets in the house.

Powell River

(north of Vancouver; see also Gibsons, Roberts Creek, Heriot Bay)

Schulz, Erwing and Renate (Cedar Lodge Resort) ► CC
C-8 Malaspina Rd, RR2, Powell River, BC V8A 4Z3 ☎ (604) 483-4414

From Vancouver take Hwy 1 north to the ferry landing at Horseshoe Bay. Take the Langdale Ferry and then drive up the impressive scenic Sunshine Coast Hwy 101. At Earls Cove take another ferry ride to Saltery Bay and continue on Hwy 101 to 24 km. north of Powell River. Turn right on Malaspina Rd to Cedar Lodge.
$35S $35-49D $45F (and up)   🍽 Meals ► 14A,4Ch
● Cont.   ♠ Rural, acreage, view, patio, quiet   ■ 1S,8D (main and upper level), also separate house   ⊶ 1S,2T,3D,2Q,1P, crib   ⌐ 5Ensuite,2sh.w.g.   ★ TV,LF,KF (in separate house only)   ✋ Children in separate house only   ∿ German

↤ Okeover Arm Prov. Park (Gateway to Desolation Sound Marine Park), scuba diving, boating, sport fishing ⇔ Powell River, MacMillan Bloedel Pulmill Division (tours), Lund

☞ Experience the Pacific Coastal Wilderness surrounding beautiful lodge with a European touch and located at the doorstep of Desolation Sound Marine Park in a tranquil area north of Vancouver.

Prince George

(Central BC)

Welygan, Alice and Pete (Hart Hiway B&B) ↙ CC
702 Hart Hwy, Prince George, BC   V2K 2X4 ☎ (604) 564-8710/962-2063 (ask for Alice)

First house across John Hart Bridge (Nechako River) on Hwy 97 North.
$25S $32D $10Add. person ► 6A,2Ch
● Choice   ♠ Sub., acreage, view, patio   ■ 1S,1D,1Ste   ⊶ 1S,2D,R,P, crib
⌐ 2Sh.w.g.   ★ F,TV in guest room, parking, separate entrance   ∿ Dutch, Ukrainian
⇔ Fort George Regional Museum, good fishing and boating, Purden Ski Village and Tabor Mountain skiing, numerous lakes and public beaches, Quesnel, Cottonwood House and Bowron Lake Prov. Parks, beautiful public swimming pool

☞ Large modern home in the"Western White Spruce Capital"of the world. Town is built in a valley formed by the junction of the Fraser and Nechako rivers and serves as a jumping-off point for wilderness trips into the famous Peace River and Stuart Nechako region to the northwest. Hosts are very outdoorminded and love hiking, walking and cross-country skiing. There is a small Malti-Poo in residence.

Qualicum Bay

(on Vancouver Isle; see also Lasqueti Isle, Parksville, Port Alberni, Lantzville)

Cromer, Peggy Reine (Driftwood)   ⌐ B&B
RR3, Qualicum Bay, BC   V0R 2T0   ☎ (604) 757-0942/584-9325

Located on Island Hwy and 0.8 km beyond Crown & Anchor in Qualicum Bay.
$39S $45D $10Child (under age 6) $15Add.person   ▣ Meals   ► 4A,4Ch
● Full   ♠ Rural, older, 1.5 acres, oceanfront, quiet   ■ 2S,2D   ↤ 2T,2D
⌐1Private,1sh.w.g.   ★ TV,F,LF, parking
↪ Beach, good clamming, neighbourhood Pub, small restaurants and stores, Eagle
nesting grounds in surrounding Island Hwy woods
⇔ Quaint Qualicum Village, delightful shops, Qualicum Falls, Cathedral Grove, golf
course overlooking Georgia Strait, world famous salmon fishing

☛ All cedar Heritage home with real charm surrrounded by natural and formal
gardens. Adjoining annex Kennel (entire grounds completely fenced for pets)

McLeod, Shirley M. (The Geoid)   ⌐ CC
799 Canyon Cres. Box 2163, Qualicum Beach, BC   V0R 2T0   ☎ (604) 752-5759

Turn off Island Hwy in Qual.Beach by Urchin's Restaurant onto Garrett Rd, then 3
blocks.
$30S $35D $5Add.person   ▣ Meals   (Deposit required)   ► 8
✙ Summer   ● Cont. (Full on request)   ♠ Res., split-level, acreage, patio, quiet,
isolated   ■ 1S,1D,1F   ↤ 1S,2T,1D,1Q,1P   ⌐ 2Sh.w.g.   ★ Air,F, TV, sauna,
exercise equpment   ☝ Pets, children, restricted smoking
↪ Beach, well kept nature trails
⇔ Town Qualicum Bay, golf courses, churches, Urchin's Restaurant, Qualicum shopping
centre, live theatre, Legion, Arts and Cultural Centre,

☛ Located in a quiet peaceful place, the house is a very unusual museum and furnished
with antiques. "Relax and enjoy some of God's greatest beauties of the world".

Quathiaski Cove

(on Quadra Island near Campbell River; see also Black Creek)

Johnson, Joyce and Harold (Joha House)   ⌐ All Seas.B&B
Box 668, Quathiaski Cove, Quadra Isle, BC   V0P 1N0   ☎ (604) 285-2247

Take ferry from Campbell River (15 min) to Quathiaski Cove. Located 1 km from ferry
dock and end of private road. Call from Ferry parking lot and hosts will meet you.
$35-40S $55D $8Add.person   ► 6A
● Choice, homebaked   ♠ Rural, oceanfront, quiet   ■ 2D,1Ste,1F (upstairs and
garden level)   ↤ D,Q,P   ⌐ 1Private,1Sh.w.g.   ★ TV,F,parking   ☝ Restricted
smoking, pets, not safe for small children
↪ Private dock (Salmon Fishing Trips-pickup), beach walking, restaurants, shopping
⇔ Lighthouse, Indian Museum, Provincial beach park, forest trails and diving areas,
Cortes Island and Campbell River (short ferry rides)

☛ Contemporary island home with lots of wood and glass to reflect the mood of the
beautiful surroundings, overlooking the inside passage to Alaska.

Queen Charlotte Islands

(near Prince Rupert; see also Queen Charlotte City, Massett, Sandspit)

Queen Charlotte City

(on Queen Charlotte Islands; see also Massett, Sandspit)

Fortier, Patrick (South Moresby Hostel)   ✓ CC
Box 578, Queen Charlotte City, BC   V0T 1S0   ☎ Marine Operator

Ask for Prince George Marine Operator "South Moresby" N159009 Ch24, Cape
St.James. B&B is located 165 km south of Queen Charlotte City in South Moresby
National Park at Rose Harbour and only accessible by plane or boat.
$15-20S   🍽 Meals   ► 8
✚ Summer   ♠ Rural, very isolated, hist., view, oceanfront, very quiet   ■ Dormitory
in 2-floor cottage   ⇥ 8S   ⌐ 1shower share, outside outhouse   ★ KF   ⓦ Smoking,
pets, not suitable for people with medical problems or physically unfit   ⚒ Household
language is French
↔ Whaling Station remains, giant trees, heart of National Park and lots of nature, ocean
⇔ Haida village (access by boat or plane only), Sea Lion rookery

☞ Very remote and very simple home has electricity, hot water with alterntative
energy. Host's main goal is to offer a warm and happy place to stranded Kayakers in bad
weather. Travellers must phone for updated information on reservation. Guided trip by
boat in the area may by provided.

Hunter, Andrea and Keith (Misty Island Guest House)   ✓ CC
Box 503, Queen Charlotte City, BC   V0T 1S0   ☎ (604) 559-8224

Travel to the Island by ferry from Prince Rupert and Port Hardy (6 hours) or via Pacific
Western Airlines daily jet service from Vancouver. (Bus meets daily plane at Sandspit
airstrip and goes directly to guest house; or rent a car at the airport). Located on the
main street two blocks west of City Centre shopping area, across from the firehall.
$35-40S $45-50D $10Add.person (Discounts for longer stay and in off-season)   ► 4
● Full, homebaked   ♠ Res., village, view, large sundeck   ■ 1D,Ste
⇥2T,1Q,1P(Q)   ⌐ 1Private,1Sh.w.h.   ★ TV, parking, separate entrance
   ⓦ Smoking, min. stay 2nights in suite
↔ Beach on large waterfront property, hiking, birdwatching, swimming, canoeing and
kayaking (launch), City shopping,
⇔ Scuba diving, beach combing/crabbing/clamming, Haida Indian Museum and Village
with shops for silver, gold, argillite Haida jewellry and carvings, Yakoun River and world
renowned steelhead fishing, North Beach for agates and hunting for glass balls, chasing
crabs at low tide, excellent salmon and halibut fishing

☞ Modern waterfront home perches high above Skidegate Inlet with a specatucular
view of water and mountains on large property sloping down to the beach. Prior
reservation requested.

Kellie, Mary & Nancy Hett (Spruce Point B&B) ✔ CC
609-6th Ave., Box 735, Queen Charlotte City, BC V0T 1S0 ☎ (604) 559-8234

From Ferry landing drive through Queen Charlotte City to 7th St, turn left to 6th Ave.
$30-40S(Summer) $35-45D(Summer) (winter rates available) ▣ Meals ► 2A,1Ch
● Choice, homebaked ♠ Res., ranch-style, acreage, oceanview, oceanfront ■ 4D
⊷ 1D ⅂ Ensuite ★ KF,LF, parking ⋙ French
↪ Pottery studio and shop on property, fishing, hiking, local artist gallery, exceptional
bird watching, kayaking (rentals)
⇔ Downtown, Haida Museum, beautiful beaches, charter fishing and hunting

📢 Hosts are very knowledgable about the Islands and can arrange tours. Warm and
friendly atmosphere. Packed lunches available. Accommodation is in separate building
and there are also hostel facilities on the premises.

Revelstoke
(west of Alberta border near Banff; see also Parson)

Nelles, Larry and Rosalyne (L&R Nelles Ranch) ✔ CC
Hwy 23 S, Box 430, Revelstoke, BC V0E 2S0 ☎ (604) 837-3800

Located 2.2 km off Trans Canada Hwy 1 at Revelstoke on Hwy 23 South.
$25S $35D $10Child ► 6A,4Ch
● Full ♠ Rural, large Horse-Ranch, acreage, view, patio, quiet ■ 1S,2D,1F (main
and upper level ⊷ 4D,1Q,1R ⅂ 1Sh.w.h., 1sh.w.g. ★ F,TV in guest family room,
separate entrance, overnight horse accommodation
↪ Trail rides (horses), cross-country skiing, hiking, riding stables
⇔ Revelstoke Dam, Golf course, Mt Revelstoke Nat. Park (scenic drive to top),
Williamsons Lake, Mt MacKenzie ski area

📢 Very congenial hosts in spacious ranchhouse. Quiet country atmosphere and super
hospitality. Huckleberry jam a house specialty. There is a small pet poodle called
"Handsome" in residence.

Richmond
(Vancouver; see also New Westminster, Surrey, White Rock, Saltspring Isle, Delta)

Carsh, Rita L. ✔ B&B
6100 Canim Place, Richmond, BC V7C 2N2 ☎ (604) 274-1808

Located near Westminster Hwy and Gilbert Rd. Phone for directions.
$20-25S $35-40D ▣ Meals ► 6
● Full ♠ Sub., umbrella-sheltered sundeck ■ 5 ⊷ 2S,2T,1D, cot, crib
⅂ 1Ensuite, 1sh.w.g. ★ TV,F,LF, ample parking ♥ ✋ Pets ⋙ German,
Hebrew, some French
↪ Parks, shops, recreational facilities, golfing, Fantasy Gardens
⇔ International Airport, ferry terminal, universities, planetarium

📢 Well-travelled hostess understands the needs of visitors and likes to cater to them.
Conveniently located residential home situated in park-like setting..

Fomenko, Mrs. Elke
6600 Gibbons Dr., Richmond, BC   V7C 2E1

✓ B&B
☎ (604) 274-6413

Upon arrival in the area, contact hosts for directions.
$25S $35-40D

► 4

● Full   ♠ Res., acreage, quiet, patio, solarium with hot tub   ■ S,D   ⊷ T,Q
⌐ 1Private, 1sh.w.h.   ★ F,TV in guest room   ⚑ Children min. age 8-10
⤳German, Russian
↔ On bus line to downtown Vancouver, Richmond
⇔ Richmond Center, International Airport, ferries to Vancouver Island

☞ European hospitality at its best in lovely ranch-style home with small acreage of gardens, fruit trees and flowers. Hosts will pick up and return guests to Airport.

Lewis, Joyce and Bob (Joyce's B&B)
10880 Granville Ave., Richmond, BC   V6Y 1R4

✓ B&B
☎ (604) 278-8584

Located between No 4 and 5 Roads. Phone for directions.
$27S $35D

► 5

● Full, homebaked   ♠ Res., sub., split-level, acreage, patio, quiet   ■ 2D
⤙2D,1R   ⌐ 1Ensuite,1sh.w.h.   ★TV in guest room, separate entrance, parking
⚑Restricted smoking, drinking, pets, children min age 6
↔ Aquatic Centre, jogging track, Malls, live theatre, restaurants, Fantasy Gardens
⇔ Downtown Vancouver, International Airport, Hwy 99 Freeway

☞ Friendly hospitality in comfortable home situated in quiet and convenient location.

McKay, May and Alec
7180 Blundell Rd., Richmond, BC   V6Y 1J4

✓ B&B
☎ (604) 278-8928

Phone for directions.
$30 $40D $10Add.person   ▣ Meals

► 5

● Choice, homebaked   ♠ Sub., acreage, older   ■ 1S,2D   ⊷ 1D,2T,1S
⌐1Sh.w.g.   ★TV,F,KF,LF
↔ Bus stop, shopping mall, fishing marina
⇔ Airport, restaurants, parks and recreational facilities

☞ Comfortable home with country atmosphere next to the city. Hosts will pick-up and return guests to Airport if requested.

Sohn, Ken and Heidy ✓ CC
8171 Corless Place, Richmond, BC V7C 4X4 ☎ (604) 271-8566

Go west on Westminster Hwy to No. 1 Rd and south to Blundell. Turn left and take first right (Claybrook) and first right again (Corless) and to end.
$30S $35D ► 3
● Choice 🏠 Res., patio, quiet, view ■ 1S,1D (upstairs) ■ 1S,1D ⌐ 1Sh.w.g.
★ TV, parking ㊕ Restricted smoking, drinking, pets ⁂ German, French
↔ On major bus route
⇔ Downtown Vancouver, shopping, dining, International Airport, Ferry Terminals

☞ Home is situated on a delightfully quiet crescent with a lovely view of the North Shore Mountains. There is a dog and a cat in the house.

Vermegen, Ingrid and Simon (Vermegen's B&B) ✓ CC
2360 #8 Rd, Richmond, BC V6V 1S1 ☎ (604) 270-1981

Located in Richmond on the outskirts of Vancouver. Phone for directions.
$25S $40D $10Child(age 2-10) $10Add.person ► 4-6
● Cont., homebaked 🏠 Rural, older, acreage, patio, quiet ■ 2D (upstairs)
⎵ 2S,1D ⌐ 1Sh.w.g. ★ TV,LF, parking, bicycles can be available ♥
㊕Smoking ⁂ Dutch, some German

↔ Fraser River, bicycling, baseball diamond

⇔ International Airport, City of Vancouver

☞ Very unique, remodeled older home situated on 1 acre of property in rural surrounding. European hospitality. Pick-ups from Airport may be available. There is a friendly dog in residence. Host is Exec. Chef at Vancouver Trade & Convention Centre.

B&B Travel Tip: *You can stay in a B&B when you are hiking the trails. In Ontario there are many B&B's along the famous Bruce Trail and some of these hosts will even forward your car and gear for you to the next B&B on the trail.*

Salmon Arm

(near Vernon; see also Sorrento)

Bodnar, Gisela (Silver Creek Guest House)   ⌐ B&B
6820-30 Ave SW, Salmon Arm, BC   V1E 4M1   ☎ (604) 832-8870

At Flashing light west of Salmon Arm, turn off to Salmon River Rd. Follow road for 2.5 km, turn right on 30th Ave SW and drive for 1.5 km. Look for sign on left side.
$21S $28-30D $8Horses overnight $5-10Child   ◙ Meals   ► 6A,2Ch
● Choice   ♠ Small ranch, patio   ■ 1S,2D   ⌐ 2S,2D, cots   ⌐ 2Sh.w.h.
   ★TV,F,LF   ♥   ⍟ Restricted smoking   ⌁ German
↔ Bicycling, cross-country ski trails
⇔ Large Community Centre with swimming pool and hot tub, Shuswap Lake, beaches, boating, fishing, Salmon Arm, canoeing

☞ Charming spacious log house with beautiful view from deck of Mount Ida (Fly Hill mountains) and Salmon River Valley.

Moore, Marie and Ray (Cindosa)   ⌐ CC
3951-40th St.N.E., Salmon Arm, BC   V1E 4M4   ☎ (604) 832-3342

Located 4 km from downtown Salmon Arm. At 1st traffice light entering Salmon Arm from the east, turn right on 39th St NE and follow signs.
$25S $35D $10Child(under age 10)   ◙ Meals   ► 10A,4Ch
● Full, homebaked   ♠ Rural, hobby-farm, ranchstyle, acreage, quiet   ■ 1S,2D, plus cottage (2D,1S)   ⌐ 2T,4D   ⌐ 1 Private, , 1sh.w.h.   ★ Air,LF, separate entrance, TV in guest room   ⍟ Pets
↔ Quiet roads for walking or hiking, viewpoint overlooking part of Shuswap Lake
⇔ Drive-in Theatre, golfing, local fruit stands, waterslide, shopping mall, beach

☞ Comfortable modern home on 10-acre hobby farm located in a quiet rural setting. Hostess is very active with the farmer's market and doll collection. Pick-up available.

Sandspit

(on Queen Charlotte Island; see also Queen Charlotte City, Masset)

Waseyleski, Bonita (Seaport B&B)   ⌐ CC
Box 244, Beach Rd., Sandspit, BC   V0T 1T0   ☎ (604) 637-5698

Take BC Ferry from Prince Rupert to Skidegate (6 hours) and then take the 20 min. Ferry to Sandspit (Alliford Bay),(4 or more crossings in summer). Follow road into Sandspit (Beach Rd) and look for house with B&B sign on right facing ocean.
$25S $35D $4Child   ► 4A,2Ch
✚ Feb.-Nov.   ● Full (free range eggs)   ♠ Res., village, view, ocean across the street, patio, quiet   ■ 2D(in trailer) and additional guest facilities planned   ⌐ 3S,1P
⌐ Sh.w.h.   ★ TV, separate entrance, parking   ⍟ children min. age 6
↔ Airport, shopping, restaurants, Sandspit Inn, beachcombing, fishing
⇔ Ferry terminal to Queen Charlotte City and Skidegate, trout fishing in Mosquito Lake, Gray Bay beach swimming, Haida villages with old totem poles

☞ Tours to South Moresby and around the Charlottes can be arranged by private companies. Boats for rent and fishing. Hunting guides available.

Saturna Island

(near Sidney; see also Pender Isle, Fulford Harbour)

Gill, Bakhshish (Breezy Bay B&B)
Box 40, Saturna Island, BC   V0N 2Y0   ☎ (604) 539-2937

Located on Gulf Island on Ferry Route (1 transfer) between Vancouver and Victoria.
$35S $50D   ► 8A,1Ch
✚ Summer   ● Full, homebaked   ♠ Farm, hist., view, oceanfront   ■ 1S,3D,1F
(upstairs)   ⊶ 1S,3D,1R, cot   ⊓ 3Sh.w.g.   ★ F,LF, library, lounge, sunroom,
badminton court   ⊛ Restricted smoking, pets
↔ Private beach, cliff hike for panorama sunset view
⇔ Gulf of Georgia, Straits of Juan de Fuca, whale route, beaches, excellent bicycling

☞ Restored Century home surrounded by 30 acres fields, woods, cliffs and fruit trees
that create a very tranquil ambience.

Sidney

(near Victoria; see also Brentwood Bay, Sooke, Mill Bay, Saanichton,
Fulford Harbour, Duncan)

Graham, Dennis and Kay (Graham's Cedar House B&B)   ✔ CC
1825 Landsend Rd., RR3, Sidney, BC   V8L 3X9   ☎ (604) 655-3699

Located 1 km west of Swartz Bay Ferry Terminal off Hwy 17.
$30S $38-58SD $5Child $10Add.person   ► 6A,2Ch
● Full, homebaked -   ♠ Rural, acreage, patio, quiet   ■ 1D,1F   ⊶ 3D,1R
⊓Sh.w.g.   ★ KF,LF, separate entrance, parking   ⊛ Smoking, drinking,pets

↔ BC ferries to Vancouver and Gulf
Islands, restaurants, marinas, public
beach access, hiking trails, many hours
of country walking

⇔ Ferries to USA, Victoria Airport,
Butchart Gardens, golfing, tennis,
horseback riding, boating, Sooke
Harbourhouse (fine dining), entrance to
West Coast Trail

☞ Charming new cedar home in
woodsy country setting with wrapped
around deck and located in the townsite
of "Sidney by the Seas".

Sooke
(on Vancouver Island's west coast near Victoria)

Altman, Inger and Bob (Altman's B&B)
6945 Possession Pt. Rd., RR4, Sooke, BC V0S 1N0

✔ Sooke B&B
☎ (604) 642-3030

From Victoria, take Hwy 14 to Sooke. Stay on main road for 1.6 km past traffic light, turn left onto Whiffenspit Rd., left on Dufour and right to Possession Pt Rd.
$70D $5child   ► 5A,1Ch
● Full, choice   ♠ Village, view, patio, oceanfront, quiet   ■ 3D   ⊢ 2T,1Q,1P, crib
⌐ 1Sh.w.g.,whirlspool spa   ★ TV, parking   ⊛ Pets   ⌇ German
↔ Sooke Harbour House (fine dining), Whiffen Spit, year round salmon fishing
⇔ Victoria, Sooke Pothole Park, East Sooke Park, French Beach, West Coast Trail

☞ Family home by the sea with beautiful view of Sooke Harbour Basin and Olympic Mountains. Enjoy the vista from the sundeck and watch sea birds and seals. Fishing charters can be arranged. There are three cats and a dog in the house.

Clare, Diana (Malahat Farm Guest Cottage)
Anderson Rd., RR2, Sooke, BC V0S 1N0

✔ Sooke B&B
☎ (604) 642-6868

From Victoria, take Hwy 1 to Hwy 14 and travel 12.8 km west. Turn right on Anderson Rd.
$65D $15Add.person   ► 9
● Full, homebaked   ♠ Farm, hist., quiet   ■ 3D (upstairs), and cottage   ⊢ 2Q
⌐ 2Private   ★ F,KF, separate entrance, guest sitting room   ♥   ⊛ Pets
↔ Explore the farm, beachcombing, birdwatching, hiking, surfing, picnics, river
⇔ Sooke Harbour House, French Beach, salmon fishing charters,Victoria

☞ Very secluded farm with fully restored and furnished heritage house and many heritage (classified) trees including a Monkey Puzzle tree. Tranquil pastoral setting.

> **B&B Travel Tip:** *Do not expect the same service you ususally get in a hotel. The service in a B&B is completely different. It is, in fact, even better, because of all the little things the hosts will do for you and the information they will give you (many extras that cannot be bought in a hotel!). In fact, they will be happy and so proud to tell you all about the local facilities, happenings and the history of their hometown.*

Knight, Janet and Ken (Burnside B&B) ✔ Sooke B&B
1890 Maple Ave., Box 535, Sooke, BC   V0S 1N0 ☎ (604) 642-4403

Follow Hwy 14 from Victoria to Sooke Centre and continue to Maple Ave, turn right.
$35-65S $45-75D $15Child $15Add. person ► 13
● Homebaked   ♠ Village, res., hist., acreage, view, quiet   ■ 5D (upstairs)
↤2T,3D,2Q,1R, crib   ⏗2Sh.w.g.   ★F,TV in guest room, parking, separate entrance

↪ Sooke House (World Class Gourmet Dining), cozy local tea house, cafe and restaurant, fishing charters, beachcombing, Reginional Museum, 1870 Moss Cottage

⇔ Entrance to West Coast Trail, downtown Victoria, Butchard Gardens, golfing, ferries to Mainland, major shopping malls

🖐 Classic Georgian style Heritage home (1870), completely renovated and decorated with a touch of yesteryear with a commanding view of beautiful Sooke Harbour and the Olympic Mountains. There are two dogs in the house.

Morton, Betty and George (House on the Bay) ✔ Sooke B&B
7954 West Coast Rd., RR4, Sooke, BC   V0S 1N0 ☎ (604) 642-6534

From Victoria, take Hwy 1 to Hwy 14 and go 6.4 km west of traffic light in Sooke. Watch for sign on the cliff on right.
$85D $10Child $15Add.person   ▣ Meals ► 6A,1Ch
● Full, homebaked   ♠ Rural, acreage, wide ocean view, quiet, secluded   ■ 2D
↤ 2Q,1P, cot   ⏗ 2Ensuite (each with hot tub)   ★ 2F, sliding doors to individual
patio, parking   ✋ Restricted smoking
↪ Beach across the road, salmon fishing, walking and hiking in quiet country roads with
abundant wild life, watch numerous birds, giant Blue Heron, Bald Eagles, seals, sea
otters and orcas (killer whales)
⇔ World Class Gourmet Seafood restaurant, Victoria, Butchart Gardens, golfing,
entrance to Pacific Rim Park

🖐 Luxurious modern Western style home located in the south west coast area of
Vancouver Island in a secluded setting, high on a cliff and sheltered by trees and rock
bluffs with a panoramic view of Sooke Bay and the Straits of Juan de Fuca.

Sorrento
(near Salmon Arm; see also Falkland, Kamloops)

Eberle, Linda and Verna Langevin (Evergreens)   ✔ B&B
Box 117, Vimy Rd., Sorrento, BC V0E 2W0   ☎ (604) 675-2568

Located in west end of village. Phone for directions.
$25S $35D   ► 6A,3Ch
● Full   ♠ Res., large sundeck, mountain view, acreage   ■ 3D   ⊶ 3D,R
⌐1Sh.w.g.   ★ KF, lounge, separate entrance, ground level accommodation
⊛Restricted smoking, drinking, controlled pets
↔ Small shopping centre, restaurants, Shuswap Lake, boat trips, tea garden with gazebo
in back yard, small bird zoo
⇔ Golfing, Adams River Salmon Run, cross-country skiing, Okanagan Fruit Valley

🖚 New cottage-style home surrounded by evergreens in picturesque historic village.

Summerland
(near Penticton,; see also Kelowna, Oliver, Peachland)

McCuaig, Marion and Ian (Peach Valley B&B)   ✔ B&B
RR2, Summerland, BC V0H 1Z0   ☎ (604) 494-1078

Phone on arrival in Summerland and hosts will meet travellers.
$30S $40D $10Child   ▣ Meals   ► 5
● Full, homebaked   ♠ Rural, acreage, view, patio, quiet   ■ 1S,2D   ⊶ 1S,2D
⌐ 2Private, 1sh.w.h.   ★ Air,LF,F,TV, facilities for the disabled, children welcome
⊛Restricted smoking and drinking, pets by special request   ⋙ some French
⇔ Okanagan Lake beaches, boating, fishing, fish hatchery, wineries, fruit packing,
Agriculture Canada Research Station, cross-country and Apex Alpine skiing.

Ursuliak, Mary and Ernie (Lakeside Inn)   ✔ CC
Site 104, RR4 Summerland, BC V0H 1Z0   ☎ (604) 494-1825

Located 5 km south of Summerland east off Hwy 97 at Johnson St in Trout Creek. Look
for 7219 Nixon Rd.
$30S $45D   ► 5
● Choice   ♠ Res., lakefront, quiet, decks   ■ 1S,2D (main and upper level)
⊶1S,2D   ⌐ Sh.w.h.   ★ TV,2F, parking   ⊛ Restricted smoking, pets
↔ Beach, safe swimming, tennis court
⇔ Museum, Research Station, winery, golf course, library, swimming pool, town of
Summerland and major shopping, skiing (downhill and cross-country), Penticton

🖚 Located on the shore of beautiful Lake Okanagan in suburban residential area.
Hostess is a potter and has her own studio and Art Gallery on the premises.

Surrey

(near Vancouver; see also White Rock, Delta, New Westminster, Coquitlam)

Bury, Chuck and Glad (White Heather)   ⌐ B&B
12571-98th Ave., Surrey, BC   V3V 2K6   ☎ (604) 581-9797

Follow Hwy 99 to 96th Ave. Travel west to 126th St and north to 98th Ave. Turn left.
$24S $35-39D $12Child $6RV(electric hook-up)   ► 4A,2-3Ch
● Full, homebaked   ♠ Res., sub., view, patio, quiet, sunroom   ■ 1D,F   ⊣ 1D,1P
⊓ 1Sh.w.g., 2ensuite   ★ F,parking   ⊛ Smoking, pets
↔ Local bus routes connecting to all Vancouver bus lines and ski train, good restaurants
⇔ Grouse Mt.Sky Lift, golfing, downhill ski areas (Grouse Mt., Seymour, Cypress Bowl)

☞ Panoramic view of North Shore Mountains and Fraser Valley farmlands. Well travelled hosts are very knowledgeable about local area, as well as Vancouver Island. Pick-up at airport or train station can be arranged.

Cowan, Wes and Peggy (Guestdale Manor B&B)   ⌐ B&B
5639 Kilmore Cr.W., Surrey, BC   V3S-6R7   ☎ (604) 576-8230/576-8618

Located closest to Cloverdale & White Rock. From Hwy 10 travel 1 block to Kilkenny. Turn left onto Kilmore Cr E, which runs into Kilmore Cr W and look for sign.
$45-50D $60F   ▣ Meals   ► 8
● Full   ♠ Rural, res., acreage, heated swimming pool, patio   ■ 3 (main and upper floor)   3D,1Q, futons   ⊓ 3ensuite   ★ LTV in guest room, room locks, whirl pool
⊛ Restricted smoking
⇔ Historic Cloverdale (shops, antiques, flea markets, historic Transportation Centre and Raceway/Rodeo), scenic White Rock, US border, ferry terminal, Guildford shopping Centre, Vancouver International Airport, Vancouver and north shore, Abbottsford

☞ Former Ontario residents in spacious Heritage-style home on large lot with circular driveway was the original home on the acreage, now turned subdivision.

Terrace

(northern BC)

Schoenfeld, Joe and Cecile (Terrace Bed & Breakfast)   ⌐ CC
4732 Straume Ave., Terrace, BC   V8G 2C5   ☎ (604) 635-6154

Coming from the East on Hwy 16, follow the sign "City Center" to B&B between Eby and Sparks, just one block from R.E.M.Lee theatre.
$30S $35D $10Child   ▣ Meals   (Senior's Rates available)   ► 4A,2Ch
● Choice   ♠ Downtown, res., view, patio, quiet   ■ S,D,F (lower level)   ⊣ S,T,D, crib   ⊓ Sh.w.g.   ★ LF, separate entrance, parking   ⊛ Smoking, pets welcome outside or in shed   ♥(in summer)   ⋙ German, French, some Spanish
↔ Tennis courts, jogging circuit, swimming pool, hiking and nature trails, ice-skating
⇔ Mount Layton Hot Springs Resort (all year), Lakelse Provincial Park and Furlong Bay Beach, BC Heritage Museum, steelhead/salmon fishing, ocean (Kitimat), boat charters

☞ Cozy home with European atmosphere located in the Skeena Valley, world reknown for its salmon and steehead fishing, a hunters' and nature lover's paradise and situated in very quiet neighbourhood. Pick ups can be arranged. There is a cat in the house. Pets welcome outside or in the shed.

Tofino
(on Vancouver Island's west coast; see also Ucluelet)

Bristow, Joan and Jim (Park Place) ✔ CC
341 Park Street, Tonquin Park, Tofino, BC V0R 2Z0 ☎ (604) 725-3477

Please phone for directions.
$30-40S $35-45D $15Child $15Add.person ► 4A,2Ch
●Full,homebaked ♠Rural, acreage, view, patio, quiet, oceanfront ■1D,1Ste(main and upper floor) ◄2T,1D,1Q,1R, crib ⌐1Ensuite, 1sh.w.g. ★F,TVin guest room ⦿Pets
↔ Treed acreage fronting open Pacific, private sandy beach, beachcombing, exploring tidal pools, strip fishing for salmon at beach level
⇔ Miles of sandy beaches, hiking trails, rain forests, golfing, kayaking, Tofingo airport, art gallery, by boat: Hot springs, Meares Isle - fishing and whale watching charters

🖝 Contemporary oceanfront home atop the rocks with circular glassed living room and decks providing vantagepoint for viewing gray whales, dolphins seals and eagles. Enjoy the magnificient sunsets and thrilling winter storms. Relax and experience the splendor of the West Coast. There is a black Lab called "Jamie" in residence.

Mae, Olivia A (Silver Cloud) ✔ B&B
Box 249, Tofino, BC V0R 2Z0 ☎ (604) 725-3998

Take Hwy 4 across Island to Tofino. Turn right before Crab Dock Rd, past motel.
$70-75D $115Ste (Deposit required) (Minimum 3 nights) ► 6-8
●Cont. ♠Village, acreage, oceanfront, patio, quiet, sunroom ■1Ste,1D
◄1D,1Q,2T,1sofa ⌐1Sh.w.h.,2ensuite ★separate entrance, TV in guest room, parking, use of 12 ft boat ⦿not suitable for small child ∿Danish
↔ Village centre, beach in front garden, great fishing
⇔ Pacific Rim National Park, whale watching boat and air charters

🖝 Unusually decorated home with beautiful view of green islands. Watch grey whales, dolphins, bald eagles. Warmest weather all winter in evergreen playground.

Ucluelet
(on Vancouver Island's west coast; see also Tofino)

Burley, Ron and Micheline Riley (B&B at Burley's) ✔ CC
1078 Helen Rd, Ucluelet, BC V0R 3A0 ☎ (604) 726-444

Take Hwy 4 to Port Alberni, and continue across the island to Ucluelet.
$30S $35-45D $15Add. person ▣ Meals ► 8A
● Cont. (buffet-style) ♠ Village, res., acreage, oceanfront, patio, quiet ■ 6D,F
◄ 2T,2D,3Q(2 are waterbeds), cots ⌐ 2Sh.w.h. ★ TV,F, parking, boat available ⦿ Smoking, Pets ∿ French
↔ Beach and wharf, village centre, hiking, harbour and ocean, fish plants
⇔ Pacific Rim Nat. Park, Long Beach, lighthouse, logging activities, Tofino Airport

🖝 Large waterfront home overlooking Ucluelet Inlet. Watch the fishing fleet sail by. Spectacular views. Especially suitable for photographers.

Valemount

(south-east of Prince George; see also Jasper-Alta, Eagel Creek, Clearwater)

Kraemer, Anne and Bernie (Summit River Lodge)
Box 756, Valemount, BC   V0E 2Z0   ☎ Radio Operator Valemount JK Channel N690-494

Located on the Yellowhead South Hwy 5 and 21 km south of Valemount.
$45D $10Child (under age 5 free) $10Add. person   🍽 Meals   ► 10A,10Ch
●Full   🏠Rural, 40-acres, view, patio, quiet, isoltated   ■ 5D (main and upper level)
↦ 5Q,5R   ⌐ 2Sh.w.g.   ★ LF,TV (satellite)   ⊛ Pets   ⌇German
↔ Trout fishing in camp River Creek on property, fishing, hiking into mountains starts
at doorstep, hunting, snowmobiling and cross-country skiing
⇔ Mount Robson Park, Jasper National Park

☛ Spacious log cabin situated on creek with crystal clear water at the foot of Mount
Thompson at an elevation of 900 m in the Albreda Valley with a beautiful view of the
Albreda Glacier. Enjoy ultimate comfort and relaxation in an authentic log house.

Simpson, Loretta (Simpson's Farm Vacation)   ✓ B&B
Box 584, Valemount, BC   V0E 2Z0   ☎ (604) 968-4453

Located 20 km west of the Tete Jaune Cache junction on the right side of Hwy 16 (just
4.8 km beyond the rest area at Small River).
$25S $40D $5Child(under age 8) $10Add.person   🍽 Meals $10Tours   ► 6
● Full,homebaked, 160-acrea farm, split-level, view   ■ 3D   ↦ 2T,2D
⌐1Sh.w.g.,1sh.w.h.   ★TV,F, separate entrance
(walk) Walks along mountain stream flowing through property, extensive pasture land,
fishing

☛ Working farm in beautiful Robson Valley. Large white house has a stuffed grizzly
bear, shot by former host some years ago. There are three young children who enjoy
visiting with guests and showing them the farm. By special arrangement, hosts will give
2-hrs guided tours of the beautiful mountain valley cattle range.

Vancouver Island

*(see Campbell River, Chamainus, Courtney, Duncan, Ladysmith, Lantzville,
Nanaimo, Parksville, Port Alberni, Qualicum Beach, Tofino, Ucluelet*

B&B Travel Tip: *If you are on the road and decide to stay in a B&B, do
phone ahead from a nearby phone (best: take a break at lunchtime and choose the
B&B for the coming night). The hosts will appreciate your consideration and if
their rooms are booked, they can also direct you to another B&B host. (This is not
convenient, if you appear at the door in the evening without prior notice.)*

Vancouver

(see also Coquitlam, New Westminster, Richmond, Surrey, Whistler, White Rock, Gibsons)

Armstrong, Mr. & Mrs. J. (Grouse Mountain B&B)   ✔ B&B
900 Clements Ave., North Vancouver, BC V7R 2K7   ☎ (604) 986-9630

Take Trans-Canada Hwy 1 across Second Narrows Bridge and continue to Capilano Rd.
Turn right and right again at Montroyal, then left at Cedarcrest and left at Clements.
$50-60D   ▣ Meals   (please phone to reserve)   ► 4
● Full, gourmet   ♠ Res., patio, 2decks, view,   ■ 1Ste,1D   ⊷ 2D,R,P   ⸀ 1Ensuite,
1sh.w.h.   ★ LF,F, private entrance, ample parking, piano   ⓌRestricted smoking
↔ Bus stops, hiking trails, Grouse Mountain skiing, fish hatchery, suspension bridge
⇔ Stanley Park, Vancouver City Centre

🐾 Charming house at 800-metre level in park-like setting nestled at the foothills of
Grouse Mountain in quiet residential area. Relax in the deep secluded back yard. Enjoy
the island and mountains views. Home made jams a specialty. There is a dog.

Chalmers, Guy and Donna (Grand Manor)   ✔ B&B
1617 Grand Blvd., North Vancouver, BC V7L 3Y2   ☎ (604) 988-6719

From Vancouver take 2nd Narrows Bridge to Lynn Valley Turnoff. Turn left at lights
(Lynn Valley Rd) and turn into Grand Blvd. Look for house on west side.
$45-55S(Summer) $55-70D(Summer) $10Child $20Add.person (winter rates
available)   ► 8
● Full, homebaked   ♠ Res., heritage home, quiet   ■ 3D,1Ste (upstairs)
⊷D,Q,R,P, crib   ⸀ 1Private, 2sh.w.g.   ★ F,LF, TV in guest room, parking   ♥
ⓌRestricted smoking

↔ Bus across the street to Sea Bus

⇔ Downtown Vancouver, Grouse
Mountain, Dam and Fish Hatchery,
Lynn Valley Canyon, Stanley Park,
Ferry to Nanaimo

🐾 Large Stone house built in 1914
(one of the original mansions on the
Grand Blvd) provides a restful
atmosphere after a busy day of
exploring the many nearby attractions.
There is a small cockapoo dog in the
house. Minimum stay 2 nights in
summer.

Boire, Helen (Helen's B&B)   ✔ CC
302 East-5th St., North Vancouver, BC   V7L 1L1   ☎ (604) 985-4869

Follow Hwy 1 and signs to North Vancouver. Reaching Londsdale, turn to 5th St, turn
left again. House is on corner.
$40-65D $20-22Add.person   ► 6A,2Ch
● Full, homebaked   ♠ Res., older, view, patio, quiet   ■ 3D (upstairs)   ⊷ 3D,3R
⍨ 1Private, 1sh.w.g.   ★ LF, TV in guest room   ⚇ Pets   ⤳ French
↔ Local city bus and Sea Bus, Sky Train, Grouse Mountain Chair Lift and Chalet, skiing
⇔ Downtown, Ferry to Victoria, Salmon fishing, Stanley Park, Fantasy Gardens

☞ Charming Victorian home built around 1906, well kept, restored and decorated with
antiques with a beautiful view of Vancouver City and Harbour.

Cooper, Sherry and Rick (Cooper's B&B)   ✔ B&B
236 West King Edward Ave., Vancouver, BC   V5Y 2J2   ☎ (604) 879-5554

Exit Hwy 1 at Grandview. Travel west on 12th Ave and turn left on Cambie. Go south to
25th Ave (King Edward Ave) and turn left.
$30S $40D $10Add.person   ► 4A,3Ch
✥ Summer   ● Full, homebaked   ♠ Res., bungalow, patio   ■ S,D,1F
⊷ 2T,1D,1R, 2cots, crib   ⍨ Sh.w.g.   ★ TV, parking   ♥   ⚇ Pets
↔ Beautiful Queen Elizabeth Park, direct bus route to UBC, Stanley Park and
downtown Vancouver, shops, restaurants

☞ Hosts are well travelled school teachers and very knowledgable about the city. Very
convenient and easily accessible location in the heart of Vancouver.

England, Mrs. Arlene (Blue Willow B&B)   ✔ B&B
506 West 19th St., North Vancouver, BC   V7M 1X9   ☎ (604) 984-9028

From Hwy 1 exit south at Westview. Go to West 19th St, turn left
$35-40S $45-50D $15Add.person   ► 6A,2Ch
● Full, homebaked   ♠ Res., split-level bungalow, view, patio   ■ 2D,1Ste
⊷1Q,2D,2S,1R   ⍨ 1Ensuite, 1sh.w.g.   ★ TV,LF,F, parking   ⚇ Small dogs only
⤳French, German
↔ Main bus route to Seabus and downtown
⇔ Lions Gate Bridge, Grouse Mountain Skyride, Horseshoe Bay-Vancouver Island Ferry

☞ Relax in the backyard which is dominated by a huge weeping willow tree against the
blue haze of Grouse Mountain. Hosts family has travelled by B&B extensively, also in
U.K. Hostess is proud of Blue Willow China collection. There is a small dog.

> **B&B Travel Tip:** *You can stay in a B&B even if you are not travelling by
> car. Many B&B homes are situated near excellent public transportation and many
> hosts will pick up and deliver from bus terminal, railway station or airport, some-
> times at no charge.*

Evers, Allan and Dorothy (Prospect B&B)   ✔ B&B
4388 Prospect Rd., North Vancouver, BC   V7N 3L7   ☎ (604) 980-5800

Take Trans Canada Hwy 1 to Lonsdale Ave in North Vancouver. Go north to top and
left on Rockland and then right on Prospect.
$50S $55D   (Off-season and special weekly rates available)   ► 2A
● Full, homebaked   🏠 Res., sub., view, patio, quiet   ■ 1D   ⊨ 1D   ⅂ 1Ensuite
★ F, TV, telephone, radio clock in guest room, ample parking   Ⓦ Children, pets, non-
smoking preferred
↪ Shopping, pub
⇔ Grouse Mountain Skyride, Capilano Suspension Bridge, Sea Bus, City Center

☞ Comfortable modern home situated in the foothills of Grouse Mountain with a
breathtaking view of Vancouver. By prior arrangement, hosts will meet Airporter Bus.
There are 2 cats and a dog in residence.

Feist, Lillian   ✔ B&B
896-W13 Ave, Vancouver, BC   V5Z 1P2   ☎ (604) 873-0842

Centrally located near Oak-Street and 12th Ave.
$28S $38D $6Child $6Add.person   ► 10A,6Ch
● Cont.   🏠 Res., older, quiet   ■ 1D,4Stes (upper and main floor)   ⊨ 12T, 2P
⅂ 2Sh.w.g.   ★ KF,LF, TV in guest room, separate entrance, parking   Ⓦ Restricted
smoking
↪ Public transportation, Vancouver General Hospital
⇔ Queen Elizabeth Park, Van Dusen Gardens, Granville Island, Planetarium,
Chinatown, Gastown

☞ Larger older home situated in the heart of the City and very convenient location.
There are 2 dogs and 2 cats in the house.

Gibbs, Gordon and Joan (Beachside B&B)   ✔ CC
4208 Evergreen Ave., West Vancouver, BC   V7V 1H1   ☎ (604) 922-7773

Take Hwy 1 to West Vancouver, drive west along Marine Dr to Ferndale Ave., turn left
and then left on Evergreen. From Horseshoe Bay, go East on Marine Dr to Ferndale,
turn right.
$55S $75-95D $10Child(under age 12) $20Add. person   (Deposit)   ► 8
● Full, homebaked   🏠 Res., sub., view, patio, oceanfront, quiet, isolated
■ 3D,1Ste,1F   ⊨ 2S,2D,2Q   ⅂ 1Ensuite, 1sh.w.g., 1sh.w.h.   ★ TV,KF,4F,
separate entrance, parking   Ⓦ Smoking, pets
↪ Sandy beach at doorstep, Lighthouse Wilderness Park, tennis, excellent restaurants
⇔ Gleneagles Public Golf Club, Stanley Park, downtown, Museum of Anthropology,
U.B.C., Grouse Mtn, Cypress Bowl Prov. Park, Horseshoe Bay, Heritage Village

☞ Beautiful luxury waterfront home in fine residential area, tastefully decorated in
Spanish-style structure with stained glass windows and a panoramic view of Vancouver.
See daily Alaska Cruise Ships pass by on route to Vancouver Harbour. Hosts are very
knowledgeable about local history and commerce. There is a dog and a cat in the house.

Kavanagh, Janet and Bernard ✔ B&B
3340 26th Ave., Vancouver, BC   V6S 1N5   ☎ (604) 733-9072

Take King Edward Ave west to Blenheim St, turn south and right at first intersection.
$35S $45D   ▶ 4A
● Full   🏠 Res., older, quiet, sundeck   ■ S,D   ⊷ 2T,1Q   ⌐ 1Sh.w.g.
★parking   ⓦ Smoking, drinking, children, pets
↔ Bus service to downtown, very quiet and lovely for walks
⇔ University of B.C., hostpitals, Int. Airport, Stanley Park, beaches

☞ Beautifully renovated older home in quiet residential part of the City. Hosts are seasoned travellers. There is a long-haired white cat in residence.

Kininmont, Olive
3253 East 22nd Ave., Vancouver, BC   V5M 2Z1   ☎ (604) 433-7332

Exit from Grandview Hwy onto Rupert St and go south to 22nd Ave. Turn right.
$30S $45D   ▣ Meals   ▶ 2
● Choice, homebaked   🏠 Res., quiet, older, view, patio   ■ 1D   ⊷1D
⌐1Sh.w.h.   ★ parking   ⓦ Pets, smoking
↔ Excellent transportation (LRT and bus), swimming pool, park, library
⇔ Grouse Mountain, beaches, theatre, easy approach to freeways, Int.Airport

☞ Hostess loves having company and entertaining. Enjoy a vista of ocean/city from sun deck in this centrally-located home. Homebaking and preserves.

McCurrach, Bill and Norma   ✔ B&B
4390 Frances St., Burnaby, BC   V5C 2R3   ☎ (604) 298-8816

Phone for directions.
$35S $40D $10Child $15Add.person   ▶ 5
● Full (nutrional)   ● Res., sub.,, viw, quiet   ■ 1S,2D (main and upper floor)
⊷1S,2K   ⌐Sh.w.h.   ★TV in guest room, parking   ⓦSmoking, drinking pets
⇔ Downtown Vancouver, Heritage Village, Pacific National Exhibition (huge 6400 sqft map of BC), top of Seymour Mountain, Brentwood shopping Center, B.C.I.T., excellent restaurant on top of Burnaby Mountain with panoramic view

☞ White stucco house furnished for comfort and situated in an area considered the "hub" of the action and very convenient to all tourist attraction.

Nelson, Roy and Charlotte
470 W.St.James Rd., North Vancouver, BC   V7N 2P5   ☎ (604) 985-1178

From Trans Canada Hwy 1 turn north on to Westview, right on Windsor, then left.
$35S $50D   ▶ 5
●Choice   🏠Res., quiet   ■2D,1S   ⊷2D,1S   ⌐2Private   ⓦPets,smoking
⇔ Grouse Mountain Chairlift, Cleveland Dam, Fish Hatcherie, Capilano Suspension Bridge, par 3 golf course, Lonsdale Quay, Gastown, Whistler Village Ski Resort, tennis, beaches, retaurants, shopping

☞ Home is situated in garden setting on quiet tree-lined residential street. There are cats in residence.

Ordelt, Paul F. (Paul's Guest House)   ⌐ CC
345 West 14th Ave., Vancouver, BC   V5Y 1X3   ☎ (604) 872-4753

Located in the Shaughnessy area near Vancouver City Hall. Phone for directions.
$25S $35D $5Add.person   ⬛Meals   ► 10
● Full   🏠 Downtown, res., hist., quiet   ■ 6D (main and upper floor)   ⊣ S,D
⌐3Sh.w.g.   ★F,KF,LF, TV in guest room, parking, storage available, rent-a-car
specials   ✋ Pets, children by special arrangement   〰European languages, Japanese
↪ Public transportation to downtown Vancouver
⇔ Queen Elizabeth Park, City Hall, Expo grounds, Granville Island

☞ European Pension-style hospitality with international flavor. Host is a seasoned
traveller and enjoys exchanging experiences from around the world. Private sightseeing
tours can be arranged.

Peloquin, Eugene and Janet (Peloquin's Pacific Pad)
426 West 22nd Ave., Vancouver, BC   V5Y 2G5   ☎ (604) 874-4529

From Hwy 1 exit at Grandview and travel to Cambie St. Turn left and left on 22nd Ave.
$40S $50D $10-15Child $15Add. person   (Reserve please)   ► 4A,2Ch
● Full   🏠 Res., quiet   ■ 1S,2D   ⊣ 1D,R,crib   ⌐ 1Sh.w.g.   ★ KF, TV in guest
room, separate entrance, off-street parking, room for trailer or mobile home
✋Smoking, pets   〰 French, Ukrainian
↪ Numerous popular restaurants, shops, Q.E. park, Bloedel Conservatory
⇔ U.B.C., Horseshoe Bay Ferry Terminal, Oakridge shopping centre, downtown

☞ Comfortable, newly decorated and cozy suburban home in quiet central location
with easy access to Hwy 99 from USA, airport and Ferry Terminal..

Platt, Nancy and Elwood (Platt's B&B)   ⌐ Cope's Choice B&B
4393 Quinton Place, North Vancouver, BC   V7R 4A8   ☎ (604) 987-4100

From Hwy 1, turn north onto Capilano Rd, then right on Edgwood to Quinton P.
$30S $40D   ► 4A
● Full   🏠 Res., quiet   ■ 2D (upstairs)   ⊣ 2T,1D   ⌐ 1Sh.w.g.   ✋ Smoking,
children, pets
↪ Grouse Mountain, Cleaveland Dam, Fish Hatchery, Capilano Suspension Bridge
⇔ Whistler Mountain Ski area, Granville Island and Market, Gastown, Chinatown,
Robsonstrasse and fashionable shopping, pleasant ocean beaches

☞ Home is situated in quiet park-like area and close to the heart of the City.

Poole, Arthur and Doreen ✔ B&B
421 West St. James Rd., North Vancouver, BC V7N 2P6 ☎ (604) 987-4594

From Vancouver City Centre, go west on Georgia St over Lions Gate Bridge, taking right lane to North Vancouver Marine Dr. Turn left at Capilano Rd and right onto Rt1 East. Go left on Westview Dr, right on Windsor and then left.
$25S $35D (Family and children's rates) ⬛ Meals ► 4A,2Ch
● Full, homebaked 🏠 Res., view, patio ■ 2D ⊢ 1D,1Q,1S, crib ⅂ 1Sh.w.g.
★ TV,LF,F ♥ ⓦ Smoking, pets
↔ Grouse Mountain Skyride, Capilano Suspension Bridge, Cleveland Dam, Sea Bus
⇔ Stanley Park, Whistler & Blackcomb ski areas, Ferry to Vancouver Island, Royal Hudson Train

🛏 Lovely colonial-style home in quiet residential district. Retired hosts are happy to assist visitors with information about the city.

Vickers, Barrie and Connie (VickeRidge B&B) ✔ B&B
3638 Loraine Ave., North Vancouver, BC V7R 4B8 ☎ (604) 985-0338

From Hwy 1 exit Capilano Rd northbound (Grouse Mt). Past Capilano Susp. Bridge, turn right onto Edgemont Blvd and then make two sharp left hand turns, first onto Sunset Blvd, then immediately afterwards onto Loraine Ave. Look for house on right.
$40S $45-60D $10Child $20Add.person ⬛ Meals ► 7A,2Ch
● Full, homebaked 🏠 Village, res., bungalow, deck, quiet ■ 2D,1Ste
⊢ 5T,1D,2K,1R ⅂ 1Private, 1sh.w.h. ★ F,LF, parking, library ♥ ⓦ Smoking, pets 〰 French
↔ Capilano Canyon, fish hatchery and fish ladder, Edgemont village, fine dining, shops, parks, tennis, jogging, hiking, biking, swimming
⇔ Grouse Mountain Skyride (spectacular view, helicopter & chairlift rides and alpine skiing), ferries to Vancouver Island and Sunshine Coast, downhill and cross-country skiing, BC Rail Whistler and Caribou, Stanley Park, downtown Vancouver, Chinatown

🛏 Restful alpine village home nestled in the evergreens tucked away from the bustle of nearby downtown Vancouver. There is a dog in the house.

B&B Travel Tip: *On the day of departure, you should leave after breakfast and with all your belongings! It is not fair for the hosts to have to store your luggage, while you are making some side-trips before leaving town. Remember, they have to get the room ready for the next night.*

Weigum C.& G.Christie (West End Guest House)   ✓ B&B
1362 Haro Street, Vancouver, BC   V6E 1G2   ☎ (604) 681-2889

Located one block south of Robson between Broughton and Jervis Streets.
$45-65S $65-80D $15Add.person   ► 14
● Full, homebaked   ♠ Downtown, res., hist., front veranda, sundeck, quiet   ■ 6D
(upstairs)   ⊷ 2S,6Q   ⊓ 5Ensuite   ★ TV in guest room, parking, piano
      ⊕Smoking, pets, children min. age 12

↔ Stanley Park, Aquarium, English
Bay beaches, Robsonstrasse
(fashionable shopping), Art Gallery,
Chinatown, Gastown, Canada and BC
Place
⇔ Museum of Anthropology, U.B.C.,
Queen Elizabeth Park, Maritime
Museum, Granville Island and market,
Grouse Mtn Skyride, Capilano
Suspension Bridge

☛ 1906 Heritage house is nestled on a
quiet tree-lined residential street among
apartment buildings and modern
condominiums in the cities cosmopolitan West End. Hosts are transplants from rural
Alberta and have a keen interest in classical music and Heritage Preservation.

Wickens, Mr. & Mrs. J.A. (Storwick House)   ✓ B&B
1576 Nanton Ave., Vancouver, BC   V6J 2X2   ☎ (604) 738-9865

Located near Granville St and King Edward Ave. Phone for directions.
$35-45S $45-55D $5-10Child $15Add.person   ► 6
● Full, homebaked   ♠ Res., older, patio, quiet   ■ 3D (upstairs)   ⊷ 2T,2D
⊓ Sh.w.g.   ★ TV,LF, parking   ⊕ Restricted smoking, pets, children min. age 3
↔ Excellent bus service on Granville St to downtown and sea bus and ALRT, Airport
⇔ City Center, Van Dusen Botanical Gardens, Queen Elizabeth Park, Gastown and
Chinatown, Stanley Park, theatre district and hospitals

☛ Gracious and charming older style home situated on quiet treelined street in the
prestigious Shaughnessy area, ideally located for those travelling without a car. Well
travelled hosts are very knowledgeable about the Vancouver area. There is a cat.

Town & Country Bed & Breakfast in BC
Box 46544, Stn. G, Vancouver, BC   V6R 4G6   ☎ (604) 731-5942
(Helen Burich and Pauline Scoten)
Town & Country B&B in B.C. is a reservation service for Vancouver as well as a referral
system representing a network of host homes throughout BC in rural and urban areas.
Write or phone for information.
A complete listing is available in book form and can be ordered from the above (prepaid
$7.95 plus $1 for shipping). Some of the hosts are listed in this publication.

Williams, Dorothy Mae and Hugh (Kenya Court Guest House)
2230 Cornwall Ave., Vancouver, BC   V6K 1B5   ☎ (604) 738-7085

Located between Yew and Vine Streets, facing Kitsilano Beach. Phone for directions.
$55-60S $65-80D   ► 11A
● Full   ♠ Downtown, apartment, view, patio, oceanfront, quiet   ■ 1S,4D,3Ste
(main and upper floor)   ⊷ 1S,5T,2Q,2K   ⌐ 3Sh.w.g.   ★ F,TV in guest room,
separate entrance, music room with grand piano   ⊛ Smoking, pets   ∾ Italian,
French, German, Japanese
↪ Large heated outdoor salt-water swimming pool, English Bay, Kitsilano Beach tennis
courts, Granville Island
⇔ Vanouver Island and Gulf Island ferries (Horseshow Bay/Tsawwassen), Stanley Park

📪 Spacious three-storey Heritage building with gracious antique furnishings and
penthouse solarium with spectacular oceanview, where breakfast is served.

Born Free Bed & Breakfast of B.C.
4390 Frances St. Burnaby, BC   V5C 2R3   ☎ (504) 298-8815
(President Norma McCurrach)
Rates: $30-45S $45-60D $75-125Ste $5Child(under age 10) $10Child(over age 11)
Born Free B&B of B.C. is a reservation service and offers "A Home away from Home".
Choose from modest, average and luxurious classification. For reservation call the above.

Alberta & Pacific Bed and Breakfast
Box 15477, MPO, Vancouver, BC   V6B 5B2   ☎ (604) 682-4610   (8am-2pm)
(Mrs. June Brown)
Rates from: $30S $40D   (Deposit required)
Formerly called"Alberta B&B" stationed in Edmonton, Mrs. Brown now resides in
Vancouver and, as before, continues to represent Alberta Bed and Breakfast homes (see
Edmonton/Alta), as well as B&B homes in Vancouver, Kamloops, Victoria and Whistler.
For a brochure send $1 (overseas enquiries please include Int. Coupon to cover postage).
The Agency is closed during October through February.

Canada West Accommodations B&B Registry
Box 8667, North Vancouver, BC   V7L 4L2   ☎ (604) 987-9338
(President Ellison Massey)
Rates: $35-40S $45-60D   (including breakfast) (Deposit required)
Canada West Accommodations represents 18 selected quality B&B hosts in four regions
of the Province (Vancouver, Victoria, Okanagan Valley and Cariboo) and reservations for
all locations may be made by contacting the North Vancouver Number above. For skiers:
Whistler ski packages area available.

Old English Bed & Breakfast Registry
1226 silverwood Cres., North Vancouver, BC   V7P 1J3   ☎ (604) 986-5069
President Vicky Tyndall
Rates: 35-50D (including a hearty breakfast)   (Deposit required)
Old English Bed & Breakfast offers guest homes to meet every taste in city homes,
turn-of-the-century, contemporary, or traditional houses. For information and
reservation call the above.

Vernon

(see also Salmon Arm, Kelowna)

Beeby, Frank and Norma (Lakeview B&B)   ↙ Okan B&B Netw.
465 Rockland Dr., S3,C14,RR1 Vernon, BC   V1T 6L4   ☎ (604) 549-3549

From Hwy 97 in Vernon, take Hwy 6 East (toward Lumby) and exit left at Aberdeen Rd.
Located 3.2 km east of City. Details with reservation confirmation.
$30S $40D   ► 4A
✽ Summer (weekends all year)   ● Full, homebaked   ♠ Sub., view, patio, bacony,
quiet, hot tub   ■ 2D   ⊷ 1D,1Q   ℂ 1Sh.w.g.   ★ F,TV,LF, ample parking   ♥
   ⊛Smoking   ⌇ French
⇔ Okanagan and Kalamalka Lakes for beaches and swimming, orchards, historic
O'Keefe Ranch, waterslide and bobslide, Vernon Hockey School

☞ Modern, comfortable cedar home with a view of Kalamalka Lake and the
Coldstream Valley and a beautiful garden. There are 3 cats and a dog in the house.

Cullaton, David (Silverhaven Bed & Breakfast)   ↙ Okan B&B Netw.
8146 Silver Star Rd,S11,C60,RR3, Vernon, BC   V1T 6L6   ☎ (604) 545-0755

From Hwy 97 in Vernon, take Silverstar Rd for 10 km.
$ 30S $40D $15Child (under age 16)   ► 6
● Choice, homebaked   ♠ Rural, ranch-style, acreage, view, patio, quiet   ■ 3D (main
and upper level)   ⊷ 2T,1D,1Q   ℂ 1Ensuite,1sh.w.h.   ★ TV,2F, separate guest
lounge   ⊛ Smoking, pets
↪ walking along stream, hiking trails through large property
⇔ Silverstar Ski Resort (snowmobiling, downhill and cross-country skiing), Hot Springs,
lakes and Okanagan valley

☞ Comfortable and quiet mountain home in peaceful surroundings, located on wooded
acreage. Congenial hosts are avid skiers, hikers and canoeists.

LaFortune, Connie (The Windmill House)   ↙ Okan B&B Netw.
S19A, C2, RR1, Vernon, BC   V1T 6L4   ☎ (604) 549-2804

From Vernon, take Hwy 6 east to Lavington. Turn right at Henri's Arcade to Learmouth
Rd. Turn left and look for Windmill-shaped house at No.5672
$30S $35-45D $5Child(under age 14)   ▣ Meals   (Group rates)   ► 10A,2Ch
✽ May-Oct.   ● Choice   ♠ Rural, 4-story Windmill, acreage, view, quiet, balcony
■ 4D, 1Ste (upstairs)   ⊷ 2T,3D,1Q,R, crib   ℂ Sh.w.g.   ★ TV,F,LF, separate
entrance   ♥   ⊛ Smoking
⇔ Downtown Vernon, Silver Star cross-country and downhill ski resort, Cedar Hot
Tubs, Kelowna Regatta, orchards, hunting, excellent beaches and fishing

☞ Modern and unique accommodation in a Windmill (inspite of the 45 steps to the
top) with a panoramic view of the Coldstream Valley. Craft shop of native's carvings on
premises. Sour dough waffles and homemade fruit toppings a specialty.

Larson, Eskil and Sharon (Castle on the Mountain)   ✔ Okan B&B Netw.
8227 Silver Star Rd, S10, C12, RR8, Vernon, BC   V1T 8L6   ☎ (604) 542-4593

Located 10 km east of Hwy 97 on 48th Ave (Silver Star Road).
$35-45S $45-55D $5-10Child $20Add.person   📵 Meals   ► 4A,3Ch
● Full, homebaked   🏠 Rural, acreage, spectacular view, patio, quiet, isolated
■ 1Ste(3D)   ⊨ 2T,2D,2R,K,P   ⌐ 1Sh.w.g., 1ensuite   ★ KF,F,TV in guest room,
separate entrance, facilities for the handicapped, outside kennel area   ✋ Smoking
↪ Mountainside hiking, camp area on property for B&B guests
⇔ Silver Star Ski Resort, Cedar Springs (Hot Springs), water and bobsled slide, local
wineries and brewery (tours), fishing, boating, beaches, O'Keefe Historical Ranch,
lumber mills (tours)

🐾 Spacious Tudor home situated on mountainside above valley with fabulous views
over lakes, city and Okanagan Valley. Hosts are artists and craftspeople and have filled
their home with art and handcrafted woodwork.

Pringle, Rod and Colleen (Twin Willows by the Lake)   ✔ Okan B&B Netw.
7456 Tronson Rd, S10,C16,RR4, Vernon, BC   V1T 6L7   ☎ (604) 542-8293

Located 8.4 km west of Vernon. Obtain brochure with map at tourist booth.
$35-40S $45-50D $7.50-10Child $15Add.person   ► 4A,6Ch
● Full, homebaked   🏠 Rural, view, lakefront, patio, quiet   ■ 1D,1Ste,1F
⊨ 2D,2P, cot, crib   ⌐ 1Ensuite, 1sh.w.h.   ★ TV in guest room, large fridge for
guest's use, separate entrance   ✋ Smoking
↪ Swimming wharf, rowing, walks along the lakeside, tree-lined lanes, sandy beach,
pick your own peaches
⇔ Silver Star Mountain (chairlift, ski village), Kalamalka Lake Park, Swan Lake Animal
Farm, Cedar Springs Recreation (hot springs), golfing, fishing

🐾 Recently retired forester and school teacher in spacious lakefront home with each
window looking out onto the lake and situated in the beautiful Okanagan valley town.
Honeymoon special a sailboat ride. There is a double hammock strung between the
twingiant willows by the lake.

B&B Travel Tip: *Plan your trip at home in the comfort of your living room,
researching the maps of the provinces you want to visit, and then write or phone
the B&B hosts, to see if the room is available for you. When you have B&B confir-
mations, you will relax and enjoy your trip much more.*

Spencer, Jimmie and Andy
2400-23rd St., Vernon BC   V1T 4J5

 Okan B&B Netw.
☎ (604) 542-8474

Phone for directions.
$25S $35D $5Child(over age 5)   🍽 Meals

► 4A,2Ch
● Full (English)   🏠 Res., patio, quiet, swimming pool   ■ 2S,1D,1F
⊢ 2T,1Q,1P,crib   ⌐ 1Private   ★ TV,F,LF, parking   🐾 Pets   ♥   ⠧ German

↔ Downtown, Winter Carnival (Feb), sandbox for children

⇔ Silver Star Mt Resort (summer and winter), Okanagan and Kalamalka Lakes, Cedar Springs Hot Tubs, historic O'Keefe Ranch

🔫 Beautiful Okanagan Valley home, convenient to all resort activities. Arrangements can be made for transportation to Silver Star Mt Resort.

Victoria
(on Vancouver Island; see also Duncan, Chemainus, Saltsprings Isle, Mill Bay, Brentwood Bay, Sooke)

Arlidge, Rose Marie and Bruce (Charlotte's Guest House)
338 Foul Bay Rd., Victoria, BC   V8S 4G7

 CC
☎ (604) 595-3528

From downtown Victoria follow Fairfield Rd easterly to Foul Bay Rd and turn right.
$50 per room (not more than 2 persons in room)
► 4
● Choice, homebaked   🏠 Res., sub., split-level, view, quiet   ■ 2D   ⊢ 2T,1D
⌐1Private,1ensuite   ★ F,KF,LF, TV in guest room, separate entrance, ample parking, phones available   🐾 Pets, children
↔ Gonzales Bay, beautiful sea and "view" walks, Oak Bay Village, Sealand and Marina
⇔ Butchart's Gardens, downtown Victoria, Beacon Hill Park, breakwater, Fishermen's Wharf, theatres, boutiques, markets, antiqueries, neighborhood pubs

🔫 Warm and attractive contemporary West Coast Garry Oak-shaded house with spectacular views over the Straits to the snow-capped Olympics in Washington State and out over the city and Royal Roads towards Japan. Located on a meandering road in the quiet and mature Gonzales neighbourhood of Victoria. Hosts operated a B&B in Ottawa for many years before retiring to their "beloved roots" on the West Coast.

Aquarius, John and Colleen (Aquarius Guest House)   ✓ B&B
124 Goverment St., Victoria, BC   V8V 2K7   ☎ (604) 383-9009

Located at James Bay. Phone for directions.
$45S $55D $15Child   ► 6
● Full, homebaked   🏠Downtown, res., hist., patio, quiet   ⊢ 1D,1F (main and upper floor) ⊢ 1D,2Q,1R   ⌐ 1Sh.w.g.   ★ F,TV, parking   ⑩ Restricted smoking, pets, children min. age 6 (1 child at a time)
↤ Ocean and inner Harbour, Beacon Hill Park, Empress Hotel, bus depot
⇔ Downtown, Ferries to mainland, Butchart Gardens, Sealand,

☞ 1919 built home and lovely gardens, tastefully decorated with antiques. Hosts main occupation is stained glass (and there is plenty of it in the house). There are 2 cats in residence.

Baillie, Jim and Pat (Portage Inlet House)   ✓ B&B
993 Portage Rd., Victoria, BC   V8Z 1K9   ☎ (604) 479-4594

Phone for directions.
$40-55D $75Cottage   ► 6A
● Full, homebaked   🏠 Res., acreage, view, waterfront   ■ 3, also Honeymoon cottage   ⊢ T,K, crib   ⌐ Private, sh.w.g.   ★ LF, TV in guest rooms, separate entrance, street parking   ♥   ⑩ Pets
↤ Walking and strolling in an acreage of garden inhabited by an abundance of wildlife, mute swans and herons on water
⇔ Downtown Victoria, ferry terminal to Mainland

☞ Secluded waterfront home, overlooking Portage Inlet, is solar heated. Organic homegrown foods and homemade breads/scones from fresh ground wheat.

Barr, Frank and Rene (Cadboro Bay Bed & Breakfast)   ✓ B&B
3844 Hobbs St., Victoria, BC   V8N 4C4   ☎ (604) 477-6558

From Swartz Bay Ferry Terminal or Airport follow Hwy 17 to McKenzie, which continues as Sinclair, and turn left on Hobbs St.
$35S $50D   ► 4
● Full, homebaked(Gourmet)   🏠 Village, res., view, patio, quiet   ■ 2D
⊢2T,1Q,crib   ⌐Sh.w.g.   ★F,separate entrance,parking   ♥   ⑩Pets,no facilities for babies
↤ Suburban village center, first class restaurant, neighborhood pub, shops, parks, sandy beach (swimming, windsurfing), tennis, University of Victoria, bus stop
⇔ Downtown City Centre, beautiful scenic drive to Fable Cottage and Butchart Gardens

☞ Warm hospitality and homey atmosphere and quiet secluded back garden with patio in picturesque Cadboro Bay Village.

Black, Norm and Lois (Dogwood House)   ✓ VIP B&B
2429 Barbara Place, Victoria, BC   V8Z 5T6   ☎ (604) 652-2137

Take Hwy 17 to Keating Cross Rd and one block to Barbara Drive and to Barbara Place.
$30S $45D $7Child   ▣ Meals   ► 10A,2Ch
● Full, homebaked (gourmet)   ♠ Rural, res., ranch style, patio, half-acre garden
■ 5D,1F   ⊷ 4T,2D,1K,1R,2Q (waterbed), cot, crib   ⌐ 2Sh.w.g., 1ensuite
★F,LF,TV in guest room, separate entrance, facilities for the handicapped, Old
English Pub style lounge   ♥   ⊛ Pets
↪ Island View Beach, shopping centre
⇔ Butchart Gardens, BC Ferry & Washington State Ferry, Airport, downtown

☛ Expect to be spoiled in the Chef's Home with special treats for special events. Hosts
enjoy taking guests out in own cabin cruiser (by prior arrangemnt) through the beautiful
Gulf Islands for fishing or relaxing. There is a cat in the house.

Buchholz, Stana & Renato (Villa Camellia Beachfront B&B)   ✓ CC
5055 Cordova Bay Rd., Victoria, BC   V8Y 2K1   ☎ (604) 658-5254

Phone for directions.
$105D $15Child $25Add.person   ▣ Meals   ► 4A,2Ch
● Choice(banquet-size)   ♠ Res., view, oceanfront   ■ 1Ste (upstairs)   ⊷ 1D,1Q,R
⌐ Private   ★ F,KF,LF, separate entrance, parking, jacuzzi   ⊛ Pets   ≈ Italian,
Serbo-Croation

↪ Fable cottage, mini golf, tennis, restaurants, fishing, stroll along beautiful sandy beach, shopping centre

⇔ Butchart Gardens, downtown Victoria

☛ Spacious, colourful Spanish-style waterfront home with European Hospitality and breathtaking panoramic view of majestic Mount Baker and the blue waters of the Straits of Juan de Fuca situated at Cordova Bay.

B&B Travel Tip: *Do not think of giving tips. Remember this is not a hotel service.*

Gordon, Pat and Alec (Seaview B&B)   ✔ B&B
144 Dallas Rd, Victoria, BC   V8V 1C1   ☎ (604) 383-7098

Phone for directions.
$40S $55-65D $10Child $15Add. person   ► 6A,1Ch
✱ Feb.-Oct.   ● Choice, homebaked   🏠 Res., older, view, oceanfront, quiet   ■ 3D
🛏 2T,1Q,1K (or 2S)   ⌐ 1Private, 1sh.w.g.   ★ 3TV in guest rooms, parking
Ⓦ Smoking, pets, only one child at a time
↔ Beacon Hill Park, beautiful flower displays, City Centre, Seattle ferry docks
⇔ Butchart Gardens, Vancouver ferry docks, airport

☞ Enjoy the beautiful views of the Olympic Mountains and lights of Port Angeles across the Strait of Juan de Fuca and shipping from around the world passing by.

Harris, Gail and Clint (Lilac House)   ✔ B&B
252 Memorial Cres., Victoria, BC   V8S 3J2   ☎ (604) 382-2887/384-6620

Follow Fairfield Rd east from Blanshard St (past Cook and Moss St), and turn right onto Memorial Cres to 3rd house on right.
$40S $50D $15Add.person   ► 6-7
● Full, homebaked   🏠 Res., hist., quiet   ■ 3D (upstairs)   🛏 3D,2R   ⌐ 2Sh.w.g.
★ 2F, parking   Ⓦ Smoking, pets, children min. age 19   〰 some French

↔ Craigdarroch Castle, stroll along the waterfront and through Beacan Hill Park to the Parliament Buildings and the Prov. Museum

⇔ Sooke Potholes Park, Butchart Gardens, Devonian and Witty's Lagoon Parks

☞ Award-winning home (built in 1892) authentically restored to its original charm, is located near scenic Strait of Juan de Fuca in a park-like setting and beautiful residential neighbourhood of Fairfield. Experience a relaxing English-style B&B.

B&B Travel Tip: *You can go B&B if you are a single traveller (on business or pleasure). Then, you are in the company of others, and socializing with strangers is so much easier.*

Hicks, Ken and Brenda (Elk Lake Lodge)   ✓ CC
5259 Patricia Bay Hwy, Victoria, BC   V8Y 1S8   ☎ (604) 658-8879

Located right across from Elk Lake on Hwy 17 (Patricia Bay Highway).
$38S $50D $15Child $15Add.person   ► 8A,3Ch
● Full   ♠ Rural, hist., view, patio, lakefront   ■ 3D,1F (main and upper level)
⊷2T,2Q,1K,1R   ⌐2Sh.w.g.   ★ F, TV in guest room, hot tub on patio, magnificient
lounge and library   Ⓦ Children min. age 3
↪ Elk Lake sandy beach, windsurfing, sailing, trout fishing
⇔ Downtown Victoria, Cordova Bay and beaches, Fable Cottage, ferry terminals,
golfing, Butchart Gardens, riding, airport

🖝 Originally built as a chapel, Elk Lake Lodge has been beautifully restored and is
surrounded by cedar trees and gardens. There are 2 dogs in the house.

Laschuk, Tairroyn and Roy (Seabreeze)   ✓ CB&B
629 Senanus Dr., Saanichton, Victoria, BC   V0S 1M0   ☎ (604) 652-4434

Phone for directions.
$85D (and up) $20Add.person   ► 6
● Full, homebaked   ♠ Rural, quiet, oceanfront, indoor pool,   ■ 3D ⊷2T,2Q
 ⌐3Private   ★ Separate entrance, parking, moorage for guests   Ⓦ Pets
↪ Beachcombing, nature walks, swimming
⇔ Butchart Gardens, Victoria Harbour, Airport, Swartz Bay Ferries, gourmet
restaurants, dinner cruises, boat rental

🖝 Elegant home situated on 2 acres property with private beach cove. Enjoy relaxing
in the moonlight by the oceans edge or the warm water of the exotic "Hawaiian" pool
before retiring to the comforts of duvet-covered beds. There are 3 small dogs in the
house.

Lydon, Aideen (Hibernia B&B)   ✓ B&B
747 Helvetia Cres., Victoria, BC   V8Y 1M1   ☎ (604) 658-5519

Located close to junction of Patricia Bay Hwy (17) and Sayward.
$21S $42D $5-10Child $10Add.person   ► 7
● Full(Irish)   ♠ Semi-rural, acreage, patio, quiet   ■ 2S,2D (upper and main floor)
⊷ S,T,D,R, cot   ⌐2Sh.w.g.   ★ TV, parking, facilities for the handicapped
 Ⓦ Restricted smoking   ⌁ Spanish, French, some German
↪ Cordova Bay village, Fable Cottage, beaches, sea and lake, golfing, tennis
⇔ Butchart Gardens, downtown, ferries

🖝 Relaxed atmosphere in home furnished with antiques and located in secluded spot
on a cul-de-sac without traffic noise, yet a few minutes off highway. Breakfast served on
large vine-covered patio.

McMillan, Sonia and Brian (Sonia's B&B By The Sea)   ⌐ CC
175 Bushby St., Victoria, BC   V8S 1B5   ☎ (604) 385-2700

Phone for directions.
$55-65D $15Add.person   ► 8
✪ not Xmas   ● Full   ♠ Res., bungalow, view, patio, oceanfront, quiet   ■ 3D
⊷ 2Q,1K,2R   ⌐ 2Private, 1sh.w.g.   ★ TV,LF, parking, 2bicycles for guests
    ⊕Smoking, childen min. age 12   ⋙ some German
↔ Walk along ocean through Beacon Hill Park to inner Harbour, Straights of Juan de
Fuca at back door, good restaurants, English Double- Decker Bus at door
⇔ Butchart Gardens, Chemainus "a little town that did it"

☞ Hosts will take guests out on fully equipped boat for salmon fishing in the evening
or on weekends. There is a parrot and a cockatiel in residence.

Savage, Joan, Teri and Bryan (Oak Bay Guest House)   ⌐ CC
1052 Newport Ave., Victoria, BC   V8S 5E3   ☎ (604) 598-3812

From downtown Victoria, take Fort St, turn right at Oak Bay Ave, travel to end,
continue on right hand curve (Newport Ave). Look for house on right side.
$35S(and up) $55D(and up) $17Child $17Add.person   ► 24
✪ not January   ● Full   ♠ Res., quiet   ■ 2S,8D   ⊷ 4T,6D,2Q,2R,1P, crib
⌐ 8Private, 2sh.w.g.   ★ Parking, separate entrance, TV in large sunroom for guests
    ⊕Restricted smoking, pets, 2-day min. stay on holiday weekends & Christmas
↔ Sealand, golfcourse, excellent restaurants, shopping, ocean beaches, direct bus route

☞ Home is situated in one of the finest residential locations in Victoria in quiet
neighborhood with beautiful gardens. There is a cat in the house.

Shnider, Charlie and Diana (Blenkinsop B & B)   ⌐ CC
4049 Century Rd, Victoria, BC   V8X 2E5   ☎ (604) 477-5195

From Airport or Ferry, take Hwy 17 to McKenzie Ave. Turn left and continue past
Quadra St up and down the hill to Century Rd. Turn left into Cul-de- sac.
$35S $55D   ▣ Meals   (Deposit)   ► 6
● Full, gourmet   ♠ Res., view, quiet, deck   ■ 3D   ⊷ 2T,2D,P   ⌐ Sh.w.g.
★TV in guest room, woodstove separate entrance, facilities for the disabled
    ⊕Smoking, pets, children minimun age 10
↔ Shopping centre, library, Mount Douglas, bus stop
⇔ Downtown Harbour, city center, chinatown, museums, ferries, Butchart Gardens

☞ Newly bungalow overlooks Blenkinsop Valley. Complimentary evening tea and
snack, a special time for hosts and guests."Country quiet in the heart of the City".

Smith, Vicky and Bob (Rose Cottage B&B) ✓ B&B
3059 Washington Ave., Victoria, BC   V9A 1P7 ☎ (604) 381-5985

From The Empress Hotel in downtown Victoria, take Government St to Gorge Rd, turn left and continue to Washington Ave.
$43-45S $54-58D $18Add.person   (Deposit required) ► 10
● Full   ⌂ Res., older, quiet   ■ 1S,4D (upper and main floor)   ⌐ 2D,2Q,2R
⅂2Sh.w.g.   ★ F,TV in guest parlour, library, guest room keys   ⓦ Restricted smoking
↔ Sheltered bus stop, Gorge Waterway Park
⇔ Inner Harbour, Ferry Docks from Port Angeles and Seattle, Butchart Gardens

☞ Home was built in 1912 in the traditional Victorian style of the era with leaded paned windows. Originally from London, hostess has travelled extensively by B&B in England and North America and has collected much memorabelia, including an antique piano victrola and various musical instruments. There is a cat in residence.

Thompson, Jack and Nancy (Sunnymeade House Inn) ✓ CC
1002 Fenn Ave., Victoria, BC   V8Y 1P3 ☎ (604) 658-1414

Located on Cordova Bay. From Swartz Bay Ferrie on Hwy 17 go to traffic light at Sayward and turn off at Fenn.
$40S $57-65D $20Add.person ► 9A,2Ch
● Full, homebaked   ⌂ Res., village, older, patio, quiet   ■ 1S,3D,1F (main and upper floor)   ⌐ 1S,3T,2D, cot, crib, 1Q,1R   ⅂ 1Private, 2sh.w.g.   ★ TV in guest lounge, separate entrance   ⓦ Smoking, pets
↔ Beautiful beach, village shops, golfing, tennis, super Village restaurants
⇔ Butchart Gardens, downtown Victoria, Elk Lake (watersports),

☞ Old Colonial Charm in lovely new home setting. Hosts designed and decorated home especially for"B&B"and are very proud of the results and their beautiful garden.

Waibel, Peggy (Peggy's Cove) ✓ B&B
279 Coal Point Lane, RR1, Sidney, (Victoria) BC   V8L 3R9 ☎ (604) 656-5656

Phone for directions. Located approx. 28 km north of Victoria.
$95-125D $15Child $15Add.person ► 4A
● Full (Gourmet)   ⌂ Rural, view, oceanfront, large patios, outdoor hot tub, quiet, isolated   ■ 2D,1F   ⌐ 2Q,R   ⅂ 2Private   ★ F,KF,LF, separate entrance, canoe for guests, individual patios with oceanview, perfect for honeymooners
↔ Beach combing, sailing, swimming fishing, boat charters, tennis, nature walks
⇔ Golfing, horseback riding, fine dining, boating, birdwatching, dinner cruises, airport, Anacortes ferries, Butchart Gardens, Victoria, BC ferries

☞ Uniquely designed lodge-style spacious cedar home, beautifully decorated and surrounded by the ocean on three sides, with each room taking advantage of the spectacular ocean and mountain views. Sea lions may be seen at play, and killer whales may appear. Canoe in the moon- light and then relax in the hot tub under the stars.

Wait, Sally (Windlock on the Sea)   ✓ B&B
8560 West Saanich Rd., RR2, Saanichton, (Victoria) BC   V0S 1M0   ☎ (604) 652-2079

From Swartz Bay travel south on Hwy 17 to 4rd traffic light (McTavish Rd), turn right to end, turn left onto West Saanich Rd and travel 2 km. Located 27 km north of Victoria.
$35S $55D $10Child $15Add. person   ► 4
● Choice   ♠ Rural, acreage, view, oceanfront, large patio, very quiet, tennis court
■ 2D (one in separate cottage)   ⊶ 2D   ⌐ 2Private   ⓦ Pets
↪ Beach combing on own beach, watch seals and otters playing, good birding and fishing in Saanich Inlet, tennis court, canoeing
⇔ Butchart Gardens, Sidney and ferry to San Juan Isle, Swartz Bay Ferry Terminal to Mainland, downtown Victoria, airport

☞ Charming West Coast Cedar designed home located on beautiful Saanich Inlet. Lovely views and fabulous sunsets may be enjoyed at any time. Enjoy breakfast on a secluded patio amidst peaceful and quiet atmosphere.

Waters, Jack and Heather (Mount Newton Cottage)   ✓ CC
7969 West Saanich Rd., RR2, Saanichton, BC   V0S 1M0   ☎ (604) 652-5679

Located .75 km north of Brentwood Bay on Hwy 17A.
$45S $55-60D $65-75F $15Add.person   ► 7A,2Ch
● Choice, homebaked   ♠ Rural, hist., acreage, view, patio, quiet   ■ 2D (upstairs)
⊶ 3S,2D,2R   ⌐ 2Sh.w.g.   ★ F,TV, parking, library, music room with piano
ⓦSmoking, pets, children min. age 5

↪ Beach Cove, historic St. Stephens Anglican Church, stroll down a quiet country lane or along the beach

⇔ Butchart Gardens, Victoria Airport, Sidney Ferries to Vancouver and Gulf Islands, Sooke and entrance to West Coast Trail, charter fishing

☞ Renovated and reconstructed 1876-built home overlooking the valley, sea and mountains. Hosts have travelled extensively by B&B and know exactly what B&B travellers are looking for. Relax on the veranda and enjoy the beautiful panoramic views. Tea and coffee always available.

Young, Mrs. Karen (The Sea Rose) ⌐ CC
1250 Dallas Rd., Victoria, BC V8V 1C4 ☎ (604) 381- 7932

Take Trans Canada Hwy 1 or Hwy 17 to downtown Victoria, then follow Douglas St to
Dallas Rd and left.

$76D(and up) $15Add.person (Seniors discounts available) ► 11A
● Full 🏠 Res., older, oceanfront ■ 3 (main and upper level) ⊢ 2YT,1D,2Q
⅂Private ★ LF,TV in guest rooms, separate entrance, sunroom overlooking ocean
with panoramic view from sunrise to sunset ⊛ Smoking, children
↪ Beacon Hill park and ocean across the street, Art Gallery & Craigdarroch Castle, city
bus service
⇔ World famous Royal B.C. Museum, Parliament Buildings, Empress Hotel and High
Tea, excellent shopping and restaurants, Butchart Gardens, Sealand of the Pacific

🐾 Completely renovated 1921-built home is tastefully furnished and has a
commanding view of sea and mountains and the snowcaps in the distance. Watch the
hang gliders, windsurfers and sea life from front door.

V.I.P. Bed and Breakfast Company
1786 Teakwood Rd., Victoria, BC V8N 1E2 ☎ (604) 477-5604
(Joanne Ridley)
Rates vary: from $30-35S from $45D (Family rates) (No deposit required).
The VIP B&B Co. represents a small group of Victoria homeowners who will meet buses,
arrange tours and fishing trips, babysit, and share the secrets of their city and serve a big
breakfast (enough to eliminate the need for lunch), so guests can feel free to enjoy the
beautiful Vancouver Island until tea-time, which is usually 2-4pm. For reservation call
the above.

City & Sea B&B Agency
Box 421, Stn E., Victoria, BC V8W 2N8 ☎ (604) 385-1962
Rates: $45-120D (including a full breakfast)
A select group of homes located either on or near Victoria's waterfront and close to the
City Centre and Beacon Hill Park. All hosts are members of Tourism Victoria. Call or
write for free maps, brochures and detailed information.

Garden City Bed & Breakfast Reservation Service
660 Jones Terrace, Victoria, BC V8Z 2L7 ☎ (604) 479-9999
(Owner-Operator Doreen Wensley)
Rates: $30S $40D (including full breakfast)
Garden City B&B Reservation Service represents over 50 hosts, in mostly non-smoking,
comfortable and hospitable surroundings. For reservation call or write to the above.

All Seasons Bed & Breakfast Agency
Box 5511, Stn B., Victoria, BC V8R 6S4 ☎ (604) 595-BEDS/595-2337
(Maureen Vesey, Owner-Operator)
Rates: From $50-125D (including breakfast)
The all Seasons B&B Agengy is a personal Reservation Service representing homes and
small inns on Vancouver Island and the Gulf Islands. A free brochure and sample listing
is available from the above.

Whistler
(north of Vancouver)

Langtry, Stan and Shirley (Stancliff House)
3333 Panorama Ridge, Gen. Del., Whistler, BC   V0N 1B0   ☎ (604) 932-2393

Take Hwy 99 north from Vancouver and drive through old Gondola area to section (sign on Hwy). Turn right on Panorama Ridge to house on top of hill on right.
$ 40-55S $50-70D $15Add.person   ► 8
❇ Winter only (occassionaly in summer)   ● Full   ♠ Village, view, quiet   ■ 2
⊷4T,1Q, 2 sets of bunks (in winter only)   ⊓ 1Sh.w.h   ★TV,F, piano, ski room, hot tub (winter only), ample parking   ⊛ Restricted smoking, pets
↔ Whistler Village, Blackcomb/Whistler Chairlift, Valley Trail (biking, walking, golfing

🐾 Contemporary-styled comfortable home with magnificient view of mountains. Enjoy relaxing in the hot tub and camaraderie around the wood burning stove. Pick-ups and delivery to bus or train from Vancouver.

Spence-Myette, Ann (Golden Dreams B&B)
6412 Easy Street, Box 692, Whistler, BC   V0N 1B0   ☎ (604) 932-ANN'S(2667)

Past Whistler Village, take 2nd left at Whistler Cay and go down hill, then right on Balsam Way and left on Easy St. Look for house on right side.
$50S $65D $20Addd.person   (Reduced summer rates available)   ► 6A
● Full, homebaked   ♠ Resort village,mountainview, sundecks   ■ 2   ⊷ 3D
   ⊓1Sh.w.g. ★ F,TV in one guest room, off-street parking, indoor ski boot storage, large jacuzzi   ⊛ Smoking
⇔ Short walk to valley trail and along golf course to village, downhill and cross-country skiing, restaurants and shops, hiking trails, lakes

🐾 Long-time Whistler resident in newly-built home with attractive landscaping and tastefully decorated rooms located in the heart of the valley. Attentively catered cooking

White Rock
(near Vanouver; see also Coquitlam, Delta, Surrey, Saltspring Islands)

McIlvenna, Hugh and Maeve (Mount Carmel)   ↙ CC
15318-20th Ave, White Rock, BC   V4A 2A2   ☎ (604) 538-3776

Phone for directions.
$25S $40D $5Child $5Add.person   ► 6
● Full   ♠ Res., sub., quiet   ■ 3D (upstairs)   ⊷ 2S,2D   ⊓ Sh.w.g.   ★ LF,TV, parking   ♥   ⊛ Drinking, pets   ⤬ French
↔ Shopping, restaurants, parks, bus services covering White Rock and greater Vancouver area, swimming pool
⇔ Pacific coast beaches, golf course, U.S. border, downtown Vancouver, ferries to Vancouver Island , mountain hiking and skiing areas

🐾 Irish-style hospitality in old-country home located on a quiet street and close to the metropolis. Hosts operated a B&B in Ireland for many years. Children welcome.

North, David and Grace
1033 Habgood St., White Rock, BC   V4B 4W7   ☎ (604) 536-9356

From Trans-Canada Hwy 1, exit south on 152 St to White Rock. Turn left on Pacific Ave
and go 13 blocks left onto Habgood. From Vancouver Airport go south on Hwy 99. Exit
onto Hwy 99A (King George Hwy) south, and go right on 160 St, 9 blocks to Pacific Ave.
After 2 blocks, turn right onto Habgood. From US border, exit 8 Ave West for 1.6 km
and right onto Habgood.

$28S $40D   (Discount for Senior Citizens)   ► 4
● Full   🏠 Sub., quiet, view   ■ 2D   ⊷ 2T,1D   ⤒ 1Sh.w.g.   ★ TV,F   ⊛ Pets,
smoking, children min. age 12

↔ White Rock Beach, tennis court, restaurants, neighbourhood pub

⇔ City centre, Vancouver, Int. Airport, ferries to Victoria and islands, US border

☞ Friendly hospitality in very quiet residential area. There are two cats in the house.

Odin, Joe and Helen (The Odins')
15319 Marine Dr., White Rock, BC   V4B 1C7   ↙ B&B
                                                             ☎ (604) 531-9674

From Vancouver, take Hwy 99 south to the waterfront and Marine Drive. From
Trans-Canada Hwy 1, take Langley Exit to Hwys 10 and 16th Ave.

$25S $35D   ► 2A,1Ch
● Full   🏠 Res., patio oceanfront   ■ 1S,1D   ⊷ 1S,1D   ⤒ 1Sh.w.g.   ★ F, TVin
guest room, parking separate entrance   ⊛ Restricted smoking, pets

↔ Safe sandy beach and shops, White
Rock's famous pier, Semiahmoo Park,
bus stop across street

⇔ Shopping malls, fine restaurants and
shops, downtown Vancouver, Victoria
and Islands Ferry, U.S.border

☞ Hosts have welcomed B&B guests
from all over the world for many years
in their comfortable seaside home with
a beautiful ocean view in the
"Sandcastle Capital of the World" with
a beautiful ocean view. There is a dog
in residence.

Windermere
(near Kimberley; see also Invermere, Parson, Fort Steele, Fernie)

Younk Lene (Younk's B&B)
Box 52, Windermere, BC   V0B 2L0   ☎ (604) 342-6295

On Hwy 93 (from south) or Hwy 95 (from north) turn at Texaco Service. Follow main street all the way to corner of Fairmount Street. Located one block from Windermere beach.
$30S $35D $10Child   ► 4A,2Ch
✚ Jan-March and June-Sept.   ● Cont.   ♠ Village, res., acreage, view, 2patios, quiet
■ 2D,1F   ↪ 2S,2T,1Q   ↰ 1Sh.w.g.   ★ F,TV in guest living room, separate entrance   ✋ Restricted smoking   ⌇ Danish, German
↔ Lake Windermere and public beach, swimming, windsurfing, canoeing, golfing, interesting church
⇔ Fairmont and Radium Hot Springs, Panorama Ski Resort, hiking, cross-country skiing, horseback riding

☞ Chalet-style home with European atmosphere, beautifully landscaped and large garden. Hosts are ardent outdoor enthusiasts. There are two cats.

Northwest Territories
and
Yukon

Resolute Bay

Jesudason, Terry (High Arctic Int. Explorer Service)
Box 200 Resolute Bay, Northwest Territories X0A 0V0   ☎ (819) 252-3875

Fly in from Edmonton, Alberta or from Montreal Quebec.
$85S   (includes 3 meals and airport transportation)   ► 10
� Feb-Dec.   ● Full   🏠 Rural, view, isolated   ■ 1S,5D   ⊷ 10T   ⬗ Sh.w.g
★TV,LF,library   ⊛ Pets   ⌇ German
↪ Ice fishing for Arctic Char (Ap.-June), wildlife photography of birds and Arctic
flowers, historic sites, cross-country skiing, hiking, camping
⇔ Airport, snowmobile sledge trips, freighter-canoeing trips with local Inuit hunters

☞ Spend some time on top of the world and enjoy 24-hour sunshine. Observe Polar
Bears and Muskoxen in their natural habitat. Relax in the incredible beauty and serenity
of ice and land formation and the stillness of the frozen Arctic. Large Arctic library for
guests. Arctic delicacies (Arctic Char, Muskox & Caribou meats) served.

Dawson City

Hendley, John and Gail (White Ram Manor)   ⌐ Northern Network B&B
Box 302, Dawson City, Yukon   Y0B 1G0   ☎ (403) 993-5772

Phone for directions.
$60D $15Add.person   ► 4A,1Ch
✳ Summer   ● Choice (make your own from stocked cupboard)   🏠 Downtown, res.,
duplex   ■ 6 (upper and main level)   ⊷ 2D,2R   ⬗ 1Sh.w.g., 1sh.w.h.   ★ F,LF,KF,
TV in guest room, parking   ⊛ Non-smokers preferred
↪ Dawson City, stately Palace Grand Theatre (Gaslight Follies), Dawson City Post
Office (special commemorative postage stamps), Madame Tremblay's store, Robert
Service's cabin, Diamond Tooth Gertie's Gambling Hall, Spring Drama Festival
⇔ Midnight Dome, gold fields, active gold mining operations, guided trips down the
Yukon and Stewart Rivers

☞ New R2000 home with very comfortable and informal atmosphere located in the
heart of the Klondike a community designated by Parks Canada as a national historic
site. There is a Labrador in the house on occasion. Hostess is representative of Northern
Network B&B in Dawson City.

B&B Travel Tip: *You can stay in a B&B even if you are on a camping trip.*
Give yourself a treat and sleep in a comfortable bed once in a while, especially if
the weather turns miserable and the gear is soaking wet.

Whitehorse

Rowse, Jim and Sally Northern Network B&B
39 Donjek Rd, Whitehorse, Yukon Y1A 3R1 ☎ (403) 667-4315

Take downtown exit off the Alaska Hwy and follow exit route to 2nd Ave. Turn right and cross Robert Campbell Bridge over Yukon River (2nd runs into Lewes). Proceed to light, turn left onto Alsek then to Donjek Rd. Turn right to house at right near end of street.
$45S $55-65D $10-20Child $20Add.person $5Taxi service ► 6A,3Ch
● Cont. Downtown, res., split-level, patio, quiet ■ 2D (lower level)
2T,2T,1R,crib 1Sh.w.g.,1ensuite ★ TV,F,LF, parking (also for RV)
Smoking, pets limited French and Spanish
↔ Downtown Whitehorse, library, Archives, Art Gallery, museum, SS Kondile National Historic Site hiking trails and nature walks, tennis, swimming pool, bus route
⇔ Miles Canyon, Takhini Hot Springs, Yukon Gardens, Yukon River Cruise (MV Schwatka), Reindeer Farm

Spacious home furnished with antiques arranged in a country decor and located in a park-like setting provides gracious hospitality without extravangance. Relax in quiet homey atmosphere. House specialty is sourdough pancakes. There is a dog in the house. Hosts are Co-ordinators for The "Northern Network of B&B's"

Northern Network of Bed & Breakfasts
39 Donjek Rd., Whitehorse, Yukon Y1A 3R1 ☎ (403) 667-4315
(Co-ordinator Jim and Sally Rowse)
Rates 40-50S $50-60D $60-75F $15Child $15-20 Add.person (●included)
The Northern Network of Bed & Breakfasts represents homes in Watson Lake, Whitehorse, Tagish, Haines, Wasilla and Dawson City, as well as Atlin (BC) and Skagway (Alaska) in rural or city settings. Some of the homes operate all year and offer private suites, guest cabins and wilderness experience. Shuttle service from airport or bus depot can be arranged.
Some of the members are listed in this publication. Send for brochure and contact the individual hosts for reservation and direction.

B&B Travel Tip: *You can stay in a B&B if you travel with your own trailer. Many B&B's have ample room and a hook-up for that purpose, and they usually welcome guests to join them in the house for breakfast.*

Alberta

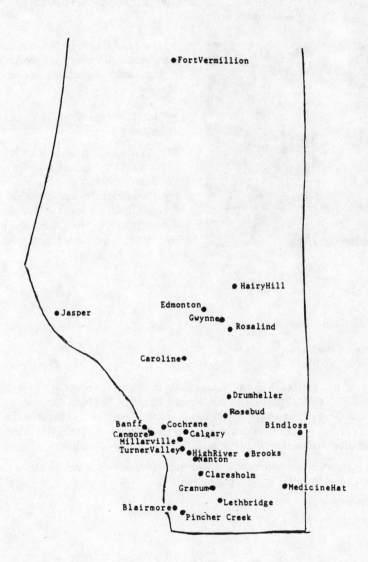

FortVermillion

HairyHill

Edmonton
Gwynne
Rosalind

Jasper

Caroline

Drumheller
Rosebud

Banff
Cochrane
Canmore
Calgary
Millarville
TurnerValley
HighRiver
Brooks
Nanton
Claresholm
Granum
MedicineHat
Blairmore
Lethbridge
Pincher Creek

Bindloss

Banff

(west of Calgary; see also Canmore, Cochrane)

Riedinger, Herbert and Fannye (Pension Tannenhof) ✔ CC
121 Cave Ave., Banff, Alberta T0L 0C0 ☎ (403) 762-4636/5660

Coming from East, cross Bow River Bridge, turn right, look for sign.. From West, at T-junction turn left, go 1 block, turn right over bridge, and right.
$50S(and up) $75D(and up) ► 35
● Full   ♠ Village, patio, quiet, view   ■ 1S,4D,2Ste,1F (3 levels) (also apt)
⊷S,T,D,Q,P, crib   ⅂ Private, sh.w.g., ensuite   ★ 2F,KF, separate entrance,
parking   ♥   ✋ Pets   ⋙ German, Spanish

↔ Cave and Basin, historic exhibition, tempered swimming pool, tennis courts, riding stables, downtown, Indian Museum

⇔ Banff Springs Hotel, Lake Louise, Johnston Canyon

☞ Very spacious home with homey, yet elegant atmosphere in quiet location and surrounded by pine trees. German style breakfast a house specialty. Unique BBQ, made out of petrified dinosaur bones (prob. the oldest one in the world) is available for guests.

Bindloss

(north of Medicine Hat)

Haas, Peggy and Wallace ✔ B&B
Bindloss, Alberta T0J 0H0 ☎ (403) 379-2300

Phone for directions. (Hosts are in and out, keep trying on the phone)
$8S $15D $2.50 ● Each(and up)   (Children's Rates)   🍽 Meals   ► 6
✤ Summer   ● Choice, homebaked   ♠ Farm, quiet, view   ■ 3D (upper and main
level)   ⊷ T,D, crib   ⅂ 1Private, 1sh.w.h.   ★ TV,KF,LF   ⋙ Some German
↔ Hiking, climbing, fishing and hunting, open prairie land, dog training

☞ Working farm with two houses and lots of space for visitors. Peaceful and quiet prairie scenery. Ideal for painting and photography.

Blairmore
(west of Lethbridge; see also, Pincher Creek)

Sara, William and Shirley.   ✔ S.Alta B&B
Box 1088, Blairmore, Alberta   T0K 0E0   ☎ (403) 628-3954

On Hwy 3 approx. 5 km west of Lundbreck, turn left at government gravel pit and follow gravel road to end.
$30S $45D $55F (of 4) $5Add. person   ▣ Meals   ► 4-6
● Full, homebaked   ♠ Farm, hist., view, quiet, riverfront, wine cellar   ■ 3D
◄ 3D, cot, crib   ⌐ 1Private, 2sh.w.h.   ★ F,LF   ⓦ Restricted pets   ⌁ some German
↔ Crowsnest River, Class A trout stream, river coulees (valley), wooded area
⇔ Frank Slide Interpretive Center (1903 mountain fall), Head-Smashed- In Buffalo Jump (world Heritage Site), Ski hills (West Castle, Fernie (beginner to expert), superb fishing, hunting, cross-country skiing, Waterton National Park, BC and US borders

☞ Period home (one of first-built in Alberta and later moved from original site) furnished in authentic style with secluded river frontage and view of Livingstone Range. Hosts are well travelled nationally and internationally and specialize in wine and gourmet cooking.

Brooks
(east of Calgary)

Douglas, Doral and Ilene (The Douglas Country Inn)
Box 463, Brooks, Alberta   T0J 0J0   ☎ (403) 362-2873

Located 6.5 km north of the thriving town of Brooks on John Ware Trail 873 and just off the Trans Canada Hwy.
$60S $75D   ▣ Meals (Weekly rates and Senior Citizens discounts available)   ► 8A
● Full, homebaked   ♠ Farm, bungalow, quiet, isolated   ■ 4D   ◄ 2T,3Q
⌐ 4Private   ★ Air,F, TV in guest room on request, separate entrance, freezer and cleaning facilities for sportsmen   ⓦ Smoking, no facilities for young children
↔ Hunting for pheasants, ducks, geese
⇔ Horticultural Research and Wildlife Centers, Dinosaur Prov. Park (World Heritage site with guided tours to restricted areas) Brooks Aquaduct, fishing, golfing, swimming

☞ "Rest easy in Casual Country Luxury" and enjoy a hearty country breakfast (including homemade sour dough bread) served in the solarium. There is a licenced Dining room on the premises and reservations are required for Saturday night Dinner. Picnic lunches can be provided. Pets are welcome to stay in heated Kennels.

Calgary
(see also Cochrane, Nanton, Millarville, High River)

Buckley, Evelyn and Clarence   ↙ B&B
RR2, Calgary, Alberta   T2P 2G5   ☎ (403) 242-9234

Located at Springbank. Phone for directions.
$25S $45D $10Child   ▣ Meals   ► 8
● Choice, homebaked (ranch-style)   ♠ Ranch, view, patio, quiet   ■ 4D
⊷ 2Q,2T,1D   ⊓ 2Sh.w.g.   ★ TV,F,LF, hot tub, trampoline   ⓦ Children min. age 6
↪ Large ranch grounds, Calaway Theme Park
⇔ Calgary, Kananaskis Prov. Park, Olympic Site, downhill and cross- country skiing,
Rocky Mountains

☛ Congenial hosts in unique, beautifully decorated ranch home specializing in western
ranch life. Convenient location, just a short drive outside the city.

Buroker, Mrs. Julene (Mrs. Buroker's B&B)   ↙ B&B
3012 Capital Hill Cres.N.W., Calgary, Alta   T2M 4C5   ☎ (403) 282-2479/288-2109

From Trans Canada Hwy, turn north on 19 St NW and continue to Morley Trail. Turn
left and go to Castle Rd and then left onto Capital Hill Cres.
$25S $35D   ► 2
● Choice   ♠ Res., sub., ranchstyle, view, patio   ■ 1D   ⊷ 1D   ⊓ Sh.w.h.
★ F,TV,LF,KF, parking   ⓦ Smoking, pets, quiet after 11pm
↪ University of Calgary, McMahon Stadium, shopping center, United Church, L.R.T.
Station (light rapid train to downtown)
⇔ City Center, hospital, Rocky Mountain foothills, Kananaskis Olympic ski area

☛ Relaxed and casual atmosphere in beautiful established north-west area of the city
and easy access from The University of Calgary campus.

DeVries, Mark and Natalie   ↙ B&B
23 Langton Drive, S.W., Calgary, Alberta   T3E 5G1   ☎ (403) 243-3193

Phone for directions.
$30S $40-50D $10Child   ▣ Meals   ► 4-5
● Choice   ♠ Res., sub., patio, quiet   ■ 2D,F   ⊷ 1D,1Q, bassinett, playpen
⊓Sh.w.g.   ★ KF,LF,TV, parking   ⓦ Pets   ⌇ Dutch   ♥
↪ Shopping centre, bus lines, restaurants, parks, swimming pool
⇔ Heritage Park, Glen Bow Museum, downtown City Centre, Calgary Tower, Calgary
Zoo, Calaway Park, Stampede(July)

☛ Young hosts with 3 small children in comfortable home offer family atmosphere in a
quiet residential area of the City. Children more than welcome.

Heerema, Joanne ✓ B&B
335-40 St., S.W., Calgary, Alta T3C 1V9 ☎ (403) 246-2443

Phone for directions.
$30S $40D   🍽 Meals ►4A
● Choice   🏠 Res., sub., patio, quiet   ■ 2D (ustairs)   ↵ 2D   ⌐ 1Private,
1sh.w.h.   ★ TV,LF, parking   ⚘ Children, pets, restricted smoking and drinking
⚬Dutch, French, some German
↔ Shopping centre, bus-lines, restaurants
⇔ Heritage Park, Glen Bow Museum, downtown, Calgary Zoo, Stampede (July)

☞ Split-level home with well-kept grounds and situated close to downtown.

MacNichol, Robin , L.J.
1639 Altadore Ave., S.W., Calgary, Alberta T2T 2P8 ☎ (403) 243-0362

Located in the south-west part of the City. Phone for directions.
$30S $40D $10Child   🍽 Meals ►4
● choice   🏠 Res., older, quiet   ■ 2D and extra space in basement   ↵ 1S,1D,R
⌐Sh.w.h.   ★ Air,F,TV,KF,LF, parking   ⚘ Smoking
↔ Bus stop(to downtown city centre)

☞ Quiet neighborhood in residential area. There is a dog in the house.

Turgeon, Eileen and Denis ✓ CC
4903 Viceroy Dr.N.W., Calgary, Alberta T3A 0V2 ☎ (403) 288-0494

Please call for directions.
$25S $40D   🍽 Meals ►4
✹ Summer (off-season by special arrangement)   ● Full, homebaked   🏠 Res.,
bungalow, patio, quiet   ■ 3D (main and lower level)   ↵ 1D,2Q,1R
⌐1Sh.w.h.,2sh.w.g.   ★ Air,TV,F,LF, street parking   ⚘ children, restricted smoking
and drinking, pets only by special request   ⚬ French
↔ Quiet park at end of street, two large shopping centres, bus line connecting with LRT
(Light Rail Transit) to downtown, University of Calgary, McMahon Stadium
⇔ Canada Olympic Park, Heritage Park, Calgary Zoo, Glenbow Museum, Kananaskis

☞ Home is located in quiet north-west residential area. Warm and friendly Western
Hospitality. Hosts will meet planes, trains and buses with prior arrangement.

Bed & Breakfast Bureau
Box 7094 Station E., Calgary, Alta T3C 3L8 ☎ (403) 242-5555/Banff:762-5070
(President: Don Sinclair)
Rates: $20-50S $35-125D $10-20Add.person $5(single night stay surcharge)
The Bureau represents a variety of excellent hosts in over sixty towns and cities in the
Province of Alberta as well as some hosts located in BC. Most of the homes are situated
along the Trans-Canada Highway, in the Foothills and Rocky Mountains. Write for free
brochure including Reservation Form. Deposit required upon reservation.

ALBERTA   77

Canmore

(west of Calgary; see also Banff, Cochrane)

Doucette, Mrs. Patricia (Cougar Creek Inn) ✔ CC
240 Grizzly Cres., Canmore, Alberta T0L 0M0 ☎ (403) 678-4751

From Trans Canada Hwy 1 exit to Canmore on Hwy 1a and continue to Benchland Trail
and Cougar Creek Dr and then to Grizzly Cres.
$35S $50D $5Child ► 8
● Full, homebaked 🏠 Res., view, patio, quiet ■ 2S,2D,1F ↦ 4T,2D,1P crib
⌐1Private, 1sh.w.h. ★ F, separate entrance, parking, private guest patio and BBQ
spit ⑭ Pets
↦ Beautiful walks along Creek to Creek head with waterfall, downtwon, quaint
mountain community, galleries (local artists), gift shops, a restaurants, elegant dining
⇔ Banff and Banff National Park, Lake Louise, Kananaskis Village, Spray River and
Spray Lakes Recreational areas, Lake Minnewanka

🕮 Quiet, rustic Cedar Chalet with beautiful mountain views in every direction.
Property borders on Cougar Creek and is surrounded by rugged mountain scenery,
which invites all types of outdoor activity. Hosts have a strong love for the mountains
and can give guests recommendations concerning local hiking, skiing (cross-country,
back country and downhill), as well as scenic drives, canoeing and mountain bike trips,
back-packing etc.

Green, Richard and Patricia (Patrick's B&B) ✔ B&B
Box 1086, Canmore, Alberta T0L 0M0 ☎ (403) 678-2358

Phone for directions from Travel Alberta Information Centre (Canmore Exit off Hwy 1)
$25-30S $40-45D $5-15Child $10-20Add.person ► 4
● Homebaked 🏠 Village, res., mountain view, patio, quiet ■ 1Ste ↦2T,1D
⌐Private ★ Separate entrance, parking ♥ ⑭Restricted smoking, pets ⸺some
Spanish
↦ Hiking trails, Bow River, fishing, cross-country and downhill skiing
⇔ Banff (shopping, dining) Banff School of Fine Arts, Sunshine Ski Resort, Winter
Olympics 88 area

🕮 Large home with art and antiques. There are two small children and a dog.

B&B Travel Tip: *All hosts are very obliging to special needs, but as a guest
you must always remember that these extras are usually given by the hosts out of
friendliness and a desire to please.*

Segstro, Jac and Sarah (Jac'n'Sarah's)
Box 1067, Canmore, Alberta T0L 0M0   ☎ (403) 678-2770

Please call for directions.
$30S $50-60D $10Add.person $5Child   (Reduced rates in spring/fall)   ► 10
● Choice, homebaked   ♠ Res., mountain views, quiet cul-de-sac, large decks   ■ 1D
with loft, 1Ste with loft (mainand upper level)   ↵ 3Q,4S   ⌐ 1Sh.w.g.1sh.w.h.
★F,LF,KF, large skylight in one guest room for starlit view from bed, separate
entrance   ⊕ smoking

↪ Quiet and scenic walks at the doorstep, downtown business center, restaurants, galleries, gift shops, dike holding back the Bow River

⇔ Nordic Centre, Hot Springs, hiking, mountaineering, cross-country skiing, Banff National Parks, downhill skiing, Kananaskis Valley, site of 1988 Olympic events, Calgary

☞ "Rooms with a difference - Hospitality with a flair". House is situated on a quiet cul-de-sac which backs onto the Bow River with a beautiful vie of the Rocky Mountains and Foothills.

Hosts have travelled B&B all across New Zealand. There are pets in the house.

Setzer, Ottmar and Ulrike (Haus Alpenrose Lodge)   ⌐ CC
629-10th St., Canmore, Alberta T0L 0M0   ☎ (403) 678-4134

Located in Canmore behind Public Libaray and near Fire Hall.
$30-35S $40-50D $50-80F   ► 20
● Choice, homebaked   ♠ Downtown, Bavarian chalet-style, view, quiet   ■4D,3FF
↵ 2Q,4D   ⌐ 3Sh.w.g.   ★ 2F,KF, TV in guest rooms, sauna   ⊕Smoking
∿German, French
↪ Variety of good restaurants, Canmore Nordic Olympic Centre, Hodoos, Bow River
dykes, Grassi Lakes and Benches, walking by rivers, hiking, climbing, trail rides, golfing,
fishing, cross-country skiing
⇔ Downhill skiing, rock and ice-climbing, Banff, Yoho, Kananaskis & Assinniboine
Prov. Parks, Kootenay and Jasper Nat. Parks, Lake Louise and Sunshine ski areas,
cross-country and biathlon trails

☞ Rustic, comfortable pension, nestled in the very heart of the Canadian Rockies at
the foot of the Three Sisters Mountain amd Chinaman's Peak; a recreation lodge for the
outdoor enthusiast. Hosts also operate The Canadian School of Mountaineering.

Caroline
(near Red Deer)

Bystrom, Burdett and Louise (Burlou Ranch) ✔ AFV
Box 106, Caroline, Alberta T0M 0MC ☎ (403) 722-2409

Take Hwy 2 to Hwy 54 interchange between Edmonton and Calgary and travel west to
Caroline. Turn south at hotel and then go 5 km to Burlou Ranch.
$30S $35D ▣ Meals (Rates for riding and trail rides) ● Full, homebaked
⌂Ranch, view ⓦ Children min. age 7
↪ Riding, fishing, hiking, swimming, boating, winter hay rides, cross-country skiing,
overnight and longer trail rides
⇔ Community activities and rodeos, Innisfail, Rocky Mountain House

☞ Visitors may stay in the ranch house and participate in regular ranch activities.
Homecooked nutritional meals are a specialty. Burlou Ranch is nestled in the foothills of
the Rocky Mountains.

Claresholme
(near Lethbridge: see also Nanton, High River, Pincher Creek, Granum)

Laing, Anola & Gordon (Anola's Bed & Breakfast) ✔ CC
Box 340, Claresholm, Alberta T0L 0T0 ☎ (403) 625-4389

Located 15 km east of Claresholm on Hwy 520 and 1.5 km north.
$20S $40D ► 4
● Full, homebaked (cater to diabetics) ⌂ 3600-acres farm, ranch-style, patio
■2D ⊢4T ⅂ Sh.w.g (old-fashioned tub) ★ F, separate entrance, TV in guest
room, indoor hot tub ⓦSmoking, pets, children min. age 12
↪ Airstrip adjacent to farm building
⇔ Calresholm Agriplex, Head-Smashed-in Buffalo Jump (UNESCO World Heritage
site), Museum at Fort MacLeod

☞ Country home is furnished with Western Canadian antiques and quilts like
"Grandma used to have". Work out on the rowing machine and soak in the hot tub.

Cochrane
(near Calgary; see also Canmore, Banff)

McDowell, Kevin and Kay
Box 955, Cochrane, Alberta T0L 0W0 ☎ (403) 932-3675

Located 13 km west of Cochrane on Hwy 1A, and 13 km north on Forestry Rd 940. Turn
left past Benchlands sign to cedar home flying Alberta flag.
$25S $30D $5Child (under age 16) ► 2A,2Ch
● Full, homebaked ⌂ Rural, acreage, patio, view ■ Ste (1D,F) ⊢ 1D,2R
⅂ 1Private ★ TV,LF,F ⓦ Pets
↪ Ghost River
⇔ Horseback riding, hiking, Kananaskis and Peter Loughead Parks, Banff Nat.Park

☞ Great hospitality and fine food. Situated high above the river with a panoramic
view of the everchanging Rockies and surrounding foothills. There is a little dog.

Drumheller

(east of Calgary: see also Rosebud)

Parsons, Sally and John (The Parson's House)   ⌐ CC
131-2nd St. W., Drumheller, Alberta T0J 0Y0   ☎ (403) 823-8524

Located in Drumheller on the main highways (56 and 9). Look for 2nd house south of
the Red Deer River bridge crossing.
$35S $40D $54F $7Child $7Add.person   ►8
● Full, homebaked $h Village, hist., 2 porches   ■ 2D,1F   ⇥ 4D,R, crib
⌐Sh.w.g.   ★ TV,LF, parking   ⓦ Restricted smoking
↔ Downtown city centre, shopping, restaurants and services
⇔ World famous Tyrell Museum of Palaentology

☞ Cozy, spacious home is tastefully decorated with antiques. Host is a commercial
Fossile Dealer and the owner of "The Fossil Shop". Formerly from North Carolina,
hostess' specialty is "Southern Hospital".

Edmonton

(see also Gwynne, New Sarepta)

Croteau, Paul and Suzanne (Suzanne's)
18603-68 Ave., Edmonton, Alberta T5T 2M8   ☎ (403) 487-2071

Phone for directions.
$30S $40D $60F $5Child $10Add.person   ▣ Meals   ► 2A,2Ch
●Choice, homebaked   ♠ Res., patio, quiet   ■ 1S,1D,1F (lower level)
⇥1S,1D,R,P   ⌐ 1Sh.w.g.   ★ F,TV in guest room, parking   ⁓ French

↔ West Edmonton Mall

⇔ Elk Island Park, downtown
Edmonton City Center, Children's Zoo,
University of Alberta

☞ Relax and enjoy the large yard
with garden after a full day of exploring
the world's biggest Mall (which has also
an indoor phantasyland, an indoor
waterpark with beach and indoor
scating rink).

Townsley, Mrs. Eileen
7311-180 St., Willow Circle, Edmonton, Alberta T5T 2T1   ☎ (403) 481-4719

From Whitemud Freeway take 178 St. Turn left to 76 Ave, then right and left again to
Willow Cresc and 3rd house on right.
$25S $35D   ⌐3A
●Full   ♠ Res., split-level, quiet   ■ 1S,1F(upstairs and lower level)   ⊢ 1S,2T
⌐1Private, 1sh.w.h   ★ TV in guest room, parking   ⊛ Smoking, drinking, pets,
children, couples or females guests only
↪ Largest shopping center in the world (West Edmonton Mall), Fort Edmonton,
Storyland Valley Zoo, Alberta museum

☞ Cozy atmosphere in quiet residential area. Beautifully furnished Duplex in west end
area of the City.

Wagner, Ellenora
8306-158 St., Edmonton, Alberta T5R 2C4   ☎ (403) 483-1517

Take 159 St Exit from Whitemud Freeway and go two blocks right, then right again.
$25S $35D   ► 2A,1Ch
● Full   ♠ Res., raised bungalow, quiet, deck   ■ 1S,1D   ⊢ 1S,1D   ⌐ Sh.w.h.
★ TV,KF,LF, parking   ⋙ German
↪ West Edmonton Mall (largest shopping center in the world)
⇔ Downtown City Centre, University of Alberta

☞ Congenial hostess in cheerful and comfortable home located in very convenient
residential area of the city.

Bed and Breakfast Alberta's Gem Reservation Agency
11216-48 Ave., Edmonton Alberta T6H 0C7   ☎ (403) 434-6098
(President: Betty and Gorden Mitchell)
Rates: $25-35S $35-45D   (including breakfast)
Alberta's Gem offers personal and inexpensive accommodation throughout the Province
and some in BC. There are approximately 50 homes registered with the Agency.
For a brochure and special information on the National Parks of Jasper, Banff and
Revelstoke write to the above including $1 for postage.

Alberta and Pacific Bed and Breakfast
Box 15477, MPO, Vancouver, BC V6B-5B2   ☎ (604) 682-4610(8am-2pm)
(Mrs. June M. Brown)
Rates $30S $40D   (Deposit required) (Agency closed during Oct-Feb)
Alberta and Pacific B&B (formerly in Edmonton, Alta) is now relocated in Vancouver.
Mrs. Brown makes reservations for Alberta (Edmonton, Calgary, Banff, Jasper), as well
as for BC (Vancouver, Kamloops, Victoria and Whistler). Brochure available for $1
(overseas enquires please include International Coupon to cover postage.

Fort Vermilion
(northern Alberta)

Fromhold, Irene and Joe (Vermilion Lodge)   ⌐ CC
Gen Delivery, Fort Vermilion, Alberta T0H 1N0   ☎ (403) 927-4470

Located 700 miles by paved road north from Edmonton via Peace River and High Level
to Fort Vermilion and situated 1.5 km east of Fort Vermilion on River Road.
$30S $35D   ●$1.50-5Each   🍴 Meals   ► 14
● Full 🏠 Village, hist., acreage, patio, quiet   ■ 6D,2F (main and upper level)
⇥10T,4D, 3cots   ⌐ 1Sh.w.h.,1sh.w.g.   ★ TV, parking, firepit and BBQ,
〰German, French, Cree
↔ Children's playground, Tipi Village, group Firepit, Frontier Farm, Trading Post,
coffee shop, Indian Museum, historic cemetery, horseshoe, mini golf, riverside,
cross-country skiing, snowmobiling, hiking trail, fishing
⇔ Alberta's oldest community (200 years) and first settlement homes, boat launch,
ecology trail, North America's northernmost agricultural region, river rafting,
Mennonite communities, Northern Boreal Wilderness (largest waterfall, accessible by
boat only)

☞ A reconstruction of a turn-of-the-Century frontier community, owned and operated
by an Indian family, specializing in Indian Lore. Hosts are very knowledgeable about
Indian History and Culture, Anthropology and Archaeology. There are pets in the house.
Accommodation (furnished) is also available in tipis, trapper's tent and homesteader's
tent for 26 people.

Gwynne
(south of Edmonton; see also Rosalind)

Glaser, Mabel (Gwynalta Farm)   ⌐ AFV
Gwynne, Alberta T0C 1L0   ☎ (403) 352-3587

From Edmonton, take Hwy 2 south to Leduc. Then take Hwy 2A past Kavanaugh to
junction Hwy 616. Go east for 1.6 km past Clover Lawn Community Hall, then south for
5 km to Gwynalta Farm. Or take Hwy 13 to Gwynne, turn north on Secondary Hwy 822
for 9.6 km, then travel 1.6 km west and then north 0.8 km and west to farm.
$20S $25D $3 ● Each $7.50Child   🍴 Meals $7Camping   ► 4
● Choice 🏠 Dairy farm ■ 2D ⇥T,Q ⌐ Sh.w.h. ★ TV,F,KF,LF 〰 German
↔ Lake for fishing, hiking, bird-watching, skiing, ice-fishing, snowmobiling
⇔ Community centre, local shopping area, Wetaskiwin, Edmonton Int. Airport

☞ Guests are invited to enjoy the quiet countryside and see the Northern Lights.
Operating dairy farm with adjoining lake. Bring your own boat.

Granum

(near Lethbridge; see also Claresholm, Nanton, Pincher Creek)

Dimm, Marilyn, Jocelyn and Cliff (Dimm's Ranch B&B) ⌣ CC
Box 228, Granum, Alberta T0L 1A0 ☎ (403(687-2274

Located off Hwy 2 northwest of Lethbridge on route to Calgary.
$30S $40D $15Child(age 6-14) $10Add.person ► 6A,4Ch
●Choice, homebaked   ♠ Ranch, split-level on hill, acreage, mountain view, patio,
quiet, large deck   ■3D1F   ⇥2T,2Q   ⌐1Sh.w.g.,1ensuite ★Air,F,LF,TV in guest
room, separate entrance, sauna, parking, corral for overnight horses   ✋Smoking, pets

↔ Ranch buildings, corrals, ranch
surroundings for walking and hiking,
Willow Creek runs through property,
artifcial lake (Dimm's Lake, also on
property) stocked with trout

⇔ Head-Smashed-In Buffalo Jump
Interpretive Centre, Fort Museum
(Musical Ride Mounted Patrol),
Claresholm Museum, Rodeos and Fair
Days, live stage production at Fort
MacLeod, Hutterite Brethern Colony,
golf courses

☞ Working ranch with cedar house built into the hills with beautiful views of the
foothills, Rocky Mountains and unsurpassed sun-sets . Huge deck-balcony on west side
and surrounded by a shelter belt of huge trees. Hosts enjoy all outdoor sports when not
involved with riding, branding etc.

High River

(near Calgary; see also Millarville, Nanton,Claresholm, Turner Valley)

McLean, Lenore and Roy (Highlandview Guest Ranch)
RR2, High River, Alberta T0L 1B0 ☎ (403) 395-2154/2149

Go south 10 km on Hwy 2A from High River to Hwy 540. Turn west and follow oiled
road for 25 km.
$30 per person   🍽 Meals ► 10
● Homecooked   ♠ Farm, view, quiet   ■ In main ranch or bunkhouse   ⇥S,T,D
⌐ Sh.w.h., sh.w.g.   ★ TV,F   ✋ Pets
↔ Horseback riding and lessons, cross-country skiing, sleigh rides

☞ Working farm and ranch in Alberta Foothills with spectacular Mountain View.
Annual branding in spring. Guided trails and rides.

Hairy Hill
(east of Edmonton near Vegreville)

Toma, Lawrence and Ann (L.A.Triple B Guest Farm) ✓ AFV
Box 21, Hairy Hill, Alberta   T0B 1S0 ☎ (403) 768-3877

From Vegreville travel 32 km north on Hwy 857 and 8 km east on Hwy 637.
$25S $40D ► 6
● Full   ♠ 1600-acres farm   ■ 2D (downstairs)
⊷2D,1D   ⅂1Private   ⑭Smoking, pets   ⌇ Ukrainian, Hungarian

↔ Trout fishing, horseshoes, table tennis, track ball, lawn darts

🖝 Working grain farm offers warm Alberta hospitality. Hosts cater primarily to farm vacationers and hunters. Guests may observe farm activities or relax in complete solitude by the outdoor fireplace.

Jasper
(west of Edmonton; see also Valemount,BC)

Dobra, Mrs. Bonnie ► CC
Box 285, 308 Balsam Ave., Jasper, Alberta   T0E 1E0 ☎ (403) 852-5637

Located 2 blocks off Connaugt Dr (Main Street). Phone for directions.
$42S $45D $5Child $5Add.person   ▣ Meals ► 4
● None   ♠ Village, older, split-level, view, quiet, large deck   ■1Ste(upstairs)   ⊷D,P
⅂Private   ★Separate entrance, KF,TV in guest room   ⑭Pets   ⌇French,Hungarian
↔ Downtown shopping area, churches, restaurants, fine dining, hiking/skiing trails
⇔ National Park, downhill ski areas, golfing, horseback riding, fishing, lakes

🖝 Very warm family oriented home. Host is a Chef and will make nutritious and delicious box lunches for hikers and skiers on request.

B&B Travel Tip: *B&B travelling can be most enjoyable, when it is planned ahead and when there is ample time to socialize.*

ALBERTA   85

Kan, Mrs. Marilyn Leslie   ✓ CC
Box 1940, Jasper, Alberta T0E 1E0   ☎ (403) 852-3009

Located in town at 1222A Cabin Creek Drive. Phone for directions.
$15-20S $25-30D $5Add.person   (Discounts for longer stay)   ► 4
● None   🏠 Res., quiet   ■ 2D   ⊨ 2T,1S   ⌐ 1Sh.w.g.   ✋ Pets, smoking.
↔ Jasper Town Center, hiking trails
⇔ Jasper National Park

☞ House is situated in a new subdivision at the west of the townsite with a partial view
of the Mountain skyline. If requested, hosts may pick-up guests by prior arrangement.

Lethbridge
(south-western Alberta; see also Pincher Creek, Lundbreck, Blairmore)

Haig, Joan and Bruce (Heritage House)   ✓ B&B
1115-8th Ave. South, Lethbridge, Alta T1J 1P7   ☎ (403) 328-9011

Phone for directions.
$29S $40D $10Add.person   ▣ Meals   ► 5
● Full, homebaked   🏠 Res., hist., patio, quiet   ■ 2D (upstairs)   ⊨ 2D,1R   ⌐ Private
↔ Walking tour of Lethbridge, Japanese Gardens
⇔ Head-Smashed-In Buffalo Jump, hist. Ft. MacLeod, Mormon Temple, Waterton Park

☞ 1937-built home is a provincial historic resource, situated on a large city lot not far
from downtown area and designated because of its architecture and hand painted inside
decorations. Breakfasts reflect western Canadian taste. Hosts are knowledgeable about
western Canadian history and operate the Trails West B&B Bureau. There is a dog.

Medicine Hat
(south-east of Calgary)

Kuntz, Betty (Betty's B&B)   ✓ CC
547 Terrill Rd. N.W., Medicine Hat, Alberta   T1A 7A8   ☎ (403) 526-2026

From Hwy 1 turn onto 3rd St NW, turn left onto Brier Park Rd. Turn right onto 12th St
NW. Turn right again on McCutcheon Dr, then left on Bassett Cres and left at Terrill.
$30S $35D   ▣ Meals   Children welcome   ► 6
✳ Summer   ● Full   🏠 Res., patio, quiet   ■ 2D (main and lower level)   ⊨ 2D,2P,
crib   ⌐ 1Private, 1sh.w.h.   ★ Air,TV,LF, parking   ✋ Pets, drinking   〰 Limited
French and German
    ↔ Shopping Centre and recreational facilities, park, several churches
    ⇔ Golfing, Waterslide

☞ Quiet and restful atmosphere. Home cooked food, including breads and pastries.
Retired Teacher hostess has travelled extensively through Canada and abroad. There is a
small gift shop on the premises.

Phillips, George and Isabelle
General Delivery, Medicine Hat, Alberta   T1A 7E4   ☎ (403) 527-0321

From Hwy 41A east out of Medicine Hat, turn right at Burnco Rock Products Lts.
Follow gravel road for 1 km. (Write or phone in advance)
$15S $25D $5Add. person $1.50 ● Each   ► 4
● Full (fix your own with food provided)   ♠ Sub, acreage, quiet   ■ Mobile home
(self-contained)   ⌣ 2D, cot   ⌐ Private   ★ KF,LF, separate entrance, parking
Ⓦ Drinking, smoking   ⌂ German
↩ Riding stable, Nature studies, bird watching
⇔ Hycroft China Co., Canadian Greenhouse and Floral Centre, Alberta Glass Plant,
Riverside Waterslide and Amusement Park, Cypress Hills Prov. Park

☞ Countryside is especially appealing to artists/photographers. Accommodation is
adjacent to host home. Children and pets welcome.

Millarville
(near Calgary; see also High River, Turner Valley)

Glaister, Dave and Lucille (Mesa Creek Ranch)   ✓ AFV
RR1 Millarville, Alberta   T0L 1K0   ☎ (403) 931-3573/3618

From Calgary, take Trans-Canada Hwy 2 south to Hwy 22X and go west to Millarville.
Continue west on Sec.Rd 549 to Sec.Rd 762, north to sawmill and then west to ranch.
$25 per person   🍽 Meals   ► 8
● Full, homebaked   ♠ 3,000-acre cattle ranch, view   ■ 3   ⌣ 4T,2D, crib
⌐ 1Sh.w.h., 1sh.w.g.   ★ TV,F, ranch library   ♥

↩ Horseback riding, hiking, fishing,
cross-country skiing

⇔ Turner Valley, towns of Black
Diamond and Bragg Creek

☞ Operating cattle ranch located in
the foothills of the Canadian Rockies
bordering on Kananaskis Country.
Enjoy the activities or just relax by the
fireplace in the rustic lodge.

B&B Travel Tip: *You can stay in a B&B when visiting a sick relative or
friend in another town. It makes for very comforting and convienent accommodation. Many hospitals keep lists of nearby B&B's for out-of-town relatives.*

Nanton

(south of Calgary; see also High River, Claresholm, Turner Valley)

Squire, Sam and Rosemary (The Squire Ranch)   ✔ B&B
RR1, Nanton, Alberta T0L 1R0   ☎ (403) 646-5789/646-2736

From Calgary, take Hwy 2 to Nanton. Just south of town turn right (west) on Hwy 533.
Go 9.6 km, turn left (south) and continue 8.7 km on winding road into hills. Turn right
off Hwy 533 on steep turn, go 1.7 km and turn left (west) to ranch.
$20-25S $35-45D   (Extra for riding)   ▣ Meals   ► 6
● Choice   ♠ Beef-Cattle Ranch, view, quiet, patio   ■ 2D,1S,F (upper and lower
level)   ⊷ 3T,1Q, mattresses for guest's own sleeping bags   ⊓ 2Sh.w.g.
★TV,F,LF, some facilities for the disabled   ♥   ⓦ Restricted smoking, drinking, pets
↔ Cross-country skiing, walking, riding for experienced riders, yard- activities
⇔ Rocky Mountains, hiking, trail-riding, canoeing, swimming, tennis, golfing, fishing,
curling, riding for beginners, Chain Lakes Provincial Park, historic sites

☞ Friendly Christian Ranch in foothills ranch country, with lovely view of mountains
and beautiful surrounding scenery. Located on route to Head-Smashed-In Buffalo Jump,
Waterton National Park, Kananaskis and Banff. There are llamas on the ranch.

Pincher Creek

(west of Lethbridge; see also Lundbreck, Blairmore, Claresholm)

Coles, Ralph and Bernie   ✔ S.Alta B&B
Box 1329, Pincher Creek, Alberta T0K 1W0   ☎ (403) 627-3443

Located 7 km west of Pincher Creek on the Christie Mines Rd.
$30-35S $40-45D   ▣ Meals   (Bag lunches available)   ► 6-7
● Full   ♠Buffalo-calf ranch   ■4   ⊷2D,1Q   ⊓ Private with jacuzzi tub   ★LF   ♥
↔ Horseback riding, fishing in stocked trout pond
⇔ Westcastle and Fernie Ski Hills, good fishing and hunting, US and Alberta borders

☞ Great western hospitatlity. Home overlooks mountains and surrounding Foothills.
The acreage is fenced and there is a large barn to accommodate horses and guests' pets.
Hostess is spokesperson for Southern Alberta B&B Booking Agency.

Sweet, Dorothy (Sweet's B&B)   ✔ S.Alta B&B
Box 1872, Pincher Creek, Alberta T0K 1W0   ☎ (403) 627-4208

Located 3.2 km south of Pincher Station. Look for house ar 1128 Bridge Ave.
$25S $30D $5Add. person $5Child   ▣ Meals   ► 3A,2Ch
● Full, homebaked   ♠ In town, quiet   ■ 1S,2F (upstairs)   ⊷ S,D   ⊓ Sh.w.h.
★ TV in guest room, LF, parking   ⓦ Smoking, drinking
↔ Downtown shopping, services
⇔ Head-Smashed-In-Buffalo-Jump, Frank Slide, Westcastle Ski Resort, Canadian
Rockies and Foothills, various fishing areas, Waterton Park and Waterton Hutterite
colony, US and BC borders

☞ Spacious older home with large grounds. Hosts offer friendly Alberta hospitality.

Rosalind
(near Edmonton; see also Gwynne)

Yuha, Steve and Marguerite (Rosalind's B&B)
General Delivery, Rosalind, Alberta   T0B 3Y0   ☎ (403) 375-3943

From Camrose travel southeast on Hwy 13 to junction 854. Turn south (right) on good
pavement for '8 km to Rosalind. Remain on paved road to the school. Turn east (left)
and 0.75 km to house on left side.
$20S $25D $40F   ◙ Meals   (Advance reservation please)   ► 8
● Choice   ♠ Village, patio, quiet   ■ 4D (mainand lower level)   ↲ 4T,2D
⌐2Sh.w.g.   ★TV,F,LF, parking   ⍦Pets in garage (by prior reservation)   ≈Polish
↔ Hockey and ball games, extensive Adventureland Playground
⇔ Grass green golf course (9hole), good fishing

☞ Semi-retired couple in bungalow in quiet village. Enjoy the peaceful atmosphere.

Rosebud
(east of Calgary, see also Drumheller)

Comstock, Bob and Rosemary (Bocoro Farm)   ↙ Big Country Reg.B&B
Box 714, Rosebud, Alberta   T0J 2T0   ☎ (403) 677-2269

From Calgary east on Hwy 1, continue east on Hwy 561 to Hwy 840 and then north to
Severn Dam sign and east to only farm on left side. From Drumheller go west on Hwy 9
to Hwy 840. Then south to sign and continue 4 km as above.
$25S $40D $10Child $5Dog ◙ Meals   (Family rates available)   ► 4A,4Ch
● Choice, homebaked   ♠ Farm, bungalow, view, sunporch   ■ 2S,2D
↲ 2S,1D,1Q,2P   ⌐ 2Sh.w.h.   ★ TV in guest room   ♥   ⍦ Restricted smoking
Theatre (Rosebud), fishing (stocked trout), Calgary

☞ Farm is set on the edge of a small ravine (coulee). There is a Kennel with a run on
the property. Hosts are involved in 4H clubs and other community activities and are
Representatives for "Big Country Bed & Breakfast Registry".

Turner Valley
(near Calgary; see also Millarville, High River, Nanton)

Lyon, Douglas and Doris (Bighorn Pension B&B) 　　　　 ✔ B&B
656 Royalite Way, S.E., Box 771, Turner Valley, Alberta　T0L 2A0　　☎ (403) 933-4714

Located in the middle of Turner Valley Golf and Country Club.
$20S　$38D　$8Child　📷 Meals 　　　　　　　　　　　　　　► 6A,4Ch
$f Full, homebaked　🏠 Rural, bungalow, view, patio, quiet　■ 1S,1D,1F (main and
lower level)　🛏 2S,2D　◥ 1sh.w.g.　★ TV,F,LF, separate entrance, parking　♥
🖐 Drinking
↔ Golfing,canoeing, kayaking, hiking, picnicking, fishing, swimming tubing gliding,
cross-country skiing, curling, skating, snowshoeing, hunting
↔ Kanaskis Country, Alberta Rockies, horseback riding, rodeoing, down-hill skiing,
mountain climbing and biking, skidooing, excellent restaurants

🐾 Home is located right in the middle of the Turner Valley Golf and Country Club just
off Fairway No 14 and offers cozy comfortable accommodation and German country
cooking. There is plenty of peace and quiet with a spectacular view of the Rocky
Mountains and foothills. Lunches packed for picnics, hiker's and skiers.

Saskatchewan

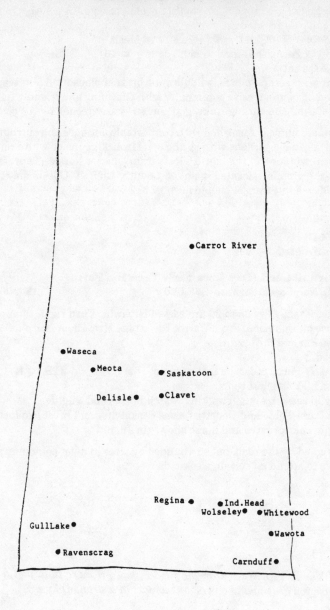

Carnduff

(in south-east part of Saskatchewan; see also Wawota)

Greenwood, Connie and Miles (Greenwood Vacation Farm)　　　✔SFV
Box 273 Carnduff, Saskatchewan　S0C 0S0　　　　　　　☎ (306) 482-3721

From Carnduff take the East road 5 km south, turn left and go 1.5 km west to farm with
white rail fence and country church.
$15S　$20D　$40F　$15Child　●$4Each　⬛Meals　　　　　►6
● Homebaked　🏠 Farm, split-level　■2D,1Ste　🛏3D　🥄2Sh.w.g.
★Air,F,KF, separate entrance　♥
↔ Native pasture with several ponds, wild flowers, birds and beautiful landscaped oasis
⇔ Town of Carnduff (a progressive community with charming and friendly folks),
swimming pool, stating and curling rinks, golf course (grass greens), tennis courts

☞ Modern 2-storey home is furnished with comfortable antiques and surrounded by
trees, flower and vegetable gardens with spring colts frolicking inside white rail fences
seen from different windows in the house. Hosts train Quarter horses. There is also an
antique store on the premises, located in an old Country Church. Guests may rent a golf
cart or bike or ride a horse (min. 4 people for lessons).

Carrot River

(east of Prince Albert)

Milligan, Dawn and Cecil (Day Dreamer's Vacation Farm)　　✔SFV
Box 635, Carrot River, Saskatchewan　S0E 0L0　　　　　☎ (306) 768-3525

From Prince Albert, take Hwy 55 to 26 km east of Nipawin. Turn right, then proceed 2
km south to house on right side. From Carrot River take Hwy 23 and turn left on grid
road. Proceed 3.5 km and turn right.
Rates not supplied　　　　　　　　　　　　　　　　　►4
● Homebaked　🏠 Farm, older, bungalow, quiet　■2S,1D　🛏2S,1Q,R
🥄Sh.w.h.　★KF,TV in guest room　♥
↔ Berry-picking in season, hiking, walking, watch horses and wildlife
⇔ Squaw Rapid Dam, Tobin and Codette Lakes, Saskatchewan Forest Product Sawmill
and Planer, wagon chariot races and horse shows (in June)

☞ House is situated by the road, but surrounded by trees in quiet community Hosts
have horse shows to attend on certain weekends.

B&B Travel Tip: *When travelling B&B, you get more than just a bed to
sleep, because you are making a personal contact in a strange place.*

Clavet

(near Saskatoon; see also Delisle)

Gallagher, Doreen and Bill (Yellowhead B&B) ⌐ SFV
Clavet, Saskatchewan S0K 0Y0 ☎ (306) 933-4986

Located 1.5km east of Clavet and .75km south from weigh scales on the Yellowhead Rt.
$15S $20D $30F $15Add.person ●$5Each ⦿ Meals ► 6A,5ch
● Full, homebaked ♠ Rural, res., acreage, patio, quiet ■ 2D (upstairs) ⊷ 2D,1P,
crib ⅂ Sh.w.g. ★ LF,F,TV in guest room, parking, telephone available in guest
room, wheel chair accessible ⓦ Smoking

⇔ Esso Chemical Plant, two Potash
mines, Saskatoon Gardens

☞ Spacious and comfortable country
home with old fashioned hospitality
and quiet country surroundings.
Popular coffee and lunch stop for
Seniors and bus tours. Camping
facilities and trailer hookups available.
Guest can explore the nearby Bee Farm.
Enjoy delicious fresh honey for
breakfast.

Delisle

(near Saskatoon; see also Conquest, Clavet)

Colborn, Keith and Norma, et al (Colborn Vacation Farm) ⌐ SFV,B&B
Box 183, Delisle, Saskatchewan S0L 0P0 ☎ (306) 493-2646

Travel 5 km north of Delisle, then 0.8 km east and 0.8 km north again.
$15S $20D ● $2.50Each ⦿ Meals ► 6
● Full ♠ Farm, view ■ D ⊷ D,R ⅂ Sh.w.h. ★ TV,F,KF,LF
↪ Horseback riding
⇔ Delisle Town Centre, golfing, shopping, boating,swimming, Saskatoon

☞ Large poultry farm with all kinds of animals. There is a pretty view of the creek and
yard. Hosts are ardent old-tyme and square dancers. Camping space on grounds.

Gull Lake
(west of Swift Current; see also Tompkins, Ravenscrage)

Magee, Tom and Beatrice (Magee's Farm) ⮕ SFV,B&B
Box 654, Gull Lake, Saskatchewan S0N 1A0 ☎ (306) 672-3970

Take Trans-Canada Hwy west from Gull Lake for 13.3 km. Turn left at"Carmichael"sign, then 6 km south to"Magee"sign. Turn left and go for 2.5 km to 1st farm on left.
$20S $30D $15Child(under age 12) ☒ Meals ► 6
✚ May-Oct.1 ● Choice, homebaked ♠ Farm ■ 2D(also modern cottage)
⊢ 3S,1D �🛏 1Sh.w.g. ★ TV,F
↪ Working grain and livestock farm grounds
⇔ Town of Gull Lake, Indian historic site, lookout, creek, trout fishing

☞ Mixed working farm. Hosts are involved in 4H and very interested in photography. Lunches packed for hunters.

Wells, Dick and Judy (Wounded Knee) ⮕ B&B
Box 527, Gull Lake, Saskatchewan S0N 1A0 ☎ (306) 672-3651

On Hwy 1 west of Gull Lake (20.8 km), turn south and travel 2.4 km to village of Carmichael. Turn right at white school to 1st house on left.
$15S $25D $10Child $15Add.person ☒ Meals ► 4
● Full, homebaked ♠ Village, res., bungalow, quiet ■ 2D ⊢ 2T,1Q
🛏 1Ensuite, 1sh.w.h. ★ Air,LF,TV in guest room
⇔ Cypress Park, Gull Lake, swimming pool, golf course

☞ Hunters welcome. There is a dog in the house. Please write or phone ahead.

Indian Head
(near Regina; see also Wolsley, Qu'Appelle, Whitewood)

Hearn, Al and Brenda (Hearn's Manor House B&B)
Box 1177, Indian Head, Saskatchewan S0G 2K0 ☎ (306) 695-3837

Located 0.8 km south of junction Hwys 1 and 56 at Indian Head.
$25S $35D $10Add.person ► 7-9
● Full, homebaked ♠ Village, older, acreage, quiet ■ 3D ⊢ 2T,1D,Q,R, crib
🛏 1Sh.w.g.,1sh.w.h. ★ TV,F
↪ Forestry farm (tours), late evening and early morning strolls
⇔ Scenic Qu'Appelle Valley, beautiful lakes for picnics and swimming

☞ Old English-style home built in 1889 with large comfortable and quiet rooms.

Meota
(near North Battleford; see also Waseca)

Sutton, June and Brian (Lakeside Leisure Farm)   ✓ SFV,B&B
Box 1, Meota, Saskatchewan   S0M 1X0   ☎ (306) 892-2145

Located 28 km north of the Battlefords (Hwy 4) and 4.5 km west on Metinota Acc. Rd.
$30S $40D $10Child $10Add.person   ◉ Meals   ► 6A,2Ch
✠ Summer   ● Choice   ♠ Farm, ranch-style, view, lakefront, patio, quiet, small plane
landing strip   ■ 3D,1F   ↦ 4T,1Q,1P   ⌐ 2Sh.w.g.   ★ TV,F,LF, separate
entrance   ⍟ Restricted smoking, pets outside   ♥
↪ Jackfish Lake with sandy beaches (fishing, swimming, sailing), Village of Meota
⇔ North and South Battleford, golf course, riding stables, Go Cart track

🐾 Spacious home situated on Jackfish Lake with a spectacular view of the water,
rolling farmland and distant hills. Hosts' interest is flying, and have own plane.

Qu'Appelle
(near Regina; see also Balcarres, Wolseley, Indian Head)

Mader, Ken and Jo (Bluenose Farm)   ✓ SFV B&B
Box 173, Qu'Appelle, Saskatchewan   S0G 4A0   ☎ (306) 699-2328

Located 4.8 km north of the Trans Canada Highway on Hwy 35. Watch for signs.
$38D $5Child $15Add.person   ◉ Meals   (Family rates available)   ► 12
✠ Mar-Dec   ● Full, homebaked   ♠ Working grain farm, indoor swimming pool,
quiet   ■ 4   ↦ 2Q,2R, crib   ⌐ 2private, 2ch.w.g.   ★ Air,TV, separate entrance,
facilities for the handicapped   ♥   ⍟ Restricted smoking

↪ Mini golf and children's playground on property

⇔ Qu'Appelle fishing lakes and resorts, boating, Regina, Dominion Experimental Farms

🐾 Accommodation is in modern guest house on large landscaped grounds. Breakfast served in old stone house main building. Hosts also cater to bus tours in daytime. There is a Country Tea Room on the premises, featuring High Tea and homebaked buns. Relax and enjoy the fresh country air and beautiful skywide sunsets.

Peebles

(near Regina; see also Wolseley)

Sugden, T.& M. Balog (Sugden Semmental Vacation Farms)   ✔ SFV B&B
Box 2, Peebles, Saskatchewan S0G 3V0   ☎ (306) 697-3169

Located south of Grenfell. Phone for directions.
$15S $25D $10Child   ● Extra   ► 6A,4Ch
● Choice, homebaked   ♠ Farm, rural, swimming pool, quiet   ■ 3D   ⊣2T,1K
⌐3Sh.w.h.   ★ TV,F   ⌁ Swedish
⇔ Peebles, Broadview Last Oak Ski Resort, Kipling

Ravenscrag

(south-west of Swift Current; see also Gull Lake)

Saville, Bill and Ann (Crystal Springs Farm)   ✔ SFV B&B
Box 44, Ravenscrag, Saskatchewan S0N 2C0   ☎ (306) 295-4121

From Maple Creek take Hwy 21 south for 40 km. Turn east on gravel road for 19 km,
right at T into Valley. Cross bridge and go south (not up hill). Cross cattle guard.
$20S $30D $7.50Child   ▣ Meals   ► 5A,2Ch
● Choice, homebaked   ♠ 6000-acre farm, quiet, isolated   ■ 1S,2D   ⊣ 1S,2D,
double bunk   ⌐1Private, 1sh.w.h.   ★ TV
↪ Small museum and country store
⇔ Town of Eastend with swimming pool, tennis, golfing, museum, Cypress Hills Prov.
Park and Fort Walsh Historical Park

☛ Working cattle and grain farm situated far from noise of cities. There are lots of
farm animals. Hosts specialize in spinning and harness leather work.

Saville, Jim (Spring Valley Guest Ranch)   ✔ SFV
Box 10, Ravenscrag, Saskatchewan S0N 2C0   ☎ (306) 295-4124

Call ahead for directions.
$20S $30D $10Child   ▣ Meals   ► 8
● Full   ♠ Farm, older, quiet, isolated   ■ 4D (upstairs)   ⊣ 4D   ⌐1Sh.w.g.
★KF,LF   ☝ Restricted smoking
↪ Pleasant wooded valley (exceptional in spring-time) and abundant wildlife
⇔ Cypress Hills Prov. Park (golfing, swimming, boating, craft shops), Fort Walsh
National Historic site

☛ Early-Century built home in ideal location for naturalists, photographers and those
who can appreciate the beauty of total darkness, silence and solitude. There is a
Tea-room on the premises (open 24 hrs - house specialty: croisssants). Also available
tipis in the wilderness camp with wood, water and washrooms supplied (guests must
bring own sleeping bags). Horseback riding can be arranged.

Regina

(see also Qu'Appelle, Wolseley, Wawota, Balcarres, Peebles)

McDowell, Jean and Bill (B & J's B&B)   ⌐ CC
2066 Ottawa St., Regina, Saskatchewan   S4P 1P8   ☎ (306) 352-8532 or 522-4575

Take Hwy 1 into Regina on Victoria Ave and turn south on Ottawa St.
$15S $25D   ► 8A
● Full   ♠ Res., older, quiet   ■ 4D (separate home)   ⊢ 4D (upstairs)
⊓1Sh.w.g.   ★KF,LF,TV in guest room, parking, separate entrance   ⊕Drinking
↪ Downtown Regina, Regina General Hospital
⇔ Centre of the Arts, R.C.M.P. Museum, Sask. Legislative Grounds

☞ Relaxed atmosphere. Maps and brochures of Regina activities available. Accommodation consists of entire two-storey house.

Waseca

(near Lloydminster; see also Meota)

Litchfield, John and Darlene (Litchfield Country Vac.Farm)   ⌐ SFV,B&B
Box 118, Waseca, Saskatchewan   S0M 3A0   ☎ (306) 893-4470

Located 6.5 km south and 1 km. east of Waseca on Hwy 16.
$15S $20D $30F $5Add. person   ● $3Each   🍽 Meals   ► 6A,4Ch
● Choice   ♠ Farm, view, patio, quiet   ■ 2 (also separate cabin)   ⊢ D,R, cot, crib
⊓ 1 Private, 1sh.w.h.   ★ KF,LF,TV in guest room   ♥   ⋙ some German
↪ Nature hikes, bird watching, berry picking, tobogganing, cross- country skiing, wiener roast pit, treehouse for children
⇔ Battle River (angling, canoeing, skating) Maska Lake, swimming, boating, waterskiing, golfing, tennis, Waseca

☞ Hobby farm in beautiful location near the Battle River in quiet area with beautiful sunsets. Hostess does "wheat weaving" and has souvenirs on hand. Children especially welcome. There is room for campers and trailers. There are pets in the house.

Wawota

(east of Regina; see also Carnduff, Whitewood)

Husband, George and Doris (Pleasant Vista Angus Farm)   ⌐ SFV,B&B
Box 194, Wawota, Saskatchewan   S0G 5A0   ☎ (306) 739-2915

Located 6.4 km east of junction Hwys 9 and 48.
$15S $20D   ● $2.50Each $1-2.50Child   🍽 Meals   ► 7
● Full, homebaked   ♠ Farm, quiet, view   ■ 3   ⊢ 1T,3D,P, crib   ⊓ 1Sh.w.h.
★ TV,F,LF,KF,   ♥
↪ Horses for riding, room for tents and campers
⇔ Kenosee Lake in Moose Mountain Prov. Park (canoeing, swimming, fishing, golfing)

☞ Welcome to small working farm in treed area with a good view of countryside. Homebaking, garden vegetables and fruits in season. Hosts enjoy working with and showing their beautiful Arabian horses. Overnight accommodation for horses. Seniors especially welcome; (also bus tours).

Whitewood

(east of Regina; see also Wolesley, Wawota, Indian Head)

Ecklund, Ken and Donalda (Pipestone View Ranch) ✓ SFV
Box 29, Whitewood, Sakatchewan S0G 5C0 ☎ (306) 735-2858

From Percival proceed 3.5 km south and 3.5 km west, then 1.5 km south again. Watch for signs.
$15S $20D $2.50Child $2.50Add. person ◙ Meals ► 2-8
● Farm, older, view, patio, quiet ■ 4 (main and upper floor and cabin for 6) ■
3T,3D ⌐ Sh.w.h. ★ TV,KF,LF,F ♥
⇔ Round and Kenosee Lakes, museums, tennis courts, swimming pool, hangliding

☞ Community minded hosts have 3 sociable children and are very knowledgeable about the area. There is a cat in the house. Families are particularly welcome.

Wolseley

(east of Regina; see also Qu'Appelle, Peebles, Whitewood, Indian Head)

Crawford, Doris and Stu (Crawford Claim) ✓ SFV
Box 44, Wolseley, Saskatchewan S0G 5H0 ☎ (306) 698-2649

Coming from east on Trans-Canada Hwy 1, turn at Summerberry and go north- west for 2 km to CPR crossing, 3.3 km north, 2 km west and 2 km north again. From west, go 3.3 km east of Wolseley to Lemberg sign. Then 5 km north, 6.6 km east, 2 km north again.
$15S $20D ● $2.50Each ◙ Meals ► 8A,4Ch
✪ Summer ● Choice ⌂ 960-acres farm, swimming pool, quiet ■ 2D (upper and main level in farm house), 2D (in separate building) ⊷ 4S (in main building, 2D,2S (in separate house) ⌐ 2Private, 1Sh.w.h. ★ KF,LF
↔ Riding horses, biking, hiking, a few farm animals
⇔ Qu'Appelle Valley, Wolseley

☞ Sit and visit and enjoy the glorious Saskatchewan sunsets. Working grain farm on rich prairie land. Hosts also cater to bus tours in daytime.

B&B Travel Tip: *You can stay in a B&B even if you are on a camping trip. Give yourself a treat and sleep in a comfortable bed once in a while, especially if the weather turns miserable and the gear is soaking wet.*

Manitoba

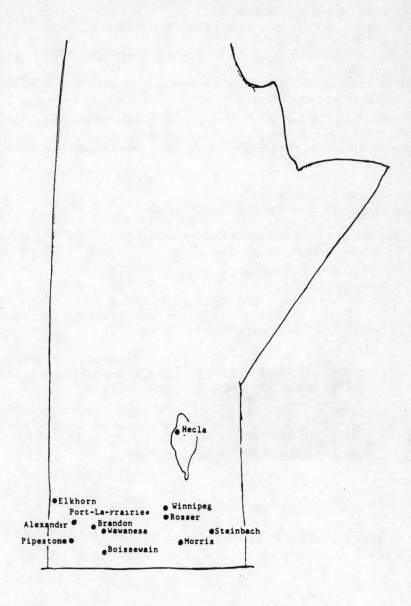

Alexander

(near Brandon; see also Wawanesa, Pipestone)

Harvey, R.A. & Family (Willeta Farm) ⟍ MFV
RR1, Alexander, Manitoba   R0K 0A0 ☎ (204) 328-7201

From Brandon on Hwy 1 travel to Junction of Hwy 250, then north to 1.5 km past
Assiniboine River, west 7 km and then north 2 km.
$20S $30D $15Child   ▣ Meals ► 4A,4Ch
● Full, choice   ♠ Farm, hist., acreage, quiet   ■ 2D (upstairs)   ⌐ 2D
⌐Sh.w.h.   ★ TV   ⓦ Pets
↔ Sleigh and hay rides, cross-country skiing, hiking, berry-picking, horse back riding,
many farm animals to see
⇔ Agricultural museums, Sioux Valley Pow Wow (in July), golf course, waterslides,
country fairs and auctions, Brandon

☞ Farm brick house, built in 1906, complete with stained glas windows and ornate
woodwork that used to be very popular in this area at that time, and situated in the
rolling hills surrounding the Assiniboine River. There are pets in the house.

Boissevain

(south of Brandon: see also Wawanesa, Pipestone)

Dueck, Hilda and Henry (Dueck's Cedar Chalet) ⟍ Man B&B
Box 362, Boissevain, Manitoba   R0K 0E0 ☎ (204) 534-6019

Located 1.5 km east of the cemetery and just north off Hwy 10.
$40S $50D   ▣ Meals ► 4
● Choice   ♠ Farm, acreage, ranch-style, view, isolated   ■ 1Ste(all cedar)
⌐1Q,1P   ⌐ Private   ★ TV and fridge in guest room, separate entrance, tea/coffee
making facilities   ⓦ Smoking,drinking   ⚭ German

⇔ International Peace Garden, several
lakes, Brandon, Turtle Mountain
Provincial Park.

☞ Large all cedar room in 100 year
old farm house. Warm and friendly
Manitoba hospitality with European
influence.

B&B Travel Tip: *Do not think of giving tips. Remember this is not a hotel
service.*

Brandon
(see also Killarney, Pipestone, Elkhorn, Dauphin, Boissevain, Glenboro)

Shwaluk, William (Bill) (Casa Maley)
1605 Victoria Ave, Brandon, Manitoba   R7A 1C1

✔ Man B&B
☎ (204) 728-0812

Located two blocks east of junction of Hyws 10 and 1A.
$30S $40D $50F   ▣ Meals
● Choice, homebaked   ⌂ Downtown, res., older, patio, quiet $i 3D (upstairs)
⊷2T,2D   ⌐ 3Sh.w.g.   ★ 2TV,3F,LF, parking for 4 cars, sinks in 2 guest rooms
♥ ⊕ Smoking, pets   ⋙ Ukrainian

► 4A,4Ch

↦ Brandon University, Daly House Museum, Architectural walking tours, antiques, Keystone Recreation Centre

⇔ Canada Winter Games Sportsplex, waterslides, parks, shopping centres

☞ 1912-built European-style,3-storey Tudor house with red brick exterior, fairy-tale Gingerbread-house appearance and spacious interior decor in beautiful quarter-cut oak and wainscotting in foyer and dining room and grand stair-case. Transportation and pick-ups by appointment can be arranged.

Slimmon, Don and Glenora (Spruce Grove)
1713-34th St., Box 811, Brandon, Manitoba   R7A 5Z8

☎ (204) 726-1992

Located 2 km south from corner of Trans-Canada Hwy 1A and 34th St, or southwest of junction Hwy 10 and 18th St in Brandon.
$15S $20D   ● $2Each   (special rates for children)
● Full, homebaked   ⌂ Rural, acreage, quiet, patio, view   ■ 2D   ⊷ 2T,1D
⌐1Sh.w.g.   ★ TV in guest rooms,F ⊕ Restricted smoking
↦ Restaurants, golf courses, airport, Brandon University, Research Station

► 4A,2Ch

☞ Retired couple with large modern home situated in a quiet area on the outskirts of Brandon, on an acreage among a large grove of spruce trees. There are 2 cats in residence. Children and pets welcome.

Smith, Joy and Keith (Gwenmar Guest Home)   ✔ MFVA
RR3, Brandon, Manitoba R7A 5Y3   ☎ (204) 728-7339

Located northwest of Brandon and 3 km off Trans-Canada Hwy. Phone for reservation
and directions.
$20S $30D   🍽 Meals   ► 8
● Full, homebaked bread   🏠 Rural, acreage, older home, quiet   ■ 1S,2D,1F (upper
and lower level) ⊷ 2D,3Q,(2R on veranda)   ⌐ 1Sh.w.h.,1sh.w.g.   ★ LF,TV,F   ♥
↔ Little Saskatchewan River, cross-country skiing, hiking, camping, berry picking
⇔ Brandon, shopping, restaurants, waterslide, air museum, Brandon U.,golf course,
airport, Agriculture Canada Research Station, Neepawa (Autho Marg.Lawrence
childhood home), famour Souris Swinging Bridge

🖙 Relax on the big screened porch in 1914 home built by former Lt. Governor J.D.
McGregor of Manitoba, and enjoy the beautiful grounds. There is a cat.

Elkhorn
(west of Brandon; see also Pipestone)

Twigg, Mrs. Margaret (Windyhill Farm)   ✔ MFV
Box 248, Elkhorn, Manitoba R0M 0N0   ☎ (204) 845-2101

Turn off Trans-Canada Hwy just past Esso Stn. Go west on Elkhorn's main street to
Post Office, turn left across railway tracks, then right for 3 km, then left and 6 km south.
$29S $25D $5Child   🍽 Meals   ► 6-8
● Choice, homebaked   🏠 800-acres farm, quiet, swimming pool (summer)
■ 1S,3D, (upper and lower level), also small cabin for 4   ⊷ 1T,3D, double bunks, cot,
cribs   ⌐ 1Sh.w.h.   ★ TV   ⓦ Drinking
↔ Ravines, strolling and hiking, swimming, room for camping
⇔ Elkhorn, Sask. border

🖙 Very casual atmosphere in spacious two-storey modernized stone house in mixed
farming country. There is a cat in the house.

Emerson
(south of Winnipeg; see also Morris, Steinbach)

Ewens, Sharon-Ann (Tanglewood)   ✔ Man B&B
99 Assiniboine, Emerson, Manitoba R0A 0L0   ☎ (204) 373-2210

Located on Hwy 75 at US/Canada border. Turn left at 4th St and follow the bend in the
road to house.
$25S $35D   🍽 Meals   (please call in advance) ✠ starting June88 ●Choice
🏠Hist., rural, quiet   ■ 1D,1F (upstairs)   ⊷ 1D,1S, crib   ⌐ 1Sh.w.g.
★TV,F,KF,LF, parking   ⓦ Pets
⇔ US (Min/ND) borders, Morris Stampede,

🖙 Historic home built in 1881 with lovely large property and located on the bank of
the Red River in interesting town with many century homes. Hostess is Interior
Decorator and Gourmet cook. There are pets in the house. Camping facilities available.

Hecla
(on northern part of Lake Winnipeg)

Holtz, Sharon and Dave (Solmundson Gesta Hus) ⌐ Man B&B
Hecla, Manitoba R0C 1K0 ☎ (204) Dial Operator,ask for Hecla 88

Located within Hecla Island Provincial Park in the heart of Lake Winnipeg, asseccible
via Hwy 8.
$49S $55-69D $10Child $10Add.person ▣ Meals ► 10A,4Ch
● Full, homebaked ♠ Village, hist., acreage, view, lakefront, quiet, veranda ■ 3
(upstairs) ⊢ 3D,2Q,2cots ⊓ 2Sh.w.g., 1ensuite ★ TV,KF, parking ⊛ Rest.
smoking
↪ Woodland lakeshore for walking, church in historic Icelandic fishing village.
⇔ 18-hole Golf course, beaches, interpretive programs, hiking and cross-country ski
trails, snowmobiling and skidooing

☞ European-style hospitality in newly renovated and completely modern comfortable
home located in original Icelandic settlement. Each room has view of the lake. Relax on
the veranda and enjoy the beautiful view of Lake Winnipeg and tranquil and peaceful
atmosphere.

Morris
(south of Winnipeg; see also Steinbach, Ermerson)

Jorgenson, Ed and Kathleen (Deerbank Farm) ⌐ MFV
Box 23, RR2, Morris, Manitoba R0G 1K0 ☎ (204) 746-8395

From Winnipeg, take Hwy 75 south to Morris, then Hwy 23 east to Ste Elizabeth corner
and south.
$22S $32D $7Child $10Add. person ▣ Meals ► 6A,3Ch
● Full, homebaked ♠ 320-acre farm, patio ■ 3D (upstairs) ⊢ 3D, cot, crib and
playpen ⊓ 1Sh.w.h., 1sh.w.g. ★ TV ⊛ Restricted smoking and drinking
↪ Stampede and Exhibition, horseback riding (for experienced riders), many churches
⇔ St. Malo Lake and beach

☞ Enjoy the peaceful farm country of the Red River Valley. There is a small, most
agreeable miniature poodle in the house.

Pipestone
(south-west of Brandon; see also Elkhorn, Alexander, Boissevain)

Patmore, Harry and Gladys (The Patmores) ⌐ B&B
Pipestone, Manitoba R0M 1T0 ☎ (204) 854-2584

Located at junction of Hwys 1/83, turn south for 44.8 km, or at junction of Hwys 2/83
turn south for 11.2 km. Go west on gravel road. From US border travel 56 km north on
Hwy 83. Turn at 2 mailboxes at west side.

$14S $18D   ● $2.50Each $8Child   📷 Meals   ► 4-5
● Choice   🏠 Farm (grainand livestock), view   ■ 2D, basement room   ⊢ 2D
⤒ 1Sh.w.h.   ★ Air,TV,KF,LF   ⓦ Smoking, drinking, bring sleeping bags for kids
↔ Beef and wheat farm, camping

☞ Hosts enjoy visitors from out of the country or Canada. They are proud to show off
the beautiful prairies. Lots of room for campers in yard. Hunters welcome.

Portage La Prairie
   (near Winnipeg)

Goertzen, J.L. and Dorothy (Clutters)
41-5th St.N.E., Portage La Prairie, Manitoba R1N 1J4   ☎ (204) 857-3466/857-6431

Phone for directions.
$20S $25D $2Child $3Add.person   📷 Meals   ► 3-5
● Cont.   🏠 Res., older   ■ 1S,1D,1Ste (upstairs)   ⊢2T,1S,1Q
⤒1Sh.w.h.,1sh.w.g.   ★ Air,KF,LF,TV in guest room, parking   ⓦ Pets   ⌇Low
German
↔ Island Park, Crescent Lake, paddle boat rental, Strawberry-Festival activities, Fort La
Reine Museum, golfing, Harnes Race Track, City Hall (architecturally noteworthy),
Waterfowl Research Station, Agricultural Fair and Midway

☞ Unique home remodelled over many years, hence the name "Clutters". Hosts are
keen conservationists and are in the process of cataloging flora on a private 160 acres
Sanctuary, where there are nature trails and a cabin. Enjoy the extensive house library
on diversive topics.

Rosser
   (near Winnipeg)

Krym, Fred and Geraldine (Krym's Farm)   ↙ MFVA
Rosser, Manitoba R0H 1E0   ☎ (204) 467-5716

From Winnipeg take Hwy 1 west to PR 334 at Headingley and go 10 km north to farm.
$30S $40D   55F   📷 Meals   (Special rates for Seniors and children)   ► 4A,2-4Ch
● Full   🏠 Working farm   ■ 2D (upstairs)   ⊢ 2D, crib   ⤒ Sh.w.h.
★TV,F,facilities for the disabled   ⓦ Smoking, drinking, pets (on leash only)
⌇Ukrainian, German
↔ Hike or ride your bike, farm's wide open fields and related activities, bird watching.
⇔ Lower Fort Garry, beautiful beaches, Prairie Dog Central - historic train rides, Little
Mountain Park, nature trails, Miniature railroading and golfing

☞ Guests may join in on farm activities, if they wish. Relax and enjoy the Aurora
Borealis (Dancing Northern Lights). Host family enjoy music and invite guests to bring
their own instruments for impromptu sessions. Senior and handicapped welcome.

Minaker, Mrs. Mabel
Rosser, Manitoba R0H 1E0

⌐ Man B&B
☎ (204) 633-2219

Located 10 km west off Perimeter Hwy 221 on south side.
$20S $28D $35F   ▣ Meals
▶ 2A,2Ch
● Full, homebaked   🏠 Farm, bungalow, acreage, quiet   ■ 1D   ⊢ 1D,R
⊓Sh.w.h.   ★ TV,LF, wheel chair access   ♥
⇔ Town of Rosser, Dorsey Power Station (tours), Assiniboia Downs Racetrack, Bird Hill
Park, City of Winnipeg

☞ Peaceful country home and warm hospitality. Quick access to Airport.

Steinbach
(near Winnipeg; see also Emerson, Morris)

Warkentin, George and Elma
5 Springwood Bay, Southland Pk, Box 3626, Steinbach, Man R0A2A0   ☎ (204) 326-9910

Take Hwy 12 into Steinbach and turn east at Chrysler Gate.
$25S $30D $5Child $5Add.person
▶ 6
✚ Summer   ● Full   🏠 Sub., split-level, patio, quiet   ■ 3D (lower level)   ⊢ 3D
plus playpen   ⊓ 2Private   ★ TV in guest room, separate entrance   ⊛ Smoking,
drinking pets   〰 German
↔ Downtown and business section, church
⇔ Museum, shopping mall, various restaurants

Wawanesa
(near Brandon; see also Alexander, Boissevain)

Plett, Harry and Ruth (Spruce Shadows Farm)
Box 158, Wawanesa, Manitoba R0K 2G0

⌐ MFV
☎ (204) 824-2408

Located west of the city on Hwy 2 and 21 km west from Glenboro. Take Treesbank Rd 5
km. north and then 5km east to first farm on south side.
$25S $35D $5Child $5Add. person   ▣ Meals
▶ 6
🏠 Hog farm, acreage, patio, quiet   ■ 2D (lower level)   ⊢ 2S,2D   ⊓ Sh.w.g.
★TV,KF,LF   ⊛ Smoking, drinking   〰 some German and Spanish
↔ Beautiful rural surroundings, country walks along river bank, swimming
snowmobiling, cross-country skiing
⇔ Spruce Wood Provincial Park and Spirit Sands, Souris Swinging Bridge, International
Peace Gardens, swimming pool, good deer hunting in season

☞ Active working farm located in beautiful area near the junction of Souris and
Assiniboine rivers. Well travelled hosts have 3 young children and the whole family
enjoys meeting new folks and sharing their way of life with others. Children welcome.

Winnipeg
(see also Portage La Prairie, Rosser)

Algeo, Terry and Peggy
183 Larchdale Cres., Winnipeg, Manitoba   R2G 0A3

✔ Man B&B
☎ (204) 334-7633

Travel north on Henderson Hwy to traffic light at McLeod/Rowandale, turn west and then right. From East Perimeter (Rt 20) turn west on Grassie Blvd. Proceed app. 3km across Henderson Hwy and turn north on Larchdale.
$25S $32D $10Child (up to age 12)   ◙ Meals
► 2A,2Ch
● Full, homebaked   ■ Res., quiet, large lot   ■ 1D (upstairs)   ⊷ 1D, crib
⁐2Sh.w.h.   ★ TV,LF, parking   ⍟ Controlled pets only
↪ Fraser's Grove Park and Red River, shopping, restaurants, excellent bus service to downtown
⇔ Lower Fort Gary National Park, Oak Hammock Bird Sanctuary, Canadian Mint, Birds Hill Park, Rainbow Stage, Museum of Man & Nature

🐾 Modern two-storey home located in the north-east corner of the city on large shaded lot. Hosts have keen interest in aviation and are recipients of Canadian Tourism Award. House specialty: homemade Irish Soda Bread.

Antymis, Ray (Southern Rose Guest House)
533 Sprague St., Winnipeg, Manitoba   R3G 2R9

✔ Man B&B
☎ (204) 786-3105/775-3484

Located in the centre of the City. Phone for directions.
$25S $35D   ◙ Meals
► 6
● Downtown, res., hist., swimming pool, patio, quiet   ■ 3 (upstairs)   ⊷ 2S,2T,1Q
⁐ 1Private, 1sh.w.h.   ★ Air,F,LF,TV in guest room, parking   ⍟ Smoking
↪ Walking tour around historic Wolseley area, Legislative Buildings, Polo Park Shopping Centre, arena and stadium, express bus route
⇔ St. Boniface (old French section), Osborne Village, Lower Fort Gary, Assiniboia Downs Race Track

🐾 Home is located in City's historic Wolseley area in park-like setting with Old English Decor and highly polished warm wood and brass trims. There is a Shih Tzo dog in the house.

Johnson, Paul and Trudy
455 Wallasey St., Winnipeg, Manitoba   R3J 3C5

✔ Man B&B
☎ (204) 837-3368

Located three blocks north of Portage Avenue (Hwy 1) in the St. James area of the city.
$20S $30D $5Child
► 6A,2Ch
● Choice   ⌂ Sub., bungalow, quiet, patio   ■ 2D   ⊷ D,Q   ⁐ 2Sh.w.h.
★ Air,F,KF,LF, TV in guest room, parking, screened Florida Room   ⍟ Drinking
↪ Living Prairie Museum, city transit,
⇔ City Park with excellent Zoo, downtown Winnipeg

🐾 Very quiet neighborhood. There is a private yard for sun bathing.

Jones, Arlene and Bob (Bannerman East)   ⌐ Man B&B
99 Bannerman Ave., Winnipeg, Manitoba   R2W 0T1   ☎ (204) 589-6449

Located close to Portage/Main Sts junction in central Winnipeg.
$25S $35D $10Child   🍴 Meals   ► 3
●Full   🏠 Res., patio, quiet   ■ 1S,1D (upstairs)   ⊢ 1S,1D   ⌐ 2Sh.w.h., jacuzzi
tub   ★ TV,KF,LF, parking   Ⓦ Smoking, drinking, pets, children min. age 10

↔ Excellent ethnic and continental restaurants, historic St. John Park and Anglican Church(1820), MS Lord Selkirk (floating restaurant and cruise ship), Museum of Man & Nature, Concert Hall, Ukrainian Cultural Centre, shopping, theatres, Folklorama sites (Aug), Railway Stn, bus depot

⇔ Lower Fort Garry, Steinbeck Mennonite Museum, Manitoba Stampede (Morris), Emerson (USA border), Mint Factory, Lake Winnipeg, International Airport

☞ Well travelled hosts (B&B in Europe and Eastern Canada) in comfortable home and pleasant surroundings. Enjoy warm hospitality in convenient location. There is a dog.

Lobreau, Francis and Anya   ⌐ Man B&B
137 Woodlawn Ave., Winnipeg, Manitoba   R2M 2P5   ☎ (204) 256-9789

Located in South Winnipeg, off St. Mary's Rd (Rt 52), and easy access to Trans Canada
Hwy or South Bypass (Hwy 100).
$25S $32-36D   ► 4-6
● Choice   🏠 Sub., split-level, acreage, quiet   ■ 3D   ⊢ 1Q,2D (upstairs)
⌐1Private, 1Sh.w.g.   ★TV,KF,LF,F,parking   ⒲Pets,smoking   ⌇French,Polish
↔ Large shopping mall, City transit, St. Vital Park, Riel House, restaurants
⇔ Downtown Winnipeg

☞ Spacious and comfortable home with private yard for relaxing.

B & B of Manitoba
93 Healy Cres, Winnipeg, Manitoba   R2N 2S2   ☎ (204) 256-6151
(Len and Marlene Loewen, Managers)
Rates: $20-45S $28-60D   (including full breakfast)
Host members of B&B of Manitoba are located in Winnipeg, Brandon, Morris, Killarney,
Boissevain and Lockport. For a complete listing of the hosts, send $3 for postage and
handling to the above. Some of the homes are listed in this publication.

O'Hara, Edna M.
✔ Man B&B
242 Amherst St., Winnipeg, Manitoba   R3J 1Y6
☎ (204) 888-6848

Located north of Portage Ave with quick access to Rt 90 and Int. Airport.
$22S $30D $10Child
► 2A,2Ch
● Choice   🏠 sub., older, quiet   ■ 1D   ⊢ 1D   ⌐ Sh.w.h.   ★ Air
↪ Assiniboine River crosswalk to Assiniboine Park and Zoo
⇔ Excellent city transit service to Polo Park Shopping Mall, bus depot and via rail

Paulley, Fred and Daisy
✔ Man B&B
141 Furby St., Winnipeg, Manitoba   R3C 2A4
☎ (204) 772-8828

Located south of Trans-Canada Hwy between Broadway Ave and Westminster Ave.
$25S $35D $10Child(under age 12)
► 3
● Choice, homebaked   🏠 Downtown, older   ■ 1S,1D   ⊢ 1S,1D,1Q
⌐ 1Sh.w.h., 1sh.w.g.   ★ Air, parking   ⓦ Pets, drinking
↪ Downtown Convention Centre, churches, restaurants, laundromat, art gallery,
Legislative Building, tourist information, McDonald House Museum (1895 house restored
and furnished), transit line
⇔ Assiniboine Park, newly opened North Portage Mall, Museum of Man and Nature,
Imax Theatre

☞ Hosts will meet guests at airport, train or bus if requested.

Ronald, Mr. and Mrs. A.
✔ Man B&B
3232 Assiniboine Ave., Winnipeg, Manitoba   R3K 0B1
☎ (204) 889-8317

From Trans-Canada Hwy 1, go south on Westwood Dr and west on Assiniboine Ave
$20S $30D $7Child
► 4-5
● Choice, homebaked   🏠 Res., sub., river lot, quiet   ■ 2D   ⊢ 2S,1D (upstairs)
⌐ Sh.w.g.   ★ Air,TV,F,LF, parking, private tennis court   ♥   ⓦ Smoking
〰French, German

↪ Good downtown bus, cross-country skiing, tennis

⇔ Golfing, historic sites, bird sanctuary, lakes, racetracks, dining

☞ Lovely, well-treed riverside home. Lots of birds. Homemade bread. Well travelled hosts spend time each year in Africa and they have a "Video Safari" they will show to guests, if they wish.

Ontario

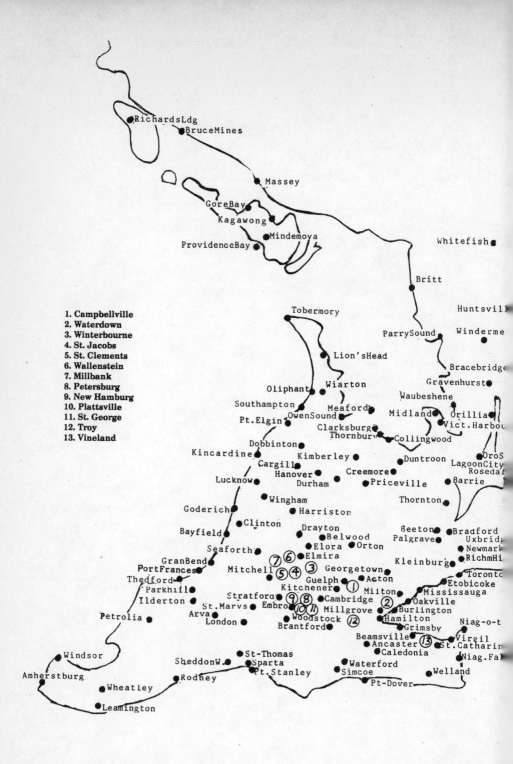

RichardsLdg
BruceMines

Massey

GoreBay
Kagawong
Mindemoya
ProvidenceBay

Whitefish

Britt

Huntsvill

1. Campbellville
2. Waterdown
3. Winterbourne
4. St. Jacobs
5. St. Clements
6. Wallenstein
7. Millbank
8. Petersburg
9. New Hamburg
10. Plattsville
11. St. George
12. Troy
13. Vineland

Tobermory

ParrySound
Winderme

Lion'sHead

Bracebridge

Oliphant
Wiarton
Southampton
Meaford
Pt.Elgin
OwenSound
Clarksburg
Thornbury
Dobbinton

Waubeshene
Gravenhurst
Midland
Orillia
Vict.Harbou

Kincardine
Cargill
Hanover
Lucknow
Durham

Kimberley
Creemore
Priceville

Collingwood
Duntroon
OroS
LagoonCity
Rosedal
Barrie

Wingham
Harriston
Goderich
Bayfield
Clinton
Seaforth
GranBend
PortFrances
Thedford
Parkhill
Ilderton
St.Marys
Arva
London

Drayton
Belwood
Elora   Orton
Elmira
Mitchell   ⑤④ ③ Georgetown
Guelph   ①   Acton
Stratford ⑨⑧ Cambridge
Embro   ⑩⑪ Millgrove
Woodstock   ⑫
Brantford

Thornton

Beeton   Bradford
Palgrave   Uxbrid
Newmark
Kleinburg   RichmHi

Toronto
Etobicoke
Milton   Mississauga
② Oakville
Burlington
Hamilton
Grimsby
Niag-o-t
Beamsville   Virgil
Ancaster ⑬ St.Catharin
Caledonia   (Niag.Fa

Petrolia

Windsor
Amherstburg
Wheatley
Leamington

SheddonW.
Rodney
St-Thomas
Sparta
Pt.Stanley
Waterford
Simcoe
Pt-Dover
Welland

⑦⑥

Ontario

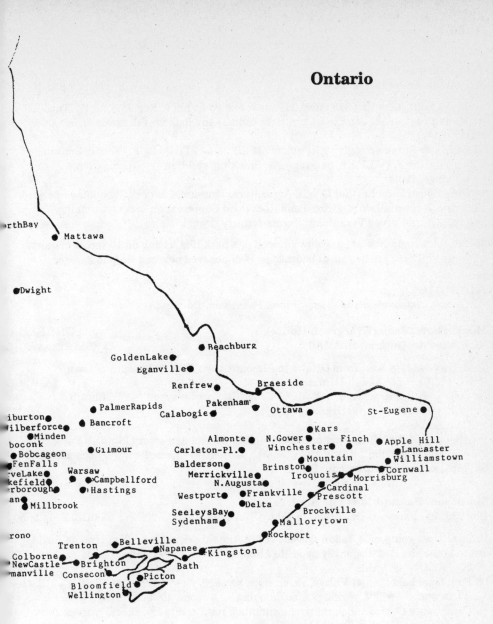

Acton
(near Toronto,; see also Guelph, Georgetown, Campbellville, MMilton)

Toth, Marg and Les
RR1, Acton, Ontario L7J 2L7   ☎ (519) 853-1065

From Hwy 401, take Exit 320 (Hwy 25) north and go 14 km to Regional Rd 12. Turn left (west) and continue to 6th Line. Turn right (north) and look for 6th house on left side.
$35S $45D   ► 4
● Full   ♠ Rural, acreage, patio, quiet   ■ 2D   ⊢ 2T,1Q   ⊓ 1Private, 1sh.w.h..
whirlpool   ★ F,TV,LF,KF, parking   ⓦ Smoking, children   ⌇Hungarian
↪ walking, biking
⇔ Olde Hyde House Leather Goods, Agricultural Museum, Mohawk/Woodbine Raceway, Glen Eden (downhill skiing), Kelso and Rockwood Conservation areas (swimming, sailing, picnics), Bruce Trail (hiking, cross-country skiing)

☞ Spacious, sunny new bungalow situated in a park-like setting on 10 acreas of quiet wilderness. There are two small housedogs. Well behaved pets can sleep in garage.

Almonte
(near Ottawa; see also Carleton Place, Pckenham, Balderson)

MacFarlane, Jean (Evergreen House)
RR3, Almonte, Ontario K0A 1A0   ONT B&B
       ☎ (613) 256-3760

Take Hwys 417/44 west from Ottawa to Almonte, then Hwy 29 to south of town.
$20S $30D $8Child $1Infants   ► 7A,3Ch
● Full   ♠ Rural, acreage   ■ 3D   ⊢ 1S,3D, 2cots, playpen   ⊓ 2Sh.w.h.
★TV,F, picnic table   ⓦ Drinking
↪ Co-op store
⇔ Almonte, Mill of Kintail historic site, Hershey Chocolate Factory (Smith's Falls), Woolen Mill (Appleton), Kitten Mill (Lanark), Balderson Cheese Factory, Packenham Ski Mts., swimming at Almonte Beach

Matheson, Pat and Ian (The Squirrels)
       ✔ CC
Box 729, 190 Parkview Dr., Almonte, Ont. K0A 1A0   ☎ (613) 256-2995

From Ottawa going west, follow Queensway to Almonte cut-off and then Hwy 44 for 14 km to house situated diagonally opposite Almonte Community Centre.
$20S $30D   ▣ Meals   ► 5
● Full, homebaked   ♠ Village, ranch style, acreage, view, quiet   ■ 1S,2D   ⊢1S,4T
⊓ 1Sh.w.g.   ★ TV, parking   ⓦ Smoking   ⌇ some French
↪ Community Centre and park, river swimming, restaurants and shops, cross-country skiing, Mississippi Valley Textile Museum
⇔ Indoor swimming pool, downhill skiing, golfing, Tait MacKenzie Museum

☞ Unique home with cathedral ceilings surrounded by almost an acre of landscaped gardens. Hosts are world travellers with many interesting experiences and memorabilia. Farm-style breakfast is served in sunroom.

Amherstburg
(near Windsor; see also Leamington, Wheatley, Pelee Island)

Honor, Robert and Debra (The Honor's) ✔ FOBBA,ONT B&B
RR2, Box 161A, Amherstburg, Ontario   N9V 2Y8 ☎ (519) 736-7737

From Amherstburg, go out Simcoe St/Pike Rd to 4th Con., turn right and look for 10th
house on east side of road. (send for detailed map)
$35S $40D $5Child ► 4A,1Ch
● Choice ♠ Farm, older, view, patio, quiet ■2D(upstairs) ▬2D, cot ⌐1Sh.w.g
★ TV ⑩ Restricted smoking, drinking, pets ⌇ French
⇔ Historic Amherstburg, Fort Malden Nat. Hist. Park, Black History Museum, Point
Pelee, birdwatching, Nature Sanctuary, Windsor shopping and dining

☛ Tree shaded cottage-style home in quiet and peaceful country setting, overlooking
farm and woods, but close to Metropolitan activities. There is a dog and a cat in the
house. Hosts are members of the executive of FOBBA.

Ancaster
(near Hamilton; see also Waterdown, Brantford, Millgrove, Jerseyville)

Wentworth, Dan and Dorothy ✔ Ham/Went B&B
1573 Butter Rd. West, Ancaster, Ontario   L9G 3L1 ☎ (416) 648-3596

From Hwys 2/53, near Duffs corner, travel south on Trinity Rd. Turn right on 2nd
Concession and continue on Butter Rd to first farm past hydro lines.
$30S $45D ► 4A
● Choice ♠ 44-acre farm, view, patio, quiet, isolated, pond with ducks ■ 2D
▬2T,1Q ⌐ Sh.w.g. ★ Air,TF, separate entrance ⑩ Restricted smoking,
drinking, children min. age 4
↪ Private museum on property (free tours), quiet country roads
⇔ Caledonia Boat Farm, Bell Homestead, Mohawk Chapel Indian Reservation. There
are two cats and a standard poodle in residence.

☛ Modern country home overlooking rolling fields and pond, situated near picturesque
Niagara Escarpment. Museum features early Canadian Artifacts.

Annan
(near Owen Sound; see also Meaford, Tara)

Piplack, Otto and Ina (Hemloch Farm) ✔ Grey Bruce B&B
RR1, Annan, Ontario   N0H 1B0 ☎ (519) 376-9142

Located 8.4 km east of Owen Sound off Hwy 26 and 4.8 km north of Conc. Rd 8.
$25S $35D ▣ Meals   (Weekend packages available) ► 6
● Homebaked ♠ Farm, hist., view, patio, quiet ■ 3D (main and upper floor)
▬ 2T,2D ⌐ 1Private, 1sh.w.h. ★ F,LF,TV in guest room ⌇ German
↪ Country lane to a beautiful waterfall, trails overlooking Georgian Bay
⇔ Safe, sandy Sauble Beach on beautiful blue Lake Huron, Leith (fishing), Owen Sound

☛ Enjoy true country living in Century stone house with old-fashioned comfort and
situated in peaceful park-like surroundings. Watch hosts train Standardbred horses.

Apple Hill

(near Cornwall; see also Finch, Lancaster, Williamstown)

McIntosh, Stewart and Christena (Tanglewood Farm)   ⌐ OFVA
RR2, Apple Hill, Ontario K0C 1B0   ☎ (613) 527-2884

From Hwy 401 take Exit 789 to Hwy 138 north to Hwy 43. Travel east for 5 km and south for 2 km to farm located 5 km west of Apple Hill.
$20S $10Child   ◙ Meals   ► 4A,2Ch
● Full   🏠 Dairy farm   ■ 2D   ⊨ 3D(upstairs)   ⊓ Sh.w.h.   ★ TV,F
🖐Smoking, drinking, pets

↤ Hiking, walking, cross-country skiing, maple bush

⇔ Glengarry Highland Games, Cornwall, Seaway Valley, St. Lawrence Parks, Upper Canada Village.

🖝 Feel the warmth and welcome of country hospitality and relax in rural tranquility. Enjoy delicious homecooking and fresh vegetables from the garden.

Arva

(near London; see also Ilderton)

Robson, Joyce and Everett (Robsons Rolling Ridge Farm)   ⌐ London B&B
RR1, Arva, Ontario N0M 1C0   ☎ (519) 666-0896

Take Hwy 4 north from London to 8th Concession (one road beyond Arva). Go west for 8.3 km to large yellow brick house on south side of road.
$30S $35D $10Add. person   ► 4A,2Ch
● Choice, homebaked   🏠 470-acre farm, view, swimming pool   ■ 2D(upstairs)
⊨ 2T,1D,R, crib   ⊓ 1Private, 1sh.w.h.   ★ Air (some)   🖐 Pets
↤ Rolling green hills, hayloft fun, see wild geese in season, maple syrup making
⇔ Antique auctions, factory outlets, tennis courts, Story Book Gardens, Stratford theatres, (ultimate shopping Masonville Mall), boutiques, country crafts, quality restaurants, Theatre 2nd City and Grand Bend, Stoybook Gardens, Lake Huron and Lake Erie Shores, Mennonite Country, Factory Outlets

🖝 Unwind in the country while enjoying the closeness of London. House specialty is homemade Maple Butter. Take some maple products home.

Balderson
(near Perth; see also Carleton Place, Merrickville, Frankville, Delta)

Miller, John and Ann (Woodrow Farm)   ⌐ CC
RR1, Balderson, Ontario K0G 1A0   ☎ (613) 267-1493

From Perth go north on Trans-Canada Hwy 1 (511) to Balderson village. Turn right onto Ferguson Falls Rd and look for third farm on left.
$30S $40D $12Child   ▣ Meals   ► 6
● Full, homebaked   ♠ 96-acre working farm   ■ 3D   ⊶ 6T,R, cot   ⊓ Sh.w.g.
★ TV,F   ♥   ⒲ Pets
↪ Village of Balderson, beaches, fishing, Prov. Parks, cross-country skiing
⇔ Glenair Kitten Factory outlet stores, Heritage Silversmiths, Balderson Cheese Factory

☞ Century old red brick farmhouse built in the lovely Ottawa Valley. Home raised roast beef and Yorkshire pudding served on request. An easy drive from Ottawa.

Bancroft
(north of Peterborough; see also Gilmour, Palmer Rapids, Haliburton, Wilberforce)

Grav, Fritz and Ingeborg (Beechmount Studio)   ⌐ ONT B&B
RR2, Bancroft, Ontario K0L 1C0   ☎ (613) 332-2329

Located 11 km west of Bancroft on old Hwy 500 or Airport Rd. Look for sign.
$25S $30D $10Child   ▣ Meals   ► 8
●Homebaked   ♠Farm, view   ■3   ⊶T,D   ⊓2Sh.w.g.,extra showers   ⸾German
↪ Hiking, cross-country skiing, fishing, boating, swimming, birdwatching

☞ New home is located on a hill with a view of lake and valley. Hosts do custom woll carding. There is a studio on the premises (spinning, weaving and craft classes). Meals served from own produce. Children welcome.

Barrie
(near Orillai: see also Thornton, Ferndale, Oro Station)

Bidgood, Marilyn (Craig Cottage)   ⌐ ONT B&B
RR1, Barrie, Ontario L4M 4Y8   ☎ (705) 726-1334

From Hwy 400 at Barrie, continue on the Hwy 400 extension to Horseshoe Valley Rd Exit. Proceed east to flashing light at village of Craighurst. Turn north on Hwy 93 to Craig Cottage on the left, after crossing railway tracks.
$25S $40D   ► 4A,1Ch
● Full, homebaked   ♠ Farm, hist., quiet   ■ 2D (upstairs)   ⊶ 1S,2D (upstairs)
⊓ 1Sh.w.h.   ★ KF,LF   ⒲ Smoking, drinking
↪ Village of Craighurst with local art shops, antiques and dining, cross country skiing, hiking, golfing, horseback riding, watch maple syrup being made
⇔ Horseshoe Valley Ski Resort, Barrie, Simcoe County Museum, Martyr's Shrine (Midland), Wasaga Beach, Copeland Conservation Area, Orillia

☞ Restored farm house decorated in a English "Country Cottage-style" and furnished with antiques situated in a quiet setting on a century farm.

Robins, Ruth and Paul (The Robin's Nest)   ✔ Orillia B&B
Craighurst, RR1, Barrie, Ontario   L4M 4Y8   ☎ (705) 726-7838

Take 400 north from Barrie to Horseshoe Valley Rd (20 km), right 1 km to Hwy 93
(Craighurst Village Centre). Turn left and go 1 km to house on right at railway crossing.
$35S $45D $15Add.person   ▶ 6A,1-3Ch
● Full, homebaked   ♠ Rural, acreage, hist., older, view   ■ 3D (upstairs)
⊷ 1S,2D,1Q,1R   ⊓ 2Sh.w.g.   ★ Air,TV in guest sitting room   ⊛ Pets
↔ Gifts, crafts and antique shop on premises (The Olde Emporium), village of
Craighurst, restaurants, shopping
⇔ Skiing, golfing, horseback riding, Wasaga beach, Martyr's Shrine, Indian Village, Wye
Marsh, Canada Wonderland, Trent Waterway

☛ Restored 1903-built home with General Store (The Old Emporium). Hosts are very
knowledgable about local history and happenings.

Bath
(near Kingston: see also Napanee, Sydenham, Picton. Bloomfield)

Crowle, Jan and Frank (Crowle's Landing)
RR1, Bath, Ontario   K0H 1G0   ☎ (613) 373-2277

Located on Loyalist Parkway (Hwy33), 11 km from Glenora Ferry (East).
$25S $35D $50F $5Add.person   ▣ Meals   ▶ 6A,4Ch
● Full   ♠ Farm, view, lakefront, deck, quiet   ■ 1S,2D,1Ste (with Nursery)
⊷ T,D,Q,crib   ⊓ 1Ensuite, 1sh.w.g.   ★ F,LF,TV in guest room,   ⊛ Smoking
↔ 1840 built and restored barn, fishing, swimming, boating
⇔ Prince Edward County, Picton, Sandbanks/North Beach Prov. Park, Glenoro Ferry

☛ Extended 2-storey cape cod with 90 ft floor to ceiling glass overlooking Adolphus
Beach located in beautiful and popular vacation area. There is a dog in the house.

Bayfield
(on Lake Huron near Goderich; see also Clinton, Seaforth, Bloomfield)

McAlister, Mrs. Leda (Gallery on the Bluff)
RR1, Bayfield, Ontario   N0M 1G0   ☎ (519) 482-9181

Located on Hwy 21 and 1.6 km north of Bayfield on the lake side at the stone gates.
$45D $10Child $20Add.person   ▶ 2
▣ not in winter   ● Choice   ♠ Rural, acreage, view, patio, lakefront, quiet   ■ 1Ste
⊷ 1D, cot   ⊓ 1Private   ★ KF,F, parking, private entrance
↔ 1.6 km long walkway along beach to Bayfield Harbour, exceptional restaurants, shops
⇔ Blyth leather and woolen mills, hiking trails, Summer theatre at Huron County
Playhouse & Blyth Festival Theatre, historic sites

☛ Perched on a bluff surrounded by fruit trees just north of the village. Paths
crisscross to Lake Huron 80ft below or through beautiful gardens with over 70 herbs.

Beachburg

(near Pembroke; see also Eganville, Foresters Falls, Renfrew, Golden Lake)

Campbell, Hazel and Alex (The Manse)
129 Main Street, Beachburg, Ontario K0J 1C0 ☎ (613) 582-3967

From Trans Canada Hwy 1 exit at Cobden to Hwy 21 North and continue to Beachburg.
$20S $28D $5Child ► 6
✚ Summer ● Full 🏠 Downtown, village, hist., quiet ■ 3D ⊷ 2T,1D,1Q
�🍴 1Sh.w.g. ★ parking Ⓦ Drinking
↔ Beachburg Fair, interesting little craft shops and restaurants
⇔ Sandy beaches, Ottawa River white-water raft rides and kayaking, good fishing,
untouched wilderness areas, prehistoric caverns

☞ Turn-of-the-Century family home, formerly a Church Manse, is airy, bright and
sunfilled and situated in quiet little village with lovely old homes.

Miles, David (Beachburg Inn) ✓ B&B
161 Main St., Beachburg, Ontario K0J 1C0 ☎ (613) 582-3585

Phone for directions.
$25S $30D   🍽 Meals ► 4
● Full, homebaked 🏠 Village, older, quiet ■ 2D (upstairs) ⊷ 2S,1D
🍴 1Sh.w.g. ★ Air,TV, private sitting room parking Ⓦ Children min. age 12
↔ Hiking, cross-country skiing, shopping
⇔ Whitewater rafting, swimming, boating, horseback riding

☞ Restored older home located in the "Whitewater Capital of Canada". There is also
an antique shop and English-style Tea room and restaurant on the premises.

Beamsville

(near St.Catharines; see also Grimsby, Hamilton, Vineland)

Bruinsma, Grace and Stewart
679 Hixon St., Box 687, Beamsville, Ontario L0R 1B0 ☎ (416) 563-8807

Take Exit 64 off QEW near Beamsville. Follow Ontario St south to stoplight at King St,
turn left to Hixon, turn right and look for white bungalow with spacious drive-way.
$20per person $10Child   🍽 Meals   (Family rates available) ► 10
● Full 🏠 Village, view, patio, quiet ■ 1S,3D ⊷ S,Q,R, cot, crib 🍴 Private,
sh.w.h. ★ Air,TV,KF,LF, separate entrance 〰 Dutch, some German and French
↔ Bruce Trail, Kinsmen Park with swimming pool
⇔ Ball's Falls, Prudhommes Miniature World (Tivoli), Niagara Falls, Welland Canal
(seven locks for ocean- going ships), city shopping Hamilton

☞ Retired hosts offer Dutch hospitality in quiet environment.

Beeton

(near Toronto; see also Bradford, Newmarket, Palgrave, Thornton)

Clark, Bill and Ruth
78 Centre St., Beeton, Ontario   L0G 1A0   ☎ (416) 729-2038

Take Hwy 27 north from Toronto to .8 km north of Bond Head. Turn west to Beeton
and right on Centre St.
$25S $30D   ◙ Meals   ► 4
● Full   ♠ Village, hist., acreage, quiet   ■ 2D (upstairs)   ⊣ 2Q, 2cot, crib
⌐1Sh.w.h.   ★ TV   ♥   ⊛ Smoking, drinking, pets
↔ Tree-lined park, race track
⇔ Honda Plant, Wonderland, Midland Martyr's Shrine, swimming, fishing,skiing areas

☛ 100-year old brick home is surrounded by many trees which attract over 20 different
kinds of birds and is an Ornithologist's delight.

Belleville

(near Kingston; see also Bloomfield, Picton, Wellington, Brighton, Consecon)

Kuntze, Charlotte and Jack   ✔ ONT B&B
240 Dufferin Ave., Belleville, Ontario   K8N 3X4   ☎ (613) 968-9972

Take Exit 543 or 544 off Hwy 401. Follow blue/yellow signs indicating route to Museum
(corner of Bridge St E/Dufferin Ave). Go north on Dufferin Ave to house with Canadian
flag.
$30S $40-45D $8Child   ◙ Meals   ► 6
● Full   ♠ Downtown, res.   ■ 3D (upstairs)   ⊣ 2T,2D   ⌐ Sh.w.g.
★Parking   ⊛ Pets, smoking, drinking
↔ Hastings County Museum, Belleville Harbour and waterfront Festival, downtown
business section, General Hospital
⇔ Sandbanks and Presquile Prov. Parks, Prince Edward County Vacation area, boating,
cross-country skiing, pick-your-own farms

Belwood

(near Guelph; see also Orton, Drayton, Elora, Acton)

Cawood, Robert (The Schoolhouse)   ✔ B&B
General Delivery, Belwood, Ontario   N0B 1J0   ☎ (519) 843-3576

Located 6.4 km east of Lake Belwood on Rd 26.
$60-85D   ◙ Meals   (Special rate for daytime coach tours)   ► 6
●Full   ♠Village, hist., acreage, patio, swimming pool, quiet, view, tennis court
■3D,plus self-contained log cabin   ⊣3D   ⌐1Sh.w.g.,hot tub   ★TV,F   ⊛Children
↔ Lake Belwood, windsurfing, canoeing, Grand River Conversation Area, large flower
and herb garden, weaving studio, excellent skiing, nature walks
⇔ Fergus, Elora, craftshops, boutiques

☛ Fieldstone former schoolhouse is surrounded by Conversation Area. Hosts are busy
with the popular gourmet restaurant on the premises and also conduct holiday spinning,
weaving, and knitting workshops. Host likes to cater to creative people.

Bloomfield
(near Belleville; see also Picton, Consecon, Wellington)

Bed and Breakfast Prince Edward County   ✔ FOBBA,ONT B&B
Box 160, Bloomfield, Ontario K0K 1G0   ☎ (613) 393-3046
(Reta Scoyne, Co-ordinator)
Rates from: $28S $38D   (includes full breakfast)
B&B Prince Edward County's host homes are located in some of the most picturesque
and historic sites, such as Lake on the Mountain, Millford, Rednersville, Bloomfield,
Wellington, Rednersville, Glenora, Waupoos, Picton and Sandbanks area. For
reservations mail money order or cheque for one night's accommodation and a stamped
self-addressed envelope. Some members are listed in this publication.

Bobcaygeon
(near Peterborough; see also Fenelon Falls, Coboconk, Rosedale)

Hume, Angela and Jim (Ambassador Inn & Restaurant)   CC
30 Front St.East, Box 598, Bobcaygeon, Ontario   K0M 1A0   ☎ (705) 738-2051

Take Hwy 36 from Lindsay to Bobcaygeon. Turn right at village sign (King St), then
right at Bolton St (3-way stop) to Swing Bridge over Lock and continue to Front St.
Turn right. (Just past the Bobcageon Inn)
$30-35 $40-55 $5Child $5Add.person   🍽 Meals   ► 8
● Choice, homebaked   🏠 Village, view, lakefront, large patio   ■ 4D (upstairs)
⌐2T,1D,1Q,1R,cot   ⌐ 2Sh.w.g   ★ Separate entrance, parking, guest lounge with
games and books   👑 Restricted smoking
↔ Public dock and marina across the street. Lock #32 on Trent/Severn Canal System,
swimming at dock or 2 beaches

☞ 80-year old home with pine plank flooring and antiques in rooms each with view of
water. Enclosed front porch is part of the restaurant overlooking the water.

Justice, Mary and Les "Bud" (Courtleigh Place)   ✔ CC
31 King St.W., Box 952, Bobcaygeon, Ontario   K0M 1A0   ☎ (705) 738-4969

Located four blocks from Hqy at corner of Sherwood. (Kings St runs west of Hwy 36)
$30-35S $40-45D $10Child   ► 6A,1Ch
● Full, homebaked   🏠 Village, older, res.   ■ 3D (upstairs)   ⌐ 2T,1D,1Q
⌐1Ensuite,1sh.w.g.   ★ Air,TV, parking, guest den   👑 Restricted smoking, pets
↔ First completed lock on Trent Severn System, fishing, swimming, shopping
⇔ Summer Theatre, Lindsay and Peterborough, golfing, horseback riding, Art Galleries,
antiques

☞ Home was built in 1890 and has tastefully decorated bedrooms ("elegant but
homey"). There are open screened porches for relaxing.

Peirson, Eloise (Lichthouse Point) $\smile$ CC
289 Riverside Dr., Bobcaygeon, Onario   K0M 1A0   ☎ (705) 738-4366

Located off Hwy 35, first street north of theTrent Canal Overpass.
$35S $45D $60Ste ☩ May-Oct   ● Choice, homebaked   ♠ bungalow, acreage,
waterfront, screened in porch, quiet   ■ 2D,1Ste   ⊷ 2S,1D,1Q   ⌐ 1Private,
1sh.w.h.   ★ TV in guest room, F, separate entrance, coffee making facilities, large
common room   ⓦ Restricted smoking, pets
↔ Private sandy beach with docking facilities and 132 ft shoreline for swimming, fishing
and walking. Village of Bobcaygeon
⇔ Fenelon Falls, Lindsay, shops, churches, restaurants, Summer Theatre, boat cruises,
art gallery, Curve Lake Indian Reserve, Peterborough lift lock

🐾 Comfortable and sunny home with large garden and screened porches faces the
lake. Canoe available. Hosts welcome boat travellers.

Bowmanville
(near Oshawa: see also Newcastle, Orono)

Cahais, William and Ruth $\smile$ Durham B&B
RR4, Bowmanville, Ontario   L1C 3K5   ☎ (416) 623-2704

From Hwy 401 east of Toronto take Exit 432 (Liberty) north to Concession Rd 3. Turn
right (east) past Mearns, Lambs, to Providence St. Look for house on corner.
$25S $40D $10Child $15Add.person   ▣ Meals   ► 6A,2Ch
● Full, homebaked   ♠ Rural, patio, quiet   ■ 3D (upstairs)   ⊷ 2T,2Q,1R, crib
⌐1Sh.w.h.   ★ F, parking   ⓦ Smoking, drinking, pets   ⤳ Dutch, German, Spanish
↔ Lovely rural countryside for walking, hiking and cross-country skiing, bird watching
⇔ Oshawa GM Canada, Bowmanville Zoo, Cullen Gardens, Peterborough Lift Locks,
Oshawa Ski club, Mossport Park car racing, Orono Exotic Cat World

🐾 Large country home, once the site of an old school, is surrounded by mature maple
trees and cedar hedges in peaceful rural setting. There is a small grey silver poodle in the
house.

Bracebridge
(see also Port Carling, Gravenhurst, Huntsville, Windermere)

Douglas, Mrs. Dorothy (Century House) $\smile$ Musk.B&B
Box 74, 155 Dill St., Bracebridge, Ontario P0B 1C0   ☎ (705) 645-3428/5510

From Hwy 11, take Bracebridge Exit. Follow signs to Hwy 118 west 4.8 km to Dill St.
$30S $40D   ► 5
● Full   ♠ Res., hist. patio, quiet   ■ 2D,1S (upstairs)   ⊷ 2T,1D,1S   ⌐ Sh.w.g.
★ TV in guest sitting room, sundeck, Victorian veranda   ⓦ Pets
↔ River (boat access and cruises available), parks, shopping, restaurants, town centre
⇔ Muskoka Summer Theatre, Santas Village, specialty craft shops, Muskoka lakes

🐾 Enjoy past Century charm and present Century convenience in lovingly restored
early Bracebridge home, located in the heart of popular vacation country.

Hillman, Jim and Euphemia (Hillford House) ✓ CC
360 Manitoba St., Box 2242, Bracebridge, Ontario P0B 1C0 ☎ (705) 645-4353

Take first entrance to Bracebridge off Hwy 11. From Hwy 118 intersection in Bracebridge follow Manitoba St two blocks north of the A&P store.
$25S $35-40D $40Unit ► 8
■ Summer (other by appointment) ● Full, some homebaked ⌂ Res, older, acreage, quiet ■ 1S,D,Ste (main and upper level) ⊏ 2T,2D,P ⌐ 1Ensuite, wsh.w.g. ★Air, F,TV in guest room, separate entrance, KF, parking, facilities for the disabled ✋Smoking, drinking, pets
↔ Scenic Falls, Bird's Historic House, golf course, shopping
⇔ Santas Village, Muskoka Lakes and public beaches, Bracebridge River, Fall "Calvacade of Colour"

☞ Native Muskoka residents in two-storey brick home. House specialty honey and maple syrup made by the host "with a little help from the bees and the trees"

McHugh, Cecile ✓ Musk.B&B
29 Wilshire Blvd., Bracebridge, Ontario P0B 1C0 ☎ (705) 645-2014

From Hwy 11 at Bracebridge, exit at Muskoka Rd 42 and follow 1.5 km to Pine St. Turn right a few blocks to Wilshire Blvd.
$20S $40D $4Child(over age 6) ► 6A,2Ch
● Full, homebaked ⌂ Res., sub., view, patio, quiet ■ 3.sp .5lnD ⊏ 2T,1D,1Q
⌐ 1Private, 1sh.w.g. ★ TV,F,LF, ceiling fans, parking ♥ ✋ Pets ≈ French
↔ Parkland, wharf for picnics, town of Bracebridge, craft shops
⇔ Santa's Village, Lady Muskoka boat cruises, Pioneer Village, swimming, golfing

☞ Modern residential home in peaceful parkland setting at center of all Muskoka activities. Enjoy breakfast on the patio in very private and friendly surroundings.

Bradford

(north of Toronto; see also Newmarket, Beeton, Barrie, Thornton)

Clubine, Shirley (Country Guest Home) ✓ OFVA
RR2, Bradford, Ontario L3Z 2A5 ☎ (416) 775-3576

Located 3.2km north of Bradford on Hwy 11.
$25S $35-40D ► 6-10
● Full, homebaked ⌂ Farm, quiet, view ■ S,D (upper and main floor) ⊏ T,D
⌐ Sh.w.g. ★ TV ✋ Pets, smoking, drinking
↔ Scanlon Creek Conservation Area, Town of Bradford
⇔ Lake Simcoe, Golf and Ski Haven at Gilford, Newmarket, Holland Marsh, Cookstown anitque markets, Canada Wonderland, Toronto

Braeside

(near Ottawa; see also Almonte, Renfrew, Calabogie, Pakenham, Shawville-Que.)

McGregor, Steve and Noreen (Glenroy Farm)
RR1, County Rd. 6, Braeside, Ontario K0A 1G0   ☎ (613) 432-6248

Located east of Arnprior. Follow River Rd 11 km. Look for sign "McGregors Produce".
$20S $35D   ▣ Meals   ► 8A,3Ch
● Full, homebaked   ♠ Farm   ■ 4 (main and upper floor)   ↳ T,D, bunks, crib
⌐ 2Sh.w.h., 1sh.w.g   ★ TV   ⓦ Pets, drinking
↔ Working farm, beef and produce
⇔ Arnprior, Renfrew, Storyland, Ottawa River Rafting, Ottawa, Bonnechere Caves

☞ Quiet setting, not near any major highways or urban area in 100- year old stone
house. Hosts also welcome parents of Arnprior Hockey School Students. Large host
family is very proud of their Scottish roots.

Brantford

(near Hamilton; see also Ancaster, St. George, Troy, Caledonia)

Kovack, Audrey and Ernest (Helm House)
152 Brant Ave., Brantford, Ontario N3T 3H7   ☎ (519) 759-4762

Phone for directions.
$20 per person $10Child   ► 9A,2Ch
✠ Mar1-Nov30   ● Full   ♠ Downtown, res., hist., patio   ■ 1S,4D (upstairs)
↳4T,1D,1Q,1P, crib   ⌐ 2Ensuite, 1sh.w.h.   ★ Air, TV in 3 guest rooms, F,LF,
parking   ⓦ Restricted smoking, pets   ⌣ French, Italian, German, Hungarian
↔ Eatons Mall, Cineplex, Showplace Gardens along the Grand River
⇔ Mohawk Chapel, Home of Alexander Graham Bell, Kitchener Farmer's Market and
Octoberfest, Elmira, Mennonite country, Stratford Festival, Lake Ontario, Toronto

☞ Well travelled couple enjoy receiving guests. "Take a step back in time and find
comfort and beauty in a turn of the Century spacious home"

B&B Travel Tip: *You can stay in a B&B even if you are not travelling by
car. Many B&B homes are situated near excellent public transportation and many
hosts will pick up and deliver from bus terminal, railway station or airport, sometimes at no charge.*

Brighton

(near Trenton; see also Colborne)

Barton, Marie & Patrick Davies (Butler Creek Inn) ⌐ FOBBA,Ont.B&B
RR7, Brighton, Ontario K0K 1H0 ☎ (613) 475-1248

Located just outside town limits. Phone for directions.
$35 $40-45D $10cot   ▣ Meals   ► 10
● Full   ♠ Rural, acreage, hist., view   ■ 3-4 (upstairs)   ⊷ 2T,2D,1Q,2R,2P
⊓ 1Private, 1sh.w.g.   ★ F, parking   ⊛ Smoking

↔ Hiking, cross-country skiing, historic house museum, excellent bird watching, orchards and roadside markets, antique shops
⇔ Presqu'ile Park, beach, camping, nature events, Kingston, Toronto

☛ Stately Victorian home situated on 10 acres with trout stream, valley and woods and an adjoining conservation area. "breakfast in a basket" provided for guests who enjoy this small Nature Paradise. There are pets in the house. Hostess operates an antique and restoration shop in the coachhouse.

Griffith, Bob and Shirley (Giuthas-Ard Choille)
RR4, Brighton, Ontario K0K 1H0 ☎ (613) 475-2485

From Hwy 401, take Exit 509 south to Brighton. Take Hwy 2 west to Cramahe- Brighton Boundary Line sign and right to top of first hill. Turn right to brown mail box.
$25S $30D   ► 2
▣ Apr. 1-Nov.1 ● Full   ♠ Rural, acreage, patio   ■ Self-contained guest home
⊷ 1D   ⊓ Private   ★ Separate entrance, KF,LF, parking   ⊛ Smoking, drinking, pets
⇔ Presqu'ile beach and Prov. Park, antique shops (Grafton and Brighton), Proctor House Museum, golfing

☛ Secluded location with beautiful view of Brighton and Lake Ontario. Excellent for birding (north-south flyway). Breakfast food provided for guests to serve.

Muir, Eleanor (Applecrest House) FOBBA
61 Simpson St., Box 1106, Brighton, Ontario K0K 1H0 ☎ (613) 475-0538

From traffic light on Hwy 2 in downtown go west. Then turn north onto Simpson St and look for first lane on right at top of hill.
$25S $40D $10Child $10Add.person ► 4A,4Ch
● Full Rural, 10 acres, quiet, hist. ■ 4D 4T,2D,1S 1Private, 1sh.w.g. ★ TV Pets, drinking, smoking
↔ Brighton, woodland walks
⇔ Presqu'ile Prov. Park, sandy beach, bird watching, water sports, cross country skiing, antique shops, Trenton, Prince Edward County vacation area

☞ Relax in large, gracious restored Victorian home surrounded by quiet woodlands and orchards with a panoramic view of Lake Ontario and Presqu'ile Prov. Park.

Brinston

(south of Ottawa; see also Morrisburg, Iroquois, Mountain, Winchester Merrickville, Cardinal)

Westervelt, Gerry and Johanna (Westergreen Farm)
RR2, Brinston, Ontario K0E 1C0 ☎ (613) 652-4241

Take Exit 738 off Hwy 401 at Iroquois. Follow County Rd 1 north for 4 km to Concession Rd 3 and turn right. Continue 4 km to stop sign on Brinston Rd (County Rd 2). Turn left. In Brinston turn right and right again on Payne Rd to first farm on left.
$20S $25D $2.50 Child (under age 12) $5Add.person Meals ● Choice, Farm, patio, quiet, a small orchard ■ 1D,1Ste,1F (main and upper floor) 1S,2D 1Private, 1sh.w.h. ★ TV,separate entrance, facilities for the disabled Drinking, pets Dutch, some German

⇔ Upper Canada Village, Iroquois Seaway Locks, Fort Wellington at Prescott, Thousand Islands vacation area, Ottawa (Capital)

☞ 1825 grey stone house on a 55 milking cows dairy farm. There are three boys in the host family who help with chores when not in school. There is a dog and a cat in the house. Hosts welcome young and old.

Britt

(north of Parry Sound)

Sangster, Alma and Harry (B&B in Britt)   ✓ Parry Sound B&B
Box 144, Britt, Ontario P0G 1A0   ☎ (705) 383-2441

Located 3.3 km west on Hwy 526 off Hwy 69.
$25-37S $33-45 $10Child or Add.person   ▣ Meals   ► 14
✚ Mar-Dec. ● Full ♠ Rural, view, riverfront ■ 7D (upstairs) ◡ 8T,3D, cot,
crib ⌐ 2Private, Sh.w.g. ∿ French
↔ Good fishing and hunting, swimming, canoeing, boating, store, marina
⇔ Parry Sound (30000 Island cruise), French River golf course, Sudbury (Science North)

☞ Also called "New Magnetawan Hotel", it's Scottish owners welcome guests to their
home located at the end of the famous Magnetawan River Canoe Routes.

Brockville

(see also Delta, Frankville, Rockport, Cardinal, Prescott, Mallorytown)

Darrach, Doli and Peter (The Webster House Inn   ✓ CC
37 James Street East, Brockville, Ontario K6V 1K3   ☎ (613) 345-4707

From Hwy 401 take Exit 696 and proceed toward centre of town. After Pearl St traffic
lights, turn left onto James. Located between Garden and Bethune Streets. From Hwy 2
(King St in the city) proceed 2 blocks north on Bethune to James. Turn left.
$40-50S $45-55D   ► 6A
● Gourmet ♠ Downtown, res., hist., ■ 3D (upstairs) ◡ 2T,2D ⌐ 2Sh.w.g.
★ F(very ornate with Belgium Tiles), parking, separate entrance ✋ Smoking, pets,
children min. age 12
↔ Waterfront parks, fine restaurants and pubs, historic homes, Centretown, 1000 Island
boat tour, Courthouse Square (New England style)
⇔ Upper Canada Village, Heritage Highway scenic drives, St. Lawrence River Biway,
golfing, swimming, cross-country skiing, bikeway

☞ Lovingly restored elegant Victorian home, former home of Senator Webster with
100-year old lace-curtains still gracing the windows and original brass gas fixtures and
accents. Experience life in beautiful home built for a gentile Victorian family. There are
two cats in the house.

B&B Travel Tip: *Most hosts do not accept credit cards or cheques, so make
sure you have cash on hand - or check about this when making your reservation.*

Miller, John and Phyllis (Burnside Inn)   ✔ CC
RR1, Heritage Highway 2, Brockville, Ontario   K6V 5T1   ☎ (613) 342-4920

Located 3.5 km east of Brockville on the riverside of Hwy 2.
$45S $50D   (Deposit required)   ► 6A
✪ May1-Oct31   ♠ Hist., older, acreage, riverfront, quiet   ■ 3D (main and upper
floor)   ⊷ 4T,1D   ⩘ 2Private   ★ TV in guest room, separate entrance   ⓌSmoking,
no facilities for young children
↔ St. Lawrence River front walking, hiking, Burnside House (fine Canadian Crafts),
workshop (decoys, shorebirds and folksart)
↔ Fort Henry, Kingston, Brockville, Ottawa (Capital), Upper Canada Village, historic
Heritage Highway No.2, fine dining

☛ 18th Century Loyalist stone cottage furnished with antiques and with an excellent
view of the St. Lawrence Seaway. Watch ships and many pleasure craft pass by the door.

Nelson-Stewart, Mrs. Connie (Brockville B&B)   ✔ B&B
331 King St.W., Brockville, Ontario   K6V 3S5   ☎) (613) 345-4600

From Hwy 401, take Exit 696 (Stewart Blvd) south to Hwy 2 (King St). Turn right.
$30S $35D $5Child $5Add.person   ► 6A,2Ch
● Full, homebaked   ♠ Downtown, res., hist., patio, quiet   ■ 3D (upstairs)
⊷4T,1Q,1R, crib   ⩘ 2Sh.w.g.   ★ Air,TV, parking   Ⓦ Outdoor smoking area, pets
↔ Historic downtown Brockville, Blockhouse Island, boat tours of the 1000 Islands, fine
parks, excellent restaurants
↔ Upper Canada Village, bridges to USA, Heritage Hwy following the St.Lawrence
River, Rideau Canal System

☛ Pleasant and relaxed atmosphere in older comfortable home. Breakfast is served in
the large eat-in kitchen, indeed a "home away from home". There is a large friendly dog.
Children welcome.

Bruce Mines
(near Sault Ste. Marie; see also Richards Landing)

Thompson, Robert and Florence (Lake Forest Farm)   ✔ OVFA
RR1, Bruce Mines, Ontario   P0R 1C0   ☎ (705) 785-3510

Phone or write for directions.
$20S $30D   ▥ Meals   (Family Rates available)   ► 4A,4Ch
● Choice, homebaked   ♠ 200-acre farm, lakefront - ■ 3D   ⊷ 1T,2D   ⩘ Sh.w.g.
★ TV,F,KF   ♥   Ⓦ Smoking, drinking
↔ Swimming and fishing in Lake Huron, cross-country skiing
↔ Sault Ste. Marie, shopping, dining

☛ Farm grounds back onto Lake Huron. Enjoy home-grown, whole-wheat bread,
maple syrup from the farm and jams and jellies. Join host when he checks his traplines.

Burlington
(near Hamilton, see also Waterdown, Millgrove, Campbellville, Milton, Oakville)

Creasey, Betty (Butterfly House)   ✔ Burl.B&B
504 Forestwood Cresc., Burlington, Ontario L7L 4J9   ☎ (416) 637-3196

From QEW take Exit 107 south on Appleby Line to New Street stoplight. Turn left. Just
before next stoplight turn left onto Pinedale. Forestwood is first street on left side. Look
for 2nd single dwelling on right side with Butterflies on house.
$28S $35D   ▣ Meals   ► 4
● Choice   ♠ Res., quiet   ■ 2S,1D   ⌣ 2S,1D   ⌐ Sh.w.g.   ★ TV   ⚇ Pets,
smoking
↪ Appleby Mall, indoor swimming pool, small library, restaurants, bicycling
⇔ Lake Ontario, golfing, Conservation Parks, cross-country skiing, Hamilton

☛ Modern quiet residential area. Hostess is an outdoor person, square dancer and
teacher of microwave cooking.

Glatz, Arlene (Cedar Croft)   ✔ Burl.B&B
3273 Myers Lane, Burlington, Ontario L7N 1K6   ☎ (416) 637-2491

From QEW take Exit 105 (Walkers Line) south to New Street traffic light. Turn right
and continue to Pine Cove Rd. Turn left to Myers Lane on right.
$30S $45D $5Child   ► 4
● Choice   ♠ Res., quiet, swimming pool   ■ 2D (main and upper floor)
⌣ 2T,1D   ⌐ 2Sh.w.h.   ★ F,TV,parking   ⚇ Smoking, drinking
↪ Small plazas, Lake Ontario
⇔ Burlington Shopping Mall, downtown Lakeside Park and trendy shopping, Royal
Botanical Gardens, Toronto, Niagara-on-the-Lake

☛ Warm and friendly "Home-away-from-home" atmosphere on a quiet court.

Jordan, Maude and Clayton (Twin Birches)   ✔ Burl.B&B
637 Wilene Drive, Burlington, Ontario L7L 2B3   ☎ (416) 637-2079

From QEW take Exit 105 (Walkers's Line) south and go to Flemish. Turn left to 1st
street on right. House is on corner.
$30S $45D $25Child   ▣ Meals   ► 4
● Full, homebaked   ♠ Res., patio,   ■ 2D (upstairs)   ⌣ 2T,1D   ⌐ 2Sh.w.h.
★ Air,TV,F   ♥   ⚇ Smoking
↪ Burlington Shopping Mall, small plaza
⇔ Lake Ontario, Bronte Creek Park picnics and cross-country skiing, Botanical
Gardens, Toronto, Niagara Falls

☛ Retired couple welcomes guests in comfortable split-level suburban home. There is a
dog in the house.

FitzSimons, Robin and Millie   ✓ Burl.B&B
598 Barons Ct., Burlington, Ontario   L7R 4E4   ☎ (416) 637-9919

From QEW take Exit 102 south on Guelph Line to Woodward Ave stoplight. Turn right.
Baron Court is first street on left side.
$30S $45D   ► 4
● Full, homebaked   ♠ Central, res., parkview, patio, quiet ■ 2D(upstairs)   ⌐ 2D
⌐ Sh.w.g.   ★ Air,F,TV,KF   ♥   ⍟ Pets, drinking   ⌣ some French and Spanish
↔ Library, tennis courts, Family YMCA with indoor swimming pool, Central Park and
Arena, quaint Village Square and exclusive shopping and dining
⇔ Lake Ontario, Hamilton, Botanical Gardens, Kitchener/Waterloo, McMaster U.

☞ Quiet, relaxing atmosphere in centrally located modern home. Hosts have travelled
extensively throughout Europe, Mexico and Canada and have welcomed many
International students visiting the city.

Kemp, Helen and Art (Strathcona Place)   ✓ Burl.B&B
4050 Apple Valley Lane, Burlington, Ontario   L7L 1E7   ☎ (416) 634-0721

From QEW take Exit 105 (Walkers Line) south and left on Apple Valley Lane. (1 block
north of Lakeshore Rd).
$30S $45D   ▣ Meals   ► 2A
● Full   ♠ Res., sub., patio, quiet, swimming pool   ■ 1D (upstairs)   ⌐ 1D
⌐Sh.w.h.   ★ Air,F,TV,LF, parking   ⍟ pets
↔ Lake Ontario, Eastway Plaza, bus service (local and to Toronto)
⇔ Burlington downtown and Spencer Park, Burlington Mall, Hamilton, Toronto,
Niagara-on-the-Lake

☞ Unique comfortable open-concept home on large property with pool and garden.
Burlington natives and now retired hosts are very knowledgeable about the City and
involved in many aspects of the community.

Oude-Reimerink, Marijke and Henk   ✓ FOBBA,Burl.B&B
5435 Stratton Rd., Burlington, Ontario   L7L 2Z1   ☎ (416) 637-0329

From QEW take Exit 109 south (Burloak) to Lakeshore Rd (Hwy2). Turn right and then
right again at Hampton Heath. Stratton is first street on right.
$25S $40D   ► 2A
● Choice   ♠ Res., patio, quiet   ■ 1D   ⌐ 2T   ⌐ Sh.w.h.   ★ Air, TV
⍟Smoking, children, pets   ⌣ Dutch
↔ Lakeside Shopping Village, Lake Ontario, Lakeshore parks, restaurants, bus stop to
Toronto and Hamilton
⇔ Royal Botanical Gardens, Toronto, Niagara-on-the-Lake, Bruce Trail, Milton
Agricultural Museum

☞ Ranch-style bungalow on quiet street. Very congenial hosts are square dancers and
have travelled extensively by B&B in Canada and USA.

Murphy, Pat (Murphy's Manor) ⌐ Burl.B&B
5112 Ashland Drive, Burlington, Ontario   L7L 3H2   ☎ (416) 532-4917

From QEW, take Exit 107 South (Appleby Line) to Spruce Ave traffic light. Turn left
and first right on Linwood. Then turn left on Ashland.
$30S $40D $60F   ► 4
● Choice, homebaked   🏠 Res, sub., patio, quiet   ■ 2D (upstairs)   ⊨ 1T,1D
⊓1Sh.w.g.   ★ Air,F,LF, parking, badminton court
↔ Lake Ontario, Lakeside Village Shopping Centre, Appleby Mall, bus service to
Toronto on Lakeshore Road
⇔ Quaint town of Oakville, Bronte Harbourfront and trendy shopping, fine dining,
Commuter Train to Toronto, downtown Burlington, Burlington Shopping Mall

☛ Lovely large well kept home on quiet tree-lined residential street. Cozy and
comfortable surroundings and very friendly neighborhood.

Pantel, Ted and Gerda ⌐ Burl.B&B, FOBBA
270 Juniper Ave., Burlington, Ontario   L7L 2T3   ☎ (416) 632-1996

From QEW take Appleby Line Exit (107) south to Spruce Ave stoplight. Turn right.
Juniper is on left side. Look for 2nd house on right. .
$30S $45D   (please phone ahead to see if the room is available)   ► 2A
✚ July & Aug.   ● Full   🏠 Res., quiet   ■ 1D(upstairs)   ⊨ 2T   ⊓ Sh.w.h.
★ Air   ✋ Pets, children   〰 German
⇔ Marina, sailing, dining, shopping, commuter train to Toronto, Bronte Prov. Park

☛ Contemporary suburban split-level home with European atmosphere.

Thomson, Carol Ann (Harmony Haven) ⌐ Burl.B&B
2051-3 Amherst Heights Crt, Burlington, Ontario   L7P 3R2   ☎ (416) 336-0294

From Toronto on QEW, take Plains Rd Exit and turn right at Brant Sreett stop-light.
Proceed past Mount Royal Plaza on right to Amherst Hts Drive. Turn right and continue
around Apt Bldg on left side to Amherst Hts Court. Turn right again and then left into
driveway by chain link fence and continue around the back.
$25S $40D $10Child   ▣ Meals   ► 4
● Choice   🏠 Townhouse, sub.,view, patio, quiet   ■ 2D(upstairs)   ⊨ 2T,1D
⊓Sh.w.h.   ★ Air,TV, parking   ✋ Smoking, pets
↔ Restaurants, golf course, shopping plazas
⇔ Niagara Escarpement, Bruce Trail, historic village of Waterdown, "Go" Commuter
Train to Toronto, downtown Burlington, Hamilton, Botanical Gardens

☛ Suburban townhouse with view of Skyway Bridge, Lake Ontario and Niagara
Escarpment. Quiet location, but close to all amenities and bus routes. Homebaking and
gourmet cooking a specialty. There is a grand piano in the Living room (hostess is
involved in "Opera Hamilton", choral singing and musical theatre.

Calabogie

(west of Ottawa; see also Renfrew Pakenham, Eganville, Carleton Place, Almonte)

Jamieson, Pam and Bill (The Pinery) ✔ B&B
RR3, Calabogie, Ontario K0J 1H0 ☎ 613) 752-2054

Located south of Hwy 17 on Hwy 508 between Arnprior and Renfrew.
$40S $45D $10Child ► 6A
● Full, homebaked 🏠 Rural, acreage, view, lakefront, patio, quiet, screened porch
■3D (upstairs) ⊷ 3D,2R ⌐ 1Private, 1sh.w.g. ★ TV,F,LF, glass-enclosed hot
tub ♥ ✋ Restricted smoking, pets ∿ some French
↔ Hike along an old railway line, village of Calabogie, boat rentals, windsurfing,
excellent restaurants, art galleries, gift shops, flea markets, cross-country skiing,
beautiful fall colour spectacles
⇔ Ski hills, Calabogie Peaks, Calabogie Highlands Golfcourse, tennis, whitewater
rafting at Beachburg

☛ Contemporary home with open concept ceilings, pine floors and view of Calabogie
Lake located at the edge of the village on the way to Calabogie Peaks ski area. Well
travelled hosts know "the Valley" and will arrange day trips anywhere. There is a dog
and a cat in residence.

Caledonia

(near Hamilton: see also Jerseyville, Brantford)

Roy, Margaret and Lawrence (Roy's Ranch)
RR2, Caledonia, Ontario N0A 1A0 ☎ (416) 765-2814

From Hwy 6 at Caledonia go west on Hwy 54 towards Brantford to County Rd 22, turn
right 1.6 km. Look for blue and red mailbox on left side.
$20S $37.50D ▣ Meals ► 3A
✚ May-Oct. ● Full, homebaked 🏠 75-acre farm, view, quiet ■ 1S,1D
⊷ 1S,1D,P ⌐ 1Private, 1Sh.w.h. ★ Air, TV
⇔ River boat trips, large shopping mall, fall fairs, African Lion Safari, Hamilton Hunt
Club, Lake Erie beaches, Niagara-on-the-Lake

☛ Hosts have travelled extensively in Canada and abroad.

B&B Travel Tip: *You can stay in a B&B when you are hiking the trails. In
Ontario there are many B&B's along the famous Bruce Trail and some of these
hosts will even forward your car and gear for you to the next B&B on the trail.*

Cambridge
(near Waterloo/Kitchener; see also Guelph, Campbellville)

Bauman, Janet and Clare (Red Door Bed & Breakfast) ✔ CC
754 Queenston Rd., Cambridge, Ontario N3H 3K3 ☎ (519) 653-9767

Located 1 km off Hwy 401. Take old Hwy 8 Exit into Campbridge. Continue down
Shants Hill and across the speed River to King St. Go one block to the west between
Westminster and Church Sts and look for house with red door.
$30S $35D $5Child $10Add.person ► 6
●Full, homebaked ⌂Downtown, res, older, quiet, outdoor swimming pool
■3D(upstairs) ⊷2T,1D,1Q,cot,crib ⌐1Sh.w.g. ★TV, parking ⊕Smoking, pets
↪ Popular factory outlets (shoes, fabrics)
⇔ Lion Safari, Kitchener Farmer's Market, Stratford Shakespear Festival, golfing, Lake
Ontario, Toronto

☞ Century old family home in the heart of Preston-Cambridge country situated on a
quiet street lined with mature trees.

Fraser, Donald and Alma
RR4, Cambridge, Ontario N1R 5S5 ☎ (519) 621-9989

On Hwy 24 south of Cambridge go south for 3.2 km, turn right and over bridge to West
River Rd. Turn left to Edgewood Cr. Look for second place on right.
$25S $35D ► 4A
● Full   ⌂ Res., acreage, patio, quiet   ■ 1D,1Ste   ⊷ 2D   ⌐ Sh.w.g.   ★ TV,
parking   ⊕ Restricted smoking, drinking, children, pets
⇔ African Lion Safari, Kitchener farmer's market, Bell Homestead (Brantford), Doon
Pioneer Village, Hamilton Place, Lake Ontario

☞ Ranch-style home in the beautiful Grand River Valley view.

Campbellford
(near Belleville; see also Peterborough, Hastings, Trenton, Brighton, Colborne)

Kibbe, Pauline and Harvey (Linden House) ✔ CC
91 Doxsee Ave., South, Campbellford, Ontario K0L 1L0 ☎ (705) 653-4406

From Hwy 401, take Exit 30 North to Campbellford. Turn right at traffic light and
continue over Bridge, then right again at Doxsee and house on left.
$30S $35D $10Child $10Add.person ► 6A,2Ch
● Full, English-style   ⌂ Res., older, quiet   ■ 3D,1F (upstairs)   ⊷ 3S,3D
⌐1Sh.w.g.   ★ Air,TV, parking   ⊕ Drinking, pets
↪ Trent Severn Waterway and Locks, Conservation area
⇔ Lake Ontario, Presqu'ile Park, Healey and Ranney Falls, Swimmers Delight at Crowe
Bridge, fleamarkets and antique emporiums abound

☞ Turn-of-the-century home situated on a quiet residential street. Complimentary
pick-up and delivery for Waterway travellers.

Campbellville

(near Burlington; see also Millgrove, Waterdown, Acton, Milton, Cambridge)

Bloss, John and Audrey (Maple Hill Farm)   ⌐ CC
548 Campbellville Rd.RR2, Campbellville, Ontario   L0P 1B0   ☎ (416) 659-1503

From Hwy 401, exit onto Guelph Line south to the Emporium in the centre of town, then go 4 km west on Campbellville Rd. From QEW exit onto Guelph Line north.
$30S $40D   ► 4A
● Full, homebaked   🏠 14-acre farm, hist., view, patio, quiet   ■ 2D (main and upper floor)   ⊷ 2T,1D   ⏗ 1Sh.w.g.   ★ TV,LF, separate entrance, guest sitting room
🖐 Smoking, drinking, pets, children

↔ Mountsberg Wildlife Centre, large apple orchard on property

⇔ Halton Region and County Railway Museums, Ontario Agricultural Museum, Rattlesnake Point, Crawford Lake and restored Indian Village, five conservation areas

🖝 Restored and refurbished 1874 home with 18in. thick stone walls and retaining its traditional country charm, situated on a hill overlooking the Niagara Escarpment. There is a dog in the house.

Cardinal

(near Brockville; see also Morrisburg, Iroquois, Prescott, Brinston)

Roduner, Walter and Margareta (Roduner Farm)
RR1, Cardinal, Ontario K0E 1E0   ☎ (613) 657-4830

Leave Hwy 401 at Exit 730 (Cardinal) and drive north to Brouseville Rd W. Look for sixth house on north side of road.
$20S $30D $5-12Child $12Add. person   ► 5
● Choice, homebaked   🏠 Dairy farm   ■ 1S,1D,F   ⊷ 2T,1D, crib, cot
⏗ 1Private, 1sh.w.h.   ★ LF,TV, two bicycles   ♥   ⤳ German, French
↔ Cross-country ski trails
⇔ Iroquois Locks, Upper Canada Village, Prescott, Thousand Islands, Ottawa

🖝 Hosts have been welcoming guest to their farm for many years and invite everyone to watch and take part in the bustling dairy farm operation. Swiss hospitality. House pet is allowed in summer kitchen only.

Cargill

(south of Owen Sound; see also Hanover, Dobbinton Kincardine, Durham, London)

Moffatt, Elaine and Jack (Corner Brook Farms B&B) ✔ FOBBA,OFVA
RR2, Cargill, Ontario N0G 1J0 ☎ (519) 366-2629

From Hwy 21, take Co Rd 15 at Tiverton and go east 14.5 km through Glammis on to farm on right side (well marked). Or travel 12 km north of Junction 4 and 9.
$25S $35D $55F 📷 Meals (Children half-price) ► 6
● Full 🏠 200-acre mixed farm, well shaded ■ 3D ↩ 2T,2D ⌐ 1Sh.w.g. ★ TV, Air (on main floor)
↔ Hiking, skiing, woodland and maple bush
⇔ Saugeen River, canoeing, fishing, swimming, Lake Huron, Bruce Nuclear Plant tours, Blyth Summer Festival Theatre

📢 Large modernized century-home in quiet, scenic surroundings and relaxed atmosphere. Enjoy Lake Huron's magnificient sunsets. Senior citizens most welcome.

Carleton Place

(near Ottawa; see also Almonte, Balderson, Pakenham, Calabogie)

Lalonde, Marjorie and Jack (Ottawa Valley B&B) ✔ CC
96 Lake Ave. W, Carleton Place, Ontario K7C 1L8 ☎ (613) 257-7720

From Bridge Street in town, turn west at the traffic light onto Lake Ave West.
$28S $34D $10Child(over age 12) ► 6
● Choice 🏠 Res., older, porches ■ 3 (upstairs) ↩ 1Q,1D,2S ⌐ 1Sh.w.g.
★TV in two guest rooms, off- street parking ♥ ✋ Pets ∼ French
↔ River and Lake, swimming, boating, Riverside Park, historic buildings, discount outlets, flea markets and auctions
⇔ Ottawa, Rideau Canal (hand-operated locks), Perth (architecturally restored)

📢 Gracious older home with large tastefully decorated rooms in restful surroundings.

McGinnes, Janet and David Somppi (Hudson House B&B) ✔ CC
7 Lorne St., Carleton Place, Ontario K7C 2J9 ☎ (613) 257-8547

Follow Lake Ave East from traffic lights at foot of Bridge St. After railway crossing, turn left at sixth street. Located at corner of Lorne St and Lake Ave East.
$25S $35D $10Add.person (weekly rates available) ► 6
● Choice 🏠 Downtown, older, new wooden porches and verandas ■ 3D (upstairs)
↩2S,3D ⌐ 2Sh.w.g. ★ TV in guest room, parking
↔ River swimming, fishing, boating, shopping area
⇔ Ottawa, Mississippi Lake, Rideau Canal waterway, gateway to Lanark County

📢 Large beautifully restored and decorated Victorian home on quiet, tree-lined street won a 1987 Heritage Restoration Award.

Cavan

(near Peterborough; see also Millbrook, Curve Lake)

Brown, Les and Louise
746 Hwy 7A, RR1, Cavan, Ontario   L0A 1C0   ☎ (705) 944-5510

Located on north side of Hwy 7A, west of Cavan village. Look for mailbox with name.
$25S $30D   ► 6
● Full   ♠ Rural, 4-acres,scenic   ■ 3D   ⊶ 3D (upper and main floor)
⁓1Private   ★ Air,TV,F   ♥ ⊛ Pets, drinking, smoking
↪ Trout stream, cedar bush
⇔ Peterborough, Bethany Ski area, Kawartha Lakes

☞ Formerly from Toronto, retired hosts enjoy visitors in winter and summer.

Hanbridge, Roger and Karen (Rokar Farms)   ⊷ B&B
RR3, Cavan, Ontario   L0A 1C0   ☎ (705) 745-5383

From Springville (on Hwy 7 south-west of Peterborough), travel 1.5 km north to first
stoplight (Cashway Lumber Store). Turn left on 12th Concession (Stewart Rd) and travel
1.5 km to 2nd farm on right.
$25S $38D $12Child
● Full, homebaked   ♠ 100-acre farm, quiet   ■ 2D (upstairs)   ⊶ 2D,1R
⁓Sh.w.g.   ★ F,TV in guest room   ⊛ Smoking
↪ Country ways in the heart of the Kawarthas
⇔ Peterborough, Kawartha Downs Harness Racing, Devils Elbow/Suregga Ski Resorts,
Whitneys Ojibwa Crafts/Art Gallery, Pioneer Village, Peterborough Festival of Lights

☞ Extensively renovated 100-year old brick farm house furnished with pleasing
combination of antiques and new furnishing. Retired Dairy Farmers enjoy curling and
gardening. There is a dog in the house.

Clarksburg

(near Owen Sound; see also Kimberley, Meaford, Thornbury, Collingwood, Palgrave)

DeNys, Dinie and Pieter (DeNys Country B&B)   ⊷ FOBBA
RR2, Clarksburg, Ontario   N0H 1J0   ☎ (519) 599-6577

Take Hwy 26 west from Collingwood toward Thornbury (22 km) to Grey Rd No 4. Turn
left and go to first stop sign, turn left again onto Grey Rd No 2 and to first home on left.
$25-35S $35-45D $10Add.person   ► 6
● Choice   ♠ Rural, acreage, quiet, porches   ■ 2D,1Ste (upstairs)   ⊶ 2T,1D,1Q,1R
⁓ 1Ensuite, 1sh.w.g.   ★ TV, woodstove   ⊛ Restricted smoking, pets   ⤬ Dutch
↪ Cross-country skiing, Beaver Valley
⇔ Wasaga Beach, Blue Mountain Ski Resort, Collingwood, Eugenia Falls, Bruce Trail.

☞ Newly-built early American-style farmhouse on 25-acre property.

Maitland, Don and Nan (Grape Grange) ↙ CC
Box 39, Marsh St., Clarksburg, Ontario N0H 1J0 ☎ (519) 599-2601

Take Hwy 26 to Thornbury stop light, turn south 1.5 km to 4th house on left at top of
hill. Look for Century Farm sign at entrance.
$30S $40D $10Child $15Add. person ▣ Meals ► 5A,1Ch
● Choice, homebaked ♠ Farm, historic, older, patio, quiet ■ 1S,2D
⊢ 1S,2T,1D, crib ⊓ 2Sh.w.h. ⇔ V,F ⓦ Pets
↪ Village shopping, Military Museum, art studios, Georgian Bay, cross- country skiing
⇔ Meaford, scenic caves, Bruce Trail, Blue Mountain & Beaver Valley Ski Resorts

☞ Small farm with large garden. Fresh eggs and bacon and homemade preserves.

Stewart, Karen and Norm (Hillside Bed & Breakfast) ↙ CC
Box 72, Clarksburg, Ontario N0H 1J0 ☎ (519) 599-5523

From Hwy 26, turn south at lights Thornbury. Follow Bruce St to Clarksburg (1.4km)
and continue up the hill from the village. Look for sign on stone pillar corner of Brook
St. From Beaver Valley on County Rd 13 drive north from Kimberley to Clarksburg.
$30S $40D $10Child $10Add.person ► 9
● Full, homebaked ♠ Village, res., acreage, hist., view, quiet, large porch, ■ 3D
(upstairs) ⊢ 1T,2T,1R,1P ⊓ 1Sh.w.g. ★ 2F,TV, parking ⓦ Smoking, pets,
children min. age 5
⇔ Several well-known ski resorts, cross-country ski trails, tennis courts and golf courses,
Bruce Trail hiking, fishing, boating, windsurfing, Georgian Bay beaches, theatre, antique
shops

☞ Stately 1880 Victorian home overlooking the Beaver Valley, situated on 3 acres of
beautifully treed and terraced lawns with natural stream. Truly a peaceful place to relax.
Hosts have gathered much information about the home and its prominent owners.

Clinton
(near Goderich; see also Seaforth, Bayfield)

Roy, Ruth E. (Maples) ↙ CC
48 Isaac St., Box 863, Clinton, Ontario N0M 1L0 ☎ (519) 482-9781

Located at intersection of Hwys 8 and 4 in Clinton, beside the Bowling Green.
$15S $20D ► 5A
✦ June-Sept 15 ● Full, homebaked ♠ Village, older, quiet ■ 1S,2D ⊢ 3
(upstairs) ⊓ Sh.w.g. ⓦ Smoking, pets, drinking ⌇ German
↪ Business section, bowling green
⇔ Blyth (Theatre), Stratford Festival, Grand Bend (Lake Huron beaches)

☞ Century Home, centrally located on a quiet shaded lot.

Coboconk

(northwest of Peterborough; see also Minden, Rosedale, Bobcaygeon, Fenelon Falls)

MacNeil, Michael and Eleanor
RR1, Coboconk, Ontario K0M 1K0 ☎ (705) 454-1018

Located 4.5km east of Coboconk on Base Line Road.
$20S $30D $5Child ●$2Each 🍽 Meals ► 2A,2Ch
●Cont, homebaked 🏠Farm, ranch-style, view, quiet, isolated ■1D ⊷1D,1cot,1R
🜂Sh.w.h. ★TV,LF, parking, facilities for the disabled ⍾Drinking, pets
↪ Trails through over 200 acres of woods and meadows (possible sild-life sighting)
⇔ Public beach and play ground, Kirkfield lift locks, Buckhorn Gallery on the Lake,
Peterborough Lift Locks, Curve Lake Indian Reserve, Fenelon Falls

Colborne

(near Trenton; see also Brighton)

Lee, Roger and Margaret (The Maples) heck
Box 743, 119 King St. E., Colborne, Ontario K0K 1S0 ☎ (416) 355-2059

From Hwy 401 take Percy St Exit into village to Hwy 2 (King St), turn left.
$30-35S $40D $10Add.person ► 5A
🈳 May-Oct. (other by special arrangement) ● Full 🏠 Village, acreage, older,
veranda, quiet ■ 1S,3D (upstairs) ⊷ 1S,2Q,1D 🜂 1Sh.w.g. ⍾ Smoking,
pets, children min. age 2
⇔ Antique and craft shops, Presqu'ile Prov. Park, Lake Ontario , Prince Edward
County vacation area and sandbanks, Bay of Quinte

🖝 Spacious red brick century home with open veranda across the front, pleasant to
relax on. There are spacious grounds to ramble over.

Collingwood

(near Owen Sound: see also Kimberley, Clarksburg, Creemore, Meaford, Palgrave)

Buchan, Peter and Pauline (Apple Hill) ⌁ CC
Box 3181, RR3, Collingwood, Ontario L9Y 3Z2 ☎ (705) 444-1352

Located 10 km west of Collingwood. Follow signs for the scenic Caves. Look for sign on
right side at first curve on road up Mountain
$40S $45D $5Child $5Add.person ► 6A,3Ch
● Full, homebaked 🏠 Farm, hist., view, patio, quiet, isolated ■ 3D,1F
(upstairs) ⊷4D,1R 🜂2sh.w.g. ★2F,TV in guest room, parking ⍾Smoking,
drinking, pets
↪ Bruce Trail, scenic caves, Blue Mountain Ski Hills, waterslide, golfing
⇔ Wasaga Beach, Scenic Beaver Valley, downhill skiing, Aquafarms, live theatre, four
season recreation area

🖝 Original 1850 Gothic farm house with panoramic view over Georgian Bay and
Collingwood has new additions, but has kept the old-style charm. Enjoy 12 acres of
interesting terrain gardens and wildlife. There are two dogs and a cat in the house.
Hosts also cater to personal retreats, artist workshops and small seminars & meetings.

Lovett-Doust, Penelope & Walter Taylor (Penelope's Overnights) ✓ CC
216 Cedar Street, Collingwood, Ontario L9Y-3A8 ☎ (705) 445-7062

Phone or write for directions.
$35S $50D $10Child ► 12
● Full, homebaked 🏠 Downtown, older, quiet ■ 4D,1S, (upstairs)
⊷1S,2T,4D,1R,crib ⌐ 2Sh.w.g. ★ TV, parking, reading room ⛔ Restricted
smoking, pets
↔ downtown Collingwood, shopping, restaurants, harbour and waterfront
⇔ Blue Mountain Recreational summer and winter activities, Georgian Bay beaches,
windsurfing, boating, antiques throughout the surrounding area

☞ Century home offers the elegance of yesterday with the convenience of the present.
Hearty breakfasts send you on your way. There are two dogs and a cat in the house.

Szelestowski, Steve and Diane (Pretty River Valley Farm) ✓ OFVA
Box 254 Collingwood, Ontario L9Y 3Z5 ☎ (705) 445-7598

Take Hwy 26 from Barrie to Stayner. Then Hwy 91 to Hwy 24. Follow north to Service
Rd 30/31. Turn left and go 8 km up mountain to farm on left.
$35-45S $40-55D   ● $2.50Each $2Child $2Cot   🍽 Meals ► 9
● Full 🏠 Res., 120-acres, resort, log home, pond, view ■ 8, plus family loft
upstairs ⊷8Q,1D,2S5P ⌐ 9Private, 1-6 person whirlpool and spa ★ TV,F,Lf
❤ ⛔ Pets, smoking
↔ Pond, stream, rock crevices and hills on property, tobogganing, skating, cross-country
skiing, hiking, biking
⇔ Collingwood, Wasaga Beach, Georgian Bay, boating, swimming, windsurfing

☞ Warm family atmosphere in Log home nestled in the Blue Mountains overlooking
scenic hills and Valley. Watch rainbow trout spawn in spring. Help make maple syrup.

Wilson, John and DorRene (Beild House) ✓ CC
64 Third St., Collingwood, Ontario L9Y 1K5 ☎ (705) 444 1522

Take Hwy 400 to Barrie and then Hwy 26 west to Collingwood. Located on the corner of
Third and Pine Sts near harbour.
$40-50S $50-60D $160Ste   🍽 Lunch for skiers. ► 28
● Full, homebaked 🏠 Downtown, res., older, patio ■ 14D ⊷4T,10D,R,P
⌐ 5Sh.w.g., 2ensuite ★ 3F, parking, separate entrance, ski locks, guest lounge with
fireplace and refrigerator, air (5rooms) ⛔ Pets, limited smoking, children under age 6
〰 some french
↔ Theatre, banks, shopping, dining
⇔ Blue Mountain and Devils Glen ski areas, cross-country skiing, Wasaga Beach,
golfing, Fall Colour Spectacle

☞ Recently renovated older home with lots of antiques and clocks. Host family
members are experienced skiers and offer special help for first time skiers. Hosts also
accommodate students from the Blue Mountain School of Lanscape Painting.

Consecon

(Quinte's Isle near Trenton; see also Wellington, Bloomfield, Picton, Brighton, Belleville, Colborne)

Banks, Rosemary (The Marsh House)   ⌐ CC
Box 143 Mill St., Consecon, Ontario K0K 1T0   ☎ (613) 394-5319

From Hwy 401 take Exit 522 at Wooler Rd and continue on Hwy 33 to Rte 29. Look for house opposite Post Office.
$30S $45D   🍴 Meals   (Deposit required)   ► 6A
● Full, homebaked   🏠 Rural, village, hist., older, acreage, patio, quiet   ■ 3D
╾ 1D,4T   ⌐ 1Sh.w.h., 1sh.w.g.   ★ TV,F, fans   ⓦ Children, pets, restricted smoking
↔ Weller's Bay, Lake Ontario , Consecon village, United Church (built 1820)
⇔ North Beach Prov. Park, excellent area for swimming and water sports, fine dining, flea markets, antiques, Sandbanks, ferry to Glenora, scenic route to Kingston

🖝 Owner's specialty is Quiche. Formerly from England hostess is proud of Prince Edward County and well informed about its history.

Harris, Bob and Pat (The Sword)   ⌐) CC
RR1, Consecon, Ontario K0K 1T0   ☎ (613) 392-2143

From Hwy 401 take Exit 522 (Wooler Rd) to Hwy 33. Turn right onto Hwy 33. and continue to house 5 km south of Carrying Place.
$28S $40D $60Ste   ► 4
✖ not Feb.   ● Choice   🏠 Rural, acreage, view, lakefront, quiet   ■ 2D,1Ste
╾4T,1Q   ⌐ Sh.w.g.   ★ TV, ceiling fans   ⓦ Restricted smoking, pets   ∿ French and German understood
↔ International famous Dining Room, Evelyn's Pantry (jams and jellies)
⇔ Prov. Parks, excellent swimming, surfing, Sandbanks, antique and craft shops, museums, golfing

🖝 Hosts operate and own dining establishment next door, featuring seafood, Cajun and creole dishes as well as special imported wines.

B&B Travel Tip: *If you stay more than one night, you can go and come at your pleasure. But do let the hosts know when you will be back, especially if you plan to be late. They might even give you a key, and then you can let yourself in quietly.*

Cornwall
(see also Finch, Apple Hill, Lancaster, Morrisburg, Williamstown, St.Anicet)

Johnson, Edward and Michelyne
1002 Pescod Ave., Cornwall, Ontario K6J 2J9   ☎ (613) 933-0398

From Hwy 401 take Exit 789 (Brookdale) and drive to traffic circle. Take 7th St west and
continue onto Queen St and then Pescod Ave.
$27S $37D   ► 6
● Full   ♠ Res., large cedar deck, quiet   ■ 2D   ⊨ 2T,1Q,1K   ⌐ Sh.w.g.
★ Air, LF, TV in one guest room   ∽ French
↪ Pitt Street Mall shopping, St. Lawrence Seaway, Wood House Museum, Robert H.
Saunders Energy Information Centre
⇔ Morrisburg (Upper Canada Village), beaches

☛ Retired hosts enjoy visitors and showing them around Ontario's most easterly City
situated right on the St. Lawrence Seaway.

Creemore
(near Barry; see also Duntroon, Collingwood, Kimberley, Ferndale)

McArthur, Robert and Sherry (Sherbert Country B&B)
RR1, Stayner, Ontario L0M 1S0   ☎ (705) 466-2380

Take Hwy 26 from Barrie to Stayner and County Rd 42 south 8.5 km. Sign on left.
$30S $40D   🍽 Meals ● Choice   ♠ 200-acre farm, 40-acres bush, quiet   ■ 2D
⊨ 2D   ⌐ Sh.w.h.   ★ TV   ⓦ Restricted smoking, pets
↪ Quiet countryside ideal for walking and cross-country skiing
⇔ Blue Mountain down-hill skiing area, waterslide, Wasaga Beach (boating, swimming,
windsurfing), spectacular fall colours

☛ Early Century home located on operating beef farm. Peaceful surroundings. Watch
Maple syrup making in March.

Curve Lake
(near Peterborough; see also Lakefield, Warsaw, Bobcaygeon, Fenelon Falls)

McCue, Clarence and Evelyn (Reflections of Beauty)   ↙ CC
Curve Lake, Ontario K0L 1R0   ☎ (705) 657-8468

Phone for directions.
$25S $32.50D   (please pay on arrival)   ► 4A
● Choice   ♠ Rural, lakefront, view, quiet   ■ 2D   ⊨ 2T,1D   ⌐ 1Sh.w.h.
★ TV   ⓦ Pets, restricted smoking
↪ Ojibwa Crafts and Art Gallery, Johnsons Floral designs, fishing, canoeing
⇔ Peterborough Liftlocks (largest in world), Severn Trent Waterway, boat cruises,
museums, Warsaw Caves, Petroglyphs, Lang Century Village

☛ Enjoy the beautiful sunsets overlooking gorgeous Buckhorn Lake with its many
Indian Legends and mysterious islands. Quiet homey atmosphere.

Delta

(near Brockville; see also Westport, Frankville, Seeley's Bay, Rockport)

Derouin, Gwen (The Denaut Mansion)

Box 209, Mathew St., Delta, Ontario K0E 1G0   ☎ (613) 928-2588

From Hwy 401 take Brockville Exit 696 (Hwy 29 north) to Hwy 42 to Delta. Or take Exit 623 (Hwy 15 N) to Crosby and then east on Hwy 42 to Delta. For scenic route from Hwy 401 take Exit 659 and paved County Rd 3 north via Lansdowne/Lyndhurst to Hwy 42 and east to Delta.

$38S $45D   ● $3.50Each $10Add.person   🍴 Meals   ► 8
● Choice,homebaked   🏠 Village, acreage, hist., patio, quiet, swimming pool   ■ 4D
(upstairs) ⊷ 2T,3D,2R   ⌐ 1Sh.w.h., 1sh.w.g.   ★ TV,LF, parking   ♥   ✋ Pets, restricted smoking
↪ Beach and campground, nature trails, cross-country skiing, bicycling, fishing, Delta Maple Syrup Festival (April), Delta Fair (July)
⇔ Westport (Rideau System), Kingston (Fort Henry), Gananoque (1000 Islands Tours)

📣 1850 heritage home frequented by Sir John A. MacDonald (first Canadian Prime Minister). Small town full of unflinching stone battlements and historic buildings. Paddle boats, canoes and boats available in village. There are household pets.

Noakes, Susan (Black Church Gardens)   ✔ CC

Box 45, Delta, Ontario K0E 1G0   ☎ (613) 928-2303

Located 3km east of Delta village on Hwy 42. Turn east off Hwy 15 from Kingston or west off Hwy 29 from Brockville.

$22S $40D $5Child $10Add.person   🍴 Meals   ► 4A,2Ch
● Full, homebaked   🏠 Rural, hist., view, patio, quiet, greenhouse dining   ■ 2D
(upstairs)   ⊷ 1D,1Q   ⌐ Sh.w.g., sink ensuite   ★ TV,LF, wood heat with stoves
↪ Fully landscaped acreage
⇔ Sandy beaches and swimming in Delta, old Stone Mill Museum, Rideau Canal locks and waterway, Kingston, Brockville, Charleston Lake Prov. Park, cross-country ski trails

📣 Gothic-style stone church, built in 1877, is entered through its high mansard steeple to reaveal a post and beam interior contructed with vintage building parts. Hostess is also the weaver at Black Church Gardens and welcomes visitors to her studio and showroom in the church.

B&B Travel Tip: *As a B&B guest you have all the privacy you want in your own room. Hosts take the cue from you - if you do not want to socialize, they will understand.*

Dobbinton
(near Owen Sound; see also Paisley, Tara, Cargill, Southampton, Port Elgin)

Abbott, Ruth and Fran Sandford (Hattie's Hideaway) ⌐ Grey Bruce Trail Assoc.
RR2, Dobbinton, Ontario N0H 1L0 ☎ (519) 363-6543

Located 10 km north of Chesley on Bruce County Rd 4 off Country Rd 10.
$25S $35D 🍽 Meals (Family rates available) ► 6A
● Full, homebaked 🏠 Rural, acreage, view, patio, quiet, isolated ■ 3D ⊢ 3D
⌐ Sh.w.g. ★ TV,F
⇔ Lake Huron and Georgian Bay Resort areas, winter and summer vacation centres

🖝 Quiet modern home located in the heart of scenic farmland. Ideal spot for Nature lovers, hikers and cross-country skiers. There are in-house pets.

Drayton
(near Waterloo; see also Elora, Elmira, Fergus, Wallenstein, Millbank)

McIsaac, Jack and Virginia ⌐ SOCVA
Box 263, Drayton, Ontario N0Q 1P0 ☎ (519) 638-2190

$25S $40D 🍽 Meals ► 4
● Choice 🏠 Village, res., acreage, patio, quiet ■ 2D,F ⊢ 2D ⌐ Sh.w.h.
★ TV,LF, parking ⊛ Restricted smoking, pets in garage
↔ Mennonite farming countryside, Conestoga River Banks, large swimming, skiing
⇔ Elmira, Kitchener farmer's market, Guelph University, Elora Gorge, Stratford

🖝 Native Village hosts are active in local agricultural society and well versed in rural life of community which is one of the best farming areas in Ontario.

Duntroon
(near Collingwood)

Eastmure, Patsy and Ian (Murecroft Farm) ⌐ $&B
Duntroon, Ontario L0M 1H0 ☎ (705) 445-3191

From junction of Hwys 24 and 91 (flashing light) go west on paved sideroad and look for first farm house on the southside of Duntroon Sideroad.
$40S $45D 🍽 Meals ► 4A,2Ch
● Full 🏠 25-acre farm, hist., view, patio, deck, quiet, pond with dock ■ 3D,1S
(main and upper floor) ⊢ 2T,2R,1D ⌐ 1Sh.w.g. ★ TV,F ⊛ Pets
↔ Swimming in pond, village of Duntroon, Bruce Trail hiking and cross- country skiing
⇔ Wasaga Beach, Ski Resorts (Blue Mountain, Georgian Peaks, Devils Glen)

🖝 Red brick farm house (1869 Ontario Gothic architecture) set among expansive lawns and spectacular view of Georgian Bay. Hosts are breeders of Reg'd Canadian Hunters for dressage and jumping. There are 2 very friendly dogs.

Durham

(near Owen Sound; see also Flesherton, Cargill, Harriston, Priceville)

Cotterell, David and Eliszabeth (Forest Edge) ✔ Grey Bruce B&B
Forest Edge, RR3, Durham, Ontario N0G 1R0 ☎ (519) 369-5661

Take Hwy 6 north and 24 km past Mount forest. Turn left after Durham sign (Bentinck
SR27 - Douglas St) and continue 1.2 km to house on right.
$30S $40D $10Add.person   🍽 Meals   ► 8
● Full, homebaked   ♠ Rural, ranch style, wooded acreage, quiet   ■ 2D,F
⊨ 2T,1D, crib   ⊓ Sh.w.g.   ★ F,LF   ♥   ⊛ Smoking, pets
↔ Town of Durham, scenic walks, cross-country skiing, snowshoeing, horseback riding
⇔ Owen Sound, Lake Huron beaches, Wellbeck Saw Mill, Collingwood and Beaver
Valley skiing areas, Guelph, Kitchener Mennonite Country

☞ Architecturally designed country retreat near delightful little friendly town and
situated on the banks of the Saugeen River, unspoiled by the advance of progress. Very
peaceful and relaxing surroundings.

Dwight

(near Huntsville; see also Port Carling, Gravenhurst, Windermere, Haliburton)

Stephenson, Margaret and George (Stephenson's B&B)
RR1, Dwight, Ontario P0A 1H0   ☎ (705) 635-2115

Located near western entrance to Algonquin Park on Spring Lake Rd. Take Hwy 60 for
1.3 km east of Junction with Hwy 35. Look for second house on left side.
$30S $40D   ► 4
✠ May-Nov (other by appointment)   ● Full   ♠ Rural, acreage, quiet   ■ 2D
(upstairs)   ⊨ 2S,1D,cot   ⊓ Sh.w.g.   ★ TV, parking   ⊛ Smoking   ⋙some
French
↔ Two fine Art Galleries
⇔ Algonquin Park, public beach on Lake of Bays, The Trading Post (shopping), Palmer
House Antiques

☞ Comfortable two-storey house in park-like setting.

B&B Travel Tip: *You can stay in a B&B when visiting a sick relative or
friend in another town. It makes for very comforting and convenient accommodation. Many hospitals keep lists of nearby B&B's for out-of-town relatives.*

Eganville
(near Pembroke; see also Beachburg, Foresters F., Renfrew, Calabogie, Golden Lake)

Verch, Miss Beatrice ⌐ FOBBA
RR2, Eganville, Ontario K0J 1T0 ☎ (613) 628-6901

Take Hwy 512 off Hwy 41 at Eganville to Strickland's store. Then take Sand Road for 5 km. Go right for 0.2 km and turn left again. Look for red plow at mailbox.
$15S $25D   ● $3Each   ☒ Meals ► 9
● Full   ♠ Farm, quiet, view   ■ 1S,2D (upstairs)   ⊷ 2D, cot   ⊓ 2Sh.w.g.
★TV,KF   ⍟ Pets   ⌇ German
⇔ Bonnechere Caves, Golden Lake

☛ Gracious hostess invites guests to spend some time in quiet and relaxed atmosphre and fall asleep to the tinkle of the cowbells and the call of the whippoorwill. Most easily reached after 6 pm and before 8 am and on weekends. Hostess is involved with Red Cross Home Support Work. There is a dog in the house.

Elmira
(near Kitchener; see also Elora, Fergus, St. Jacobs, Wallenstein, Winterbourne)

Bauman, Verna and Maurice (Bue Jay Cedars) ⌐ CC
RR1, Elmira, Ontario N3B 2Z1 ☎ (519) 669-2230

Drive north of Elmira on Rd 21 and go left on Rd 4 to 3 flagpoles by road.
$25-30S $35D   (Breakfast extra)   ☒ Meals ► 4
● Full   ♠ Rural, acreage   ■ 1S,1D   ⊷ T,Q (waterbed)   ⊓ 1Private, 1sh.w.h.
★ TV,F   ⍟ Drinking
⇔ Maple Syrup Festival, Elmira, Elora, Kitchener, Cambridge

☛ Mennonite Community in Waterloo County. The Bauman's enjoy company and a house full of people.

McDougall, Noreen and Neil (The Plaid Blanket B&B) ⌐ CC
17 William Street, Elmira, Ontario N3B 1P1 ☎ (519) 669-5361

Take Hwy 86 to Elmira and go 1 block north past Arthur/Church Sts traffic light, turn left. Located across the street from Riverside School.
$25S $35D $5Child $5Add.person   ☒ Meals ► 5A,2Ch
● Choice, homebaked   ♠ Res., older, patio, quiet   ■ 3D(upstairs)   ⊷ 2T,1Q,1R,
crib   ⊓ 2Sh.w.g.   ★ KF,TV   ⍟ Pets, restricted smoking
↝ Local restaurants, craft shops (quilts and supplies), parks, swimming pool, churches
⇔ West Montrose covered Bridge and Country Store, St. Jacobs Village, Waterloo Farmer's Market, Elora Gorge and shops

☛ Comfortable century home in tranquil community of Mennonites. There is a dog.

Milliken, Rodger and Doris (The Evergreens) ✔ SOCVA B&B
RR1, Elmira, Ontario N3B 2Z1 ☎ (519) 669-2471

In Elmira, take Arthur St. north towards Alma to Woolwich Rd 3, turn right and look for house on right.
$30S $35D $10Child(age 5-16) $10Add.person ► 4A,2Ch
● Full, homebaked 🏠 Rural (fruit farm), bungalow, acreage, view, patio, inground swimming pool, quiet, isolated ■ 2D ⊸ 2D ⌐ 2Sh.w.g. ★ F,TV,LF, parking
🖐 Smoking
↪ Wooded walks, 300 acre forest, cross-country skiing
⇔ Elmira, shopping, Elora tourist attractions, St. Jacobs, Stratford Festival, Kitchener (Octoberfest and famous farmer's market)

☛ Retired hosts in quiet location in the heart of Old Order Mennonite Country. There is a dog in the house.

Smith, Vivian and Gerrie (Teddy Bear B&B Inn) ✔ SOCVA,FOBBA
Wyndham Hall, RR1, Elmira, Ontario N3B 2Z1 ☎ (519) 669-2379

From Elmira take Hwy 86 west to Hwy 19. Turn right and continue through village of Floradale to house on left.
$30S $40D $5Child $10Add. person ▦ Meals ► 8A,2Ch
● Cont. 🏠 Hist., bungalow, acreage, quiet ■ 3D,1Ste,F ⊸ 1S,4T,2D,1K,R, also Ste downstairs ⌐ 2Private, 1ensuite, 1sh.w.g. ★ F,LF, TV in guest room, separate entrance ♥ 🖐 Smoking

↪ Antiques, Canadiana display gift and collection shoppe, hiking, cross-country skiing, boating, swimming

⇔ Elora Gorge, Seagram Museum, Fergus Highland Games, Guelph Music Festival

☛ 1907 Schoolhouse right in the heart of Mennonite countryside, portraying many of Ontario's heritage and cultural hideaways. Reservations please.

B&B Travel Tip: *Traditionally, B&B is overnight accommodation only, but nowadays people stay longer, sometimes even up to a week.*

Elora

(near Kitchener; see also Elmira, Fergus, Belwood, St. Jacobs, Drayton, Orton)

Eastep, Sandra and Steven (Eastep Farms)
RR1, Elora, Ontario N0B 1S0   ☎ (519) 846-5874

Located 4.3 km north of Elora on Wellington County Rd 7 (Elora Rd).
$30S $0D $10Child   10Add.person   ▣ Meals   ► 4
● Full   ♠ 200-acre farm, quiet, extensive lawns   ■1D,1Ste   ⊷ 2D   ⌐1Sh.w.g.
★ Air,TV,F   ⑩ Drinking, smoking, pets   ⌇ French
↔ Hog operation on premises, country lanes for walking and bicycling
⇔ Elora, Elmira and Mennonite Community, Kitchener Farmer's Market

☞ Large modern home with African wood carvings and artifacts throughout.

Grove, Dorothy (Grove House of Elora)
           ↙ SOCVA B&B
Box 905, Elora, Ontario N0B 1S0   ☎ (519) 846-0640/0295

From Hwy 6 take County Rd 7 into Elora. Turn right at 2nd flashing light and look for
36 David St East.
$25S $35D $5Child $5Add. person   ▣ Meals   ► 4A,2Ch
● Full, homebaked   ♠ Village, older, patio, quiet   ■ 2D   ⊷ 1D,2S, crib
⌐ Sh.w.g.   ★ parking   ⑩ Restricted smoking
↔ Elora Gorge, boutiques and craft shops, cross-country skiing in Gorge Park
⇔ Elmira, St. Jacobs, Mennonite Country, Kitchener Farmer's Market, Kleinburg
"Group of Seven" Gallery, Guelph

☞ Spacious Victorian-style home with large lot and prize winning vegetable garden.
Hostess is well informed about Mennonite culture.

Lent, R. & P.Danahy (Desert Rose B&B)
           ↙ CC
60 Mill Street West, Elora, Ontario N0B 1S0   ☎ (519) 846-0685/9600

From Hwy 40l, take Hwy 6 North, turn left at Elora Rd to town. Cross over bridge and
turn left to first block on river side. Look for house adjacent to Victoria foot bridge
which crosses the Grand River.
$45S $60D $15Child(free under age 5) $20Add.person   ▣ Meals   ► 10
● Cont, homebaked   ♠ Village, hist., view, riverfront, patio   ■ 5D,1Ste (upstairs)
⊷ 4T,3D,1P (antique brass)   ⌐ 3Sh.w.g.   ★ F,TV,KF, parking, separate entrance
⑩ Pets
↔ Crafts and antique shops, restaurants, vegetarian gourmet dining (all on the
premises), limestone quarry for swimming, hiking or skiing through Elora Gorge,
historical village walking tour
⇔ Mennonite countryside, Three Centuries Festival (classical and popular music),
Kitchener and Waterloo (famous farmer's markets), Guelph University

☞ Gracious quarried stone building erected in 1867 has cheerful inviting ambiance
with sunny back deck and garden overlooking the river. Deposit required.

Smith, Jane and Bryan (Ponsonby Inn Antiques)   ✓ B&B
RR2, Elora, Ontario N0B 1S0   ☎ (519) 846-5827

Take Hwy 6 north to Elora Side Rd (County Rd 7) and turn left to house on left side (7.4 km). Watch for signs.

$50S $60D $5Child $10Add.person   ◙ Meals   ► 9
● Full, homebaked   ♠ Rural, hist., acreage, view   ■ 4D(main and upper floor)   ⊷5S,2D,crib   ⌐ 2Private, 1sh.w.g.   ★ Separate entrance, KF, parking, guest sitting room   ♥
↪ beautiful garden and yard, antique showroom
⇔ Elora Gorge Conservation area and boutiques, Elmira, St Jacobs, Kitchener Farmer's Market, Music Festival, Fergus Highland Games

☞ 2-storey red brick home, built in 1827 as an Inn has restored servants quarters as guest rooms furnished with antiques and is a showroom by day and a B&B by night. Hosts are well informed about the Inn's history and the area around it. There is a dog.

Steane, Doug and Carolyn (Salem Falls Retreat)   ✓ B&B
Box 1034, Elora, Ontario N0B 1S0   ☎ (519) 846-0566

Located in the village of Salem 2.2 km north of Elora. From Hwy 401 take Hwy 6 from the east or Hwy 24 from the west and travel north. Just north of Guelph, turn left onto the Elora Rd (Wellington County Rd) and continue 16 km to the 2nd flashing amber light in Salem at the intersection of Hwys 7 and 18. Then look for 75 Washington St.

$40S $50D $80F   ► 6A,2CH
● Full, homebaked   ♠ Village, acreage, spectacular views, quiet, riverfront, indoor swimming pool, grotto with a pool table (recreation room), private swimming hole in the river below falls   ■ 2D,1Ste   ⊷ 1K,2P,1D,2T   ⌐ 1Sh.w.g., 1ensuite   ★ F,TV, separate entrance,   Ⓦ Restricted smoking
↪ Lover's Leap, historic churches and buildings, downtown, Elora Mill Inn, fine dining, arts and crafts shops, Elora Gorge Park, hiking, and nature experiences, canoeing, kayaking, beach and quarry, cross- country skiing
⇔ Fergus Farmer's market, Guelph, Kitchener/Waterloo, Mennonite country

☞ Spacious, very unique home (historic limestone grotto) situated on a very picturesque site on the Irvine River overlooking the river gorge and falls and located in a beautiful pre-confederation village that is rich in Canadian history. Hosts can accommodate small groups for workshops and special occasions.

B&B Travel Tip: *You can stay in a B&B when taking part in acitivity groups, such as whitewater rafting, bicycling and wilderness tours etc. Ask for information when signing up for a trip.*

Embro
(near Woodstock; see also Londong, St. Marys, Plattsville)

Matheson, Jean (Jean's Bed & Breakfast)
RR3, Embro, Ontario N0J 1J0   ☎ (519) 475-4507

Take Hwy 7 out of Stratford towards St. Marys. At the Embro Rd turn left to
Brooksdale. Turn right and continue to 3rd Rd (Happy Hills Campground). Turn left
and go to 2nd farm on left.
$40D   ► 4
✷ Summer   ● Full   ♠ Farm, hist., quiet   ■ 2D (upstairs)   ⊷ 2D   ⊓ Sh.w.h.
Ⓦ Smoking, drinking, pets
⇔ Stratford Shakespeare Festival, Kitchener Farmer's Market, Mennonite Country,
quaint village of St. Marys, Woodstock

☛ Grand older home, built at the turn-of-the-Century by local carpenters who left
their mark in the community, is situated in quiet surroundings and clean countryside.
Enjoy the beautiful colours in spring, summer and fall. There is a cat in the house.

Fenelon Falls
(northwest of Peterborough; see also Rosedale, Coboconk, Orton)

Brooks, Gillian and Homer (Marle Green)   ⤳ FOBBA,CC
RR1, Rosedale Rd., Fenelon Falls, Ontario K0M 1N0   ☎ (705) 887-5576

From Hwy 401 exit east of Oshawa (436) onto Hwy 35 and then Hwy 121 to Fenelon
Falls. Go west at lights near Falls (Helen St) and look for large house with stone
chimney and sign. From Trent Severn Waterway, Cameron Lake, dock at Kings Marina.
$25 per person   ▣ Meals   ► 10
● Full   ♠ Village, older acreage, lakefront, patio   ■ 5D,F (upstairs)   ⊷1T,2D,1Q
(waterbed)   ⊓ 2Sh.w.g., spa   ★ TV,F, separate entrance, solarium, evening VCR
movies   ♥   Ⓦ Pets, restricted smoking   ⤳ French
↪ Marina, golfing, swimming, tennis, marina, shopping, movie theatre.

☛ Comfortable older home originally used as a lumber company staff house, and later
as a small rustic lodge, completely renovated and modernized as a private family home.
Located in the Kawartha Lakes District with access to the Trent-Severn Waterway.
There is a dog in the house. Relax in the solarium with spa.

> **B&B Travel Tip:** *B&B travelling can be most enjoyable, when it is planned
> ahead and when there is ample time to socialize.*

Nyberg, Don and Kathy (Gazebo Corner) ⌐ CC
72 Francis St. W., Box 878, Fenelon Falls, Ont. K0M 1N0   ☎ (705) 887-6800

Located 2 blocks west of main intersection stop light (Francis and Colborne Sts).
$45S $60D   ► 8
● Full, homebaked   ♠ Village, res., hist., acreage, patio, quiet   ■ 4D (upstairs)
⊢ 4T,2D   ⊓ 2Sh.w.g., 1sh.w.h.   ★ Air, TV in guest lounge, separate entrance,
parking   ⊛ Restricted smoking, drinking, pets, children min. age 13
↔ Museum, sandy beaches of Cameron Lake and Sturgeon Lake, Trent Canal Lock,
shops, restaurants, movie theatre, golfing, fishing, cross-country skiing, ice skating in
arena, tennis, bowling

🐾 Century home is located very conveniently in the center of the village, which is
called "the jewel of the Kawarthas". There is a dog in the house. House specialty
homemade jams and muffins. Enjoy fresh eggs and fruit. Second floor exclusive for
guests. Hosts will pick up guests who come by bus or boat to the village.

Finch
(near Cornwall; see also Apple Hill, Morrisburg, Williamstown)

MacLean, Mrs. Duart A. (Wayside Welcome House)
RR1, Finch, Ontario   K0C 1K0   ☎ (613) 984-2352

Located on north side of Hwy 43 at Goldfield cross road 4.2 km west of Finch
$14S $15D   ● $2Each $10Child $10Add. person   ► 3-4
● Full   ♠ Rural, acreage, duplex   ■ 1S,1D   ⊢ 1D,1S,3R,   ⊓ 1Sh.w.h.
★TV, ground floor access for wheelchair   ⊛ Pets, drinking
↔ Surrounding farmland, strolling, walking
⇔ Upper Canada Village, Morrisburg, Cornwall

🐾 Hostess asks to please phone on weekend ahead, so rooms can be heated in winter.
If her rooms are booked, a friend will help out.

Foresters Falls
(near Pembroke; see also Beachburg, Eganville, Renfrew)

Bennett, Mrs. Norma A. ⌐ B&B
RR1, Foresters Falls, Ontario   K0J 1V0   ☎ (613) 646-7951

Take Rt 21 exit off Hwy 17 to Forester's Falls and continue south for 4.8 km. Look for
yellow stucco house on left side.
$20S $25D   ● $4Each   ► 2
✴Summer ●Full   ♠Farm   ■1D (upstairs)   ⊢1D   ⊓Sh.w.h.   ★TV   ⊛Pets
↔ Presbyterian Church, Ottawa River, whitewater rafting
⇔ Cobden, fishing and boating (Ottawa River and Muskrat Lake near Cobden), good
shopping (Renfrew and Pembroke)

🐾 Very picturesque pastoral setting; quiet modest farmhouse. Cool in summer.

Frankville
(near Brockville; see also Delta, Westport, Prescott)

Gibbons, Anna and Bill
RR1, Frankville, Ontario K0E 1H0   ☎ (613) 275-2893

Take Hwy 29 north from Brockville off Hwy 401 (Exit 696) to Frankville. Turn right and travel 3.3 km to fork in road. Take left road and look for first farm on right.
$20S $30D   ► 3A,2Ch
● Full, homemade   ♠ 300-acre farm   ■ 1S,1D,F   ⊨ 1S,1D, cots, crib
� Sh.w.h.   ★ F,KF   ⍟ Smoking, pets sleep outside   ⚏ Polish
⇔ Thousand Islands eastern gateway, oldest railway tunnel in North America

☞ Working dairy farm. Young host family in stone century- farmhouse.

Georgetown
(near Toronto; see also Milton, Campbellville)

Bowhay, Peggy and George (Peg's Place)   ✔ CC
RR3, Georgetown, Ontario L7G 4S6   ☎ (416) 876-419-09

From 401 exit at Trafalgar Rd north (328) and continue until first cross road after Steeles Ave. Turn left by church. Look for 5th house past 6th Line on north side.
$20S $35D   ◉ Meals   ► 4A
● Full   ♠ Rural, acreage, view, quiet   ■ 2D   ⊨ 2T,1D   face Sh.w.h.
★ TV,F,LF, parking   ⍟ Smoking, children
↔ Cross country skiing, hiking
⇔ Agriculture Museum, Terra Cotta Inn (fine dining), Old Hyde House (leather goods), Ski slopes, Lake Ontario, Canada's Wonderland, Bruce Trail, Caledon Scenic Route

☞ Cozily decorated bungalow is located in the heart of Ontario's fruit and farming country. Hosts are organic gardeners and they are also very knowledgeable about reflexology. Vegetarian meals a speciality. There is a friendly German Shepherd.

Gilmour
(north of Peterborough near Bancroft)

Vandersanden, Kay and Gerry (Greenbush Acres)   ✔ CC
RR2, Gilmour, Ontario K0L 1W0   ☎ (613) 474-2606

Located 26 km south of Bancroft. From Belleville, take Hwy 62 north (about 82 km). Turn east on Limerick Lake Rd, then 0.9 km to Art Studio on Rd and house set back.
$25S $30D $15Child $15Add. person   ◉ Meals   ► 6
● Full   ♠ Rural, hist., acreage, view, quiet   ■ 3D   ⊨ 1S,3D   face Sh.w.g.
★ TV,F   ♥   ⍟ Smoking, pets   ⚏ Dutch
↔ Country skiing and walking trails, sugar bush and hut for spring- time fun
⇔ Limerick Lake, marina, public beach, Bancroft, large craft show (Dominion Day), winter festival (February), sleigh-rides.

☞ 110-year old, fully restored log house with modern facilities. There is an a-la-carte dining room with old fashioned charm and excellent fine dining on the premises.

Goderich
(on Lake Huron; see also Kincardine, Clinton, Millbank, Bayfield)

Beauchemin, Eileen (The Beauchemins)   ↙ CC
88 Blue Water Beach, RR2, Goderich, Ontario N7A 3X8   ☎ (519) 524-2897

Located off Hwy 21 and 3 km south of junction of Hwys 8 and 21. Phone for directions.
$25S $30-36D   ► 4
● Choice 🏠 Rural, ranch-style, acreage, patio, quiet ■ 2D ⊨ 2S,1D,1K cot
⊓1Sh.,w.h. ★ F,TV in one guest room separate entrance, parking, bicycles
↔ Quiet roads for walking/bicycling/hiking, Blue Water Beach, x-country ski trails
⇔ Downtown Goderich, museum, sandy beach and long board walk to harbour, Bayfield
Little Inn and shops, Huron Country Playhouse, Blyth Festival Theatre

☞ Home is surrounded by lovely wooded area with a view of nearby Lake Huron and
close to charming historic town.

Blanchard-Hublet, Tom and Nicky (La Brassine)   ↙ OFVA
RR2, Goderich, Ontario N7A 3X8   ☎ (519) 524-6300

Located 8.3 km south of Goderich on Hwy 21 at Kitchigami Camp Road.
$30S $45-50D 🍽 Meals   ► 12
● Full, homebaked 🏠 103-acres horse farm, quiet, view ■ 4 (on main and upper
floor) ⊨ 1Q,4S,3D ⊓ 4Sh.w.g. ★ Air,TV,F, private access to beach
🐾Pets ⁓ French
↔ Private access to beaches (Lake Huron), jogging, windsurfing, cross-country skiing
⇔ Excellent dining at Victorian Village in Bayfield, Blyth Theatre Grand Bend, beach

☞ Large renovated Century home with European atmosphere on farm stretching from
highway to beach. Breathtaking view of water and sunset. Hosts invite guests to watch
trotting horses being groomed and exercised. French gourmet dining available. There
are pets in the house.

Stadelmann, Louis and Joan
RR4, Goderich, Ontario N7A 3Y1   ☎ (519) 524-6380

From Goderich, drive north on Hwy 21 across Maitland River. Turn right on County Rd
31 and continue through Saltford to first road on top of hill. Go left to forth house on
right side.
$25S $30D $7Add. person 🍽 Meals   ► 3
● Choice, homebaked 🏠 Rural, patio ■ 1D (upstairs) ⊨ 1D,1T ⊓ Sh.w.h.
⁓German, French
↔ Cross-country skiing from back door
⇔ Goderich, Lake Huron beaches, Grand Bend, Blyth Festival

☞ Hosts serve own honey, yoghourt. House overlooks decorative pond and small park.

Tyler, Linda and Paul Johnston (The Inn at the Port)   SOCVA
RR3, Goderich (Port Albert), Ontario N7A 3X9   ☎ (519) 529-7986

Take Port Albert Cut-ff Hwy 21. Located in the hollow across from Petries General
Store just north of Goderich.
$35S $45D $5Child - 410Add.person   ●3Each in cottage   🍽 Meals   ► 12A,3Ch
● Full   🏠 Village, acreage, older, riverview, quiet   ■ 4D,1F (upstairs), 3D (in
lakeview cottage)   ⊨ 2T,3D,2R, bunkbeds   ⅂ Sh.w.g.   ★ Separate entrance,
parking, guest sitting area   ♥   🖐 Restricted smoking, pets   ∾ French

↪ Lake Huron and beautiful beaches,
Nine Mile River, fish ladder,

⇔ Goderich, Bayfield, Van Egmond
House (Seaforth), theatre (Blyth and
Grand Bend) CNR School on Wheels
(Clinton), Historic Lighthouse (Point
Clark)

☛ Originally the general store and
Post Office in a bustling milltown,
spacious Georgian home has been
lovingly restored to offer contemporary
comfort in the atmosphere of another
era. Enjoy the quiet village setting.

Golden Lake
(near Pembroke; see also Eganville, Beachburg, Palmer Rapids, Renfrew)

Carnochan, Don and Greta (Golden Gables Guests)   ⌣ B&B
RR2, Golden Lake, Ontario K0J 1X0   ☎ (613) 625-2314

Located on Hwy 60, between Golden Lake Village and Village of Killaloe, at Deacon.
$40S $45D   ► 6A,1Ch
● Choice, homebaked   🏠 Rural, lakefront, super view, quiet   ■ 3D,1F   ⊨ 4T,1D
⅂ 1Sh.w.g.   ★ TV, parking   🖐 Pets, drinking
↪ Sandy beach, "Golden Sands" (homecooking) and "Deacon Chinese" restaurants
⇔ Eganville, Bonnechere Caves, Renfrew, Storyland, Wilno Lookout, Madawaska Ski
area, Kaminiskeg Lake, whitewater rafting

☛ Early retirees in beautiful waterfront home with spectacular view of lake and
mountains - as pretty in the fall and winter as in summer. Inhouse Artisan boutique.

Gore Bay

(on Manitoulin Islands; see also Providence Bay, Mindemoya, Kagawong)

Hill, Francis and Catharine (Hill House B&B)   ✔ B&B
6 Borron St., Gore Bay, Ontario   P0P 1H0   ☎ (705) 282-2072

Take ferry from Tobermory to South Baymouth, then drive on Hwy 6 north and 542 to
Gore Bay. From Espanola drive south on Hwy 6 south to Little Current and then take
Hwy 540 to Gore Bay. On main street (Meredith St), go to end, turn left up hill.
$30S $35D   ► 6
✜ May-Oct. ● Full, homebaked ♠ Village, older, veranda ■ 3D (upstairs)
⊷ 3D ⊓ 1Sh.w.g. ⊕ Smoking, pets
↔ Tennis court, C.Y.C., beach, store, restuarant
⇔ South Bay Ferry Terminal to Tobermory, Gore Bay Marina and Yacht Basin,
museum, Western Manitoulin Isle, quaint waterside village of Kagawong

🖝 Charming island home in woodland setting overlooking Gore Bay and situated on a
hill surrounded by maples. House specialty: memorable breakfasts.

Grand Bend

(on Lake Huron, near Sarnia; see also Parkhill, Thedford)

Bloch-Gower, Barbara (For Goodness Sake B&B)
12 Ontario St.,Grand Bend, Ontario   N0M 1T0   ☎ (519) 238-8489

Located just south of main intersection on Hwy 21 (also called Ontario St).
$45S $50D $10Child   (winter reduced rates) ⊠ Meals   ► 6
● Choice, homebaked (Also European Muesli) ♠ Farm, view, patio, quiet ■ 3D
⊷ 4D ⊓ Sh.w.g., private sinks ★ Air, separate entrance, guest lounge
⊕Restricted smoking

↔ Bakery and Specialty shop on
premises, downtown shopping, Lake
Huron and soft sandy beaches, Huron
Country Playhouse, Pineridge Zoo,
cross-country skiing

🖝 Home is located on very large
property with extensive beautiful
gardens in one of Lake Hurons major
resorts. Rooms are decorated in French
Canadian Decor.

Gravenhurst
(near Orillia; see also Bracebridge, Port Carling, Severn Bridge)

Annala, Helena (HAV Bed & Breakfast)　　　　ー Muskoka B&B
510 Bay St., Box 2489, Gravenhurst, Ontario　P0C 1G0　☎ (705) 687-8966

From Hwy 11 exit into Gravenhurst and follow signs for Hwy 169 through town. Look
for white house located 4 blocks past the Post Office.
$30S　$40D　🍴 Meals　　　　　　　　　　　　　　　► 4
✚ July/Aug (other on weekends only)　● Full, homebaked　🏠 Res., older, view,
screened Muskoka room　■ 2D (upstairs)　⊷ 2T,2D　⁊ 1Sh.w.g.　★ F,.TV,LF,
parking　🐾 Pets, restricted smoking　〰 Finnish
↔ Seguin Steamship Cruises, historic Bethune House, Muskoka Summer Theatre
⇔ Lake Muskoka beaches, water sports, golfing, tennis, horseback riding, Santa's
Village, Georgian Bay, superb dining

☞ Unique and comfortable Nantucket Colonial home. Hosts aim to "pamper" their
guests. There is a dog in the house. Picnic hampers available.

Allen, Karen (Allen's B&B)　　　　　　　　ー Musk.B&B
Box 2276, 581 David St.,E., Gravenhurst, Ontario　P0C 1G0　☎ (705) 687-7368

From Toronto, take Hwy 400 to Hwy 11 and Gravenhurst Exit 169. Continue to David
Sreet East and turn right.
$30S　$40-48D　　　　　　　　　　　　　　　　► 6
● Full, homebaked　🏠 Res., deck, quiet　■ 3D (upstairs)　⊷ 2T,1D,1Q
⁊1Ensuite, 1sh.w.g.　★ F,TV, parking　🐾 Restricted smoking, pets　〰 Danish
↔ Gull Lake Park (beach and band concerts on the barge), station, downtown, Summer
Theatre, Bethune Memorial House
⇔ RMS Segwun Steamship Cruise, beautiful Muskoka Tourist area

☞ Spacious new home with Danish influence on quiet street and close to Gull Lake.
Deck overlooking attractive garden and large Muskoka Rock. Located in popular center
at the Gateway to the Muskoka Lakes.

Dudley, Brad and Debbie (Dudley Home on Lake Muskoka)　　ー Musk.B&B
RR2, (Walker's Point), Gravenhurst, Ontario　P0C 1G0　☎ (705) 687-5452

Enter Walker's Point Rd from Hwy 169. Go past Marina to stop sign, turn left. House is
on lakeside.
$25 per person　　　　　　　　　　　　　　　　► 5
●Full　🏠Rural, older, lakefront, quiet　■ 3D(upstairs)　⊷3D　⁊Sh.w.h.　★TV,F
↔ Private beach for swimming, cross-country skiing
⇔ Gravenhurst, Bala, summer theatre, fine restaurants, boat tours (Segwun steamship)

☞ Enjoy the country setting in a century farmhouse on Lake Muskoka in popular
four-season vacation area.

Milne, John and Marg (Milne's B&B)
270 Hotchkiss St., Gravenhurst, Ontario   P0C 1G0
⌣ FOBBA,Musk.B&B
☎ (705) 687-4395

Take Hwy 169 into Gravenhurst on Muskoka Rd. Turn left on Hotchkiss St at
Toronto-Dominion Bank corner.
$25-30S $40D   (Family and group rates)   ► 5A,2Ch
✚ Summer (winter by reservation) ● Full   ♠ Resort, older, sundeck   ■ 1S,2D
◅ 3T,1D,R, crib   ⌐ 1Sh.w.g.
↔ Beach, Muskoka Theatre, Bethune House, steamboat cruises, restaurants, gift shops
⇔ Muskoka beach, Santa's Village, Bracebridge, cross-country skiing,

☞ Comfortable home on pleasant tree-lined street in Muskoka resort area. Hosts are
Chairpersons for Muskoka B&B Association.

Peltier, Joyce and Al Terryberry (B&B on the Bay)
326 Bethune Drive N., Box 45, Gravenhurst, Ontario   P0C 1G0
⌣ Muskoka B&B
☎ (705) 687-7416

From Hwy 11, take Gravenhurst Exit at Hwy 169, which runs into Bethune Drive.
Continue to 2 blocks north of traffic light at Railroad Station.
$35S $45D $10Child   ► 6A,1Ch
● Full   ♠ Res, downtown, view, lakefront, patio   ■ 3D (upstairs)   ◅ 1D,2Q,1R
⌐ 2Sh.w.g.   ★ TV,F, parking, gallery   ⚇ Smoking, pets
↔ Gull Lake Park (swimming, boating, band concerts), downtown shopping, summer
theatre, 100 year-old cruiseship "Seguin", Bethune National House
⇔ Golf course, cross-country skiing, antique stores, Santa's Village, Algonquin Park,
Huntsville Ski downhill areas

☞ Spacious 2-storey home with large gallery for quiet reading or relaxing and large
deck facing Lake Muskoka.

Muskoka Bed and Breakfast Association
Box 1431, Gravenhurst, Ontario   P0C 1G0
⌣ Ont B&B
☎ (705) 687-4395
(John and Marg Milne, Chairpersons)
Rates: $25-40SS $40-60D   (including breakfast)
Muskoka B&B Association has 20 member hosts scattered throughout Muskoka in the
communities of Gravenhurst, Bracebridge, Huntsville, Port Carling, Rosseau,
Windermere, Dwight, Baysville and Honey Harbour. Some are situated in towns, others
on country roads or by lakes.
A brochure, containing a description of each B&B with directions, is available from the
above address. Some of the homes are listed in this publication.

Grimsby

(near Hamilton; see also Beamsville, Vineland, St. Catharine)

Lowell, Ted and Muriel ⌐ CC
12 Melrose Ave., Grimsby, Ontario   L3M 1G7 ☎ (416) 945-5079

From QEW, take Christie St Exit and go east on Main St for 2 blocks to Kingsway Blvd
(Esso Station on corner). Turn right and continue one block to Melrose Ave.
$30S $35D ► 4
● Downtown, res, patio, quiet   ■ 1D,den   ⊷ 2T,1P   ⁷Private
★Air,TV,F,parking   ✋ Smoking, pets   ⋙ some French

↔ Lake Ontario, shopping, restaurants
⇔ Niagara Falls, Niagara-on-the-Lake,
Hamilton, Toronto

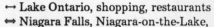 Well travelled young retired couple
assure a warm welcome. Relax in
screened gazebo or small solarium after
a day of sightseeing at Niagara Falls.

Guelph

(near Kitchener/Waterloo; see also Belwood, Fergus, Cambridge, Winterbourne)

Thomas, Betty and Al (Bonderrabi)
RR1, Guelph, Ontario . N1H 6H7 ☎ (519) 824-0247

Farm is located in Erasmosa Township, 7 km from Guelph on C 2-3 off Hwy 24.
$20S $35D ► 5
● Choice   ♠ Farm, patio, quiet, swimming pool   ■ 1S,2D   ⊷ 1S,2D
⁷ Sh.w.g.   ★ TV   ✋ Pets, children min. age 4
⇔ Guelph Lake Conservation Area, University of Guelph, Elmira Mennonite country,
Kitchener farmer's market.

☞ Bungalow-style home on 10-acres farm in a very pretty setting in Mennonite
country. Hosts make wooden rocking horses and are very interested in live theatre.

Haliburton

(north of Peterborough; see also Minden, Bancroft, Wilberforce)

Gillespie, Lenore and Hadden (Lengillinn)   ↙ CC
Kashaga Drive, Haliburton, Ontario K0M 1S0   ☎ (705) 457-2060/2061

From Hwy 401 (east of Oshawa), take Hwy 35 north all the way to Minden. Then take
Hwy 121 East and go 19 km to Kashaga Dr. Turn south to second driveway on left.
$28S $40D $9Child   ► 6A,2Ch
● Full   ♠ Rural, acreage, view, lakefront, quiet   ■ 3D (upstairs)   ⊢ 4T,1D
⌐ Sh.w.h.   ★ 2F,TV, parking
↔ Golfing, swimming, boating, fishing, tennis, cross-country skiing and snowmobiling
on well groomed trails
⇔ Haliburton village, crafts and art shops, museum, surrounding Highlands and Lake
country, downhill skiing

☞ Beautiful cut-field-stone home situated on 500 ft of lakefront on Lake
Kashagawigamog, surrounded by acres of lawns and woods in the heart of Haliburton
Highlands. Hosts are interested in antiques and refinishing furnitue. There is are two
cats called "Jack" and "Anthony".

Towns, Harry and Joanne (Dell-Haven)   ↙ CC
RR2, Haliburton, Ontario K0M 1S0   ☎ (705) 457-2545

Coming from Toronto on Hwy 401 exit at Newcastle to Hwys 35 and Hwy 121. From
Kingston on Hwy 401 take Hwys 62, then 28 and 121.
$30-35S $40-45D $5Child $5Add.person   ► 12A,2Ch
● Full (English style)   ♠ Rural, res, village, acreage, view, lakefront, quiet   ■ 1S,6D
(upstairs)   ⊢ 1S,2T,5D,R,crib   ⌐ Sh.w.g., 1Ensuite   ★ TV, parking, paddle boat
and canoe for rent   Restricted smoking, pets
↔ Haliburton Highlands vacation area, Nordic and Alpine skiing, golfing,
⇔ Sandford Fleming School of Fine Arts, water slide, Sky Glider, Guild of Fine Arts,
museum, shopping, alpine skiing

☞ Country-style home is set on spacious grounds on the shores of Lake
Kashagawigamog with pleasant airy rooms. There is a dog in the house. Hosts are well
informed about the Haliburton area. Relax on the screened in porch.

B&B Travel Tip: *Most guests find it more convenient to pay in the morning
at breakfast, when there is usually more time. Some hosts will ask for this to be
settled upon arrival. It is wise to ask the hosts what they would prefer.*

Hamilton

(see also Burlington, Millgrove, Waterdown, Brantford, Grimsby, Ancaster)

Gilchrist, Christine (Downtown B&B)
406 King William St., Hamilton, Ontario   L8L 1P7   ☎ (416) 526-9845

From Hwy 403, take Main St East Exit to Victoria St. Turn left and continue across King
St to King William St. Turn right and go 2 blocks to house on corner of Tisdale.
$30S $45D   ► 4
● Full   🏠 Downtown   ■ 2D (upstairs)   ⊷ 1D,1Q   � 1Sh.w.g.   ★ TV in
guest room   ⊕ Pets   ⌇ French
↪ Hamilton Place, Copps Coliseum, Convention Centre, Art Gallery, Football Hall of
Fame, bus routes, two major hospitals
⇔ Niagara Falls, NOTL, Toronto, Guelph, Kitchener and Mennonite country

☞ Older home located very near the downtown core. There is a dog in the house.

Kennedy, Diana and Ron (Haddo House)   ✓ Ham/Went B&B
107 Aberdeen Ave., Hamilton, Ontario   L8P 2P1   ☎ (416) 524-0071

Phone for directions.
$35S $50D   ► 4
● Choice   🏠 Downtown, res., hist., large front porch, quiet   ■ 2D (upstairs)
⊷1D,1Q   � Private   ★ TV,F, parking   ⊕ Restricted smoking, pets, children
↪ Downtown Hamilton, shopping, restaurants, Art Gallery, Hamilton Place and
Convention Centre, Copps Coliseum, City Hall
⇔ McMaster University and Hospital, Dundurn Castle, Royal Botanical Gardens, Lake
Ontario shoreline, Niagara Falls

☞ Turn of the Century home located in one of the most distinctive areas of the city.
Breakfast is served in formal dining room or large country kitchen. There is a cosy
library with fireplace and a poolside patio.

Mordue, Bruce and Betty (East Mountain B&B)   ✓ Ham/Went B&B
61 East 43 St., Hamilton,Ontario   L8T 3B7   ☎ (416) 383-9517

From Hwy 403 take Mohawk Rd East exit and continue to 2nd street after Upper Gage
St. Turn left (East 43rd St), and follow almost to end to house on right.
$35S $50D   ▦ Meals   ► 3
● Full, homebaked   🏠 Res., patio, quiet   ■ 1S,1D   ⊷ 1S,1D   � 2Sh.w.h.
★ TV   ⊕ Pets
↪ City Park, Mountain Brow, shopping plaza, major city bus routes
⇔ Downtown Hamilton, Convention Centre, V.Copps Arena, Football Hall of Fame,
Jackson Square Shopping Mall, Dundurn Castle, Royal Botanical Gardens.

☞ Home is located a few blocks from Mountain Brow, which offers a panoramic view
of the city and Niagara escarpment. Hosts have travelled extensively by B&B on their
motorcycle and enjoy meeting people and exchange travel experiences.

Mulvihill, Velma
1405-100 Bay Street S., Hamilton, Ontario   L8P 3H3 ☎ (416) 528-6025

Phone for directions.
$50S $50D ► 2
● Choice   🏠 Downtown, apartment, patio, view   ■ 1D   ⇥ 1Q,1R   ⌐ Ensuite
★ Air, LF, indoor and outdoor parking   ⑩ drinking, children, pets
↔ Hamilton City Hall, Art Gallery, Hamilton Place, Copps Coliseum, Eatons and downtown area
⇔ McMaster University, Dundas, Niagara Falls, Toronto, African Lions Safari

📢 Fourth floor apartment in very quiet and exceptionally clean building right in the heart of Hamilton. Hostess is an ardent bridge player.

Stoddart, Thomas and Grace (West Mountain Guest Home)   ✓ Ham/Went B&B
76 Mohawk Rd. West, Hamilton, Ontario   L9C 1V7 ☎ (416) 388-1355

From Hwy 403 west take Mohawk Rd Exit East and travel to West 5th St (6th stop-light). Look for 2nd house on left side past light.
$35S $50D ► 3
● Full   🏠 Res., patio   ■ 2D,1S   ⇥ 1D,1S   ⌐ Sh.w.h.   ★ Air,TV,LF, parking   ⑩ Smoking, pets
↔ Major bus routes (downtown and Chedoke Hospital), plaza, banks, library
⇔ Shopping centre, Dundurn Castle, Botanical Gardens, Mountain Brow

📢 Hostess is an artist and very involved in local organizations. Formerly from Britain, hosts have welcomed many B&B guests in their comfortable bungalow.

Watson, Marina and George (Bangor B&B)   ✓ Ham/Went B&B
54 Monte Drive, Stoney Creek, Hamilton, Ontario   L8G 4M5 ☎ (416) 560-3055

Located near King St. East and Hwy 20 (Centennial Parkway).
$35S $50D ► 4A
● Full, homebaked   🏠 Res., view, patio, quiet   ■ 2S,1Ste (upstairs)   ⇥ 2S,1D
⌐ 1Ensuite, 1sh.w.g.   ★ Air,TV,F, parking   ⑩ Smoking, drinking, children, pets
↔ Historic Battlefield Park, shopping, restaurants, golfing, Stoney Creek Monument, popular Stoney Creek Dairy Bar
⇔ Niagara Falls, Niagara-on-the-Lake, 50-Point Conservation area and marina, Wild Waterworks Wave Pool, Lake Ontario shores, Toronto

📢 Home is situated in peaceful, but very accessible location on the outskirts of the City and overlooks the historic Battlefield Park (re-enactment of 1812 War held every June). Hosts are formerly from Ireland and the house specialty is Irish Wheaten bread and home made jams. There is a Siamese cat in the house. Weather permitting, hosts will serve breakfast on the patio.

Hanover

(south of Owen Sound; see also Durham, Priceville, Dobbinton)

Lemm, Kerstin and Ray Smith (The Nut Tree Inn) ↙ Durham B&B
399-9th St., Hanover, Ontario   N4N 1L6 ☎ (519) 364-1182

Phone for directions.
$35S $40D $5Child   ◉ Meals   (weekend and weekly rates available)   ► 6A,2Ch
● Full,homebaked   ♠ Downtown, res., older, quiet   3D (upstairs)   ⊢ 2D,1Q,cot
⼮ 2Sh.w.h.   ★ TV,F,LF,KF, parking   ♥   ⌇ German
↔ Centre of town, Hanover horseraces, ski trail, Allan Park
⇔ Wellbeck Saw Mill (historic place), Southampton, Port Elgin, Owen Sound, Bruce
Trail hiking, Collingwood and Walkerton ski hills

☛ Century home beautifully decorated in central location with a fine touch of quality.
There is an office available for business travellers.

Harriston

(near Mount Forest, see also Durham)

Schaming, Judy (The Country Place) ↙ Grey Bruce B&B
RR1, Harriston, Ontario   N0G 1Z0 ☎ (519) 323-1008

Take Hwy 89 west from Mount Forest to 3rd Rd on left (Minto Side Rd 1, after big iron
bridge). Turn left and go to house on left past second bend in road.
$25S $35D $17Add.person   ◉ Meals   (special diets)   ► 6
● Full, homebaked   ♠ Farm, view, patio, quiet   ■ 3D (main and upper floor)
⊢ 1D,1P,1Q (waterbed)   ⼮ 1Sh,.w.h., 1sh.w.g., sauna, whirl pool   ★ TV,KF,LF,
parking, facilities for the handicapped, dunking tub   ⓦ Restricted smoking
↔ Quiet back roads for walking, cross-country skiing, bird watching, tobogganing
⇔ Downhill skiing, golfing, outdoor swimming pool, Bruce Trail, Guelph, Kitchener

☛ Hand-built house of unique design, built of log and stones gathered from coast to
coast and surrounded by 21 acres of rolling fields and woods. There is a dog in the house.
Travelling pets can be accommodated.

Hastings

(near Peterborough; see also Warsaw, Lakefield)

Forde, James and Joan
RR3, Hastings, Ontario   K0L 1Y0 ☎ (705) 696-2617

Located west of Hastings on County Rd 2. Phone for directions.
$20S $30D   ► 4
● Full, homebaked   ♠ Rural, ranch style, quiet   ■ 2D   ⊢ 2D   ⼮ 1Sh.w.h.
★ Air,TV, parking   ⓦ Restricted smoking, pets
↔ Small park over the fence, country store, golfing, fishing
⇔ Hastings, good restaurants, Peterborough, Hydraulic Lift Lock

☛ Comfortable red brick house near pretty little town on the Trent River System.

Huntsville

(see also Port Carling, Gravenhurst, Windermere, Emsdale)

MacConnell, Betty (Edelweis House Betty's B&B)   ✓ Musk.B&B
Box 1285, 57 Main St.W., Huntsville, Ontario   P0A 1K0   ☎ (705) 789-5455

Travel north on Hwy 11 to Huntsville and turn right on Muskoka Rd 3. Go 2.5 km
towards town center and look for Betty's B&B on right.
$25S $39D $49F   ► 8A,2Ch
● Full, homebaked   🏠 Sub., older, view, patio, quiet   ■ 1S,2D,1F (upstairs)
◄ 1S,2T,3D, cot, crib   ⌐ 1Sh.w.h., 2sh.w.g.   ★ TV in guest room, parking   ♥
Ⓦ Drinking   ⌇ German
↔ Downtown Huntsville, shopping, dining
⇔ Arrowhead and Algonquin Parks, Pioneer Village Muskoka, golfing, boat trips

🐾 Relaxed atmosphere in quiet neighborhood with friendly service.

Struyk, Ton and Cathy (Falcon Lodge)   ✓ Musk.B&B,FOBBA
RR1 Falcon Rd., Huntsville, Ontario   P0A 1K0   ☎ (705) 789-2603

From Hwy 11 North take Muskoka Rd .near2 Exit. Turn left and go over highway, then
immediately turn left on Falcon Rd. and follow to end.
$38S $48D   (Child free under age 6) $5Add.person   🍴 Meals   ► 24
● Full, homebaked   🏠 Historic lodge, acreage, view, lakefront, patio, quiet
■ 4S,5D,5Ste (some in separate cabins)   ◄ S,D,R,P, cots, crib   ⌐ All ensuite
★Air,TV,KF, separate entrance, hot tub   Ⓦ Pets   ⌇ Dutch
↔ Private sandy beach, swimming, boat rentals, playground, cross-country skiing
⇔ Huntsville town centre, Algonquin and Arrowhead Nat. Parks, down- hill skiing

🐾 Historic lodge with modern facilities on Lake Vernon. Rustic lounge with fireplace
and scenic tranquil grounds. Discover the magic of Muskoka. Children welcome.

Ilderton

(near London; see also Denfield, St. Mary's)

Corsaut, Ray and Margaret   ✓ London B&B
RR3, Ilderton, Ontario   N0M 2A0   ☎ (519) 666-1876

From London, take Hwy 4 north for 10 km to Concession 12 and west for 0.8 km.
$25S $30D $40F(and up)   ► 2A,2Ch
Choice, homebaked   🏠 Rural, quiet   ■ 2S,1D   ◄ 2T,1D   ⌐ Sch.w.h.
★ Air,TV   ♥   Ⓦ Smoking
↔ Walking in quiet countryside
⇔ London (shopping, restaurants, theatres, parks, museums), Stratford, Lake Huron

🐾 Attractive 1869's farmhouse set in a large shaded yard.

Iroquois
(near Brockville; see also Cardinal, Morrisburg)

Groeniger, Karel and Mary (Weeberault Farm)   ✔ OFVA
RR1, Iroquois, Ontario K0E 1K0   ☎ (613) 652-4615

From Hwy 401, take Exit 738 at Iroquois onto Carman Rd and drive north for 3 km to
Conc RD Matild 3, turn right and after crossing Brinston Rd look for 5th house on left.
$20S $25D $5Child(in crib) $15Add. person   ► 6
● Choice   🏠 200-acre farm   ■ 2D,1S (upstairs)   ╾ 2D,1S, crib   ⌐ 1Private,
1sh.w.g.   ★ TV,LF   ᔫ Dutch
⇔ Public beach and golf course, Iroquois Lock, Morrisburg (Upper Canada Village),
Cornwall (Power Station)

☛ New cash crop and purebred Holstein heifer farm located in vacation paradise.

Ryan, Tammy and Mike (Ryan's Place)   ✔ CC
RR2, Iroquois, Ontario K0E 1K0   ☎ (613) 652-2472

From Hwy 401, take Exit 738 and north on Carman Rd. past school bus station. Turn
left on dirt road marked "Matilda"(Concession 2) and continue to 2nd house on right.
Sign on front.
$24S $30-34D $10Child   ► 6A,2Ch
● Full   🏠 24-acre farm, hist., acreage, view, quiet   ■ 1S,2D (upstairs)   ╾ 2S,2D,
cot, crib   ⌐ Sh.w.h.   ★ TV, parking   ♥   ✋ pets   ᔫ French
⇔ Upper Canada Village and Playhouse, golfing, public beach, Iroquois Locks

☛ Hobby farm with house built in 1849. There are 2 cats and a friendly dog named
"Boots" who will be there to greet visitors on arrival.

> **B&B Travel Tip:** *Do tell the hosts all about yourself and where you come
> from and what you do day in and out. They will be eager listeners. After all that's
> why they are inviting people into their homes – so the world comes to them!*

Jerseyville
(near Brantford; see also Hamilton, Ancaster, St. George, Troy)

Plas, Marie (Ancaster Farm B&B)
2114 Jerseyville Road West, Jerseyville, Ontario L0R 1R0   ☎ (416) 648-2795

From QEW, take Hwy 403 to Brantford. Turn right on Hwy 52 to Jerseyville Rd and 1st farm on south side past Alberton Side Rd.
$30S $40D $10Child   ► 7A,2Ch
● Full, homebaked   ♠ Farm, older, acreage, view, patio, quiet   ■ 1S,3D (upstairs)
◡ 1S,4T,1D, cot   ⌐ Sh.w.g.   ★ TV, parking   ⊛ Pets   ∾ Dutch

↦ Aquatic Centre, Dunmark Park, shopping malls

⇔ Bell Homestead, Shopping Malls, Ancaster Old Mill, Bruce Trail

☛ Cosy, homey atmosphere in the dairy country. Enjoy the quiet countryside. There is a dog in the house.

Kagawong
(on Manitoulin Islands; see also Providence Bay, Mindemoya, Gore Bay)

Park, Ken and Shirley (Park's Folly)
Box 8, Kagawong, Ontario P0P 1J0   ☎ (705) 282-2791

Phone for directions.
$30S $35-46D   ► 4
● Full, homebaked   ♠ Village   ■ 2D (upstairs)   ◡ 2D   ⌐ 1Sh.w.h.,1sh.w.g.
★TV,separate entrance   ⊛ Smoking, pets, children min. age 8
↦ Lake across the road with beach, dock for boating, swimming, fishing, hunting, restaurant, library, nature trails to Bridal Veil Falls, Marine Church, x-country skiing
⇔ Manitoulin Island day excursions, historic points of interest, villages, museums

☛ Older remodelled home with Widows Walk balcony overlooking beautiful Bay and the North Channel of Lake Huron. There is also a spacious housekeeping cottage available on a weekly basis.

Kars

(near Ottawa; see also North Gower, Mountain, Winchester, Merrickville)

Chewpa, Marta (Rideau Pines B&B)　　　　　　　⌐ B&B
RR1, Kars, Ontario　K0A 2E0　　　　　　　　　☎ (613) 692-3942

Located on corner of Hwy 416 & Century Road.
$25S - $35D　$8Child　🔲 Meals　　　　　　　　► 4
✦ Summer (Fall by appointment)　● Full　🏠 Rural, acreage, quiet　■ 2D
(upstairs)　⊸ 2D, cot　⊓ 1Sh.w.g.　★ Air,TV,F, parking　Ⓦ Smoking, drinking,
children min. age 2　⌁ German, Polish
↔ Take a leisurely stroll or cross-country ski in pine forests, neighboring farms
⇔ Manderly Golf & Country Club, downtown Ottawa, Manotich Village with crafts,
shops, tea room, Stittsville Fleamrket, excellent dining

🐾 Quiet and serene home with warm hospitality. Wake up to a hearty breakfast.
There is a friendly dog in residence.

Kimberley

(near Owen Sound; see also Clarksburg, Flesherton, Priceville, Crawford Bay, Meaford, Palgrave

Lamont, Graham and Mary (Lamont Guest Home)　　⌐ Grey Bruce B&B
Kimberley, Ontario　N0C 1G0　　　　　　　　　☎ (519) 599-5905

Phone for directions.
$30S　$40D　$20Child　$20Add.person　🔲 Meals　　　► 12
● Full, homebaked　🏠 Village, ranch-style, acreage, view, swimming pool, patio,
quiet　■ 3D　⊸ 3T,2D,2R,2cots -　⊓ 1Sh.w.g.　★ TV, parking　♥　Ⓦ Restricted
smoking, pets
↔ Bruce Trail, hiking, walking, downhill skii hills, cross-country skiing
⇔ Lake Eugenia and Eugenia Falls, Flesherton, Georgian Bay, Blue Mountain, summer
theatre, museums, antique and craft shops, Ontario's Chief apple district

🐾 Located on the famous Bruce Trail with view of ski hills and cliffs overlooking
beautiful Beaver Valley.

B&B Travel Tip: *You can go B&B for a weekend. You might want to go to the country for a good rest, or you might want to go to the city for a shopping spree or a cultural event.*

Kincardine

(on Lake Huron; see also Goderich, Tiverton, Port Elgin, Cargill)

Poag, Don and Lynnette (Country B&B) ✓ CC
RR1 Kincardine, Ontario N2Z 2X3 ☎ (519) 395-3613

Located on Hwy 21 and 13.5 km south of Kincardine near the crossroad of Hwy 86.
$25S $35D $5Child $42F $10Add.person ► 6A,3Ch
● Full, homebaked   ♠ Rural, res., quiet, patio   ■ S,D,F (upstairs)   ⊷ 1S,3D,2R,·
playpen   ⬝ 1Sh.w.g.,1sh.w.h.   ★ TV, parking   ⓦ Restricted smoking
⇔ Public beaches, Blyth Theatre, Bruce Nuclear Power De., Kincardine, golfing

☛ Comfortable century house with modern convenience and lovingly restored guest
rooms with original pine floors and furnished with antiques throughout. Homemade
jams and bisquets a specialty.

Kingston

(see also Sydenham, Westport, Rockport, Seeley's Bay, Bath, Lansdowne)

Sharpe, Shirley E. (B&B "The Alternative") ✓ FOBBA
715 High Gate Park Dr., Kingston, Ontrio K7M 5Z7 ☎ (613) 384-3197

From Hwy 401 take Exit 611 or 613 to Hqy 2, turn right at the lights, to Collins Bay Rd.
High Gate Park Dr. is just off Prince Charles Dr., turn right.
$35S $45-50D $5-10Child   ▣ Meals ► 5A,3-5Ch
● Choice, homebaked   ♠ Sub.,leevated bungalow, deck, quiet   ■ 1S,2D
⊷1S,1D,1Q,cribs   ⬝ 1Ensuite, 2sh.w.g.   ★Air,F,TV in guest rooms, parking   ♥
ⓦ Pets
↪ Collins Bay, marinas, fishing, local Legion, churches
⇔ Thousand Island Cruise Ships, (daily), historic Fort Henry, Pump and Marine
Museums, historic homes, art galleries

☛ Hosts offer warm hospitality and sumptuous breakfasts. There is a dog and a cat in
the house. Business travellers very welcome.

The Marine Museum of the Great Lakes (Alexander Henry B&B)
55 Ontario St., Kingston, Ont. K7L 2Y2 ☎ (613) 542-2261

On the Waterfront, located close to the Kingston downtown core.
$30S $50D ► 40
✚ Summer (till Lab-Day)   ● Cont.(fix your own)   ♠ Ship (moored icebreaker)
■ All outside cabins with view   ⊷ S,D, Captains cabin   ⬝ Private (toilets), sh.w.g.,
sinks in some cabins   ⓦ Smoking
⇔ Downtown Kingston, restaurants, shops, entertainment, marinas, tourboats and
other heritage attractions, car ferry to Wolfe Isle and to US, Old Fort Henry

☛ "Floating B&B" on authentic working ship with basic no-frills cabins and built-in
wooden bunks, former Coast Guard Icebreaker on the St.Lawrence Seaway. Listen to the
water and experience the restful lullaby of the waves washing against the hull.

Bed and Breakfast Kingston Area　　　　　　　　　　　　　　✔ FOBBA
10 Westview Rd., Kingston, Ontario　K7M 2C3　　　　　☎ (613) 542-0214
(Mrs. Ruth MacLachlan, Manager)
$35-40S　$45-53D　(including afull breakfast)　(Family Rates available)
Bed and Breakfast, Kingston Area is a Referral Service serving Kingston and the
surrounding area, as well as Sydenham, Westport, Seeley's Bay, Bath, Gananoque,
Harrowsmith, Prescott, Upper Canada Village. There are approximately 35 homes.
French, Dutch and German is spoken by some members. To guarantee accommodation,
send a deposit (cheque or money order) to cover the first night's lodging. A brochure
describing host homes is available for $1.

Kitchener
*(see also Elmira, Elora, St. Clements, Cambridge, New Hamburg, St. Jacobs,
Wallenstein, Plattsville, Guelph, Petersburg, Winterbourne)*

Holl, Frank and Maria (Austrian Home)　　　　　　　　✔ SOCVA
90 Franklin St.N., Kitchener, Ontario　N2A 1X9　　　　☎ (519) 743-5077

From Hwy 401 take Exit Kitchener Hwy 8 West to Exit Fairway/Weber. Turn onto
Weber and then turn right at 3rd stoplight.
$30S　$40D　$10Child　　　　　　　　　　　　　　　　　▶ 4
● Full　🏠 Res., patio　■ 2D (upstairs)　⊷ 2T,1D　⌐Sh.w.h.　★ TV, parking
🖐Smoking, pets

↤ Restaurants, bank, store

⇔ Stratford Festival, St.Jacobs and
Elmira Mennonite country, Lake
Ontario, Toronto International Airport

🐾 Austrian-Canadian hosts welcome
visitors to their Austrian-style home
with flower baskets and large backyard.
Enjoy the well-known October Fest
activities in traditional style.

　　B&B Travel Tip: *You can stay in a B&B when relocating to another city. Is
there a better way of getting the feeling of a new area than talking to the local
people?*

Kleinburg

(near Toronto; see also Newmarket, Richmond Hill, Palgrave)

Clark, John and Rosalind (Humber House)   ✔ FOBBA
10555 Islington Ave., Kleinburg, Ontario L0J 1C0   ☎ (416) 893-9108

From the QEW, take Hwy 427 north to Hwy 27 and continue to the village. Islington
Ave is the main street.
$25S $35D $7.50Child   ► 5
● Full   ♠ Village, older, patio, quiet   ■ 3D (upstairs)   ↵ 1D,2T,1Q,P, crib
⌐1Ensuite, 1sh.w.g.   ★ TV   ✋ Pets, non-smokers preferred
↔ Art Gallery (McMichael Canadian Collection), good restaurant, shops
⇔ Canada's Wonderland, Kortright Centre for Conservation, Toronto Int. Airport

☞ 80-year old home in charming village, very close to the Metorpolis.

Lagoon City

(near Peterborough; see also Rosedale, Coboconk, Fenelon Falls, Bobcaygeon)

Igras, Florence
Box 19, Site 1, RR1, Brechin, Ontario L0K 1B0   ☎ (705) 484-5818

Turn west at flashing amber light in village of Brechin on Hwy 12 south of Orillia and
north of Beaverton. Go 1.6 km, then right at Lagoon City entrance. Turn left at Resort
Centre, cross 4 bridges to black/white house on left corner at 1 Willow Cres.
$30-35D $3Child $5Add.person   ► 4A,2-4Ch
● Cont.   Resort res., bungalow, view, patio, lagoon waterfront, quiet   ■ 2D
↵1D,1Q   ⌐1Sh.w.g,1sh.w.h.   ★KF,TV in guest room, parking ❤ ✋Smoking
〰Polish, Ukrainian, French German
↔ Swimming, sandy beaches, sailing, fishing, canoeing (throughout a network of canals
and lagoons, tennis, golfing, fine dining at the Harbor Inn (complete with relaxing
Health Spa), snowmobiling, cross-country skiing
⇔ Huronia country (historic attractions), Horseshoe Valley Ski area, scenic waterways

☞ Unique resort retirement community ("Venice of the North"). Fishing and boating
at the foot of garden on Canal or Lagoon which leads to Lake Simcoe and Trent Canal
System ("and can lead to anywhere in the world from there!").

Lakefield

(near Peterborough; see also Warsaw, Hastings, Bobcaygeon, Fenelon Falls)

Ballantine, Anne   ✔ CC
2077 Dummer Lake Rd.W., RR2, Lakefield, Ontario K0L 2H0   ☎ (705) 877-2062

From Lakefield, take Hwy 28 north for 2.5 km and turn right onto County Rd 6 (Stoney
Lake Rd). Continue for 19 km (passing McCracken's Landing), and turn right at bottom
of steep hill.

$25S $35D   ▣ Meals
● Full   ⌂ Rural, bungalow, lakefront, quiet   ■ 1D   ⌐ 1D   ⌐ Sh.w.h.
★ TV,F   ⓦ Smoking
↔ Swimming, boating, bird watching, skating, skiing and skidooing
⇔ Petroglyphs, Peterborough Lift Locks, Stony Lake cruises, Indian Gallery, Lang
Century Village, good fiddle music and fine dining

☛ Home is situated on the picturesque shores of Dummer Lake amid pine, spruce and
silver birch trees with relaxed and cosy atmosphere and a small antique shop on the
premises. Hosts enjoy Blue Grass Music. There is a cat called "Maggie" in the house.

Killeen, John and Magaret (The Killeen's)
RR3, Lakefield, Ontario   K0L 2H0   ☎ (705) 652-6369

North of Peterborough, take Hwy 28 towards Lakefield and then Hwy 507 to Selwyn.
Turn left towards Bridgenorth. Drive southwest for 1.5 km on Bridgenorth. Turn right
at B&B sign.
$30S $40D $5Child $5Add.person   ▣ Meals
● Full,homebaked   ⌂ Farm, raised bungalow, acreage, view, patio quiet, sundeck
■1S,2D (upper and main floor)   ⌐ 2D,1P, crib   ⌐ 1Private, 1sh.w.h.
★Air,F,TV,separate entrance, parking   ⓦ Smoking, pets
↔ Beautiful rural magnificient scenery, Chemong Lake, fishing, boating
⇔ Art Gallery, flea markets, boat cruise

☛ Friendly, comfortable surroundings. Home is situated 1.5 km from Selwyn. There is
a cat in the house. Breakfast with homemade breads and muffins served on the sundeck
weather permitting.

Wilkins, Joan and Wally (Windmere)   ↙ ONT B&B
Selwyn, RR3, Lakefield, Ontario   K0L 2H0   ☎ (705) 652-6290

From Peterborough go north on Hwy 28 and then Hwy 507 to Selwyn. Turn right at
Selwyn and left at the first farm gate. (18.5 km from Peterborough)
$29S $37-42D $12Add.person   ► 14
● Choice   ⌂ 100-acres farm, hist., quiet   ■ 2D (upstairs) (also apt)
⌐4D,2R,2P   ⌐ 1Ensuite, 1sh.w.g.   ★ Air (in apt),TV,F, separate entrance, parking
ⓦ Smoking, pets   ⌇ some French
↔ Large, deep and clear spring fed swimming pond, quiet walks around the grounds,
hike to the back of the farm, cross-country skiing and snow- shoeing
⇔ Four sparkling lakes, fishing, swimming, sailing, Trent Canal System (world's highest
liftlock), Indian Petroglyphs, Century Village, Warsaw Caves, summer theatres, art
galleries, golfing

☛ Spacious orginal stone homestead built in 1839 and lovingly renovated and restored
– an oasis of country comfort – situated in the heart of the Kawarthas. Hosts enjoy to
tour the back roads with their own horse and buggy. Hostess is spokesperson for "B&B
Registry of Peterborough & Area".

Lancaster

(near Cornwall; see also Green Valley, Apple Hill, Williamstown)

Highet, Marjorie and Malcolm
RR1, Lancaster, Ontario   K0C 1N0

⌐ CC

☎ (613) 347-3550

From Hwy 401 take Alexandria Lancaster Exit No 814 and follow north through the village to Pine St. Turn left to second house before bridge with cream- colored fence.
$25S $36D   ▣ Meals   (Please phone ahead)

► 4

✚ May-Oct. (Winter by arrangement)   ● Full   ♠ Rural, riverview, in-ground swimming pool   ■ 2D   ⊢ 2D   ⊓ Sh.w.g.   ★ Guest sitting room   ⓌPets

⇔ Seaway Valley attractions, Morrisburg (Upper Canada Village)

☞ Century home on the banks of the Raisin River backed by a 10-acre tree farm. Enjoy a refreshing dip in the pool when feeling travel-weary upon arrival.

Lavigne

(near Sudbury; see also North Bay)

Smits, Adrian and Mary (Chelms Glen Farm)
RR1, Lavigne, Ontario   P0H 1R0

⌐ OFVA

☎ (705) 594-2859

From Hwy 17 take Hwy 64 south at Verner for 8 km. Look for name on mail box.
$20S $30D $5Child   ▣ Meals

► 4A,2Ch

● Choice   ♠ Farm, view   ■ 1S,1D,F   ⊢1S,1Q, cot   ⊓Sh.w.g.
★TV,KF,LF,F   ⓌSmoking, drinking, pets   ∾Dutch
↔ Hunting, skiing, hiking, fishing, swimming, hayrides
⇔ Lavigne (Lady of Lourds Shrine), Sudbury, North Bay, Algonquin Prov. Park

☞ Located in friendly farming village on the shore of West Nipissing Lake.

Leamington

(on Lake Erie south of Windsor;see also Pelee Isle, Amherstburg, Wheatley,Palgrave

Cowan, Bruce and Margaret (Farm House B&B)
RR5, Leamington, Ontario   N8H 3V8   ☎ (519) 326-8384

Go 10 km north of Leamington on Hwy 77 to County Rd 14. Turn west 1.6 km.
$30S $40D   ▨ Meals   ► 6A,2Ch
● Full,homebaked   ♠ Farm, view, patio, quiet   ■ 3D (upstairs)   ⊷ 3D,R,P crib
⌐ 1Sh.w.g. ★ F,TV, parking   ⊛ Pets
⇔ Point Pelee Nat. Park, Jack Miners Bird Sanctuary, Colasanti's Tropical Gardens,
Pelee Island Ferry, Windsor, Detroit

☞ Large country home and warm hospitality. There is a dog in the house.

Tiessen, Harry and Agatha (Home Suite Home)   ✓ FOBBA
115 Erie St., South, Leamington, Ontario   N8H 3B5   ☎ (519) 326-7169

Located by Point Pelee National Park. Phone for directions.
$37S $43-53D   (Deposit)   ► 6
▣ Not Feb.   ● Full   ♠ Res., patio, screened porch, sundeck, swimming pool
(in-ground)   ■ 3D (upstairs)   ⊷ 2T,3D,1Q   ⌐ Sh.w.g.   ★ TV   ⊛ Smoking,
pets   ᵥᵥ German
↪ Downtown, fine shops and restaurants
⇔ Point Pelee Nat. Park and lovely beaches, Marsh Board Walk, Jack Miners Sanctuary,
Tropical Gardens, marinas, boat launches, biking, canoeing, fishing, cross country skiing

☞ Spacious Victorian home is located on a shaded street and furnished with antiques
and wicker. Hostess is also spokesperson for Point Pelee B&B Association.

Lion's Head

(near Tobermory; see also Wiarton, Oliphant)

Bard, Ann and Don (Cape Chin North Connection)   ✓ Grey Bruce B&B
RR4, Lion's Head, Ontario   N0H 1W0   ☎ (519) 795-7525

From Wiarton take Hwy 6 to Lindsay Rd 5, to second road on left, turn left to second
road on right (Cape Chin North Rd). Follow to farm on right. From Tobermory take
Hwy 6 to Dyer's Bay Rd. Turn right at Brinkman's Corners to first road on left and
continue as above.
$30S $35D - $5Child $10Add.person   ▨ Meals   ► 6
● Full, homebaked   ♠ Farm, hist., acreage, view, patio, quiet, isolated   ■ 1S,1D
(main and upper floor)   ⊷ 2T,1D,1Q   ⌐ 2Sh.w.g.   ★ TV,F,separate entrance,
parking, facilities for the disabled   ⊛ Restricted smoking, pets
↪ 18 km ski trail on site, Bruce Trail hiking, Devils Monument, Georgian Bay
⇔ Wiarton (shopping), Ferry to Manitouling Island, St. Marargarets Historical Chapel,
Tobermory, scenic Lions Head Harbour

☞ Home was built in late 1800's and is nestled in Maple Woods with rolling meadows,
quiet, peaceful countryside. Hosts have retired from operating a resort and now have lots
of time to enjoy B&B guests in their peaceful country home.

Butchart, Faye (Touchstone and Wood)   ✔ Grey Bruce
RR2, Lion's Head, Ontario N0H 1W0   ☎ (519) 793-3182

Follow Hwy 6 north of Wiarton, turn right at Ferndale onto the Stokes Bay Rd. Turn
left at first stop sign, and go 1 km. Turn left onto laneway through the wood.
$25S $35D - 🍽 Meals   ► 4A,2Ch
● Full, homebaked   ♠ Rural, acreage, view, patio, quiet   ■ 1D,1F (main and upper
floor)   ⊷ 2T,1D,cot   ⌐ Sh.w.h.   ★ F,TV in guest room, LF,KF, parking
⇔ Beautiful beach at Georgian Bay, village of Lion's Head, Dorcus Bay and Nature
Reserve, Tobermory and Ferry to Manitoulin Islands

☛ Cedar-slab house with large deck nestled in a sunny meadow beside a maple bush.
Fruits and vegetables from garden with homemade breads and jams. Enjoy the quiet and
relaxing homey atmosphere. There is a cat in the house.

Gwizdala, Anna and Jim (Cape Chin Crafts B&B)
RR4, Lion's Head, Ontario N0H 1W0   ☎ (519) 795-7892

Located 8 km N of Ferndale. Turn right from Hwy 6 at Lindsay Rd 5. Follow the paved
road past St. Margaret's Church and continue onto the gravel road to Cape Chin N
junctions (7km), then another 8 km to Cape Chin N Rd, turn left to 5th house on right.
$25S $35D   🍽 Meals   ► 4
✚ May-Oct   ● Full, homebaked   ♠ Rural, bungalow, acreage, view, patio, lakefront,
quiet   ■ 2D   ⊷ 2T,1D   ⌐ Sh.w.h.   ★ TV,F,LF, parking, facilities for the
disabled   ⓦ outside smoking preferred   ⤬ Polish
↪ Walk and hike on the Bruce Trail which runs through the property, good swimming
(water is cold), rocky beach
⇔ Tobermory, Ferry to Manitoulin Islands, Owen Sound, Georgian Bay beaches

☛ Simple home in beautiful surroundings with spectacular seascape and peaceful
rolling countryside. Hosts are conservationists and lead a full but quiet life. Fruits and
vegetables from the garden.

White, Ivan and Elaine (The Butchart House)   ✔ CC
Box 293, Lion's Head, Ontario N0H 1W0   ☎ (519) 793-3129

Take Hwy 6 and turn right at Ferndale.
$25S $30D   🍽 Meals   ► 6
✚ Summer (other by appointment)   ● Choice, homebaked   ♠ Village, older, patio,
quiet   ■ 2D (upstairs)   ⊷ 2D,1P   ⌐ 1Sh.w.g.,1sh.w.h.   ★ parking
↪ Bruce Trail (walking, hiking, cross-country skiing), Georgian Bay (swimming,
boating, fishing)
⇔ Tobermory and ferry to Manitoulin Islands, Owen Sound, Wiarton, Lake Huron
beaches

London
(see also Denfield, St. Mary's, Woodstock, Ilderton, Arva, Embro)

Burket, Paul and Beverley (Trillium)　　　　　　✔ London B&B
71 Trillium Cres., London, Ontario　N5Y 4T3　　　　☎ (519) 453-3801

From Windsor take Hwy 401 and Exit 189 North. Continue past 7 lights, to crosswalk
opposite Montcalm High, turn left on Fuller St, right on Regal, left on Trillium.
$25S　$35D　$10Child　◙ Meals　　　　　　　　　　　　　► 4
● Full　🏠 Res., bungalow, quiet　■ 2D　⊢ 2S,1Q　⌐ Sh.w.g.　★ Air,F,TV,
parking　⚉ Smoking, pets
↔ U.W.O., bus route, good shopping, trout farm
⇔ Fanshawe Pioneer Village, Theatre London, Children's Museum, Huron County
Playhouse, Kettle Creek Canvas Company, Museum of Indian Archaeology

☞ Restful modern with warm and friendly atmosphere is situated on a very quiet
crescent with mature trees in a large backyard. There are plenty of birds which are fed
all year round.

Herbert, Theresa and John　　　　　　　　　　✔ London B&B
87 Askin St., London, Ontario　N6C 1E5　　　　　　☎ (519) 673-4598

Exit Wellington Rd off Hwy 401 (Exit 186). Turn left at Commissioners Rd, right onto
Wharncliffe and right onto Askin.
$28S　$35D　$10Child　　　　　　　　　　　　　　　　► 5A
✚ Summer　● Full　🏠 Downtown, hist.　■ 1S,2D (main and upper floor)
⊢ 1S,1D,1Q　⌐ 2Sh.w.g.　★ KF,LF　⚉ Pets　〰 French
↔ Downtown shopping, restaurants, parks
⇔ Fanshawe and Springbank parks, Stratford Festival, Grand Bend, Lake Huron

☞ Extensively renovated 1871 spacious Victorian home surrounded by many old
churches & historical landmarks. Nutritious Canadian breakfast served. There is a cat.

Humberstone, A. (Annigan's B&B)　　　　　　　✔ London B&B
194 Elmwood Ave. East, London, Ontario　N6C 1K2　☎ (519) 439-9196

From Hwy 401 take Exit 186 (Wellington Rd) and go north to Grand Ave. Turn left.
Turn right at Ridout and immediate left onto Elmwood (one way).
$30S　$45D　$5Child　　　　　　　　　　　　　　　　► 6
● Cont., homebaked　🏠 Downtown, res., hist., verandah　■ 3D　⊢ 2T,2D
(upstairs)　⌐ 1Sh.w.h., 1sh.w.g.　★ F,Air (in guest rooms) parking (off street)
⚉Restricted smoking, pets, children min. age
↔ Downtown, Grand Theatre, Art Gallery, Thames Park, Wortley Village
⇔ University of Western Ontario, Fanshawe College, Guy Lombardo Museum, Stratford
Festival, Lake Erie and Lake Huron beaches

☞ Charming, turn-of-the-century house with turret, interesting architecture owned by
Interior Designer. "A taste of home with a touch of class".

James, Jesse and Joanne (Ferndale West)   ✔ London B&B
53 Longbow Rd., London, Ontario   N6G 1Y5   ☎ (519) 471-8038

From Hwy 401 take Exit 186 (Wellington Rd N) to Commissioners Rd. turn left to
Wonderland (5km). Turn right and continue to Lawson Rd (6.5km). Turn right and first
left (Wychwood and then immediatedly right into Longbow.
$30S $40-45D $50F $10 Add.person   ► 6A,2Ch
● Full   🏠 Res., sub., view, swimming pool, patio, quiet   ■ 2D,1F (upstairs)
🛏2T,1D,2Q   ⚟ 1Ensuite, 1sh.w.g.   ★ Air,F,TV,LF, parking   🐾 Pets
↔ University of Western Ontario, cross-country skiing at bottom of street
↔ Downtown London, Grand Bend on Lake Huron

☞ Lovely redecorated house is situated in a very prestigious part of the City in the
beautiful North London area.

Odegaard, Eileen   ✔ London B&B
433 Hyde Park Rd., London, Ontario   N6H 3R9   ☎ (519) 471-1107

From Hwy 401 take Exit 186 North (Wellington Rd)to Queen's Ave.Turn left and go 6.5
km to Hyde Park Rd (Queen's Ave becomes Riverside Dr at bridge). Turn right.
$25S $40D   ► 6
● Full, nutricious, homebaking   🏠 Res., sub., acreage, swimming pool, patio, quiet
■ 3D (upstairs)   🛏 4T,1D   ⚟ 1Sh.w.h.,1sh.w.g.   ★ Air,TV,parking   🐾 Pets
↔ Shopping plaza, Springbank Park, Storybook Gardens, Thames Valley golf course,
Thames River
↔ London Regional Art Galleries, museums, University, Grand Theatre Company
(renovated opera house)

☞ Red brick Cape Cod home set amid an acre of oaks and evergreens in country-like
setting. There is a dog in the house.

Rose, Doug and Betty   ✔ London B&B
526 Dufferin Ave., London, Ontario   N6B 2A2   ☎ (519) 433-9978

Take Exit 186 Wellington Rd N to Duffering Ave. Turn right and go past City Hall.
$30-40per room   ► 4
● Full   🏠 Downtown, quiet   ■ 3D   🛏 2D,2T   ⚟ 1Private, 1sh.w.h.   ★ Air,
free parking   🐾 Pets, children min. age 12, smoking
↔ Downtown shopping, dining, Richmond Row, parks, sports facilities, Art Gallery
↔ University of Western Ontario, Fanshawe College, Pioneer Village, Stratford
Shakespeare Festival Theatres

☞ 120-year old home located in most desirable residential area of century homes in
North Central London.

Warren, Earl and Serena
720 Headley Dr., London, Ontario   N6H 3V6

✓ London B&B,FOBBA
☎ (519) 471-6228

Take Exit 126 Highbury Ave off Hwy 401 to Oxford St. Proceed across town, turn left and go west to Headley Dr., turn left again.
$25 $30-35D $8Child (under age 12) $15Add. person   ► 7
● Full, homebaked   🏠 Res., patio, summer room   ■ 3   ⊷2T,2D,1R   �1Sh.w.g.
   ★ Air, TV   🕭 Restricted smoking
↔ Springbank Park, shopping malls
⇔ Downtown London

☛ Comfortable Oakridge Park home in prestigious residential area of West London. Host is co-ordinator for London & Area B&B Association.

Longbow Lake
(near Kenora north-west of Thunder Bay)

Janke, Betty and Emil (Heritage Place)
Longbow Lake, Kenora, Ontario   P0X 1H0   ☎ (807) 548-4380

Located on Hwy 17 (TransCanada) and 14.5 km east of Kenor. Look for sign.
$33S $40D $5Child(over age 6) $10Add.person   🍽 Meals (Tax extra)   ► 16
● Full   🏠 Lodge, acreage, pond, view, balconie, patio, quiet   ■ 8D,F (upstairs)
⊷ T,D,R, crib, cots   �4Private, 4sh.w.g.   ★ Air,TV,F,LF, pool table, camping hook-ups and playground   🕭 Smoking, drinking pets   ⌇ German
↔ Cross-country skiing, hiking
⇔ Kenora, Lake of the Woods, fishing, boating, Int. sailing regattas, hunting, Lake cruises (M.S.Kenora), US border (Min)

☛ Home offers family atmosphere and home baking in attractive and prosperous pulp and paper town and major tourist center both to the wilderness country in the north, and to the lake activities to the south.

Lucknow
(near Goderich; see also Kincardine, Wingham)

MacLean, Marjorie and Ewan (Maple Shadows Farm)
RR3, Lucknow, Ontario   H0G 2H0   ☎ (519) 395-5060

Located on south side of Hwy 86 and 12.8 km west of Lucknow. Look for sign.
$25S $30D   🍽 Meals   ► 4
✚ April-Oct.   ● Choice, homebaked   🏠 Rural, acreage, quiet   ■ 2D   ⊷ 2D
�1Sh.w.g.   ★ TV   🕭 Pets
⇔ Public beach, churches, Blyth Theatre

☛ Relax in the shade of the big maple trees in this quiet spot and enjoy the beautiful sunsets. Plenty of strawberries and raspberries in season.

Mallorytown
(near Brockville: see also Rockport, Seeley's Bay, Delta)

DeWolfe, Kent and Sue (The Birches Inn B&B)   ✔ CC
RR2, Box 179, Mallorytown, Ontario   K0E 1R0   ☎ (613) 659-2025

Located 1.5 km east of 1000 Island Bridge on 1000 Island Parkway.
$60S $60D   ► 28
✦May-Oct. ●Cont, homebaked ♠Rural, hist., view, quiet, riverview, patio in front of
all rooms ■8 ⊷3S,13D ⊓13D,3S ⊓8 Private ★ Air, TV, separate entrance,
parking ⑩pets
↔ 1000 Island Bridge, 36 km bicycle path
⇔ Old Fort Henry, Rideau Canal, boat tours, river museums

📣 Fresh baked continental breakfast served in guest room or on the deck overlooking
the St. Lawrence River.

Massey
(near Sudbury; see also Webbwood, Whitefish, Spanish)

Emiry, Mack and Beth   ✔ CC
RR2, Massey, Ontario   P0P 1P0   ☎ (705) 865-5249

Phone for directions from Massey or ask at the tourist bureau.
$20S $30D $50F   ▣ Meals   ► 5
● Choice, homebaked ♠ 600-acres farm, quiet, isolated ■ 2S,2D (upstairs)
⊷2S,2D ⊓ 1Sh.w.g. ★ TV,F ⑩ Smoking, drinking, pets
↔ Dairy farm grounds with fields and bush and lake
⇔ Prov. Park, Science North in Sudbury, Elliott Lake

📣 Perfect location for nature lovers. Tranquil surroundings for relaxing and listening
to the country quiet. Hosts have travelled extensively by B&B.

Mattawa
(east of North Bay)

Levitan, Mrs. Mary (Bear Creek Farm)   ✔ OFVA
RR2, Mattawa, Ontario   P0H 1V0   ☎ (705) 744-2423

From North Bay take Rt 17 east to rue Dorion and follow up hill for 4.8 km. Keep to
right at fork in road. Continue keeping right and look for 2nd farm on left with red roof.
$30S $45D   ▣ Meals (Weekly rates available)   ► 4A
● Full,homebaked ♠ 260-acre sheep farm, older, view, patio, quiet ■ 2D
⊷ 4T, futon ⊓ 1 Ensuite, 1sh.w.h. ★ TV,F,KF, 100-year old wood stove, spinning
wheels, artesian well water ⑩ prefer non-smokers
↔ Wool carding facilities on premises, hiking, bush, waterfall
⇔ Pretty town of Mattawa on river, dining shopping, beaches at Lakes Papineau and
Champlain and Mattawa Rivers, Algonquin Prov. Park

📣 Century old log home with lots of ambience and charm situated on scenic hill with
large organic vegetable garden. Former art teacher spins, dyes and weaves wool from
own sheep raised on hillside.

Meaford

(near Owen Sound; see also Clarksburg, Kimberley, Thornbury, Collingwood)

Allen, Joan and Doug (The Cheshire Cat)   ✓ CC
32 Nelson St., Box 1809, Meaford, Ontario   N0H 1Y0   ☎ (519) 538-3487

In Meaford, turn towards the Harbour at Townhall lights. Located next to Fire Hall.
$35S $40-45D $10Child $10Add.person   🍽 Meals   ► 6A,4Ch
● Full   ♠ Downtown, older, Harbour view, large old fashioned porch   ■ 1S,3D
⇥ 1S,2T,2D,2R, 4cots   ⌐ 3Sh.w.g.   ★ F,LF,TV in guest room, separate entrance,
parking   ⚘ Pets, smoking
↔ Harbour and beach, downtown Meaford, restaurants, summer theatre, large craft
show, antique and gift shops, museum
⇔ Blue Mountain/Beaver Valley (downhill skiing), cross-country skiing, scenic caves

☞ Old country atmosphere in gracious old home with oak woodwork and leaded
windows. Good location from which to explore the pretty town. There is one cat.

Merrickville

(near Ottawa; see also North Augusta, Frankville, North Gower, Mountain)

Brownell, Neil and Joyce (Cherry Hill B&B)   ✓ CC
Box 76, 218 Lewis Street East, Merrickville, Ontario   K0G 1N0   ☎ (613) 269-3133

Phone for directions.
$35S $40D $10Add.person   ► 7
●Full,homebaked   ♠Village, older, quiet, sunroom/veranda, quiet ■2D,1Ste
(upstairs) ⇥1S,2D,1R   ⌐1ensuite,1sh.w.h.   ★TV,F, parking ⚘Smoking, pets
↔ Rideau Canal, Blockhouse Museum beside Lock 21, artists studios, craft and antique
shops, tea room, excellent restaurants
⇔ Brockville, Ivy Lea Bridge from USA,Perth, Kingston, Upper Canada Village

☞ Older solid brick house with pine and maple floors, a veranda with Wicker furniture
and antiques throughout the home. Located on a large lot with plenty of parking space.
There is a cat named "Holly" in residence.

B&B Travel Tip: *Do remember that you are entering a private house as a
guest – (even though you are paying something) – the hosts are still doing you a
favour by inviting you into their homes and you must observe whatever house rules
exist. If you keep this in mind, your stay will be very enjoyable.*

Midland

(on Georgian Bay near Orillia; see also Elmvale, Honey Harbour, Waubaushene)

Calvert, James and Patricia
476 Yonge Street E., Midland, Ontario   L4R 2C3   ☎ (705) 526-0306

Follow Hwy 400 to Hwys 12 or 93 to King St in Midland and to Yonge St East.
$35S $45D $10Child   ► 4A,2Ch
●Choice   ♠Downtown, older, verandas   ■2D,1F (upstairs)   ⊷2T,1Q,1P
⁊1Sh.w.g., 1sh.w.h.   ★TV in guest sitting room, parking   ♥   ⓌRest.smoking,pets
↔ Midland docks, 30 000 Island Boat Cruises, Little Lake and park
⇔ Martyr's Shrine, St. Marie Among the Hurons, Wye Marsh Wildlife Center, sandy
beaches of Georgian Bay, scenic caves, Collingwood downhill skiing and winter activities

🐾 Warm welcome in turn-of-the-Century red brick home with natural pine floors,
stained glass windows and furnished with antiques.

Siddall, Gwen and Bill   ↙ FOBBA
670 Hugel Ave., Midland, Ontario   L4R 1W9   ☎ (705) 526-4441

Take Hwy 400 north from Barrie to Hwy 93; then north to Midland, right on Hugel.
$35S $45-50D   ► 5
✚ Summer (also Ski season Jan/Feb)   ● Full, homebaked   ♠ Res., older, large
veranda   ■ 2D (upstairs)   ⊷ 1S,2T,1Q   ⁊ 1Sh.w.g.   ★ TV, parking, 2 adult
bicycles   Ⓦ Smoking, pets
↔ Midland Harbour, Island Cruises, Little Lake Park, Huronia Museum, Indian Village,
restaurants, theatres, downtown shopping antiques and boutiques
⇔ Downhill skiing, Horseshoe Valley, Mt. St. Louis, cross-country groomed trails,
Martyrs' Shrine, beautiful Georgian Bay beaches including Wasaga

🐾 Former teacher hosts in large, turn-of-the-Century home, located in residential
Midland in an area known as Huronia country which is full of Huronia History.

Southwestern Ontario Countryside Vacation Association & B&B   ↙ FOBBA
RR1, Millbank, Ontario   N0K 1L0   ☎ (519) 595-4604
(Mrs. Alveretta Henderson, Secretary Treasurer)
The Association represents approximately 35 homes at the time of publication. Members
are located in Platsville, St. Clements, Millbank, Wingham, Goderich, New Hamburg,
Drayton, Elmira, Elora, Thorndale, Cambridge, Harriston, Parkhill, Wallenstein,
Waterloo, Seaforth, Breslau, St. Jacobs, Kitchener, Sebringville, Port Stanley and
Leamington. For information phone or write to the above. Some of the hosts are listed
in this publication.

Millbank

(near Kitchener; see also St. Clements, St. Jacobs, Elmira, Stratford, Wallenstein)

Henderson, Jack and Alveretta (Honeybrook Farm) ∠ SOCVA,FOBBA
RR1, Millbank, Ontario N0K 1L0 ☎ (519) 595-4604

Write for map or telephone for specific directions.
$25S $40D $10Add.person   ▣ Meals   ► 6A
●Choice, homebaked   ♠160-acre farm, hist., view, riverfront, quiet   ■2D(upstairs)
⊷2T,2D   ⌐ 1Private, 1sh.w.g.   ★ TV in guest room, F,LF   ⊛ Smoking, pets, not
suitable for children   ⌇ Some French

⇔ Kitchener, Waterloo, Elmira and
surrounding Mennonite country,
Stratford

☛ Restored 1866 stone house situated
on rolling land by the Niyth River with
large comfortable rooms each with own
heat control. Choose breakfast from
extensive menu..

Snyder, Lorne and Mabel (Lomar Farm)
RR1, Millbank, Ontario N0K 1L0   ☎ (519) 595-8347

From Hwy 401, take Exit 278 to Hwy 8. Follow Hwy 86 north to County Rd 15. Go west
through Crosshill to Rd 18 south, located 3.3 km east of Millbank. Look for 1st farm on
right. From Stratford, take Hwy 19 north to Millbank exit and Rd 18 south as above.
$25S $35D   ► 5
● Full, homebaked   ♠ 200-acre farm   ■ 1S,2D (upstairs)   ⊷ 1S,2D, crib
⌐1Sh.w.h.   ★ TV   ⊛ Smoking
⇔ Stratford Festival, Wellesley, Apple Butter Cheese Festival, Elmira Maple Syrup
country, Kitchener-Waterloo farmer's markets

☛ Century-old farmhouse in Waterloo Country (built in 1854) is comfortably furnsihed
with some family heirlooms.

Millbrook

(near Peterborough; see also Cavan, Lakefield)

Jackson, David and Judy (Westmacott House) ✔ CC
60 King Street W, Box 386, Millbrook, Ontario L0A 1G0 ☎ (705) 932-2957

From Hwy 401 take Hwy 115 or 28 (Exits 436 or 464) north to Millbrook.
$30S $40-45D $65F ► 11
●Full,homebaked ♠Village,historic,acreage,patio,swimming pool ■1S,2D,1F
(upstairs) ⌙1S,3D,1T ⁊2Sh.w.g. ⬤Rest.smoking,pets,child min. age 7
↔ Historic walking tour, Mill and pond, theatre, anitque shops, fine dining
⇔ Boating on Trent Canal, Kawartha Lakes, downhill and cross-country skiing

☛ Charming restored Victorian heritage home was once occupied by A.G.E.
Westmacott, an Anglican Min. Host operates antiquarian book store on the premises.

Millgrove

(near Hamilton; see also Waterdown, Burlington, Campbellville, Milton)

Lovegrove, Nancy and Barry ✔ Flamb.B&B
862 Millgrove Side Road, Box 3, Millgrove, Ontario L0R 1V0 ☎ (416) 689-5730

From QEW, take Hwy 403 and Hwy 6 and continue 4 km north of Hwy 5 (Clappisons
Corner) to Millgrove and turn on Millgrove Side Rd.
$25S $35D ▣ Meals ► 4A
● Choice ♠ Village, rural, older, acreage, view, patio, quiet ■ 1D, 1Ste (main and
upper floor) ⌙2T,1D,1R ⁊ 1Privte, 1sh.w.h. ★ TV in guest room, parking ⬤
Children, pets
↔ Millgrove flea markets, country store
⇔ African Lion Safari, quaint town of Waterdown, antique shops, Flamborough Downs
Race Track, Dundas Cactus Festival, Botanical Gardens, Burlington, Lake Ontario

☛ Century farm house plus recent addition with bright sunroom and patio surrounded
by large treed lot with trout stream, yet located close to the city. Hosts enjoy natural
country living and organic gardening. There is a cat in the house.

Milton

(see Burlington, Campbellville, Oakville, Georgetown, Waterdown)

Sandlohken, Horst and Ille (Red Maple House)
RR3, Milton, Ontario L9T 2X7 ☎ (416) 878-5716

From Hwy 401 take Exit 320 (Hwy 25) north and go 8 km to Reg Rd 15 (Shell Station on
corner). Turn left and look for house 2 km down road on left.
$25S $35D ► 2A
● Choice ♠ 40-acre Maple Bush farm, quiet, isolated, heated swimming pool
■ 1D ⌙2T ⁊ Ensuite ★ Air,TV,F,separate entrance ⬤ Pets 〰 German
↔ Maple bush, Bruce Trail for hiking and cross-country skiing
⇔ Agricultural Museum, Glen Eden and Bronte Conservation areas (summer and winter
recreation), Crawford Lake restored Indian village, Campbellville quaint village shopping

☛ Contemporary, spacious country home on the Niagara Escarpment with own maple
bush at backdoor. Watch maple syrup being made in the Spring.

Minden

(northwest of Peterborough; see also Koboconk, Rosedale, Bobcaygeon, Fenelon Falls, Haliburton, Wilberforce)

Redgrave, William C. and Family (Hunter Creek Inn) ⌒CC
Box 765, Minden, Ontario K0M 2K0 ☎ (705) 286-3194

From Hwy 401 take Exit 436 north to Hwy 35 through Lindsay and Moore Falls. Before village, turn left on Hunter Creek Rd and follow signs to house.
$34-81per person ► 10A,2Ch
● Full, homebaked ♠ Rural, acreage, view, riverfront, patio, quiet, isolated, pond, docks ■ 3D,1Ste,F ↤ 2S,2T,2D,1Q,R, cot, crib ⌐ 2Private, 1sh.w.g., 1ensuite
★ F, TV in some rooms, separate entrance, sauna, whirlpool, guest breakfast room, lounge ⓦ Pets, non-smokers preferred
↦ Gull River (swimming, boating), fishing, skating, cross-country skiing, hiking
⇔ Dorset Lookout and Forestry School, Haliburton Skyslide, Minden Whitewater Reserve, museum and Cultural Centre, Algonquin Prov. Park

📯 Intimate and informal, yet truly exquisite beauty in a unique home of elegant class, design and charm. Special package for Newleyweds. Brunch-style breakfast served.

Mindemoya

(on Manitoulin Island south of Sudbury; see also Providence Bay, Massey, Gore Bay, Mindemoya, Tobermory, Kagawong)

Williamson, Harold and Sally (Mindemoya Lake View Farm) ⌒ AOFVA
Mindemoya, Manitoulin Island, Ontario P0P 1S0 ☎ (705) 377-5714

From Hwy 17, take Hwy 6 to Little Current. Then take Hwy 540 to West Bay and Hwy 551 to Mindemoya. Take Hwy 542 west to Lake Mindemoya, turn right onto gravel road and look for 4th house on the right with lake on left. From South Baymouth ferry docks take Hwy 6 to Hwy 542 and follow as above.
$25S $30D ●$3Each (Special rates for children) ► 6A,2Ch
● Full ♠ 1000-acre farm, lakefront, patio ■ 3D ↤ 3D, cot, 2cribs
⌐ Sh.w.g. ★ TV,F ⓦ Pets
↦ Sandy beaches, excellent fishing, swimming and beautiful sunrises and sunset
⇔ Providence Bay, Bridal Veils Falls, Ten-Mile Point scenic lookout

📯 Located on on the South-East shore of beautiful Manitoulin Island, world's largest fresh- water island and picturesque coastline. With permission to hunt on property, hunting guests are welcome in Deer Hunting Season (November).

Mitchell

(near Stratford; see also Seaforth, St. Mary's, Millbank)

Hoffmeyer, Ollie and Jean (Spruce Hill Farm)
RR3, Mitchell, Ontario N0K 1N0

✔ CC

☎ (519) 348-8688

Located west of Stratford. Take Hwy 8 to approx. 2km west of Mitchell. Turn right
(north) at first corner and continue 1.5 km to farm.

$20S $30D $10Child

► 4

✚Summer ● Choice ⌂Farm, acreage, older, quiet ■4(main and upper level)
↦1S,2D,1P,1cot,1crib ⌐Sh.w.g. ★TV,LF ⓌRestricted smoking,drinking
⇔ Stratford Shakespearean Festival, Blyth Summer Playhouse, beaches of Lake Huron,
Grand Bend

☞ Quiet country home and friendly hospitality. Families welcome.

Scott, Jim and Betty (Pinewood Country Inn B&B)
RR2, Mitchell, Ontario N0K 1N0

✔) CC

☎ (519) 348-8760

From Stratford take Hwy 8 to Fullarton Sideroad 20 (last road before Mitchell). Turn
left and go over 2 crossroads. Look for house on right just past curve sign.

$35S $40D

► 10

● Full ⌂ Rural, 27-acres, swimming pool, quiet ■ 5D (upstairs) ↦ 2T,4D
⌐2Sh.w.g. Ⓦ Smoking, drinking, pets, children
↦ Walking along creek which winds its way through the property, interesting bird
watching
⇔ Stratford Shakespearean Festival, Blyth Festirval, Huron Country Playhouse, Lake
Huron beaches

☞ Home is nestled in the natural surroundings of a quiet woodland setting in the rural
area of Mitchell. A Bird watchers paradise. Each guest room has sliding glassdoors out to
adjoining balconies.

B&B Travel Tip: *You can stay in a B&B if you travel with your own trailer.
Many B&B's have ample room and a hook-up for that purpose, and they usually
welcome guests to join them in the house for breakfast.*

Mountain

(near Ottawa; see also Winchester, Brinston, Merrickville, North Gower, Kars)

Butler, Helen and Tom (Lilac Bower)
RR2, Mountain, Ontario   K0E 1S0   ☎ (613) 989-5347

Located 6 km East of Kemptville off Hwy 43.
$20S $35D $40F $10cots   🍽 Meals   ► 4A,1-2Ch
● Choice, homebaked   🏠 140-acres tree plantation, older, quiet   ■
1S,2D(upstairs)   ⊑ 1S,2D,P,cot   ⌐ Sh.w.g.   ★ Air,F,TV in guest room,LF, parking
Ⓦ Smoking

↔ Walking on quiet country roads, cross-country skiing,

⇔ village of Mountain, post office, fishing (Rideau River and St. Lawrence), KCAT College in Kemptville, Ottawa (Capital City)

🐾 There are 46000 pine trees planted on over 100 acres of land. Friendly old fashioned and homey hospitality. 2 cats are in residence.

Morrisburg

(near Cornwall; see also Cardinal, Finch, Iroquois, Brinston, Winchester)

Keyes, Glenn and Kay (Upper Canada B&B)   ✓ CC
Box 247, Morrisburg, Ontario   K0C 1X0   ☎ (613) 543-3253

From Hwy 401 take Exit 750 south (Hwy 31) and go to Lakeshore Dr. Turn right to
Mariatown and Cherry St. Look for second house on left.
$40D   ► 10
✚ May-Oct.31   ● Full, homebaked   🏠 Village, res., sub., view, patio, quiet   ■ 3D
(upstairs) ⊑ 3   ⌐ 1Sh.w.h., 1sh.w.g.   ★ TV,F   Ⓦ Smoking, drinking
↔ Lake St. Lawrence small park, Mariatown
⇔ Ingleside, Morrisburg center, Upper Canada Village and golf course, Prehistoric
World, Bird Sanctuary, Seaway Locks and Generating Station, Fort Wellington.

🐾 Quiet, comfortable home with a view of the Seaway System and Lake. Cooked
cereal made from freshly ground wheat a speciality.

Napanee

(near Kingston; see also Bath, Belleville)

Dupré, Lyle and Sharon (Beechwood Farm ✔ OVFA
RR6, Napanee, Ontario   K7R 3L1   ☎ (613) 354-5770/354-2234

From Hwy 401, take Hwy 41 north 1 km to Richmond Township Rd 3. Turn left and
travel 3 km to stop sign. Turn right and continue 1 km to farm with name on mailbox.
$25S $40D $6Child   Children welcome.   ▶ 6
● Full   🏠 260-acre farm, hist., isolated   ■ 3D   ⊷ 2Q,1D,2S, 1crib   ⬲ 1Private,
1sh.w.g.   ★ TV   ⚘ Smoking, drinking, pets   ⌇ Some French
↪ Cross-country skiing
⇔ Town of Napane, museums, Picton on Quinte's Isle, Sandbanks, Provincial Park

🐾 Large 1882-built brick home with pine floors and gingerbread exterior.

New Hamburg

*(near Straford; see also St. Clements, Millbank, Plattsville, Petersburg, St.Jacobs,
Kitchener/Waterloo, Cambridge)*

Kerr, Lucille (The White Birches) ✔ B&B
331 Bleams Rd. W., New Hamburg, Ontario   N0B 2G0   ☎ (519) 662-2390

Located in the village, just off Hwys 7 and 8, west of Kitchener.
$25S $40D   ▶ 5A
✪ Summer   ● Choice, homebaked   🏠 Res., bungalow, canopied canopied sundeck,
view   ■ 1S,2D   ⊷ T,D,Q   ⬲ 1Sh.w.g.   ⚘ Pets, smoking, drinking, children
under age 12
↪ Town center, shopping, restaurants, river bed for strolling
⇔ Stratford Festival, Kitchener, Mennonite area

🐾 Cheerful spacious home on quiet street in thriving picturesque village. There is an
unobstructed view of quiet meadows, bordering the meandering River Nith.

McMillan, Mrs. Ruby (Glenalby Farms) ✔ B&B,OFVA
RR1, New Hamburg, Ontario   N0B 2G0   ☎ (519) 625-8353

Situated 16.6 km east of Stratford. Phone for directions.
$35S $50-60D $10Add. person   ▣ Meals   ▶ 10A,4Ch
● Full, homebaked   🏠 Dairy farm, hist.   ■ 4D,F   ⊷ T,D,P,R   ⬲ 2Sh.w.g
★ TV,F, facilities for the disabled   ⚘ Pets, restricted smoking
↪ Conservation area with lake and picnic grounds, woodland trails
⇔ Stratford Festival, Mennonite country, antique auctions and shopping

🐾 Picturesque 5th Generation dairy farm surrounded by hills and woods. Hot cider
served around fieldstone fireplace. Hosts keep registered Lassie Collies and offer
handmade quilts, jams and homemade bread for sale. Picnic lunches packed. There are
lots of pets.

Ziegler, Barry and Anne (The Station House)   ✓ SOCVA B&B
216 Steinman Street, New Hamburg, Ontario   N0B 2G0   ☎ (519) 662-2957

Phone for directions.
$35S $40D $5Child $15Add.person   ► 6
●Cont.   🏠Village, hist., open sunporch   ■3D (upstairs) ⊷2D,1Q,1P ⌐2Sh.w.g.
★Air, separate entrance, ample off-street parking   🖐Restricted smoking, pets
↪ The Waterlot Restaurant
⇔ Charming City of Stratford and Shakespearean Festival, Kitchener- Waterloo famous
farmers' markets

☞ Beautiful Victorian home, full of charm and character with extensive use of fine
natural woodwork, stained glass windows and impressive foyer with winding stairs.

Newmarket
(near Toronto; see also Bradford, Kleinburg, Uxbridge)

Lovell, Phyllis and Jack (Glen Gullach)
RR3, Newmarket, Ontario   L3Y 4W1   ☎ (416) 836-6328

Take Hwy 401 north to Aurora Rd. Turn East to 1st lights (Woodbine), then turn north.
Go 2km and turn east at St.Johns sideroad, then 1.5km east to entrance (sign). - or -
Take Hwy 11 (Yonge St) south to Aurora. At Wellington St (lights) turn east. Continue
over Hwy 404 to Woodbine Ave, turn north and proceed as above.
$25S $35D $5-15Child   🍽 Meals   ► 4
● Choice, homebaked   🏠 Rural, acreage, view, elevated deck, quiet, isolated
■2S,1D(main and upper floor) ⊷ 2S,1D ⌐ 2Sh.w.h. ★ TV,F,LF, parking with
power hook-up ♥
↪ Hiking/cross-country skiing on large property with stream and reforestation area
⇔ Direct link on Hwy 404 to downtown Toronto, Lake Simcoe

☞ House was designed by hosts and set in own grounds with a view across the fields to
the south. Weather permitting, meals are served on deck. There is a dog in the house.

Newcastle
(near Oshawa; see also Bowmanville, Millbrook)

Allin, Bob and Esther   ✓ Durham B&B
RR2, Newcastle, Ontario   L0A 1H0   ☎ (416) 987-4487

Go 1.5 km north of Newcastle village to 3rd concession, then follow sign which says
"Clarks 3rd Concession West". Located 1.5 km west of Hwy 115.
$25S $40D $6Child $6Add.person   ► 4
● Full, homebaked   🏠 Rural, bungalow, 9-acres, view, quiet ■ 2D
⊷2S,1D,cot ⌐ Sh.w.g. ★ TV,F, parking 🖐 Smoking, drinking
↪ Walk along Wilmot Creek, bird watching
⇔ Lake Ontario, cross-country and downhill skiing areas, museums, Toronto Zoo,
antique shops, Oshawa GM Canada, Peterborough

☞ Home is situated on a well-treed lawn on a quiety country road bordering on Wilmot
Creek. Hosts are enthusiastic bird-watchers and look after several bird feeders.

Beaucage, Mrs.R.L. (Beau Villa Bed & Breakfast)
General Delivery, Newcastle, Ontario   ☎ (416) 885 7367

Located on Hwy 2 East. Call for directions.
$60D $10Child $15Add.person   ► 6
● Cont.   ♠ Rural, res, acreage, patio, quiet   ■ 2D (upstairs)   ⊢ T   ⌐ Private,
sauna   ★ F, parking   ⊛ Smoking, pets, children min. age 10   ⤳ German
⇔ Metropolitan Tornto, Port Carling, Port of Newcastle, Lake Ontario

☞ Home is situated on 5 acres of land and surrounded by beautiful landscaped garden. There is a dog in the house.

Niagara Falls

(see also Niagara-on-the-Lake, St.Catharines, Welland, Beamsville, Vineland, Virgil

Burke, Carolyn and Gary (Park Place B&B)   ✔ B&B
4851 River Rd., Niagara Falls, Ontario   L2E 3G4   ☎ (416) 358-0279

Take QEW to Rainbow Bridge and continue to Clifton Hill. Turn left and go to River Rd, left again and 1.9 km to house on corner of Ellis St (entrance on Ellis St).
$40S $50D $10Child $15Add.person   ► 8A,2Ch
✚ Summer (other by special arrangement)   ● Full,homebaked   ♠ Downtown, res.,
hist., view, patio   ■ 3D,1Ste (upstairs)   ⊢ S,T,D   ⌐ 1Private, 1sh.w.g.   ★ F,
parking, cater to special diets   ♥   ⊛ Smoking

↩ Niagara Falls, shops, restaurants and entertainment, Maid of the Mist cruise, Greenhouse, many churches, Victoria Park and Gardens, railway station
⇔ Niagara on the Lake and Shaw Festival Theatre, Art Park (Lewiston NY), Fort Erie, Welland Canal and Locks, Outlet Mall at Niagara Falls NY

☞ 103 year old Queen Ann Style Victorian home (designated historic) located on the Niagara Parkway. Everyone in the host family tries to make guests feel comfortable. There is a dog in the house.

B&B Travel Tip: *When travelling B&B, you get more than just a bed to sleep, because you are making a personal contact in a strange place.*

Gardiner, Stan and Marg (Gretna Green   ⌐ B&B
5077 River Rd., Niagara Falls, Ontario   L2E 3G7   ☎ (416) 357-2081

From QEW take Hwy 420 into Niagara Falls and turn left on Stanley St. At 2nd set of
traffic lights turn right onto Morrison St, go to end, turn right onto River Rd.
$40S $50D $5Child $10Add.person (Winter rates available)   ► 8A,2Ch
●Full 🏠Res., older, view, quiet ■3D,2F(upstairs) ╸2S,4D,1R ⌐4Ensuite
★Air, TVin guest room, separate entrance, parking, bicycle rental   🖐Pets
↪ Falls, Niagara Gorge
⇔ Skylon Tower, Rose Gardens and Floral Clock, Imax Theatre, Marineland, Shaw
Festival at Niagara-on-the-Lake, Fort Erie Race Track

☛ Scottish hosts welcome visitors to their home with a view of the Niagara Gorge.

Moncur, Vi and John (Glen Mhor House)   ⌐ B&B
5381 River Rd., Niagara Falls, Ontario   L2E 3H1   ☎ (416) 354-2600

Phone or write for a map and directions.
$35-40S $52-65D $10-15Add
● Full, homebaked   🏠 Downtown, res., older, view, patio   ■ 1S,3D (main and
upper floor)   ╸ 1S,3D, 3daybeds   ⌐ 1Private, 1Sh.w.g.   ★ Air, separate
entrance, ample parking   🖐 Children, pets
↪ Horseshoe Falls, tourist attractions & shops, restaurants, business area
⇔ Quaint old-world town of Niagara-on-the-Lake, Shaw Festival Theatre, Welland ship
canal and locks, Niagara Parks Commission (most beautiful gardens, parks and
Horticultural Center)

☛ Older Canadian home surrounded by beautiful flower garden overlooking the
Niagara River Gorge and situated on a street with carefully restored houses. Ideal
location for visitors travelling without cars. Tours are arranged for pick-up at home.

Niagara-on-the-Lake
(see also Niagara Falls, Welland, St.Catharines, Vineland, Virgil)

Coakeley, Claire and Michael (Rose Corner)   ⌐ CC
760 Charlotte St., Box 1048, Niagara-on-the-Lake, Ontario   L0S 1J0   ☎ (416) 468-5361

Take QEW and Hwy 55 to N-o-t-L, turn right on John St and right on Charlotte St.
Look for house on corner facing Promenade.
$55S $65D $10Child $10Add. person   ► 4A,2Ch
✪ Summer   ● Full, homebaked   🏠 Split-level, patio, quiet   ■ 2D (upstairs)   ╸
2T,1D,1R   ⌐ 1Private   ★ Air,F, parking, coffee and tea making in guest rooms   🖐
Smoking, pets, children min. age 12   ∾ French
↪ Military Museum
⇔ Shaw Festival Theatres, historic downtown N-o-t-L, Lake Ontario, Fort George,
wineries (tasting tours), scenic Parkway to the Falls, Welland Canal

☛ Elegant accommodation in new home furnished with charming antiques with
spacious and comfortable guest rooms. Generous breakfast is served either in the garden
or D-room (cont.breakfast in guest room if preferred). There are 2 dogs.

Hiebert, Otto and Marlene   ⌐ NOTL B&B
Box 1371,275 John St., Niagara-on-the-Lake, Ontario   L0S 1J0   ☎ (416) 468-3687

Phone for directions and reservation.
$50S $55D $5Child $15Add. person   ► 6A,4Ch
● Full, homebaked   ♠ Village, bi-level, patio, quiet   ■ 3D   ⊣ T,Q, sofabed,
playpen   ⌐ 1Sh.w.g., 1 sh.w.h.   ★ Air, F,TV in guest 1 guest room, parking   ♥
⊛ Smoking, drinking, pets
↔ Shaw Festival Theatre, quaint village centre, Lake Ontario
⇔ Niagara Falls, Buffalo U.S.A.

☛ Browse through the many craft and boutique shops or relax at the waterfront
viewing the many sailboats drifting down the Niagara River.

James, Ursula and Cliff (Butler's Grove)   ⌐ CC
30 Colonel Butler Cres., Box 584, Niagara-on-the-Lake, Ont.   L0S 1J0   ☎ (416) 468-5247

From QEW, take Hwy 55 to NOTL, turn left onto Lakeshore at Mary St stoplight, turn
left onto Garrison Village Drive and left immediately onto Colonel Butler Cres.
$39S $44-59D $9Add.person   ► 4A,2Ch
● Generous Cont., homebaked   ♠ Res., swimming pool, patio, quiet   ■ 2D,1Ste
(upstairs)   ⊣ 4T,1Q,1P   ⌐ 1Private, 1sh.w.g.   ★ Air, parking, separate entrance
⊛ Smoking, pets, children min. age 8   ～ German, Dutch, some French

↔ Two Mile Creek, jogging, walking,
Colonel John Butler resting place in a
pleasant grove

⇔ Shaw Festival Theatre, old town,
shops and restaurants, historical sites,
Lake Ontario

☛ Comfortable, modern home set in
a large garden backing on the
conservation area of Two Mile Creek
and located in Garrison Village, a quiet
area adjacent to the old town.

       B&B Travel Tip: *All hosts are very obliging to special needs, but as a guest
you must always remember that these extras are usually given by the hosts out of
friendliness and a desire to please.*

Jones, Louise and Trevor (Tudor Rose)   ✔ CC
14719 Niagara River Parkway, Niagara-on-the-Lake, Ontario L0S 1J0 ☎ (416) 262-5006

Take QEW to Hwy 405, then follow the sign to Niagara River Parkway. Turn left.
Located between Queenston and Niagara-on-the-Lake.
$60S $75D $25Add.person   ► 8
✠April-Oct. ●Full, homebaked ⌂Rural, hist., view, riverfront, patio, quiet ■4D
(upstairs) ⊢2T,3D,2R ⌐2Ensuite, 1shw.g. ★F, parking ⊛Smoking, pets
↝ Laura Secord Homestead in Queenston Village, scenic paths along the river
⇔ Shaw Festival (Niagara-on-the-Lake), Niagara Falls, Art Park in Lewiston, wineries
(tours), fine dining, golfing, antiques, crafts and gift shops

☞ Charming turn-of-the-century home situated on the Niagara River bank and
furnished with antiques. Congenial hosts are well informed about the local area.

King, Helen and Mike (The King's Way)   ✔ B&B
308 Nassau St, Box 684, Niagara-on-the-Lake, Ontario L0S 1J0   ☎ (416) 468-5478

From QEW take the exit for N-O-T-L (Hwy 55) and follow through Virgil to Williams
Street. Turn left, go 2 blocks to Nassau Street, turn right.
$55-75D - $10Child $15Add.person   (weekend rates available)   ► 6A,2A
● Full ⌂ Res, acreage, swimming pool, patio, quiet ■ 3D (upstairs)
⊢1S,3Q,1cot ⌐2Private, 1shw.g.   ★ Air,F, parking, guest room balconies, guest
parlor ⊛Restricted smoking, pets
↝ Shaw Festival Theatres, golf course, shopping, restaurants
⇔ Art Park (Lewiston), US border, Fort Erie, Lake Ontario, hiking, cross-country
skiing, Niagara Escarpment, Niagara District Airport

☞ Young and hospitable host family in spacious modern home located on a quiet street
minutes from downtown. Guests are encouraged to use the outside pool and deck area.

Knapp, Mrs. Lynda Kay   ✔ CC
390 Simcoe St., Niagara-on-the-Lake, Ontario L0S 1J0   ☎ (416) 468-3935

Simcoe Street runs off Queen Street.
$45S $55D $5Add.person   ►) 6
● Cont ⌂ Res, shaded ■ 2 ⊢ 2T,1D,1cot ⌐ 2Private   Parking, private
entrance ♥ ⊛ Pets, smoking ∿ some German
↝ Shaw Festival Theatres, downtown Niagara-on-the-Lake, Fort George

☞ New home and friendly atmosphere in historic town. Children welcome.

Koppert, Mrs. Helene   ✔ NOTL B&B
RR2, Hwy 55, 1301 Niag.Stone Rd., Niagara-on-the-Lake, Ontario L0S ☎(416) 468-7039

From QEW take Exit 55 and drive 10 km east to fifth house on right past "Virgil" sign.
Look for blue house with cream shutters. From downtown Niagara-on-the-Lake, go west
on Hwy 55 past Virgil intersection.
$45D $5Child   ► 6A,2Ch
●Full, homebaked ⌂Rural ■D ⊢T,D ⌐Sh.w.h. ★TV,Air ∿German, Polish
↝ Village of Virgil
⇔ Niagara-on-the-Lake, Niagara Falls, St.Catharines, Lake Ontario

Moyer, Marybeth and Matt (House on the River)   ✓ CC
14773 Niagara River Parkway, Niagara-on-the-Lake, Ontario   L0S 1J0 ☎ (416) 262-4597

Located 1 km north of the village of Queenston on the Niagara River Parkway.
$65-70S $70-75D $100Ste $5Child $15Add.person   ► 4A,2CH
● Choice, homebaked   ♠ Rural, hist., view, patio, quiet, riverside   ■ 2D,1Ste,1F
⊷2D,1R   ⌐ 1Ensuite, 1sh.w.g.,1sh.w.h.   ♠ Air,F,TV,LF, parking   ⓌSmoking,
pets, children min. age 10
↪ Extensive recreational trail from Lake Erie to Lake Ontario (walk, bike, cross-country
ski), historic Village of Queenston
⇔ Shaw Festival Theatres, marina, River Cruise, golfing, museums, Adam Beck Power
Plant, historic forts, Niagara wineries, Welland ship canal, Art Park (Lewiston, NY),
boutique shopping, fine dining
☞ House is situated 300 ft from the Niagara River behind the stone wall. Breakfast is
served on the patio overlooking the river. Enjoy the beautiful views by day or night.

Padovani, Karen and Enzo (Kingsborough House)   ✓ CC
86 Prideaux St., Box 1206, Niagara-on-the-Lake, Ontario   L0S 1J0   ☎ (416) 468-7605

From QEW, take Hwy 55 Exit to Niagara-on-the-Lake. Upon reaching the golf course,
turn right and then first left. Located between Regent and Victoria Streets.
$55-60S $60-65D   ► 6A
● Full, homebaked   ♠ Downtown, res., older, quiet, veranda   ■ 3D (upstairs)
⊷ 2T,1K,1Q   ⌐ Sh.w.g., vanity in guest rooms   ★ Air,F, parking, guest parlour,
fridge for guests   Ⓦ Smoking, children, pets
↪ Main Street shopping and restaurants, Shaw Festival Theatre, lake and river
⇔ Niagara Wineries (tasting tours), Welland Canal, Niagara Falls, Queenston Heights
☞ Located in the heart of historic Niagara-on-the-Lake. Sit and relax in the popular
front parlour between sightseeing and the theatre performance.

Shah, Brenda and Inder (Waverley)   ✓ CC
471 Queenston Rd., RR4, Niagara-on-the-Lake, Ontario   L0S 1J0   ☎ (416) 684-0949

From Hwy 55 turn left at Reg. Rd 81. Go to Townline Rd, turn left and look for house on
right side. From Niagara Falls take Hwy 38 and then as above.
$50D $5Child $10Add.person   ► 8
● Full   ♠Rural, acreage, view, patio, quiet, swimming pool   ■ 2D   ⊷4T,2Q, crib
⌐ 2Sh.w.g.   ★ Air,TV, games room, parking   Ⓦ Pets
⇔ Niagara-on-the-Lake towne, Shaw Festival Theatres, Niagara Falls, Art Park New
York, Niagara Wineries (tours)
☞ Comfortable and cozy rural home in quiet and relaxing surroundings with view of
Niagara Escarpment. Reservations pleae.

Shankula, Mary (Amberlea)   ⌐ NOTL B&B
285 John St., Box 1724, NOTL, Ontario L0S 1J0   ☎ (416) 468-3749

From QEW, take Hwy 55 to NOTL. Upon entering town, turn left at first cross street
(John St) and look for 4th house on right.
$45S $50-65D   ► 6
● Full   ♠ Downtown, raised bungalow, patio, treed setting, quiet   ■ 2D (lower
level)   ⊷ 4T,1K   ⏲ 2   ★ Air,F, separate entrance, TV in one guest room, parking
⊛Smoking, pets, children min. age 13

↦ Unique shops, Shaw Festival and
Courthouse Theatres, historic sites of
Old Town, Lake Ontario picnic areas,
walking, biking, Yacht Basin

⇔ Niagara Falls, Welland Canal, Fort
Erie Race Track, Art Park (NY),
Hamilton

☞ Located in a quiet, park-like
residential area. Hostess is an
ccomplished artist and Stained Glass
Artisan, whose works are on view
throughout the home. There is a cat in
the house

Stamp, Marjorie and Bill   ⌐ CC
17 Coach Drive, Niagara-on-the-Lake, Ontario L0S 1J0   ☎ (416) 468-4785

From QEW take Hwy 55 to N-O-T-L. Turn right onto John St, cross over King St and
turn right onto Charlotte St. Then turn left into the Promenade and right into driveway.
$50S $60D $10Child $15Add.person   ► 4A,1Ch
● Full (English)   ♠ Res, quiet   ■ 2D (upstairs)   ⊷ 2T,1R,1Q   ⏲ Sh.w.g.   ★
Air, plenty of parking, bicycles for guests   ⊛ Smoking, pets, children min. age 10
⇔ Niagara Falls, Queenston, Lewiston Art Park, golfing, boating, theatres, wineries,
historic sites

☞ New home with extra large rooms furnished beautifully. If arriving by boat
transportation to and from the marina is available. Hosts will make dinner reservation
for guests with advance notice.

B&B Travel Tip: *You can stay in a B&B when attending a wedding in
another town. Many churches have lists of B&B's located nearby.*

Taylor, Bert (Taylor House) ✔ CC
135 King St., Box 1087, Niagara-on-the-Lake, Ontario L0S 1J0   ☎ (416) 468-7256

Take Hwy 55 to end. Turn right on Queen St and proceed to King St (4-way stop). Turn
left to 2nd house. - or - Take Niagara River Parkway north to King St. Turn right.
$45S $55D   ► 4A
● Choice 🏠 Res. older ■ 2D (upstairs) ⇥ 2T,1D ⌐ Sh.w.g. ★ Air, TV,
parking ✋ Children
↔ Shaw Festival/Courthouse/Royal George theatres, historical Fort George
⇔ Queenston Heights Park (Brock Monument), Niagara Park Horticulture School and
Gardens, Niagara Glen, River Whirlpool, Niagara Falls, Welland Canal Viewing Site

☞ 1920 vintage house with old fashioned front porch, ideal for just relaxing. Host is a
retired Public Servant from Canada Post.

Taylor, Cec and Anne Forest (Varey-Hendrie House) ✔ CC
105 Johnson St. Box 1438, Niagara-on-the-Lake, Ontario L0S 1J0   ☎ (416) 468-3154

From QEW take Hwy 55 to Queen St (end of road). Turn right and proceed 3 blocks to
Victoria Street. Turn right to Johnson. Look for house on corner.
$60S   70-85D   ► 4
● Full, homebaked 🏠 Downtown, hist., patio, quiet ■ 2S,2D (main and upper
level) ⇥ 4T,1D,1Q ⌐ 2Private, 1sh.w.g. ★ 2F, separate entrance, parking
✋Smoking, pets
↔ Shaw Festival theatres, Lake Ontario and Niagara River, shopping, historic Fort
George, many restaurants
⇔ Niagara Falls, Queenston Heights, St. Catharines, wineries with tours, golfing

☞ 1837-built house is set in a quiet tree-lined street and surrounded by English-style
garden with beautifully furnished rooms. One guest room has a four-poster bed and
crewel-work curtains. There is a cat in residence.

Theriault, Mark & Heather (The Therilynne) ✔ CC
312 Orchard Dr., Box 1572, Niagara-on-the-Lake, Ontario L0S 1J0   ☎ (416) 468-7541

Take QEW Niagara to Hwy 55. Turn left on Johnson, left on Palatine and then right.
$50S $75D   ► 4A
✚ Summer ● Full 🏠 Res., split-level, patio, quiet ■ 2D (main floor) ⇥ 2D
⌐ 1Sh.w.g. ★ TV, parking ✋ Children, pets ⌇ French
↔ Shaw Festival Theatre, downtown Queen Street, restaurants and fine dining
⇔ Niagara Falls (Canadian and US side), St. Catharines, Welland Canal

☞ Comfortable home in quiet residential area of historical and picturesque town.
Congenial hosts invite guests for a daily "Happy Hour".

Wiens, Arnold ✓ NOTL B&B
189 William St., Niagara-on-the-Lake, Ontario L0S 1J0 ☎ (416) 468-2091

From St. Catharines, take Hwy 55 into Niagara-on-the-Lake. Turn right on first street
after stoplight.
$30S $35-40D $50-60F ► 6-8
● Full 🏠 Res., porch, quiet ■ 3D ⊷ S,D,T,K ⚲ 1Private, 1sh.w.g.
★ Air,TV,KF,LF, separate entrance, parking. table tennis, badminton ⚓ Restricted
smoking, pets ∾ German, Spanish
↪ Shaw Festival Theatres, Lake Ontario, marina, downtown quaint village
⇔ Niagara Falls, Marineland, Inniskillin Winery, Welland Canal

Witt, Dietlinde CC
341 Dorchester St., Niagara-on-the-Lake, Ontario L0S 1J0 ☎ (416) 468-3989

From QEW take Exit 38 to Niagara Stone Rd, then proceed to Centre St. Turn north to
Dorchester and then right.
$30S $40D $2.50Child $5Add.person (Off Season rates available) ► 6
● Full (German) - 🏠 Res., acreage, patio, quiet ■ 2D ⊷ 4T ⚲ Sh.w.g.
★Air,TV,KF,LF, private parking ♥ ⚓ Smoking ∾ German
↪ Shaw Festival Theatres, Lake Ontario, Harbour, Fort George, Main Street
⇔ Marineland, Horticulture School, Flower clock, Welland Canal, whirlpool

☞ Relax in quiet and shady garden.

North Augusta
(near Brockville: see also Frankville, Merrickville, Prescott)

Haupt, Eileen and Caspar (Gosford Place) ✓ CC
RR1, North Augusta, Ontario K0G 1R0 ☎ (613) 926-2164

From Hwy 401 take Exit 698 (North Augusta Rd) at Brockville and proceed 13 km north
on Rt 6 to Gosford Rd. Turn right to house on right side.
$50S $55D ► 8
✪ Not at Christmas time ● Full, homebaked 🏠 Rural, older, acreage, view, patio,
swimming pool, quiet, isolated ■ 4D,1Ste,2F (upstairs) (some in log cabin guest
house) ⊷ 2T,3D,2R ⚲ 3Private, 1sh.w.g.,1Ensuite ★ Air,F,TV in guest room,
seprarate entrance, parking ⚓ Smoking, pets, children min. age 12 ∾ French
↪ Cross-country skiing/jogging/walking/hiking on country roads, watch maple syrup
being made, church suppers, neighboring Asparagus and Honey Farm
⇔ 100 Islands, Gananoque, Upper Canada Village, auctions, cheese factories, antique
dealers, golfing, fine dining, Ottawa, Kingston

☞ Rambling 150 year-old English country home with plenty of privacy for guests and
situated in secluded quiet country setting with English gardens. Hosts are seasoned
travellers and cross-country trail blazers. There are two friendly dogs in residence.

North Gower
(near Ottawa; see also Kars, Mountain, Winchester, Carleton Place, Almonte)

McDonald, Alfred and Madeleine (Carsonby Manor) ⮕ CC
RR3, North Gower, Ontario K0A 2T0 ☎ (613) 489-3219

From Hwy 401 take Hwy 16 turn off at "Carsonby old Hwy 16".
$25S $35D $8Child $10Add.person ► 5
● Choice   ⌂ Village, acreage, quiet   1S,2D (upstairs)   ⇥ 1S,2D   ⌐ Sh.w.g.
★F,TV in guest room, separate entrance, parking   ⑮ Smoking, pets   ⦙⦙ French
↔ Manderley Golf Course, cross-country skiing
⇔ Stittsville flea market, village of Manotick, Ottawa (Nation's Capital)

🖝 Warm and cozy hospitality in B&B in charming pastoral setting. Enjoy fresh
products from the garden. There is a dog in the house.

North Bay
(see Palgrave: Country and Ski Host; see also Mattawa, Temagami)

Burak, Bill and Flo ⮕ CC
653 Lakeshore Dr., North Bay, Ontario P1A 2G1 ☎ (705) 472-4734

Located near Ramada Inn on Lakeshore Drive (formerly Hwy 11B). Phone for directions.
$30-35S $40-50D   (Off-season rates available)   ▣ Meals ► 6A
● Choice   ⌂ Downtown, view, lakefront, patio   ■ 3D   ⇥ T,Q   ⌐ 3Sh.w.g.
★ F,TV in guest room, parking   ⑮ Moderate drinking, children, pets   ⦙⦙ French,
Ukrainian
↔ Swimming on own beach (Lake Nippissing), downtown commercial area, churches
⇔ Sturgeon Falls

🖝 Friendly hospitality in new home. Hosts enjoy playing bridge with guests.

Oliphant
(near Owen Sound; see also Wiarton, Lion's Head, Southampton)

Poste, Doug and Clare (The Oliphant Poste) ⮕ Grey Bruce B&B
Oliphant, Ontario N0H 2T0 ☎ (519) 534-0557

Phone for directions.
$35S $40D $10Child $15Add.person ► 6
● Full   ⌂ Rural, ranch-style, 27-acres, swimming pool, patio, quiet
■2D,1Ste   ⇥1Q,2D,2P   ⌐1ensuite,1sh.w.g.   ★Air,F,TV,   ⑮Pets,child min. age 8
↔ Lake Huron beaches, swimming boating
⇔ Tobermory ferry to Manitoulin Islands, Owen Sound, Georgian Bay beaches/coves

🖝 Cozy ranch-style house situated in the beautiful Bruce Penninsula. (home for the
retired hosts since childhood). Both are very knowledgeable and proud about the area
and enjoy sharing their enthusiasm with their guests.

Oakville

(near Toronto; see also Milton, Burlington, Georgetown)

Odenbach, Alan and Marg ⌐ Burl B&B
2527 Dundas Hwy West, Oakville, Ontario L0P 1L0 ☎ (416) 825-4074

From Hwy 401 take Exit 320 south all the way to corner of Hwy 5 (Dundas Ave). House is situated on left (north) corner lot. From QEW take Exit 111 north to Hwy 5.
$25S $40D ► 4A
● Full, homebaked   ♠ Rural, hist., small acreage, patio   ■ 2D (upstairs)   ⌐ 2D
⥌ 1Sh.w.g.   ★ Ceiling fans, separate entrance, TV in guest sitting room and balcony, parking   ⊕ Smoking, children, pets

↔ Glen Abbey Golf Course, quaint town of Oakville, Oakville Mall, popular Bronte Harbourfront (fine dining, shops and active marina), Bronte Creek Prov. Park (cross-country skiing, swimming, picnics), downtown Burlington, Botanical Gardens, Bruce Trail hiking, Toronto International Airport.

☞ Spacious, comfortable turn-of-the-Century home beautifully decorated and furnished with antiques. Hosts have a small hobby antique shop on the premises.

Orillia

(see also Barrie, Gravenhurst, Oro Stn, Waubaushene, Victoria Harbour, Midland)

Laity, Eleanor (Sim-View) ⌐ Orillia B&B,FOBBA
RR2, Lakeshore Rd., Hawkestone, Orillia, Ont L0L 1T0 ☎ (705) 487-7191

Take Hwy 11 north from Barrie for 25 km, turn right at Oro Line 9, continue towards Lake (1.6 km) and take first sharp right turn on Lakeshore Rd to first mail box on left.
$30S $39D $8Add. person ► 4A,2Ch
● Full   ♠ Rural, res., lakefront, sundeck, view, quiet   ■ 2D   ⌐ 4T
⥌ 1Private, 1sh.w.h.   ★ TV,F   ⌇ Some French
↔ Safe, clean, sandy beach, park, swimming, boating, ice fishing, bicycling, hiking
↔ Three ski resorts, boat cruises, theatres, Stephen Leacock Home (Orillia), Muskoka area and Ste. Marie-Among-the-Hurons Heritage site, Lake Couchiching.

☞ Very private, large modern home has a pleasant country atmosphere, yet is located close to Orillia and Barrie. Come and listen to the quiet. There is a small dog who loves company. Hostess is Co-ordinator for Orillia B&B.

Moreland, Bill and Anna (Henmore Acres)   ⁓ Orillia B&B
RR1, Orillia, Ontario L3V 6H1   ☎ (705) 325-1261

Take Hwy 11 north to Hwy 12 west. Follow Prov. Park signs and turn left off Hwy 12.
Go to top of hill (SRd 5/6), turn right. Cross Oro-Orillia Townline to house on right.
$35S $35D   ●$3.50Each(full) $5Crib/Cot   🍽 Meals   ► 6A,2Ch
● Cont.   🏠 46-acre farm, view   ■ 2D (upstairs)   ⊢ 2D,1K, cot, crib
⌐1Sh.w.g.   ★ TV,F, separate entrance   Ⓦ Smoking, drinking, pets
↔ Langman Bird Sanctuary, Bass Lake, trout pond, maple bush, winter sports
⇔ Bass Lake Prov. Park, Couchiching Park and Lake, Ste. Marie-Among- the-Hurons

☛ Host is a retired minister and chaplain. Cozy remodelled farm home with all the
charm and nostalgia of days gone by, has a huge eat-in kitchen with full wall sized
fireplace. There is a small friendly Pug dog called "Mr.Jiggs" who loves to welcome
guests. Enjoy the beautiful fall colour spectacle all around.

Peterson, Lois and Erik (Villa Costa)   ⁓ B$B
168 Heyden Ave., RR1, Orillia, Ontario L3V 6H1   ☎ (705) 326-0725

Take Hwy 400 north towards Orillia. From Hwy 11 north, take second turn-off (No 12
By Pass) east to Gill St. Turn right to Victoria Cres and right onto Heyden Ave.
$45S $50-55D   ► 4
■ 2 (upstairs)   ⊢ 2T,1D   ⌐ 1Sh.w.g., 1private   ★ F,TV in guest room, parking,
guest room balcony   Ⓦ Children, pets, restricted smoking
↔ Waterfront city Park (tennis, swimming, walking), lovely old main street
⇔ Horse Shoe Valley Ski Resort, Orillia opera house, S.M.S. Segwin Steam Boat
(cruises), beautiful marina facilities for boaters

☛ Uniquely designed new house with slightly Spanish flair and tastefully decorated
located in a lovely setting of mature maple trees right on the water's edge and located in
the heart of this popular tourist region.

Orillia and District Bed and Breakfast
c/o E. Laity, RR2, Lakeshore Rd, Hawkestone, Orillia, Ont L0L 1T0   ☎ (705) 487-7191
(Mrs. Eleanor Laity, Co-ordinator)
Orillia B&B has a listing of approximately 10 host homes located in Orillia and
surrounding area, including Craighurst, Coldwater, Hawkestone. Many of the guest
homes are situated by the water, while some are conveniently located in town. Most are
suitable for a weekend away from Toronto. For information call the above.

> **B&B Travel Tip:** *As a B&B guest you have all the privacy you want in your
> own room. Hosts take the cue from you - if you do not want to socialize, they will
> understand.*

Oro Station
(near Barriw and Orillia)

Bedford, Doug and Betty (Betty's Bed & Breakfast)
RR1, Oro Station, Ontario L0L 2E0   ☎ (705) 487-2706

From Barrie travel 18 km on Hwy 11. Turn right on Simcoe County Rd 27 and (4 km) to Lakeshore Rd, turn right.
$28S $38D   ◙ Meals   ►4
● Full   ♠ Rural, village, older, view, lakedront   ■ 2D (upstairs)   ⊷ 2D
⌐1Sh.w.g.   ★ TV, parking   ⦿ Smoking, pets   ⋘ limited French
↔ Lake Simcoe, park with playground equipment, marina, icefishing, hut rentals
⇔ Martyr's Shrine, Midland, Ski facilities, Horseshoe Valley and Moonstone), Georgian Bay beaches, cross-country skiing, Toronto

Orono
(near Toronto; see also Newcastle, Bowmanville, Millbrook)

Hebditch, Mr. & Mrs. D (The Rhoden House)
RR1, Orono, Ontario L0B 1M0   ☎ (416) 983-5196

Located on the west side of Hwy 35/115. Take Main St Orono turn-off and circle back onto Hwy 35/115 south. Located south of Cango Gas Station.
$25S $40D $15Child(age 10-16)   ◙ Meals   ► 6A,2Ch
● Full   ♠ Rural, hist., acreage, greenhouse conservatory   ■ 1S,3D (upstairs)
⊷ 1S,2T,1D,1Q, cot   ⌐2Sh.w.g.   ★ TV, parking   ⦿ Smoking, drinking
⇔ Mossport Park (car racing), Oshawa Ski Club, Bowmanville Zoo, Exotic Cat World

☞ Former British hosts. Century brick farmhouse recaptures the charm of yesterday and is furnished with antiques and Colonial furniture. There are 2 cockotiels and a dog.

Orton
(near Guelph; see also Belwood, Elora, Acton)

Tyler, Barry, Carol and Family (Amblewood Farm)   ↙ OFV
RR1, Orton, Ontario L0N 1N0   ☎ (519) 855-4705

Located 6 km north of Ospringe (N/E of County Rd 22 and 2nd Line of Erin Township).
$35S $30D   ◙ Meals   ►4-6
● Full, homebaked   ♠ 82-acres working farm, hist., hilltop view, quiet   ■ 1F (upstairs)   ⊷ 2S,2D,1Q,1P, crib   ⌐2Sh.w.g.   ★ TV,LF,6F, facilities for the handicapped   ⦿ Smoking, drinking, pets
↔ Farm activities, horse trails, walks, cross-country skiing, fishing
⇔ Fergus, Elora, Salem, Elmira, Guelph, museums, galleries, flea- markets and auctions, unique cultural events

☞ 1820 built log home of unique structure has been painstakingly restored by Erin Township's craftsmen, neighbours, friends and host family. Very spacious guest room can be arranged into flexible sections (suitable for one party).

Ottawa

(see also Almonte, Braeside, Carleton Place, Renfrew, North Gower, Kars, Winchester, Mountain; see also Prov. Quebec: Ouyon)

Brunet, Luce and Lawrence Mason (Marlborough House)   ✔ Ott.B&B
80 Marlborough Ave., Ottawa, Ontario   K1N 8E9   ☎ (613) 238-6906

Take Nicholas Street Exit off Hwy 417 (Queensway) to Laurier Ave East. Turn right and
then right again on Malborough Ave.
$40-50S $44-54D   ► 8
●Full, homebaked   ♠Downtown, res, patio, quiet   ■4D (ustairs)   ⊷2T,2D,1Q
⊓1Sh.w.h., 1sh.w.g   ★F,TV   ⓦRestricted smoking, pets, children min. age 12
⋙French
↪ Wayward Market, National Art Centre, Museum of Civilization, Canadian Mint
⇔ Gatineau Park, Kingsmere (McKenzie King Estate), Lanark

🐾 Tastefully restored Queen Ann-style home in the exclusive downtown area of Sandy
Hill with guest rooms individually decorated to compliment a particular performing art
form (music, dance, theatre, cinema). Hosts' membership tickets to the Ottawa Film
Society are often available for guests during season.

Bycroft, John and Beth (Appletreewick)   ✔ CC
58 Marlborough Ave., Ottawa, Ontario   K1N 8E9   ☎(613) 237-2753

Located 1.6 km from Hwy 417 via Nicholas St exit and off Laurie East in the Sandy Hill
area. Turn right onto Marlborough Ave from Laurie East..
$30S $40D $10Child $10Add. person   ► 11A,5Ch
●Choice, homebaked   ♠ Downtown, res, hist., quiet   ■ 1D,1Ste,2F (main and upper
floor)   ⊷ 3T,1D,3Q,1R, cot   ⊓ 1Ensuite,1sh.w.h.,1sh.w.g.   ★ Air,F,TV in 3 guest
rooms, separate entrance   ⓦ Restricted smoking   ⋙ some French
↪ National Art Gallery, boat tours on Ottawa River/Rideau Canal, Parliament
Buildings, museums of Science and Technology, Byway Market area and restaurants,
Embassies
⇔ Gatineau Park, skiing, hiking, swimming, William Lyon MacKenzie King Estate

🐾 80-year old very relaxed and comfortable home is named after a small village in
Yorkshire Dales, England, the ancestral home of the Bycroft Clan and is a restored
classic residence in Sandy Hill, an area of Ottawa boasting tree-lined streets, a peaceful
park on the Rideau River where one can view feeding ducks, geese & swans.

Charlebois, Nicole Faubert & Jean-Jacques (L'Auberge du Marche   ✔ CC
87 Guigues Ave., Ottawa, Ontario K1N 5H8   ☎ (613) 235-7697

Phone for directions.
$34S $44D $10Add.person   ► 10A,3Ch
● Full, homebaked   ♠ Downtown, older, patio   ■3D,1Ste (main and upper floor)
◄┘ 1D,4Q, crib   ⌐ 1Private,1 shw.g.
↪ Parliament Hill, National Gallery, Byward Market, Rideau Canal and River, National
Arts Centre, Canadian War Museum, Notre Dame Basilica, Major's Hill Park, specialty
shops and restaurants
⇔ Skiing, walking,hiking in Gatineau Hills, golf course, beaches

☞ Completely renovated turn-of-the-Century home with truly Canadian ambiance is
located in the historic part of the city called "Byward Market", a 25 square block area
containing all the interesting tourist attractions of Canada's Capital City.

Delroy, John and Cathy (Albert House)   ✔ FOBBA
478 Albert St., Ottawa, Ontario K1R 5B5   ☎ Toll free 1-800-267-1982

Located downtown. Phone for directions.
$48-55S $43-65D $10Add.person   ► 34
● Full   ♠ Downtown, hist.   ■ 3S,13D,1Ste (main and upper levels)   ◄┘ 5Q,5D
⌐ 17Private ★ TV and telephone in guest rooms, Air, parking, LF   ✋ Pets, children
min. age 12   ⚬ French
↪ Parliament Hill, Public Archives, Supreme Court, Public Market, shops, bicycle path

☞ 1875 Victorian Mansion built by a noted Architect and located in the heart of
downtown. There are two large dogs in the house.

Ferguson, Sheena (Cartier House Inn)
46 Cartier Street, Ottawa, Ontario K2P 1J3   ☎ (613) 236-4667

From Hwy 41, take Metcalfe St Exit, proceed north to Somerset St W. Turn right and go
to Cartier (2nd cross street). House is located on northwest corner.
$79-119 per room   ► 22
● Extended Cont.   ♠ Downtown, hist., quiet   ■ 8D,3Ste (second and third floor)
◄┘ 11Q   ⌐11Ensuite (including 3 jaccuzzis)   ★ F,TV in guest rooms   ⚬French,
Spanish
↪ Parliament Bldgs., Nat. Arts Centre, Rideau Canal, Convention Centre, shopping
facilities, restaurants, well-known market, outdoor cafes, live theatre
⇔ Scenic Gatineau Hills on Quebec side of Ottawa River with rolling woodlands, clear
lakes, Village of Wakefield and 19th Century restored flour mill

☞ Intimate luxury brick mansion Inn is ideally situated in the city and has been
meticulously restored to preserve the historic charm. Very convenient but quiet
residential location provides for an inviting tranquil retreat.

Goulding, Gwen (Gwen's Guest Home - A Home away from Home)   ⌐ CC
2071 Riverside Drive, Ottawa, Ontario   K1H 7X2   ☎ (613) 737-4129

Located two blocks east of Bank Street (Hwy 31) at corner of Pleasant Pk Rd.
From 40S   From 45D   (Weekly rates available)   ▣ Meals   ► 6
● Choice, homebaked   ♠ Central, quiet, hist., view of park and river, porches, garden
■ 1S,2D,F   ↤ 5T,2R   ⌐ 1 Sh.w.g. (old deep lounging tub)   ★ TV in guest sitting
room, free parking (entrance of Pleasant Park Rd), garden picnic-area
↔ Rideau River, Park, bicycle path and cross-country skiing across the road, major
shopping centre, Billings Heritage Estate, Civic Centre
⇔ Parliament Hill, Universities, Byward Market, Convention Centre

☛ 1900-built French style home has atmosphere of gracious comfort, created by
antique Canadian furniture, stained glass, hand-crafted pottery, native Indian art and
textiles. Superb dining. "Dessert Magnifique" always the "piece de re'sistance".

Hartsgrove, George (Rideau View Inn)   ⌐ FOBBA
177 Frank St., Ottawa, Ontario   K2P 0X4   ☎ (613) 236-9309

Take Metcalfe Exit from Queensway. Go right at Museum of Civilization to Elgin St.
Turn left and go 3 blocks to Frank St, turn right.
$46-51S $51-56D $5Add.person   ► 14
● Full   ♠ Downtown   ■ 7D (upstairs)   ↤ 4D,3Q   ⌐ 4Sh.w.g.   ★ F,TV,
parking   ✋ Restricted smoking, pets   ∿ French
↔ Parliament Hill, National Arts Center, National Gallery, Rideau Center, Byward
Market, Rideau Canal, Sparks Street Mall, public tennis courts
⇔ Gatineau Hills, Gibsons Flea Market

☛ Large Edwardian home built in 1907 situated in the heart of the Capital.

Haydon, Mary and Andy (Haydon House)   ⌐ FOBBA
18 The Driveway, Ottawa, Ontario   K2P 1C6   ☎ (613) 230-2697

Follow Information signs to Information Office and then to the Rideau Canal (facing the
Canaal at the corner of Queen ELizabeth Driveway and Somerset St).
$35S $45D $10Child   ► 6
● Cont.   ♠ Downtown, res., hist., canal-view, porch   ■ 3D   ↤ 2T,2D
(upstairs)   ⌐ 2Sh.w.g.   ★ Air,TV,F, parking, separate entrance, private outdoor
portico sitting areas   ∿ French
↔ Parliament Buildings, Rideau Canal, Arts Centre, National Library and Gallery, boat
canal tours, Museum of Man, Ottawa University
⇔ Embassies, Governor General and Prime Minister Residences, Experimental Farm

☛ Victorian area mansion with traditional pine decor nestled in tranquil residential
downtown district, beside the historic and picturesque Rideau Canal (put skates on
inside and walk over to the longest skating rink). There is a dog and a cat in residence.

Hunter, John and Pat (Blue Spruces) ✔ FOBBA
187 Glebe Ave., Ottawa, Ontario   K1S 2C6 ☎ (613) 236-8521

Take Bronson Exit off Queensway. Go south to Powell (first stoplight). Turn left and go
to Percy, turn right and continue to Glebe and turn left.
$40S $50D $10Add. person ► 6
●Choice, homebaked   ♠Downtown, older, quiet   ■3D (second floor exclusive for
guests)   ⊷2T,1Q,1D   ⌐1Private, 1Sh.w.g.   ★ Air, TV, guest sittings rooms,
parking   ♥   ⊌Pets, restricted smoking, children minimum age 6
↪ Dow's Lake, Rideau Canal, Lansdowne Park, Carleton University, restaurants,
antique shops, Civic and Conference Centre, bus routes
⇔ Gatineau Hills, Fall Colour Spectacle, hiking, cross-country skiing

☞ Restored Edwardian house, located in the Glebe (the heart of downtown Ottawa)
and furnished with antiques. There is friendly old Cocker Spaniel in residence.

Leclerc, Clemence (Leclerc's Residence) ✔ FOBBA
253 McLeod St., Ottawa, Ontario   K2P 1A1 ☎ (613) 234-7577

Take Metcalfe Exit on Hwy 417 east or west and go around the National Museum of Man
and Natural Sciences. Located in front of the Museum on McLeod
$45S (and up) $55D (and up) $15Add.person   ▣ Meals ► 6
● Full, homebaked   ♠ Downtown, hist., res., views, flowered porches and balconies,
quiet,   ■ 3D (upstairs)   ⊷ 2T,2D   ⌐ 2Sh.w.g.   ★ TV,F,Air, parking   ⊌ Pets,
children min. age 16, restricted smoking   ⊸ French
↪ Parliament buildings, Nat. Museum of Natural Sciences, Nat. Art Gallery and Arts
Centre, Rideau Canal, historical Byward Market, tennis courts, Sparks Street, bus
station, arts and antique shops, Convention Center, Somerset Village
⇔ Experimental farm, Hull/Gatineau Park (Quebec), Museum of Science/Technology,
Airport, Train Stn., Dow's Lake, Embassies, Aviation/Civilization Museums

☞ Lovely Victorian home (1871) in super central location on a quiet shaded street
facing park decoratd with French flair, nice paintings and prints all over the hosue.

Lyon, Beatrice (Beatrice Lyon Guest House) ✔ Ott.Downt.B&B
479 Slater St., Ottawa, Ontario   K1R 5C2 ☎ (613) 236-3904

Take Bronson Exit off Queensway north to Slater St. Look for 2nd house from corner
$30S $35D $15Add. person   (Special rates for children and families) ► 7
● Full, Canadian   ♠ Downtown, older   ■ 1S,3D   ⊷ T,D   ⌐ 2Sh.w.g.
★ TV, Air   ♥   ⊸ some French
↪ Parliament buildings, downtown shopping, restaurants, Sparks Street Mall, Museum,
National Library, National Archives, Arts Center

☞ Home has been in the family since it was built around 1890 and is the only single
dwelling left in the downtown core of the city. Hostess also operates the Downtown
Ottawa B&B Association. Pets welcome.

Peterson, E. & N. Haramis (Constance House)   ‿ FOBBA
62 Sweetland Ave., Ottawa, Ontario K1R 7T6   ☎ (613) 235-8888

From Hwy 417 take Nicholas St Ramp to Laurier Ave. Turn right to Sweetland Ave.
$40-48S $48-54D $80-88F $5Add.person   (plus tax)   ► 10A, 2Ch
● Choice, homebaked   ♠ Downtown, res., hist., patio   ■ S,D,Ste (upstairs)
⊷ 2S,2D,1Q,1R, cot   � 1Private, 1sh.w.g. (sinks in each room)   ★ Air,F,TV in
guest rooms, parking, terry cloth robes in each room, balconies   ⚉ Restricted smoking
↔ Parliament Hill, Rideau Canal (boating and skating), bicycling, downtown market,
shopping and restaurants, museums and galleries, Convention Centre, Ottawa U
⇔ Experimental Farm, Gatineau Hills (walking and cross-country ski trails and fall
foliage spectacle), Pinoeer Log Farm, Maple Sugar Bush

🐾 Award-winning restored Victorian Home located in Ottawa's Sandy Hill area. Hosts
are professional photographers whose works are displayed throughout the house. Each
room is named after a famous hotographer.

Schutte, Anne and Unger, Mary (McGee's Inn)   ‿ FOBBA
185 Daly Ave., Sandy Hill, Ottawa, Ontario   K1N 6E8   ☎ (613) 237-6089

From Hwy 417 take Nicholas St exit to Laurier Ave E. Turn right and proceed to Nelson,
turn left and continue to Daly. Look for large brick Victorian house with green roof on
north west corner.
$52-102S $58-108D $15Add. person   ► 24
● Choice, homebaked   ♠ Downtown, res., hist., quiet   ■ 14
⊷3T,2D,6Q,1K,3R,crib   � 2Sh.w.g., 10ensuite, 1Jacuzzi ensuite   ★ Air, F, TV, free
downtown parking, telephone in all rooms   ⚉ Pets   ～ French, Spanish

↔ Parliament Hill, Byward (outdoor
market), museums, U of Ottawa, bicycle
path network, Rideau Shopping Centre,
Rideau Canal (skating and boating)

⇔ Camp Fortune/Gatineau Park
(skiing and hiking), steam train to
Wakefield (Maple Syrup Run in March),
Stitsville Flea Market

🐾 Historic Victorian mansion built in
1886 and centrally situated in
distinguished heritage area. Each room
has comfortable brass bed and some
have fireplaces. Featured in various
magazine articles.

Waters, Carol and Brian (Australis Guest Home)   ✔ B&B
35 Marlborough Ave., Ottawa, Ontario K1N 8E6   ☎ (613) 235-8461

From Hwy 417 west bound, take Nicholas St Exit. From Hwy 16 go to Sandy Hill area.
$29S (and up) $36-38D (and up) $10Add.person   ► 5
● Full   🏠 Downtown, older, view   ■ 2D,F   ⊷ T,D   ⌐ 1Private,2sh.w.g.
★TV   ♥   ✋ Pets, drinking
↔ Downtown, Parliament buildings and all tourist attractions
⇔ Gatineau Hills (skiing, beautiful foliage scenery in autumn)

📢 60-year old home with fireplaces and leaded windows situated in beautiful older part
of the City and convenient to all tourist attractions.

Capital Bed and Breakfast Reservation Service
2071 Riverside Drive, Ottawa, Ontario K1H 7X2   ☎ (613 737-4129
(Gwen Goulding)
Rates: from $40S and $45D (including superb homecooked or gourmet breakfast).
Capital is a personalized booking service. Homes are located in downtown city
residential areas, quiet suburbia close to public transportation, in the country or on
farms, good roads and easy short drives to downtown attractions. Most hosts will gladly
drive guests to and from points of entry, if they travel without a car. Write or phone to
discuss and arrange your personal requirements.

Ottawa Area Bed and Breakfast   ✔ FOBBA
Box 4848, Stn. E, Ottawa, Ontario K1S 5J1   ☎ (613) 563-0161
(Mr. Robert Rivoire)
Rates: $34S $44D   (including a full homecooked breakfast)
Ottawa Area B&B offers a professional reservation service and represents older homes
situated right in the heart of the city, as well as suburban homes. The Agency represents
65 rooms in Ottawa and surrounding areas, including Hull (Quebec). For more
information or to make a reservation, please contact the above.

Ottawa Centertown B&B Association
253 McLeod St., Ottawa, Ontario K2P 1A1   ☎ (613) 234-7577
(Mrs. Clemence Leclerc)
Rates from: $45S (and up) $55D (and up)   (including full Canadian breakfast)
The Association consists of a few private heritage homes all located in Centertown and
in walking distance from all major points of interest. The hosts work together to assist
visitors coming to the Capital. They are in constant contact with each other and will
refer guests when their own rooms are booked.

Owen Sound
(see also Cargill, Clarksburg, Port Elgin, Southampton, Wiarton, Meaford,
Kimberley, Thornburg, Collingwood, Oliphant, Lion's Head, Palgrave)

Ackermann, Bernice and Hermann (Hazeldean House)   ✔ Grey Bruce B&B
347-10 St. West, Owen Sound, Ontario N4K 3R4   ☎ (519) 376-5435

Located west of Sydenham River in Owen Sound bewteen 3rd and 4th Ave. W-10th St
becomes Hwy 6 & 21 going to the Bruce Peninsula.
$32S $40-45D $10Add. person   ◙ Meals   ► 4A,2Ch
● Full (Canadian and European)   🏠 Res., view, quiet, veranda   ■ 3D,1S (upstairs)
   ⊷ 2D,2T,1S,R   ⌐ 1Private,1Sh.w.g.   ★ TV,LF,off street parking
ⓌSmoking, pets   〰 German, Swiss-German
↩ Downtown, Harrison Park, Tom Thomson Art Gallery, waterfront, bus station
⇔ Bruce Trail, golf course, marina, antique stores, Lake Huron (Sauble Beach,
swimming, boating), Southampton, Harrison Park, Indian reservation, cross-country
skiing, ice fishing, snomobiling

☛ Lovingly preserved Victorian home built in 1904, with original oak trim and
fireplaces situated on a shady street and nestled under the bluffs (east side of the Owen
Sound Valley). Host is a Swiss Pastry Chef and specializes in homemade croissants,
breads and truffels. Office available for business travellers. Packed lunches available and
hosts will drive guests to Bruce Trail.

Bart, Mrs. Wanda (Pine Lane Haven)   ✔ Grey Bruce B&B
606-14th St. West, Owen Sound, Ontario N4K 3Y4   ☎ (519) 376-7831

Phone for directions. Situated on the banks of the Potawatomi River.
$25S $35D   ◙ Meals   ► 4
● Full   🏠 Res., older, patio, quiet   ■ 2D (upstairs)   ⊷ 2T,1D   ⌐ Sh.w.g.
★TV,KF,LF Ⓦ Smoking, drinking, pets
↩ Downtown, Tom Thomson Art Gallery, library, churches, restaurants, bus service,
Mall on Sunset Strip, Heritage Mall on East Hill, ice-fishing in Georgian Bay
⇔ Sauble Beach on Lake Huron, Tobermory (ferry to Manitoulin Isles), skiing

☛ Spacious, quiet home very informal atmosphere and a large backyard to stroll down
to the banks of the Potawatomi River. Tours of the city area offered.

B&B Travel Tip: *You can stay in a B&B even if you are not travelling by
car. Many B&B homes are situated near excellent public transportation and many
hosts will pick up and deliver from bus terminal, railway station or airport, sometimes at no charge.*

Moses, Bill and Cecilie (Moses Sunset Farm's B&B)   ✔ Grey Bruce B&B
RR6, Owen Sound, Ontario   N4K 5N8   ☎ (519) 371-4559

From Hwys 6 & 10 take 8th St E to dead-end (past Georgian College and hospital). Turn
right on gravel road amd go 1.4 km to mail box No S578.
$25S $35D $10Child $10Add. person   ◙ Meals   ▶ 6A,6Ch
● Choice, homebaked   ♠ Rural, acreage, view, patio, quiet   ■ 1S,1D,F ⊶
1D,1S,1Q,1P,2R cots   ⊓ Sh.w.h., sh.w.g.   ★ TV,4F,KF,LF, woodstove, some
facilities for the disabled   ♥   ⓦ Smoking   ⌇ Some German and French
↔ Cross-country skiing at back, walk along creek, riding school next door
⇔ Hibou Beach and Conservation Authority Park, Bognor Wildlife Marsh, City Centre,
shopping mall, hospital, Georgian College, Bruce Trail, boat launching ramps, golfing

☛ Host family has travelled around the world and stayed at many B&B places.
Uniquely designed home to suit outdoor life-style. Gourmet cooking teacher makes meals
from homegrown fresh garden herbs/ vegetables. Host is hobby beekeeper.

Piplack, Otto and Ina (Hemloch Farm)   ✔ Grey Bruce B&B
RR1, Annan, Ontario   N0H 1B0   ☎ 519) 376-9142

Located 8.4 km east of Owen Sound off Hwy 26 and 4.8 km north of Concession Rd 8.
$30S $40-45D   ◙ Meals   (Weekend packages available)   (cap
●Homebaked   ♠Farm,hist.,view,patio,pond,quiet   ■3D (main and upper floor)
⊶2T,2D   ⊓1Private, 1sh.w.h.   ★F,LF,V in guest room   ⌇German
↔ Country lane leading to beautiful waterfall, trails overlooking Georgian Bay
⇔ Safe, sandy Sauble Beach on beautiful blue Lake Huron, Leith (fishing), Owen Sound

☛ Enjoy true country living in Century stone house with old-fashioned comfort
situated in peaceful park-like setting. Watch hosts train Standardbred horses.

Pakenham
(near Ottawa; see also Braeside, Renfrew, Calabogie, Carleton Place,Almonte)

Pugh, Robert and Thora (Stonebridge)
RR4, Pakenham, Ontario   K0A 2X0   ☎ (613) 624-5431

Take Hwy 17 west of Ottawa to Antrim intersection. Turn left and proceed 6.5 km over
Mississippi River to house on left. Look for 5-Span stone bridge at entrance.
$25S $40D   ◙ Meals   ▶ 8
●Full, homebaked   ♠Hist., 8.5-acres, riverfront, quiet   ■3D,1F (upstairs)
⊶3T,2D,1Q   ⊓2Sh.w.g.   ★F,TV, separate entrance, parking   ⓦChildren min. age 12
↔ 300m of riverfront, Limited Edition collectors shop (dolls, plates, prints) on premises
⇔ Mt. Pakenham Ski area, Fulton's Sugar Bush (Maple products year round), CMP
Ranch (home of Musical Rides), boat launching, Mill Outlets at Appleton

☛ Gracious Heritage home (1860 "Breezy Heights") set on a wooded hill overlooking
the Missisippi River and stone bridge,with unspoiled woodwork. Enjoy the Tea Room on
the premises serving afternoon teas and light refreshing lunches. There is are pets.

Palgrave

(near Orangeville; see also Kleinburg, Beeton, Bradford, Pelee Island)

Country Host and Ski Host
RR1, Palgrave, Ontario L0N 1P0   ☎ (519) 941-7633

(Mrs. Grace Cronin, President)
Rates $30-35S $40-45D (including a hearty breakfast)
COUNTRY HOST is a Reservation Service for quality, year-round B&B homes located in
2 areas. The northern network follows the Niagara Escarpment from outside Toronto
north-west to Tobermory. The southern network has homes near Point Pelee National
Park. Additional homes are on Lake Nipissing at North Bay, Bolton, Mono Mills and
Orangeville areas.
SKI HOST is a reservation service for homes offering B&B to downhill/x-country skiers
N/W of Toronto near conservation areas, Beaver Valley, Collingwood and Blue Mt.

Palmer Rapids

(south of Pembroke near Bancroft, Eganville, Gilmour)

Creaghan, Barbara and Family (Wingle Inn)   ✔ B&B
RR2, Palmer Rapids, Ontario   K0J 2E0   ☎ (613) 758-2072

Located 2 km off Hwy 515, halfway between Quadeville and Palmer Rapids.
$22-45S $25-50D   🍽 Meals   ► 14
● Homebaked   🏠 Rural, 250-acres, hist., view   ■ 7D (upstairs)   ⊨ 8T,3D,R
⌐ 4Private, 1sh.w.g.   ★ TV,F in one guest room   ♥
↪ Rolling wooded hills, trout pond, fine dining
⇔ Lake swimming, cross-country and Mt. Madawaska downhill skiing, numerous craft
shops, Wal-Gem Lepidary, Madonna House

☞ Century-old stone house situated in beautiful rolling hills, surrounded by lakes and
easily accessible to summer and winter sport activities. There are pets in the house.
Recommended by the book "Where to eat in Canada, 1986/7".

Parkhill

(west of London; see also Grand Bend, Ilderton, Arva)

Sadler, Wilfred and Grace (WesLayne Farms B&B)   ✔ SOCVA B&B
RR2, Parkhill, Ontario   N0M 2K0   ☎ (519) 294-6578

Located on Hwy 7 between Thedford and Parkhill at West Williams side-road 2 sign.
$30-35   ► 6
● Choice, homebaked   🏠 Farm, older, quiet   ■ 3D (main and upper floor)
⊨ 1D,2Q   ⌐ 1Private,1sh.w.g.   ★ Air,F,TV,KF, separate entrance, facilities for the
handicapped   ⊛ Smoking, drinking, pets, children min. age 6
⇔ Grand Bend and Pinery Prov. Park (swimming and nature trails), Arkona fruit
orchards, Lambton Heritage Museum, good restaurants and shopping

☞ Comfortable older home with shady lawns is situated in a picturesque community.

Parry Sound
(see also Port Carling, Britt, Emsdale)

Douglas, Shirley and Cameron (Malkin House) ↙ Parry Sound B&B
RR3, Parry Sound, Orrville, Ontario P2A 2W9 ☎ (705) 732-2994

From Hwy 69, at 3.2 km south of Parry Sound, take Hwy 518 and continue 16 km to
Orrville. Turn left at General Store to 3rd house on left.
$28S $35D $5Child $10Add.person ► 8
✚not winter ●Choice, homebaked ♠Village, hist., acreage, quiet,screened/open
porches ■3(main and upper floor) ⊷4D,1Q,1P, crib ⊓2Sh.w.g. ★TV,F, separate
entrance, parking, facilities for the handicapped ⍟Rest. smoking, pets
↪ General store, antique shopping, lakes, safe sandy beach, Sequin snowmobil trail
⇔ Parry Sound (Festival of Sound, Rainbow Theatre), Lake Rosseau, 30 000 Island
cruises, Burk's Falls, Lake Manitouwabing (tennis school), golfing

🖝 Very cozy country atmosphere in restored Century home with huge country kitchen
and surrounded by large pine trees and beautiful landscaped grounds.

Keates, Tom and Joanne (The Sound House) ↙ FOBBA,Parry S.B&B
67 Church Street, Parry Sound, Ontario P2A 1Y8 ☎ (705) 746-8806

From Hwy 69 take North 69B entrance into town, past the shopping mall and High
School and traffic lights. Look for house on left just past hospital.
$25-30S $40D $10Add. person ► 6A,3Ch
● Full ♠ Downtown, older ■ 1S,2D,F ⊷ 2T,1D,1Q,R, crib ⊓ 1Sh.w.h.,
2sh.w.g. ★ TV,LF, parking, picnic lunches provided ♥
↪ Downtown, beach, Festival of Sound and Rainbow Theatre, Sound Boat Cruises
⇔ Killbear Prov. Park (fabulous beaches), Parry Island Indian Reserve, Native craft
shop, Loon Artists Studio, boat rentals

🖝 Hosts offer comfort, convenience and conviviality. Home is located in very popular
vacation country and offers something interesting for everyone, young and old. There is
a cat in the house. Host is president of the Parry Sound & District B&B Association.

Wallenius, Shirley and Anders (Evergreen) ↙ Parry Sound B&B
Box 223, Parry Sound, Ontario P2A 2X3 ☎ (705) 389-3554

Located 19 km east of Parry Sound on Hwy 124 and 1 km south of McKellar village.
$35S $44D $10cot ► 6
✚ May15-Sept15 ● Full ♠ Rural, res., acreage, view, lakefront, quiet ■ 3,plus
separate cottage ⊷ T,D ⊓ Sh.w.g. ★TV in guest room, parking, separate
entrance, guest lounge and sun room ⍟ Pets ⌇ Swedish
↪ Village of McKellar, safe, sandy beach with float to swim, fish from private dock
⇔ Parry Sound, Festival of the Sound, 30,000 Island Cruise, Rainbow Theatre

🖝 Elegant cedar log home surrounded by spacious deck overlooking park-like grounds
on the shore of Lake Manitou-Wabing with spiral staircase and large billiard room
(professional size table) and walk-out to lawn.

Pelee Island
(on Lake Erie south of Windsor: see also Leamington, Wheatley, Amherstburg and Palgrave: Country Host)

Tiessen, Ron and Lynn (Tiessen's B&B on the Lake)
Pelee Island, Ontario N0R 1M0 ☎ (519) 724-2068

Call (519) 724-2115 for ferry information (2-3 schedules daily out of Leamington or Kingsville). On Pelee Island go 3.2 km west from Scudder Dock or 4.8 km north from West Dock along West Shore Rd.
$35S $45D ● Full   ♠ Farm, older, lakefront, quiet, veranda   ■ 2D (upstairs), also guest cabin for 4 ⊨1D,2T,R ⌐2Sh.w.h. ★TV,fridge priv. ⌇German,French
↔ Lake Erie, fishing, swimming, birding, nature hikes, vineyard
⇔ Restaurants, docks and harbours, beaches, historic sites, Nature Reserve

☞ 1911-built white frame island house situated on own vineyard-farm in quiet rural community. Watch Lake Erie's sensational sunsets from large veranda.

Peterborough
(see also Cavan, Warsaw, Lakefield, Fenelon F., Millbrook, Hastings, Bobcaygeon)

Crofts, Susan & Bruce (Fairview B&B House on the Otonabee)   ⌐ Peterb. B&B
Box 2457, Peterborough, Ontario K9J 7Y8 ☎ (705) 743-9788

Take Hwy 28 aprox. 8.5 km north of Peterborough and turn right on the 5th Line of Smith Township and continue to yellow mail box.
25S $35D ► 7
✚ May-Sept   ● Farm, hist., 27-acres, view, riverfront, quiet   ■ 3S,2D (upstairs)
⊨ 7T   ⌐ 1Private,1sh.w.g.,1ensuite   ★ TV,KF,LF, parking, separate entrance
⊛Smoking, pets
↔ Trent University, Arbor Theatre, forest meadow, wetland and shore for walking
⇔ Peterborough, Riverview Zoo, Lift Lock & Acitvity Centre, museum, archives, Ontario Waterways cruises, Lakefied, Curve Lake Whetung Gallery, Buckhorn Wildlife and Craft Festivals, Warsaw Caves, Petroglyphs and Provincial Park

☞ Large no-nonsense Gothic-style house built in the 1860's is furnished in keeping with the period and situated on the West bank of the river. Relax by the soothing quiet sound of water tumbling over the adjacent dam.

Konopaski, Mrs. Lana (Rest-A-While B&B)   ⌐ ONT B&B
80 Kawartha Heights Blvd., Peterborough, Ontario K9J 1N7 ☎ (705) 748-5545

Take Lansdowne St west to Kawartha Heights Blvd. Turn right to white brick house.
$30-40S $40-45D ► 6
● Full, homebaked   ♠ Res., sub., deck, quiet   ■ 3D (main and upper level)
⊨2D,1Q   ⌐ 2Sh.w.h.   ★ Air,TV,LF   ⊛ Pets, smoking
⇔ World's largest Hydraulic Lift Locks, downtown shopping/dining, beaches, Gallery on the Lake (Buckhorn), Warsaw Caves & Petroglyphs, Hutchinson House Museum

☞ Quiet residential side-split home in park-like setting and large private deck. Breakfast served in formal Dining Room. Homemade muffins a house specialty.

Pittman, Sharyn (Chelsea)   ✓ CC
319 Pearl Ave., Peterborough, Ontario   K9J 5G4   ☎ (705) 748-0332

In Peterb. go 7 blocks west of George St (main street) along Charlotte St. Turn left.
$30S $40D $10Child   ◉ Meals   ► 5
● Full, homebaked   ♠ Downtown, older, patio   ■ 1S,1D,1Ste (main and upper
level)   ⊷ 1S,1D,1Q (waterbed)   ⌐ 1Ensuite, 1shw.w.h.   ★ TV,F,KF,LF, parking
⊕ Smoking, pets
↔ Downtown, shopping, restaurants, Little Lake Marina, Hydraulic Lift Locks and
cruises, Theatre Guild, Artspace
⇔ Theatre, Gallery on the Lake (Buckhorn) and Whetung Art Gallery, Riverview Park
and Zoo, Warsaw Caves, Petroglyphs

☛ Relax in a home with old world charm and warm and friendly atmosphere located in
the heart of Peterborough. There is a cat in the house. Weather permitting, breakfast is
served on the patio.

Bed & Breakfast Registry of Peterborough and Area
Box 2264, Peterborough, Ontario   K9J 7Y8   ☎ (705) 652-6290
(Contact person: Wally Wilkins)
Rates: $29-39S $40-50   (Full breakfast included)
Bed Breakfast hosts in the Kawartha Lakes area welcome visitors all year round. The
homes are situated in rural settings, on the lakefront or on quiet streets in a village or
town. For information call or write to the above.

Petersburg
(near Waterloo/Kichener; see also New Hamburg, St.Clements, St.Jacobs, Plattsville)

Scott, Ted and Bernice (Scott's Country Home)   ✓ SOCVA
RR2, Petersburg, Ontario   N0B 2H0   ☎ (519) 634-8370

From Kitchener take Hwy 7/8 west to Reg Rd 12 and turn right to Petersburg. Turn
right again at Reg Rd 6. Situated east of Blue Moon Hotel.
$30S $35D   (Children's rates available)   ► 4
● Full, homebaked   ♠ Rural, acreage, view, quiet   ■ 2D   ⊷ 2T,1D   ⌐ 1Private,
1sh.w.h.   ★ TV, separate entrance   ⊕ Restricted smoking
↔ Bush trails, famous Blue Moon Hotel
⇔ Mennonite Country, St. Jacobs, Elmira, Kitchener/Waterloo Octoberfest, Farmers
Market, Seagrams Museum, Elora Gorge and shops,

☛ Quiet, spacious country setting. Provisions for preparing light lunches available.
There is a cat in residene.

Petrolia

(near Sarnia; see also Thedford, Parkhill)

MacLachlan, John and Becky (Rebecca's B&B)   ✔ SWOTA
4058 Petrolia St., Box 1028, Petrolia, Ont N0N 1R0   ☎ (519) 882-0118/ Becky 882-0244

Travelling on Hwy 402 from Sarnia or London take Hwy 21 south to Petrolia.
$30S $35D $10cot or Add.person   ► 2-3
● Cont.   ♠ Res., older, porch, quiet   ■ 2D (upstairs)   ⊢ 2D, cot   ⊓ 3Sh.w.g.
   ★ Air,F,LF,TV in guest room, century player piano, parking   ♥   ⊛ Pets,
restricted smoking, drinking
↩ Victoria Playhouse (live theatre), town arena, fairgrounds, out-door public pool,
churches, shops and restaurants, art gallery, Twilight Haven Seniors Home hospital
⇔ Petrolia Oil Discovery (famous working oil museum), cross country skiing or hiking,
Sarnia, London, Chatham, Grand Bend on Lake Huron

🐾 Young host family in pacious century brick Victorian home situated in beautiful
historic town (Canada's first oil boom town). There are 2 young daughter who take
piano lessons. Hosts are very knowledgeable about their small home town, which has so
much to offer. Homemade jams and muffins a specialty.

Picton

(near Belleville; see also Bloomfield, Wellington, Consecon, Brighton, Trenton)

Flake, Glen and Catherine (Woodville Farm)   ✔ OFVA
RR2, Picton, Onario K0K 2T0   ☎ (613) 476-5462

From Hwy 401, take Exit 566 to Hwy 49 and proceed for 19 km to farm.
$40S $50D $15Child   ► 4A,6Ch
● Full, homebaked   ♠ 200-acre farm, lakefront   ■ 3D (upstairs)
⊢ 2T,1D,1Q,2R,2P, 2cribs   ⊓ 1Sh.w.h., 1sh.w.g.   ★ TV,LF,KF   ⊛ Drinking,
drinking, pets
↩ Hiking, fishing, swimming, horseback riding, wagon rides, cross-country skiing, lots
of farm animals
⇔ Golfing, swimming, auctions, Lake-on-the-Mountain and Sandbanks Prov. Parks

🐾 Modern farm home overlooks magnificient Bay of Quinte. Home baking with own
farm produce. There are 3 cats in the house. Farm tours and activities available.

B&B Travel Tip: *B&B travelling can be most enjoyable, when it is planned
ahead and when there is ample time to socialize.*

Holm, Ms.H. (Rose Hall Guest House)　　　　　　　　　　　　　　ⵑ CC
1 Agnes St., Box 2398, Picton, Ontario　K0K 2T0　　　　　☎ (613) 476-3767

Call for directions.
$30-35S　$40-45D　$10Add.person　▣ Meals　　　　　　　　► 6
◨May-Dec.　●Choice, homebaked　♠Res., hist., quiet　■2D,1F(upstairs)
⤙3D,1P　⌐Sh.w.h.　★TVin guest room ⓌSmoking,drinking,pets,children　⤳German
↔ Craft shops, antiques, museum, galleries, historic buildings, Archives, Courthouse,
shops, restaurants, shopping, Quinte Summer Music Festival, sailing school
⇔ Sandbanks Beach and Dunes, Lake on the Mountain, berry picking farms, Provincial
Park, golfing, hiking and cross-country skiing trails, Mohawk Indian Gift Centre,
historic sites and churches

☛ Century-old (1851) country house with pink shutters, rose garden and hollyhocks at
the front is situated on a quiet cul-de-sac in a community of older homes and historic
buildings surrounded by unspoiled nature and agricultural landscape, woods, lakes, bays
and dunes. Hostess is artist and cook offering special dinners.

House, Anne and Brian Clark (Butternut Cupboard)　　　　　　　ⵑ CC
East Lake Rd, RR1, Picton, Ontario　K0K 2T0　　　　　　☎ (613) 476-7744

From Picton turn at the LCBO onto Lake St. Go south 5km to County Rd 11. Turn right
and continue 3 km to house on left side.
$40S　$55D　$15Child　$15Add. person　▣ Meals　　　　　　► 8
● Full, homebaked　♠ Farm, hist., view, lakefront, quiet　■ 2D,1Ste (upstairs)
⤙ 2D,2S ⌐ 3Sh.w.g.　Ⓦ Smoking
↔ Frontage on East Lake
⇔ Macaulay Heritage and Sandbanks Prov. Parks, Black River Cheese Factory, sailing,
windsurfing, cross-country skiing, antiques and auctions

☛ 1840's United Empire Loyalist farm house furnished with period antiques. Gourmet
breakfasts of imaginative menus supplied from own organic kitchen garden.

Whitney, Jean and Keith (The Poplars)　　　　　　　　　　　ⵑ CC
RR2, Picton, Ontario　K0K 2T0　　　　　　　　　　　☎ (613) 476-3513

From Exit 566 on Hwy 401 go south on Hwy 49 to Northport Rd. Turn right and proceed
1.5 km to large white house.
$25S　$35-45D　$10Add.person　▣ Meals　　　　　　　　► 8
● Full　♠ Rural, acreage, view, lakefront, patio, dock, quiet　■ 4D (upstairs)
⤙4T,1D,1Q,1R　⌐ 1Sh.w.g., 1ensuite　★ TV, parking　Ⓦ Pets, restricted smoking
↔ Excellent fishing, private dock for 2 boats
⇔ Belleville, Kingston, Picton, Sandbanks Provincial Park

☛ Old-fashioned hospitality in renovated Century home located in very popular
vacation area.

O'Neill, Gerald and Joan (Ginkgo Tree Place) ✔ CC
352 Main St. E, Box 3117, Picton, Ontario K0K 2T0 ☎ (613) 476-7275

For scenic road from Kingston, take Hwy 33 west to Glenora Ferry.
$40-45per room   ●$2.50Each(Full)   📷 Meals   ►8
● Cont, homebaked   🏠 Res., older, patio   ■ 3D (upstairs)   ⊢ 2T,3D
⌐ 1Sh.w.g, 1sh.w.h.   ★ Air, parking, TV in guest room   Ⓦ Smoking, pets, children
min. age 10

↔ Historic museums, shopping, yacht club, tennis, anitque shops

⇔ Sandbanks beaches, excellent bicycling and cross-country skiing, ice fishing, skating

☞ Classic, very large Victorian home has recently undergone some major restoration. There are lanscaped grounds and gardens including a large "Ginkgo" tree.

Port Bruce
(on Lake Erie ner St. Thomas; see also Port Stanley, Shedden, Rodney)

Pineo, Mel and Lynn (Loma Linda) ✔ B&B
RR1, Sparta, Ontario N0L 2H0 ☎ (519) 773-3335

From Gwt 401 take Hwy 73 south to Pt Bruce. Go over bridge and turn right to farm.
$30S $40D $10Child   📷 Meals   ► 6A,1Ch
🔀 May 1-Oct31   ● Full,homebaked   🏠 Farm, view, indoor swimming pool,
lakefront, patio, quiet   ■ 3D   ⊢ 2T,2D,1R   ⌐1Sh.w.g.   ★ F,TV in guest room,
separate entrance   Ⓦ Restricted smoking
↔Beach at Pt. Bruce, fishing pier, marina, boat rentals, charters for Salmon and Walley
⇔ Port Stanley, Sparta, Aylmer (quaint shops, tea rooms, artist studios) fine dining

☞ Country living at it's best. See the tobacco harvest and marketing operations.

B&B Travel Tip: *If you are on the road and decide to stay in a B&B, do phone ahead from a nearby phone (best: take a break at lunchtime and choose the B&B for the coming night). The hosts will appreciate your consideration and if their rooms are booked, they can also direct you to another B&B host. (This is not convenient, if you appear at the door in the evening without prior notice.)*

Plattsville

(near Woodstock; see also Petersburg, New Hamburg, Kitchener/Waterloo, Millbank)

Dobson, Barbara and Henry (The Albion)   ↙ SOCVA B&B
Box 37, 66 Albert St., Plattsville, Ontario N0J 1S0   ☎ (519) 684-7434

From Hwy 401 take Exit 268 west of Kitchener, and Road 97 to Oxford Road 8.
$25S $40D $5Add.person   ► 12
✚ May-Oct.31 (other by arrangement) ● Full 🏠 Village, 2nd level of commercial
building, verandah, large shaded yard ■ 6D (upstairs) ⌐ 2T,5D ⅂ 2Sh.w.h.
★ TV, anitque shop ⓦ Pets, restricted smoking

↪ Family style restaurant and
sandwich shop, covered park pavillion,
tennis
⇔ Community farm of Brethren,
Emporium (English cream tea), New
Hamburg (French Dining at Waterlot
or Tama Inn), Pennsylvania-German
area

☛ Former Victorian Country Inn
provides atmosphere of English
hospitality. Rooms are furnished with
antiques. There is a Collie named
"Albert" in the house. Hosts are in the
Antique business and live above the
commercial establishment.

Port Dover

(on Lake Erie near Simcoe; see also Waterford)

Lewis, Ms. Barbara-Anne (1885 House)   ↙ B&B
57 Prospect St., RR1, Port Dover, Ontario N0A 1N0   ☎ (519) 583-2459

From Hwy 6 in Port Dover, take Main St to Chapman St. Turn north, then over bridge
to crest of hill and left again.
$38-45S $45-65D $10Add. person 🍽 Meals(Gourmet)   ► 8
❄ Appointment nessessary during winter months ● Full, homebaked
🏠 Res.,hist., acreage, view, lakefront, patio, quiet ■ 3 ⌐ 4D (upstairs)
⅂1Sh.w.g. ★ TV,F, parking, indiv. thermostates in guest rooms ⓦ Restricted
smoking, pets, children minimum age 13
↪ Lowland meadow, Silver Lake (canoe available), Port Dover Beach, fishing port,
Lighthouse Festival Theatre
⇔ Lake Erie Shoreline, Long Point Conservation area, Backus Historical Complex,
antique stores, museums, ice fishing, cross country skiing

☛ Century-old home is decorated and furnished in a style in keeping with its age and
located on a hill-side overlooking Silver Lake. There are two lovable wolfhounds in the
house. Hostess is a seasoned B&B traveller and Teddy Bear collector.

Port Carling
(near Bracebridge; see also Huntsville, Gravenhurst, Windermere)

Elliott, Mrs. Mary E. (Windover Hill B&B)   ⌐ ONT B&B,Musk. B&B
Box 116, Port Carling, Ontario P0B 1J0   ☎ (705) 765-5950

Turn off Hwy 118 at Bailey St in Port Carling just off Main Street..
$20S $40D $60 (for 3)   ► 8A,2Ch
✠ Easter-Thanksgiving   ● Cont.   ♠ Village, res., bungalow, acreage, view, patio,
lakefront, quiet, isolated   ■ 2   ⊷ 1S,2D   ⊓ Sh.w.h.   ★ TV,LF, parking, box
lunches for hikers/skiers   ♥   ⊛Restricted smoking, drinking, children min.age 4
↪ Swimming in river (area cordoned off by floats), Seguin boat ride (Muskoka
Steamship), summer theatre
⇔ Pioneer Museum, locks, Gravenhurst (Bethune Memorial), Music on the Barge

☛ Picturesque summer and winter vacation village in the "Hub of the Lakes".

Stafford, Shirley and Bill (Blue Heron House)   ⌐ Musk. B&B
RR1, Pennwood Rd., Port Carling, Ontario P0B 1J0   ☎ (705) 765-5961

Travel west from Bracebridge on Hwy 118 to Port Carling. Upon entering the village
take Pennwood Rd and follow signs
$35S $50D $10Add.person   ▣ Meals (in winter only)   ► 4,2Ch
✠ June-Mar 1   ● Choice   ♠ Village, lakefront, view   ■ 2D (upstairs)
⊷2S,2T,1D   ⊓ 1Sh.w.g.   ★ TV,KF, parking   ⊛ Smoking, pets, child min. age 8
↪ Large wooded lot, natural sandy beach
⇔ Live theatre, Museum and historic churches, shopping, restaurants, boat cruises

☛ New home situated on 440 ft of waterfront in beautiful scenery amid the pine, birch
and sparkling water of magnetic Muskoka. The restored steamship, R.M.S. Segwun, sails
past the house (cruises available from May to Oct). For a fishing experience with the
hosts advance reservation must be made. There are 2 cats.

Port Elgin
(near Owen Sound; see also Dobbinton, Southhampton, Oliphant, Kincardine)

Gowanlock, Kenneth and Janet (The Gowanlocks)   ⌐ Grey Bruce B&B
RR2, Port Elgin, Ontario N0H 2C0   ☎ (519) 389-5256

Located 5.8 km east of Port Elgin and west of Burgoyne just off County Rd 17
$25S $30D $10Child   ▣ Meals   ► 4A,2Ch
● Full   ♠ 87-acre farm, older, patio, riverfront   ■ 2D,1F (main and upper floors)
⊷ 3D,P, crib   ⊓ 1Sh.w.g, 1sh.w.h.   ★ TV   ⊛ Restricted smoking, pets
↪ Creek for fishing, bush area, dairy barn tours, cross-country skiing, hiking
⇔ Southampton, golfing, beach, theatre, boating, tennis, Owen Sound, museum

☛ Comfortable home with hardwood floors and antique flavour. Hosts are dairy
farmers and show poultry. Enjoy this busy tourist town from the quiet friendly
atmosphere of a century home. "Plenty to do all year, but summer does it best". Tea and
coffee served each evening on the lovely deck. There is a cat in residence..

Port Franks
(on Lake Huron near Grand Bend: see also Thedford, Parkhill)

Rose, Pat and Malcolm (The Good Old British)   ⌐ CC
4 Ransford St., Port Franks, Ontario N0M 2L0   ☎ (519) 243-3694

Take Reg. Rd 3 into Port Franks, then 2nd left onto Ontario Rd and first right onto
Ransford to 3rd house with blue shutters on left.
$25S $35D $5child $5Add.person   (Mid-week reduced rates for Seniors)   ► 2A,2Ch
● Full, homebaked   ♠ Village, rural, split-level, swimming pool, patio, quiet
■2S,1D,1F ⌐2S,1D,1P ⌐2Sh.w.g. ★TV,KF,F, separate entrance ♥ ⓌPets
↪ Lake Huron shores and beaches, marina, docking, childrens play area
⇔ Grand Bend, Pinery and Ipperwash Provincial Parks, Karner Blue Butterfly
Conservation area, Sarnia, US border

☞ Home is located in a forested area of Port Franks and projects relaxed and friendly
atmosphere with lots of privacy. There is a dog in the house.

Port Stanley
(on Lake Erie south of London; see also Port Bruce, Rodney, St.Thomas, Shedden)

Palmer, Ken and Ellen (Spruce Grove Farm)   ⌐ SOCVA B&B
RR1, Port Stanley, Ontario N0L 2A0   ☎ (519) 769-2245

Go west of St. Thomas to Fingal, turn left and go to paved sideroad. Turn right and
follow to end of road, then curve right to 4th house on right.
$20S $30D   ► 2
●Choice ♠Farm, on lakeshore ■1D(upstairs) ⌐2S ⌐Sh.w.h. Ⓦ Smoking
↪ Walking trails on farm property and woods, maple syrup production in March
⇔ Lake Erie and long sandy beach at Port Stanley, boutiques, summer theatre

☞ Located on west side of Lake Erie Port Community on quiet lakeshore road. Watch
migration of birds along the shores of Lake Erie in the fall.

Seaton, Mrs. Carman (Windjammer)   ⌐ B&B
324 Smith St., Box 852, Port Stanley, Ontario N0L 2A0   ☎ 519) 782-4173

From Hwy 401 take Exit 177 south and continue on Hwy 4 to Port Stanley. Look for
house on corner of William and Smith Sts (main road to beach).
$30S $40D $10Add. person   (Children's Rates available)   ► 6A,2Ch
● Full   ♠ Village, hist., large veranda ■ 3D ⌐ 2T,2D,2R, crib ⌐ Sh.w.g.
★ Air,TV, parking   Ⓦ Pets, restricted smoking
↪ Top notch restaurants, sandy beach, Summer Theatre, unique Port Stanley Terminal
Railway (round trips), fishing boats and marinas, antique and boutique shops
⇔ Village of Sparta (early 1800's Quaker settlement with outstanding early Ontario
architecture), Hawk Cliff (observaton of annual migration of raptors)
☞ 1854-built spacious home in popular Lake Erie Port Community, which is located
alongside the Talbot Trail. It was originally occupied by a Sea Merchant and has retained
most of the architectural features of Victorian Gothic.

Prescott

(near Brockville; see also Cardinal, Frankville, Morrisburg, N Augusta, Brinston)

Allan, June & M.Carrick (Daze End)　　　　　　　　　↙ Kingston B&B
RR4, Prescott, Ontario　K0E 1T0　　　　　　　　　　☎ (613) 925-3172

From Hwy 401, take Domville Exit 716 and drive north on Hwy 18 for 5 km. Look for
4th house past church on left side at cross road.
$27S　$38-45D　$5Child　$10Add.person　　　　　　　　► 4A,3Ch
● Full, homebaked　　🏠 Rural, acreage, patio, quiet　　■ 1D,1F (up- and downstairs)
　⊢ 1S,1D,2T,1P　　⌐ 1Private, 1sh.w.h.　　★ TV,F,LF　🖐 Pets
↔ Spacious lawns and woods for walking
⇔ Fort Wellington, Upper Canada Village, US border (bridge at Ogdenburg), Prescott
Glove Factory and Hathaway Shirt Outlet, live theatre, museums and anitque shops

📟 Relax in the solarium and enjoy the peaceful country atmosphere. Hosts are
collectors of antiques and ardent bridge players. There are two dogs in the house.

Priceville

(near Owen Sound; see also Kimberley, Flesherton, Durham)

Hutchinson, Bill and Jean (Lakeside Farm)　　　　　　↙ B&B
RR3, Priceville, Ontario　N0C 1K0　　　　　　　　☎ (519) 924-2506

From Flesherton (south of Owen Sound), go west on Hwy 4 to Ceylon , turn left on
Wilcox Lake Dr and to 2nd stop, turn right to 1st farm on left.
$30S　$40-45D　$10Child　　　　　　　　　　　　► 6A,3Ch
● Choice, homebaked　　🏠 300-acre farm, view, patio, quiet, isolated　■ 3D
(upstairs)　　　⊢ 2S,3D, cot, crib　⌐ 1Sh.w.g.　★ TV　🖐 Smoking, pets
↔ Scenic nature trails marked for walking on farm grounds
⇔ Beaver Valley, Bruce Trail, Eugenia Falls, golfing, swimming, skiing, unique small
town with craft shops, antiques and boutiques, restaurants

📟 Turn-of-the-Century farmhouse with a complimentary blend of modern furniture
and anitques in a picturesque setting with mapleshade trees overlooking a spacious lawn
deck and patio. Hosts' family has lived in the area since 1850 and are well informed
about the community history.

B&B Travel Tip: *You can go B&B all year around. Of course, it is most
popular when on vacation. And there are many more B&B's available in the summertime.*

Providence Bay
(on Manitoulin Island: see also Mindemoya, Gore Bay, Kagawong)

Wilson, Gordon and Nellie
Providence Bay, Ontario P0P 1T0 ☎ (705) 377-4575

From north take Hwy 540 to West Bay and Hwy 551 to Mindemoya. At junction of Hwy 542 turn west for 9.6 km and take Concession Rd 12 for 1.6 km. From south take fery to South Baymouth and drive to Providence Bay, then north for 4 km and turn left.
$25S $35D $5Child ► 6A,2Ch
✚ May-Oct   ● Full   🏠 100-acre farm, quiet   ■ 3D (upstairs)   ⊷ 1D,2T
⍒1Sh.w.g.   ★ TV,games   ⦿ Pets, drinking, restricted smoking
⇔ Shopping, restauratns, sandy beach (Lake Huron), Assiginack Historical Museum, Little Red Schoolhouse (South Baymouth), Bridal Veil Falls

☞ Cosy farm house is surrounded by lawns, gardens and flower beds Hosts are active with Dairy farming and very knowledgeable about the Manitoulin Islands.

Renfrew
(near Ottawa; see also Braeside, Forester's Falls, Calabogie, Golden Lake)

McVeigh, Lee (Stretch & Yawn)
RR3, Golf Course Rd, Renfrew, Ontario K7V 3Z6 ☎ (613) 432-8163

From Hwy 417 in Renfrew take Bruce Street Exit to Hwy 60, turn right and continue 6 km to Golf Course Rd. Turn right again.
$28S $37-39D $10Add. person ► 7
● Full, homebaked   🏠 Rural, acreage, view, lakefront, quiet   ■ 3D   ⊷ 1S,2T,2D
⍒ 1Ensuite, 1sh.w.g.   ★ TV, pool table   ♥
↪ Renfrew Golf Course, swimming, kayaking, fishing, cross-country skiing, dining
⇔ Whitewater rafting, Boneshere Caves, Storyland, Logosland, Calabogie Peaks

☞ Enjoy the beautiful scenery "out of this world". There is a friendly cat in residence.

Scharfe, Clayton and Audrey (Red Door Ranch) ⌐ CC
RR5, Renfrew, Ontario K7V 3Z8 ☎ (613) 432-8767

From Renfrew, take County Rd 20 to Castleford at river, turn left to farm on right.
$35S $40D $10Child   🍽 Meals ► 8
✚not winter   ●Full, homebaked   🏠Farm, view, lakefront, sunroom, quiet
■3-4(upstairs)   ⊷2T,2D,1Q   ⍒1Sh.w.g.   ★TV,F,LF,DF   ♥   ⦿Smoking
↪ Swimming, boating, fishing, hiking, cross-country
⇔ Storyland, Logos Land, giant water slide, whitewater rafting, golfing, antique and craft shops and Valley Carver, excellent restaurants, Bonnechere Caves

☞ Stone house with oak floors and windows set in 3ft deep walls, overlooking the magnificient river and fields and surrounded by huge overhanging Maple Trees. Watch tug pulling logs to Arnprior Mill. There are beef cattle and wild turkeys.

Richards Landing

(on St.Joseph Isle near Sault Ste. Marie; see also Bruce Mines, Manitoulin Isle)

Henderson, Vi and Norm (The Lookout)

Sailors Encampment, RR1, Richards Landing, Ontario   P0R 1J0   ☎ (705) 246-2707

Take Hwy 548 off Hwy 17 onto St. Joseph Island. Proceed over bridge to intersection at Shell Gas and Trading Post. Turn right and continue to stop sign (11.5km). Turn right and go to 1st home on right side of hill facing waterfront.

$30D   ► 2

✠ June-Sept   ● Full   ♠ Rural, acreage, patio riverfront   ■ 2D   ⌐ 2D
⌐Sh.w.h.   ★ TV,F, picnic table, Hummingbird feeder
↔ Shore of the Great Lakes shipping traffic to Lake Superior

☞ Comfortable home overlooks channel between Canada and St.Joseph Island and Neebish Isle (USA). All ocean and lake freighters pass within 1000 ft of the patio deck, on their way to Sault Ste. Marie, Thunder Bay and Duluth. Enjoy breakfast where you appear to be a stone's throw from the Captain's wheel.

Smith, Phyllis and Murray (The Anchorage)   ↙ FOBBA

RR1, Richards Landing, Ontario   P0R 1J0   ☎ (705) 246-2221

45 km east of Sault Ste. Marie take Hwy 548 to St. Joseph Island. Go through Richards Landing where the Hwy turns left. Continue for 6.4 km to the water where Hwy 548 turns left again. Continue along the shore around the curve to large yellow house on (right) shoreside of highway.

$20S $24D $7Add.person   ► 10

✠ Summer   ● Choice   ♠ Rural, acreage, view, seaway-front, quiet   ■ 1S,1D,1Ste
⌐4T,4D,1Q,R,P, crib   ⌐ 2Sh.w.g.   ★ TV in one guest room, separate entrance
☮Restricted smoking
↔ Walking trails (wildlife), miniature golf, sandy beach (private)
⇔ Fort St. Joseph Nat. Hist. Park, Island Museum, excellent shopping in Sault Ste. Marie,"Su/Locks"

☞ Quiet, friendly B&B is on the Seaway where ships from all over the world pass right in front of the house.

B&B Travel Tip: *When travelling B&B, you get more than just a bed to sleep, because you are making a personal contact in a strange place.*

216   ONTARIO

Rockport

(near Kingston; see also Seeley's Bay, Mallorytown, Delta)

Bergen, Pieter (Amaryllis)   ✔ ONT B&B,Kingst.B&B
P.O. Box, Rockport, Ontario K0E 1V0   ☎ (613) 659-3513

Take Hwy 2 (1000 Island Parkway) to Rockport. Proceed to town dock for parking.
Water Taxi available at Andress Boatworks - or possibly via host's boat or boat rental.
$50S $80D $15child $15Add.person ◙ Meals(Gourmet) ► 8
✛ July 1-Oct. 15 ● Cont. ♠ 100-ft houseboat on private island, acreage, view,
decks (screened) ■ 4D,1Ste ⊶ 4S,4D, cot, crib ⅂ 3Private, 1sh.w.g. ★ F
Ⓦ Smoking, pets ⋙ French, Spanish
↪ Swimming, sailing, boating, tennis, golfing, boat tours, walking
⇔ Wild Kingdom Park, 1000 Island summer resorts

☞ Built as a hunting and fishing camp to float along the St. Lawrence River.
Houseboat offers very unique environment of simple elegance. Small group tours
available with cultural and educational immersion of the region.

Rodney

(south-west of London; see also Port Stanley, Port Bruce, Shedden)

Stan, John and Hazel (A Touch of Home)   ✔ CC
184 Furnival Rd., Rodney, Ontario N0L 2C0   ☎ (519) 785-0823

From Hwy 401, take Exit 129 south and continue on Furnival Rd for 4.8 km
$28S $35D $10Child $10Add.person ◙ Meals ► 5A,2Ch
● Full ♠ Village, res., older, patio, quiet ■ 1S,2D (upstairs) ⊶ 1S,1D,1K,1R
⅂ 1Sh.w.g. ★ TV, parking Ⓦ Pets
↪ Shopping, restaurants
⇔ Chartered fishing, Lake Erie (sandy beach, boating and marina)

☞ Hosts have travelled extensively by B&B in Britain and New Zealand. Renovated
1893-built house is situated in pretty little village with a lot of old world charm.

VanAsten, Theo and Dorothy (Serene Acres)   ✔ OFVA
RR2, Rodney, Ontario N0L 2C0   ☎ (519) 785-0218

From Hwy 401 take interchange 129 for 3 km south and 4 km west on County Rd 4.
Look for Vacation Farm sign.
$28S $38D $10Child 12Add.person (Senior Citizen Rates) ► 6
●Choice ♠200-acres farm, swimming pool, patio, quiet ■3D(in separate 2-storey
building) ⊶1S,3D,1crib,1R ⅂TV in guest room,KF,parking ⋙Dutch
↪ walk in 30-acre woodlot rich with flora and fauna, ideal for hiking and bird watching
⇔ Lake Erie (lovely beaches and charter boat), fishing, City of London (theatres,
museum, galleries, shopping), Point Pelee National Park (most southerly point in
Canada), Swain Greenhouses (acres of tropical plants & flowers

☞ Join the hosts for breakfast in 100-year-old farm house

Rosedale

(northwest of Peterborough; see also Coboconk, Fenelon Falls)

Geist, Lothar and Laila (The Artisan's Den)   ⌐ CC
Rosedale, Gen. Del., Fenelon Falls, Ontario   K0M 1N0   ☎ (705) 887-5642

From Hwy 401, take Exit 436 and follow Hwy 35 to Rosedale. At Rosedale turn left at
Bakers Rd, go streight down and follow sign to "Tack Shop.
$25S $35D $10Child   ▣ Meals   ► 6A,1Ch
● Full   ♠ Rural, chalet, quiet   ■ 3D   ⊷ 2T,2D,R   ⌐ Sh.w.g.   ★ TV,
parking   ⓦ Smoking, pets   ⌁ Finnish, German
↪ Balsam Lake (cleanest/clearest in Kawartha, ideal for swimming), skiing
⇔ Fenelon Falls (Jewel of the Kawartha), Lindsay

🖙 Beautful Chalet-type country retreat. Wake up to bird song (Oriole, Robin and
others). See the artisan at work. Hosts will pick up guests who come by boat from any
marina, government dock, or lock in Rosedale.

Rossport

(east of Thunder Bay on northern shore of Lake Superior)

Basher, Ned and Shelagh (Rossport Inn)
Bowman Street, Rossport, Ontario   P0T 2R0   ☎ (807) 824-3213

Located 0.4 km off Trans Canada Hwy on Rossport loop.
$48S $59D   ▣ Meals   ► 12A
✜ May 1-Oct. 31   ● Choice, homebaked   ♠ Village, hist., balcony   ■ 6D
(upstairs)   ⊷ 6D,1S   ⌐ Sh.w.g.   ★ Separate entrance, Finnish type log sauna
ⓦ Well-behaved pets accepted   ⌁ Icelandic

↪ Hiking trails, Charter Fishing from
main dock, Kayak and boat rentals

⇔ Rainbow Falls Prov. Park,
Aquasabon Gorge, ghost town of
Jackfish, steelhead and salmon fishing
rivers (Spring), bird hunting for ruffled
grouse (Fall)

🖙 Home was originally built by the
Canadian Pacific Railway in 1884.
Restored and refurnished with period
antiques and has a licenced Dining
Room which specializes in local fish and
has a magnificient view of picturesque
Rossport Harbour (sometimes referred
to as the "Peggy's Cove of Ontario").
Ideal spot to sail around with many islands, off shore and sheltered coves and isolated
harbours. Well behaved pets welcome.

St.Catharines

(see also Beamsville, Niagara Falls, Niagara-on-the-Lake, Vineland, Welland, Virgil, Grimsby)

Cripps, Fran (Cripps Cosy Corner)   ↙ CC
2 Queens Court, St. Catharines, Ontario L2T 2A9   ☎ (416) 688-2306

From QEW west of St. Catharines, take Hwy 406 to Glendale Ave. Exit, turn right and
past Pen Centre to Valerie Drive, turn left (at church) one block and right on Queens Ct.
$50D $15Child   ⊡ Meals   ► 2A,1Ch
● Full, homebaked   ♠ Res., ranchstyle, view, patio, quiet   ■ 1D   ⊷ 1D
⌐ Private   ★ Air,F,TV, parking, bicycles for guests   ⓦ Smoking, pets
ᵚ Aaustrian German
↔ Brock University, shopping centre, Bruce Trail, Niagara Escarpment, Burgoyne
woods, tennis courts, park
⇔ Niagara Falls, Marineland, Welland Canal Locks, Queenston Heights, historic
Niagara-on-the-Lake, Lake Erie and Lake Ontario beaches

📢 Cosy home is nestled on a quiet residential circle below the Niagara Escarpment.
Canadian-Austrian hospitality. Pick-up service is available for train or bus travellers.

Miller, Mrs. Zita
3 Brian Ave., St. Catharines, Ontario L2T 3H5   ☎ (416) 684-4063

From QEW, take exit Ontario St south to Hwy 406. Turn right on Glendale and go past
the Pen Centre, then turn on Valerie, follow to Brian and turn left again.
$25S $40D   ► 2
● Cont.   ♠ Res., sub, bungalow, patio, quiet   ■ 1D   ⊷ 2T   ⌐ Private
★ Air,TV,KF   ⓦ Smoking
↔ Five churches, Brock University, Pen Centre shopping, Burgoyne Woods, Bruce Trail
and merrit Trail
⇔ Niagara-on-the-Lake, Niagara Falls, wineries, Toronto, Lewiston NY

📢 Modern colonial home located in quiet residential area nestled just below the
Niagara Escarpment. Retired travel agent hostess enjoys helping guests with plans.

B&B Travel Tip: *You can go B&B for a weekend. You might want to go to
the country for a good rest, or you might want to go to the city for a shopping spree
or a cultural event.*

St.Clements

(near Kitchener; see also St. Jacobs, Millbank, New Hamburg, Wallenstein, Elmira)

Hergott, Marguerite (Maple Front Farm)   ✓ SOCVA B&B
RR1, St. Clements, Ontario N0B 2M0   ☎ (519) 699-5730

From Kitchener, take Hwy 86 (Conestoga Expressway) to Northfield St. Turn left and
continue to Weber St, then right to Benjamin Rd. Turn left and go to end. Make a right
and then a left at Wellsley Rd 5E and through 2 intersections to farmhouse on right.
$25S $40D   (Family rates negotiable)   🍽 Meals   ► 6
●Choice, homebaked   🏠200-acre farm   ■4(upstairs)   ⇥T,D,P,crib   ⌐3Sh.w.g.
★TV,KF,LF, facilities for the disabled   �🚭Restricted smoking   ⚡German
↔ Large wood lot and walking areas, cross-country skiing, hiking trails, parks,
conservation areas
⇔ Mennonite country, Kitchener farmer's market and Octoberfest, Elora Gorge,
Stratford (Shakespearean Festival)

☞ Large comfortable stone house in mixed farming country. Enjoy quiet times with a
freiendly hostess who loves to cook and entertain. Children welcome.

Shantz, Henry and Edna (Evergreen Lawns)   ✓ SOCVA B&B
RR1, St. Clements, Ontario N0B 2M0   ☎ (519) 699-4453

Located on Reg. Rd 15 first farm west of Heidelberg.
$25S $35-40D $10Child $2Crib   ► 6A,3Ch
● Full   🏠 96-acres farm   ■ 2D (upstairs)   ⇥ 2T,2D, crib   ⌐ 1Sh.w.g.
⚡Smoking, drinking, pets   ⚡ some German

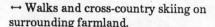
↔ Walks and cross-country skiing on
surrounding farmland.

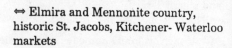
⇔ Elmira and Mennonite country,
historic St. Jacobs, Kitchener- Waterloo
markets

☞ Large two-storey house with three
porches and spacious lawns with
evergreen trees and many Mennonite
neighbors. Well travelled hosts are busy
with family and grand children,
gardening, woodworking and quilting.

St.Eugene
(east of Ottawa)

Seaman, Margaret and Ross (Windover Farm)   ✔ OFVA
RR1, St. Eugene, Ontario   K0B 1P0   ☎ (613) 674-2980

From Hwy 417, take Exit 5 and drive south to Concession Rd. At the red brick church
turn right and continue for 3.6 km to sign on mailbox.
\$15S   \$25D   \$7.50Child(under age 14)   \$15Add.person   (Reservations)   ► 4
● Full, homebaked   ♠ 100-acre farm, semi-isolated   ■ 2S,1D (upstairs)   ⊷2S,1D
   ⊓ 1Sh.w.g.   ★ TV,F   ⁓ French
⇔ Hawksbury, Carillon Prov. Park, excellent beaches, boating, groomed ski trails)

☞ Quiet, century-old brick house on farm. Breakfast served on screened porch. There
are friendly pets in residence. Hosts are keen Elderhostelers. There are horses and cows
in the pasture.

St.George
(near Brantford; see also Troy)

Brown, Gloria and Susan (Inn St. George)
16-18 Main St., St. George, Ontario   N0E 1N0   ☎ (519) 448-1481

From Hwy 5 turn onto Main St and look for Inn St. George half a block down.
\$30S   \$45-55D   ▣ Meals   ► 4-6
● Cont., homebaked   ♠ Downtown, hist., acreage, quiet   ■ S,D,Ste (upstairs)
⊷ S,T,D   ⊓ 2Sh.w.g.   ★ KF, parking   ⊛ Pets
↪ Downtown historic village of St. George
⇔ Brantford, Paris, Cambridge, Kitchener Mennonite country, African Lions Safari,
southern Ontario's finest apple orchards

☞ 1850 former small hotel, renovated for B&B is warmly decorated in "Country
Victorian". Mrs. Brown's gift shop (with old General Store feeling) is on the premises.

St.Jacobs
(near Waterloo; see also Elmira, St.Clements, Millbank, Wallenstein, Winterbourne)

Sikorski, Eunice and George (Country B&B)   ✔ CC
24 Young Street, St. Jacobs, Ontario   N0B 2N0   ☎ (519) 664-2880

From Waterloo, take Hwy 86 north to St.Jacobs. Look for central location.
\$30S   \$40D   ► 5-6
● Choice, homebaked   ♠ Village, hist., patio, quiet   ■ 1S,2D   ⊷ 1S,2T,1D
⊓ Sh.w.h.   ★ Separate entrance   ⁓ Polish
↪ Mennonite village, shops, antiques, auctions, artisan studios
⇔ Kitchener/Waterloo (Octoberfest, Glockenspiel), Woodside Nat. Hist. Park

☞ Large Victorian farmhouse in Mennonite country. Discover the fascinating history
of the Mennonite people in the Meeting place Museum. There is a cat in residence.

St.Marys
(near Stratford; see also Denfield, St.Paul, Thorndale, Ilderton)

Bosman, Tony and Sharon (Bowmore Manor)   ✓ CC
Box 363, 265 Jones St. E., St. Marys, Ontario N0M 2V0   ☎ (519) 284-1768

Coming from Stratford, turn left at the Water Tower (Queens & James) to house on first
corner on the right (Jones St).
$40S $45D   ▶ 6
● Full   ♠ Hist., res., patio, veranda   ■ 3D (upstairs)   ⊢ 2T,2Q   ⊓ 2Sh.w.g.
★ TV,F,ceiling fans in guest rooms, sunroom, parking   ⓦ Restricted smoking, pets
⌇ Dutch, German, some French

↔ Downtown shopping and dining,
Post Office, golf course, train Station,
parks, churches

⇔ Stratford Festival Theatres, London,
Goderich

🖝 Large Victorian home, tastefully
furnished and decorated, reflects the
architectural charm of the period and
located in quaint town with friendly
people and old stone homes, churches
and bridges. Breakfast is served in the
sunroom or formal dining room.

Burgin, Leanne & Jill & Jennie (Green Arbour B&B)   ✓ CC
RR1, St. Marys, Ontario N0M 2V0   ☎ (519) 229-6671

From Kirkton on Hwy 23 (north-west of St Marys), turn east on Perth County Rd 24 and
look for 1st farmhouse on north side.
$35S $45D   ▣ Meals   (Family rates available)   ▶ 4A,4Ch
✚ Summer (other times by reservation)   ● Full, homebaked   ♠ 100-acres farm,
patio, quiet   ■ 2D (upstairs)   ⊢ 2D,1D (futon), 1cot   ⊓ 1Sh.w.g.   ★ Air,TV
ⓦ Smoking, drinking, pets
↔ Sugar bush, village of Kirkton
⇔ St. Marys, Community Center, pool, playground, sportsfield, Miller's Barn, Stratford
Festival, Lake Huron, Country Playhouse, Blyth Summer Theatre

🖝 100-year old farmhouse has been renovated and lovingly maintained, is set well
back from the paved road on 3 acres of carefully tended lawns and surrounded by
thousand trees planted on the property by the hosts' family. Sour dough waffles and own
maple syrup is a house specialty served with free range eggs and homemade jams and
jellies. There are many animals including llamas.

Gibson, Janet M. (Montrave Guest Home)   ⌐ CC
RR7, St. Marys, Ontario   N0M 2V0   ☎ (519) 393-5529

Take Hwy 7 to Stratford and continue on Hwy 8 west to County Rd 19. Then go south to
5th intersection (Con.11/12) and past church and cemetery to 3rd laneway on left.
$40 per room   ●$4Each   ►4
● Choice, homebaked   🏠 Farm, older, acreage, view, quiet   ■ 2D (upstairs)   ⊢2D,
crib   ⌐ 1Sh.w.h.,1sh.w.g.   ★ TV,F, parking   🤚 Smoking, drinking, pets
↔ Quiet rural landscape ideal for walking
⇔ Lake Huron beaches, swimming, fishing, Stratford Shakespearean Festival, Blyth
Theatre, Huron County Playhouse, golfing, shopping, Saturday night dancing, antique
shops, flea markets,

🖐 Enjoy the quiet country hospitality and comfortable rooms. Ideal place from which
to explore the heart of Southwestern Ontario.

May, Doris and Harold (Park Street Maples)
242 Park Street, St. Marys, Ontario   N0M 2V0   ☎ (519) 284-3672/284-3080

Take Hwy 7 S/W of Stratford to St.Marys Exit at Wildwood Conservation intersection.
$45 (flat rate) $15 Cot   ►6
● Cont., homebaked   🏠 Res., patio   ■ 3D (upstairs)   ⊢ 3D, cots   ⌐ Sh.w.g.
★ air, parking   🤚 Smoking, children min. age 10
↔ Town centre, museum, park, churches
⇔ Swimming, tennis, Stratford theatres

🖐 Large, air-conditioned and allergy free atmosphere. Weather permitting, breakfast
is served in shaded garden with mature maple trees.

St.Thomas
(near London: see also Shedden, Port Bruce, Rodney)

Main, June & Bill (Rosebery Place   ⌐ SWOTA
42 Rosebery Place, St. Thomas, Ontario   N5R 2H7   ☎ (519) 631-1525

From Hwy 401 take Exit 164 or 177 south.
$38S $48D $10Add.person ●Full   🏠Res, hist, acreage   ■1S,2D(upstairs)   ⊢5T
⌐1Sh.w.g.,sink in one guest room   ★TV,F,parking   🤚Restricted smoking
↔ Elgin County Museum, Military Museum, Jumbo Statue, County Court House,
downtown shopping, churches
⇔ Lake Erie, Port Stanley, Sparta, Hawk's Cliff, Stratford

🖐 Unique large Copper Beech Tree and large garden surrounding 135-year-old home,
completely redecorated in keeping with the Victorian era and furnished with fine pieces
of antiques.

Sault Ste. Marie
(see also Bruce Mines, Richards Landing)

Brauer, Mrs. Margaret & Bert
40 Broos Rd, Sault Ste.Marie, Ontario P6C 5S4   ☎ (705) 253-9041

Folow Hwy 17 (Second Line) and airport signs to Goulais Ave and continue west for
3km. to Broos Rd. Look for sign. Reservations requested.
$30S $40D $10Child ► 4
● Cont, homebaked (Choice on weekends)   🏠 Sub., acreage, view, patio, quiet
■2D   ⊷ 2S,1Q   ⁀Sh.w.g.   ★ F,TV,LF, parking, solarium with indoor fish pond
⌇ German
↔ Hiking and walking along creek and bush, Lily pond with fish
⇔ Agawa Canyon tour train, swimming, fishing, boating,hiking, cross-country ski trails,
downhill skiing, Sault Locks and tour boats, shopping plazas, restaurants, untouched
wilderness and tumbling crystal clear waterfalls, cliffs of the Canadian shield

☞ Unique home is surrounded by picturesque garden and tranquil European
ambience. Hosts enjoy nature and are seasoned travellers.

Heinzel, Mr. and Mrs. Hans
29 Parasol Cresc., Sault Ste. Marie, Ontario P6B 3S4   ☎ (705) 253-7419

Take McNabb St (Hwy 17) to Pine St, turn north to Passmore, right to Palace, right to
Princess and left to Parasol Cresc.
$20S $30D   (Phone for reservation) ► 4
● Choice   🏠 Res., split-level, sub., patio, quiet   ■ 2 (upstairs) ⊷ 2S,1D
⁀1Sh.w.g.   ★TV in guest room,parking 🖐Pets,smoking,drinking ⌇German
↔ Shopping plaza, restaurants, YMCA health centre
⇔ Int. Bridge to USA, Sault Locks, ski resorts, Algoma Central Railway tour-train

Wilson, Pauline (Pauline's Place)   ↙ CC
72 Cathcart St., Sault Ste. Marie, Ontario P6A 1E1   ☎ (705) 254-2575

Write or phone for directions.
$28S $35D ► 6A,2Ch
● Full   🏠 Downtown, older, veranda   ■ 3D (upstairs)   ⊷ 2T,2D, crib,R
⁀1Sh.w.g.   ★ Air, TV, separate entrance, parking   ♥   🖐 Smoking
↔ Downtown, International Bridge, USA border
⇔ Agawa Canyon Train Tours, indoor Mall, downhill and cross-country skiing, beaches,
swimming, boating

☞ Spacious older home in the City surrounded by water. Children and pets welcome.

Seaforth

(near Stratford; see also Clinton, Mitchell, Millbank)

Patterson, John and Gwen (Holmsted House B&B)   ⌣ SOCVA,FOBBA
RR2, Box 1125, Seaforth, Ontario N0K 1W0   ☎ (519) 522-2040

Write or phone for directions.
$30-45S $45-60D $15Add.person (Reservations requested)   ► 8A,1Ch
● Full ♠ Rural, res., older, acreage, patio, quiet ■ 4D mainand upper floors)
↤ 1S,1T,2D,1Q ⌐ 1Private, 1sh.w.g. ★ TV,F, separate entrance, large guest
sitting room, bicycles ♥ ⓦ Restricted smoking
↔ Quiet country road for strolling and jogging, cross-country skiing, snowmobiling
⇔ Golf course, tennis, swimming pool, conservation area, Stratford theatres, Blyth
Summer theatre and shops, Lake Huron, charter fishing

☞ Comfortable and distinctive Century home furnished with antiques and located in
beautiful country setting in Harperhey, a friendly rural hamlet on the edge of Seaforth.
There is a cat in residence.

Seeleys Bay

(near Kingston; see also Delta, Westport, Sydenham, Rockport, Mallorytown)

Milligan, Janet and Donald (Milligan's Country B&B)   ⌣ FOBBA,Kingst.B&B
RR1, Seeleys Bay, Ontario K0H 2N0   ☎ (613) 387-4081

From Hwy 401 take Exit 623 and continue north on Hwy 15 for 25.6km. Look for B&B
sign on left side, just before turn-off to Burnt Hills Rd.
$27S $37D $10Child(under age 12) $15Add.person   ► 7
✠ M1-Oct.31 (winter by arrangement) ● Full, homebaked ♠ Rural, 5-acres, older
■ 3D (ustairs) ↤ 12D,1Q,1T ⌐ Sh.w.g. ★ TV,KF, woodstove, piano ♥
ⓦ Smoking, pets outside

↔ Brass Point Bridge on Rideauy, bike
tours

⇔ Kingston, Gananoque, 1000 Islands,
Rideau System, Charleston Lake
Provincial Park

☞ Spacious, turn-of-the-Century
brick farm house. Enjoy a relaxed
family atmosphere in country-style
home. Muffins and blueberry pancakes
with farm-fresh eggs a specialty. There
are two young daughters "Jessica" and
"Laura" in the host family, who also
enjoy travelling B&B.

Simcoe

(near Lake Erie south of Brantfort; see also Waterford, Port Dover)

McManis, Richard and Sylvia
356 Norfolk Street South., Simcoe, Ontario   N3Y 2W9   ☎ (519) 426-6719

Phone for directions.
$25S $30D   ► 6A
● Cont.   ♠ Downtown, older, acreage, swimming pool, patio, quiet   ■ 3D   ⊷ T,D,R
⌐ Sh.w.g.   ★ Air, TV in guest room, reading area   ⊛ Smoking, children, pets
↔ Conservation area across street, Christmas Light Panorama, Lynwood Art Centre
⇔ Lake Erie, Port Dover, Lighthouse Festival and Simcoe Little Theatres, Museum

☞ Comfortable family home surrounded by spacious grounds. There is a dog and a cat.
Guided cross-country ski tours can be arranged. Hostess is involved in Simcoe Little
Theatre and invites guests to attend, if interested.

Shedden West

(near London; see also St. Thomas, Port Bruce, Rodney)

Walker, Jack and Pat (Walnut Grove)   ↙ SWOTA
RR3, Shedden West, Ontario   N0L 2E0   ☎ (519) 764-2337

Take Union Rd cuoff Exit 164 from Hwy 401 and turn west on Hwy 3 to 1.5 km west of
Shedden.
$45 per room   ▣ Meals   ► 6
● Cont, homebaked   ♠ Rural, hist., acreage, swimming pool, patio, quiet   ■ 3D
(upstairs)   ⊷ T,D,Q,   ⌐ Sh.w.g.–   ★ F,TV in guest room, parking, guest lounge,
screened porch   ⊶ Spanish
↔ Peaceful rural setting ideal for walking
⇔ Lake Erie, beautiful beaches, Port Stanley, fishing, great restaurants, London, Art
Gallery, Museums, Pioneer Village, Springbank Park, Sparta (oldest Quaker settlement
in Canada) interesting boutiques and craft shops

☞ Heritage home (1864) with Cathedral windows and cozy corners provides an aura of
peace and contentment and is set back on more than an acre of land and surrounded by
a grove of Walnut trees. Enjoy silver service breakfast in the dining room or on the
screened porch.

B&B Travel Tip: *You can stay in a B&B when relocating to another city. Is
there a better way of getting the feeling of a new area than talking to the local
people?*

South Gillies
(near Thunder Bay)

Nobel, David and Arlan (Unicorn Inn)   ✔ FOBBA
RR1, South Gillies, Ontario P0T 2V0   ☎ (807) 575-4200

From Thunder Bay go south on Hwy 61 to Hwy 608 (20 km from airport). Turn right
and continue for 16 km. Look for signs for Unicorn Rd and Unicorn Inn.
$38S $48D $5-15Child   🍽 Meals (Thurs-Sun only)   ► 6
✚ Wed's to Sat's   ● Full, homebaked   ♠ Rural, 440-acres, view, quiet, isolated
■2D, bunk room   ⊷ 2D, bunk   ⌐ 2Sh.w.g.   ★ F, eclectic library, plug-ins for
vehicles   ✋ Smoking, pets, children min. age 10
↔ Walking, hiking, cross-country skking on 400 acres of property, Award-winning
dining room on premises
⇔ Lake, swimming, boating, Old Fort William, Amethyst caves, country stores,
Kakabeka Falls, major ski areas

🖙 European pension-type B&B is surrounded by cliffs of the Canadian Shield. Host is
an award-winning chef and accomplished musician. Entire first floor exclusive for
guests' use. Host is spokesperson for Thunder Bay Area B&B.

Southampton
(near Owen Sound; see also Dobbinton, Port Elgin, Oliphant, Palgrave)

Higgins, John and Hazel (Hollingborne House)   ✔ Grey Bruce B&B
48 Grey Street North, Southampton, Ontario N0H 2L0   ☎ (519) 797-3202

Located in Southampton (3rd house behind hospital).
$25S $30D   (Book early to avoid disappointment)   ► 4A
● Full   ♠ Res., view   ■ 2D   ⊷ 2T,1D   ⌐ Sh.w.g.   ★ TV   ✋ Pets,
restricted smoking, children, accessibel for the handicapped   ⊶ Armenian
↔ Inland Lake, nature walks, shopping areas
⇔ Sauble Beach, swimming, boating, Bruce Trail hiking, Georgian Bay, Douglas Point
(Nuclear Energy Plant tours), Collingwood (skiing)

🖙 Modern home, furnished with antiques, overlooking beautiful Fairy Lake. Hosts are
busy with furniture re-finishing and caning chairs.

> **B&B Travel Tip:** *Do not think of giving tips. Remember this is not a hotel
> service.*

Stratford

(see also N.Hamburg, St.Mary's, Millbank, Mitchell, Embro)

Dunn, Verna and Allan (Dunn-Drae-Homes) ✓ B&B
150 Douglas St., Stratford, Ontario   N5A 5P6 ☎ (519) 273-0619

From Toronto take Hwy 7/8 west and enter Stratford on Ontario St. Turn on Huron
St(Hwy 8), go 1 block to Petro Canada Stn, turn left onto Douglas.
$30-34S $34-54D $54F ► 16
● Cont., homebaked   🏠 Res., hist., patio, quiet   ■ 3D (main and upper floor)
⊨4T,3D,1Q,1R,1P   ⊓ 2Private, 3sh.w.g.   ★ Air (in guest rooms), F,TV in guest
room, parking   Ⓦ Smoking, pets, children min.age 8
↔ Festival Theatre, Shakespearean Gardens, uptown, River, paddle boats/canoes
⇔ Shakespeare Antique Stores, cross-country ski trails, Seagram Museum, Elmira and
Mennonite country, Montrose covered Bridge, Elora Gorge and Canyon

☛ Home, dating back to the 1880's, has large and small rooms, each in a different
decor. Retired hosts have time to visit with guests and help plan day trips to interesting
sights in the area.

Hunsberger, Joanne (Joanne's Guest House) ✓ CC
269 Ontario St., Stratford, Ontario   N5A 3H6 ☎ (519) 273-4960

Located on south side of Hwy 7/8 between Front and Nile Streets.
$45-50D ✓ 6
● Full   🏠 downtown, older   ■ 3D (upstairs)   ⊨ 2D,1D,1Q   ⊓ Sh.w.h.
★Off-street parking, ceiling fans in guest rooms, cosy sitting room   Ⓦ Smoking, not
equipped for toddlers or babies

↔ All theatres, retaurants, shops and
boutiques

⇔ Grand Bend on Lake Huron,
Kitchener Farmer's Market and
Mennonite Country, St. Jacobs

☛ Central and conveniently located
home with beautifully decorated and
cheerful rooms. There is a front
veranda with porch swing for relaxing.

Mieczkowski, Linea and Ed (The Maples)　　　　　　ⱽ SWOTA
220 Church St., Stratford, Ontario　N5A 2R6　　　　☎ (519) 273-0810

Follow Ontario St (Hwy 7/8) to Court House, turn left on Church St to 3rd house.
$32S　$39-48D　●$4.50Each(full English)　(plus Tax)　(Deposit required)　　► 12
● Cont., homebaked　♠ Downtown, older, quiet, veranda　■ 5D　┅ T,D
⌐3Sh.w.g.　★ Ample parking　ⓦ Pets, children min. age 12　ᴡᴡ Polish, German
↔ Festival theatres, downtown shopping, dining, railway station, bus depot
⇔ Mennonite Country, Elora Gorge, Blyth Festival, Lake Huron beaches

🐾 Charming 1890's home with warm oak-wood and winding staircase and pleasant
furnishings situated on quiet tree-lined street. House specialty is a "delicious Continental
or English Breakfast" served on large veranda in a relaxing atmosphere..

Wilker, Lester J (Burnside Guest Home)　　　　　ⱽ Strat.B&B
139 William Street, Stratford, Ontario　N5A 4X9　　☎ (519) 271-7076

From Toronto enter on Hwys 7/8 to Ontario St. From Detroit on Hwy 401 exit at Embro
Rd to Erie St. From Sarnia on Hwy 7 exit at Erie St. Take Huron Street bridge and keep
in right lane for Willam St.
$30S　$45D　$10Child　●$3Each (Full)　　　　　► 8A,4CH
● Cont, homebaked　♠ Downtown, res, hist., acreage, view, lakefront, quiet　■2S,2D
(upper and lower level)　┅4S,4T,1K,3D,3R,P, crib　⌐2Sh.w.g.,1sh.w.h.　★ Air,TV,
separate entrance, parking, high chair　♥　ⓦ Smoking, pets
↔ Bus and train station, theatres (Stage 3, Shakespeare, Avon), The Gallery Stratford
⇔ Shakespear Antique Shop, Listowel Mills Yarn Outlets, Elmira Mennonite country

🐾 Victorian turn-of-the-Century home situated on the north shore of Lake Victoria in
central location was built in 1851 by family's Great-grandfather on site of Stratford's
first mill and has beautiful landscaped gardens a block long. There is a dog in residence.
Host is Chairman of The Ontario Genealogical Society.

Worden, Mrs. Dorothy (Avonlea Woods)　　　　　ⱽ SWOTA
RR3, Stratford, Ontario　N5A 6S4　　　　　　☎ (519) 271-3732

Located 1 km south of Hwy 8 at the westerly city limits at 330 O'Loane Avenue South.
$25-30S　$35-40D　$15Add. person　(Family rates)　　　► 8A,4Ch
● Choice, homebaked　♠ Rural, acreage, view, patio　■ 4D,F (main and upper
floor)　┅ 4T,2D, cot, crib　⌐ 2Sh.w.g.　★ Air,TV, separate entrance, parking,
limited camping facilities　ⓦ Smoking, pets　ᴡᴡ German
⇔ Festival Theatres, Lake Huron beaches, farmer's market, Mennonite country

🐾 Award-winning home for "Beautification in Perth County 1988", has rose gardens,
fountain and waterfall with gold fish, plus other gardens and wood. Relax and enjoy the
surrounding natural beauty and park-like setting. Breakfast features fresh fruits,
homebaked muffins and more.

Ambassador B&B Guest Homes ✓ B&B
266 Ontario St., Stratford, Ontario N5A 3H5 ☎ (519) 271-5385
(Co-ordinator Grace Brunk)

Rates: $35S $58D (including breakfast)
Gracious older homes located close to theatres, restaurants, downtown shopping and
lovely park system, bus and train depots. Some homes have private bath, balcony,
sunporch, locks on doors and off-street parking. Restricted smoking.

Sudbury
(see also Lavigne, North Bay, Whitefish, Webbwood)

Cull, Kathryn and Michael (Paris Guesthouse)
60 Red Cross Blvd., Sudbury, Ontario P3B 2N3 ☎ (705) 671-2230

Located on the corner of Paris and Larch Streets. Phone for directions.
$35S $42-50D $10Add.person $70Ste (Weekly rates available) ► 13
● Full, homemade 🏠 Downtown, res., older, deck, quiet ▦ 4D,2Ste
↦ 5D,1P,1R ⌐ 1Private, 3sh.w.g. ★ TV,F,LF, off street parking ♨ Restricted
smoking, pets
↔ Sudbury Theatre Centre, City Shopping Complex, YMCA, Lake Ramsey, Bell Park,
Science North, Civic Center, Train Station
⇔ Cambrian College and Laurentian University, Big Nichol Mine

☞ Large English Tudor-style home is situated in an old residential area adjacent to the
downtown core and furnished with traditional and contemporary pieces which enhance
the relaxed atmosphere.

> **B&B Travel Tip:** *Do not expect the same service you ususally get in a hotel.
> The service in a B&B is completely different. It is, in fact, even better, because of
> all the little things the hosts will do for you and the information they will give you
> (many extras that cannot be bought in a hotel!). In fact, they will be happy and so
> proud to tell you all about the local facilities, happenings and the history of their
> hometown.*

Sydenham

(near Kingston; see also Westport, Seeleys Bay, Napanee)

Roberts, Ron and Betty (The Old School House)   ✔ Kingston B&B
RR1, Sydenham, Ontario K0H 2T0   ☎ (613) 376-6859

From Hwy 401 at Kingston, take Exit 613 (Sydenham Rd North) for 16.7 km. At flashing
red light, turn right onto County Rd 5 and go 3.3 km to house on south side of road.
$30S $45D $15Rollaway   🍴 Meals   ► 4A
● Full   🏠 Rural, acreage, bungalow, quiet   ■ 1S,1D   ⇌ 2T,1K   ⍽ 1Sh.w.g.
★ TV in guest room   ✋ Smoking, pets

⇔ Village of Sydenham and
Harrowsmith, unique shops, picnic
spots and conservation areas, Kingston,
1000 Islands, Frontenac Prov. Park,
Rideau Canal

☛ Century-old limestone school
house is situated near the historic
village of Sydenham. House specialty is
black current jam. There is a cat in the
house.

Thedford

(near Grand Bend; see also Parkhill, Petrolia, Ilderton)

Stewardson,Don and Dona (Donview Farms)   ✔ Sarnia/Lambt B&B
RR3, Thedford, Ontario N0M 2N0   ☎ (519) 786-5469

Easy access off Hwy 402 from south. Hwy 21 from north, call for directions.
$25S $35D $5Child   ► 4
● Choice,   🏠 Dairy farm, older, view, patio, swimming pool   ■ 2D   ⇌ 1Q,1SD
⍽ 2Sh.w.h.   ★ TV,F   ✋ Pets
⇔ Grand Bend, Ipperwash and Pinery Prov. Parks, Huron County Playhouse, museums,
excellent beaches, dining, golfing, US border, cross- country skiing

☛ Modern working farm with spacious 85-year old farmhouse.

Thornbury
(near Owen Sound; see also Clarksburg, Meaford, Collingwood, Duntroon, Creemore Kimberley)

Salmon, Joan and Gord (Golden Apple B&B)   ✓ CC
78 Bruce St., Thornbury, Ontario   N0H 2P0   ☎ (519) 599-3850

Phone for directions.
35-40D $60F   ► 8-10
● Full   🏠 Village, older   ■ 3D and family loft (upstairs)   ◄ 2T,1D,2Q, crib
⌐Sh.w.g.   ★ TV in guest room, parking   ♥   Ⓦ Smoking, pets
↔ Georgian Bay, Beaver River, fishing, rerstaurants, shops
⇔ Beaver Valley and Blue Mountain Ski Resorts, Collingwood, Meaford, Owen Sound

☞ Spacious older home in A-1 condition. Enjoy a special hearty country breakfast.
There is a quiet friendly Bichon Frise dog call "Jodi" in the house.

Thornton
(near Barrie; see also Bradford, Beeton)

Small, Louise and Rodney (Birch Lane)   ✓ CC
262 Barrie St., Thornton, Ontario   L0L 2N0   ☎ (705) 458-4816

Located on Hwy 27, south of Barrie. Phone for directions.
$30S $35D $5Child   ●$2Each   ► 6
● Full, homebaked   🏠 Village, older, patio, quiet   ■ 3D (upstairs)   ◄ 3D
⌐ Sh.w.g.   ★ F,TV in guest room, parking   Ⓦ Drinking
⇔ Molson Park (outdoor concerts), Balloon Festival, fishing, swimming, boating,
golfing, shopping, skiing, snowmobiling, skating

☞ Comfortable early Century home with antique furnishing and large wrap around
veranda with cool breezes. There is a dog in the house.

Thunder Bay
(see also South Gillis, Rossport)

Maier, Ed and Margaret   ✓ CC
331 Belrose Rd, RR17, Thunder Bay, Ontario   P7B 6C2   ☎ (907) 767-2254

From Hwy 17, take Oliver Rd Exit west to Belrose (1 km). Turn right to house on left.
$20S $30D $5Child $10Add.person   (Seniors welcome)   ► 6
● Full   🏠 sub., bungalow, acreage, quiet   ■ 4S,1D,1Ste   ◄ 4S,1D,1R
⌐ 3Sh.w.g.   Ⓦ Smoking, pets
↔ Five acres park-like setting for walking
⇔ Downtown Thunder Bay, Terry Fox Monument, Mt McKay lookout, Old Fort
William, Harbour Cruises, Centennial Park, Amethyst Mines, Airport

Tobermory

(north of Owen Sound, see also Lion's Head, Oliphant, Wiarton, Providence Bay, Mindemoya, Gore Bay, Kagawong, Palgrave)

Johnstone (Hidden Valley Lodge)   ↙ Grey Bruce B&B
RR2, Tobermory, Ontario N0H 2R0   ☎ (519) 596-2610

From Wiarton, take Hwy 6 north to Hidden Valley Road.
$35S $55D   ◉ Meals   (Off-season Rates)   ► 16
● Full, homebaked   ♠ 1200-acre farm   ■ 4D (separate units)   ⊷ 8D
⌐ 2Ensuite, 1sh.w.g.   ★ TV in guest room, separate entrance   ⊛ Pets
↔ Farm and bush land, snowmobiling or cross-country skiing, trout stream
⇔ Ferry to Manitoulin Isle., boat cruises, diving and underwater activities, Lions Head, Tobermory, Wiarton

☞ A paradise for the naturalist and photographer. Located near the "picture postcard" village of Tobermory on the tip of the Bruce Peninsula and next to Canada's newest National Park. Please specify when booking for "B&B accommodation".

Toronto

(see also Oakville, Georgetown, Kleinburg, Richmond Hill, Newmarket, Uxbridge)

Baldwin, Arlene and Wendal Selman (The Shaw House) ↙ B&B Homes Toronto
442 Shaw St., Toronto, Ontario M6G 3L3   ☎ (416) 533-9111

Take Spadina Exit off Gardiner Expressway. Go north to College St, west on College to Shaw St (One way south). Travel around the block at Crawford.
$35S $50-60D $10Add.person   ●$5Each(friends of guests)   ◉ Meals   ► 7
● Full   ♠ Downtown, older   ■ 3D   ⊷ 2T,2D,1Q   ⌐ 1h.w.h., 1sh.w.g.
★Piano, on site-parking   ⊛ Smoking, pets, children min. age 12
↔ Street-car service (24hr) to all of Metro's areas, Bloor St. Subway, Queen St, Kensington Market, Queen's Park, laundromats, branch library across street
⇔ Eaton Centre, Art Gallery and ROM, Sick Children's and other hospitals

☞ Recently renovated spacious Victorian home in lively west-end Toronto neighborhood just steps away from "Little Italy". Host, originally from Trinidad, represented Toronto in Canadian Living magazine (Sept.1985) for breakfasts in B&B and his famous cheese-walnut loaf recipe was included. Congenial hosts are very musical and enjoy jazz sessions every Friday night in the L-room. Guests are invited to join in, if they wish.

B&B Travel Tip: *You can stay in a B&B when relocating to another city. Is there a better way of getting the feeling of a new area than talking to the local people?*

Bolton, Elinor (Lowther House) ↙ FOBBA
72 Lowther Ave., Toronto, Ontario   M5R 1C8   ☎ (416) 323-1589

Located in the Bloor/University area.
$50S (and up) $65-855D   ► 4-5
● Full (Gourmet)   🏠 Central, res., older, hist.   ■ 1D,1Ste   ⊷ 2T,1Q
⫬1Private, 1ensuite   ★ Air,TV,F   ⊛ Smoking, pets, children min. age 9
↔ St. George Subway Stn., Royal Ontario Museum, U of T, Parliament Buildings, Casa Loma, Yonge/Bloor shopping, Yorkville,
⇔ Pioneer Village, Metro Zoo, Wonderland, Kleinburg

🖝 Spacious and lovingly restored 1890 Queen Anne-Richardson Romanesque home has turretted front with some magnificient leaded glass windows and a grand staircase made of maple and oak woodwork and located in a gracious neighborhood of stately homes, just two short blocks away from all the excitement of the commercial areas of Toronto. House is furnished with antiques and art.

Boonstra, Simen and Susan ↙ B&B
28 Athabaska Ave., Toronto, Ontario   M2M 2T7   ☎ (416) 225-5510

From Hwy 401, take Yonge Street Exit north. Located near Steeles and Yonge.
$35S $45D   ► 4A
● Full   🏠 Res, sub., patio, quiet   ■ 2D (upstairs)   ⊷ 2S,1D, 1cot   ⫬ 1Private,
1sh.w.g.   ★ Air, TV in guest room, parking   ⊛ Children min. age 10

↔ Finch Subway Station, restaurants and shopping mall

⇔ Downtown Toronto, Science Center, Ontario Place, Shouldice Hospital, York University, Pioneer Village, Canada's Wonderland

🖝 Very conveniently located home situated in the northern part of the city. Walk 1 block over to famous Yonge Street (longest street in the world) or relax on sundeck off the den.

B&B Travel Tip: *You can go B&B for a weekend. You might want to go to the country for a good rest, or you might want to go to the city for a shopping spree or a cultural event.*

Brown, Mirella & Garnet McPherson (Beaches B&B)   ↙ B&B Homes Toronto
Leuty Ave., Toronto, Ontario   M4E 2R2   ☎ (416) 691-6996

Located near Queen St and Lee Ave in Toronto East end. Phone for directions.
$39 $49D $10Add.person   ► 4
● Cont., homebaked   ♠ Res.   ■ 2   ↵ 2D   ⅂ Sh.w.h.   ★ Air,TV, F in common
room   ⓦ Smoking, pets   ⌇ French, Italian
↔ Lake Ontario, famous Lakeside Boardwalk, tennis courts, jogging, bicycle trails, lawn
bowling, windsurfing, Olympic sized swimming pool, wide sandy beaches, concerts in the
part, Kew Gardens, excellent public transportation
⇔ Downtown Toronto, Metro Zoo, Ontario Science Centre

🐾 Hosts are spokespersons for the "Bed and Breakfast Homes of Toronto"
Association and they will cater to special diets if requested. Bicycles for rent.

Conklin, William
237 Lee Ave, Toronto, Ontrio   M4E 2P4   ☎ (416) 690-9688

Located in the Toronto Beaches area. Take Hwy 2 to Queen St and right on Lee Ave.
$40S $50D $15Child $15Add.person   ▣ Meals   ► 6A,2Ch
●Cont, homebaked(large)   ♠Downtown, res, bungalow, patio, quiet
■1S,2D,1Ste(main and upper floor)   ↵2T,2D,2cots   ⅂1Private,1sh.w.h.,1ensuite
★Air,2F, TV in guest room, separate entrance,parking, outdoor jacuzzi   ⓦSmoking,
pets   ⌇French, Spanish
↔ Lake Ontario, beach and boardwalk, parks, windsurfing, bicycle rentals, 30
interesting restaurants, Harness Racetrack, shops, public transportation
⇔ Downtown Toronto, Science Centre, Harbourfront, Ontario Place, R.O.M.

🐾 Comfortable home is surrounded by lovely garden with many roses and located in
popular and interesting area of East Toronto, yet close to all of the city's major
attractions. There are pets in residence.

Dallimore, Joyce and Rob (Dallimore Residence)   ↙ B&B Homes Toronto
2110 Varency Drive, Mississauga, Ontario   L5K 1C3   ☎ (416) 822-3540/823-5212

Phone for directions. Located West of Toronto.
$35S $45D $5Child   ► 6
● Full   ♠ Res., sub., acreage, patio, quiet   ■ 3D (upstairs)   ↵ 2T,1D,1Q
⅂Sh.w.g.   ★ Air, parking   ⓦ Restricted smoking
↔ Large shopping Centre, good restaurants, excellent local bus service to City Centre
⇔ Lake Ontario shoreline and parks, "GO" Commuter train to Toronto, International
Airport, Kitchener Mennonite Country, Niagara Falls

🐾 English-style hospitality in large modern home located on large treed porperty.
There is a dog in the house. Well travelled hosts enjoy discussing mutual adventures
from all over the world. Pick-up from Airport with advance bookings, min.stay 2 nights.

Dew, Edith and John (By the Creek)　　　　⌐ B&B Homes Toronto
1716 Lincolnshire Blvd., Mississauga, Ontario　L5E 2S7　　☎ (416) 891-0337/278-5937

Located West of Toronto. Phone for directions.
$40S　$45D　$60F　$15Add.person　▨ Meals　● Choice, homebaked　♠ Res.,
sub.,view,patio,quiet,on Etobicoke Creek　■ D,Ste,F (main and lower
floor)　⊷2T,1D,1QR, crib　⌐ Sh.w.g.　★ F,TV in guest room, KF, separate
entrance, parking　⊛ Smoking, pets
↤ Sherway Gardens Shopping Mall, Dixie Value Mall, public golf course, tennis courts
↔ Pearson International Airport, downtown Toronto City Centre, Metro Zoo, Art
Gallery, Royal Ontario Museum, Eaton's Centre, Ontario Place, Exhibition

☛ Comfortable and quiet home in the outskirts of the big City. Hosts will pick up
guests from Commuter train. Business people, bus travellers and all children welcome.

Evans, Enid (Beaches B&B)　　　　⌐ B&B Homes Toronto
174 Waverly Rd., Toronto, Ontario　M4L 3T3　　☎ (416) 699-0818

Located in East end of City. Phone for directions.
$38S　$48D　$10Child　$15Add.person　　　　　　　► 12A,5Ch
● Homebaked　♠ Res., hist., semi-detached　■ 5D,1Ste (upstairs)
⊷ 2T,4D,1Q,1R, 2cribs, cot　⌐ 1Ensuite, 4h.w.g.　★ parking　⊛ Smoking　♥
↤ Streetcar to downtown, Lake Ontario, popular Lakeside Boardwalk, quaint shops,
boutiques, art galleries and cafes, Olympic pool, Greenwood Race Track
↔ Scarboro Bluffs, Science Centre, Toronto City Center, CNTower, Ontario Place

☛ 90-year old home newly decorated and furnished with antiques situated in quaint
and popular California-style neighborhood right by the lake. Breakfast served under the
trees in the pretty garden, weather permitting. There are 4 cats and a dog in the house.

Flindall, Vern and Jean
78 Smithwood Drive, Etobicoke, Ontario　M9B 4R9　　☎ (416) 239-1351

Take Hwy 427 to Burnhamthorpe Road East. Turn right on Laurel Ave and left on
Lorene, then right on Smithwood.
$50S　$55D　$5Child　　　　　　　　　　　► 2A,1Ch
● Homebaked　♠ Sub., bungalow, patio, quiet　■1S,1D　⊷ 1D,P　⌐ Sh.w.g.
★TV, parking　⊛ Smoking, pets, children min. age 4
↤ Excellent service to Toronto, subway station, shopping area, two golf courses
↔ Downtown Toronto

☛ Homey atmosphere in home located in the East end of Toronto. Hosts are ardent
bridge players and antique collectors and will be happy to have guests join them on one
of their "jaunts" in the country.

Friedrichkeit, Burke and Kenneth D. Bosher (Burken Guest House) ⌐ FOBBA
322 Palmerston Blvd., Toronto, Ontario   M6G 2N6   ☎ (416) 920-7842

Situated 2 blocks west of Bathurst St and 4 houses north of College St.
$45-55S $50-65D $25Add. person   (Weekly Rates available)   ► 15
●Cont.   ♠Downtown, res., older, patio, quiet, small deck   ■3S,4D,F   ⊢5S,5D,R
⌐3Sh.w.g.   ★F,TV-lounge, separate entrance, parking   ⓌSmoking
⋙German,French
↔ Public transportation, Kensington Market, Chinatown, U of T, Queen's Park, Eaton's
Centre, CN Tower, Museum and Art Gallery

☞ Very attractive neo-classical stately home with period furniture is situated in
residential area with tree-lined streets and old-fashioned lamp-posts recalling the
grandeur of the turn-of-the-century. Hosts are owners of Toronto B&B.

Kavanagh, Pat and John
1208 Greening Ave., Mississauga, Ontario   L4Y 1H5   ☎ (416) 277-2696

From QEW take Dixie exit and go north to Queensway Ave (first light), turn left to
Stanfield and left to Greening.
$35S $35D $10Child $15Add.person   ► 4A,2Ch
● Full, hombaked   ♠ Sub., res., patio, quiet, swimming pool   ■ 2D   ■ 2S,1D,2R,
crib   ⌐ Sh.w.g.   ★ TV,F,LF,KF, parking   ♥   Ⓦ   Smoking, pets
⇔ Downtown Toronto, Ontario Place, C.N.E., Science Centre, Metro Zoo, Lake Ontario

Kolkman, John and Margaret   ⌐ B&B Homes Toronto
20 Westwoodlane, Richmond Hill, Ontario L4C 6X9   ☎ (416) 889-1357

Take Hwy 400 or Yonge Street north to first traffic light past Hwy 7.
$35S $45D $15Child   ► 4A,2Ch
● Cont.   ♠ Suburban, res., split-level, acreage   ■ 2D   ⊢ 2S,1D   ⌐ Sh.w.g.
★Parking   Ⓦ Smoking   ⋙ Netherlands Flemish
↔ Large shopping Mall, restaurants, banking, public transportation
⇔ Shouldice Clinic, Canada's Wonderland, York University, York Central Hospital,
Beaver Creek Industrial Park, Pioneer Village, Lake Ontario shoreline

☞ Home is located in the North end of Toronto and close to major Highways
eliminating traffic jams. Weather permitting breakfast is served in the garden.

Kratochvil, V.J.
85 Garden Ave., Richmond Hill, Ontario   L4C 6L6   ☎ (416) 889-6516

Located just north of Hwy 7 and west off Yonge Street.
$35S $40D   ► 2
● Full   ♠ Res., sub., bungalow, swimming pool, patio, quiet   ■ 1D   ⊢ 2S
⌐Private   ★ TV, parking   Ⓦ Pets, children   ⋙ Dutch, Czech.
↔ Public transportation to downtown Toronto
⇔ Wonderland, Pleasure Valley Ski Centre, Science Centre, Ontario Place, CN Tower

☞ Home is surrounded by towering evergreens and situated in a quiet area in the
North end of Toronto with a resort-like relaxing atmosphere.

Martyniuk, Bernice and Dan (Martyniuk)   ✔ B&B Homes Toronto
56 Bellevue Ave., Toronto, Ontario   M5T 2N4   ☎ (416) 365-0428/364-7726

Located between Bathurst and Spadina south of College. (Fire Hall on west corner and
St. Stephen's Church on east corner).
$35-38S $45-50D $10Child $10Add.person   🍽 Meals   ► 5A,1Ch
● Full, homebaked   ♠ Downtown, res., older, quiet   ■ 1S,2D (upstairs)
⊨ S,T,D, cot   ⌐ 3Sh.w.g.   ★ Air,LF, TV in guest room, parking across the road in
public parking lot   Ⓦ Drinking, pets   ～ Ukrainian, Polish, German
↪ Chinatown, European style restaurants, entertainment, Spadina Outlet shopping,
Kensington Market, Ontario Art Gallery, Toronto Transit (buses, streetcars and subway)
⇔ CN Tower, Eatons Center, Ontario Place, Toronto Harbourfront, Pioneer Village

☛ Very central location in the popular Kensington area.

Oppenheim, Susan (Oppenheim's)   ✔ FOBBA
153 Huron St., Toronto, Ontario   M5T 2B6   ☎ (416) 598-4063

Located one block east of Spadina, south of College Street.
$40S $50-65D   (Triple rate available)   🍽 Meals   ► 7A
● Full, homebaked   ♠ Downtown, hist., patio, quiet   ■ 4D   ⊨ 1S,3D, futon
⌐ 2Sh.w.g.   ★ TV,F, parking   Ⓦ Smoking, pets, children min. age 12   ～ Some
French, German
↪ Kensington Market, Parliament Bldgs, major hospitals, U of T, City Hall
⇔ St.Lawrence Centre, Roy Thomson Hall, Sci.Centre, Harbourfront, Casa Loma

☛ Multi-ethnic Gourmet cooking (fresh produce from Kensington Market).
Champagne breakfast in bed with the New York Times on request. Live musical
evenings and soirees. Access to Health Club for female guests.

Ricciuto, William (Beverley Place)   ✔ B&B Homes Toronto
235 Beverley St., Toronto, Ontario   M5T 1Z4   ☎ (416) 977-0077

Located in the University Ave and College St area. Phone for directions.
$40S $50-60D   ► 4
● Full   ♠ Downtown, hist.   ■ 2D(upstairs)   ⊨ 1D,1Q   ⌐ 1Private, 1Ensuite
★ Air,F,KF,LF, private parking   Ⓦ Restricted smoking, street shoes left in vestibule
↪ Yorkville, Eatons Center, Museum, Art Gallery, restaurants, shopping, public
transportation (bus, streetcar and subway)
⇔ Toronto Harbourfront, Ontario Place, Science Centre, Canada Wonderland

☛ Warm hospitality in restored Victorian home. Very congenial hosts have welcomed
B&B guests for many years and have received Ambassador Award from the Provincial
Tourism Department.

238   ONTARIO

Bed & Breakfast Homes of Toronto

Box 353, 31 Lakeshore Rd.E., Mississauga, Ontario   L5G 4L8   ☎ (416) 363-6362
(Co-Ordinators: Garnet McPherson and Mirella Brown)
Rates: $30-39S $40-55D   (including breakfast)   (Deposit required)
Bed & Breakfast Homes of Toronto is a group of quality independent B&B homes
located in many prime locations spread over the city and close to Toronto's excellent
public transit system or in country settings with easy access to main highways.
For a brochure of listings send self-addressed stamped envelope to the above. For
reservation call the hosts direct or the central number above. Some of the hosts are
listed in this publication.

Downtown Toronto Association of B&B Guest Homes   ⌐ FOBBA

Box 190, Stn. B, Toronto, Ontario   M5T 2W1   ☎ (416) 977-6841/598-4562
(Susan Oppenheim, Co-ordinator)
Rates $40S $50-65D
The B&B Association of Toronto is comprised of more than 12 downtown restored older
host homes located in fascinating neighbourhoods of the city, all non-smoking with
parking on the premises. The association is universally unique and the hosts try to
assure an experience which their guests will always remember. Call for reservation.

Toronto Bed and Breakfast (1987) Inc.   ⌐ FOBBA

322 Palmerston Blvd., Toronto, Ontario   M6G 2N6   ☎ (416) 961-3676 (Mon-Fri 9-6)
(Burke Friedrichkeit, President)
Rates $40-85S $50-85D   (including full breakfast)
A professional reservation service for quality Bed and Breakfast accommodation
throughout Metropolitan Toronto. Canada's longest running urban bed and breakfast
service (10 years). Advance reservation recommended. Free brochure on request.

Metropolitan Bed and Breakfast Registry of Toronto   ⌐ FOBBA

72 Lowther Ave., Toronto, Ontario   M5R 1C8   ☎ (416) 964-2566/928-2833
(Elinor Bolton, President)
Rates $35 - $85   (Prices vary from home to home)
Metropolitan B&B represents over 50 homes, located in Downtown Toronto. Most have
parking, give delicious breakfast(some gourmet) and are close to public transit.
A charming, comprehensive booklet outlining most of the homes is available by mailing
a request with $3 to the above address. Guests may call the chosen homes directly to
reserve or telephone the Registry.

B&B Travel Tip: *You can stay in a B&B when visiting a sick relative or
friend in another town. It makes for very comforting and convienent accommodation. Many hospitals keep lists of nearby B&B's for out-of-town relatives.*

Trenton

(near Kingston; see also Belleville, Brighton, Wellington, Consecon, Picton)

Wallace, Erma and Bill (Wallace House B&B)
82 Queen St., Trenton, Ontario K8V 4X9 ☎ (613) 394-4592

Phone for directions.
$30S $35D ► 4
●Choice,homebaked   🏠Downtown, res., hist., acreage, quiet   ■2D(upstairs)   ⊶2T,1D
⌐Sh.w.g.   ★Air,TV,parking   ⓦPets, rest.smoking   ∾German
↔ Trenton Canal System (boating and fishing), marina, churches, theatres, Trent Tiver
↔ Sandbanks and Presqu'ile Prov. Parks, Kingston, Lake Ontario, 1000 Islands, antique
shops, Bird Sanctuary

🐾 Lovely older Loyalist-style brick home in beautiful setting among rock gardens.
Hostess loves to cook and breakfasts are a house specialty. There is a dog in the house.

Troy

(near Hamilton; see also Ancaster, Brantford, St. George)

Nisbet, Winston and Jessie ⌐ OFV,Ham/Went B&B
RR1, Troy, Ontario L0R 2B0 ☎ (519) 647-3323

Take QEW west and continue on Hwy 403 to Hwy 6. Go north to Hwy 5 (Clappison
Corner) turn left towards Troy. Look for stone house on right side well back from road.
From 401, take Hwy 6 south to Hwy 5 (Clappison's Corner), turn right.
$25S $50D   (Family rates available)   (Phone for reservation) ► 4
✠ Mar-Dec.   ● Choice, homebaked   🏠 200-acre farm, view   ■ 2D   ⊶ 2D
(upstairs)   ⌐ 2Sh.w.h.   ★ TV,2F   ⓦ Restricted smoking, drinking, pets
↔ Stratford, Lion's Safari, Pottery & Antique Village, wholesale mill outlets, country
flea markets, Flamboro Downs Racetrack, giant country restaurants

🐾 Dairy farm located in the heart of The Golden Horseshoe is a crown land settlement
with historic 1825 stone house overlooking beautiful orchard containing several varieties
of apple and pear trees, and is one of very few 6th generation farms. Children welcome.

Uxbridge

(near Toronto; see also Newmarket, Richmond Hill)

Barton, Ollie (Barton's B&B)
23 Church St., Box 343, Uxbridge, Ontario L0C 1K0 ☎ (416) 852-5197

Phone for directions.
$30S $48D ► 4A,2Ch
● Full, homebaked   🏠 Downtown, patio, quiet   ■ 3D (upstairs and main floor)
⊶ 1D,1Q,1R, cot   ⌐ 1Private, 1sh.w.h.   ★ TV,F, parking, facilities for the
handicapped   ⓦ Drinking, pets
↔ Downtown, several good restaurants, Country Heritage and Uxbridge-Scott Museums
↔ Downtown Toronto, Oshawa, Lake Simcoe

🐾 Interesting Century home on a very quiet street in convenient location and close to
the Metropolis. Hostess is proud of her large doll collection of 100 dolls.

Victoria Harbour
(near Orillia; see also Midland, Waubauchene)

Bartosik, Gail and Henry (Victoria Manor B&B)
Box 27, Victoria Harbour, Ontario L0K 2A0   ☎ (705) 534-3951

Drive north on Hwy 400 past Barrie to Waubaushene. Then take Hwy 12 West towards Midland and first exit into Victoria Harbour to corner of Artha and Richard Sts.
$35S $45D   (Family rates available)   ► 7A,5Ch
● Choice, homebaked   ♠ Res., quiet, hist.,view, veranda   ■ S,D,F   ⊢ T,D,R,P,
crib   ⌐ Sh.w.g.   ★ TV,F   ♥   ⌢ Polish, some French
↔ Georgian Bay, water sports, cruise boats, delightful restaurants
⇔ Midland (Ste.Marie-Among-the-Hurons Martyr's Shrine), Naval and Military Establishment., Huron Indian Village, Wye Marsh Wildlife Centre

☛ Beautifully preserved estate home overlooking scenic Georgian Bay and located in the centre of a very popular winter and summer resort area.

Vineland
(near St. Catharines; see also Beamsville, Grimsby, Niagara Falls)

Dunnink, Janet and Bert (Travellers Home)
2924 Victoria Ave., Jordan, Ontario L0R 1S0   ☎ (416) 562-5656

From QEW in St. Catharines, turn off on Victoria Ave towards Vineland. Go through stoplight and look for house on corner of Springscreek Rd.
$20S $35D $10Child $10Add. person   ► 5A,2Ch
● Full   ♠ Rural, res., split-level, acreage, view, swimming pool, patio, quiet   ■ 1S,2D
(lower level)   ⊢ 1S,1D,1Q,1R   ⌐ Sh.w.g.   ★ Air,F,KF,TV in guest room, separate entrance, parking, private guest sitting room   ⓦ Smoking, drinking, pets   ⌢ Dutch
↔ Balls Falls historic park, Bruce trail hiking, Prudhommes Landing (Tivoli Miniature World and Wet & Wilds) golfing
⇔ Niagara Falls, Marineland, quaint town of Niagara-on-the-Lake, Welland Canal Locks

☛ Spacious home with Dutch hospitality on quiet property located in Ontario's "Fruit Belt" with plenty of fruits in season. There are pets around the house.

Virgil
(near St. Catharines; see also Niagara-on-the-Lake, Niagara Falls)

Neufeld, Laura and Peter (Laura's Bed & Breakfast)   ⤳ N-o-t-L- B&B
Box 85, Virgil, Ontario L0S 1T0   ☎ (416) 468-7347

Take Hwy 55 through Virgil towards N-o-t-L. Turn left on Hunter Rd to No. 286.
$45S $50D   ► 4
● Cont., homebaked   ♠ Rural, hist., bungalow, acreage   ■ 2D   ⊢ 2T,1D
⌐Sh.w.g. ★Air,TV,area/fruit farm tours ⓦSmoking,pets ⌢German
⇔ Quaint town of Niagara-on-the-Lake and Shaw Festival Theatre, Niagara Falls
☛ Beautifully decorated spacious home situated in residential area on a large lot amidst the most productive (peach) fruit farms of the Niagara.

Wallenstein
(near Kitchener; see also Elmira, St. Jacobs, St. Clements, Drayton, Millbank)

Roe, Jim and Anne (Roewood Farm)　　　　　　　　　　✔ SOCVA
RR3, Wallenstein, Ontario　N0B 2S0　　　　　　　　　　☎ (519) 698-2278

From Kitchener, take Hwy 86 and County Rd 17 through Linwood. Go east and then onto Wellesley Rd 12. Continue north and look for first farm on right.
$25S　$40D　$10Child(under age 5)　📷 Meals　　　　　　　► 6
● Full, homebaked　🏠 143-acre farm, view, patio, quiet　■ 2S,2D,1Ste
🛏 5S,1T,2D,R,P, crib,　🍴 2Sh.w.g., 1sh.w.g.h.　★ TV,F　♥　🐾 Pets
🐾German, Austrian
↔ Linwood village, horse and buggy and sleigh rides and repair shops, hayloft fun
⇔ Kitchener farmer's market, Waterloo U, scenic Hawkesville (a photographer's dream), Linwood (handcrafted quilts and folk art), quaint village of Heidelberg (unique 150-year old former stage coach stop), Stratford Festival Theatre

🐾 Genuine Austrian/Canadian hospitality in the "horse and buggy" area of Waterloo County. Wiener Schnitzel and Strudel a specialty. Each child gets a calf to look after during stay on the farm.

Warsaw
(near Peterborough; see also Lakefield, Bobcaygeon, Fenelon Falls, Hastings)

McMullen, Mr. and Mrs. Glen
Warsaw, Ontario　K0L 3A0　　　　　　　　　　☎ (705) 652-3024

From Peterborough, proceed north-east on Warsaw Rd. In the village of Warsaw turn left at United Church on mill pond and go to top of the hill.
$25S　$35D　📷 Meals　　　　　　　　　　　► 3A,2Ch
● Homebaked　🏠 110-acre farm, hist., view　■ 1S,1D,F　🛏 1D,1S,P
🍴 2Sh.w.g.　★ TV　♥　🐾 Smoking
↔ Village of Warsaw, swimming in river, farm animals and herd of charolais
⇔ Golfing, Petroglyphs for amateur archaeologists, Kawartha Lakes region

🐾 Artifacts from hosts' life in Ghana blend with rich pine woodwork in century brick home. Unique setting in very popular resort area. Hostess spins and dyes fleece.

> **B&B Travel Tip:** *Contacting the B&B hosts ahead of time is a big advantage. You will not only have a bed waiting for you that night, but you have already "broken the ice." The hosts will be welcoming you at the door and you are not a stranger any more.*

Waterdown
(near Hamilton; see also Burlington, Millgrove, Campbellville, Dundas)

Millar, Mrs. Jean   ✔ Burl.B&B
551 Evans Rd., RR1, Waterdown, Ontario   L0R 2H0   ☎ (416) 689-5360

On Hwy 5 go 3.5 km west of Brant Street and turn right at Evans Road.(well marked)
$35D $10Child   ⦿ Meals   ► 2A,2Ch
● Full, hombaked   ⌂ Rural, ranch-style, acreage, patio, quiet   ⊛ 1D, ⌐ 1D,
crib   ⌐ Sh.w.h.   ★ Air,TV, LF, parking   ⊛ Couples or females only, smoking, pets
↔ Quiet country walks, lookout with panoramic view over Escarpment and Burlington
⇔ Downtown Burlington, Lake Ontario, Hamilton, Lion's Safari, several golf courses,
Bruce Trail, Crawford Lake, Bronte Creek Park, Toronto

☛ Congenial well travelled hostess is very active with hand crafts and frequently
exhibits her works at craft shows. Cozy country atmosphere. Enjoy breakfast in large
sunny plant-filled country room.

Payne, George and Helen   ✔ Flamb. B&B
56 Barton St.,Box 141,Waterdown, Ontario   L0R 2H0   ☎ (416) 689-6710

Take QEW to Hwy 403 and go north on Hwy 6 to Hwy 5 (Clappison's Corner). Turn
right on Hamilton St, and then left on Barton St.
$25S $35D $10Child (up to age 10)   ► 4
●Full,homebaked   ⌂Village, suburb., ranch-style, view, swimming pool, patio,
quiet ■2D ⌐2D   ⌐1Private, 1ensuite ★Air,TV,F ⊛smoking, pets
↔ Stores, boutiques and craft shops, Post Office, shopping plaza, restaurants and tea
rooms, golfing, Bruce Trail hiking
⇔ Downtown Burlington, Lake Ontario shore line, Hamilton, Toronto, Guelph

☛ Comfortable home and warm hospitality in quaint town of Waterdown,
conveniently located near major urban centers. Enjoy breakfast by the pool.

Wickens, Stan and Ann (Griffin House)
Box 282, 261 Mill Street North, Waterdown, Ontario   L0R 2H0   ☎ (416) 689-5225

From Hamilton travel east on Hwy 403 to Waterdown Rd cut-off and go north, continue
on Mill Street north of Hwy 5 (Dundas Rd). From Toronto on Hwy 5 enter village of
Waterdown and turn right on Mill Street.
$30S $40D ● Full, homebaked   ⌂ Village, older   ■ 2D (upstairs) ⌐ 2S,2
⌐Sh.w.g.   ★ Air, parking   ⊛ Smoking, drinking, children, pets
↔ Antique shops, craft and collectibles, quality clothing stores, restaurants, Folk Art
⇔ Burlington, Lake Ontario, Dundurn Castle, agricultural Musuem, Art Galleries
Crawford Lake Indian Village, Theatre, Royal Botanical Gardens, Flamborough Downs
Raceway, African Lion's Safari

☛ Country furnishings, antiques and reproductions, fluffy pillows and handmade
quilts create a cozy atmosphere in 1851-built home situated in quaint little village, near
tea-rooms and unique stores and close to the surrounding cities.

Waterford

(south of Brantford; see also Simcoe, Port Dover)

Kerr, Jean and Fred
150 Main Street S., Waterford, Ontario N0E 1Y0 ☎ (519) 443-5165

Located 3.2 km east of Hwy 24 on Reg Rd 24. Look for house opposite the Church.
$30S $35D   ●$3Each ► 5
● Choice   🏠 Village, hist.   ■ 1S,2D (upstairs)   ⊢ 1S,2D,R   ⊓ 1Sh.w.g.
★F,TV, parking   ⊛ Restricted smoking, pets
↔ Village centre, shopping, park area, restaurant
⇔ Lake swimming, fishing, Bell Homestead (Brantford), museum, Lake Erie resorts

🐂 Designated Heritage House in small village surrounded by tobacco farm country.

Waubaushene

(near Orillia; see also Midland, Victoria Harbour)

McPhail, Arvilla and Dick (3-Trees on the Bay) ⌐ FOBBA
Long Point Road North, Waubaushene, Ontario L0K 2C0 ☎ (705) 538-2630

On Hwy 69 from a point 0.5 km north of Waubaushene, take Duck Bay Rd. Turn left on
Bayway and go 0.5 km to Long Point Rd. Turn right and watch for sign.
$44S $49D ► 4A
✚ June 1-Sept.30   ● Choice   🏠 Rural, bungalow, lakefront, view, quiet   ■ 2D
⊢ 2T,1Q   ⊓ 1Sh.w.g.   ★ F, parking, boat and bicycles for guests
↔ Excellent swimming, bicycling, boating, fishing, birding
⇔ Golfing, Martyr's Shrine and Papal Alter, St-Marie-Among-the-Hurons, Naval and
Military Establishments, Trent Severn Waterway, Budd Watson Gallery

🐂 Comfortable summer home situated directly on Georgian Bay. Hosts are retired and
enjoy sharing the natural beauty and interesting historic attractions of the area.

Welland

(near Niagara Falls; see also NOTL, Vineland, Virgil, Beamsville, Grimsby)

Schafrick, Herbert and Martha
27 Eastdale Cres., Welland, Ontario L3B 1E6 ☎ (416) 732-3170

Proceed East on Lincoln Street (Reg.Rd 29). Turn left at 8th street past stoplight at
Southworth Street.
$30S $35D $10Child   ◙ Meals ► 6
● Full   🏠 Res., sub, patio, quiet   ■ 3D (main and upper floor)   ⊢ 2S,2D, crib
⊓ 1Private, 1sh.w.h.   ★ Air,LF, parking, separate entrance   ⊛ Smoking, drinking,
pets   ⌇ German, Polish
↔ New Welland Canal, public swimming pool and playground
⇔ Niagara Falls, Crystal Beach, Niagara-on-the-Lake, Thorold Locks, wineries

🐂 Relaxed and friendly atmosphere and bright spacious rooms. House specialty is a
selection of homemade jams from local fruits

Rose City Bed & Breakfast Association
102 Aqueduct St., Welland, Ontario L3C 1C1   ☎ (416) 788-9054
(Co-Ordinator: Rita Donohue)
Rates: $30S $40D   (including breakfast)
The Rose City B&B Association offers a variety of accommodations in friendly and
pleasant well-situated homes in and around the Welland area, between Lake Ontario and
Lake Erie and provide truly "A home away from home among the roses and waterways".
For information phone the above.

Wellington
(on Quinte's Isle, near Belleville; see also Picton, Consecon, Trenton, Brighton)

Chapman, Eric and Karen (Chappie's Place)   ⌐ CC
53 Main Street, Wellington, Ontario K0K 3L0   ☎ (613 399-2579

Phone for directions.
$30-34S $40-45D $10Add. person   ⬕ Meals   ► 9
● Choice, homebaked   ⌂ Village, older, res., swimming pool, view, lakefront, patio,
quiet   upper and lower deck   ■ 3   ⊢ 4T,1P,2Q (one is waterbed), cot   ⅂
2Sh.w.g.   ★ TV,F, separate entrance, LF, parking   ♥
↪ Swimming, fishing, Village of Wellington, craft and gift shops, museum, harbour
⇔ Quinte Isle vacation area, Picton, Sandbanks Dunes, Provincial Parks, beaches

🐾 Friendly and warm hospitality in late 1800's home situated on scenic West Lake.
There is cross-country skiing from the back door and ice-fishing in the winter. House
Motto is "Come as a guest and leave as a friend". There is a cat in residence.

Dancey, Gordon and Jennifer (Chelsea House)   ⌐ CC
236 Main Street, Box 535, Wellington, Ontario K0K 3L0   ☎ (613) 399-2407

Take Wooler Rd off Hwy 401 (Loyalist Parkway) and then Hwy 33 south to Wellington.
$40S $46D   ⬕ Meals   ► 6A
● Cont   ⌂ Village, older, view, patio, wrap-around veranda   ■ 3D (upstairs)   ⊢
2T,1D,1Q   ⅂ Sh.w.g.   ★ F,TV in guest room, off-street parking, bicycles available
⊛ children, pets, restricted smoking
↪ Local sandy beach, fishing, hiking, bicycling, boating, museum, antiques
⇔ Sandbanks Provincial Park, antique and craft shops, Picton, scenic drives around
Prince Edward County, golfing, cross-country skiing, fine dining

🐾 Turn-of-the-Century home with warm and friendly atmosphere. Hosts' motto is "A
friend is just a stranger... you haven't met yet"."

Fisher, Luella and John (Three Gables)

Box 570, 505 Main Street, Wellington, Ontario K0K 3L0

⌣ FOBBA

☎ (613) 399-3236

Located at the western limits of the village of Wellington and on the south side of the Loyalist Parkway (Hwy 33). Look for sign.

$35S $50D

► 8

● Full   ♠ Village, view, quiet, decks   ■ 4D (upstairs)   ⊶2T,1D,1Q   ⊓2Sh.w.g. ★F, plenty of parking, ceiling fans in each room, spacious west lounge   ⊛Smoking ↔ Lake Ontario shoreline, country lane walks, downtown Wellington, shops, Dairy Bar, restaurants, museum, library, church ⇔ Sandbanks Provincial Park, Lake of the Mountain area, North Beach, Black River Cheese Factory, town of Picton, ferry to Kingston

🔫 Unique 2-storey Cape Cod-style home with guest rooms overlooking Lake Ontario and the famous Sandbanks located in quiet section of the village. Relax on the rear deck or in the shady courtyard overlooking the water. Free day-pass to Sandbanks Provincial Park available with a minum stay of 2 nights. There is a dog. Hosts are seasoned B&B travellers and Presidents of FOBBA (Fed. of Ontario B&B Associations).

Smyth, Joanne and Tommy (Shamrock B&B)

171 Main St., Box 562, Wellington, Ontario K0K 3L0

☎ (613) 399-2261

From Hwy 401, take Exit 522 (Waller Rd) east on Hwy 33 to house opposite Sunoco Stn.

$40D $10Child $15Add.person   ▣ Meals

► 10

● Full, homebaked   ♠ Village, hist., acreage, lakefront, patio   ■ 2D (upstairs) ⊶ T,D,R,P, cot, crib   ⊓ 1Sh.w.h.   ★ TV, facilities for the handicapped   ⊛ Pets ↔ Swimming, boating, surfing, fishing from private docks, antique and craft shops, auctions, flea markets and art galleries

🔫 "A home away from home". Homemade muffins, rolls and jams for breakfast.

Steeves, Beth and Carl

299 Main St., Wellington, Ontario K0K 3L0

⌣ CC

☎ (613) 399-2569

Take Exit 87 off Hwy 401, then Wooler Rd and Hwy 33 South to Wellington.

$30S $40D

► 7

● Choice   ♠ Village, res., view, patio   ■ 3D (upstairs)   ⊶ 2D,3S, crib ⊓1Sh.w.g.   ★ TV,F   ⊛ Pets ↔ Local beach area, museum, library, arts and crafts places in village, cross-country skiing, fishing, hiking and bicycling ⇔ Trenton, Picton, Prov. Parks and historic sites

🔫 Older home in centre of village, backing onto Lake Ontario. Hosts operate a pottery studio on the premises. Relax in garden and deck and in front of the fire in winter. There is a Lab Retriever in the house.

Westport

(near Kingston; see also Delta, Frankville, Seeleys Bay)

deBruyn, Lorraine (Spring Street B&B)
Spring Street, Westport, Ontari K0G 1X0

↙ Kingston B&B
☎ (613) 273-5427

Located 1/2 block west on Spring Street off Regional Rd 10.
$35S $30D $15Child $15Add.person ▣ Meals (48 hr notice) ▶ 6A,2Ch
●Full ♠ Village, quiet ■ 3D (upstairs) ⊢ 1K,2Q, cot ⊓ 1Sh.w.g. ★TV,F in
guest lounge, parking ⊎ Restricted smoking ᷣ French
↔ Village dock (Upper Rideau in Rideau Canal System), shops, churches, bank, Post
Office, Rideau Trail walking, Foley Mountain cross-country ski trails

☛ Warm and friendly hospitality in comfortable old red brick farm-type house, newly
decorated with "furniture from Grandfather's day".

Wheatley

(on Lake Erie, near Windsor; see also Leamington, Amherstburg, Pelee Island)

Burton, Harold and Mary Lou (Burton House)
RR3, Wheatley, Ontario N0P 2P0

↙ CC
☎ (519) 825-4956

Located 8 km east of Leamington on the north side of Hwy 3.
$30S $38D $5Child $10Add.person ▶ 6A,4Ch
● Full (cater to special diets) ♠ Rural, older, quiet ■ 1S,3D ⊢ 3S,2D,1Q,2R
⊓ Sh.w.g. ★ TV in guest room, packed lunches prepared ⊎ Pets
↔ Kopegaron woods with large variety of wildflowers, trees and birds, nature walks,
roadside fruit and vegetable stands, artist studio on premises
⇔ Lake Erie, Point Pelee National Park, Hillman Marsh, Jack miner Bird Sanctuary

☛ Unwind and relax in warmth of spacious red brick Victorian farmhouse surrounded
by many nature and conservation areas to be discovered and explored. Hostess is proud
of her large collection of antique dolls displayed throughout the house.

Koop, Elsa (Royal Harbour View)
16 Kay Ave, RR2, Wheatley, Ontario N0P 2P0

↙ B&B
☎ (519) 825-7955

Located 10 km from Point Pelee and 1.6 km south of Wheatley stoplight, across from
world's largest fresh water Harbour.
$40S $6D $20Add.person ▶ 8
● Full (German/Swedish) ♠ Sub., ranch style, view, lakefront, patio, quiet ■ 4
⊢ 2T,3Q ⊓ 4Ensuite ★Air,F,TV, parking ⊎Smoking, pets, children min. age 10
ᷣ German
↔ Fisherman's Cove Restaurant, Bird Watching Lagoon, marches, conservation area
⇔ Point Pelee Na. Park, Colasanti Tropical Gardens, Windsor, Detroit (Mich),
Kopegaron Woods

☛ Home is situated on Lake Erie with a panoramic view of water on 3 sides. Located
across from the World's largest Fresh Water Fishing Harbour with boats at anchor.

Manery, Bob and Gloria (Nature View)
RR2, Wheatley, Ontario N0P 2P0

⚲ B&B
☎ (519) 825-7086

Take Hwy 3 to Wheatley stop-light. Turn south and continue to County Rd 4. Turn right, and drive over harbour bridge to first house on right.
$25-30S $35D $10Child $20Add. person   ► 6
● Choice ♠ Rural, acreage, patio, very quiet, isolated ■ 2D,2S ⊢ 2S,2D,R
ℂ 1Sh.w.h., 1sh.w.g. ★ TV,KF,LF ⍟ Restricted smoking, drinking, pets
↔ Small river, lakefront, swimming, boating, fishing harbour, good restaurant
⇔ Point Pelee, Wheatley Prov. Park, antique shops, Kopegaron Woods

🐾 Home is situated in total privacy and surrounded by large treed lot with bushland and winding river. Relax on the deck and watch and listen to a variety of birds.

Whitefish
(near Sudbury; see also Webbwood)

Svensk, Ruth
RR1 Whitefish, Ontario P0M 3E0

☎ (705) 866-2323

From Sudbury or Espanola leave Hwy 17 on Reg Rd 55. Continue to Reg. Rd 10 (Penage Rd), turn south and drive 6 km. Look for house on right before crossing Vermilion River.
$25S $35D $5-10Child $10Add. person ▣ Meals (Rates for bicyclists) ► 4
◘ May-Oct.31 ● Full, homebaked ♠ Rural, view, river, rapids ■ 2D (upstairs)
⊢ 2D, crib ℂ 1Sh.w.h., 1private ★ rowboat for guests ⍟ Smoking
↔ Swimming (deep water), golfing on adjacent property, beavers at work in their beaver lodge and other waterfowl in their natural habitat, bird watching
⇔ "Science North" Centre at Sudbury, town of Lively (Anderson Farm Heritage Home)

🐾 Home was built in 1915 by family ancestors from logs of the property and is located next to rapids which sparkle and roar year round. There are two cats. House specialty is "Ruth's four-grain bread" and Finnish braided "coffee breads".

Wiarton
(near Owen Sound; see also Southampton, Lion's Head, Oliphant, Palgrave)

Christensen, Jorn and Elsie (Bruce Gables)
410 Berford St., Box 448, Wiarton, Ontario N0H 2T0

⚲ Grey Bruce B&B
☎ (519) 534-0429

Hwy 6 passes through Wiarton and is known as Berford Street. Located at north-east corner of Berford and Mary Streets. Parking off Mary Street.
$30S $40D $5Child $10Add.person   ► 9
● Full ♠ Village, view ■ 2D,1F (upstairs) ⊢ 2,1D,1Q, cot
ℂ 1Sh.w.h.,1sh.w.g. ★ F,TV, parking (off Mary Street) ⍟ Smoking ⌇ French,
German, Spanish, Danish
↔ Bruce Trail, swimming in Colpoy's Bay, sailing, fishing, golfing
⇔ Bruce Penninsula National Park, Tobermory and Manitoulin Island Ferry

🐾 Spacious, turn-of-the-Century Victorian home restored to its Victorian splendour with bay windows overlooking Wiarton and the clear blue waters of Colpoy's Bay.

Glassford, Bill and Judy (McIvor House   ✔ Grey Bruce B&B
RR4, Wiarton, Ontario N0H 2T0   ☎ (519) 534-1769

Located 35 km northeast of Wiarton and 3.5 km north of Purple Valley.
$28S $35D $5Child (under age 12)   ▣ Meals   ► 6A,2Ch
● Full, homebaked   ♠ 788-acre farm, hist., swimming pool, patio, quiet, isolated
■2D,1Ste (upstairs)   ⊨ 2T,1D,1Q, crib   � 1Ensuite,1sh.w.g.   ★ TV, parking
↔ Bruce Trail hiking, Cape Croker Indian Reserve
⇔ Sauble Beach, swimming and water activities, Lion's Head, Tobermory and Ferry to
Manitoulin Island, Bruce Peninsula National Park, gift and antique shops, cross country
ski trails

☛ Warm country hospitality and informal atmosphere in large turn-of-the-Century
renovated farm house. Homemade preserves and maple syrup from own maple woods.

Last, Marielle (Hillcrest B&B)   ✔ Grey Bruce B&B
394 Gould St., Wiarton, Ontario N0H 2T0   ☎ (519) 534-2262

Enter Wiarton from south and pass through the "gates". Turn left at the first street and
go to top of hill. Located at first intersection (Gould, southwest corner).
$30S $40D   (Children's rates available)   ► 4
● Full   ♠ Rural, village, hist.   ■ 2D,F upstairs)   ⊨ T,D   touch 1Sh.w.g.   ★ F
    ⊕ Pets, smoking   ∿ French, Spanish, some German
↔ Bruce Trail, Niagara Escarpment, Colpoy Bay, Bluewater Park, Wiarton
⇔ Oliphant (sandy beach), warm shallow water

☛ 1880's timber baron's house with antiques. Hosts are very knowledgeable about the
area's history and geography. Good base for interested naturalists and travellers who
would like to explore the many attractions in this part of the Peninsula.

Kibbler, Arlene and Jim (Maplehurst)   ✔ Grey Bruce B&B
277 Frank Street, Wiarton, Ontario N0H 2T0   ☎ (519) 534-1210

When arriving in Wiarton, pass through the gates and down a hill. Turn left at Frank St
and continue to top of hill to house across from Anglican Church.
$30S $35-40D $10dd.person   ▣ Meals   ► 6A,2Ch
✖ Not April   ● Full, homebaked   ♠ Res., older, view, patio, quiet   ■ 2D,1Ste,1F
(upstairs)   ⊨ 2D,1K,1R   touch 1Ensuite,1sh.w.g.   ★ F,LF,TV in guest room, parking
♥   ⊕ Children min. age 4
↔ Bruce Trail hiking (Nature lover's and photographers' paradise), shopping, tennis,
swimming pool, good restaurants
⇔ Tobermory and ferry to Manitoulin Island, Bruce Peninsula, Sauble Beach (swimming
and water activities), Rankin Trail (cross-country skiing), Owen Sound, Blue Water Park
(indoor and outdoor skating)

☛ Hosts are long-time residents whose resourcefulness and knowledge of the region
will contribute immensely to visitors' stay. Fishing charters are available in the summer
from the Bay and fish huts in the winter. There is a dog in the house.

Morrison, Ann L. & Peter G. Manning (Briars Nest Inn)   ⌐ Grey Bruce B&B
Box 432, 415 Frank St., Wiarton, Ontario   N0H 2T0   ☎ 519) 534-0039

Upon entering Wiarton through the "Gate" on Hwy 6N, continue down the hill to Frank
St., turn right and go to southwest corner of Brown St.
$30S $40D $5Child $10dd.person   ◙ Meals $4Each (packed lunch)   ► 6
◙ Not Nov.   ● Choice, homebaked   ♠ Res., older, patio, quiet   ■ 3D (upstairs)
⌐ 2T,2D, cot, crib   ⌐ 2Sh.w.g.   ★ TV,LF, parking, fans in guest rooms, ski-rack
↔ Colpoy's Bay, Bluewater Park, playground, tennis courts, downtown Wiarton, marina
↔ Sauble Beach, Tobermory (Chi-Chemaun Ferry), Cape Croker Indian Reservation,
Larkswhistle Herb/Flower Garden, Bruce Peninsula National Park, Grieg's Caves
(where "Quest for Fire" was filmed), antiques and craft shops, cross-country ski trails

🐾 Recently renovated 80-year old home in spacious surroundings of rose hedges,
herbs, various flowers, many trees and a small vegetable garden. Host enjoys playing the
Saxophone. Enjoy good conversation and a hearty breakfast with hosts originally from
England. There are 2 cats in residence.

Wilberforce
(north of Peterborough; see also Bancroft, Haliburton, Minden, Gilmour)

Clark, Hilda (The House in the Village)   ⌐ CC
Box 63, Wilberforce, Ontario   K0L 3C0   ☎ (705) 448-3161/448-2018

From Peterborough take Hwy 28 north. Turn left on Dyno Rd (North of Apsley) and left
on Hwy 121. Turn right on Hwy 648. Located in the village across from General Store.
$25S $35D $10Child $10Add.person   ► 4
◙ Not Nov.and April   ● Full, homebaked   ♠ Village, older, acreage, patio, quiet
■ 7D (main and upper level)   ⌐ 2T,5D,1Q   ⌐ 1Sh.w.h.,2sh.w.g.   ★TV,
parking   ⍟Pets, restricted smoking
↔ General store, Anglican Church, Lake and Government Dock, fishing, walking, public
tennis courts
↔ Public beach, many lakes and scenic roads, Rail's End Gallery, Haliburton County
Museum, local craft and art shops, golfing, downhill and cross-country skiing, Rock shop
and Bancroft "Rockhound Gemborrie", Haliburton School of fine Arts, Maple Sugar
Festival, Winter Carnivals

🐾 Renovated comfortable former boarding house, originally established in 1905 by
family's Ancestors, and located in quiet village in popular Eastern Haliburton Highlands.
Nearby family farm provides plenty of opportunity for hiking, birdwatching,
cross-country skiing and rock collecting.

B&B Travel Tip: *You can go B&B if you are a single traveller (on business
or pleasure). Then, you are in the company of others, and socializing with
strangers is so much easier.*

Williamstown

(near Cornwall; see also Lancaster, Apple Hill, Morrisburg, Finch)

Caron, Mary and Michael (Caron House)
Box 143, Williamstown, Ontario K0C 2J0 ☎ (613) 347-7338

From Hwy 401, take Exit 814 north to Lancaster Village and west on Pine St. Go 7 km
(and 2 centuries) through Williamstown to four corners, turn left and continue over
bridge, then left again to 3rd house across from St. Mary's Church.
$32S $40D   (Reservations please) ► 4A
●Full(Gourmet)   ⌂Village, hist., acreage, veranda, quiet   ■2D(upstairs)   ⌐2D
⌐Sh.w.h.   ★2F,TV, parking   ⓌRestricted smoking, children, pets   ⌐French

↔ Ideal area for bicycling, stroll
through the village of Williamstown
with it's historic sites, The
Bethune-Thompson House (1805), Sir
John Johnson's Manor House (1784),
Nor'Westers and Loyalists Museum
(1862), village library

↔ St. Raphael's Ruins (1821), Upper
Canada Village, Morrisburg, Cornwall,
Inverarden Regency Cottage and
Museum (1816), Ottawa, Montreal

🖝 1837 brick home with old
fashioned elegance and lots of anitques,
overlooking the historical village of
Williamstown in Glengarry County. La
"piece de resistance" is gourmet
breakfast.

Winchester

(near Ottawa; see also Mountain, Kars, North Gower, Finch, Brinston)

Harkin, Dianne and Dan (Harkhaven Farm) ╱ Ottawa B&B
RR1, Winchester, Ontario K0C 2K0 ☎ (613) 774-3418

Phone for directions.
$15-20 $30-40D $5-10Child   ▣ Meals ► 4A,2Ch
● Choice, homebaked   ⌂ 150-acres farm, older, inground swimming pool, patio,quiet
■2S,2D(upstairs)   ⌐2S,2D,1P   ⌐Sh.w.g.   ★TV,LF   ⓌSmoking, pets, child min. age 3
↔ Cabinet making shop and lumber yard on property
↔ Historic Upper Canada Village, Dinosaur Park, Challies Trout Pond (stocked, free
fishing) Country Fairs and Steam Shows, golfing, Migratory Bird Sanctuary, Greely
Water Slide, Caldwell Factory Outlet, McHaffies Flea Market, Ottawa (Capital City)

🖝 Home is quiet, cosy, fully restored and renovated and located on grain farm. All
meals are served in charming Dining room. Hosts' son and young family live across the
yard. There are pets in the house. Camping rates are available.

Windermere

(near Huntsville; see also Port Carling, Bracebridge)

Rountree Pat & C. Bahrey (Rowntree Cottage)　　　　　⌐ Musk.B&B
RR2, Utterson, Windermere, Ontario　P0B 1M0　　　　☎ (705) 769-3640

From Hwy 118, take Muskoka Rd 25 for 8.5 km to Dawson Rd. Or: From Muskoka Rd 4
west, take Rd 25 for 1.2 km to Dawson Rd. Once on Dawson Rd, travel 1 km to cottage.
$35S - $60D　$20Add.person　　▣ Meals　　　　　　　▶ 9
▣ Late Spring to early Fall　　● Full　　🏠 Rural, village, hist., acreage, view, lakefront,
quiet, screened porch　　■ 3D (upstairs)　　⊶ 1D,3D　　⌐ 1Sh.w.g.,1private, basins in
two rooms　★ TV,F,video　　Ⓦ Smoking, pets, children min. age 6
↔ Swimming in Lake Rosseau, scenic nature walks
⇔ Summer resort area, golfing, tennis, gift shops, Summer Theatre, restaurants

📢 Modernized turn-of-the-Century cottage has been in host's family for over 60 years
(the original ice house and chicken house are still on the property) and located on
sparkling Lake Rosseau, which is well known for beautiful scenery and quiet elegance.

Windsor

(see also Leamington, Amherstburg, Wheatley, Pelee Island)

Ottrin, Clarea and Joseph (The Ottrins)　　　　　　　⌐ CC
841 Villaire Ave., Windsor, Ontario　N8S 2J3　　　☎ (519) 944-2875

Ending at Hwy 401 take Essex County Rd 19 to Lauzon Parkway. Go north to Tecumseh
Rd, then left to Wyandotte, left again, then to Villaire. House is on right.
$25S　$35D　$5Child　　▣ Meals　　　　　　　　　▶ 2
● Full　　🏠 Sub, older, patio, quiet　　■ 1D (upstairs)　　⊶ 1D　　⌐ 1Sh.w.h.
★Air,LF, TV in guest room, parking, separate entrance　　Ⓦ Smoking, drinking　　〰
Hungarian, German
↔ Detroit River, Coventry Garden with Peace Fountain
⇔ Lake Erie beaches, Amherstburg, Point Pelee National Park

📢 Retired hosts enjoy meeting people and help them with sightseeing, travel and
entertainment plans. There is a cat in residence. Seniors welcome.

> **B&B Travel Tip:** *On the day of departure, you should leave after breakfast
> and with all your belongings! It is not fair for the hosts to have to store your
> luggage, while you are making some side-trips before leaving town. Remember,
> they have to get the room ready for the next night.*

Wingham
(near Goderich: see also Lucknow, Clinton)

Henderson, John and Mary (Stone Away) ✔ SOVCA
RR4, Wingham, Ontario N0G 2W0 ☎ (519) 357-3607

From Kitchener-Waterloo follow Hwy 86 East and drive through Listowel to south edge
of Wingham and look for house on left side with sign on gate.
$20S $28D   ●$2.50Each ► 6
◪ Summer   ● Choice, homebaked   ♠ Farm, hist., view, patio, quiet   ■ 3D
(upstairs)   ⊣ 3D   ⌐ 1Sh.w.g.   ★ KF,TV in guest room, separate entrance
⊛ Pets, children min. age 6
↔ Scenic Maitland River, tennis courts
⇔ Blyth Festival Theatre, antique shops and boutiques, golfing, Lake Huron beaches

🔫 Stone house, well maintained and surrounded by beautifully grounds.

McClenaghan, Ms. Mildred
RR3, Windham, Ontario N0G 2W0 ☎ (519) 357-2528

Located on Hwy 86 and 1st farm west of village store in Whitechurch. Look for older,
white brick farm house surrounded by large evergreen trees.
$15 per person ► 4A
● Choice, homebaked   ♠ Farm, quiet   ■ 2D   ⊣ 1D,2T   ⌐ 1Private, 1sh.w.h.

🔫 Opportunity for perfect respite from daily frustrations and activities. Spacious
lawns and peaceful atmosphere. Various places of worship nearby.

Woodstock
(near London; see also Plattsville, Embro)

Burrill, Bruce and Margaret (Broadlea Farm) ✔ FOBBA
RR6, Woodstock, Ontario N4S 7W1 ☎ (519) 462-2716

Located on Hwy 59, half-way between Woodstock and Tavistock. Look for farm house
north of Hickson on right.
$25S $35D   ◧ Meals ► 4A,2Ch
◪ May-Oct.   ● Full, homebaked   ♠ Farm   ■ 2D   ⊣ 2D   ⌐ 1Private,
1sh.w.h.   ★ TV,LF   ⊛ Smoking, drinking
↔ Small village of Hickson
⇔ Stratford (Theatre), London, Kitchener farmers market, Mennonite country.

🔫 Hosts raise registered Clydesdale Horses. Enjoy peaceful comfort in tranquil rural
surroundings.

Quebec

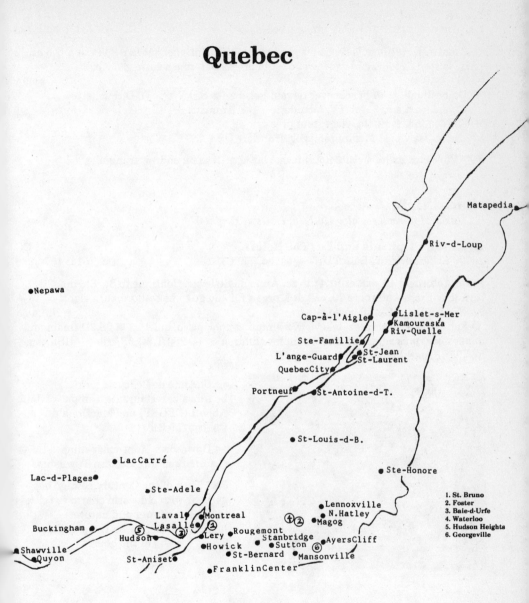

Please note that the hosts listed in French in this section all welcome
English speaking guests to their homes as well as French speaking guests.

Ayer's Cliff

(près de Magog; voir aussi Mansonville, North Hatley, Sutton, Magog, Lennoxville)

Lauzier, Cécile et Robert
Chemin Audet, RR1, Ayer's Cliff, Québec J0B 1C0   ☎ (819) 838-4433

De Montréal, rte 10, puis rte 55 jusqúa Ayer's Cliff, continuer sur la rte 141 et à 2.5 km passé la rte 143 tournez à gauche et c'est la première ferme a votré gauche.
$25S $40D   ► 9A
● Domestique   🏠 Ferme avec terrain boisé   ■ S,D,F   ⊨ J,D,couchette
⊓ Compl.,part.a.h.   ★ TV, buanderie   🐾 Animaux
↔ Ski de fond, raquette, plage, tout près
⇔ Lac Massawipi et Memphrémagog, frontière USA

🐾 Vous etes invité à visite notré ferme laitiére dans un endroit tranquille.

Baie d'Urfe

(near Montreal; see also Hudson, Hudson Heights)

Rybinski, Stephanie and Ed (The Ecles)   ↙ CC
20799 Lakeshore Rd., Baie d'Urfe, Quebec H9X 1S1   ☎ (514) 457-3986

From Autoroute 40, exit at Rt 41 to St. Anne de Bellevue. Continue to St. St.AnnsSt, turn left. From Autoroute 20, exit at Morgan Rd and go to Lakeshore, turn right.
$25S $40D $10Add.person   ► 6A,4Ch
● Full   🏠 Res, acreage, lakeview, swimming pool, patio, quiet   ■ 2S,2D (main and upper floor) plus adjoining mini-room for children   ⊨ 2S,2T,2Q,3R,crib   ⊓1Sh.w.g.
★ TV,LF, parking   🖐 Smoking   ♥

↔ St.Anne de Bellevue, locks, boardwalk, restaurants, campus of John Abbott (CEGEP) and MacDonald College (McGill)

⇔ Downtown Montreal, skiing (Laurentians and Eastern Townships)

🐾 Turn of the Century cottage has gardens with old world charm to relax in. Pressed flower and nature handicrafts display on the premises. There is a dog in the house.

Buckingham
(near Ottawa-Ont; see also Quyon, Lac des Plages, Shawville)

Deland, Michel & Herta Fleck (Sejour)
RR3, Buckingham, Quebec J8L 2W8   ☎ 819) 986-9219

Located in Mayo near Buckingham. From Ottawa, take Quebec Hwy 50 towards
Montreal and exit at Masson. Take Hwy 309 north to Buckingham, then Hwy 315 to
Mayo. Look for sign on the right side (1.5km).
$30-45 $40-55 $5Child $10Add. person   🍽 Meals   ► 10A,3A
● Choice   ♠ 52-acres farm, view, riverfront, patio, pond, quiet, isolated
■3D,2Ste,1F (upstairs)   ⊷ 3S,3D,1Q,1K,2P, crib   ⍁ 2Private, 1sh.w.h.,1sh.w.g, spa
(whirlpool)   ★ 2F,Tv in guest room   ♥   ⍟ Pets   ⊷ English, German (host
language is French)
↪ Swimming pond, picknic area, fishing, nature walks
⇔ Ottawa (Capital of Canada), Montebello (riding etc.), golfing, cross-country skiing

☛ Very large Tudor Home in secluded, quiet and restfull location. Dining Soireé.

Cap-à-l'Aigle
(near St. Simeon; see also Kamouraska, Riviere Quelle)

Villeneuve, Claire   ⌣ B&B
215 Rue St. Raphael, Cap-à-l'Aigle, Quebec G0T 1B0   ☎ (418) 665-2288

Located on north side of St. Lawrence River. On road 138 at La Malbaie cross the bridge,
turn right and continue to village.
$25S $40D $13Child(over age 5)   ► 14
● Full, homebaked   ♠ Village, hist., view, oceanfront, quiet   ■ 7D (main and
upper floor)   ⊷ 6T,4D   ⍁ 2Sh.w.g.   ★ TV,KF, separate entrance, parking   ♥
⊷ English (household language is French)
↪ St. Lawrence River, beach, wharf and marina, oldest thatched barn in Quebec
⇔ La Malbaie, famous Manoir Richelieu

☛ Very quiet and relaxing surroundings include the oldest thatched barn in Quebec
(over 150 years). There is a dog and a cat in the house.

B&B Travel Tip: *As a B&B guest you have all the privacy you want in your
own room. Hosts take the cue from you - if you do not want to socialize, they will
understand.*

Foster
(near Magog; see also Waterloo, Sutton, Mansonville)

McAviney, Chantal & Bernard Brochen (Le Vire-Vent B&B) ⌐ CC
728 Lakeside Rd., Lac Brome (Foster), Quebec   J0E 1R0   ☎ (514) 539-0127

From Montreal on Autoroute 10, take Exit 90 (Lac Brome) and go south 3 km on Rt 243
to white house on left.
$35S $45D $10Add.person   ► 9
● Full, homebaked   ♠ Hist., rural, acreage, view, patio, covered gallery   ■ 4D
(upstairs)   ⊢ 1T,3D,2cots   ⅂ Sh.w.g.   ★ Separate entrance, parking, TV for
guests available   ⋘ French
↔ Knowlton, Victorian-style village, fine boutique-antique-craft shops, watersports on
Lake, super windsurfing, Eastern Township Trails, Alpine and cross-country skiing

🐾 Cozy and comfortable Victoria-style home warmly decorated and situated at the
centre of Eastern Township's summer and winter attractions. Hosts' specialty: crêpes
bretonnes (his mother's recipe).

Georgeville
*(near Magog; see also North Hatley, Ayer's Cliff,
Sutton,Mansonville,Waterloo,Foster)*

Greenhough, P.& S. Martin (Martin House)   ⌐ Estrie B&B
Chemin de l'est, Bx 1, Georgeville, Quebec   J0B 1T0   ☎ (819) 843-3150

Phone for directions.
$25-45S $50-80D $20Child $20Add.person   ⊡ Meals(Gourmet)   ► 12
● Full, homebaked, gourmet   ♠ Farm, hist., view, patio, quiet, pond, stream
■ 1S,3D,1Ste   ⊢ 1S,2D,2T,1Q,1P,1R   ⅂ 2Sh.w.g.   ★ TV,F   ♥   ⑁ Pets,
children min. age 5   ⋘ French
↔ Cross-country skiing and nature trails, duck and beaver pond, beautiful gardens,
berry patch and orchards, picturesque village of historical Georgeville
↔ Lake Memphremagog (boating, fishing, sailing, windsurfing), Mt. Orford (downhill
skiing, hiking, Jeuness Musicale in summer), Magog (Int. tourist area, restaurants,
boutiques), Owl's Head and Jay Peak (Vt) for excellent downhill skiing.

🐾 Historic farmhouse with hand-hewn beams, spectacular views, lovingly decorated
with antiques and local handicrafts and quiet country elegance. Gourmet candlelight
dinners available (bring your own wine).

B&B Travel Tip: *Most hosts do not accept credit cards or cheques, so make
sure you have cash on hand - or check about this when making your reservation.*

Franklin Centre
(south of Montreal; see also Ste Bernard-de-Lacolle, Lery)

Goldie, Constance & Clairmont Faille (Hillspring Farm)   ~ Agricotours
1019 Rt202, Franklin Centre, Quebec J0S 1E0   ☎ (514) 827-2565

From Montreal take the Mercier Bridge and then Hwy 138 to Ormstown. Then go on
Hwy 201 south to Rt 202 and continue west for 8 km.
$25S $35D $7Child $10Add.person   ◙ Meals   ► 5A,3Ch
● Full, homebaked   ■ Farm, hist., view, swimming pool, patio, quiet   3D (upstairs)
⊢ 1S,2D,1 cots, crib   ⁋ Sh.w.g.   ★ TV   ⋙ French
↪ Walking in maple bush on property, pond, many animals
⇔ Parc Safari, NY State border

☛ 150-year old stone house set amongst apple trees and maple bush. Enjoy a good
country breakfast which includes homebaked bread and muffins. There are 2 cats and a
dog in the house.

Howick
(near Montreal; see also St. Bernard de Lacolle)

O'Hanlon, Shirly and Desmond (Tulloghgorum)
1110 Rang 3, Howick, Quebec J0S 1G0   ☎ (514) 825-2794

From Montreal, take Rt 138 to Rt 203 and follow the signs to Howick. Cross the bridge
and bear left at church. Cross Colville Street to Rang 3 and look for house on right.
$25S $35D $5Child   ◙ Meals   ► 6A,2Ch
● Choice, homebaked   ⌂ Farm, hist., quiet   ■ 3D (upstairs)   ⊢ 2D,2T,2cots
⁋ 1Sh.w.g.   ★ TV,LF   ⋙ French
⇔ New York State Border, scenic Covey Hills, Apple Country, Montreal

☛ 100-year old Victorian farm house situated in a pastoral setting. Visits to a goat
cheese farm and a dairy farm can be arranged.

Hudson
(near Montreal; see also Hudson Heights, Westmount)

Henshaw, Naomi and Fred (Riversmead)
245 Main Rd, RR1, Hudson (Como), Quebec J0P 1H0   ☎ (514) 458-5053

Take Hwy 40 west from Montreal towards Ottawa and any Hudson Exit to Main Rd.
$45S $60D   ► 6A
● Full (English)   ⌂ Village, acreage, hist., view, lakefront, patio, swimming pool,
quiet   ■ 3D   ⊢ 2T,2D   ⁋ 2Sh.w.g.   ★ 2F, bicycles for guests   ⊛ Smoking,
drinking   ⋙ French
↪ Fine restaurants, swimming, golfing, tennis, bicycling, cross- country skiing, excellent
shops, hiking, riding, sailing, maple syruping

☛ Fine Century-old Georgian brick home furnished with antiques situated on large
grounds with access to Lake of Two Mountains.

Hudson Heights
(near Montreal; see also Hudson, St-Anicet, Westmount)

Rowland, Jeanette   ✔ B&B
76 Oakland Ave., Hudson Heights, Quebec   J0P 1J0   ☎ (514) 458-5893

Take Trans-Canada Hwy west from Montreal to Exit 22, then north on Co.name te
St-Charles Rd to Main Rd. Turn right on second road on right. From Toronto take 401
and Exit "Ottawa North", then take Exit 22 and continue as above.
$34S $40-45D $10Child $10Add.person   ► 4A,4Ch
● Full, homebaked   🏠 Rural, very quiet, older, screened porch   ■ 2D,F   ⊷ 2D
� 1Ensuite, 1sh.w.h.   ★ TV,F, wheel chair entrance   🖐 Pets
↔ Village of Hudson, Ottawa River, Lake of Two Mountains, "Finnegan's" flea market
⇔ Marina, lakeside dining, antiques and craft shops, horseback riding, bicycling

🐾 Spacious older home surrounded by beautiful large grounds in rural residential area.
Breakfast is served on large sunny porch. There is a pet cat called "Charlie".

Ile Nepawa
(Lake Abitibi)

Wille, Hermann and Helene   ✔ B&B
Ile Nepawa, Abitibi Quest, Quebec   J0Z 2T0   ☎ (819) 333-6103

Located 28.8 km south-west of La Sarre and 16 km from St. Hele ne. Look for house on
right after covered bridge.
$20S $30D   ● $2.50Each $10Child   🍽 Meals   ► 10-12
● Full   🏠 1000-acre farm, quiet   ■ 3D (in house) and 4 cottages   ⊷ D,P
breakfast 1Private, 1sh.w.g.   ★ TV,F,KF,LF   ⌇ French, German
↔ Own private beach, wooded surroundings for hiking, fishing all year

🐾 Hosts organize excursions and hunting trips for bear, moose, bird and game.
Campers welcome. Peaceful and quiet place.

Kamouraska
(near Rivière-du-Loup; see also L'Islelet Sur Mer, Cap- à-l'Aigle)

Dionne, Laurence   ✔ Agricotours
92 ave Morel, CP118, Kamouraska, Quebec   G0L 1M0   ☎ (418) 492-2916

De Quebec, route 20 est, sortie 465 pour Kamouraska. A l'ave Morel tournez à gauche.
$20S $30D $7Enfant $10Add person   ► 7A,5E
❉ Ete   ● Par gout   🏠 Res., fleuve St. Laurent   ■ 3D   ⊷ 3D   Part.à.h.
★TV en chambre   🖐 Animeaux   ⌇ Anglais
↔ Artisanat, Musée de Kamouraska, visite a l'église, randonnees pedestres.
⇔ Moulin Paradis, l'aboiteau de la seigneurie de Kamouraska, seigneurie des aulnaies.

🐾 Au coeur de Kamouraska, la maison est située près du fleuve Saint-Laurent. Les
visiteurs ont le loisir de se détendre à l'éxterieur sur le grand parterre paysagé qui borne
à la mer. A Kamouraska les couchers de soleil sont remarquables.

LeBlanc, Mariette (Gite du Passant)   ⌐ B&B
81 Ave Morel, Kamouraska, Quebec G0L 1M0   ☎ (418) 492-2921

From Hwy 20 take Exit 465 to Kamouraska. In the village turn left on Morel Ave to 2nd
house on left after passing church.
$20S $30D $7Child $10Add.person   ► 8A,2Ch
✚ May 1-Nov. 1   ● Full, homebaked   ♠ Village, older, seafront, patio, quiet
■ 2S,2D,1Ste (main and upper floor) ⊷ 2S,2T,2D   ⅂ 1Private, 1sh.w.g.   ★ TV,
parking   Ⓦ Restricted smoking   ⋙ English (household language is French)

↔ Panoramic road along the St.
Lawrence River, museum

🖝 19th Century home situated on a
patch of land named "K'Amouraska"
on the southshore of the St. Lawrence
River. Watch the glorious sunsets.

Lac Carré
(north-west of Montreal; see also Lac de Pages, St. Adele)

Vaillancourt, Louisette & G. Piche   ⌐ CC
Lac Carré, Quebec J0T 1J0   ☎ (819) 688-2852

From Montreal, take Rt 15 north to Ste-Agathe and continue to St-Faustin. Then turn
right, drive 1.6 km to village and look for Gerard Piche Electrician sign.
$25S $40D $10Child $15Add.person   ▣ Meals   ► 14
✚May 15-Nov.   ●Full, homebaked   ♠Village, res., ranchstyle, view, swimming pool,
patio, lakefront, quiet ■5D,1Ste(main and lower level) ⊷2T,5D,1K   ⅂1Sh.w.g.,
1sh.w.h., whirlpool and therapeutic sauna   ★KF,2F,TV in guest room, separate
entrance, facilities for the handicapped   ♥   ⋙English (household language is French)
⇔ Mt. Tremblant Park, several downhill and cross-country ski areas

🖝 Warm welcome in large ranch-style home with cathedral ceilings and beautiful
gardens and heated swimming pool.

B&B Travel Tip: *Traditionally, B&B is overnight accommodation only, but
nowadays people stay longer, sometimes even up to a week.*

Lac des Plages
(near Ottawa and Montreal: see also Buckingham, Saint Adele, Lac Carre)

Boissonneault, Jean-F. & Luc Martin (L'auvent Bleu) $\quad$ ⌐ Agricotours
6 Chemin Vendée, Lac des Plages, Quebec J0T 1K0 $\quad$ ☎ (819) 687-2981

Phone for directions.
$25S $40D $10Add.person ◐Meals $\quad$ ► 12
● Full ♠ Rural, older, acreage, swimming pool, view, patio, lakefront, quiet ■4D,1F
(main and upper level) ⊷ 4S,4D ⌐ 1Sh.w.h.,1sh.w.g, sinks in all rooms ★TV,
solarium for guests, parking ⊛ Dogs ⋙ English (household language is French)
↪ Hiking trails, walking and cross-country skiing on large acreage, Maskinonge River,
canoeing and canoe rentals
⇔ Lac des Plages (windsurfing), St Jovite (shopping, restaurants), Mont-Tremblant
Lodge, Gray Rocks and Mont-Blanc (downhill/x-country skiing), Chateau Montebello

☛ Comfortable country home in the Laurentian Mountains situated on the banks of
the Maskinonge River. Sit back and relax in the peaceful atmosphere and country
surroundings. Vegetarian dishes available. There is a cat in the house. Cook-out meals
can be arranged and camping space is available on the property.

L'ange Gardien
(near Quebec City: see also St. Laurent, Ste. Famille, St. Jean)

France, Maes (Maison LaBerge)
24 De La Marie, L'Ange Gardien, Quebec G0A 2K0 $\quad$ ☎ (418) 822-0152

From Quebec City take Rt 138 east past the Ile D'Orleans Bridge to traffic light. Turn
north and drive into L'Ange Gardien to first stop (Ave.Royal) and on to Rue de la Marie.
$45S $60D $10Child $15Add. person $\quad$ ► 12A,4Ch
● Full, homebaked ♠ Village, rural, acreage, hist., view, swimming pool, riverfront,
patio, quiet ■4D (main and upper floor) ⊷ 6D, crib ⌐1Private,1sh.w.g.,1sh.w.h.
★F,LF ⊛Pets ⋙English (household language is French)
↪ Hillsite overlooking Saint Lawrence River
⇔ Quebec City, Island of Orleans, Mount Ste Anne and Charlebois County ski centers

☛ Traditional Quebecois red-painted, thick-stone farmhouse-turned-Inn with a rustic
look, exposed beams and rafters and country antiques situated on a hillside overlooking
the Saint Larence River and has been designated a "monument historique" by the
Quebec government.

Lennoxville
(near Sherbrooke; see also North Hatley, Ayers Cliff)

Murray, Monique and John (La Maison Quebecoise)
2 Amesbury Street, Lennoxville, Quebec J1M 1C5

✔ Agricotours
☎ (819) 563-5771

From downtown Sherbrooke take Rt 143 south to Lennoxville. Turn right to Charlotte
St and left to Amerstbury.
$30S $40D $15Child (unde age 12)

► 5

● Full   ♠ Village, swimming pool, patio, quiet   ■ 2D (upstairs)   ⊢ 1S,2T,1D
⌐1Sh.w.h.   ★ TV,F, parking   ✋ Smoking outside only   ⌁ English (French is
household language)
↔ Centre of town (stores, restaurants, churches), Bishop University, theatre, golfing
⇔ Lakes, ski hills, theatres, Sanctuary

☞ Quiet tranquil surroundings. Enjoy breakfast around the big "refectory table".
There are dormers on the guest room windows which overlook peaceful fields and woods.
Hosts are well informed about the area's happenings and take pleasure in helping guests
with their travel plans.

Lery
(near Montreal; see also Franklin Center, St. Bernard-de-Lacolle)

Raymond, Claire
32 Chemin du Lac, Lery, Quebec J6N 1A1

✔ Agricotours
☎ (514) 692-6438

Phone for directions.
$25S $40D $7-10Child

► 4A,1Ch

●Choice   ♠Rural, res., older, acerage, view, lakefront   ■2S,1D (upstairs)   ⊢2S,2T
⌐Sh.w.g.   ★F,TV in guest room   ✋Restricted smoking, drinking, pets, children min.
age 12 (one child only)   ⌁English (household language is French)
↔ Board walk (strolling, bicycling along the lake), sailing, golfing
⇔ Chateauguay battle field (Allen's Corner), Hydro Quebec Power Plant (Beauharnois),
"The Lock" on the Seaway

☞ Century home with a panoramic view of Lake St Louis with huge screened veranda
and stylish furniture facing the lake. Ideal place for cyclists.

L'Islet Sur Mer
(near Quebec City; see also Riviere Quelle, Kamouraska)

Caron, Marguerite and Denis (La Marguerite)   ✔ Agricotours
88 Des Pionniers Est, CP 101, L'Islet Sur Mer, Quebec G0R 2B0   ☎ (418) 247-5454

On Hwy 20 East (from Montreal), travel past Quebec City and Montmagny and exit at
Hwy 285 North. Travel 4 km to intersection of Rd 132, turn right and continue for 1 km.
$25-30S $40-50D (Children's rates available)   ► 10A,2Ch
● Full   ♠ Village, historic, acreage, view, patio, quiet   ■ 4D,1F (upstairs)
⊷ 4T,2D,1Q   ⌐ 2Private, 2sh.w.g.   ★ TV,F, separate entrance, parking
⊛ Smoking, pets   ∾ Household language French-English
↪ Scenic St. Lawrence River, museum and historical church
⇔ Quebec City

☞ 180-year old home, well kept and pretty with large garden to walk, read and relax
in, is located in the heart of a 300-year old historic village on the St. Lawrence River.

Magog
*(near Sherbrooke; see also Ayer's Cliff, Sutton, Mansonville, Waterloo, Foster,
Lennoxville, Georgeville,*

Fear, Marion and Paul Carignan (New Age Farm)   ► Agricotours
RR1, ch Bunker, Magog, Quebec J1X 3W2   ☎ (819) 843-1742

Fromt Montreal take Autoroute 10 to exit 121, past Magog and Rt 55 south to Exit 21.
Turn right 1 km and left on Ch.Colline Bunker-Ste Anne, and continue 4km. -Or- phone
from Magog for direction along picturesque backroad route.
$30-35S $40-50D $10Child   ► 8A,1Ch
▦ May1-Nov.1   ● Choice, homebaked   ♠ 65-acre farm, rural, view, quiet   ■1D,1F
(upstairs)   ⊷ 2T,2D,1P, crib   ⌐ 1Ensuite, 1sh.wh.   ★ Separate entrance   ⊛
Smoking, pets   ∾ French
↪ Organic gardens and hardwood forest, country road for walking with fine view of
mountains, bird and wildlife watching
⇔ Riding School, swimming, sailing, windsurfing and cruise ships on international lake,
Parc Mont Orford (golfing, hiking, outdoor concerts, English/French summer theatres

☞ Escapees from the big City, hosts live in harmony with nature in energy efficient
handcrafted home. Delicious, low-cholesterol, vegetarian breakfasts served from small
organic farm producing vegetables, herbs and berries.

Mansonville

(near Magog and Sherbrooke; see also Ayer's Cliff, Sutton, Stanbridge East, Foster)

Keith-Ryan, Heather & Family (B&B le pied-a-terre) ✔ Estrie B&B
Bellevue St., Box 404, Mansonville, Quebec   J0E 1X0   ☎ (514) 292 5684

From Autoroute 10 take Exit 106 (Eastman). Go south on Hwy 245 to South Bolton, and Hwy 243 south to Mansonville. At town Hall turn left toward Mt. Owl's Head and then to house opposite bridge.
$27S $40D $10Child $10Add. person   ► 15
● Full, homebaked   🏠 Village, hist., view, patio   ■ 3D,2F (main and upper level)
   ⊷ 6S,3D, cots   ⏻ 3Sh.w.g.   ★ TV,KF, parking, separate entrance   ♥
⚬ French
↪ Shopping, churches, restaurants, round barn
⇔ Vermont border (5km), 5 ski resorts, Lake Memphremagog, English and French summer theatres, Orford Prov. Park and Jeunesse Musicale

☛ Century old home in quiet corner of Quebec's Eastern Townships. perfect spot for relaxing, sight-seeing, hunting and skiing. Hostess is well informed about most of the local region. There is a cat in residence.

Matapedia

(west of Bonaventure near Campbelltown (NB)

Chartrand, Michel (Cafe L'Entracte)
50 Blvd Perron, CP 235, Metapedia, Quebec   G0J 1V0   ☎ (418) 865-2734

From Riviere du Loup, take Rt 132, follow signs for Ste-Flavie to Matapedia. At 5 km before the village and facing Matapedia river, follow sign to house.
$30S $45D $15Add.person   ⊠ Meals   ► 6A,3Ch
● Homebaked   🏠 Village, riverfront, patio   ■ 2D,2F (upstairs)   ⊷ 2S,4D
⏻ 3Sh.w.g.   ★ parking   ⚲ Pets   ⚬ English (Household language is French)

↪ River boating, salmon fishing, wild orchards, walking in woods, maple syruping, hunting, cross-country skiing

☛ Young hosts in beautifully renovated former Railway station situated along the CN tracks in the valley and on the shores of the Matapedia river. There is a little cafe called "L'entracte".

Montreal

(see also Ste. Anne de Bellevue, Hudson, Hudson Heights, Coteau-du-Lac, St-Anicet, Howick, Baie d'Urfe)

Allaire, Denise and Lucien
10840 Avenue d'Auteuil, Montreal, Quebec   H3L 2K8   ☎ (514) 382-4807

par l'autoroute metropolitaine, sortie Saint-Hubert Nord pres du Pont Viau (Riviere des Prairies) ou telephoner pour itineraire.
$35S $50D   ► 6
●Full, homebaked   ♠ Res., sub. duplex, quiet   ■ 3D   ⊸4T,1D   ᑠ 1Sh.w.g.
★Separate entrance, parking, solarium   ⓦ Smoking, drinking, children, pets
➳English (household language is French)
↔ 3 parcs (Ahuntsic, Nicolas Viel, Stanley), Riviere des Prairies, Metro Henri Bourassa, Terminus Autobus Laval, choix de restaurants

⇔ Apprecierez le calme de la maison situee dans un paisible quartier residentiel (Ahuntsic), desservi par le metro a permettra de rejoindre le centre ville.

Blondel, Lena (Montreal Oasis - Forever Green B&B)   ⌐ B&B
3000 Breslay Rd., Montreal, Quebec   H3Y 2G7   ☎ (514) 935 2312

Follow directions to downtown Montreal, do not take the Bonaventure Express Rd but Exit at Atwater and continue to Breslay Rd/Chemin de Breslay, turn left to 1st house.
$35-50S $34-60D $15Child $25Add.person   ► 10
● Choice   ♠Downtown, res., quiet, large garden   ■4D(upstairs)   ᑠ2Sh.w.g.
★TV   ♥(winter only)   ⓦPets, moderate smoking   ➳Swedish, French, Spanish,German
↔ Various restaurants and fine dining, Montreal Forum, Mount Royal Park (a short hike up hill), Westmount Galleries (most exclusive shopping center in the city), Alexis Nihon Plaza (part of underground City), subway stop
⇔ Old Montreal, The Latin Quarter

☛ Spacious home located in what is known as the "Priest Farm district" (once a holiday resort for priests) with original lead windows and slanted ceilings on the third floor, situated in a beautiful neighborhood with interesting houses, large trees and pretty gardens. Swedish hostess is well travelled and loves all kinds of music and African Art. There is a blue-cream Siamese cat called "Spoket" in residence. Hostess also operates a small B&B Network of good quality homes located in the west end of downtown.

B&B Travel Tip: *You can stay in a B&B when visiting friends and relatives (if they do not have enough room for you). There is probably a B&B around the corner.*

266   QUEBEC

Campbell, Carmelle & Bernard (Gite du Passant)   ✔ Agricotours
7 rue Jerome, Laval, Quebec H7C 2G7   ☎ (514) 661-3215

Located north of Montreal. Take Pie IX Blvd and over Pie IX Bridge then across Blvd
Concorde to Vanier and Dymont, left on Suzanne St to St. Joseph and Park Jerome.
$30S $40-45D $7Child $10Add.person   ► 8
✪ Apr.15-Feb.1   ● Choice, homebaked   ♠ Res., large big bungalow, patio, quiet
   ■ 1S,2D,1F   ⌐ 2T,3D   ⌐ 2Private, 1sh.w.h.   ★ Air,LF,TV in guest room
🐾 Pets   ⋙ English (household language is French)
↔ Olympic swimming pool and park "Centre de la Nature", winter ski trails
⟷ Place Ville Marie (Centre of the City of Montreal), Botanical gardens, Olympic
Stadium, Mirabel Airport, Laurentians (St Adele and Val David winter and summer
activities)

🐾 Large bungalow in very quiet surroundings with easy access to the Metropolis.

Coliton, Paul and Yolande (Le Relais du Village des Rapides)
7695 Lasalle Blvd, Lasalle, Quebec H8P 1Y4   ☎ (514) 366-5492

Take Hwy 20 to Exit 62 (marked Verdun, De l'Eglise, La Verendrye) and take Verendrye
West. Continue to 11th traffic light (4 km) to Bishop Power Blvd. Go south to Lasalle
Blvd (river road) and to house on left.
$30S $40D $5Add.person   (Family rates available)   ► 7
● Full   ♠ Res., sub.,duplex, view, patio, quiet   ■ 2S,2D (main and upper floor)
⌐ 2S,2D,1P   ⌐ 1Private, 1sh.w.g.   ★ TV,LF, parking   ♥   ⋙ French
↔ St. Lawrence River across the street (excellent bicycle path), Lachine Rapids,
Waterfowl Sanctuary
⟷ City of Montreal (Centre of French Culture in Canada)

🐾 Semi-retired hosts in brick duplex with oak wood and stained glass windows and
facing park with the St. Lawrence River. Situated on the south shore of the Island of
Montreal, between the Champlain and Mercier Bridges.

B&B Travel Tip: *You can go B&B if you are a single traveller (on business
or pleasure). Then, you are in the company of others, and socializing with
strangers is so much easier.*

A Downtown B&B Network

3458 Laval Ave., Montreal, Quebec   H2X 3C8 ☎ (514) 289-9749
(Bob Finklestein, Co-Ordinator)
Rates vary from $25-40S and from $35-50D   (Deposit rquired) (Family rates available)
Montrealer-at-Home represents more than 70 homes (most of them in the "Latin
Quarter" of the City. Some hosts offer airport service. For reservation send a stamped
self-addressed envelope to the above for illustrated brochure and reservation form.
The Agency also represents homes in Westmount, Outremont, Quebec City and
out-of-town areas.

Bed and Breakfast de Chez Nous

5386 Ave. Brodeur, Montreal, Quebec   H4A 1J3 ☎ (514) 485-1252
(Jaqueline Boulanger, Co-Ordinator)
Rates: $35-45S $45-60D   (includes full breakfast)   (Deposit required)
B&B de Chez Nous is an agency that provides residential lodging in typical Quebecois
homes. Each home has been selected in areas well serviced by an excellent Transit
System. Most of the hosts are fluently bilingual.
For detailed information and reservation form write to above.

Agricotours

4545 av. Pierre-de-Coubertin, CP 100, Succursale M,
Montreal, Que. H1V 3R2 ☎ (514) 252-3138
(Odette Chaput)
Rates: $20-25S $30-40D
The Federation des Agricotours du Quebec produces a listing of B&B's and Farm
Vacations which are located in the Province of Quebec. Some of the hosts are fully
bilingual. Write or phone the above for information and booklet.

Bed and Breakfast Montreal

4912 Victoria, Montreal, Quebec   H3W 2N1 ☎ (514) 738-9410
(Marian Kahn, Co-Ordinator)
Rates $30S(and up) $50D(and up)
Marian's extensive Bed and Breakfast network, built up since 1980, concentrates on
downtown and central Montreal locations. Homes vary from a three-storey Victorian
beauty in the "Latin Quarter" or a bright, spacious luxury apartment near McGill
University. For reservation call the above.

New Carlisle
(near Bonaventure in Gaspe area)

Sawer, Helen and Garnett (Manoir Bay View)   ⌐ Agricotour
Box 21,395 N.Carlisle W.(Fauvel),New Carlisle, Que G0C1Z0   ☎ (418) 752-2725/6718

From Quebec City follow Autoroute 20 east, then Rt 132 past Bonaventure to Fauvel.
Look for the big house next to the Fauvel Golf Course.
$25S $35D $5Child $10Add.person   ◙Meals   ► 19A,4Ch
● Full   🏠 Rural, acreage, view, quiet, oceanfront   ■ 6D,2F (main and upper floor)
⇥7S,5D,P, cots, crib   ⌐1Private, 1sh.w.h.   ★TV, parking   ♥   ⓦPets   ∿ French
↔ Golf course, quiet sandy beach across the street, fishing in Bay, Folk Festival
⇔ Archaeological Caves of St.Elzear, museum, historic sites at Paspebiac Beach, tennis
court, cross-country and downhill skiing

☞ Spcaious home in quiet coutry sea-side surroundings, yet situated on main highway
in predominantly English community. Old fashion country comfort at its best with
meals from home-grown products.

North Hatley
(near Sherbrooke; see also Ayer's Cliff, Magog, Lennoxville)

Bardati, Bob and Sonya (La Casa Del Sole)   ⌐ Agricotour
RR1, North Hatley, Quebec   J0B 2C0   ☎ (819) 842-4213

Take Hwy 55 and turn on Rt 108 to town. Take Sherbrooke Rd to Rt 143 South and then
5 km to house on left.
$25-30S $40-50D $15Add. person   (Childrens rates available)   ◙ Meals   ► 6
● Full, homebaked   🏠 26-acre farm, view, patio, quiet   ■ 2Ste   ⇥ 2T,2D,P, cot
⌐ 2Private   ★ KF, separate entrance   ♥   ⓦ Smoking, pets, children mininum
age 3   ∿ French, Italian
↔ Cross country skiing, snowshoeing, bicycle route, nature walks, hiking, birdwatching,
maple sugar parties
⇔ North Hatley, Alpine skiing, summer theatres (French and English), unpolluted Lake
Massawippi and water sports activities, good fishing, golfing

☞ Mini farm in beautiful Eastern Townships with a commanding view of the
Appalachian mountain range, including Jay Peak (Vt). Very peaceful and relaxing
atmosphere with fantastic autumn colour surroundings. Corn roast in season. There are
cats, dogs and canaries in residence.

Bouchard, Marie-P & P Ammann (Les Trois Etangs - 3 Ponds)   ✔ B&B
Hatley Center, North Hatley, Quebec   J0B 2C0   ☎ (819) 842-4111

Phone for directions.
$25S(weekdays) $40S(weekends) $60D   ► 6
● Full (Swiss specialty)   ♠ Res., bungalow, acreage, view, swimming pond, patio,
quiet, organic gardens   ■ 1S,2D   ⊶ 1S,2D,1Q,1K   � 1Sh.w.h., 1sh.w.g.
★F,TV, separate entrance, parking   ⍟ Pets, children by special arrangement
～French, German, Swiss German
↔ Golf club, Lake Massawippi, Village of North Hatley, beautiful paths
⇔ Mt. Orford (all year sports), St. Benoit du Lac (Old Abbey and Monastery)
☞ Quiet and restful location located directly on the golf of North Hatley with a view of
unparalleled beauty. Enjoy magnificient sunsets and flowers from the deck. Healthful
breakfasts: muesli and creme budwig à la suisse, whole wheat French toast or crepes.

Fleischer, Ann and Don (Cedar Gables)   ✔ B&B
Box 355, 4080 Magog Rd., Rt 108, North Hatley, Quebec   J0B 2C0   ☎ (819) 842-4120

From Sherbrooke, Montreal, points west and north, take Autoroute 55 South and exit Rt
108 East to house before center of village. From Eastern USA, take Interstate 91 North
to Quebec Autoroute 55 North and continue as above.
$45-75S $55-85D   (Deposit required)   ◙ Meals   ► 8-10
● Homebaked, something special   ♠ Res., village, older, view, lakefront, patio, dock,
lakeside deck, sunporch   ■ 3D,1Ste   ⊶ 3K,D,P   � 1Ensuite, 1sh.w.g.,2sh.w.g.
★ VCR, 2canoes, sail- and motorboat, parking   ♥   ～ some French
↔ Unique pub (eliminate microbrewery), village centre, watersports, swimming,
gourmet and casual dining, boutiques, unique microbrewery and pub, tennis, ice fishing
⇔ Piggery Theatre, Alpine ski areas, Oxford Festival, Jay Peak (Vermont-US), Bishop's
U and Sherbrooke U, horseback riding, golfing, sleigh rides
☞ Large, tastefully appointed turn-of-the Century home on Lake Massawippi in the
beautiful Eastern Township. Hostess is an exper spinner and weaver and has an
extensive frog collection. Hosts operates own microbrewery (mostly on weekends)

Matte, Monique and Jean (La Montagnarde)   ✔ B&B
McFarland Rd,, RR1, North Hatley, Que J0B 2C0   ☎ (819) 842-2576

In the village of North Hatley, take Capelton Rd to MacFarland Rd.
$45S $65D $80F $20Add.person   ► 8A,4Ch
● Full, homebaked   ♠ Village, hist., lakeview, patio, quiet, isolated   ■ 5 (main and
upper level)   ⊶ 3S,4D,1K (round)   � 1Private, 1sh.w.g., 1sh.w.h.
★TV,2F, separate entrance, facilities for the handicapped   ⍟ Children min. age 2
～English (household language is French)
↔ North Hatley village, Sky Centre, shopping center
⇔ Health Centre, Sherbrooke, Magog
☞ Spacious home located in the center of the village. House specialty: hot brunch with
special pancakes called "Moniquoise's pancakes", served with maple syrup.

270   QUEBEC

Ross, Mary Lynn & Sally Provencher (North Hatley Trillium) ‿ B&B
2165 Lake Rd., North Hatley, Quebec J0B 2C0 ☎ (819) 842-2269

From Montreal take Eastern Township Rt and Exit 121 (Hwy 55 South) and follow signs
to North Hatley. Phone for directions.
$45S $70D $15Child(under age 16-20) ► 16
● Full, homebaked ⌂ Village, acreage, view, lakefront, patio, quiet ■ 4D,2Ste
⊷ 4T,2D,2Q, crib ⊓ 2Private, 2sh.w.g. ★ F(large), separate entrance, parking,
wood burning stove, ♥ ᵚ French
↪ Private sandy beach, swimming, excellent watersports, fishing, tennis, antique and
artisan shops, restaurants and pub, cross-country skiing
⇔ Downhill skiiing, English and French summer theatre, hiking, Sports Center

☛ Home is situated on a quiet road on Lake Massawippi with a private beach and
surrounded by acres of woods bordering the Massawippi golf course in back and lake in
front. Hosts serve own pressed apple juice. House-trained pets welcome.

Winn, Antonia (Sunset View) ‿ B&B
1044 Massawippi St., North Hatley, Quebec J0B 2C0 ☎ (819) 842-2560

Take Autoroute 10 east from Montreal to Sherbrooke and Rt 55 south (Exit 121) to Rt
108 (Exit 29) and continue to North Hatley. Continue through village centre to east side
of lake. Pass the Town Hall on the right side and take next street on left.
$50-65D per room meals ► 14A
● Full ⌂ Village, hist., view, quiet ■ 7 ⊷ 6T,1D,3Q ⊓ 1Private, 2sh.w.g.
★ F, separate entrance, parking ⍟ Pets ᵚ French, German
↪ 9-hole golf course, cross-country skiing, Public beach, summer theatre and concerts,
tennis, windsurfing and boat rentals and water activities, wintersports, historic sites
⇔ Mount Orford (challenging ski slopes), Magog, Sherbrooke (shopping/restaurants), St.
Benoit du Lac Abbey (wines and cheeses), Bishop's and Sherbrooke University

☛ Charming turn-of-the-Century farmhouse, designated by Quebec Government of
historcal interest, overlooks Lake Massawippi and golf course. Sunday concerts.

Portneuf
(near Quebec City; see also St-Antoine-de-Tilly)

Farnsworth, Mary and Tam (Edale Place) ‿ Agricotour
Portneuf, Quebec G0A 2Y0 ☎ (418) 286-3168

From Autoroute 40, take Exit 261 (Portneuf) right to Hwy 138. Turn left 1 km Chemin
Neuf (toward St.Basile). Turn left on Chemin Neuf 1 km. Immediately after overpass
(1km from 138) turn left on country lane to 1st house on right.
$27S $40D $12Child $10Add. person ▣ Meals ► 6A,2Ch
●Full, homebaked ⌂Rural, acreage, patio, quiet, isolated ■2D,1F,1S (upstairs)
⊷2D,4T, 1R ⊓1Sh.w.g., 1sh.w.h. ★LF, TV in guest living room ⍟Pets ᵚFrench
↪ Wooded lanes, country walks, cross-country skiing
⇔ Historic Quebec City

☛ Victorian homestead; a quiet relaxed country home with antiques.

Quebec City
(see also St.Ant.-de-Tilly, St. Laurent, Ste. Famille, St. Jean, L.Gardien, Portneuf)

Begin, Francois (B&B in Old Quebec)
35 Rue Des Remparts, Quebec City, Quebec   G1R 3R6   ☎ (418) 655-7685

Coming from Montreal on Hwy 20, cross bridge before city. Take Boulevard Laurier
straight for 9 km to walls of the Old City.
$40S $50D   (Off season rates)   ► 12
●Full   ♠ Downtown, res., hist., older   ■ 5 (main and upper floor)   ■D,Q
⌐Private   ★ Reading and sun room for guests, coffee making facilities   ⓦ Pets
↪ Chateau Frontenac

🖝 Completely restored stone home, built in 1831 with view of marina, the St.
Lawrence River, Island of Orleans and the Laurentian Mountains. Also available studios
and apartments in the city.

Lajoie, Dolores (Battlefields B&B)   ⌐ CC
820 Eymard St., Quebec City, Quebec   G1S 4A1   ☎ (418) 527-0481

Phone for directions.
$35S $50D   ► 8
● Full   ♠ Res., older, quiet   ■ 4D,1F   ⊶3D,1Q   ⌐ 1Sh.w.g.   ⓦ Pets
⌇ English, Spanish, Chinese (household language is French)
↪ Plains of Abraham, Old Quebec and Old Port, Cartier Street
⇔ Baie St. Paul (Charlevoix, Isle d'Orleans, Montmorency Falls

🖝 Home is situated in front of the Battlefields (which is a huge park in the City).
There is a cat in the house.

Poissant, Claude & Lili Perigny (B&B Bienvenue a Quebec)   ⌐ B&B
1067 Maguire, Sillery, Quebec   G1T 1Y3   ☎ (418) 681-3212

Sillery is in the center of Quebec City. Take Blvd Laurier from East and turn left on
Maguire Ave. Look for signs.
$30S $50D $60F $10Add.person   ⍾ Meals   ► 7
● Choice, homebaked   ♠ Centretown, res., townhouse, patio, very quiet   ■ 2D,1F
(main and upper level)   ⊶3T,1D,1K   ⌐ 1Private, 1sh.w.h.   ★ Air,TV in guest
room, parking   ♥   ⓦ Pets   ⌇ English (household language is French)
↪ Laval University, Chateau Frontenac, Abraham Plaines, shopping centre, bus route
⇔ Charlevois (Baie St-Paul), Ste Anne-de-Beaupre

🖝 Home is located in very desirable area of Quebec City and very convenient to all
attractions. Hosts are very knowledgeable of the city and delight in helping guests to
discover Quebec.

B&B Bonjour Quebec
3765 Blvd Monaco, Quebec City, Quebec   G1P 3J3   ☎ (418) 527-1465
(Denise and Raymond Blanchet, Managers)
Rates: 30-40S $40-60D $10Child $10Add.person   (Family rates)
B&B Bonjour Quebec represents 11 homes which are located a few minutes drive or less
to the heart of Old Quebec and whose hosts speak some or fluent English. Upon receipt
of a reservation, along with a deposit for $10, Mr.and Mrs. Blanchet will forward
information as well as a city map with directions. For reservation write/phone the
above.

Quyon
(near Ottawa (Ont); see also Buckingham and Ontario: Fitzroy Harbour, Braeside)

Prior, Blair and Laura (Memory Lane Farm)   ↙ Agricotour
RR1, Quyon, Quebec   J0X 2V0   ☎ (819) 458-2479

From Hull, go west on Hwy 148 to Aylmer and continue for 37 km. At railway overpass
turn north on Hammond Rd to end. Turn right and go to 3rd house on right. Crossing
Ontario via ferry to Quyon, go east on Hwy 148 to overpass.
$25S $35D   ▣ Meals   ► 4A,3Ch
● Full   ♠ 100-acre working farm, view, veranda   ■ 2D(upstairs)   ⊶ S,D,R, crib
   ⚲ 1Sh.w.g.   ★ TV in guest room, F   ⚓ Pets
↔ Hiking and snowmobile trails (Quebec system), sugar bush
⇔ Pond fishing, swimming, golfing, riding stables, hunting

🐾 Relaxed farm life in traditional country home. Hosts are antique car enthusiasts.

Rivière Ouelle
*(northeast of Quebec City; see also Kamouaska, Rivière du Loup, L'Islet Sur Mer,
Cap-à-l'Aigle)*

Lizotte, Mme. Alice   ↙ Agricotours
144 Ch de la Pointe, Riviere Ouelle, Quebec   G0L 2C0   ☎ (418) 856-1391

From autoroute 20 East, take Exit 444 to Riv. Ouelle, turn left after bridge and take
chemin de la Pointe, which follows the river.
$20S $30D $10Child(over age 5)   ► 7A,2E
🔹 Summer   ● Homebaked   ♠ Rural, res., older, view, oceanfront, quiet   ■ 3D
(upstairs)   ■ 1S,3D,1R   ⚲ Private   ★ F,TV,KF, parking   ⚓ Pets   ∽ some
English (household language is French)
↔ Windsurfing, fishing, waterskiing, swimming
⇔ Quebec City, Riviere-du-Loup, Montreal

🐾 Large white and blue ancestral home situated near the shore of the Ouelle River
with a magnificient view.

Rivière du Loup

(northeast of Quebec City; see also Kamouraska, Cap-à-l'Aigle)

Levesque, Louiselle (Le Nouveau Jardin)   ✔ B&B
280 Anse Au Persil, Rivière du Loup, Quebec   G5R 3Y5   ☎ (418) 862-9494

From Rt 20 take last Exit for R-d-Loup turn right (132 East). Continue until there are no more houses close to the road and look for pink mail box well on the left.
$25S $40D $10Child(under age 12) $13Add.person   ▣ Meals   ► 6A, 2Ch
● Full   ♠ Rural, older, view, patios, quiet   ■ 2S,2D (upstairs)   ⊷ 4T,1D, divans
⌐ 1Sh.w.g.   ★ parking   Ⓦ drinking, pets, children min. age 6   ⋙ English
(household language is French)

↔ St. Lawrence River (watersports including swimming), foot paths in surrounding wooded areas, promenade in fields in quiet solitude on private road, heated sea-water pools, golfing, summer theatre, galleries, whaele watching cruises, antiques many gourmet restaurants, bird-watching cruises

⇔ Ferry to St. Simeon, horse riding ranch, New Brunswick and Maine borders, Centre Scientific d'Observation Astronomique,

☞ Retired hosts with universal mind and spirit in typical Quebecois home, which has a panoramic view embracing the city, fields, wharf and river. Enjoy the constant fresh breeze off the river. There are two cats in the house.

Rougemont

(near Granby; see also Ste. Bruno-de-Montarville)

Turgeon, Lili   ✔ Agricotour
1340 Grande Caroline, Rougemont, Quebec   J0L 1M0   ☎ (514) 469-3818

Located on Rt 231 and 5 km north of junction Rt 112.
$25S $40D $10Child $10Add.person   ▣ Meals   ► 6
● Choice, homebaked   ♠ Farm, view, quiet   ■ 4D (main and upper level)
⊷ 1S,2T,3D, crib   ⌐ 1Private, 1shw.h., 1sh.w.g.   ★TV,LF, facilities for the disabled
⋙ English (household language is French)
↔ Cross-country and night skiing
⇔ Zoo, summer theatres, downhill skiing

☞ 150-year old home with Victorian antiques and old fashioned and warm hospitality. Enjoy a campfire at night with music loving hosts.

St. Anicet

(see also Cornwall, Ont)

Leduc, Bernard and Solande (La Ferme Chez Nous)
1128 Ch La Guerre, St-Anicet, Quebec   J0S 1M0   ☎ (514) 264-6533

From Montreal, take Hwy 132 east and Hwy 236 at St. Barbe and Cazaville and look for
number on mailbox. From Toronto, cross river via toll bridge at Cornwall to Fort
Covington, then take Rt 132 to Cazaville.
\$18S   \$25D   ● \$3Each   \$5Add. person   ▣ Meals   ► 6A,4Ch
● Choice, homebaked   ♠ 150-acre farm, quiet, hist., view, patio   ■ S,D
⊷ 2T,2D,R,P, crib   ⌐ 1Sh.w.g., 1sh.w.h.   ★ TV,F,KF,LF   ∿ French
↔ River fishing on property, golfing, bicycling, swimming, hunting, cross-country skiing,
⇔ St. Anicet village

🖛 Farm is situated on the shores of beautiful Lake St-Francois, with the river running
throughout the property. "Feel at home in our home". Hosts are interested in music.

St-Antoine-de-Tilly

(near Quebec City)

Gagnon, Jocelyne and Majella (Auberge Manoir de Tilly)
3854 Chemin de Tilly, St-Antoine-de-Tilly, Quebec   G0S 2C0   ☎ (418) 886-2407

Located just north of the Church in village. From Rt 20, exit 291 north.
\$75D(and up)   ▣ Meals (Deposit)   ► 12
✚ Apr.1- Dec.31   ● Choice   ♠ Village centre, hist., acreage, patio, view, swimming
pool   ■ 6 (S,D,Ste,in main building and annex)   ⊷ T,D, cot   ⌐ 1Private, 1sh.w.h.,
1sh.w.g.   ★ TV,F   ♥   ∿ French

↔ Village, tennis courts, bicycling,
historic church

⇔ Quebec bridge (gate to Quebec City),
Old Quebec

🖛 Home was built in 1786 and is
situated in the beautiful 250-year old
village on the south-shore of St.
Lawrence River. Quebec-style cooking
is a specialty.

St. Bernard de Lacolle
(near Montreal; see also Howick, Franklin Center, Lery)

Kennedy, Gail and Stan (The Old Smoothing Board) ✔ Agricotour
336 Roxham Rd., St. Bernard de Lacolle, Quebec J0J 1V0 ☎ (514) 247-2092

From Montreal, on Hwy 15 south take Exit 11 at Henrysburg and turn right off exit and
travel west. Turn left at Bogton Rd (runs into Roxham Rd) and look for sign on gate
approx. 3 km past Parc Safari entrance.
$25S $40D $8Child $10Add. person   ▨ Meals   ► 5A,2Ch
● Choice, homebaked   ♠ Rural, hist., acreage, view, verranda, quiet, isolated
■ 2D   ⊷ 1S,2D, cots   ⤒ 2Sh.w.h.   ★ TV,F,LF, library, grand piano
ⓌSmoking   ⤳ French, German, Dutch, Spanish, some Italian
↔ Indian Trail Marker, cross-country ski and nature trails
⇔ Park Safari African, Hemmingford Golf and Country Club,, historic battle sites and
museums, US border, Montreal

🖙 Old country home furnished with antiques and pottery gift shop on the premises.

St. Bruno de Montarville
(near Montreal; see also Lasalle, Rougemont)

Richard, Dominique (Gite du Passant St. Bruno) ✔ Agricotours
1959 Montarville, St. Bruno de Montarville, Quebec J3V 3V8 ☎ (514) 653-2149

From Montreal, follow Hwy 116 to St-Bruno. Take Rabastaliere St and turn right on
Montarville. From Hwy 20, take St-Hubert Exit and follow Montarville Blvd.
$25S $40D $5Child $10Add.person   ▨ Meals   ► 12
✠ Apr 1-Oct 31   ● Full, homebaked   ♠ Res., sub., bungalow, acreage, quiet
■ 1S,2D   ⊷ 3S,1D,1Q,1P,3R, crib   ⤒ Sh.w.g.   ★ F,TV, parking   ⤳ Dutch,
English (host language is French)
↔ Swimming pool, tennis, playground
⇔ Downtown Montreal, Mount St. Bruno

🖙 Comfortable and quiet home with spacious grounds where children can play safely.
There is a cat in the house.

B&B Travel Tip: *Breakfast is almost always memorable! Most hosts will
ask in the evening what you would like for breakfast and at what time (you can
sleep in if you wish!). Go ahead and tell them if you would like porridge or something special. You will be pleasantly surprised.*

St. Honoré-de-Beauce
(Comte Beauce près de St.Georges-de-Beauce)

Carrier, Yvonne et Gorges
Rang 6 nord, St. Honoré-de-Beauce, Québec G0M 1V0 ☎ (418) 485-6510

De Sherbrooke, Rt 143 sud pour Lennoxville, pois Rt 108 est jusqu'à la Guadeloupe.
Prenez la Rt 269 est jusqu'à St-Honoré. 4km passé le village prenez à gauche le rang 6,
direction Lac Poulin et rouler 4 km.
$20S $30D   ◙ Meals   ► 4A
● Compl.   🏠 Ferme   ■ 2   ⊐ 1S,2D, lit pliant, 1couchette   ⎺⏋ 1Compl.part.à.h.
★ TV, cuisine   ∾ Francais seulement

🐾 Vacance tranquille dans cette région pittoresque qu'est la Beauce.

St. Jean
(on Isle d'Orleans near Quebec City; see also St Laurent, Ste Famille, L'Ange Gardien)

Godolphin, John and Lorraine (The Pilot's Lookout)   ✔ CC
170, Ch des Ormes, St. Jean, Isle d'Orleans, Quebec   G0A 3W0   ☎ (418) 829-2613

From Hwy 20 take Exit Quebec City then Hwy 73N and exit Ste-Anne de Beaupre
continuing over Orleans Island Bridge. Proceed straight on through villages of St.
Laurent and St. Jean to house past church.
$40S $50D   ► 6
✚ May1-Oct.31   ● Full   🏠 Rural, acreage, view, patio, quiet   ■ 2D,1Ste
(upstairs)   ⊐ 3D   ⎺⏋ 3Ensuite   ★ Separate entrance   🖐 Smoking   ∾ English
(household language is French)

↔ Surrounding wooded areas, farms, beach

⇔ Island tour, river cruises, historic Quebec City, Montmorency Falls, Ste-Anne de Beaupre Shrine, golfing, swimming pool

🐾 Spacious Island home with peaceful and relaxed atmosphere on beautiful Orleans Island and quiet country surroundings. Enjoy the magnificient views over the St. Lawrence River.

St. Laurent

(on Isle d'Orleans near Quebec City; see also Ste. Famille, L'Ange Gardien, St. Jean)

Fradet, Rolande and Raymond (La Vieille Maison Fradet)   ⏎ Agricotour
1584 Royal St.Laurent, Ile d'Orleans, Quebec G0A 3Z0   ☎ (418) 828-9501

Take Rt 20 from Quebec City to Ile d'Orleans Bridge and follow Rt 11.
$30S $50D $12Child   ► 12A,2Ch
● Full   ♠ Village, hist., patio, quiet   ■ 1S,3D,1F (upstairs)   ⊷ 6S,2T,3D
⊓2Private, 1sh.w.g.   ★ TV and fans in guest room, parking   ✋ Pets   ∾ little
English (household language is French)
↔ Marina, restaurants, fruit picking, tennis court, craft shops
⇔ Quebec City, summer theatre, bicycle rental, golfing, museum, swimming, boat cruise,
downhill and cross-country skiing,

☛ Warm and cozy atmosphere in charming house more than a century and a half old
"which reveals its past through the creaking floors over which a thousand feet have
danced frantic jigs".

St. Louis de Blandford

(south of Quebec City; see also St-Antoine-de-Tilly)

Bastien, Margot and Andre (Domaine La Piniere)   ⏎ Agricotours
St. Louis de Blandford, Quebec   G0Z 1B0   ☎ (819) 364-3653

From Trans Canada Hwy, take Exit 235 to Rt 263 south. Go 2.5 km to bridge of
Becancour River, turn left to house on left side.
$20S $30D $2-12Child $10Add.person   ► 10A,3Ch
❏ May-Sept   ● Cont.   ♠ Rural, riverfront, inside heated swimming pool, quiet,
ponds   ■ 2S,3D   ⊷ 5S,4D,1R   ⊓ 1Private, 1sh.w.g.   ★ TV in guest room, 2F,
separate entrance, outside shuffle board   ∾ English (household language is French)
↔ 5 km foot path with trout ponds on property, fishing, paddle boat
⇔ Princeville and Victoriaville (shopping, restaurants), Quebec   City

☛ Retired hosts in spacious home situated on lovely 30-year old pine plantation beside
the Becancour River.

B&B Travel Tip: *You can stay in a B&B even if you are on a camping trip.
Give yourself a treat and sleep in a comfortable bed once in a while, especially if
the weather turns miserable and the gear is soaking wet.*

Ste. Adele

(north of Montreal near Ste. Agate; see also Lac-des-Plages, Lac Carée)

Piché, Estelle (L'Auberge Bonne Nuit) ✔ CC
1980 Blvd Ste. Adele, CP2168, Ste. Adele, Quebec   J0R 1L0   ☎ (514) 229-7500

From Montreal take Rt 15 north to Ste. Adele and ask for directions at the Tourist
Kiosque beside Hwy.
$45S $70D $10Add.person   ► 14
● Full, homebaked   ♠ Village, outdoor swimming pool, patio, quiet   ■ 6D (main
and upper levels)   ■ 5D,2T,1P,2cots   ⌐1 3Private,3sh.w.g.   ★ F,TV Den, whirlpool
spa, glassed-in sitting room, parking   ⊎ Pets, children min. age 4   ∾ English
(household language is French)

↔ Ski resorts, golfing, sport center,
historic village (Seraphin), summer
theatre

⇔ Waterslides, ice-skating,
pedal-boating, fine food restaurants

🐾 Home is located in a wooded
setting and projects a calm and serene
atmosphere for relaxing, yet close to
most recreational activities. "Come and
discover the old in the new and partake
of the warm hospitality".

Ste. Famille

(on Isle d'Orleans near Quebec City; see also St. Laurent, L'Ange Gardien, St. Jean)

Desert, Loulette (Les Tanaudes) ✔ Agricotours
3616 Royal, Ste. Famille, Isle d'Orleans, Quebec   G0A 3P0   ☎ (514) 829-2894

From Quebec City, take Rt 360 E and exit to Isle d'Orlean Bridge, turn left on Rt 368 and
continue through St Pierre to Ste Famille.
$30S $50D $12Child $20Add.person   🍴Meals   ► 9A,1Ch
● Full   ♠ Rural, res., bungalow, view, riverfront   ■ 1S,2D,1F (upstairs)
↦1S,2T,3D, cot   ⌐1 Sh.w.g.   ★ TV,F,LF, parking   ⊎ Pets outside   ∾ some
English (household language is French)
↔ Museum, church, fruit picking
⇔ Quebec City, swimming, antiques, arts and craft shops, golfing, museum, summer
theatre, bicycle rentals, boat cruise, sleighrides, cross-country and downhill skiing

🐾 Home is surrounded by beautiful panorama of Quebec and Mount Ste. Anne and
furnished with old-fashioned furniture from France. Hosts have a passion for the Island
and hostess enjoys showing off her handmade embroideries.

Shawville
(near Ottawa; see also Buckingham, Quyon, Renfrew,Braeside, Foresters Falls)

MacDougall, Rolly and Beulah (Macador Farms) ⌐ B&B
Box 16, Shawville, Quebec J0X 2Y0 ☎ (819) 647-3628

From Hull take Hwy 148 west to Shawville. Turn left at flashing light and proceed on Rt 303 to 4th line, turn right on dirt road for 2km. - From Hwy 17 in Ontario turn at Haleys Stn and proceed to Portage du Fort, Quebec. Then follow Rt 303 for 8 km, turn left at 4th line on dirt road and as above.
$15S $25D $10Child ⬕ Meals ► 4A,3Ch
● Full ♠ Farm, view, patio, outdoor swimming pool, quiet ■ 2D ⊶ 2D,R,P
⌐ Sh.w.g. ★ TV,LF ♥ ⬱ Pets outside only
↔ Swimming, hiking, maple sugar bush, sleigh rides, snowmobile and ski trails
⇔ Renfrew (Ontario), white water rafting, Storyland

🖝 Newly renovated brick house on working dairy farm. Relax on the deck by the pool or watch or participate when host gathers maple sap with his Belgium team of horses at neighbors sugar bush. Breakfast served in large cheerful kitchen.

Stanbridge-East
(near Cowansville; see also Sutton, Mansonville)

Bilodeau, Danielle & Robert Lapalme (A Fleur d'Eau) ⌐ Agricotour
6 Bunker, Stanbridge-East, Quebec J0J 2H0 ☎ (514) 248-7008

From Montreal take Hwy 10 and Exit 22 (St.Jean). Proceed on Rt35 south Rt 133 south, and Rt 202 east to Stanbridge East. Turn at the flashing lights (Rt 237 S) to second house on right.
$26-28S $40-42D $8Child $15Add.person ⬕ Meals ► 5A
● Choice, homebaked ♠ Village, older, rural, swimming pool, patio ■2D(upstairs)
⌐Sh.w.h. ★F,TV ⬱Smoking ⇝English (household language is French)
↔ Discover the water gardens on the premises, Missisquoi Museum in the village, excellent for biking
⇔ Vinyard (apple orchards), Ski resorts (Sutton, Bromont), Lake with beach, good restaurants, Vermont USA boder

🖝 1865's little house is cozy and comfortable. Hosts are the first aquatic plant growers in Quebec. There are 2 cats and a dog in the house.

> **B&B Travel Tip:** *Do tell the hosts all about yourself and where you come from and what you do day in and out. They will be eager listeners. After all that's why they are inviting people into their homes – so the world comes to them!*

Sutton

(near Cowansville; see also Mansonville, Ayer's Cliff, Waterloo, Stanbridge East, Foster)

Potvin, Denise & G. Mainville (Le Pic-a-Bois)
389 Mt. Echo Road, Sutton, Quebec J0E 2K0

↙ B&B
☎ (514) 538-3776

Take Exit 68 from Eastern Township Autoroute and follow Rt 139 towards Sutton. Take Rt 215 to Sutton Junction (5 km), and then continue ahead on Mt Echo Rd.
$32-37S $50-55D $12.50Child(under age 12)   ◙ Meals   ► 11
● Choice, homebaked   ♠ Rural, large acreage, view, quiet, isolated   ■ 1S,5D (main and upper floor)   ⊢ 1S,4T,3D   ⍨ 2Private, 2sh.w.g.,1sh.w.h.   ★ F, parking, separate entrance   ∿ English (household language is French)

↪ Cross-country skiing, swimming pool, trout fishing, wooded trail

⇔ Mt. Sutton, Lake Brome, Owl's Head/Jay Peak Ski Stations, Lake Memphremagog

☛ Comfortable and very warm atmosphere and fine foods. Hosts specialty is duck, rabbit, lamb, wild boar and trout dishes.

Sorger, Clara (Pine Gable)
45 Main St.South, Box 218, Sutton, Quebec J0E 2K0

↙ B&B Estrie
☎ (514) 538-2401

From Eastern Township Rt 10 take Exit 68 at Granby and then Rt 139 south to Sutton.
$30(per person)   ◙ Meals(wholesome Bavarian)   ► 10
●Full   ♠Village, res., quiet   ■5D(main and upper floor)   ⊢5D,2S   ⍨2sh.w.g.
★ TV,F, parking   ⍟ Smoking, pets   ∿ German, some French
↪ Art Gallery, Museum of Communications, restaurants, stores, boutiques
⇔ Mt. Sutton Ski area and golf course, Bromont and Jay Peaks (VT) Ski Resorts, excellent hiking and cross-country ski trails, tennis, horseback riding, swimming

☛ 1885 house depicts Victorian charm, filled with antiques creating the cosy atmosphere of years gone by. Advance reservation necessary. Small groups welcome.

Waterloo
(near Granby; see also Bonsecours, Sutton, Foster)

Perras, Rita & Amedee
1552 RR1, ch Bromont, Rt 241, Waterloo, Quebec   J0E 2N0   ☎ (514) 539-2983

Coming from Montreal, take Rt 10 and then Rt 241 north for 3 km.
$23S $40D $70F $12Add.person   ▣ Meals   ► 6
● Full, homebaked   ♠ Rural, bungalow, acreage, view, quiet   ■ 3D   ⊢ 2T,2D
⌐ Sh.w.h.   ★ TV,KF,LF, parking
↩ Beautiful farm land, bicycling, walking, cross-country skiing
⇔ Waterslide, downhill skiing, Zoological Garden, shopping center, fishing, hunting

☞ Hostess loves to cook for her guests. House is surrounded by beautiful flowers.

Williams, Ginette and Paul (Le Coureur des Bois Enr)
51 de la Montagne, Box 1454, Waterloo, Quebec   J0E 2N0   ☎ (514) 539-0404

From Eastern Township Autoroute 10 take Exit 78, turn right to traffic light and left
onto Rt 241. Continue to next traffic light, turn left.
$235S $55D $10Child $15Add. person   ▣ Meals   ► 10A,4Ch
● Full, homebaked   ♠ Bee-farm, hist., view, patio, quiet   ■ 1S,2D,F
⊢ 2S,4D,3R   ⌐ 2Sh.w.g.   ★ TV,2F   ♥   ⓦ Restricted smoking   ∿ French
↩ Cross-country skiing on property, swimming
⇔ Alpine skiing, Brome Lake, golfing,surfing school

☞ Victorian Mansion built in 1850 and elegantly positioned amongst numerous
majestic and brilliantly coloured ancient trees, giving the feeling of stepping into the past
of the grand aristocratic century.

New Brunswick

"Dial-A-Nite "

New Brunswick offers an In-Province Accommodation Reservation System:

This free telephone service is available only in Tourist Information Centres
located in the province. It allows the traveller to make advance
reservations with Bed and Breakfast hosts located throughout the province.

Albert

(near Moncton; see also Riverside)

Tingley, Cyril and Mary (Florentine Manor) ✔ NB B&BA
RR2, Albert (Harvey), Albert Co., NB E0A 1A0 ☎ (506) 882-2271

Take Rt114 at Moncton towards Fundy Nat.Park. At Riverside-Albert take Rt915 past old Bank of NB for 3.5km. Located at Harvey Corner.
$30S $40-45D $5Child ◨ Meals ► 16A,4Ch
● Full,homebaked ♦ Rural, acreage, historic, quiet ■) 3D,1Ste,F (main and upper floor) ⊷ 5T,5D,1Q,1R,crib ⊓ 1Private, 2sh.w.g,2ensuite ★ F,TV,LF,KF, parking ⦸ Smoking, pets
↔ Country lanes for leisure walks
⇔ Shepody Bay Hemispheric Shore Bird Reserve at Mary's Point, Fundy National Park, Hopewell Cape Rocks (world's largest flower pots), Magnetic Hill and Magic Mountain, water Theme Park

🐾 House speaks of the grandeur of a past era when sailing ships were built and launched in the shipyards nearby. It was used as "Customs Office" at that time and was visited by Sea Captains from all over the world. Hosts enjoy sharing their home and the lovely country-side with others.

Apohaqui

(near Saint John; see also Bloomfield, Cody's, Cambridge Narrows)

Beatty, C.Jane & son Aaron (Apohaqui Inn) ✔ B&B
Foster Street, Apohaqui, NB E0G 1A0 ☎ (506) 433-4149

Located 6.5 km west of Sussex on Trans Canada Hwy 1.
$28S $35D $8Child ◨ Meals (Special weekend Ski-rates) ► 5A,2Ch
● Full, homebaked ♦ Village, acreage, older, patio, very quiet ■ 2D,1S (upstairs) ⊷ 1S,2T,1D,cot ⊓ 1Sh.w.h.,1s.w.g. ★ TV,parking, ♥ ⦸ Restricted smoking

↔ Fish pond in yard and pet goat, excellent deer and moose hunting, fly fishing and salmon/trout fishing in Kennebecasis River, Town of Sussex, Poley Mountain Ski area, Sussex Golf Club, Fish Farm

⇔ Digby Ferry, Fundy National Park, Saint John's, Hopewell Rocks and Tides

🐾 Spacious stately home in quiet village with large cool rooms decorated with antiques.

Very large pillers on 3 sides span two floors enclosing bay windows on both floors. Special relaxing area for well-behaved pets. Please call for reservation.

Bathurst

(see also Beresford)

Babin, Ken and Jean (Ingle-Neuk Lodge)   ✔ NB B&BA
Box 1180, RR3, Bathurst, NB E2A 4G8   ☎ (506) 546-5758

From Rt 11, take Vanier Blvd Exit to Rt 134. Travel north to Youghal Dr and right 4km.
$28S $34-38D $9Add. person   ► 12
✠ Summer   ● Full, homebaked   🏠 Rural, res., older, acreage, sea-view, quiet
■ 3D (upstairs)   ⊷ 1S,2T,3D,2R, cot   ⌐ 2Sh.w.g.   ★ TV,F   ⚯ French   ✋ Pets
↔ Chaleur Bay, salt water swimming at private safe, sandy beach, sandbars at low tide
⇔ Golfing, shopping, dining, deep-sea fishing, Acadian Village at Caraquet

🐾 Spacious old-fashioned accommodation in family home that once catered to summer tourists in the 1930's.

Beresford

(near Bathurst; see also Tracadie)

Schwarz, Marianne (Les Peupliers)   ✔ CC
RR1, Site 11, Box 16, Beresford, NB E0B 1H0   ☎ (506) 546-5271

On Hwy 134 follow signs to Danny's Motor Inn. Then go north 200 ft and take Kent
Lodge Rd. Look for "The Poplars" on left before Beresford-Youghal Beach.
$25S $32-35D $9Add. person   ► 7
✠ May-Oct.31   ● Choice, homebaked (croissants and muffins)   🏠 Semi-rural,
acreage, view, oceanfront, patio, quiet, large gazebo, tidal grounds   ■ 3D   ⊷ 2T,2D
⌐ Sh.w.g.   ⚯ French, German, Italian
↔ Bay of Chaleur, sandy beach and good swimming, Peters River
⇔ Acadian Village and Peninsula, Gowan Brae Golf and Country Club, shopping malls

🐾 Extensive grounds with waterfowl habitat. Hostess is originally from Switzerland
and well informed about both countries. Quiet and informal home atmosphere. There is
a cat in the house and a very large gentle dog in the back yard who likes to be petted.
Enjoy tasty berries from the garden and outstanding delicious honey from the behives.

> **B&B Travel Tip:** *Plan your trip at home in the comfort of your living room,
> researching the maps of the provinces you want to visit, and then write or phone
> the B&B hosts, to see if the room is available for you. When you have B&B confir-
> mations, you will relax and enjoy your trip much more.*

Bloomfield

(near Saint John; see also Apohaqui)

Cassidy, David and Evelyn (Evelyn's B&B & Farm Vac)   ✓ NB B&BA
Bloomfield, RR1, Kings Co., NB   E0G 1J0   ☎ (506) 832-4450

From Saint John, take Hwy 1 and exit at Bloomfield. Go through the covered bridge and take the next turn on left. Look for signs.
$25S $30D $8Child   ► 6A,1Ch
● Full, homebaked   ♠ Farm,hist., river view, quiet   ■ 3D (upstairs)   ⊷ 3D,cot
⌐ 1Sh.w.g.   ★ TV,separate entrance   ♥
↔ Walking in the peaceful surrounding contryside, two churches, covered bridge, variety store and vegetable stands
⇔ Fredericton (NB Capital city), Saint John (NB largest city), Moncton, Sussex (NB Dairy Center), CN Ferry to Nova Scotia, US border (Maine)

🐾 150-year old farm house overlooking the Kennebecasis River. Enjoy a restful night in a newly renovated room decorated with antiques. Take a stroll out to the barn to see the animals and watch the milking.

Cambridge Narrows

(east of Fredericton; see also White Cove, Codys,L.Jemseg, Apohaqui)

Samuels, Dorothy and Ken (Evergreen Manor B&B)   ✓ B&B
Lakeview Rd, Cambridge Narrows, NB   E0E 1B0   ☎ (506) 488-2614/2800

Take Rt 695 to Cambridge Narrows, then Lakeview Rd and look for house on lakeside.
$20S $35-37D   ▣ Meals   ► 6A,2Ch
● Choice, homebaked   ♠ Rural, hist., acreage, view, lakefront, patio, quiet
■ 3D (upstairs)   ⊷ 4S,1D,R   ⌐ 2Sh.w.g.   ★ TV in guest room   ♥   ⊛ Pets
↔ Private beach, good swimming, excellent boating
⇔ Village of Gagetown with well-known Craft Centre, Fredericton University, Sussex Dairy Capital, historic Seaport of Saint John

🐾 Well travelled hosts in 1878 lovely heritage house with spacious grounds extending down to the shores of beautiful Washademoak Lake. Candlelight dinners are a house specialty and can be arranged with prior reservation.

B&B Travel Tip: *You can stay in a B&B when attending a wedding in another town. Many churches have lists of B&B's located nearby.*

Waldow, Ursula and Achatz (Norwood Farms)   ✔ NB FV
RR1, Cambridge Narrows, NB   E0E 1E0   ☎ (506) 488-2681

From Trans Canada Hwy2, take Rt 695 at Jemseg and proceed to Cambridge Narrows.
Turn right before bridge. Norwood Farms is 12 km from turn on left hand side. Look for
signs. Phone for shorter and scenic alternate route.
$22S $35-38D $5Add. person   (Weekly rates)   ► 14
● Choice, homebaked   ♠ 300-acre farm, quiet, view   ■ 1S,6D,2F, (upstairs) self
contained apartment   ⊷ 1T,5D,3Q,2R, crib   ⌐ 1Private, 2sh.w.g.(basins in 5 rooms)
★ 2TV,F,KF,LF, private entrance   ⋙ German, Spanish, some French

↪ Washademoak Lake, private sandy
beach, wharf with boat ramp,
swimming, boating, waterskiing,
horseback riding

🐾 Very central location in the
Province (between Saint John,
Fredericton, Moncton and Sussex).
Century-old colonial-style farmhouse
beautifully kept and situated on shore
of Washademoak Lake. Working farm
specializing in poultry and beef. Large
porch with beautiful view.

Campbellton
(Northern border of New Brunswick)

Ayles, Shirley and Richard (Aylesford Inn B&B)   ✔ Herit.Inn NB
8 MacMillan Ave., Campbellton, NB   E3N 1E9   ☎ (506) 759-7672

In Campbellton on RT 134, exit at Arran St and take 2nd left (Macmillan).
$40S $45D $5Child $5Add.person   ▣ Meals   ► 14
● Full   ♠ Red,hist,view, patio, quiet   ■1S,6D (upstairs)   ⊷ 1S,2T,5D   ⌐ 1Private,
2shw.g.   ★ F,TVin guest rooms,parking   ⋙ French
↪ Waterfront promenade, restaurants, shopping Mall, Restigouche Art Gallery,
excursions on Restigouche River and picnic on the islands
⇔ Sugarloaf Prov. Park (summer Alpine Slide, paddle boats etc. and winter Alpine and
cross-country skiing), scenic cruises and deep sea fishing in Bay of Chaleur aboard
"Chaleur Phantom", Battle of Restigouche Nat. Historic Site, golfing

🐾 Spacious home is situated in the shade of chestnut, lilac and pine trees overlooking
Restidouche River. Young host family has two boys, Michael age 9, and Adam age 7.

Campobello Island

(see also Deer Island, St. Andrews, St. Stephen, Grand Manan Isle)

Centreville

(near Woodstock; see also Plaster Rock, Grand Falls, Hartland)

Reid, Ken & Shirely (Reid's Farm Tourist Home)   ⌐ NB FV
RR1, Centreville, NB   E0J 1H0   ☎ (506) 276-4787

From Trans Canada Hwy 2, take Knoxford Exit (Rt 560), and follow signs (8.4 km).
$25S $30D   ◨ Meals   ► 8A,4Ch
● Full, homebaked   🏠 Farm, view, quiet   ■ 1S,4D (upper and main floor)
⊷ 1S,3D,1Q   ⌐ 1Private, 1 sh.w.h.   ★ KF,LF,TV in guest room   Ⓦ Smoking,
drinking
↔ 20-acre natural lake stocked with trout, groomed trails for cross- country skiing,
snowmobiling and snowshoeing
⇔ Golf course, worlds longest covered bridge, US border (Maine) and downhill skiing

🏴 Log cabin overlooks Lake-with-4-Beds in scenic St. John Valley Potato Country.

Codys

(near Fredericton; see also Cambridge Narrows, White Cove,Apohaqui)

Morrow, Claudette and Don (The Grapevine B&B)   ⌐ B&B
Codys, NB   E0E 1E0   ☎ (506) 362-5307

From Trans Canada Hwy 102, take Rt 710 for 3.2 km and look for signs.
$30S $35D   ► 6A,1Ch
✪ Summer   ● Full, homebaked   🏠 Rural, hist., lakefront, patio, quiet
■ 3D (upstairs)   ⊷ 2T,2D, cot   ⌐ 2Sh.w.g.   ★ F,TV, canoes for guests   Ⓦ Pets
↔ Lake Washademoak, beaches, swimming, exclusive and charming tea room - craft
boutique - gift shop (on premises)
⇔ Restaurants, Saint John, Moncton, Fredericton

🏴 Recently renovated 1862 home is nestled on the banks of scenic lake. Breakfast is
served in tea room or sun deck overlooking private pond.

B&B Travel Tip: *If you stay more than one night, you can go and come at
your pleasure. But do let the hosts know when you will be back, especially if you
plan to be late. They might even give you a key, and then you can let yourself in
quietly.*

Deer Island

(near St. Andrews; see also Campobello Island, St. Stephen)

Cline, Audre and Ralph (West Isles World)   ‭ B&B
Lambertville, Deer Island, NB   E0G 2E0   ☎ (506) 747-2949

From St. George, follow Rt 772 and ferry signs to L'etete landing. On Deer Island, drive
1 km and turn right, then 1 km to West Isles World.
$30S $40D $5Child $5Add.person   ◙ Meals   ► 10
● Full, homebaked   ♠ Island village, older, view, quiet, oceanfront   ■ 2D,1Ste
(main and upper floor)   ⌐ 2S,2T,2D, 1P(double)   ⌐ 1Ensuite, 1sh.w.g.   ★ KF,
separate entrance, parking   ⊛ Children min. age 12, small pets accepted
↪ Working lobster pound, scenic beaches and wharfs, rock hounding, scuba diving,
ocean kayaking,Bird and Whale-watching in historic West Isle Archipelago waters at
mouth of Passamaquoddy Bay.
↔ Largest whirlpool in Western Hemisphere, scenic waterfront and shore drives, car
ferry to Campobello Island, Roosevelt Int. Park and Eastport (Maine), US border

🖙 Semi-retired Island natives in small guest house with elegant interior decor. Award
winning hospitality in small fishing community in Lambert's Cove on Bay of Fundy
island. There is a dog in the house.

Fredericton

(see also Cambridge Narrows, White's Cove, Lower Jemseg)

Gorham, Frank and Joan (Carriage House Inn B&B)   ‭ B&B,CC
230 University Ave., Fredericton, NB   E3B 4H7   ☎ (506) 452-9924/454-6090

Located off Hwy 2 and 102. Take Exit 295. Phone for directions.
$30-40S $35-45D $5Child $10Add.person   ► 20
● Full, homebaked   ♠ Downtown, res., hist., quiet, open and screened verandas,
adjacent river   ■ 2D,5F (main and upper levels)   ⌐ 4T,10D,1R, 1cot, playpen
⌐ 2Private, 2sh.w.g., 1sh.w.h.   ★ Air exchanger, TV, F, KF,LF, parking, solarium

↪ Saint John River and riverfront
walking/biking pathway, farmer's
market, Art Gallery, Prov. Legislature,
Playhouse, Pioneer Princess (luxury
paddle wheel cruises)

↔ Kings Landing (1780-1830 re-created
village), Woolastook Park, Mactaquac
Prov. Park (swimming, boating,
golfing), Crabbs Mountain Ski Resort

🖙 3-storey Victorian mansion built in
1875 is surrounded by huge Elm trees.
Spacious rooms are furnished with
antiques. Gracious mahagony staircase winds to 3rd floor and new sky-lit library.
Breakfast is served in Solarium. There is a dog and a cat.

Hamilton, Margaret and Angus (Happy Apple Acres)   ✔ NBFV,NB B&BA
RR4, Fredericton, NB   E3B 4X5   ☎ (506) 472-1819

From Fredericton, take Rt 105 north across Westmoreland Bridge and continue 11 km to
farm on right - or phone for directions.
$25-35S $40-50D   ► 11
● Full, homebaked (gourmet)   ♠ 34-acre farm, quiet, view   ■ 5(2in separate house)
plus loft   ⊢ 3T,1D,3Q,2R, crib   ⌐ 2Private, 1sh.w.g., 1sh.w.h.   ★ TV in guest
lounge, VCR, Video library, Funny Pool, outdoor play area, room refrigerators, fans,
sauna, heart-shaped whirlpool bath available with some rooms   ⊛ Restricted smoking
   ⁓ little French   ♥ with notice
↔ Clean, shallow stream on property, nature trails, cross-country skiing, Currie Mt.
⇔ King's Landing, Mactaquac Prov. Park, Crabbe Mountain Ski Resort, Fredericton
(Provincial Capital), University of New Brunswick, the Provincial Archives, Woolastook
Wildlife Park, and a variety of restaurants

🖛 Sample gourmet breakfasts and relax in the peace and serenty of spacious grounds
overlooking beautiful Saint John River.

Myshrall, Elsie and Ed (Appelot B&B)   ✔ NB B&BA
RR4, Fredericton, NB   E3B 4X5   ☎ (506) 472-6115

Located west of Fredericton on Rt 105 (Douglas).
$30S $35-40D $10Add.person   ► 7
● Full, homebaked   ♠ Rural, older, riverfront, view, sunporch, quiet   ■ 2D,1S
(upstairs)   ⊢ 1Q,2T,(extra length),2R   ⌐ 1Sh.w.g.   ★ TV, parking   ⊛
Smoking,drinking,pets
↔ Orchards and woodlands, pick-yourself apple orchards, St. John River

🖛 Completely renovated 1905-built attractive farmhouse situated on hillside with
lovely view of river and surrounding countryside. Hosts also grow Christmas trees. Full
breakfast served on spacious sunporch with view of valley. Enjoy homemade apple cider.

Grand Falls
(south of Edmundston; see also Plaster Rock, Centreville)

McCarthy, Eugene and Magaret (Old Farm House)   ✔ NBFV
RR1, Grand Falls, NB   E0J 1M0   ☎ (506) 473-2867/473-5461

Located on Rt 2 south of Grand Falls. Phone for directions.
$20S $30D $8-15Child $7Add. person   ► 6A,3Ch
● Homebaked   ♠ Farm, quiet, view   ■ 1S,2D,F   ⊢ 1S,1T,2D, crib
⌐ Sh.w.g.   ★ Separate entrance   ⊛ Restricted smoking
↔ Dairy barns, draft horses
⇔ Falls in Grand Falls

🖛 Well kept spacious century farm house with bright red barn situated high with
peaceful view of surrounding pastoral and wooded areas.

Grand Harbour
(on Grand Manan Island)

Ells, Phil and Doris (Woosters Guest House)
Box 101, Grand Harbour, NB   E0G 1X0

⌐ CC

☎) (505) 662-3454

Take ferry from Black's Harbour to North Head on Grand Manan Isle. Crossing time 1.5 hours (5 crossings daily in summer), then drive to Grand Harbour.
S32S $40D $6Add.person

► 15

● Full, homebaked   🏠 Village, hist., acreage, patio, quiet, oceanfront
■5D   ↦1S,5D,R   ⌐1Sh.w.g.,1sh.w.h.   ★ TV in guest room, F,LF, parking, separate entrance   ♥   🖐 Pets
↔ Playground, swimming pool, tennis courts, stores, museum, churches
⇔ Beaches, hiking trails, boat tours, bird and whale watching

🔫 150-year old Cape Cod-style island home with ocean view. Bicycle and canoe rentals available.

Fleet, Gerry and Sheila (Hillcrest Lodge)
Woodwards Cove, Box 37, Grand Harbour, NB   E0G 1X0

⌐ CC

☎ (506) 662-3639

Phone for directions.
$25S $35D $5Child $5Add.person

► 12

● Full, homebaked   🏠 Hist., acreage, sundecks, quiet   ■ 3D,2F (main and upper floor)   ↦5D,1R, 2cots, crib   ⌐1sh.w.g.   ★ TV,F,KF, separate entrance, parking
🖐 Smoking
↔ Smoked Herring Industry, Rainbows End gifts and boutique, sandy beach, public wharf, view of Bay of Fundy from cove below house
⇔ Museum, light houses, Dulse Plants, view points from 300 feet cliffs

🔫 Native Island hosts in very cozy Cape Cod-style home, built in 1860 as a lodge, and is surrounded by beautiful grounds. There is a dog in the house.

Grand Manan Island
(see Grand Harbour, North Head; see also Campobello Island, Deer Island)

B&B Travel Tip: *Most guests find it more convenient to pay in the morning at breakfast, when there is usually more time. Some hosts will ask for this to be settled upon arrival. It is wise to ask the hosts what they would prefer.*

Hartland

(near Woodstock; see also Centreville)

Campbell, Rosemary and Howard (Campbell's Tourist Home)   ✓ NBFV
RR1, Hartland, NB   E0J 1N0   ☎ (506) 375-4775

From Rt 2 (Trans Canada) take Exit 170 to Rt 105 north for 2km.
$30S $35D $5Child $5Add.person   ► 8A,4Ch
● Cont, homebaked   ♠ Farm, riverview, quiet   ■ 3D,1F (main and upper level) also
private camper available   ⊢ 3S,4D,2R,crib   ⌐ 1Private,1sh.w.g   ★ Air,TV in guest
room, separate entrance, LF,KF   ⍟ Pets, restricted smoking   ⌁ some French

↔ Saint John River, canoeing, fishing, hunting, hiking, snowmobiling, cross country skiing, bird watching

⇔ World's longest covered bridge, Fredericton (Prov. Capital), US Border (Maine), golfing, tennis and swimming facilities, waterslide, alpine ski hills, restaurants and several points of historical interest.

☛ 500-acres family farming operation situated along the Saint John River Valley in New Brunswick's "Potato" Belt. Large rooms are decorated with family antiques and there are homemade quilts and crafts for sale.

Hopewell Cape

(near Moncton; see also Riverside)

Rossiter, Eric and Marla (Dutch Treat Farm)   ✓ NB B&BA
RR1, Hopewell Cape, NB   E0A 1Y0   ☎ (506) 882-2552

Take scenic Rt114 through Fundy Nat. Park and along Chignecto Bay to Hopewell Cape
$22S $28-30D $6Add. person   ► 8
● Full, homebaked   ♠ Farm, hist., view, quiet   ■ 2D,F (upstairs)   ⊢ 4D, crib
⌐ 1Sh.w.g.   ★ TV in guest room, LF   ♥
↔ Hiking trails to Salt Marsh on Bay of Fundy, all purpose woodland trails for day use
and primitive camping, 18th Century Acadian dykes, cross-country skiing, snowmobiling
⇔ Mary's Point waterfowl santuary, the Rocks Light Houses, covered bridges, salmon
fishing, Tidal Bore, Moncton, Magnetic Hill, Steam Train excursions

☛ Century home with view of Bay of Fundy. Host was Lobster fisherman and hostess
is gardener at Fundy Nat. Park. Both are active in local curling club. Area hiking trails
include guaranteed best view in Albert County.

Lower Jemseg

(east of Fredericton; see also White's Cove, Cambridge Narrows)

Wolfe, Max M. & Willi Evans (Oakley House)   ✔ B&B
Lower Jemseg, NB   E0E 1S0   ☎ (506) 488-3113

Located 55 km east of Frederiction and 5 km off the Trans Canada Hwy. Take Rt 695
exit at the foot of the Jemseg bridge and turn right past Lion's Hall onto Ferry Rd.
$27S $45D $60F   🍽 Meals   (Deposit required)   ► 6A,3Ch
● Choice, homebaked   🏠 Rural, acreage, older, riverfront, quiet   ■ 3D (upstairs)
◡ 3T,2D   ⌐ 2Sh.w.h., 2sh.w.g.   ★ Extensive library, piano, harpsichord, parking
🖐 Smoking   ⌇ French, Spanish
↔ Jemseg River, canoeing, sailing, swimming, birdwatching, cross- country skiing
⇔ Ferry across Saint John River to Gagetown, crafts, churches, restaurants,
Fredericton, Sussex

🐾 Graciously rebuilt 150-year old farmhouse in the heart of strawberry country,
surrounded by tall acacia trees. Quiet lifestyle allows peaceful relaxation. In July guests
can pick strawberries from organic garden. There are pets in the house. Hosts offer
special canoeing, birdwatching or cross-country skiing packages for two or more days.

Moncton

(see also Hopewell Cape, Shediac, Riverside)

Lutes, Frank and Gladys (Lutes B&B)
RR1, Moncton, NB   E1C 8J5   ☎ (506) 852-3507

Located north-west of Moncton on Hwy 2 at Berry Mills, west of Hwy 128 T.
$25S $30D $8Rollaway   ► 6A,1Ch
◧ June to Oct.   ● Choice, homebaked   🏠 Rural, split-level home, view, patio
■ 1S,2D (lower level)   ◡ 2T,2D,2R   ⌐ 1Sh.w.h., 1sh.w.g. (one with whirlpool)
★ Air exchanger, TV in guest room, parking   🖐 Smoking, drinking
↔ Downtown and Magnetic Hill, Game Farm, Magic Mountain (water theme park with
slide, wave pool and riverboat)
⇔ Hopewell Cape Rocks, Bay of Fundy, Shediac Beaches (warmest water north of the
Carolinas), Prince Edward Island Ferry, NS Border, Hillsborough (ride back in history
on the railroad)

🐾 Hosts have recently retired from dairy farming. Modern split-level home surrounded
by maples and birches and lots of beautiful flowers. Children welcome.

> **B&B Travel Tip:** *You can stay in a B&B when taking part in acitivity
> groups, such as whitewater rafting, bicycling and wilderness tours etc. Ask for
> information when signing up for a trip.*

Nelson-Miramichi
(near Chatham; see also Tracadie)

Doucet, Liane & Joseph (Miramichi Manor)   ↙ NB B&BA
Box 23, Nelson-Miramichi, NB   E0C 1T0   ☎ (506) 622-8837

Located directly across from Newcastle on the south side of the Miramichi River 3.5 km west of the Morrisey Bridge on the corner of Main & Station Streets and in the historic village of Nelson-Miramichi.

$30S $40D $5Child   📷 Meals   ► 6A,2Ch
📷 Summer only   ● Full   🏠 Village, hist., view, upstairs and downstairs balconies, riverfront, quiet   ■ 3D (upstairs)   ⊷ 3D   ⌐ 1sh.w.g.   ★ TV,LF,KF,parking
🐾 Pets   ⋙ French

↔ Nature trails, fishing in Miramichi River, sandy beaches, boat trips to Nat. Historic Site of Beaubear Island

⇔ Kouchibouguac National Park, Salmon Fish Hatchery, McDonald's Farm Historic Site, Middle Island, Miramichi Golf & Country Club, Double D Horseback Riding Stables

🐾 Historic 100-year old Victorian home with balconies overlooking the world famous salmon fishing Miramichi River. Watch the beautiful sunsets and the salmon jump upstream. Canoe rentals to make short trip to Beaubear Island. There is a cat in the house.

North Head
(on Grand Manan Island near Saint John)

Shelton Family (The Fundy Folly)   ↙ B&B
Box 23, North Head, Grand Manan Island, NB   E0G 2M0   ☎ (506) 662-3731

From Saint John or Calai Mo. Follow Hwy 1 to Blacks Harbour to ferry dock. Crossings are every 2 hrs. with 6 trips week days and 4 on Sundays.

$22S $36-40D   ► 7
● Choice, homebaked   🏠 Island village home, acreage, view, patio, oceanfront
■ 3D   ⊷ 3D,1S   ⌐ 2Sh.w.g.   ★ TV,F, parking, separate entrance   🐾 Pets
↔ Sandy beaches, restaurants, tennis courts, boat tours can be arranged
⇔ Museums, sardine canneries, fishing industry

🐾 Hosts are private tour guides and very knowledgeable of local areas.

Plaster Rock
(near Grand Falls; see also Centreville)

Linton, Bill & Sheila (Northern Wilderness Lodge) ✓ NBFV
Box 571, Plaster Rock, NB   E0J 1W0 ☎ (506) 356-8327

Located near the village of Plaster Rock. From Grand Falls, take Hwy 108 and then Hwy
380. From Fredericton, take Hwy 2 north, then Hwy 109 and Hwy 390.
$40S $45D $5Add. person   ● Extra   ▣ Meals   ► 12A,2Ch
● Choice   ♠ 75-acre mixed farm, view, quiet, isolated   ■ 12   ⊢ S,D,R
⊓ 12Private   ★ TV in each guest room, parking   Ⓦ Conditional deposit for pets
↔ Hiking, fishing, hunting, rockhounding, canoeing on river and lakes
⇔ Grand Falls (one of largest cataracts east of Niagara)

🐾 Lodge is surrounded by the Tobique River Country, an unspoiled wonderland for
sportsmen, artists, rockhounds, bird watchers, backpackers - anyone who enjoys clear
fresh air, spring-like waters and being at one with nature.

Port Elgin
(near Sackville)

Allen, Olive & Dorothy Kern (Allen's Holiday Farm) ✓ NBFV
Baie Verte, RR 3, Port Elgin, NB   E0A 2K0 ☎ (506) 538-2597 or 538-2693

Located on Hwy 16, west of junction Hwys 15/16 (8 km west of Port Elgin traffic circle).
$20S $30D $10Child(under age 12)   ► 22
● Full   ♠ Working mixed farm, older   ■ 1S,3D   ⊢ S,D,R, crib   ⊓ 2Sh.w.h.
★ TV,LF

↔ Beach and swimming on property,
Port Elgin, shopping, wooden foot-
bridge

⇔ PEI Ferry Terminal (Cape
Tormentine), Fort Beausejour, Sackville
shopping mall

🐾 Century country farm home in the
village. Hosts offer sleigh rides to their
nearby sawmill. Old-time music a
favorite, and all the family takes part.
Hostess is president of NB Farm
Vacation Association.

Riverside

(near Moncton; see also Hopewell Cape, Albert)

Cail, Hazen and Eunice (Cail'swick Babbling Brook) ✔ B&B
Riverside, Albert Co., NB E0A 2R0 ☎ (506) 882-2079

Coming from Moncton follow Rt 114 to Riverside - from Sussex (on Hwy 1), take Hwy
114 and follow all the way through Fundy National Park to Riverside.
$22S $30D $42F   🍽 Meals ► 10
● Full, homebaked   🏠 Village, acreage, older, view, patio, quiet   ■ 2S,4D,1F
(upstairs)   🛏 2S,4D,1R, crib   🍳 1Sh.w.h., 1sh.w.g.   ★ TV,F, separate entrance,
parking   ⚬ French
↔ Running brooks, trees, flowers and spacious land
⇔ Hopewell Cape Rocks, Nat. Fundy Park, Moncton, Chignecto Bay, Fundy Bay

🐾 Relax on the large patio of Century old Victorian home overlooking Shepody Bay.

Saint John

(see also St. Andrews, Bloomfield, Apohaqui)

Gates, Linda and Peter (Five Chimneys B&B) ✔ NB B&BA
238 Charlotte St. West, Saint John West, NB E2M 1Y3 ☎ (506) 635-1888

Located four blocks from Digby Ferry Docks. Coming from Harbour Bridge, take Exit
109 to Market Place and drive 6 blocks to Charlotte Street.
$35S $40D $10Add.person ► 6
● Full, homebaked   🏠 Res., hist., quiet, patio   ■ 2D (upstairs)   🛏 1T,2D,2R
🍳1Sh.w.g.   ★ F,fans, TV, parking, library   Ⓦ Smoking, pets, children min. age 5

↔ Carleton Martello Tower, Bay of
Fundy, The Reversing Falls Rapids

⇔ Fort Howe Lookout, Loyalist House,
Barbour's General Store, museum,
market, Cherry Brook Zoo

🐾 Recently renovated Greek Revival
Home (1850's) located in unique setting
with 5 chimney stacks and italianate
dormer has comfortable homey-style
decorated rooms. There is a 4year old
boy "Aaron" in the young host family.

New Brunswick B&B Association
238 Charlotte St.,W., Saint John, NB, E2M 1Y3   ☎ (506) 635-1888
(Peter Gates, contact person)
The New Brunswick B&B Association is a newly-formed group of hosts from all over the
province and they have put together a list of members. For more information phone or
write to the above. Some of the members are listed in this publication.

St. Andrews
   (west of Saint John; see also Deer Isle)

Lazare, Kathleen and Michael (Pansy Patch)   ⌐ CC
59 Carleton St., Box 349, St. Andrews, NB   E0G 2X0   ☎ (506) 529-3834

Phone for directions.
$60S $65D $12Add. person $10Child   ► 8A,2Ch
✖ May 15-Oct.1   ● Full, homebaked   ♠ Village, hist., view, acreage, patio, quiet,
30ft. deck   ■ 4   ⊢ 3D,2T,3R   ⌐ 2Sh.w.g.   ★ F, parking   ⑭ Pets, children
min. age 6   ⋙ French
↩ Tennis, golf and pool privileges at Algonquin Hotel across the street, Passamaquoddy
Bay, public beach, St. Andrews village
⇔ Campobello Island, Grand Manan Island, Saint John

☞ Turreted home with unusual shop on first floor, called "the most photographed
home in Canada". All rooms are furnished with antiques and overlook the Bay.
Breakfast is served on deck overlooking lovely garden, weather permitting.

Noseworthy, Daphne (Shady Maples)   ⌐ B&B
132 Sophia St., St. Andrews, NB   E0G 2X0   ☎ (506) 529-4426

Located on the Passamaquoddy Bay. Phone for directions.
$30S $35-45D $6Add.person   (plus tax)   ► 7A
● Full, homebaked   ♠ Village, res., hist., deck, quiet   ■ 1S,2D,1F (upstairs)
⊢ 1S,2T,1D,1Q,P   ⌐ 1Sh.w.g.   ★ TV in most guest room, parking   ⑭ Smoking,
pets, not suitable for children
↩ Downtown, whale watching tours, hiking and nature trails, Harbour and market
wharf, charming boutiques and interesting beaches

☞ Artist hostess in charming turn-of-the-Century home situated on a quiet tree lined
street near centre of pretty town, which displays many splendid examples of buildings of
that era when high plastered ceilings and shining hardwood floors were in vogue.

Parke, Bob and Eleanor (Pippincott)   ✔ NB B&BA
208 Prince of Wales, Box 318, St. Andrews, NB   E0G 2X0   ☎ (506) 529-3445

Located at corner of King Street.
$50-60S $55-65D   ► 4A
● Generous cont., homebaked   🏠 Res., village, hist., screened porch, quiet
■1D,1Ste (upstairs)   ⊷ 2T,1D   ⌐1Ensuite, 1 private   ★ F, separate entrance,
parking   ✋ Restricted smoking, children, pets   ⋙ some French
↔ Historic homes and churches, museums, shopping, golfing, seashore, town wharf,
boat cruises (scenic and whale-watching), cross-country ski trails, Algonquin Hotel
⇔ Campbello and Deer Islans, beaches, nature trails, downhill skiing, Oak Bay and New
River Beach Provincial Parks, Huntsman Marine Aquarium200

🐾 Comfortable and spacious historic (1860) home located in an area of private estates
with charmingly furnished guest rooms and grounds enclosed by high cedar hedge.
Hostess is President of NB B&BA (New Brunswick Bed & Breakfast Association).

St. George
(see also St. Andrews, Deer Island and Campbello Island)

St. Stephen
(west of Saint John; see also Welshpool, Grand Harbour, North Head, Deer Isle)

Juneau, Elizabeth (Liz's Place B&B)   ✔ B&B
14 Watson Street, St. Stephen, NB   E3L 1Y5   ☎ (506) 466-3401

Located off Rt 1. On King St, turn right at third traffic light (Union St) and continue to
Watson St. Turn left.
$30S $36-40D $10Add.person   ► 6A,2Ch
■ May-Nov.   ● Full   🏠 Res., patio, quiet, open and screened-in porches   ■ 2D
(upstairs)   ⊷ 2T,2D, 2cots   ⌐1Sh.w.g., 1sh.w.h.   ★ Air-cooled, TV,F, parking,
smoking area
↔ US border, shopping, new Airport, golfing, tennis, swimming, sandy beaches
⇔ St. Andrews by the Sea, Campobello and Deer Islands, trail walks, deep sea fishing,
whale watching

🐾 Friendly N.B. hospitality in a home-away-from-home located on quiet street.

> **B&B Travel Tip:** *You can stay in a B&B when visiting friends and relatives
> (if they do not have enough room for you). There is probably a B&B around the
> corner.*

McGeachy, Duncan and Flo (Bay's Edge)   ✔ B&B
RR3, St. Stephen, NB   E3L 2Y1   ☎ (506) 466-5401

Follow Rt1 East from St. Stephen for 6.4 km and take first right just after Weigh Station (Dufferin/Ledge Rd). Turn right at end of road and continue 6 km to house on point overlooking Oak Bay. Sign on left.
$30S $35-37.50D $5Child   ► 4A,2Ch
● Cont.   🏠 Rural, hist., view, swimming pool, patio, quiet   ■ 3D (main and upper floor)   ⊨ 2D,2T   ⫠ 1Private, 1sh.w.h.   ★ Satellite TV, parking   ♿ Limited smoking   ♥
↪ Shore walks (beach, birdwatching, wild flowers)
⟷ Deep-sea fishing, Dolphin and Whale watching, covered bridges, Campobello Island (NB), historical museum, Eastport and Luebec (Maine), cross-country skiing, St.Andrews-by-the-Sea

🐾 Home is situated on edge of Oak Bay overlooking Tidal Bay. Hostess is a retired nurse and both are very involved in the annual Chocolate Festival (beginning of August).

Schwarz, Dianna and Rudy (A Touch of Country)
61 Pleasant St., St.Stephen, NB   E3L 1A6   ☎ (506) 466-5056

Take Hwy 1 from St. John or Hwy 3 from Fredericton and Hwy 9 from Calais. Located off Milltown Blvd (main street in St.Stephen), and two blocks from the Milltown border crossing.
$30S $35D   ► 5A,2Ch
● Choice, homebaked   🏠 Res., older, double corner lot   ■ 1S,2D (upstairs)
⊨ 1S,2D,2P   ⫠ 1Sh.w.g.   ★ TV,parking   ♿ smoking
↪ Charlotte County Museum, Milltown Generating Station (tours), tennis courts
⟷ Campobello Island, Rosevelt Park, Kings Landing, Woolastock Wildlife Park, Huntsman Marine Laboratory, St. Andrews, golfing, skiing

🐾 Victorian 2-storey home furnished with antiques and situated on large property. There are lots of activities for children (3 children in host family). There is a dog in the house.

B&B Travel Tip: *All hosts are very obliging to special needs, but as a guest you must always remember that these extras are usually given by the hosts out of friendliness and a desire to please.*

Whittingham, Betty and Bryan (Blair House) ⟋ NB B&BA
38 Prince William St., Box 112, St.Stephen, NB   E3L 2W9   ☎ (506) 466-2233

Located near Tourist Information Centre and 3rd house east of Christ Church
$37S $49-53D $10Add.person   🍽 Meals   ▶ 6A,3Ch
● Full English, Vegetarian on request   ♠ Res, acreage, hist., quiet, patio, riverview
■ 3D,1F (main and upper floor)   ⊢ 1S,2T,2D   ⌐ 2Ensuite,1sh.w.g.,1sh.1.h.
★ F,TV,parking, ceiling fans   ⓦ Smoking, pets outside only

↔ Canadian-US border crossing, Tidal River St. Croix, fishing, boating, Duty-Free store, Commercial St. Stephen, churches, library, Annual Int. Festival with Calais (Maine)

⟷ Fundy Tides (28ft), Fundy Isle, Deer Isle, Campobello Isle, Whale- watching, beaches, ferry to Grand Manan, McGraw Hill Ski area, golfing, hunting, fishing, white-water kayaking, Moosehorn Nature Refuge. Kayak/Canoe trips by advance booking

☛ Elegant home standing back on treed grounds was built in 1850 and overlooks the historic St. Croix River near the International Bridge linking St.Stephen, NB and Calais, Me.

Ideal base for exploring, on wheels or water, the Fundy Isles of Passamaquoddy Bay and the river system on both sides of the international border. There is a dog.

Ste-Anne-de-Kent
(near Moncton; see also Shediac)

Caissie, Rita (Au Bord de la Mer) ⟋ B&B
RR2, Ste-Anne-de-Kent, NB   E0A 2V0   ☎ (506) 743-5329

From Moncton, take Rt 15 to Shediac, then Rt 11 to Ste-Anne Exit, and Rt 505 for 3 km.
$35S $40D   ● $2Each   ▶ 4
● Full, homebaked   ♠ Rural, bungalow, acreage, view, quiet   ■ 1D,1Ste   ⊢ 2D
⌐ 1Sh.w.h.   ★ Air,KF,LF,TV in guest room, separate entrance, parking   ♥
⌄ English (household language is French)
⟷ Sandy beaches, Pays de la Sagouine, Magnetic Hill, Magic Mountain

☛ French Acadian hosts enjoy meeting people and take guests to points of interest.

Shediac

(near Moncton; see also Ste-Anne-de-Kent)

Chance, David and Beverly (Edgewater B&B)   ⌐ CC
Edgewater Road, Box 88, Shediac, NB   E0A 3G0   ☎ (506) 532-2889

Phone for directions.
$35-40S $45-50D $65-75Ste $5Child(under age 6) $10Add.person   ► 6A,2Ch
● Full   ♠ Rural, res., acreage, view, large deck, quiet   ■ 3D,1Ste (main and upper
floor)   ⊶ 2T,2D,1K,1R, crib   ⌐1Ensuite, 2Sh.w.g.   ★ Air,TV,F,sitting area in
suite, packed lunches available   ⓦ Smoking   ⋓ some French
↦ Beach area, walks and long neck clam digging, observe the Great Blue Heron and
other shore birds, there is a craftshop on the premises
⇔ The Rocks at Hopewell Cape, National Parks at Fundy and Kouchibouquac

🐾 Hide-away by the Sea overlooking the water. Cape Cod style home surrounded by
trees in beautiful wooded cottage area and furnished with quilts and antiques. There is a
cat in the house. There is also a large gift shop "Grannys Trunk" on the premises
specializing in Atlantic Region handcrafted items.

Tracadie

(near Bathurst; see also Nelsen-Miramichi, Beresford)

Losier, Jocelyne (Chez Prime)   ⌐ CC
RR3, Site 32, Box 6, Tracadie, NB   E0C 2B0   ☎ (506) 395-6884

Located in the Acadian Peninsula north-east coast on route 11 and 5 km from the village
of Tracadie on the Gulf of the St. Lawrence.
$25S $35D $7Child   ▧ Meals   ► 8A,1Ch
▨ June15-Sept15   ● Full, homebaked -   ♠ Rural, acreage   ■ 1S,3D (upstairs)
⊶ 2T,3D,cot   ⌐1Sh.w.g.   ★ TV,parking   ⓦ Pets, restricted
smoking   ⋓Household language is French.
↦ Peaceful blueberry farm surroundings, country walking
⇔ Acadian Museum at Caraquet, Marine Museum at Shippagan, Bird Sanctuary at
Miscou, public beaches, fishing

🐾 4th Generation Losiers (family has been on property since 1854), is taking great
pride in preserving their heritage and keeping the original decor in the house. There is a
great collection of books and historic documents. Discover Acadian history and
traditions firsthand.

White's Cove

(east of Fredericton; see also Cambridge Narrows, Codys, Lower Jemseg)

Gunter, Lucille (Gunter's Family Farm) ✔ NBFV
White's Cove, Queens Co.,NB E0E 1S0 ☎ (506) 488-2037

Located on Rt 2 and east of Jemseg bridge, next to Red Schoolhouse Shop.
$25-30S $30-35D (Rates for children) ► 6
● Full, homebaked ♠ Farm, lakefront, view ■ 3D (upstairs) ⊷ 3D
⌐ 2Shw.g. ★ TV,F ⋙ some French
↔ Little Red School House (shop featuring NB crafts), Grand Lake (fronts on
property), swimming, boating, fishing, cross-country skiing,
⇔ Fredericton, Theatre New Brunswick, art gallary, University of NB , airport, riding
stable, duck hunting, golfing

🖝 Working farm specializing in Simmental beef cattle purebread. Large comfortable
home furnished with several antique conversation pieces. There is a magnificient view of
rural setting and superb sunsets across the lake. Hosts also grow early garden products.

Woodstock

(see also Hartland, Centreville)

Froehlich, Elfriede and Edgar (Froehlich's B&B Swiss Chalet) ✔ NB B&BA
RR2, Box 1983, Woodstock, NB E0J 2B0 ☎ (506) 328-6751

Take Trans Canada Hwy 2and exit at Woodstock or Upperwoodstock. Cross the Saint
John River on Grafton Bridge, turn right (south) and drive 9 km on Hwy 105 to Chalet.
$25S $30D ► 4A,1Ch
▣ Summer only ● Homebaked ♠ Rural, acreage, view, quiet ■ 2D ⊷ 4T
⌐ 2Private ★ TV,separate entrance, parking ⋙ German
⇔ Covered bridge (Hartland), Kings Landing historical settlement, US border,
Fredericton, Woodstock Wildlife Centre

🖝 Enjoy a quiet and relaxing atmosphere in Swiss-style Chalet with a beautiful view
over the Saint John River Valley. There is a dog in the house. Hosts enjoy "serving
special people in a special way".

Prince Edward Island

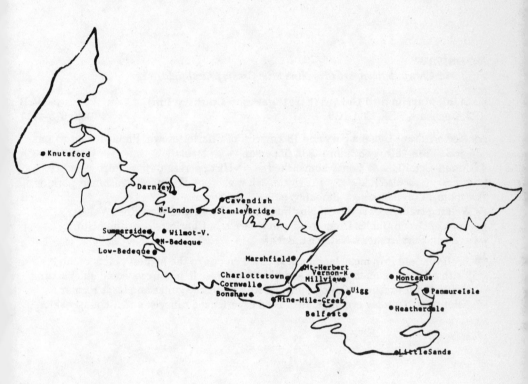

"Dial-the-Island"

Prince Edward Island free reservation service.   (902) 892-2457
From Nova Scotia or New Brunswick only.   Toll-free: 1-800-565-7421

For CN Marine ferry schedules and rates contact:
Prince Edward Island Visitors Services
Box 940, Charlottetown, PEI C1A 7M5   (902) 892-2457

Belfast

(south of Montague; see also Uigg, Heatherdale, Little Sands)

Ross, Mrs. Marion (Lazydays Farm Tourist Home) ✓ B&B
RR1, Belfast, PEI C0A 1A0   ☎ (902) 659-2823/2267

Located at Garfield. Take Rt 207 from Trans Canada Hwy at Eldon (4km).
$15S $20D   ●$2.50Each $5Add.person   ► 9
◻ June-Sept.   ● Homebaked   ♠ Tobacco farm, quiet   ■ 4 (upstairs)
⊢ 1S,2T,3D, cot, crib   ⌐ 1Sh.w.h., 1sh.w.g.   ★ TV   ♥
↪ Private beach
⇔ Licenced restaurant, Charlottetown, Montague

Bonshaw

(near Charlottetown; see also Nine Mile Creek, Marshfield)

Gabriel, Martha and Gerald (Strathgartney Country Inn) ✓ B&B
RR3, Bonshaw, PEI C0A 1C0   ☎ (902) 675-4711

Located on Trans Canada Hwy and 18 km west of Charlottetown. Phone for directions.
$35-45S $38-48D $8Child $8Add.person   ◙ Meals   ► 16A,4Ch
◻ June 1-Oct.10   ● Cont., homebaked   ♠ Hist., acreage, view, quiet   ■ 8D
(upstairs)   ⊢ 6D,2R,2Q   ⌐ 1Private, 3sh.w.g.   ★ F, separate entrance, parking,
Tea room on premises   Ⓦ Smoking, pets   ⌇ French
↪ Walking trails, scenic view of Northumberland Strait and West River Valley
⇔ Anne of Green Gables Homestead, sandy beaches, Charlottetown and historic
waterfront, Fort Amherst Nat. Hist. Park

☞ 140-year old Provincial landmark situated on one of the highest points of land in
PEI with 32 acres of open meadow and hardwood trees in picturesque and quiet setting.
Opportunity for excellent photography. Hostess plays the guitar and leads regular
sing-alongs on Tuesday evenings. Host is an experienced canoeist and X-country skier.

B&B Travel Tip: *Breakfast is almost always memorable! Most hosts will
ask in the evening what you would like for breakfast and at what time (you can
sleep in if you wish!). Go ahead and tell them if you would like porridge or something special. You will be pleasantly surprised.*

MacKinnon, Jeanette and Waldron (Churchill B&B) ✓ FV
RR3, Bonshaw, PEI C0A 1C0 ☎ (902) 675-2481

Bonshaw is located on Trans-Canada Hwy 1, 19 km southwest of Charlottetown.
$18S $20-25D $4Child ●$2.50Each $4Add. person ► 12
● Full, homebaked hot muffins ♠ 50-acre farm, view, patio ■ 5D (upstairs)
⊷1T,5D,P, cot, crib ⊐ 2Sh.w.g. ⊛ Pets, smoking

⇔ North and south shore beaches, fishing, golfing, shopping, dining cross-country skiing

🔫 Mixed working farm with large home in quiet location in the centre of Prince Edward Island.

Brackley Beach
(near Charlottetown; see Marshfield, Cavendish, Stanley Bridge)

Huck, Joan and John (Windsong Farm B&B)
Brackley Beach, RR1, Winsloe, PEI C0A 2H0 ☎ (902) 672-2874/(508) 842-2688

Located on Rustico Bay on Rt 6 between Rts 15 and 7.
$30-45S $45-55D plus tax ▣ Meals ► 8A
✚ June-Sept ● Full, wholesome ♠ Rural, quiet, acreage, hist., view, guest
sunporch, long private lane ■ 4D ⊷ 2S,4D ⊐ 1Private,1sh.w.g. ★ TV,
woodstove for cool days ⊛ Pets, children, smoking
↔ Bay shell fishing, wild berry picking, birding, cycling
⇔ Rustico Bay, ocean beach and dunes, deep sea fishing, Cavendish (Ann of Green
Gables house), Charlottetown Airport, Borden ferry, canoeing, lobster suppers, dining

🔫 Unique atmosphere in renovated 130-year old farmhouse furnished with antiques.

Cavendish

(near Kensington; see also Brackley Beach, Stanley Bridge, New London)

Clark, Barry and Judy (Shining Waters Lodge & Cottages)   ↙ B&B
Cavendish, PEI   C0A 1N0   ☎ (902) 963-2251

Located on Rt 13 in Cavendish, just before entrance to National Park.
$40-48D $5Add.person   (Off season rates available)   ▶ 21
● Full   ♠ Village, centre, quiet, swimming pool, indoor whirlpools ■9T,5D,R,crib
↱ 10Private   ★ TV, table tennis, library, piano, campfires ⌇French
↔ Anne of Green Gables House, golfing, tennis, Cavendish Beach and National Park
⇔ Charlottetown, Woodleigh Replicas

🔫 Beautiful rustic lodge with ocean-view sundeck.

Charlottetown

(see also Cornwall, Brackley Beach,.Mt.Herbert, Marshfield, Millview, Vernon River, Bonshaw, Nine Mile Creek)

Hay, Anne (Anne's Ocean View)   ↙ B&B
Box 2044, Charlottetown, PEI   C1A 7N7   ☎ (902) 569-4456

Located on Kinlock Hill near downtown.
$40(per room) $10Add.person   ▶ 11
● Full   ♠ Rural, res., ranch style, view, oceanfront, patio, quiet ■ 4 ⌐4T,2Q,
daybed   ↱ 4Private   ★ TV in all rooms, use of fridge, separate entrance ♥
✋ Smoking

↔ Tea Hill Prov. Park, ocean (clam-digging, picnics, surfing), cross-country skiing

⇔ Downtown Charlottetown, all major central and eastern Island attractions

🔫 Attractive home by the ocean with a panoramic view of the beautiful Northumberland Strait. There are three cats and a dog in the house.

B&B Travel Tip: *Do remember that you are entering a private house as a guest – (even though you are paying something) – the hosts are still doing you a favour by inviting you into their homes and you must observe whatever house rules exist. If you keep this in mind, your stay will be very enjoyable.*

MacDonald, Judy and Gary (Barachois Inn) ✓ B&B
Box 1022, Charlottetown, PEI C1A 7M4 ☎ (902) 963-2194

Located in South Rustico on Church Rd, Rt 243.
$45-60D $15Child $15Add.person ● $3Each (Off-Season Rates) ► 13
◨ May 1-Oct.31 ● Full ⌂ Village, historic, acreage, view, quiet ▣ 5D,1Ste,1F
(upstairs) ⊨ 6T,3D,2Q,2R ⌐ 1Ensuite, 2sh.w.g. ★ Parking ⓦ Smoking,
pets ⋙ French
↪ Seashore, clam-digging, golfing, horseback riding, historic Farmer's Bank of Rustico
(1869) and St. Augustine's Church (1838)
⇔ Charlottetown City Centre, theatres, Province House Nat. Historic Site,

☛ Spacious Victorian house has lovely vistas, including a view of Rustico Bay, Winter
River and surrounding countryside located in a beautiful historic community. Built in
1870, and restored to its former graciousness without sacrificing modern comforts.
Deposit required.

Cornwall
(near Charlottetown; see also Nine Mile Creek, Bonshaw)

Gallant, Sandi and Paul (Chez Nous) ✓ B&B
Route 248, RR4, Cornwall, PEI C0A 1H0 ☎ (902) 566-2779

Located west of Charlottetown off Trans Canada Hwy on Ferry Road.
$30-35S $38-45D $15Add.person ► 8A,3Ch
◨ June 1-Oct.31 ● Full, homebaked ⌂ Rural, acreage, view, patio, quiet ▣ 2D,
1Ste (main and upper floor) ⊨ 2T,3D,1Q,1R ⌐ 1Private, 1ensuite, 1sh.w.g.
★ F,TV in guest room, separate entrance ♥ ⋙ some French
↪ Bonnie Brae Restaurant
⇔ Charlottetown Harbour, Cavendish and Brackley Beaches, Nat. and historic parks

☛ Secluded retreat, nestled amongst tall birches and mature maples. Stay two nights
and the third night is half price.

MacFadyen, Mrs. Dingwell (MacFadyen's Farm Tourist Home) ✓ B&B
RR2, Cornwall, PEI C0A 1H0 ☎ (902) 566-2771

Located on Meadow Bank Rd., on Rt 1, west of Charlottetown.
$22D $5Add. person ● Extra ► 12
◨ Summer ● Cont. ⌂ 98-acre farm, view ▣ 4 ⊨ 2S,5D,3cots
⌐ 2Sh.w.g. ★ TV,KF, separate entrance ⓦ Small pets only
↪ West River beach on property
⇔ Licensed dining, fishing, golfing, Cavendish beaches, Borden ferry

☛ Mixed working farm with spacious farm house on scenic West River. Hostess will be
happy to help plan day's activities.

Darnley
(near Kensington)

Hickey, Erma and James (Sherwood Acres Guest Home)   ∟ B&B
Darnley, Kensington RR1, PEI C0B 1M0   ☎ (902) 836-5430

Located on Rt 20 in Darnley and 14 km north of Kensington.
$25S $40D   ●$3.50Each   ▣ Meals (Cots extra)   ► 14
● Homebaked   ♠ 500-acre farm   ■ 8   ⊢ T,D,Q, crib, cots   ⼍ 3Sh.w.g.   ★ TV

↔ Beautiful private sandy beach, red country roads for walking/jogging/bicycling

⇔ Cabot Prov. Park, Burlington Go Carts, Woodleigh Replicas, Malpeque Gardens

🔫 Family operated potato and grain farm located near world-famous oyster beds at Malpeque. Hosts will conduct farm tours. Children welcome to join in farm activities.

MacKinnen, Fraser and Lorraine (Fralor Farm Tourist Home)   ∟ B&B
Darnley, RR1 Kensington, PEI C0B 1M0   ☎ (902) 836-5300

Located along Blue Heron Scenic Drive on Rt 20; 14 km north of Kensington.
$20per person   ●$3.50Each   ► 8
▣ Summer   ● Full, homebaked   ♠ 200-acre farm, quiet   ■ 4(upstairs)   ⊢ 6D,R
⼍ 1Sh.w.g.   ★ TV   ♥
⇔ Malpeque Cabot Prov. Park, excellent beaches, Kensington, restaurants, scenic country roads, deep sea fishing and world renouned lobster suppers

🔫 Large working farm located on picturesque Blue Heron Drive with remodelled century farmhouse and easy going rural atmosphere.

B&B Travel Tip: *You can go B&B all year around. Of course, it is most popular when on vacation. And there are many more B&B's available in the summertime.*

Emerald
(near Kensington)

Mayne, Leland and Violet (Woodland View Farm Tourist Home)   ✓ B&B
Emerald, RR6, Kensington, PEI   C0B 1M0   ☎ (902) 886-2732

Located in Emerald on Rt 232 and 12 km south-east of Kensington.
$18D   ●$3Each $4Add. person   ► 10-12
● Full, homebaked   🏠 250-acre farm, quiet   ■ 2D (and housekeeping unit)
⊨ 4D,2R,2P, 2cribs, cots   ⊓ 1Private, 1sh.w.g.   ★ 2TV,KF, private entrance and
wheelchair access   ♥
↦ Emerald

🔫 Picturesque century farm house in mixed farming area. Guests are welcome to help
out with farm chores and small animals. There are several cats in the house.

Heatherdale
(near Montague; see also Uigg, Little Sands, Belfast)

Brydon, Mrs. Mary (Brydon's B&B)   ✓ B&B
Heatherdale, RR1, Montague, PEI   C0A 1R0   ☎ (902) 838-4747

Located 8 km south-west of Montague on Rt 316 and off Rt 315.
$20S $22D   ●$1.50-3Each   (Family rates available)   ► 6A,2Ch
❑ Summer   ● Choice   🏠 Rural, acreage, view   ■ 2D   ⊨ 3D,cot   ⊓ Sh.w.g.
★ TV, Private entrance
↦ Woods for walking, brook for trout fishing
⇔ Sandy beach, Wood Island Ferry, Charlottetown, restaurants, park

🔫 Quiet, rural area with woodland behind house and a beautiful view. There are three
adorable cats in the house. Host family is very involved in local United Church activities.

Hebron
(south of Tignish near O'Leary)

Lanoue, Muriel Morrison (Hebron B&B)   ✓ B&B
Hebron, Coleman, RR1, PEI   C0B 1H0   ☎ (902) 859-2834

Take Rt 2 to Rt 14 and then Rt 164.
$20S $25D $9Child   ◖ Meals(light)   ► 4
❑ June-Nov.30   ● Full, homebaked   🏠 Rural, acreage, quiet   ■ 2S,1D (upstairs)
⊨ 2T,1D, cot   ⊓ 1Sh.w.h.   ★ TV, wood stove in kitchen, stained glass studio
⇔ Egmont Bay beaches, fishing, golfing

🔫 Comfortable cottage-type home overlooking warm waters of Egmont Bay. A private
setting off "Lady Slipper Drive".

Kensington

(see also Darnley, Emerald, Stanley Bridge, North Bedeque)

Blakeney, Velma   ✔ B&B
15 MacLean Ave., Kensington, PEI C0B 1M0   ☎ (902) 836-3254

From ferry at Borden, take Rt 1 to Albany, Rt 1A to Reads Corner, and then Rt 2.
$17S $22-25D   ●Extra $5cots   ► 8
● Full, homebaked   🏠 Res., town house, view   ■ 4 (main and lower level)
▬2D,4S, cot   ⌐Sh.w.g.   ★TV,F   ⓦSmoking, pets, drinking, children min. age 5
↔ Via Rail Depot, stores, churches
⇔ Cabot Prov. Park and beach, Malpeque Gardens, Woodleigh Replicas, Cavendish,
Green Gables House, deep sea fishing

🐾 Sunny home on large lot with lots of flowers located in quiet residential area
overlooking Malpeque Bay.

Little Sands

(near Montague; see also Murray Harbour North, Heatherdale, Belfast)

Perkins, Don and Nancy (Bayberry Cliff Inn B&B)   ✔ B&B
RR4, Little Sands, Murray River, PEI C0A 1W0   ☎ (902) 962-3395

From Wood Islands Ferry turn right on Rt 4 (East) and follow 8km to house on right.
$27-40D $8Child $8Add. person   ► 17A,11Ch
● Full, homebaked   🏠Rural, acreage, view, oceanfront, quiet, balcony   ■7D (3 with
sleep lofts)   ▬ 10T,8D, cots   ⌐2Sh.w.g., 1sh.w.h.   ★ Small guest refrigerator
ⓦ Pets, smoking

↔ Private stairs leading to beach, craft
shop on premises

⇔ Northumberland Prov. Park, Wood
Island Ferry, Murray River boat cruises,
restaurants, Charlottetown

🐾 Two post and Beam Barns
decorated with antiques and marine art,
situated on 40ft cliff above waters of
Northumberland Strait.

Knutsford

(south of O'Leary)

Smallman, Arnold and Eileen (Smallman's B&B) ✓ B&B
RR1, Knutsford, PEI C0B 1V0 ☎ (902) 859-3469

Located on Hwy 142 midway between Hwys 2/14. Look for split level home.
$10S $20-25D ●$1.75-3Each $5Child $5Add.person ► 10
● Cont, homebaked 🏠 Rural, patio ■ 4 ⊨ 2T,2D,1Q, cot, crib ⌐ 2Sh.w.g.
★ TV,LF Ⓦ Restricted smoking, pets sleep in attached garage
⇔ Beaches, church, restaurants, craft shops, flour and wollen mills

🔫 Country home in beautiful farming area. Large children's play area.

Lower Bedeque

(near Summerside; see also North Bedeque, Wilmot Valley)

Waugh, Willard and June (Waugh's Farm B&B) ✓ B&B
Lower Bedeque, PEI C0B 1C0 ☎ (902) 887-2320

Located on Rt 112 and 3 km north of the village store in Bedeque.
$25D ●$3Each $5Add.person ► 10A,3Ch
✪ May 1-Oct.1 ● Full 🏠 300-acre farm, view, lakefront, quiet ■ 4D (upstairs)
⊨ 1S,4D,2R,1Q (waterbed) ⌐ 1Private, 2sh.w.g. ★ TV in cozy sitting room
ⓌDrinking, Pets

↔ Bedeque Bay, churches

⇔ Excellent warm water beaches, Charlottetown

🔫 Active potato and cattle farm. Century-old farmhouse overlooking Bedeque Bay is equipped with modern conveniences.

B&B Travel Tip: *Do not expect the same service you ususally get in a hotel. The service in a B&B is completely different. It is, in fact, even better, because of all the little things the hosts will do for you and the information they will give you (many extras that cannot be bought in a hotel!). In fact, they will be happy and so proud to tell you all about the local facilities, happenings and the history of their hometown.*

Marshfield

(near Charlottetown; see also Mt. Herbert, Oyster Bed Bridge, Brackley Beach)

Wood, Wallace and Doris (Mill Creek B&B)   ✔ B&B
Marshfield, RR3, Charlottetown, PEI C1A 7J7   ☎ (902) 894-7833

Located 8 km from Charlottetown on Rt 2East.
$25D $5Child $5Add.person   (Off-season rates available)   ► 8A,3Ch
◼ May15-Oct.15   ● Full   🏠 Large farm, quiet   ◼ 3D (main and upper floor)
🛏 4D, 2cots   ⌐ 2Private, 1sh.w.h.   ★ TV, separate entrance for one room   ⊛ Pets
⇔ Harness racing, golfing, lobster suppers, theatre and excellent beaches

📢 Relax in century-old farm house.

Millview

(near Montague; see also Vernon River, Uigg)

Smith, Mrs. Louise (Smith's Farm B&B)   ✔ B&B
Millview, Vernon Bridge P.O., PEI C0A 2ED   ☎ (902) 651-2728

Located on Rt 3,2 km off Trans-Canada Rt 1, and 21 km east of Charlottetown.
$20S $22-26D   ●$3Each $4Add.person $3Child   ► 14
● Full,. homebaked   🏠 250-acre farm   ◼ 2D,3S,F (main and upper floor)
🛏 6D,1S, crib, cots   ⌐ 1Private, 1sh.w.g.   ★ TV, sitting room for guests   ♥
⊛Drinking
⇔ Charlottetown, Montague, North Shore beaches

📢 Long time B&B hosts in century old farm house. Relax, share a cup of tea, and enjoy a visit with fifth generation farm family. Guests are welcome to use the organ and piano.

Mt. Herbert

(near Charlottetown; see also Millview, Marshfield)

Wood, Winston and Marguerite (Just Folks B&B)   ✔ B&B
Mt. Herbert, RR5, Charlottetown, PEI C1A 7J8   ☎ (902) 569-2089

Situated on Rt 215. Cross Hillsboro Bridge, turn left on Bunbury Exit onto Rt 21, go 4 km and turn right at T intersetion, then left on Bethel Rd. Watch for B&B signs.
$20-24D   ●$2-3.25Each $5-8Add. person   ► 10-12
● Choice, homebaked   🏠 99-year old farm   ◼ 3D,F   🛏 4D,2S, cots, crib
⌐ 1Sh.w.g.   ★ TV
⇔ Confederation Centre Art Gallery and Museum in Charlottetown

📢 Quiet location and large grounds. Children and trained pets welcome.

Murray Harbour North
(near Montague; see also Panmure Islands)

Currie, Catherine (Lady Catherine's B&B)   ✔ B&B
RR4, Montague, Murray Harbour North, PEI   C0A 1R0   ☎ (902) 962-3426

Located on Rt 17 (Kings Byway) in Murray Harbour North, midway between Montague and Murray River.
$29S $38D   ► 12
● Full   ♠ Rural, older, acreage, ocean view, 3 verandas, quiet   ■ 4D (main and upper floor)   ⊷ 2T,2D,1Q,1P   ⌐ 3Sh.w.g.   ★ TV,F,LF, parking   ⊌ Restricted smoking, children min. age 7

↔ Long beach for swimming, walking and beach combing

⇔ Provincial Park, craft shops, fishing villages, fine restaurants, golfing, seal watching tours, deep sea fishing

☞ Large Victorian-style home on scenic Kings Byway and overlooking Northumberland Strait. Bicycles and fishing rods available for rent. Hosts invite guests to watch a movie from the film library.

New London
(near Kensington; see also Stanley Bridge, Cavendish)

Mikita, Marion and Andrew (New London B&B)   ✔ B&B
New London, RR6, Kensington, PEI   C0B 1M0   ☎ (902) 886-2091

Located in the village of New London on Rt 6.
$20S $24D   ●$3Each   ► 4A
● Choice, homebaked   ♠ Former farmstead, village, older, view, glassed-in porch
■ 2D   ⊷ 2D   ⌐ Sh.w.g.   ★ TV   ⊌ Smoking   ⌁ Hungarian, Spanish
↔ Island crafts, L.M.Montgomery's birthplace, fisherman's wharf, canoeing (Southwest River and New London Bay)
⇔ Northshore beaches, lobster suppers, Cavendish, Charlottetown, Summerside

☞ Home is in a quiet northshore country village setting overlooking gently rolling fields of grain and water views in the heart of "Anne of Green Gables" country.

Nine Mile Creek
(near Charlottetown; see also Cornwall, Bonshaw)

MacLaine, Florence and Milton (Laine Acres Tourist Home B&B)   ✔ B&B
Nine Mile Creek, RR2, Cornwall, PEI C0A 1H0   ☎ (902) 675-2402

Located on Rt 19 (Blue Heron Dr) and 20 km east of Charlottetown.
$20S $22D   ●$1.25-3.75Each   plus tax   ◙ Meals $3Air mattress   ► 6
◨ June 1-Oct 15 (other by arrangement)   ● Choice   ♠ 126-acre farm, patio,
waterfront   ■ 3D(upstairs)   ⊣2Q,1D   ⌐ Sh.w.h.   ★ TV, picnic table
⊕Pets on leash outside
⇔ Ocean, beach, golfing, licensed dining

🐾 Quiet country home set back from highway overlooking beautiful countryside and
Hillsborough Bay. Central location for daytrips to either end of the Island.

North Bedeque
(near Summerside; see also Emerald, Wilmot Valley, Lower Bedeque)

Wright, Carl and Vivian (Wright's B&B)   ✔ B&B
North Bedeque, RR3, Summerside PEI C1N 4J9   ☎ (902) 436-9879

Located off Trans-Canada Rt 1A on Taylor Rd in North Bedeque and 7 km east of
Summerside.
$17S $20D   ●$1.75-3Each $5Add. person   ► 10
● Full   ♠ Rural, patio   ■ 4D   ⊣ 4D, cot, crib   ⌐ 2Sh.w.g.
⇔ Lobster suppers, beach, craft shops, Ann of Green Gables house, golfing

🐾 Modern two-storey home overlooking Wilmot river with large lawns, picnic table
available for guests. "A right place to stay whether you want a quiet evening to youself,
or to chat with the family in the living room".

Oyster Bed Bridge
(near Charlottetown; see also Brackley Beach, Marshfield)

MacPherson, D.& R.(MacPherson's Farms Tourist Delight B&B)   ✔ PEIFV
Oyster Bed Bridge, RR2 Winsloe, PEI   C0A 2H0   ☎ (902) 964-2032

Located on Hwy 251 and 25 km from Charlottetown.
$20S $25D $5Child $5Add. person   ●$3.50Each   ► 16
● Full, homebaked, preserves   ♠ 115-acre mixed farm, view   ■ 6D   ⊣ 8D,3P,
crib   ⌐ 2Sh.w.g.   ★ TV, separate entrance   ♥   ⊕ Smoking, drinking, pets
↔ River beach, golfing, store and coffee shop, laundromat
⇔ Ocean beach, Cavendish, theatre, lobster suppers

🐾 100-year old home on the Wheatley River, with 500 m scenic country lane.

Panmure Island
(near Montague; see also Murray Harbour North)

Partridge, Gertrude and Lee (Partridge's Panmure Island B&B's)
Panmure Island, RR2, Montague, PEI C0A 1R0   ☎ (902) 838-4687

Located 26 km east of Montague on east coast of PEI.
$30-40D $8Add. person (Off season rates)   ► 9
● Full, homebaked   ♠ Two island homes, rural, acreage, view, oceanfront   ■ 5D
▬ S,D,R, cot, crib   ⌐ Private   ★ TV,F,LF,KF, library, separate entrance, facilities
for the disabled   ♥   ⌇ French
↔ Woodland walks to beaches, lighthouse, clam digging, berry picking
⇔ Georgetown (summer stock theatre), Graham's Lobster factory, Wood Island Ferry

☛ Beautiful sandy beaches, organic vegetable and flower garden, lots of raspberries in
season. Canoe, rowboat and bicylces available. There are two cats. Pets permitted.

Stanley Bridge
(near Kensington; see also Cavendish, New London)

Simpson, David and Dorothy (Gulf Breeze Tourist Home)   ✓ PEI B&BA
RR2, Stanley Bridge, PEI C0A 1E0   ☎ (902) 886-2678

Located on Rt 224 and 1.5 km off Rt 6.
$20S $20-25D $3-5Add.person ●$2.50-3Each   ► 10A,4Ch
◩ Ma1-Oct30 (other by reservation)   ● Full, homebaked   ♠ Farm, quiet   ■1D,3F
(upstairs)   ▬ 2S,5D,2cribs   ⌐ Sh.w.g.   ★ TV, parking   ♥   ⊕ Pets
↔ Ocean beaches, clam digging, deep sea fishing, gift shop, restaurant, service station,
grocery store
⇔ Cavendish Beach, lobster suppers, golfing, Ann of Green Gables House, National
Park, Charlottetown Festival

☛ 150-acre hog farm. There is a playground for children. If guests are lucky, they
might see pigs being born.

Weeks, Adelaide and Milton (Blue Heron Tourist Home)   ✓ B&B
Stanley Bridge, RR1, Breadalbane, PEI C0A 1E0   ☎ (902) 886-2319

Take Rt 238 off Hwy 6 in Stanley Bridge
$18S $25D ●$2Each   ► 6A
◩ Reservation required after Sept.   ● Choice   ♠ Res., acreage, view, patio
■ 3D (main and upper level)   ▬ 3D   ⌐ 1Private, 1sh.w.g.   ★ F,TV in one guest
room, separate entrance, parking, pool table
↔ Stanley River beach, Marineland Aquarium, licenced dining room
⇔ Cavendish, Lobster suppers (June-Oct), deep-sea fishing

☛ Long time B&B hosts make visitors feel right at home. Relax and enjoy the beautiful
view overlooking the Stanley River.

Summerside

(see also North Bedeque, Wilmot Valley, Emerald)

Oulton, Faye and Eric (Faye & Eric's Tourist Home)   ✔ B&B
380 MacEwen Rd., Summerside, PEI   C1N 4X8   ☎ (902) 436-6847

Phone for directions.
$35-45D $50and75Ste   ● (Full Extra)   ► 22
● Cont.   ♠ Downtown, res., sundeck   ■ 1Ste,5D (also basement apt-1D)
⊷ 7D,T,P,2R, waterbed, canopy beds   ⌐ 4Sh.w.g., 2private, jacuzzi whirlpool in suite
★ TV,KF in rec- room, private entrance
⇔ Town centre, restaurants, shopping malls, churches
⇔ Borden Ferry to mainland, Cavendish Beach, Charlottetown

☛ Rooms are beautifully decorated in a variety of styles designed to suit guest's personal needs.

Smallman, George and Helen (Smallman's B&B)
329 Poplar Ave, Summerside, PEI   C1N 2B7   ☎ (902) 886-2846/436-5892

Phone for directions.
$15S $25D $5Add.person   ●$2.50-3.50Each   ► 5A
✚ Summer   ● Choice   ♠ Rural, bungalow, acreage, view, patio, quiet   ■ 1S,2D
beds 1S,2T,1D,R   ⌐ Sh.w.h.   ★ F,TV, parking   ⊛ Pets
⇔ Boating, bird-watching, swimming, private floating dock
⇔ Cavendish, lobster suppers (New London), Charlottetown

☛ Enjoy breakfast in sunny dining room which has a beautiful view through the unusual large window. Also available housekeeping unit for weekly rental.

Uigg

(near Montague; see also Heatherdale, Vernon River, Millview, Belfast)

MacLeod, Malcolm and Margie (MacLeod's Farm B&B)   ✔ B&B
Uigg, Vernon PO, PEI   C0A 2E0   ☎ (902) 651-2303

Located east of Charlottetown on Rt 24. Look for signs on Trans-Canada Hwy 1 at Orwelll and Hwy 3 at Vernon River.
$25-30D   ●$2.50Each $2Child $4Add. person $5 cots   ► 4A,3Ch
✚ May1-Sept30   ● Full, homebaked   ♠ 100-acre mixed farm, quiet, view
■1S,3D,F and housekeeping unit   ⊷ 2T,2D,1Q,R, 4cots   ⌐ 3Sh.w.g.   ★ TV,F,KF
in unit, wheelchair ramp   ♥   ⊛ Pets
⇔ Trout fishing in brook, glass blowing shop, historic village of Uigg large playground with tree house
⇔ Drive-in theatre, canoeing, tennis, sandy beaches, lobster suppers, shops

☛ Enjoy a peaceful yet fun-filled holiday in a modern farm home in the scenic community of Uigg and watch the mixed farming operations. There are kittens, bunnies and a friendly Newfoundland dog. Children welcome.

Vernon River
(near Montague; see also Uigg, Millview)

Lea, Ralph and Dora (Lea's Farm B&B)　　　　　　　　　ↆ B&B
Vernon River, PEI　C0A 2E0　　　　　　　　　☎ (902) 651-2501/2051

Located off Rt 3 on Rt 216 east of Charlottetown, 32km from Wood Isle ferry.
$18S　$20-26D　●$3Each　$4Add. person　(plus tax)　　　▶ 14
● Full, homebaked　🏠 25-acre farm　■ 5 (upstairs), also housekeeping unit
🛏D,S,R, cot, crib　🍳 1Private, 1sh.w.g.　★ TV　🐾 Pets
↪ Churches, stores, dining, there are rabbits, pheasants and a Bird Dog
⇔ Charlottetown, lobster suppers, beaches, golfing, deep sea fishing

🐾 A "home away from home". Hosts are active with bowling and are very busy with family and 15 grandchildren. Delicious cinnamon rolls and scones a house specialty.

Wilmot Valley
(near Summerside; see also North Bedeque, Emerald, Kensington, Lower Bedeque)

Dyment, Wanda (Dyment B&B)　　　　　　　　　　ↆ B&b
Wilmot Valley, RR3, Summerside, PEI　C1N 4J9　　　☎ (902) 436-9893

Located on Rt 107 off Trans-Canada Rt 1A and 7km from centre of Summerside.
$25-29D　●$1.50-3Each　$3Child　$4Add. person　　　▶ 4
● Choice, homebaked　🏠 Rural, older, acreage, view　■ 3(upstairs)　🛏 3D
🍳 Sh.w.h.　★ TV　🚭 Restricted smoking

⇔ Bay and beach swimming, golfing, horseback riding, deep sea fishing, Summerside Lobster Carnival, Borden ferry to NB

🐾 Home is on Blue Shank Road in picturesque farming area. Hosts have enjoyed B&B visitors for more than 14 years. Children welcome.

Nova Scotia

(including Cape Breton Island)

Check Inns Reservation Service

Nova Scotia offers a free Accommodation Reservation Service. Bed and Breakfast homes which are registered with this service have such a notation in their listing.

For general information and reservation in Nova Scotia call the Toll-Free numbers. (see "Government Tourist Offices in Canada" listed in the back of this book). Marine Ferry schedules can also be obtained from this service.

Annapolis Royal

(near Digby; see also Middleton, Weymouth)

Susnick, Donna and Michael (The St. George House B&B)   ✔Annap.R.B&B
548 Upper St. George Street, Annapolis Royal, NS   B0S 1A0   ☎ (902) 532-5286/425-5656

Turn off Hwy 101 at Annapolis Royal Exit or: off Hwy 1, 1 km from light.
$38S $42D $6Add.person   ► 10
🔳 June 25-Lab.Day   ● Cont.   🏠 Res., hist., acreage, view   ■ 4,Ste   ⊷ S,D,
cot, crib   ⌐ 1Sh.w.g.   ★ F   ⓦ Smoking
↝ World's highest tides, wharf and waterfront walkway, restaurants, antique shops,
Fort Anne, Historic Gardens, Tidal Power Project, King's Theatre, Via Rail Station

🐾 1868 restored spacious Victorian home (designated a "Registered Heritage
Property"), is comfortably furnished in antiques, ornately carved fireplaces and leaded
glass windows. Antique shop adjoining home.

Williams, Syd and Iris (The Poplars B&B)   ✔Annap.R.B&B
124 Victoria St., Annapolis Royal, NS   B0S 1A0   ☎ (902) 532-7936

Look for large yellow house located one block east of traffic light in town.
$28-43S $30-45D $8Add.person   ► 18
● Cont.   🏠 Downtown, res., hist., large sunporch   ■ 9D (main and upper floor)
⊷ 6D,4P, 2cots, crib   ⌐ 6Private, 2ensuite, 1sh.w.g.   ★ F,TV, parking, facilities for
the handicapped, 3 separate entrances   ⓦ Smoking, pets
↝ Historic gardens, Fort Anne, train and bus stops, downtown center
↭ Tidal Power Project, Habitation and North Hills Museum, Digby Ferry

🐾 Located in the heart of picturesque and historic town on a large treed lot with huge
300-year old poplars. Hostess makes sweaters and quilts for sale.

Williams, Floyd and Sandra (Hillsdale House)   ✔CC
519 St.George St., Box 148, Annapolis Royal, NS   B0S 1A0   ☎ (902) 532-2345

Located in the center of town and next to Annapolis Royal Historic Gardens.
45S $50-60D $5Child $5Add.person   🍴 Meals   ► 8
● Full   🏠 15-acres, older, view, lakefront, patio, quiet   ■ 9D,1Ste (2nd and 3rd
level)   ⊷ 2T,8D,1Q, cot, crib   ⌐ 10Private   ★ F,TV, parking   ⓦ Pets
↝ Historic Gardens, Duck Sanctuary on property, historic Fort St. Anne, craft stores,
restaurants, NS Tidal Power Plant, watch the tides rise and fall
↭ Port Royal Habitation (1st settlement in Canada - ca1605), NS Theme Park,
Kejimkujik National Park

🐾 Hillside house built in 1849 and fully restored to its former grandeur with crystal
and regal touches, has been host to kings and numerous leading politicians over the past,
and is a place of great comfort and pleasure.

Aylesford
(near Kentville; see also Middleton, Canning, Kingsport)

Haworth, Brad and Ingrid (The Doctor's House) ✓ B&B
63 Main St.West, Aylesford, NS B0P 1C0 ☎ (902) 847-9622

FromHwy 101 take Exit 16 at Aylesford. Turn right at main intersection in town and
travel 1 km to large light grey house with sign.
$32S   37-39D $5Add.person ► 9
● Choice, homebaked ♠ Village, hist., quiet ■ 2D,1Ste (upstairs)
⊷1S,2D,2T,1P, cot �🖱 1Ensuite,1sh.w.g ★ TV,2F, parking ⚋ German
↪ Antique shop on property
⇔ Annapolis Royal, Digby Ferry to Saint John NB, Acadia University Wolfville),
National Park (Grand Pre), shopping district (New Minas), swimming (Lake George)

🐾 Greek Revival-style spacious Victorian home situated in quiet village and tastefully
decorated with appropriate antiques. Hosts operate own antique shops on premises and
are publishers of the Nova Scotia Antique Dealers Directory. Children, cyclists and pets
are very welcome.

Baddeck
(on Cape Breton Island near Sydney; see also North Sydney)

Drinnan, Philip and Laverne (An Seanne Mhanse) ✓ CB Dev.B&B
RR2, Baddeck, NS B0E 1B0 ☎ (902) 295-2538

Located on Trans-Canada Hwy 105, east of Exit 10 (to Baddeck).
$25S $30D $9Child $9Add. person (Reservation please) ► 7
● Choice (trout, if desired) ♠ Rural, older, acreage, view ■ 3D ⊷ 3D,1S, cot
🖱 1Sh.w.g., 2private sinks ★ Separate entrance ✋ Pets, restricted smoking
↪ Gaelic College, Alexander Graham Bell Museum
⇔ Cabot Trail, Bras d'Or Lakes, North Sydney (ferry to NflD), Fortress of Louisbourg

🐾 Young hosts in 1906 built former Presbyterian Church Manse. Cyclists and children
welcome. Breakfast special is Rainbow Trout.

B&B Travel Tip: *If you are on the road and decide to stay in a B&B, do
phone ahead from a nearby phone (best: take a break at lunchtime and choose the
B&B for the coming night). The hosts will appreciate your consideration and if
their rooms are booked, they can also direct you to another B&B host. (This is not
convenient, if you appear at the door in the evening without prior notice.)*

Edwards, Harold and Patricia (The Bay Tourist Home)   ⌐ NSFV
General Delivery, Baddeck, NS   B0E 1B0   ☎ (902) 295-2046

Located 6.5 km west of the village on Hwy 205. Take Exit 10 from Trans Canada Hwy
onto Rt 205.
$25S $30D $5Add.person   ► 4
● Cont   ♠ Rural, 31-acres, view, quiet   ■ 1S,2D (upstairs)   ⊢ 2S,1D   ⅂ Sh.w.g.
★TV,F, separate entrance   ⊛ Drinking, pets

⇔ Graham Bell Museum, Gaelic
College, town of Baddeck, restaurants,
St.Annes Bay, boat tours, Sydney, ferry
to Newfoundland, Fortress of
Louisburg, Ingonish

🖝 Home overlooks Baddeck Bay.
Hosts is a lobster fisherman and there
are 2 young teenagers in the family.
Very quiet and relaxed atmosphere.

Roberts, Joan and William   ⌐ CB Dev.B&B
Shore Rd., Baddeck, NS   B0E 1B0   ☎ (902) 295-2807

On Rt 205 (Shore Rd), proceed west of Baddeck for 0.4 km.(Exit from Hwy 105).
$25S $30D   ► 8
▣ Summer   ● Choice, homebaked   ♠ Rural, acreage, view, patio   ■ 3D
⊢ 2D,2T,1Q, crib   ⅂ 1Sh.w.g.   ★ TV   ⊛ smoking
↔ Beaches, Alexander Graham Bell Museum
⇔ Gaelic College, square dancing, St.Ann's, Bras d'Or Lakes, water sports

🖝 "A lovely place to live and especially nice to visit". Home in this small village is a
good base for discovering beautiful Cape Breton Island.

> **B&B Travel Tip:** *Plan your trip at home in the comfort of your living room,
> researching the maps of the provinces you want to visit, and then write or phone
> the B&B hosts, to see if the room is available for you. When you have B&B confir-
> mations, you will relax and enjoy your trip much more.*

Bear River
(near Digby; see also Barton, Annapolis Royal)

Dockrill, Doug and Nancy Onysko (Inn Bear River)   ✔ B&B
Bear River, Annapolis Royal, NS   B0S 1B0   ☎ (902) 467-3809

Take Exit 22 off Hwy 101 and travel 6.4 km to village. Cross bridge and then turn right on first street.
$28S $32-38D   ● Full, homebaked   ♠ Village, hist., view, riverfront   ■ 3D
╾3D   ⊓ 1Private,1sh.w.g.   ★ F, parking   🖐 Pets
↪ Nova Scotia's only windmill, craft stores, tidal river
⇔ Town of Annapolis Royal and historic sites, whale and bird watching

🐾 Spacious Gothic Revival home with cheerful country decor and surrounded by flower gardens and fruit trees. Hosts serve outstanding breakfast on the veranda with emphasis on unusual pancakes, especially European.

Boutiliers Point
(near Halifax/Dartmouth; see also Chester Basin)

Rennie, Muriel (Oceanview Bed & Breakfast)   ✔ B&B
501 Islandview Dr., Boutiliers Point, NS   B0J 1G0   ☎ (902) 826-2887

From Halifax take Exit 5 to Hwy 213 and proceed west on Hwy 3 for 8.5 km to Islandview Drive. Watch for B&B sign.
20S $30D   ●$3Each   🍴 Meals   ► 5
▣ Summer (other by appointment)   ● Cont, homebaked   ♠ Villge, acreage, res., view, quiet   ■ 1S,1D (upstairs)   ╾ 1S,1D,1K   ⊓ Sh.w.g.   ★ parking, separate entrance   🖐 Smoking, pets
↪ Local church and general store
⇔ Halifax/Dartmouth, Peggy's Cove, Lunenburg (Fisherie's Museum), several area beaches, lobster supper

🐾 Warm Nova Scotien hospitality in home with large rooms and ocean view and a beautiful glassed-in sun porch.

Breton Cove
(on Cape Breton Island's north-east coast near Ingonish)

MacLeod, Effie (MacLeods Tourist Home)
Breton Cove, RR1, Englishtown, NS   1B0 1H0   ☎ (902) 929-2719

Located 36 km south of Ingonish (Cape Smokey).
$19S $22D $3Add. person   ●Extra   🍴 Meals   ► 11
▣ June-Nov.1   ● Choice, homebaked   ♠ Rural, oceanfront, quiet   ■ 1S,4D
╾ 4T,3D   ⊓ 1Sh.w.g.   ★ TV
↪ Seashore, Cabot Trail
⇔ Ingonish, Bras d'Or Lakes, ferry to Newfoundland, Graham Bell Museum

🐾 Lovely old home in quiet location on the Cabot Trail with beautiful ocean view.

Bridgewater

(see also Chester Basin, Mahone Bay, Petite Riviere, Lunenburg)

Conrad, Mrs. Mary (The Conrad Home)   ✓ S.Shore B&B
Bridgewater RR3, Dayspring 178, NS   B4V 2W2   ☎ (902) 543-2033

Located just 1.7 km from Bridgewater on Hwy 3 towards Lunenburg.
$18 per person $15Child(age 3-12)(free under age 3) $18Add.person   ► 6
✚ June-Oct.15   ● Full, homebaked   ♠ Sub., hist., quiet, acreage   ■ 2
⊷ 2D,2S   ⌐ 2Sh.w.h.   ★ TV   ✺ Pets
↔ Shipyard, pottery shop
⇔ Downtown Bridgewater, Lunenburg, Mahone Bay, modern shopping centre, dining.

☛ Quiet, old country heritage home occupied by adults only, near many interesting places and surrounded by beautiful scenery.

Brookfield

(near Truro; see also Hilden, Masstown, Newport Station, Maitland))

Geddes, Shirely (Bidia Bed and Breakfast)   ✓ CC
RR3, Brookfield, NS   B0N 1C0   ☎ (902) 673-2016

From Hwy 102, take Exit 12 at Brookfield to Hwy 289 East and continue 13 km from flashing light to house on left side. (Two houses past Kenrick's General Store).
$25S $30D $10Child (under age 10)   ► 6
✚ Summer   ● Full, homebaked   ♠ Village, rural, view, quiet   ■ 3D (upstairs)
⊷ 4T,1D   ⌐ 1Sh.w.h., 1sh.w.g.   ★ TV,F, parking   ✺ Smoking

↔ Rural dairy farm surroundings, salmon and trout fishing, hunting in the fall

⇔ Truro, Shubenacadia Wild Life Park, cities of Darmouth and Halifax, Halifax Int. Airport, Pictou (ferry to PEI), Cobquid Bay (beaches), Fundy Tides

☛ Home is situated in a tranquil rural setting in the beautiful Stewiacke Valley and in the town of Middle Stewiacke.

Canning

(near Wolfville/Kentville; see also Aylesford, Kingsport)

Barkhouse, George and June (Country Corner)   ⌐ B&B
Kingsport, RR2 Canning, NS B0P 1H0   ☎ (902) 582-3293

From Halifax on Hwy 101 take Exit 11 and follow Hwy 358 to Canning and then Hwy 221 to Kingsport.
$18S $28D $5Child $5Add.person   ● Full, homebaked   ♠ Village,older, quiet
■2D(upstairs)   ⊷ 2T,1D,R, cot, crib   ⌐ Sh.w.g.   ★ TV, parking
↔ Clean and sandy beach, view point of Fundy Tides (highest in the world)
⇔ Local craft shops and restaurants, Cape Split hiking trail, historic sites, Grand Pre

🖝 Completely renovated 125-year old home located in peaceful valley. Retired hosts have time to visit. There is a large bottle collection. All food served from homegrown products. There is a dog and a cat in the house. Children welcome.

MacDonald, Bill and Lynda (Pilgrims Rest)   ⌐ B&B
1023 Main St., Canning, NS B0l 1H0   ☎ (902) 582-3258

Take Exit 12 from Halifax Hwy 101 and then take Hwy 358 north to Canning.
30S $40D $10Add.person   ► 6A,2Ch
● Full   ♠ Village, acreage, hist., inground swimming pool, patio, quiet   ■ 3D
(upstairs)   ⊷ 3D, cot   ⌐ 2Sh.w.g.   ★ TV, parking   ⓦ Smoking   ⌇ Welsh
⇔ Prescott House, Kingsport Beach, Scotts Bay, historic sites, Grand Pre

🖝 Large Century home furnished with European Antiques and seven black marble fireplaces. Pool and large patio are surrounded by trees and flower gardens and provide comfort and privacy.

Cherry Hill

(near Bridgewater; see also Petite Riviere)

Talbot, Bob and Margaret (Talbot's B&B)   ⌐ S.Shore B&B
Cherry Hill, Lunenburg, County, NS B0J 2H0   ☎ (902) 677-2465

Located on Rt 331 (Lighthouse Rt) in Cherry Hill. Look for B&B sign.
$20S $30D $10Child $15Ad. person   ► 3
◪ June-Oct. 15   ● Choice   ♠ Farm, quiet, view   ■ 1D   ⊷ 2T,1R   ⌐ Private
★ TV, separate entrance
↔ Charming fishing village surroundings on scenic Lighthouse Route
⇔ Sandy beach

🖝 180-year old restored farm house with beamed ceilings, massive fireplace and extensive interesting library.

Chester Basin

(near Bridgewater; see also Mahone Bay, Lunenburg)

Oxner, Cliff and Ruth (Big Oaks Inn by the Sea) ✓ CC
Chester Basin, NS B0J 1K0 ☎ (902) 275-4542

Located west of Chester on Hwy 3. Take Exit 9 and proceed towards village stop sign.
$35-40D $6Add. person ●Extra ► 10
May 1-Oct.31 ● Choice, homebaked Village, acreage, view, patio, oceanfront, quiet ■ 4D (upstairs) 1S,2T,3D,R 4Private (powder rooms), 1Ssh.w.g. ★ TV in guest room, parking Pets, smoking some French
↔ Quiet walks along seashore, churches, store
⇔ Halifax, Peggy's Cove, Grand Pré National Park, Annapolis Valley, LeHavre River scenic way

☞ Magnificient view and scenery. Hosts will help with choice of restaurants, gift shops and scenic attractions.

Church Point

(near Yarmouth)

Gaudet, Louise and Herman (Golf Course View B&B) ✓ CC
Box 217 B, RR1, Church Point, NS B0W 1M0 ☎ (902) 769-2065

Located on P.F. Comeau Rd in Comeauville. Watch for Clare Golf & Country Club sign.
$18S $24-28D $10Add. person Meals ► 6A,2Ch
● Full Farm, res., quiet ■ 3D,1F 2T,2D 1Sh.w.g. ★ TV
Restricted smoking English (household language is French)

↔ Stroll around grounds, beach, golf course

⇔ Digby and Yarmouth Ferry Terminals

☞ Enjoy the quiet and relaxing surroundings. Very convenient location near St. Mary's Bay and Evangeline Trail. There is a friendly dog in the house.

Dartmouth
(near Halifax; see also Musquodoboit Harbour)

Christie, Chris and Isabel (Riverdell)   ⌐CC
68 Ross Rd., RR1, Dartmouth, NS   B2W 3X7   ☎ (902) 434-7880

Located on Hwy 328 (Marine Drive), o.4 km from Hwy 7 on the outskirts.
$30-35S $40-50D $15Add. person   ►8
● Full, homebaked   ♠ Rural, acreage, patio, quiet, solarium, river-frontage
■ 4(upstairs)   ⊶ 3T,3Q,1D   ⊓ 2sh.w.g.,sinks in 2rooms   ★ F,TV in guest room
Ⓟ Pets, smoking
↔ Little Salmon River (bubbling brook), country walks, bird watching, corner store
⇔ Fishing, sailing, golfing, sandy ocean beaches, Halifax City Centre, Ferry, theatres

🐾 Spacious modern Cape-Cod home. Outstandingly prepared cuisine served in country
kitchen or solarium. Part of accommodation completely private on second floor. Close to
Halifax International Airport.

De Molitor, Bill (Sterns Mansion Inn)   ⌐B&B
17 Tulip St., Dartmouth, NS   B3A 2S5   ☎ (902) 465-7414

Take Rt 118 to Victoria Rd and turn left (south). Go through 2 sets of lights, then take
first left on Tulip St and look for sign.
$35-40S $40-45D $55-65Suite $5Child   🍽 Meals   ► 12A,2Ch
● Full, homebaked   ♠ Downtown, res., hist., patio, quiet   ■ 6 (main and upper
floor)   ⊶ 2S,5D, 2cots   ⊓ 3Private, 3sh.w.g., 5-seater Jaccuzzi Spa   ★ F,TV in
guest room, parking, picnic lunches provided   Ⓟ Smoking, pets

↔ Restaurants, Brightwood Golf &
Country Club, Halifax Ferry, Sportsplex
facilities, lake swimming and boating.

⇔ Mic Mac Mall, Halifax Bridge,
Citadel Hill, historic properties, Peggy's
Cove

🐾 Beautifully restored and decorated
Victorian turn-of-the-Century home,
complete with high ceilings and brass
chandeliers throughout. Situated close
to everything in Metro. Hosts are
expertise at Honeymoon and special
occasion packages.

Debert

(near Truro; see also Masstown, E.Earltown, Tatamagouche, Hilden, Brookfield)

Eisses, James and Eileen (National Bed & Breakfast)   ↙B&B
RR1, Debert, NS B0M 1G0   ☎ (902) 662-3565

From Truro on Hwy 104 take Exit 12 to Masstown and travel 3 km to Debert.
$30S $38-53 $10Child   ► 6A,3-5Ch
● Full   ♠ Farm, patio, quiet, outdoor swimming pool   ■ 3D,1Ste,2F (upstairs)
⊶3D,1,1P (waterbed)   ↗ 1Private,1sh.w.h., whirlpool bath   ★ TV,F,LF, piano room,
libray   ♥   ⌇ Dutch
↔ Woodland walking trails, extensive farm grounds

🔫 Working Dairy farm with large farm house in rural Nova Scotia. Guests are welcome
to view and visit farm activities. House specialty is candlelit breakfast.

Dingwall

(on Cape Breton Island near Cape North)

McEvoy, Hansel and Sharon (Oakwood Manor)   ↙ B&B
Box 19, Dingwall, NS B0C 1G0   ☎ (902) 383-2317

At Cape North, take road to Bay St. Lawrence for 1.6 km and Northside Rd (0.4 km)
$25S $30D $6Child $6Add.person   ► 8A,3Ch
✚ Summer   ● Full, homebaked   ♠ 150-acres farm, view, quiet, isolated   ■ 2D, 1F
(upstairs)   ⊶ 4D,1S   ↗ 1Sh.w.g.   ★ Air,TV, separate entrance   ✋ Pets
↔ Enjoy the vast surrounding farmland and tranquil countryside

🔫 Unique home was built from local wood and milled by hosts' father and is situated
at the foot of a mountain in a pretty valley. Longtime B&B hosts.

East Earltown

(near New Glasgow; see also Pictou, Debert, Tatamagouche, Westville)

Matheson, Joyce and Don (Windy Acres)   ↙ NSFV
East Earltown, NS B0K 1V0   ☎ (902) 657-2358

20 km from village of Tatamagouche on paved Hwy 326, off Sunrise Trail.
$25S $35D $8Child (under age 12)   ► 2A,2Ch
✚ June-Sept.30   ● Full   ♠ 100-acre farm   ■ 1D,F (upstairs)   ⊶ 2T,1D,cots
↗1Sh.w.h.   ★ TV
↔ Historic Balmoral Grist and Sutherlands Steam Mills, Brule' beach, Tatamagouche
Bay, Sandpoint beaches, Northumberland Strait, Truro, Bavarian Garden restaurant

🔫 Located halfway between Earltown and Brule. There is a chinese pug dog in the
house and a pony called "Trigger" available for rides. Hostess has her crocheted and
knitted crafts on display throughout the home.

Falmouth
near Windsor; see also Canning, Newport Station)

Draper, Jerry and Ruth   ✔B&B
Mount Denson, RR1, Falmouth, NS B0P 1L0   ☎ (902) 684-3844

From Hwy 1 take exit 7 and proceed across 2 railway crossing in Mount Denson. Look
for 3rd house on right after crossing 2nd railway track.
$30D $10Add.person   ► 4A,1Ch
● Choice   ♠ Rural, 11-acres, older, view, quiet   ■ 2D (upstairs)   ⊷ 2D,1R
⌐Sh.w.g.   ⦿ Smoking, drinking
↪ Two churches (Baptist and United), community Hall
⇔ Appleblossom Festival in May, historic homes, Martock Ski and Windsor Forks ski
area, Grand Pre, restaurants

☞ Hosts will provide free chair lift passes for ski guests and will serve breakfast out
door in the summer if weather permits. There is a dog in the house. Watch pheasants
come to the feeders.

Glace Bay
(on Cape Breton Island; see also Sydney)

Grand Pre'
(near Wolfville; see also Windsor)

Chodakowski, Mrs. June (Gowanbrae Farm)   ✔ NSFV
Box 42, Grand Pre', NS B0P 1M0   ☎ (902) 542-4277

From Hwy 1, take Exit 10. Past Evangeline Farm Market, take first road on right and
continue to T-junction. Turn left and look for 4th property on right.
$25S $35-40D   ► 4
▣ Summer/Fall   ● Full   ♠ 40-acre hobby farm, view, patio, full size riding ring
■2D   ⊷ 2T,1K   ⌐ 1Sh.w.g.   ★ TV   ⦿ Restricted smoking
↪ Adjacent dykelands, walking, jogging, bicycling, horseback riding, Evangeline
National Historic Site, museums, antiques, restaurants, winery
⇔ Acadia U, Nat. historic homes, Bloomidon Look-Off, Fundy beaches

☞ Large, fully restored Century farmhouse on hobby farm.

> **B&B Travel Tip:** *Most guests find it more convenient to pay in the morning
> at breakfast, when there is usually more time. Some hosts will ask for this to be
> settled upon arrival. It is wise to ask the hosts what they would prefer.*

Halifax
(see also Dartmouth, Chester Basin, Musquodoboit H., Windsor)

Crowe, Michal (The Apple Basket)
1756 Robie St., Halifax NS   B3H 3E9   ☎ (902) 429-3019

Located on corner of Cedar & Robie St, opposite Camp Hill Hospital.
$40S $45-50D   ► 6A
● Homebaked   ♠ Downtown, res., older   ■ 3D   ⊷ 2T,2D   ⌐ Sh.w.g.
⊛ Smoking, children, pets
↔ Shops, restuarants, museums, Universities, Citadel
⇔ Beaches, Peggy's Cove

☛ Turn-of-the-Century Victorian home furnished with antiques and art collection.
Honeymoon special with champagne breakfast and "Apple Basket" marmalade gift.
Hosts are widely travelled professionals.

Lock, Carolyn (Old 362)   ✓ H.Metro B&B
1830 Robie St., Halifax, NS   B3H 3G3   ☎ (902) 422-4309

Phone for directions.
$30-35S $45D $15Add. person   ► 7
● Full, homebaked   ♠ Downtown, res., older, view   ■ 1S,3D(upstairs)
⊷1S,2T,2D,R   ⌐ Sh.w.g.   ⊛ Smoking
↔ Citadel Hill, Prov. Museum/Gardens/Archives, Dalhousie U, YMCA, tennis
⇔ Peggy's Cove, southshore beaches, Point Pleasant Park

☛ 100 year old home in excellent central city location. Breakfast is always special and
lively, eaten family style with other guests. There are two friendly and well-behaved dogs
in the house. Halifax-born hostess will help plan trips, if desired.

MacDonald, Innis and Sheila (Fresh Start B&B)   ✓ B&B
2720 Gottingen St., Halifax, NS   B3K 3C7   ☎ 902) 453-6616

Located 1 block north of MacDonald Bridge, across from Maritime Command Museum.
$30-40S $35-50D $10Child $10Add.person   (Off-season Rates available)   ► 14
● Full, homebaked   ♠ Downtown, hist.   ■ 3D,1Ste (2D) (upstairs)   ⊷ 2T,4D,3R
⌐ 2Private, 1sh.w.g.   ★ TV,F,LF,KF, parking, facilities for business meetings
⌇ some German
↔ Maritime Command Museum, Citadel Hill, historic Halifax waterfront, shopping, fine
restaurants, site of Halifax Explosion, public swimming pool
⇔ Picnic area, fresh/saltwater beaches, windsurfing, Peggy's Cove, Fundy Tidal Bore

☛ Very modest Victorian Mansion which has retained much original woodwork and
glass. Though close to downtown, the location is very quiet. There is a friendly dog in
the house. Business travellers welcome.

Mills, Mrs. Diana (Birdland) ✔ B&B
14 Bluejay St., Halifax, NS B3M 1V1 ☎ (902) 443-1055 (summer only)

From City, take Bedford Hwy 102, turn left on Flamingo to top of hill, right on Dove, right on Nightingale, left on Bluejay. From Airport, take Hwy 102 to Exit 2, turn left on Kearney Lake Rd, right on Dunbrack St, left on Bridgeview South, right on Meadowlark, right on Flamingo, left on Dove and as above.
$25S $35D $10Child $15Add.person ► 6
✿ Summer ● Full, homebaked ♠ Res., quiet ■ 3D (upstairs) ⊨ 2S,1D,3R
⌐1Sh.w.g. ★ Parking ♥ ⓦ Smoking, pets
↔ Back yard Birdwatching, Clayton Park Shopping Centre, restaurants
⇔ Mount Vincent University, Crystal Crescent and Lawrencetown beaches, downtown Halifax, The Citadel, public gardens, museums, Int. Airport

🐾 Contemporary tree-shaded split-level house located at the end of a cul-de-sac in an extremely quiet residential neighborhood. Hostess is co-author of "A Guide to NS B&B" and available as guide or tour planner. Fresh raspberies in season.

Saulnier, Alfred J. (Queen Street Inn)
1266 Queen St., Halifax, NS B3J 2H4 ☎ (902) 422-9828

Located south of Spring Garden Road.
$30-35S $40-45D (plus tax) ► 14
● No ♠ downtown, hist., quiet ■ 2S,6D,1Ste (upstairs) ⊨ 2S,6D
⌐1Private, 2sh.w.g. ★ KF, parking
↔ Restaurants serving breakfast, Public Gardens, Citadel, museums, University, downtown shopping, dining

🐾 Old Halifax stone house built in 1870 for the Justice of Supreme Court. Comfortable home with Nova Scotia antique furnishings. There is a very quiet Yorkshire Terrier.

Hilden
(near Truro, Brookfield, Masstown, Maitland, Debert, Stewiake)

Castell, Judith and Desiree (Julaine's Chalet) ✔ NSFV
Edward Rd., Hilden, Box 203, Truro, NS B2N 5C1 ☎ (902) 895-3723

Take Exit 12 or 13 off Hwy 2 and follow signs to Hilden. Turn left at Edwards Rd to 4th house on left.
$30S $33-35D $38-40F(of4) $5Add. person (Seniors & Off-season Rates) ► 12
May1-Sept30 ● Cont., homebaked ♠ Rural, res., acreage, view, quiet ■ 4D,F
⊨ 2T,3D,R, cots ⌐ 1Sh.w.g., 1sh.w.h. ★ TV,KF,LF, separate entrances, lounge, telephone available ♥ ⓦ Smoking, pets
↔ Wood, brook, Meditation Gardens, Village ball field, confectionary store
⇔ Tidal Bore, Prov. Wildlife Park, beaches, Teacher's and Agricultural Colleges

🐾 New house set in woods in quiet country surroundings. Lots of things to do outside and inside. Seniors discount rates available. Check Inns Reservation.

Louisbourg
(on Cape Breton Island near Sydney)

Cross, Mrs. Greta
81 Pepperell Street, Louisbourg, NS B0A 1M0

⌐CB Dev.B&B
☎ (902) 733-2833

Take Rt 22 to Louisbourg. Look for 2nd street on right side of Main St.
$25S $30D   ▣ Meals
► 10A,4Ch
● Full, homebaked ♠ Downtown, older, view, quiet ■3D,F ⊨ 3D,2cots
⌐1Sh.w.h.,1sh.w.g. ★ TV,LF,KF, separate entrance to apartment, ample parking
♥ ⤳ some French

Levy, Ed and Annie (Levy's Bed & Breakfast)
20 Marvin Street, Louisbourg, NS B0A 1M0

☎ (902) 733-2793

Take Rt 22 off Hwy 125.
25S   30D
► 6
● Full, homebaked ♠ Downtown, raised bungalow, view, quiet, oceanfront ■ 3D
(upstairs) ⊨ 3D ⌐ Sh.w.g. ★ TV, parking ⓦ Smoking, drinking
↪ Craft shops, general stores, historic light house and beautiful ocean view
⇔ Ferry at N. Sydney, Miners Museum at Glace Bay, Fortress of Louisbourg
🐾 Homey atmosphere in historic town. Guest may use the electric organ and join in
an evening sing-song.

MacLeod, Harvey and Mona (MacLeod's B&B and Cottage) ⌐Cape Breton B&B
RR1, Louisbourg, NS B0A 1M0
☎ (902) 733-2456

Located 10 km before Louisbourg on Rt 22 and 23 km from Sydney.
$25S $30D
► 6
● Full ♠ Rural, acreage, patio, quiet ■ 3D (upstairs) ⊨ 3D ⌐1Private,
1sh.w.g., 1ensuite ★ TV,F, parking ⓦ Restricted smoking, pets
⇔ Fortress of Louisbourg, Miners Museum, Newfoundland Ferry, Sydney Airport
🐾 Ambassador Award winning new Cape Cod home in a very quiet area in the
country. Hosts are proud of display of artifacts and coins recovered from the 1st French
Pay Ship "Chameau".

Peck, Mrs. R.Camilla (Peck Tourist Home B&B) ⌐ B&B
RR1, Louisbourg, NS B0A 1M0
☎ (902) 733-2649

Located in Catalone and 10 km from Louisburg on Rt 22. Phone for directions.
$25S $30D $42F $10Add.person
► 9A,4Ch
● Full, homebaked ♠ Farm, older, hilltop view, quiet ■ 3D,1F (upstairs)
⊨ 4D,1P,1T ⌐ 1 Private for guests, 1sh.w.h. ★ TV
↪ Walking and hiking
⇔ Louisbourg, Glace Bay, North Sydney (ferry to Nfld), Bras-d'Or Lake
🐾 Comfortable, quiet hospitality. Complimentary tea or coffee in lounge at any hour.

Lunenburg
(see also Mahone Bay, Chester B., Bridgewater, Petete Riviere, Pleasantville)

Callan, Nancy (Snug Harbour B&B) ✔ CC
9 King St., Box 1390, Lunenburg, NS B0J 2C0 ☎ (902) 634-9146

Drive through the business section of Lunenburg to the Post Office. Turn downhill one block to house across from the Bank of Commerce.

$30-35S $35-45D $10Add.person ► 8A,3Ch

✪ Summer ● Full, homebaked ♠ Downtown, hist., view, oceanfront, sundeck
■ 3 (upstairs) ⊨ 2S,2D,1Q,1R ↰ 1Private, 1sh.w.g. ★ F,KF,TV,VCR, parking
〜 French, German, some Dutch and Russian

↦ Lunenburg Academy (National Historic Site), 10 art galleries, many gift and craft shops, oldest Lutheran & Presbyterian Churches in Canada, historic Lunenburg Harbour, Fisheries Museum

⇔ Mahone Bay, Antique auto mueseum (Blockhouse), Ross Farm Museum, Petite Riviere, Stonehurst, Blue Rocks

☛ Century-old home located in the centre of Lunenburg (Canada's oldest German settlement) seconds walk from the town's best restaurants. Third floor sundeck has the best view of the tall ships in the harbour.

Murray, Margaret (Margaret Murray's B&B) ✔ S.Shore B&B
20 Lorne St., Box 1197, Lunenburg, NS B0J 2C0 ☎ (902) 634-3974

Located one street directly behind Falkland Street.

$25S $45D ► 6A

● Full, homebaked ♠ Downtown, view, quiet ■ 2 (upstairs) ⊨ 2D,1Q
↰ Sh.w.h. ★ F,parking, garage for bicycles Ⓦ Smoking, children, pets
↦ Fisherie's Museum of the Atlantic and ship tours, art galleries, good shopping, dining
⇔ The Ovens Natural Park, Blue Rocks (picturesque fishing village and favourite spot for photographers and artists)

☛ Relax in spacious garden area and enjoy friendly Nova Scotia hospitality. Very convenient location in one of Canada's most important fishing ports.

Mahone Bay
(near Bridgewater; see also Chester B., Lunenburg, Petite Riv., Pleasantville))

MacKenzie, Shirley K. (Book Barn and B&B)   ✔ S.Shore B&B
255 West Main St., Box 564, Mahone Bay, NS B0J 2E0   ☎ (902) 624-9843

From Rt 103, exit on Hwy 10 or 11 down Nova Scotia's south shore.
$30S $40D $5Add.person   ► 4A,1Ch
✚ June-Sept.   ● Full, homebaked   🏠 Village, hist., acreage, quiet ■ 2D
(upstairs)   ⊢ 2T,1D,1R   ⌐ Sh.w.h.   ★ TV,LF, parking 🖐 Smoking
↪ Historic town of Mahone Bay, forest walks, used book store on premises
⇔ Town of Lunenburg, Fisheries museum, Halifax

🐾 Lovely old (1860) Cape Cod house in the center of town. Hostess loves animals and has two Labs and three cats in the house. Hostess buys and sells used books.

Norklun, Curt and Nancy (Bayview Pines Country Inn)   ✔ S.Shore B&B
RR2, Indian Point, Mahone Bay, NS B0J 2E0   ☎ (902) 624-9970

From Hwy 103, take Exit 10. Go right to Mahone Bay, turn left at Indian Point sign and 5.7 km to house.
$41S $45-55D $6Child $6Add.person ●$3-5Each   Meals   ► 12A,2Ch,1Inf
● Full, homebaked   🏠 21-acres farm, hist., view, oceanfront, quiet, porches
■ 6D(main and upper floor)   ⊢ 2T,3D,2Q, cot, crib, 2 sleeping bags   ⌐ 6Private
★TV, boat and bicycles available for guests   ♥   🖐 Restricted smoking

↪ Spacious pastureland and woods to roam, long walking and cross- country ski trails, quiet country waterfront roads, small beach and boat launch

⇔ Mahone Bay, Oak Island, Halifax, Annapolis Valley

🐾 Century home has been carefully restored by hosts to keep it's historical value and the heritage of the original Andrews Family (1776) alive. Enjoy the spectacular water views and magnificient sunsets in quiet and peaceful surroundings.

Redden, Ron and Mabel (Sou'Wester Inn)
Box 146, 788 Main Street, Mahone Bay, NS B0J 2E0

⮡ S.Shore B&B
☎ (902) 624-9296

Located in Mahone Bay on Hwy 3 West (towards Lunenburg). Phone for directions.
$33-38S $43-48D $9Add.person   ► 10
❖ May-Oct.   ● Choice, homebaked   🏠 Res., oceanfront, quiet   ■ 4D(upstairs)
    ⇀ 2S,4D   ⍁1Private, 1sh.w.g.   ★ TV, parking   ⍦ smoking
↔ Fine shops, collectables, antiques, exquisite dining
⇔ Halifax, Peggy's Cove, beautiful fishing hamlets, Lunenburg, beaches

🐾 Victorian shipbuilder's home with antique period furnishings and large veranda
overlooking Bay. Bicycles, canoe and dory available for guests. Hosts build woodcrafts
and superior quality doll houses styled as Victorian Mansions on premises.

Maitland
(near Truro; see also Hilden, Brookfield, Stewiake)

Hill, Freda and Roy (Hilltop)
RR1, Maitland, Hants County, NS B0N 1T0

⮡ NSFVA
☎ (902) 261-2042

Located west of Truro on Rt 236 to 215. Take Exit 10 near Shubenacadie and travel west
on Rt 215.
$25S $35D $15Child   ► 3
● Full   🏠 Rural, village, bungalow, acreage, view, patio, quiet, oceanfront, enclosed
veranda sunporch off kitchen   ■ 1S,1D   ⇀ 2T,1S   ⍁ 2Sh.w.h.   ★ TV, parking
↔ Cobquid Bay beach, trails in wooded area, adjacent farm and grounds belonging to
son and family
⇔ Local museums, town of Truro, golfing, shopping

🐾 Comfortable and warm home with lovely view of Bay in the background from the
picture window at the rear. Hostess is past President of Canadian Country & Farm
Vacation Association and has travelled extensively across Canada by B&B. There is a dog
in the house. Reservations please.

Masstown
(near Truro; see also Brookfield, Debert

⮡ NSFCV

Mingo, Keith and Jennie (Bayview Guest Home)
Masstown, RR1, Debert, NS B0M 1G0

☎ (902) 662-2561

Located 1km from Masstown Exit 12 off Trans Canada Hwy 104 west of Truro.
$25S $35D $10Child   ► 6
● Choice, homebaked   🏠 Rural, view, patio, quiet   ■ 2D (upstairs)   ⇀ 2T,2D,1R
    ⍁ 1Sh.w.g.   ★ TV,F   ⍦ Drinking
↔ Restaurants, church, fruit and vegetable market
⇔ Wentworh Ski Hill, Debert Military Base, Bird Sanctuary, Tidal Bore

🐾 Brick house with view of Bay, relaxing backyard and circular driveway. There is a
cat in the house.

Middleton

(near Annapolis Royal; see also Aylesford)

Hanan, Gary and Charlene (Victorian Inn B&B)   ✔ B&B
Box 1065, 145 Commercial St., Middleton, NS   B0S 1P0   ☎ (902) 825-6464

Turn by 2 banks on Main St (on Trans Canada Hwy 1 onto Commercial Street.
$30S $35D   ●3Each $4Add. person   ► 9
● Full   ♠ Downtown, older, patio, swimming pool   ■ 5   ⊷ 1T,4D
⌐Sh.w.g.   ★ TV,F, guest parlour, TV lounge
↔ Walking trails, restaurants, shops, theatre, Post Office
⇔ Bay of Fundy, scenic areas in Annapolis Valley, amusement park

🐾 Relax on spacious sundeck by the pool. Home is completely furnished with antiques.
Check Inns Reservations.

Morse, Dick and Barbara (Morse Century Farm B&B)   ✔ NSFVA
Box 220, Middleton, NS   B0S 1P0   ☎ (902) 825-4600

Take Exit 18 off Hwy 101 to Middleton and Hwy 10 to Hwy 201. Turn right and
continue 1.6 km to house on right in the community of Nictaux West.
$25S $35-40D   ► 6
● Cont., homebaked   ♠ Farm, hist., view, patio   ■ 3D ⊷ 2T,2D   ⌐ Sh.w.g.
★ TV   ⓦ Pets, smoking
⇔ Bridgetown, historic Holy Trinity Church, Annapolis Royal Hist. site, Bay of Fundy
Shore, local arts, crafts and antiques, two golf courses

🐾 Working fruit and vegetable farm operated by host's family since 1760. Spacious
farm home has large guest rooms.

Musquodoboit Harbour

(east of Dartmouth; see also Halifax)

Kent, Mildred and Ivan (Seaview Fisherman's Home)   ✔ NSFV
RR1, Musquodoboit Harbour, NS   B0J 2L0   ☎ (902) 889-2561

Located east of Dartmouth at Pleasant Point. Travel 12 km on the Ostrea Lake Rd off
Hwy 7 (Marine Drive) to road sign Kent Rd and to second house.
$30S $35D $5Child $10Add.person   ► 6A,1Ch
✚ May1-Nov.1   ● Full, homebaked   ♠ Village, acreage, view, oceanfront, quiet,
isolated   ■ 1S,3D (upstairs)   ⊷ 1S,1T,2D   ⌐ Sh.w.g.   ★ TV, parking
ⓦ Smoking, pets
↔ Lighthouse on property, seashore , watch fishing boats come in with catch.
⇔ Two beaches, restaurants, Dartmouth, Halifax, historical sights

🐾 Fourth and Fifth Generation home (built in 1861) in pretty fishing village and very
quiet secluded island (20 acres) with a view of the sea from every room in the house.
There is a cat and a dog in the house.

New Glasgow

(see also Pictou, New Glasgow

Cameron, Margaret and Robert G (Willow Tree Cottage)   ✔ NSFV
Irish Mountain, RR2, New Glasgow, NS   B2H 5C5   ☎ (902) 752-8519

Take Exit 25 off Hwy 104 at New Glasgow and Rt 348 at left of Esso Station. Go south to
Irish Mt. Eureka sign, left and past Churchville Hall up dirt road to 3rd house on right.
$25S $30D   (Special family 7 childrens rates)   📧 Meals   (Deposit required)   ► 5
● Full, homebaked   🏠 Farm, very quiet   ■ 2   ⊢ 2D   ⌐ Sh.w.h.   ★ TV
↩ Walking trails, beautiful view from top of hill
⇔ Fishing, museum, shopping areas, restaurants, New Glasgow, beautiful beaches,
Annual Lobster Carnival and Festival of Tartans, P.E.I. ferry, Antigonish Elderhostel

🐾 Home was built in 1834 on an original grant of land at 200 metres above sea level
and is in excellent condition with a magnificient view. So quiet, you can hear it. No
reservations held after 5pm, unless confirmed.

Hughes, Stan and Florence (Highland View)   ✔ NSFV
RR2, New Glasgow, NS   B2H 5C5   ☎ (902) 752-8862

From Hwy 104, take Exit 25 to Hwy 348 south to Sunnybrae Rd. Proceed for 5.8 km to
Mountville. Turn left and look for third mailbox on the right.
$25S $35D $7.50Child   📧 Meals   ► 6
● Choice, homebaked   🏠 Rural, acreage, view, patio   ■ 3D   ⊢ 4T,1Q, cot, crib
⌐ 1Private, 1sh.w.g.   ★ TV, F   ✋ Pets
↩ Walking trails and peaceful countryside
⇔ Melmerby Beach, Abercrombie golf course, Pictou (ferry to PEI)

🐾 Modern country home with Scottish Canadian atmosphere situated on 130 acreage.
Enjoy the Gathering of the Clans. Scottish oatcakes and muffins served for breakfast.

MacKay, Mrs. Evelyn (MacKay's)   ✔ B&B
44 High St., New Glasgow, NS   B2H 2W6   ☎ (902) 752-5889

From Trans-Canada Hwy 104, take Exit 25 and drive along East river Rd to traffic lights
at Temperance St. Turn right and continue to Mountain Rd. Turn left onto High Street.
$25S $30-35D $2Child $10Add. person   (Off season rates)   ► 6A,2Ch
● Cont., homebaked   🏠 Res., older, large veranda   ■ 3D (upstairs)   ⊢ 2T,2D,P
⌐ Sh.w.h.   ★ TV,F, piano, parking   ♥   ◠ some French
↩ Stewart House museum and first steam locomotive on steel rails.
⇔ Melmerby, Caribou and Big Island beaches, MacPherson's Mills, Pictou

🐾 Relax on the large veranda after a day on the beach or golf course.

Newport Station
(near Windsor; see Falmouth)

Stevens, Pierre and Jane (Wavertree Inn)   ✓B&B
Newport Station, Hants County, NS B0N 2B0   ☎ (902) 798-5864

From Hwy 101 take Exit 4 to Hwy 1 and turn west and proceed 3 km to house not visible from road.
$30S $35D $5Child   5Add.person   ▨ Meals   ► 2A,2Ch
● Choice, homebaked   🏠 Mini-farm, acreage, older, quiet   ■ 2D,1F (upstairs)
⌐2T,3D,1R, crib   ⌐1Sh.w.h.,1sh.w.g.   ★ F,TV, separate entrance, parking
♥ ⑩Pets ▰ Dutch, French, Spanish
↔ Tranquil farm grounds and peaceful surroundings
⇔ Windsor, Haliburton House, Grand Pre Park, Halifax, Chester, Peggy's Cove

🐖 Relaxed informal comfort and friendly hospitality. Enjoy a quiet moment in the enclosed sunroom and den. Hosts are proud of many collectibles and antiques that fill the rooms. There are two dogs and two cats in the house.

Nova Scotia Farm and Country Vacations Association
Newport Station, Hants County, NS B0N 2B0   ☎ (902) 798-5864
Secretary Jane Reid Stevens
Rates: $25-30S $30-40D   (including a hearty breakfast)
The Nova Scotia Farm and Country Vacation Association is a non-profit organization representing members of one to four bedroom properties, scattered around rural Nova Scotia and it is a pre-requisite to membership, that the property either be a farm or country home. There are 75-80 members at the time of publication. Some of the properties are working farms, some hobby farms, and some strictly B&B properties, but all share one thing, good old "Downeast Hospitality".
A brochure is available upon request from the above. Hosts should be contacted directly.

Petite Riviere
(near Bridgewater; see also Cherry Hill)

MacLennan, Theresa P. (Tannery Hollow Lodge)   ✓S.Shore B&B
RR1, Petite Riviere, Lunenburg Co, NS B0J 2P0   ☎ (902) 688-2186

From Hwy 103 take Exit 15 and proceed 10 km on Rt 331.
$30S $40D $5Child $10Add.person   ► 9
● Full   🏠 Rural, acreage, view, quiet, veranda   ■ 2D,1F ⌐4D
⌐1Sh.h.,1sh.w.g.   ★ Tv, separate entrance, parking, VCR and radio in guest rooms
⇔ Ocean beaches, fishing, canoeing, quiet countryside

🐖 80-year-old home, once a Tannery in the late 1800, is located on peaceful country road on Nova Scotia's beautiful South Shore. The house is restored to its original atmosphere and filled with antiques throughout. The back veranda overlooks a babbling brook and meadow. A warm welcome and a hearty country breakfast are guaranteed.

Pictou

(near New Glasgow; see also East Earlton, Westville)

Ferguson, Jack and Kathleen (Ferguson's Guest Home)   ✓NSFVA
RR1, Pictou, Bayview, NS B0K 1H0   ☎ (902) 485-4837

Located 3.5 km from Pictou en route to PEI Ferry Terminal in Caribou.
$25S $35D   ► 6
● Full   🏠 130-acres farm, older, quiet   ■ 3 (upstairs)   ⌐ 2S,1D,1Q   ⌐ 1Sh.w.g.
★TV   🖐 Smoking, drinking, pets
↔ Pretty fields of flowers and trees, large Holstein Dairy farm (in-laws) on adjacent
property, Caribou Park and beach
↔ Ferry to Prince Edward Island, Pictou

🔫 Friendly Nova Scotia Hospitality in beautiful big old home in quiet surroundings
with a duck pond and many animals outside.

Sellers, Johnson and Fern   ✓ CC
96 Faulkland St., Pictou, NS B0K 1H0   ☎ (902) 485-5113

Take downtown exit from Pictou Rotary. Turn left at Dairy Bar on second street on left
side. Continue to first intersection. Look for large white house with semi-circle driveway
at corner of Prince St.
$25S $30-35D $40F(for 4) $5Add. person   ●Extra(Full)   ► 8
✚ May1-Nov30   ● Homebaked   🏠 Res., quiet, hist.   ■ 1D,1F main and upper
floor   ⌐ 2T,3D   ⌐ 2Sh.w.g.   ★ TV,F (in each room)   ★ KF, large veranda for
guests   🖐 Pets, drinking, restricted smoking

↔ Live theatre, restaurants, swimming,
wharf fishing

↔ Beaches, New Glasgow shopping
mall, ferry to Pictou Island and P.E.I.

🔫 Beautiful century home with high
ceilings and spacious rooms in quiet
area on large treed lot. Hostess has
beautiful handcrafted quilted items for
sale. Enjoy a quiet moment in the cozy
place by the window in the large
hallway.

Pleasantville
(near Bridgewater; see also Petite Riviere)

Harris, Bob and May (Harrises at Mt.Pleasant)   ⌐ S.ShoreB&B
RR1, Pleasantville, NS B0R 1G0   ☎ (902) 688-2234

From Rt 103 eastbound, take Exit 15 to Rt 331 to West Dublin. From Rt 103 westbound, take Exit 12 to Rt 331 to West LaHave.
$25S $32-35D   🍽 Meals   ▶ 4
✜ Summer   ● Choice, homebaked   🏠 Rural, quiet, view   ■ 2D (upstairs) ⊷2D
⌐ Sh.w.g.   ★ F,TV,parking   Ⓦ Pets,children, smoking   ⋙ French
⇔ Beaches, yacht club, museums, churches, golfing, scenic points, birdwatching,
Lunenburg Fisheries Museum

🐾 Hosts are knowledgeable about history and background of area. Comfortable and friendly atmosphere. House is located on Huey Lake with attractive lawns and garden for relaxing.

Port Clyde
(near Shelburne; see also Port Saxon, Barrington, Blanche)

Haeghaert, Eva (MacLaren Inn)   ⌐B&B
Port Clyde, NS B0W 2S0   ☎ (902) 637-3296

From Rt 103 (Lighthouse Route), take Exit 28.
$25S $35D $10Child $10Add.person   ▶ 5
✜ Summer   ● Full   🏠 Rural, hist., acreage, view, oceanfront, quiet   ■ 1S,2D
(upstairs) ⊷ 2D,1S,1R, crib   ⌐ Sh.w.g.   ★ TV   Ⓦ Restricted smoking

↔ Golf course, Clyde River at back of property, canoeing, fishing, hiking

⇔ Shelburne, Cape Sable and Cape Negro Islands, Beaverdam Lake

🐾 Mid 19-Century Gothic mariner's and shipbuilder's home, located at the Head of Cape Negro Harbour and the mouth of the Clyde River with exceptional view of water surroundings and natural environment. There are two cats in the house.

Pugwash
(near Amherst)

Bond, Bonnie and John Caraberis (Blue Heron Inn)   ✔ Cent.NS B&B
Box 405, Sunrise Trail, Pugwash, NS B0K 1L0   ☎ (902)243-2900/2020

Located on Rt 6 (Durham St) in village and just past bridge.
$34-38S $36-42D $40-46F $7Add. person   ► 13
📅 June1-Lab.Day   ● Cont, homebaked   🏠 Res., quiet, hist.   ■ 3D,1Ste (for 4)
🛏3T,4D,2P, cots, crib   🍴1Private, 2sh.w.g.   ★TV, 2sitting rooms,   ♥   🖐Pets
↪ Village centre, harbour
⇔ Warm water beaches, golf course, Pugwash River and tennis courts

☛ Restored 1880 home, tastefully decorated. Check Inns reservations.

St.Peters
(on Cape Breton Island near Port Hawkesbury)

Tobin, Lawrence and Carmel   ✔ CB Dev.B&B
RR1, St. Peters, Richmond Co., NS B0E 3B0   ☎ (901) 535-2061

Located on Rt4 near Barra Head Church and east of the St. Peters Canal.
$25S $30D $4Child $5Add. person   🍽 Meals   ► 5A,2Ch
📅 May 1-Oct. 30   ● Full, homebaked   🏠 Rural, acreage, view, quiet   ■
1S,2D(upstairs)   🛏 1T,2D,cot   🍴Sh.w.g.   ★ TV in guest room, separate entrance
↪ Bras D'Or Lakes
⇔ Manually operated locks, tidal activity, Mount Granville, Battery Park, Port
Hawkesbury, Baddeck, Bell Museum

☛ Home is located near small village siutated on a narrow strip of land separating
Atlantic Ocean and the Bras D'Or Lakes.

Stewiacke
(near Truro; see also Brookfield, Maitland, Hilden)

Caldwell, Ian and Jean (Riverside View Farm)   ✔NSFVA
RR2, Stewiacke, Colchester County, NS B0N 2J0   ☎ (902) 639-2198

$25S $35D $10Child   🍽 Meals   ► 4A,2Ch
● Full   🏠 Rural, acreage   ■ 3D   🛏 2D,1Q,R,crib   🍴 1Sh.w.g.   ★ TV,F
↪ Shubenacadie River with famous Tidal Bore
⇔ Halifax International Airport, Provincial Wildlife Park

☛ Quiet stop for a night or longer. Country-style living with modern conveniences.

Sharples, Lloyd and Elinor (Cloverdale Inn)
RR2, Stewiacke, NS B0N 2J0

⌐CC

☎ (902) 673-3313

From Hwy 102 take Exit 12 to Rt 289. Go through flashing light and continue through Brookfield (13 km). Turn right on Cloverdale Rd to first house on right over the bridge. Look for sign.

$25S $34D   ◙ Meals

► 6

● Choice, homebaked   🏠 Rural, view, quiet   ■ 3D (upstairs)   ⊨ 2T,2D
⌐1Sh.w.h.   ★ TV, parking, VCR, in-house movies, grade A water   ⚓ Pets, children

↔ Church, general store, Stewiacke River, greenhouses and nursery, hunting fishing

⇔ Truro, Pictou, Halifax

☛ 1870 Farmhouse overlooking the Stewiacke River with spacious and comfortable guest rooms and furnished entirely with antiques (which are for sale). Hosts have been in the antique business for over 20 years. They know the Province well and take pleasure in assisting guests with touring plans.

Sydney
(on Cape Breton Island; see also Baddeck, Louisbourg)

McEwen, Evanel (Park Street B&B)
169 Park St., Sydney, NS B1P 4W7

⌐CB Dev. B&B

☎ (902) 562-3518

$25S $30D $5Child $5Add.person ● Full, homebaked   🏠 Downtown, res., hist.,
patio   ■ 2D   ⊨ 2D   ⌐ Sh.w.g.   ★ TV   ♥   ⚓ Pets
↔ Park, shopping centre, hospital, Steel Mills
⇔ Louisbourg, Glace Bay, Miner's Museum

☛ Interesting 1910-built home with curved walls in front hall and living room.

B&B Travel Tip: *Most hosts do not accept credit cards or cheques, so make sure you have cash on hand - or check about this when making your reservation.*

Sydney Mines
(on Cape Breton Island near North Sydney; see also Baddeck)

Matthews, Clifford, J. (Gowrie)   ✔ Innk.Gld.NS
139 Shore Rd., Sydney Mines, NS B1V 1A6   ☎ (902) 544-1050

From Rt105 (Trans-Canada Hwy) take Exit 21 and follow Rt305 north for 3 km.
$38S $45D $8Add. person ◪ Meals   ► 12
◘ May-Oct.   ● Full ♠ Hist., acreage, quiet ■ 6D(upstairs) ⊷ 1T,4D,1Q
⤒ 2Sh.w.g. ★ Parking Ⓦ Small pets only
⇔ Louisburg Fortress, Glace Bay Miner's Museum, Nfld Ferry Terminal, Cabot Trail

🐾 Large rooms in 1825-built home filled with antiques. Each room has been decorated to enhance the feeling of comfortable elegance. There are two cats in the house. Dinner reservations required for four course repast which may include delicacies from the waters, fields and gardens of Nova Scotia.

Tatamagouche
(near Pictou; see also Debert, East Earltown, Truro)

Cockburn, Helen (Barrachois Harbour B&B)   ✔NSFVA
RR1, Tatamagouche, NS B0K 1V0   ☎ (902) 657-3009

From Amherst take Hwy 6 East to Tatamagouche, turn left on Sand Point Rd. Then turn right on east (gravel) "Shore Road" and go 1.5 km to house on left side across from Lobster Pound.
$25S $30-35D $8Child (Deposit required)   ► 4A,2Ch
● Full ♠ Rural, 15-acres, oceanfront, quiet, view ■ 1D,1Ste ⊷ 1S,2D,1R
⤒1Private,1sh.w.h. ★ TV in guest room, separate entrance Ⓦ Restricted smoking
↬ Swim in warm salt water, walk the shore collecting driftwood, bird watching,
⇔ Golf Course, craft shops, museum, excellent eating places

🐾 Scottish-Canadian Hospitality in home overlooking the fisherman's wharf. Enjoy a fresh cooked lobster from the Lobster Pound (May/June). Scenic views all around - an Artists delight. There is a dog in the house.

B&B Travel Tip: *You can stay in a B&B if you travel with your own trailer. Many B&B's have ample room and a hook-up for that purpose, and they usually welcome guests to join them in the house for breakfast.*

Truro

(see also Hilden, Masstown, Brookfield, Tatamagouche, Westville)

Jennings, Doug and Enid (Blue House Inn) ✔ Truro B&B
43 Dominion St., Truro, NS   B2N 3P2   ☎ (902) 895-4150

From Hwy 102, take Exit 13 and proceed to lights, turn left and continue to next lights,
turn right and go two blocks to Dominion St, then left again.
$25S $35D $5Child(age 4-12) $10Add.person   ► 9A,2Ch
✚ June/July/Aug.   ● Full   ⌂ Downtown, hist., sunporch   ■ 3D (main and
upper floor)   ◡ 2S,2T,1D,1Q, 2cots, also extra mattresses for small children
⌐ 2Sh.w.g.   ★ KF, TV in guest room   Ⓦ Smoking, drinking, pets
↔ Victoria Park (pool, tennis, picnic areas), walking trails, Bay of Fundy Tidal Bore
⇔ Northumberland Strait (picnic and beach area), Halifax International Airport

☞ 100 year old Colonial style mansion located in older section of town,"The Hub of
Nova Scotia". Hosts are retired church workers. Early reservation recommended.

Rogers, Carol and Family (The Marigold Inn) ✔NSFVA
75 Truro Heights Rd., Lower Truro, NS   B2N 5A9   ☎ (902) 895-9722

$25S $35D $45F $5Add. person   ► 6A,4Ch
● Choice, homebaked   ⌂ Res, acreage, older, patio   ■ 3D (upstairs)   ◡3,3D,1cots
⌐ Sh.w.g.   ★ F,TV in guest room, separate entrance, parking   ⒲Smoking, pets
↔ Bay of Fundy Tidal Bore, shopping malls, Dairy farm grounds
⇔ Halifax and South Shore, PEI Ferry Terminal, Victoria Park for fishing, Wentworth
Ski area, Teacher's and Agricultural Colleges

☞ Comfortable restored Victorian farmhouse with spacious shaded lawns and garden.
Good and warm hospitality for a home away from home.

Westville

(near New Glasgow and Pictou; see also East Earltown, Truro)

Hatfield, Lorna (Lorna's Bed & Breakfast) ✔ CC
2195 Spring Garden Rd., Westville, NS   B0K 2A0   ☎ (902) 396-3877

From Rt 104 take Exit 21 to Westville onto Cowan St. Drive approx. 25 km, turn left on
MacKay St and go to large corner lot at end on left side; or phone for specifics.
$30S $35D $5Child   ► 4A,1Ch
✚ Summer   ● Choice, homebaked   ⌂ Res., acreage, quiet   ■ 2D (upstairs)
◡2T,1D,1P   ⌐ Sh.w.h.   ★ TV in guest room, parking
↔ Town of Westville, restaurant, laundromat and small stores
⇔ Shopping Mall, Ferry to Prince Edward Island, beaches

☞ Ideal location for a stop over and relax on route from Halifax to Cape Breton.
Located on the outskirts of a small town with lovely garden. Hostess enjoys a friendly
game of "scrabble" and good conversation. Fresh muffins and scones a house specialty.

Windsor
(near Halifax; see also Grand Pre', Canning, Falmouth, Kingsport)

Connelly, Veronica and Dennis (Clockmaker's Inn)
1399 King St., Windsor, NS B0W 1H0   ☎ (902) 798-5265

Located west from Halifax (Rt 101). Take Exit 5 (follows into King St) and look for house at junction 14 for Chester.

$30S $35D $10Add. person   ► 10

● Full, homebaked   🏠 Rural, hist., acreage, sunroom and veranda   ■ 4D (upstairs)

⊷ 2T,4D,1R   ⌐ 1Sh.w.g.   ★ TV,F in guest rooms

↪ Local and Haliburton (Sam Slick) museums, Fort Edward Blockhouse (1750) windsurfing on Lake Piziquid, Teddy Bear Jamboree (July), Giant Pumpkin Weigh-Off

⇔ Tidal Bore, Halifax, Peggy's Cove, Grand Pre Nat. Park, beautiful Mahone Bay, free tours through winery

🐾 Grand Victorian (1894) house with stained glass windows and ornate victorian fireplaces has beautiful grounds for pleasant walking and is situated in quiet small historic town. Handpainted decorated rooms are filled with antiques. There is a cat in the house. Hostess is President of the local Historial Society.

Young, P.R (Youngs's B&B)
231 Wentworth Rd., Box 461, Windsor, NS B0N 2T0

↙ CC
☎ (902) 798-2516

Take Exit 5A off Hwy 101 onto Wentworth Rd. Proceed to town past Exhibition Grounds. Look for 4th house on right past entrance to shopping mall.

$20S $30D   ●$2Each   ► 4A,1Ch

● Choice, homebaked scones and muffins   🏠 Res., older, quiet   ■ 2D,1S   ⊷2D,1S
cot ⌐ Sh.w.h.   ★ TV, parking   ♥

↪ Agricultural Fair Grounds, museum, hospital

⇔ Tidal Bore (Bay of Fundy), Halifax, Grand Pre' Nat. Park, Peggy's Cove

🐾 Older Residence built in 1800's situated at the Gateway to Annapolis Valley. Ideal location for travellers wishing to see the Valley and South Shore.

Yarmouth

(see also Church Point

Colbeck, James and Lori (Murray Manor Guest House) ✔ CC
225 Main St., Yarmouth, NS B5A 1C6 ☎ (902) 742-9625

Take either of Rts 101 or 103 to Yarmouth. Located where the Evangeline Trail (Rt 1) and the Lighthouse Route (Rt 3) meet. Look for 17 Forest Street.
$25-40D   (plus tax) (weekly and off-season rates available) ► 17
● Cont. 🏠 Downtown, acreage, view, quiet ■ 8D in guesthouse ⊨ 3T,7D,P ⌐
1Private,2shw.g. ★3F,TV in guest room on request, ample parking space, common room with TV and library, garages for securing bicycles, ⓦ Pets, smoking
↝ Ferry (Bar Harbour/Portland), bus/train depots, Tourist Bureau, fine dining
⇔ Digby (ferry to NB) Annapolis Valley historic sites, South Shore of NS

📣 Built in 1824, the home is surrounded by 2 acres of beautiful landscaped grounds and is one of Yarmouth's oldest and most attractive properties, set apart from the bustle of the rest of the community by its stone wall and bordering trees, and just steps from the the ferry docks.

Whittaker, Albert and Evelyn (Whittaker's B&B) ✔ NSFV
RR5, Box 1238, Yarmouth, NS B5A 4A9 ☎ (902) 742-7649

Take Chegoggin Rd off Rt 1 in Dayton and drive 1.6 km to South Chegoggin. Turn left and continue 0.5km to first house past church.
$20S $30D $8Child(age 5-12) ► 6A,2Ch
✚ May 1-Oct.15 ● Full 🏠 200-acre farm, quiet ■ 1S,2D,1F (upstairs) ⊨3D,1Q
⌐ 1Sh.w.g., 1sh.w.h. ★ TV in guest rooms, parking
↝ Long hiking trail to hills on property with view of ocean & surrounding communities
⇔ Ferry to Bar Harbour and Portland (Maine), Firefighters museum and historical museum, Yarmouth Lighthouse, Tin Mine, airport

📣 170/180-year old, remodeled home on dairy farm of 60 Holsteins. There are Canadian and African Geese and numerous animals to pet.

Newfoundland

For CN Marine Ferry schedules and rates contact:

Reservation Bureau, CN Marine
Box 250, North Sydney, Nova Scotia B2A 3M3
or call toll-free information for your area toll-free number: 1-800-555-1212

Bay Bulls
(near St. John's; see also Portugal Cove, Brigus)

Gatherall, Rosemary (Gatherall's Hospitality Home)   ⌐ B&B
North Side Rd., Bay Bulls, Nfld A0A 1C0   ☎ (709) 334-2887

From Ferry Terminal (2hrs by car), take Trans Canada Hwy to Route 13 and left on
Route 10 to Bay Bulls or phone for directions.
$35S $40D $7Add.person   ▣ Meals   ► 6
◘ May 15-Sept.30   ● Cont.   ♠ Rural, village, hist., bungalow, oceanfront, view,
quiet   ■ 3D   ⊷ 3D   ⼉ 2Sh.w.g.   ★ parking
↪ Hiking, bird watching, see icebergs and whales in spring, jigging for cod and squid
amon spetacular ocean scenery, watch fishermen at work
⇔ City of St. John's (shopping, museum, Univerity) Nat. Historic Sites at Cape Spear &
Signal Hill, guided boat tours to Witless Bay Seabird Sanctuary (largest nesting colonies
of Puffins and other seabirds in N.A.), St.John's Airport

🐾 Canadian Tourism Ambassador Award winning host family in bungalow home right
on ocean's edge has a dining room with panoramic ocean view. Host family enjoys a long
tradition as a "sea people" and they take pride and delight in sharing their heritage with
others. Historic and quiet fishing village, where the sea enters intimately into the lives of
the people. Hosts operate Sanctuary Boat Charters. Newfoundland Cousine. Centrally
located and ideal home base for day trips. No air pollution.

Boyd's Cove
(near Lewisporte)

Thoms, June (Thoms Hospitality Home)
Boyd's Cove South, Nfld A0G 1G0   ☎ (709) 656-3301

Take Rt 330 and 331 from Gander or Rt 340 from Lewisporte. At Boyd's Cove South
sign, turn right and look for Thoms Hospitality Home sign.
$12S $17D   ● $3Each   (Children half rate age 6-12)   ▣ Meals   ► 5
● Full   ♠ Rural, quiet, view   ■ 1S,2D,F   ⊷ 3T,1D   ⼉ 1Sh.w.g.   ⚅ Pets, drinking
↪ Cove for walking and strolling
⇔ Dog Bay Pond, public beach, cod jigging

🐾 Enjoy a quiet rest in peaceful surroundings and the lovely sunsets across the bay.

B&B Travel Tip: *On the day of departure, you should leave after breakfast
and with all your belongings! It is not fair for the hosts to have to store your
luggage, while you are making some side-trips before leaving town. Remember,
they have to get the room ready for the next night.*

Brigus

(near St.John's; see also Portugal Cove, Heart's Delight, Bay Bulls)

Tennant, Pam & Reg Sherren (Seaport Cottage)   ✓ B&B
Brigus, Nfld ADA 1K0   ☎ (709) 528-4943

Take Trans Canada Hwy to Roache's Line Exit and go to Cupids, turn off to Brigus. OR
Take the more scenic road (old Conception Bay Hwy) to Brigus.
$35S $50D $55F $5Add.person   🍽 Meals   ► 10
● Choice   🏠 Village, hist., view, patio, quiet   ■ 2Ste,2D (upstairs   ⊨ 3D,1Q,1P
(double)   🚽 2Private, 1sh.w.g   ★ F,TV, separate entrance, parking, stereo   🐾 Pets
〰 some French
↪ Captain Bob Bartlett's Monument & Tunnel, Rockwell Kent's cottage,
⇔ Salmonier Nature Park, Communities of Cupids, Harbour Grace, many historic sites
in the Avalon Penninsula, St. John's (Prov. Capital)

☛ 110-year old Seaport cottage home in small historic community (400-year old
fishing village). Large 3-storey dwelling built in traditional Newfoundland style with
modern conveniences, while still maintaining its rustic appeal. Very quiet surroundings.

Cormack

(near Deer Lake and Corner Brook)

Lush, Daisy and Bruce (Lush's Bed & Breakfast)   (check) CC
Box 581, Cormack, Nfld A0K 2E0   ☎ (709) 635-2070

Take Hwy 1 to Rt 430 (Viking Trail) and then Rt 422. Continue 3km to Lush's B&B.
$27S $35D $5Add.person   ► 4A,4Ch
● Choice   🏠 Farm, view, patio, quiet   ■ 4D (main and upper floor)   ⊨2T,4D,4R
🚽 2Sh.w.g.   ★F,TV in guest room, KF, parking
↪ Funland Resort, swimming pool, water slides, strawberry picking in season
⇔ Gross Morne National Park, Sir Richard Squires Prov. Park, salmon fishing

☛ Enjoy friendly Newfoundland hospitality in comfortable home situated on a hill
with very long driveway and surrounded by trees. There is a small store on the premises

Corner Brook

(see also Woody Point, South Branch)

Brake, Mrs. Howard (Brake's Hospitality Home)
25 Cooper's Rd., Corner Brook, Nfld A2H 3Y8   ☎ (709) 785-2077

Located on scenic South Shore Drive. Phone for directions.
$24S $29D $2.50Child $5Add.person   🍽 Meals   ► 4A,3Ch
● Full, homemade   🏠 Res., farm type house, view, quiet   ■ 2D (upstairs)
⊨1S,2T,2D   🚽 1Sh.w.g., 1sh.w.h.   ★ TV, parking
↪ Seashore and scenic view, marina, park, bus route
⇔ Gros Morne Park, Port-Aux-Basques (Marine Atlantic Ferry to mainland)

☛ Hosts serve true Newfoundland meals and homebaked bread and rolls. Boat tours of
Bay of Islands and Cod Jigging trips can be arranged.

French, Mary and Bill (Delightful Guest Home)
1 Elswick Rd., Corner Brook, Nfld   A2H 2W3   ☎ (709) 634-2165

From Trans-Canada Hwy 1, make a left turn at Irving Self Service Stn onto West Valley
Rd (main western entrance to the city). At about 0.5 km bear left into Elswick Rd. Or
phone for directions.
$30S $35D $3Child   ► 4A,3Ch
✪ Summer   ● Cont.   🏠 Res., patio, quiet   ▪ 2D,F   ⇁ 4S,1R,P   ⌐ 1Sh.w.g.
★ TV in guest room, parking   ✋ Pets
↔ Excellent dining (Old Inn), ball park, shopping centres, golfing, skiing
⇔ Sandy beaches, swimming, scenic drives on north and south shores of Bay Islands,
quaint fishing village, airport, Bay of Islands Yacht Club

🐾 Spacious family home. Hosts are very knowledgeable about Newfoundland history
and points of interest. Convenient location for noon ferry at Port-aux-Basques (225 km).

Grand Bank
(on south shore near Burin; see also Saint Pierre et Miquelon)

Fizzard, Elva and Garfield (The Thorndyke)
33 Water Street, Grand Bank, Nfld   A0E 1W0   ☎ (709) 832-0820

Situated 1.6 km from first turn-off coming from Route 210 into Grand Bank.
$25S $30D   ● $2-4.50Extra   ► 10
✪ Summer   ● Choice, homemade   🏠 Hist., view, oceanfront   ▪ 5D (upstairs)
⇁ 6S,2D, 2cots   ⌐ 2Sh.w.g.   ★ TV, parking   ✋ Restricted smoking
↔ Grand Bank downtown, harbour, Seaman's Museum, beaches, hiking trails
⇔ Ferry to French Islands of Saint Pierre et Miquelon

🐾 Recently restored turn of the Century Sea Captain's home has excellent view of bay
from sunporch and from "Widows Walk" on roof. Located on Fortune Bay in quiet and
comfortable surroundings. Hosts are well informed of area's history. Ideal location from
which to take a trip to the nearby French Islands of Saint Pierre.

B&B Travel Tip: *Contacting the B&B hosts ahead of time is a big advantage. You will not only have a bed waiting for you that night, but you have already
"broken the ice." The hosts will be welcoming you at the door and you are not a
stranger any more.*

Heart's Delight
(near Carbonear; see also Brigus)

Sooley, Mrs. Shirley (Farm House Hospitality Home) ✔ CC
Box 72, Heart's Delight, Trinity Bay, Nfld   A0B 2A0   ☎ (709) 588-2393

Coming from St. John's, take Rt1 to Whitbourne intersection and take Rt80 to Heart's Delight. Coming from Argentia Ferry, take Rt1 East to Whitbourne intersection and turn left onto Rt80. Look for signs.
$25S $30D $2Child $5Add.person   📧 Meals   ► 6A,5Ch
✚ May15-Oct30   ● Choice, homebaked   🏠 Village, bungalow, acreage, view, oceanfront, patio, quiet   ■ 2D,1Ste,1F   ⊷ 3D,1R,1P   ⌐2Private, 1Ensuite   ★ TV in guest room, LF, parking   ♥   ✋ Smoking, pets

↔ Marshland on back of property, ocean scenic walks, supervised swimming pool

⇔ Moose-watching, Trans Atlantic Museum, Rainbow Trout Farm, cod-jigging, whale-watching, craft shop

🐾 Home overlooks Trinity Bay and is surrounded by marshland abundant with beautiful flowers and birds and where moose can be seen frequently. Hosts have spent many years in Canada's Eastern Arctic & Labrador, before retiring and they sometimes take visitors out in their fishing boat to cod-fish or whale-watch.

L'Anse aux Meadows
(near St. Anthony on northern tip of Newfoundland)

Hodge, Bella (Valhalla Lodge)
Gunners Cove, Nfld   A0K 2X0   ☎ (709) 632-2018(summer) 896-5476(winter)

Located 8.5km from L'Anse aux Meadows National Historic Park. Phone for directions.
$35S $45D $10Child $10Add.person   ► 12A,2Ch
✚ Summer   ● Cont.   🏠 Hist., view, quiet, oceanfront   ■ 3S,3D (main and upper level)   ⊷ 4S,4D,1P, cot   ⌐ 2Private, 2sh.w.g.   ★ F,TV, separate entrance, KF, parking, facilities for the disabled   ♥
↔ Hiking trails, beach combing, restaurant
⇔ Unesco World Heritage Site of the Vikings, L'Anse aux Meadows, Grenfell museum and handicrafts, Viking shopping mall, St. Anthony

🐾 Home is decorated with pine furniture and hand made quilts. From the comfortable wicker furniture on the Balcony, overlooking the ocean and light-houses, see whales, icebergs, ships and watch the fishermen at work.

Portugal Cove
(near St.John's; see also Bay Bulls, Brigus)

Roe, Fiona C (Broad Cove House)   ⌐ B&B
Box 223, RR1, Old Broad Cove Rd., Portugal Cove, Nfld   A0A 3K0   ☎ (709) 895-3684

Phone for directions. Hosts will send map with sufficient notice.
$34S $45D   ◙ Meals (Vegetarian Cuisine)   ► 4
● Full   ♠ Rural, splet-level house, acreage, view, quiet   ■ 2S (upstairs)   ⊢ 1D,1Q
⌐ 1sh.w.g.   ★ F, parking   ⓦ smoking   ∾ basic French and Italian
↔ Hiking and cross-country ski trails, woods, ponds, convenience store
⇔ Historic downtown St. John's, Memorial University, Bell Island (by ferry), bird- and whale-watching, Botanical Gardens

🖝 Warm welcome to comfortable home located in rural surroundings. There are European comforters on the beds. Enjoy a hot cup of tea and a chat after a busy day of travelling and sightseeing.

St. John's
(see also Bay Bulls)

Wall, Marie (Fireside Guest Home)   ⌐ B&B
28 Wicklow Street, St. John's, Nfld   A1B 3H2   ☎ (709) 726-0237

Phone for directions.
$30S $35D   (plus tax)   ► 5
● Choice   ♠ Res., townhouse, patio   ■ 1S,1D   ⊢ 2D,1P   ⌐ 1Sh.w.g.
★ TV, parking   ⓦ Pets
↔ Memorial University of Newfoundland, shopping mall
⇔ City Centre, restaurants, Pippy Park Children's Farm, Signal Hill Nat. Historic Park, Commissariat House, Quidi Vidi Battery historic site

B&B Travel Tip: *If you stay more than one night, you can go and come at your pleasure. But do let the hosts know when you will be back, especially if you plan to be late. They might even give you a key, and then you can let yourself in quietly.*

South Branch

(near Port-au-Basques; see also Corner Brook)

Muise, Zita and Norman (Muises Tourist Home)   ✔ B&B
South Branch, Nfld   A0N 2B0   ☎ (709) 955-2471

From Route 1 turn left at South Branch Intersection and continue for 2.4 km to brown
and white house with white fence. (57 km from Port au Basques)
$25S $30D $3Child $5Add.person   ▥ Meals   ► 6A,3Ch
✚ June 1-Sept 30   ● Full   ♠ Village, bungalow, acreage, view, patio, quiet   ■ 3
⊷ 3D,1S,2R   ⊓ 1Sh.w.g., 1sh.w.h.   ★ TV,LF, separate entrance
✋ Restricted smoking, drinking

↔ Excellent salmon fishing, Grand
Codroy River

⇔ Restaurant, craft shop, night club,
Port Aux Basques, shopping, Ferry to
Mainland, Stephenville Festival, Gross
Morne Nat. Park.

🖙 Enjoy genuine Newfoundland
hospitality in south coast home with
spacious yard and beautiful view of
Long Range Mountains and Cape
Anguille Mountains. Hosts serve early
breakfast for guests who have to catch
the ferry out of Port Aux Basques (ferry
to Mainland). Delicious homemade
breads a house specialty.

Woody Point

(near Corner Brook)

Parsons, Mr. & Mrs. Stan (Victorian Manor Hospitality Home)   ✔ B&B
Box 165, Woody Point, Bonne Bay, Nfld   A0K 1P0   ☎ (709) 453-2485

At Deer Lake on Trans Canada Hwy 1, take Rt 430 to Wiltondale and then Rt 431.
$32S $38D $5Add. person   ● $4.75Each   ▥ Meals   ► 7
● Choice, homebaked   ♠ village, hist., acreage, view, oceanfront, sunporch
■ 1S,3D   ⊷ 1S,3D   ⊓ Sh.w.g.   ★ TV in guest room, F, separate entrance,
parking   ✋ Pets, restricted smoking
↔ Seashore, cod jigging, whale watching
⇔ Gros Morne Mountain and trails (Green Garden's Trail with Sea Caves and Table
lands trail with rare plants), Trout River, swimming pool

🖙 4th Generation owners in Unique Victorian Home still contains many artifacts and
is rich in history and Newfoundland culture with scenic panorama of Gros Morne and
Bonne Bay. Ocean cruising can be arranged.

Government Tourist Offices in Canada

Note: When using a pay phone, ask the operator to place the toll free call.

Canadian Government Office of Tourism   (613) 956-3852
235 Queen Street, 4th Floor East,
Ottawa, Ontario   K1A 0H6

Alberta
Travel Alberta,   (403) 427-4321
Box 2500, 14th Floor, Capital Square,   toll free from Alberta 1-800-222-6501
Edmonton, Alberta   T5J 2Z4   from BC & rural Sask. 112-800-661-6543
toll free from anywhere in N.A   1-800 661-8888

Travel Alberta,
455-6th St. S.W., Calgary, Alberta   T2P 4E8

British Columbia
Tourism British Columbia,
1117 Wharf Street, Victoria, BC   V8W 2Z2   (604) 387-1642

Travel Information Centre,
562 Burrard St., Vancouver, BC   V6C 2J6   (604) 683-2000

Manitoba
Travel Manitoba,
Department 2020, Legislative Building,   (204) 944-3777
Winnipeg, Manitoba   R3C 0V8   (204) 268-3420

New Brunswick   (506) 453-2377
Tourism New Brunswick,   toll free from NB 1-800-561-0123
Box 12345, Fredericton, New Brunswick   E3B 5C3   from BC 112-800-561-0123
   from USA 1-800-343-0812
Dial-a-Nite reservation from Tourist Information Centres within the Province

Newfoundland
Tourism Division, Department of Development,   (709) 737-2830
Box 2016 St. John's, Newfoundland   A1C 5R8   toll free 1(800) 563-1353

Northwest Territories
Travel Arctic,   (403) 873-7200
Yellowknife, Northwest Territories X1A 2L9   toll free 1-800-563-6353

Nova Scotia   (902) 424-5000
Department of Tourism,   Check-Inns-Reservation toll-free:
Box 130, Halifax, Nova Scotia B3J 2M7   from Ontario 1-800-565-7140
                          from Quebec, Newfoundland 1-800-565-7180
                     from New Brunswick, PEI, and NS 1-800-565-7105
                               from rest of Canada 1-800-565-7166
                                    from U.S.A. 1-800-341-0286

Ontario   from Toronto(English) (416) 965-4008
Ontario Travel,   (French) (416) 965-3448
900 Bay Street, Queen's Park,   toll free from Canada(English) 1-800-268-3735
Toronto, Ontario   M7A 2E5   Canada (French) 1-800-268-3736
                                   from New York State 1-800-462-8404
                                        from USA 1-800-828-8585

Prince Edward Island
PEI Visitor Services Division,
Box 940, Charlottetown, Prince Edward Island   C1A 7M5   (902) 892-2457
Dial-the-Island-Reservation toll free from NB and NS   1-800-565-7421

Quebec   (418) 643-5070
Tourism Quebec,from Montreal   toll free from Quebec 1-800-361-5405
CP 20000, Quebec City, Quebec   G1K 7X2   from Ontario 1-800-361-6490

Saskatchewan
Saskatchewan Travel,
3211 Albert Street,   (306) 565-2300
Regina, Saskatchewan   S4S 5W6   toll-free from Saskatchewan 1-800-667-7191

Yukon
Tourism Yukon (CG)
Box 2703, Whitehorse, Yukon   Y1A 2C6   (404) 667-5360

Bed & Breakfast Registries, Reservation and Referral Services, Information Centres, Associations,and Organizations in Canada

There are various types of groups interested in Bed and Breakfast, most are profit making establishments.

Some registries act as a reservation service (just like a travel agent (they make all the arrangements for the unlisted member hosts).

Some are referral agencies only (they will print a list of member hosts to be contacted by the travellers directly).

Most will require a non-refundable deposit upon reservation.

Then there are many non-profit associations which are formed within a given area by the local hosts mainly as a co-operative effort to promote the B&B's and to refer guests to each other, when unable to accommodate them.

Some of the following are also listed under their respective locations in this book.

Alberta

Banff
Banff/Jasper Central Reservation
204 Caribou St., Banff, Alberta,
mailing: Box 1628, Banff, Alberta   T0L 0C0   (403) 762-5561

Banff B&B Bureau
Box 369, Banff, Alberta T0L 0C0   (403) 762-4636

Calgary
Hospitality Centre, Calgary Tourism and Convention Bureau,
1300, 6th Ave. S.W., Calgary, Alberta T3C 0H8   (403) 263-8510

Welcome West Vacations Bed and Breakfast Agency,
1320 Kerwood Cr. S.W., Calgary, Alberta   T2V 2N6   (403) 258-3373

Edmonton
Alberta Pacific Bed and Breakfast,
Box 15477, MPO Vancouver, BC   V6B 5B2   (604) 682-4610

Gibbons
Alberta Ranch and Farm Vacations
Box 966, Gibbons, Alberta   T0A 1N0   (403) 921-2490

Jasper
Jasper/Banff Central Reservations,
626 Connaught Ave., Jasper, Alberta
mailing: Box 1628, Banff, Alberta   T0L 0C0   (403) 762-5561

Jasper Park Chamber of Commerce,
Box 98, Jasper, Alberta   T0E 1E0   (403) 852-3858

Lethbridge
Trails West B&B Bureau
1710-31 St.N., Lethbridge, Alberta   T1H 5H1   (403) 328-9011

Pincher Creek
Southern Alberta B&B Booking Agency
Box 1329, Pincher Creek, Alberta   T0K 1W0   (403) 627-3443

Rosebud
Big Country B&B Registry
Box 714, Rosebud, Alberta   T0J 2T0   (403) 677-2269/2333

British Columbia

Burnaby
Vancouver B&B Ltd.,
1685 Ingleton Ave., Burnaby, BC   V5C 4L8   (604) 291-6147

Born Free B&B of BC Ltd.,
4390 Francess St., Burnaby, BC   V5C 2R3   (604) 298-8815

Kaslo
Kootenay Lakes B&B Association
Box 884, Kaslo BC V06 1M0   (604) 353-7134

New Westminster
Royal City Bed and Breakfast
628-10th St., New Westminster, BC   V3M 3Z8   (604) 521-5733

Richmond
Westway Accommodation Registry
Box 23124 AMF, Richmond, BC   V7B 1V6   (604) 273-8293

Sooke
Hosts of the Southwest Coast B&B Ass.
RR4, Sooke BC   V0S 1N0   (604) 642-6534

Surrey
Family Care Bed and Breakfast
6104 172A Street, Surrey, BC   V3S 5M3   (604) 574-3133

Vancouver
Greater Vancouver Convention Bureau,
Box 11142, Royal Centre, 1055 West Georgia St. No.1625,
Vancouver, BC   V6E 4C8   (604) 682-2222

Alberta & Pacific Bed and Breakfast
Box 15477, MPO, Vancouver, BC   V6B 5B2   (604) 682-4610

Bairich Bed and Breakfast
805-7241 Cambie St., Vancouver, BC   V6P 3H3   (604) 324-5159

Best Canadian Reservations for B&B
1030 West King Edward Ave., Vancouver, BC   V6H 1Z4   (604) 738-7207

Canada West Accommodations B&B Registry
1383 Mill St., North Vancouver, BC   V7K 1V5   (604) 987-99338

Cope's Choice B&B
4808 Skyline Dr., North Vancouver, BC   V7R 3J1   (604) 987-8988

First Choice B&B Int. Inc.,
658 East 29th Ave., Vancouver, BC   V5V 2R9   (604) 875-8888

Home away from Home B&B Agency Ltd.
4228 Windsor St., Vancouver, BC   V5V 4P4   (604) 873d-4888

Hosts International B&B Reservation Ltd.
1478 Gordon Ave., West Vancouver, BC   V7T 1R6   (604) 926-0004

Old English Bed and Breakfast,
Box 86818, North Vancouver, BC   V7L 4L3   (604) 986-5069

Town & Country Bed and Breakfast in B.C.,
Box 46544, Stn. G, Vancouver, BC   V6R 4G5   (604) 731-5942/261-0569

Western Comfort Bed and Breakfast,
180 E. Carisbrooke Rd., North Vancouver, BC   V7N 1M9   (604) 985-2674

Vernon
Okanagan Bed and Breakfast Network
Site 19A, C2, RR1, Vernon, BC   V1T 6L4   (604) 549-2804

Victoria
Accommodation West B&B Res. Service
Box 6161, Stn.C, Victoria BC   V8P 5L5   (604) 479-1986

All Season Bed and Breakfast Agency,
Box 5511, Stn. B, Victoria, BC   V8R 6S4   (604) 595-BEDS/5952337

City & Sea B&B Agency
126-790 Topaz Ave., Victoria BC   V8T 2M1   (604) 385-1962

Garden City B&B Reservation Service
Box 6398, Stn C, Victoria, BC   V8P 5N7   (604) 479-9999

Greater Victoria Visitor & Convention Bureau,
812 Wharf St., Victoria, BC   V8W 1T3   (604) 382-2127

Heritage Homes B&B Registry
829 Fort Street, Victoria, BC   V8W 3A9   (604) 384-4014

Old Victoria B&B Registry,
Box 5093, Stn B, Victoria, BC   V8R 6N3   (604) 592-5038

Traveller's B&B Registry
1840 Midgard Ave., Victoria, BC   V8P 2Y9   (604) 477-3069

Victoria Bed and Breakfast, Inc.
1054 Summit Ave., Victoria, BC   V8T 2P5   (604) 385-2332

Victoria Hospitality Club,
1240 Gladstone, Victoria, BC   V8T 1G6   (604) 384-8033

V.I.P. Bed and Breakfast,
1786 Teakwood Rd., Victoria, BC   V8N 1E2   (604) 477-5604

White Rock
Bed and Breakfast by the Sea,
15047 Marine Dr., White Rock, BC   V4B 1C5   (604) 536-6844

Manitoba

Winnipeg
Bed and Breakfast of Manitoba,
93 Healy Cres., Winnipeg, Manitoba   R2N 2S2   (204) 256-6151

Manitoba Farm Vacations,
525 Kylemore Ave.,
Winnipeg, Manitoba   R3L 1B5   (204) 475-6624

New Brunswick

Fredericton
New Brunswick Farm Vacations, Dept. of Tourism,
Box 12345, Fredericton, NB   E3B 5C3   use toll free numbers

Harcourt
New Brunswick Farm Vacations
RR1, Harcourt, Kings Co, NB   E0A 1T0   (506) 785-4361

Saint John
New Brunswick B&B Association
238 Charlotte St.,W., Saint John, NB   E2M 1Y3   (506) 635-1888

Nova Scotia

Annapolis Royal
A.R. Tourist Bureau & Bed and Breakfast Places,
Box 2, Annapolis Royal, NS   B0S 1A0   (902) 532-5769

Bridgewater
South Shore Bed and Breakfast Association,
Box 82, Bridgewater, NS   B4V 2W6   (902) 543-5391

Halifax
Halifax Metro Bed and Breakfast,
Box 1613, Stn. M, Halifax, NS   B3J 2Y3   (902) 374-3546

Middleton
Annapolis Valley Bed and Breakfast,
Box 1149, Middleton, NS   B0S 1P0   (902) 825-4344/6777

New Glasgow
Northumberland Shore Bed and Breakfast Homes,
Box 782, New Glasgow, NS   B2H 5G2   (902) 755-5180

Newport Station
Nova Scotia Farm Vacations
Newport Station, Hants Co., NS B0N 2B0   (902) 798-5864

sp 1ln
Parrsboro
Central Nova Bed and Breakfast,Parrsboro Tourist Office
Box 263, Parrsboro, NS   B0M 1S0   (902) 254-3266

Sydney
Cape Breton B&B (Cape Breton Development Corp),
Box 1750, Point Edward, Sydney, NS   B1P 6T7   (902) 562-6300

Ontario

Alma
Ontario Farm Vacation Association
RR 2, Alma, Ontario N0B 1A0

Beachburg
Beachburg and Area Bed & Breakfast Association
Box 146, Beachburg, Ontario K0J 1C0   (613) 582-3585

Bloomfield
Guest Homes B&B Prince Edward County
Box 160, Bloomfield, Ontario K0K 1G0   (613) 393-3046

Burlington
Bed and Breakfast Burlington
270 Juniper Ave., Burlington, Ont. L7L 2T3   (416) 632-1996/634-0721

Fergus
Elora B&B Association
550 St. Andrew St. E., Fergus, Ontario NiM 1R6   (519) 846-0640/843-2584

Hamilton
Bed and Breakfast in Hamilton/Wentworth,
61 East 43rd St., Hamilton, Ontario L8T 3B7   (416) 383-9517

The Bruce Trail Association,
Box 857, Hamilton, Ontario L8N 3N9   (416) 689-7311

Kingston
Bed and Breakfast Kingston Area,
10 Westview Rd., Kingston, Ontario K7M 2C3   (613) 542-0214

Leamington
Point Pelee B&B Association
115 Erie St., S, Leamington, Ont N8H 3B5   (519) 326-7169

London
London and Area Bed and Breakfast,
720 Headley Dr., London, Ontario N6N 3V6   (519) 471-6228

Millbank
Southwestern Ontario Countryside Vacation Assoc.& B&B,
RR1, Millbank, Ontario N0K 1L0   (519) 595-4604

Millgrove
Flamborough Bed and Breakfast,
Box 75, Millgrove, Ontario L0R 1V0   (416) 689-5937

Missisauga
All Seasons Bed and Breakfast Inc.,
383 Mississauga Valley Blvd.,
Mississauga, Ontario   L5A 1Y9   (416) 276-4572

Muskoka/Gravenhurst
Muskoka B&B Association
Box 1431, Gravenhurst, Ontario   P0C 1G0   (705) 687-4395

Niagara Falls
Niagara Region Bed and Breakfast Service
(Le Gite d'Accueil de la region du Niagara),
2631 Dorchester Rd., Niagara Falls, Ontario   L2J 2Y9   (416) 358-8988

Niagara-on-the-Lake
Guest Homes in Niagara-on-the-Lake,
CC Box 1043, Niagara-on-the-Lake, Ontario   L0S 1J0   (416) 468-2326

Shaw Festival Theatre,
Box 774, Niagara-on-the-Lake, Ontario   L0S 1J0   (416) 468-2153

Orillia
Orillia and Area Bed and Breakfast,
c/o Laity, RR2 Hawkestone, Orillia, Ontario   L0L 1T0   (705) 487-7191

Ottawa
Capital Bed and Breakfast Association Ottawa,
2071 Riverside Dr., Ottawa, Ontario   K1H 7X2   (613) 737-4129

Downtown Ottawa Bed and Breakfast Association,
479 Slater St., Ottawa, Ontario   K1R 5C2   (613) 236-3904

Ottawa Centertown B&B Association
253 McLeod St., Ottawa, Ontario K2P 1A1   (613) 234-7577

Ottawa Area Bed and Breakfast,
Box 4848, Stn. E, Ottawa, Ontario   K1S 5J1   (613) 563-0161

Owen Sound
Grey Bruce Bed and Breakfast Association
c/o Grey Bruce Tourist Association,
RR5, Owen Sound, Ontario   N4K 5N7   toll free 1-800-265-3127 or (519) 534-2422

Palgrave
Country Host and Ski Host,
RR1, Palgrave, Ontario   L0N 1P0   (519) 941-7633

Parry Sound
Parry Sound & District B&B Association
67 Church St., Parry Sound, Ontario   P2A 1Y8   (705) 746-8806

Penetanguishene
Centre d'activities Francaises,
CP 1270, Penetanguishene, Ontario   L0K 1P0   (705) 549-3116

Peterborough
B&B Registry of Peterborough & Area
Box 2264 Lakefield, Ontario   K9J 7Y8   (705) 652-6290

St. Catharines
Region Niagara Tourist Council
Box 3025, St. Catharines, Ontario   L2R 7E9   (416) 685-1571

St.Catharines B&B Association
489 Carleton St., St. Catharines, Ontario L2M 4W9   (416) 937-2422

Simcoe
Simcoe Information Centre,
85 Pond Street, Simcoe, Ontario   N3Y 2T5   (519) 426-6655

Stratford
Stratford & Area Bed and Beakfast,
256 Albert St., Stratford, Ontario   N5A 3K9   (519) 273-1112

Stratford Festival Accommodations,
Box 520, Stratford, Ontario   N5A 6V2   (519) 271-4040

Stratford Bed and Breakfast 2,
208 Church St., Stratford, Ontario   N5A 4B3   (519) 273-4840

Thorold
Region Niagara Tourist Council
2201 St. Davis Rd., Box 1042, Thorold, Ontario   L2V 4T7   (416) 685-1571

Thunder Bay
Thunder Bay Area B&B Association
RR1, South Gillies, Ontario   P0T 2V0   (807) 577-1034

Toronto
FOBBA, Federation of Ontario B&B Associations
72 Lowther Ave., Toronto, Ontario   M5R 1C8   (416) 964-2566/(613) 399-3226

Bed & Breakfast Homes of Toronto
Box 353, 31 Lakeshore Rd.E., Mississauga, Ontario   L5G 4L8

(416) 363-6362

Downtown Toronto Association of B&B Guest Houses,
Box 190, Stn. B, Toronto, Ontario   M5T 2W1

(416) 977-6841

Metropolitan Bed and Breakfast Registry of Toronto,
72 Lowther Ave., Toronto, Ontario   M5R 1C8

(416) 964-2566/928-2833

Toronto Bed and Breakfast (1987) Inc.,
Box 74, Stn M, Toronto, Ontario   M6S 4T2

(416) 233-3887/4041

Welland
Rose City B&B Association
102 Aqueduct St., Welland, Ontario   L3C 1C1

(416) 788-9054

Wellington
Quinte's Isle B&B Association
Box 570, 505 Main St., Wellington, Ontario   K0K 3L0

(613) 399-3236

Prince Edward Island

Bonshaw
PEI Farm Vacations
RR3, Bonshaw, St. Catherines, PEI   C0A 1C0

(902) 675-2989

Charlottetown
Visitor Services PEI,
Box 940, Charlottetown, PEI   CIA 7M5

(902) 892-2457

Kensington
Kensington and Area Tourist Association,
RR1, Kensington, PEI   C0B 1M0

(902) 836-3031/4206

Quebec

Cowansville
Townshippers Association
203 Main St, Cowansville, Quebec   J2K 1J3

(514) 263-4422

Montreal,
La Federation des Agricotours.
4545 Ave Pierre-de-Coubertin
CP1000, Succ M, Montreal, Quebec   H1V 3R2   (514) 252-3138

Bed & Breakfast de Chez-Nous,
5386 Ave. Brodeur, Montreal, Quebec   H4A 1J3   (514) 485-1252

Downtown B&B Network (Montrealers at Home),
3458 Laval Ave., Montreal, Quebec   H2X 3C8   (514) 289-9749

Bed and Breakfast Montreal,
4912 Ave Victoria, Montreal, Quebec   H3W 2N1   (514) 738-9410

Quebec City
Bed and Breakfast in Old Quebec,
300 Rue Champlain, Quebec City, Quebec   G1K 4J2   (418) 525-9826

B&B Bonjour Quebec
3765 Boul. Monaco, Quebec, Quebec   G1P 3J3   (418) 527-1465

Gite Quebec Bed and Breakfast,
3729 Ave Le Corbusier, Ste-Foy, Que'bec   G1W 4P3   (418) 651-1860

Saint-Laurent
Gites du passant Saint-Laurent (Ile d'Oreleans)
1415, Chemin Royal, Saint-Laurent, Que   G0A 3Z0   (418) 828-9442/2671/9501

Sherbrooke
Les Gites L'Estrie,
2883 West King Street, Sherbrooke, Quebec   G1L 1C6   (810) 566-7404/(418) 567-6981

Townshippers Association
2313 King St. W., Ste 308, Sherbrooke, Que   J1J 2G2   (819) 566-5717

Saskatchewan

Bateman
Saskatchewan Farm Vacations,
Box 24, Bateman, Saskatchewan   S0H 0E0   (306) 648-3530

Yukon

Whitehorse
Northern Network of Bed & Breakfasts
39 Donjek Rd., Whitehorse, Yukon   Y1A 3R1   (403) 667-4315

Index

Last Minute Additions

Delta (BC)
(near Vancouver; see also White Rock, Surrey, Richmond, New Westminster)

Joe and Adeline Posh (Posh House)
6285 Sunwood Drive, Delta, BC   V4E 3A7   ☎ (604) 596-6512

From Trans Canada Hwy 1 exit onto Hwy 10 and go to 120St (Scott Rd). Turn right and continue to Sunwood Dr (very first street on left side).
$25S $35D $10Child   ► 6
● Choice   🏠 Res., patio   ■ 3   ⊷ 2T,2Q   ⌐ 1Sh.w.g.   ★F,TV,KF,LF
♿Restricted smoking
↔ Small shopping centre, public transportation
⇔ US-border, Tswassen Ferry Terminal to Vancouver Island, downtown Vancouver

🐾 Hosts are former Albertans. On extra beautiful mornings, breakfast is served on outdoor deck. There is a trailer pad on the property (with water and electric hook-up including access to washroom facilities).

Niton Junction (Alta)
(west of Edmonton near Edson)

McLellan, Linda and Dale Dickson
Box 181, Niton Junction, Alta   T0E 1S0   ☎ (403) 795-3793/795-3782

Located on Hwy 16 about 150 km due west. Turn right at Niton Jucntion (north) and travel to end of pavement past school on right side. Look for first trailer on left directly behind Fire Hall.
$15S $20D $5Child   🍽 Meals   ► 2A,2Ch
● Choice, homebaked   🏠 Farm, acreage, swimming pool, patio, quiet   ■ 1D,1S
⊷1D,1S   ⌐ Private   ★ TV,LF,KF
↔ Skating rink, arcade, satellite
⇔ Silver Summit Ski Hill

🐾 Accommodation is in spacious house-trailer in very convenient location on the famous Yellowhead Hwy. Hosts enjoy meeting and helping visitors on their way heading West. Children are welcome to tour the farm. Guests may bring pets.

Jasper (Alta)
(see also page 85)

Mellace, Wendy and Tony
Box 932, 907 Pyramid Lake Rd., Jasper, Alta   T0E 1E0   ☎ (403) 852-3851

Take Yellowhead Hwy 16 into Jasper. Turn right on Pine Ave for 5 short blocks and turn left. House is third on left side.
$30D   ► 2A,2Ch
● None   🏠 Res., quiet   ■ 1D (downstairs)   ⊨ 1D,1Q   ⤄ Private   ★ Private entrance   ✋ pets   〰 Italian
↪ Downtown Jasper, restaurants, shopping, entertainments
⇔ Jasper Park Lodge, lakes, fishing, Jasper Sky Tram, horseback riding, downhill and cross country skiing, tours

🐾 Centrally-located home in beautiful and popular year-round resort town.

Elora (Ontario)
(see also page 146)

Veveris, Petra (Ginger Bread House)
22 Metcalfe St.S., Elora, Ontario N0B 1S0   ☎ (519) 846-0521

From Guelph take Hwy 6 north and SR 7 to Elora. Continue to stop sign at Elora Bus section and to last house before bridge across from the LCBO (stone building).
$60S $65D   ► 8A
● Full   🏠 Hist., view   ■ 4 (upstairs)   ⊨ 2T,3D   ⤄ 1Sh.w.g.,1sh.w.h.
★TV,parking   ✋ Smoking   〰 German
↪ Bridge across the Grand River leading to shopping district on Mill Street, parks, famous Elora Gorge
⇔ Fergus (Highland Games), Mennonite Country

🐾 Completely renovated and updated home was built around 1833 is situated on a slab of Rock, which has remained intact; with 3 brick-deep field stone construction and original glass panes in the windows and reflecting the elegance of years past.

Paisley (Ontario)
(near Owen Sound; see also Dobbinton, Cargill, Hanover, Port Elgin, Kincardine)

Grice, Alice and Larry (The Country Touch)   ↙ Grey Bruce B&B
RR5, Paisley, Ontario N0G 2N0   ☎ (519) 353-5464

Located 3.5 km west of Paisley on Bruce County Road 11.
$25S $35D $8Child $10Add. person   ► 6A,3Ch
● Full   🏠 Farm, ranch-style, swimming pool, patio, quiet   ■ 3D   ⊨ 2D,1Q,1P
⤄ Sh.w.g.   ★ Air,F,TV in guest room   ✋ Smoking, drinking, pets   〰some German
↪ Saugeen River (good fishing and canoeing), Treasure Shest Museum (Paisley)
⇔ Bruce County Museum (Southampton), Nuclear Power Station (Douglas Point)

🐾 Home is situated in quiet location and a good area for hiking and bird-watching.

Notes

Reader's Comments

To the Reader of the Canadian Bed & Breakfast Guide:

Do take a moment to send me a few words if you like this book. I would very much appreciate receiving comments about your own experiences while planning and travelling with The Canadian Bed & Breakfast Guide. Your personal input will be useful for future editions. I am always open-minded to new suggestions and improvements. Don't forget to give me your address and phone number – I may want to hear more from you. Thanks so much. G.P.

_____

_____

_____

_____

_____

_____

_____

_____

_____

How to list your Bed & Breakfast Home

Gerda Pantel, 270 Juniper Avenue, Burlington, Ontario L7L 2T3

I am a Bed and Breakfast Host and I would like to be included in the next edition of The Canadian Bed and Breakfast Guide. Please send me a questionaire.

Name:_____.

Address:_____.

City:_____ Prov._____ Code:_____.

Please submit cancellation, correction or new entry by Nov.15, 1989.

Order Form

Fitzhenry & Whiteside, 195 Allstate Parkway, Markham Ontario L3R 4T8

Please send me a copy of The Canadian Bed & Breakfast Guide. I am enclosing **$ 12.95**   plus **$ 2.00**   for postage and handling for each copy I order.

Name:_____.

Address:_____.

City:_____ Prov._____ Code:_____.